Practicing Democracy

Practicing Democracy

ELECTIONS AND
POLITICAL CULTURE IN
IMPERIAL GERMANY

MARGARET LAVINIA ANDERSON

PRINCETON UNIVERSITY PRESS

PRINCETON, NEW JERSEY

Library of Congress Cataloging-in-Publication Data

Anderson, Margaret Lavinia.
Practicing democracy : elections and political culture in Imperial Germany
/ Margaret Lavinia Anderson.
p. cm.
Includes bibliographical references and index.
ISBN 0-691-04853-3 (cloth : alk. paper) — ISBN 0-691-04854-1 (pbk. : alk. paper)
1. Elections—Germany—History—19th century.   2. Elections—Germany—History—
20th century.   3. Germany—Politics and government—1866–1871.   4. Germany—Politics
and government—1871–1918.   5. Authoritarianism—Germany—History—19th century.
6. Democracy—Germany—History—19th century.   I. Title.

JN3838.A54   2000
324.7'0943'09034   21—dc21   99-045803

This book has been composed in Times Roman

The paper used in this publication meets the minimum requirements of
ANSI/NISO Z39.48-1992 (R1997) (*Permanence of Paper*)

http://pup.princeton.edu

Printed in the United States of America

P

(Pbk.)

FOR JIM

IL MIGLIOR FABBRO

CONTENTS

LIST OF FIGURES

ACKNOWLEDGMENTS

THIS BOOK owes so much to so many people over such a long period of time that the pleasure of thanking them is somewhat diminished by the fear that I have overlooked someone.

Let me gratefully acknowledge first of all the National Endowment for the Humanities for a summer stipend and support for a full academic year, as well as Swarthmore College and the University of California at Berkeley for research support; Stephen Lehmann, now of the University of Pennsylvania Library; the staffs at the Staatsbibliothek in Berlin and in Munich; Frau Gesine Bottomley at the Wissenschaftskolleg and Frau Eleanore Liedtke at the Theologisch-Pädagogische Akademie Bibliothek in Berlin; Herr Gotthard Klein, director of the Berlin Diocesan Archiv; and especially the archivists at the former Federal Archives at Potsdam and Merseburg, who allowed me to use their collections even as they were busy packing them away; Dr. Andreas Daum of the German Historical Institute in Washington, who tracked these files down for me after they had been moved to the new Bundesarchiv at Lichterfelde and the Geheimes Staatsarchiv Preußischer Kulturbesitz; and the staffs at those institutions who then helped me figure out what the new signatures would be.

Thanks also to the Dietz Verlag, Berlin, for permission to reprint the maps in figures 5 and 6, and to the Institute of Latin American Studies at the University of London to reprint part of my article "Clerical Election Influence and Communal Solidarity: Catholic Political Culture in the German Empire, 1871–1914," from Eduardo Posada-Carbó, ed., *Elections Before Democracy: The History of Elections in Europe and Latin America* (London, 1996).

I owe a special debt to Jonathan Sperber for sending me the galleys of his own election book; to Helmut Walser Smith, for generously sharing copies of material from the Generallandesarchiv in Karlsruhe and the Landesarchiv in Koblenz; and to Dr. Josef Hamacher of Haselünne, who gave me tea and sympathy, and his large collection of documents from the Niedersächsisches Staatsarchiv in Osnabrück, copies of Windthorst letters now in private hands, and copies of his own research.

For bibliographical and other help I owe a great deal to Benjamin Lazier, Michael Printy, Daniel K. Rolde, Julia Schneeringer, and Jonathan Sheehan. Gerhard A. Ritter offered trenchant criticism of an earlier version of these ideas. Hans-Ulrich Wehler tried to keep me from falling behind by sending me recent work from the Federal Republic. Kenneth D. Barkin, Henry A. Turner, and Vernon Lidtke read all of the manuscript and offered important suggestions. During the years that I was writing this book, Josef and Ruth Becker have nourished me with their help, friendship, and unfailing support. Finally I am especially indebted to four people: Lisa Fetheringill Swartout and Chad Bryant of Berkeley, whose intelligence and resourcefulness solved insoluble problems and kept this book from taking another decade; Marcus Kreuzer of Villanova, who went over several chapters with a fine-tooth comb and to whose epistolary tutorial over the years I owe what little political science I know; and to my husband James J. Sheehan of Stanford, who worked his way through all of it many times and was able to see the skeleton beneath the skin.

A NOTE ON USAGE

LIBERAL with a small "l" designates the persuasion, as well as liberal parties collectively and candidates for whom any closer party designation is impossible to ascertain. "Liberal" capitalized is short for National Liberal. "Left liberals" refers to the following parties, singly or collectively: the South German Volkspartei (1848–1910); the Progressives (1862–84); the National Liberal's Secession—later named the Liberale Vereinigung (1880–84); the Deutsche Freisinnige Partei (also referred to as Freisinnige or Freisinn, created in March 1884 from a union of Progressives and Liberale Vereinigung, and lasting until 1893); the Freisinnige Volkspartei (= the Richterites: 1893–1910); the Freisinnige Vereinigung (1893–1910); and the Fortschrittliche Volkspartei (1910–19).

"Conservative" capitalized refers to the Deutsch-Konservative Partei; uncapitalized, it includes the Reichspartei (referred to here by its more common Prussian name, the Free Conservatives, or FK) or the persuasion generally.

Antisemite/antisemitic, unless otherwise noted, refers to any of the antisemitic parties.

I use Socialist and Social Democrat interchangeably, but SPD only after 1891, when it became the official name of the party.

To avoid confusion with a place on the political spectrum, I refer to the Center Party by its contemporary name: Centrum. In footnotes I use the abbreviation "Z".

"Provincial Saxony" and "provincial Hessen" refer to Prussian provinces, in contrast to "royal Saxony" (= the Kingdom of Saxony) and Grand Ducal Hessen, which were separate federal states. Hessenland refers to both Hessens.

In order to save space, titles in footnotes that also appear in the bibliography will include only the first noun.

AA	Auswärtiges Amt (Foreign Affairs); MAA: Minister of Foreign Affairs
AL	Alsace-Lorraine
AnlDR	Anlageband des Deutschen Reichstags
APSR	American Political Science Review
Arns.	Arnsberg
BAK	Bundesarchiv Koblenz
BAT	Bistumsarchiv Trier
BdL	Bund der Landwirte, Farmers' League
BH	Bethmann Hollweg
BK	Bonifacius Kalender
Bl.	Blatt = page
BR	Bundesrat
BrZ	Breslauer Zeitung
BT	Berliner Tageblatt
CEH	Central European History
DA	Deutsches Adelsblatt
DGZ	Deutsche Gemeinde-Zeitung
DN	Dresdner Nachrichten
DNJ	Das Neue Jahrhundert
DS	Drucksache
DZJ	Das Zwangzigste Jahrhundert
Els.	Elsaß, regional Alsatian Party
F	Before Mar. 1884: Fortschrittspartei (Progressive Party); Mar. 1884–Jun. 1893: Freisinn or Freisinnige Partei
Fhr.	Freiherr
FK	Free Conservative (= Reichspartei)
FrankZ	Frankfurter Zeitung
FrVp	Freisinnige Volkspartei
FrZ	Freisinnige Zeitung
FtVp	Fortschrittliche Volkspartei
GA	Görlitzer Anzeiger
GG	Geschichte und Gesellschaft
GLA	Generallandesarchiv Karlsruhe
GSR	German Studies Review
GStA PK	Geheimes Staatsarchiv Preußischer Kulturbesitz
Gumb.	Gumbinnen
Han.	Hanover
HJ	Historical Journal
HVZ	Hagener Volkszeitung

HZ	Historische Zeitschrift
HZtg	Hallische Zeitung
IM	Minister of Interior
JIH	Journal of Interdisciplinary History
K, KP	Conservative[s], Conservative Party, German Conservative Party
KölnZ	Kölnische Zeitung
KrZ	Kreuz-Zeitung
KVZ	Kölnische Volkszeitung
LHAK	Landeshauptarchiv Koblenz
LL	Left Liberals: used generically
LP	Legislature Period
LR	Landrat
LRA	Landratsamt
LT	(Prussian) LT
LV	Liberale Vereinigung
MdI	Ministry of Interior
MK	Märkisches Kirchenblatt
ND	National Democrats (radical Polish nationalists)
NL	National Liberal
Oberb.	Oberbayern
Oberf.	Oberfranken
P	Polish Party
PVB	Preußisches-Verwaltungsblatt
RdI	Reichsamt des Innern
RefP	Reform Party (Antisemitic)
RJA	Reichsjustizamt
RKA	Reichskanzleramt
RP	Regierungspräsident
RR	Regierungsrat; ORR = Oberregierungsrat; Geh. RR = Geheimer Regierungsrat
RT	Reichstag
SaaleZ	Saale-Zeitung
SAO	Niedersächsisches Staatsarchiv-Osnabrück
SBDR	Stenographische Berichte des deutschen Reichstages
SBHA	Stenographische Berichte des Haus der Abgeordneten
SBNDR	Stenographische Berichte des Norddeutschen Reichstags
SchlZ	Schlesische Zeitung
S-H	Schleswig-Holstein
SD	Social Democrat; Social Democratic
SM	Staatsministerium, or (when preceding a name) Staatsminister
SS	Staatssekretär
SVZ	Schlesische Volkszeitung
VossZ	Vossische Zeitung
VP	Volkspartei
VS	Victorian Studies

W	Guelf Party
WPK	Wahlprüfungs-kommission
Z	Centrum
Ztg	Zeitung

PART ONE

The Framework

Introduction

> Many of the current theories about democracy seem to imply that to promote democracy you must first foster democrats. . . . Instead, we should allow for the possibility that circumstances may force, trick, lure, or cajole non-democrats into democratic behavior and that their beliefs may adjust in due course by some process of rationalization or adaptation.
>
> —*Dankwart Rustow (1970)*

In 1882, the Imperial Council (*Bundesrat*) of the German Empire received a letter from a sixty-year-old schoolteacher, begging it to abolish universal suffrage. Franz Pieczonka, from Mikorzyn in Posnania, recalled the days before 1848, when his peasant neighbors had known nothing of parliaments, were undisturbed by religious and ethnic differences, and lived in peace with their fellow men. The introduction of parliamentary institutions had completely destroyed this tranquillity. Hostile parties were now whipping up mutual hatred among the rural population, and if the war of words that was now part of every election ever spilled over into a war of blood and iron—then God help us! Pieczonka begged the Imperial Council not to consider it an impertinence if he suggested a change in Germany's voting law. Instead of universal suffrage, it should introduce a lottery. The choice of deputies would be no less democratic, he insisted (perhaps recalling the argument of Aristotle), since just as with the ballot, "so too with lotteries, all sorts and conditions of men can play. They win or they lose. But"—and this was the point—"they don't pillory and hate each other as a result."[1]

The schoolmaster's advice of 1882—shortly after national elections that were an unprecedented disaster for the government—was one of the many unsolicited letters that over the years arrived on the desks of Germany's leaders. Exasperated, obsequious, naive, and sophisticated, again and again they rang changes on the same themes: how to square divisive competition with community, freedom with authority, representation of the many with a voice for the few—in short, how to negotiate what the political scientist Dankwart Rustow calls "the transition to democracy." It is the beginning of this process—in which Germans practiced for a debut that had not yet been announced—that is the subject of this book.

---

[1] 8 Jan. 1882, BAB-L R1501/14693, Bl. 110.

DEMOCRACY AND THE REICHSTAG FRANCHISE

Democracy and its dangers was *the* theme of the nineteenth century, provoking agitation, speculation, and debate at least since the 1830s. Alexis de Tocqueville's *La Démocratie en Amérique* (1835, 1840), France's February revolution in 1848, and Britain's Reform Bills of 1832 and 1867 are all, in their different ways, landmarks for this preoccupation. Grave misgivings had been expressed even by radicals like John Stuart Mill about "the extreme unfitness [of] the laboring classes . . . for any order of things which would make any considerable demand on either their intellect or their virtue," and in Britain both extensions of the vote had come only after monster meetings, cabinet changes, and political crises drawn out over two years. Although "more than one member" of Disraeli's cabinet in 1867 ". . . spent a miserable arithmetical Sunday," as Asa Briggs put it, "making precise calculations of what the government's proposals implied" for the future composition of the House of Commons, the Second Reform Bill was denounced by its opponents as a "revolution," and even its cosponsor, Lord Derby, conceded that it was a "leap in the dark."[2]

How different across the channel! No popular agitation preceded Bismarck's far more daring leap to universal male suffrage that same year, and its possible ramifications sparked no extensive public debate. The contrast should not surprise us. Parliament, since time out of mind, had been the stage of the British national drama. Who could play and who could not was bound to be a question of greatest moment. But during the years when Chartism had been making democracy in England a household word, most residents of the German lands had "known nothing of parliaments"—as Schoolmaster Pieczonka, our advocate of the lottery, pointed out. Public interest had been fragmented among guilds, towns, and the corporate estates (*Stände*) of a multitude of provinces and states. Before 1848, statewide consultative assemblies had existed only in Baden, Bavaria, Hessen, and Württemberg. In central and eastern Germany, even these modest bodies were lacking. The year 1848 had indeed marked a caesura: nationally, with the gloriously democratic Frankfurt parliament; locally, with the *Stände* reforming themselves into more or less popular legislatures, and with new parliaments springing up elsewhere. But the glory had been brief. The Frankfurt Assembly, with its democratic suffrage law, disappeared in 1849, and although the state legislatures remained, in the following decade the revived monarchies revised them back into somnolence. By the sixties, with military and political earthquakes rocking Europe, there were other, more pressing, claimants for public attention.

For all these reasons, when the Prussian government submitted an article establishing manhood suffrage to the Constituent Reichstag of the North German Confederation in 1867, its reception was curiously neutral. Only three

---

[2] A. Briggs, *People* (1955), 272; Mill, *Representative Government* (1861), quoted on 247. Lord Cranborn ("revolution") and Derby quoted in Robert Blake, *Disraeli* (New York, 1967), 474f. Contrast M. Cowling, *1867* (1967), which rejects any connection between the reform and "revolution."

deputies outside of the constitutional commission explicitly supported it, but only two bothered to oppose it outright.[3] People did not expect much to change. Bismarck, after all, was its sponsor.

What *was* the German chancellor thinking of? We shall return to this question in our conclusion. For now it suffices to note that his dismal experience with elections during Prussia's constitutional conflict had left Bismarck with no love for a suffrage calibrated by wealth. Believing that modern principles were gaining ground with public opinion, yet confident that the masses were still moved by "monarchical needs and instincts," Bismarck's hunch was that simple manhood suffrage would in fact prove "more favorable to the conservative principle" than any franchise that favored the well endowed.[4] The gratifying results of its first test, in the elections of 1867, suggested that his gamble had paid off. It was left to a Pomeranian nobleman, Alexander von Below, a man whose consciousness of six centuries of Junker forebears may have sharpened his perception of just what was conservative and what was not, to point out the flaw in Bismarck's speculation: "It is impossible to win a Battle of Königgrätz before every election."[5]

Direct, equal, and—for "every German" who had reached the age of twenty-five—universal suffrage: this was the Frankfurt Assembly's revolutionary franchise that Bismarck had nailed to Prussia's banner in his struggle with Austria over dominion in Central Europe and then wrote into the electoral laws of the North German Confederation and the German Empire.[6] In its democratic sweep, the franchise was practically a novum for Europe. Although "every German" did not, as these words were then understood, include any women, even so Germany's precocity can be measured against the dates at which other European states acquired a suffrage similarly broad: Spain, 1890; Norway, 1906; Austria and Finland, 1907; Sweden, 1909; Italy, 1912; Denmark, 1915; Iceland, 1916; the Netherlands, 1918.[7] Only Greece, since 1844, and France (after earlier trials) since 1852 boasted a voting law as inclusive as Germany's.[8]

[3] G. v. Below, *Wahlrecht* (1909), 2–5; G. Meyer, *Wahlrecht* (1901), 239–40. T. Hamerow, "Origins" (1973), 105–20.

[4] Bis. to SM, 23 May 1866, BAB-L R43/685, Bl. 13f, 16v; these lines were cited by Finance Minister Bodelschwingh in his dissent: ibid., Bl. 18; Prussia's motion to reform the confederation in E.-R. Huber, ed., *Dokumente* (1964) 2: 192.

[5] Quoted by Below, *Wahlrecht*, 60.

[6] Bis.'s memo to the Prussian Ministry, 23 May 1866, BAP Reichskanzlei 685, Bl. 13–16v. Background: K. E. Pollmann, *Parlamentarismus* (1985), 73. Usefully emphasizing the franchise's role in the "national" project: Andreas Biefang, "Modernität wider Willen. Bemerkungen zur Entstehung des demokratischen Wahlrechts des Kaiserreichs," in *Gestaltungskraft des Politischen*, edited by W. Pyta and L. Richter (Berlin, 1998), 239–80.

[7] The Finnish franchise in 1906 and Danish and Norwegian in 1909 included women, but Denmark and Norway still had a property requirement. S. Rokkan and J. Meyriat, eds., *International Guide to Election Statistics* (The Hague, 1969), vol. I. A. Przeworski and J. Sprague, *Stones* (1988), 36, put Denmark's manhood suffrage in 1849. E.-R. Huber, *Verfassungsgeschichte* (1963) 3: 862n. 8 gives slightly different dates for female suffrage. France: J.-P. Charnay, *Le Suffrage* (1965), 83–91.

[8] Switzerland, whose franchise varied according to canton, is only a partial exception. That the exclusion of women did not automatically follow from the law's grammatical inflection ("Jeder

The United States, conventionally considered to have crossed the threshold to democracy in the 1830s, in practice barred those of African descent even after the Civil War had emancipated them. True, the Fifteenth Amendment, enacted only a year before Bismarck's manhood suffrage and Disraeli's Second Reform Bill, granted freedmen the vote. But by 1903 the eleven southern states, where most African-Americans lived, had effectively disfranchised them. The numbers of those excluded were not small. In six of these states, they made up more than half of the population; in only one were their numbers below 20 percent. The exclusion persisted until the invalidation of the white primary in 1944 and the passage of the Voting Rights Act in 1965.[9] And it is worth remembering that measures introduced to bar black Americans worked, quite intentionally, to exclude large numbers of the white poor as well. Morgan Kousser estimates that in the south the *white* males disfranchised ranged from nearly 25 percent in Virginia to nearly 60 percent in Louisiana. In the north, he maintains, large numbers of the foreign-born were also shut out.[10]

Britain, whose democratic *agon* long qualified as the master narrative of her nineteenth century, also experienced a major franchise extension in 1867.[11] But this Second Reform Bill, while doubling the electorate, was far from including most of Britain's adult population within what Gladstone called "the pale of the constitution."[12] In 1884, the third and last of the great nineteenth-century reform bills expanded voting rights still more, and commentators began to refer to Britain as a democracy (indeed "the most democratic of European nations").[13] Yet in spite of continuing Liberal efforts to broaden Britain's franchises (of which there were seven, uncodified and operating concurrently), as late as 1911 only an estimated 59 percent of male adults were able to vote. Moreover, plural franchises, repeatedly protected by a hereditary House of Lords, bestowed up to thirty (some said eighty!) *extra* votes on 200,000 to 600,000 men. As late as 1910, seventy-eight Conservative seats were attributed to the ability of some

---

Deutsche") is evident from the appearance of the same phrase in Art. 41 of the constitution of the Weimar Republic. R. Schuster, *Verfassungen* (1992), 179. The Prussian municipal ordinance of 1808, which proclaimed unmarried women citizens, had felt it necessary to be explicit in excluding "citizens of the female sex" from voting. Reprinted in B. Vogel et al., *Wahlen* (1971), 318.

[9] J. M. Kousser, *Shaping* (1974). Less pessimistic: G. M. Pomper, *Elections* (1968), 213–18. Figures for the African-American population were extrapolated from *Statistics of the Population of the United States Embracing the Tables of Race, Nationality, Sex, Selected Ages, and Occupations* (Washington, D.C., 1900), 40f.

[10] Kousser, *Shaping*, esp. chaps. 2 and 3; Louisiana, 49, 60f, 70f; Virginia, 71.

[11] This narrative was fundamentally challenged for the decades between 1832 and 1867 as early as 1953 by N. Gash, *Politics*, and more radically, in a Habermasian, Foucaultian vein, by J. Vernon, who maintains that "English politics became progressively less democratic during this period. . . ." Yet even he describes the debate over the *discourse* of "popular constitutionalism" as the "master narrative" of England's nineteenth century. *Politics* (1993), 9f (quotes), 38f, 107, 160, 320, 328f, 338.

[12] Briggs, *People*, 226. Because of the property qualification, the number of eligible voters after the Second Reform Bill is impossible to calculate with certainty.

[13] C. Seymour, *Reform* (1915), 2–5, 523f; G. Hermet et al., *Elections* (1978), xii; C. O'Leary, *Elimination* (1962), 2.

men to vote more than once.[14] A suffrage as egalitarian as Germany's was passed only in late 1918. And even that franchise was less democratic, for not only did it exclude until 1928 unmarried women under thirty (included in Germany after 1918), but plural voting, now limited to two per citizen, continued until 1949.

The egalitarianism of the German Empire's national franchise not only contrasted with the restrictions of other nations, it stood in equally sharp contrast to the various arrangements for electing representatives to the assemblies of her member states. In Prussian Landtag elections, for example, the tax bill in each precinct was divided into thirds, with the voters necessary to make up each third segregated accordingly. Here the biblical injunction that the last shall be first was strictly observed. The multitude of small taxpayers in the third class came forward to vote, orally, under the watchful eyes of the first two; then the thinner ranks of the second; and finally, in splendid isolation, the wealthy few of the first class. Within each class, this order was reversed. The heaviest taxed would be called upon to announce his choice, and others would follow, single file, each in order of his taxpaying importance, until the least of the voting brethren had been accommodated. Thus did elections to the Prussian state legislature visibly replicate the social hierarchy of each precinct. And this was only the first stage of a two-stage process that then required those elected from each class to select their respective district's deputies. The system endured until the fall of the monarchy in 1918. Small wonder that so many Prussians opted out of this particular ritual of inclusion. The election code for the German *national* parliament, however, put every male adult who was not a convicted felon, a bankrupt, a soldier or sailor on active duty, a ward of the court, or a charge on public charity on the same footing as the most blue-blooded baron, the most puissant factory owner in the land.[15]

The Reichstag franchise not only ignored all hierarchy, it was also radically individualizing. Although constitutional scholars insisted that voting was not the "right" of an individual, but a "public office entrusted in him by the whole," direct elections with secret balloting implied that a man's political decision was indeed a private one.[16] This was a revolutionary assumption. To vest the *commonweal* in the decisions of individuals, to displace matters of state into the private realm, implicitly reversed the values Germans were used to ascribing to public and private activity. It also reversed the direction of legitimate political influence. Open balloting, required in many countries and in most state elec-

---

[14] Edward Porritt, "Barriers Against Democracy in the British Electoral System," *Political Science Quarterly* 26/1 (Mar. 1911), 1–31; esp. 8; N. Blewett, "Franchise" (1965), 31, 44–51.

[15] Although the 1871 constitution did not say "equal," equality was implied by the distribution of one deputy for every 100,000 residents. O. Merkt, "Einteilung" (1912), col. 59; F. Naumann, "Ungleiches Wahlrecht" (1903), 580–82. Explaining the exclusion of military personnel: W. v. Tzschoppe, *Geschichte* (1890), 47f, 52. French soldiers were excluded until 1944–45.

[16] Quote: Huber, *Verfassungsgeschichte* 3: 864. The public aspect of the franchise was argued by theorists as different as P. Laband, G. Jellinek, and J. Hatschek. Hatschek, *Kommentar* (1920, completed in 1914), 184f.

tions in Germany, implied that the act of voting was a public trust, for which each voter could and should be held accountable by the other members of his community.[17] Secrecy, on the other hand, implied at least a potential separation of the individual's interests from those of his neighbors. What happened when this egalitarian, individualistic franchise was suddenly injected into a world whose assumptions and structures were still both hierarchical and communal? That is the question the following work will explore.

Did the Franchise Matter?

Historians have not taken the revolutionary implications of Bismarck's franchise as seriously as did Schoolmaster Pieczonka or the Junker Below. Mass enfranchisement is, after all, associated with democracy, and democracy is a term that one rarely encounters in descriptions of Imperial Germany. For the past fifty years teachers have written "No Experience With Democracy" on their blackboards—just under Versailles, Inflation, Depression, and Article 48—when listing the causes of the demise of Germany's first parliamentary regime in 1933. Prewar Germany was certainly no democracy. But can it be true that Germans came out of the empire with "no experience" with democratic practices?[18] From 1871 until 1893, national elections were scheduled every three years. Only the Scandinavian countries voted so often; in Britain seven years was the legal norm.[19] Moreover, unlike Britain, where as late as 1910 approximately 25 percent of the seats in the House of Commons went uncontested, only eight Reichstag candidates were unopposed in 1871, and virtually none thereafter. By 1893 an average of four candidates were competing for every seat.[20] Even when a district's "demographics" precluded a victory—

[17] Bismarck's view: Johannes Penzler, *Fürst Bismarck nach seiner Entlassung. Leben und Politik des Fürsten seit seinem Scheiden aus dem Amte auf Grund aller authentischen Kundgebungen*, 4 Bde. (Leipzig, 1897), 4: 344; similarly, Gash, *Politics*, 21, and Vernon, *Politics*, 138.

[18] William Carr's popular textbook, *A History of Germany* (London, 4th ed. 1991), which avoids the worst stereotypes, characterizes Germany on the eve of the Great War as an "autocracy" (181) and concludes its discussion of the Empire (145) by quoting Max Weber in 1917: "Bismarck left behind him a nation without any political education. . . . a nation accustomed to submit, under the label of constitutional monarchy, to anything which was decided for it, without criticising the politial qualifications of those who now occupied Bismarck's empty place." Cf. H. A. Winkler on Germany's "special path" (*Sonderweg*): "There can no longer be any doubt that Germany's deviance from the secular and normative process of democratisation is at the bottom of the catastrophies of the 20th century." "Bürgerliche Emanzipation und nationale Einigung. Zur Entstehung des Nationalliberalismus in Preussen," in H. Böhme, *Probleme der Reichsgründungszeit 1848–1879* (Berlin, 1968), 226–42; 237. More recently, "Abweichung" (1998).

[19] L. Bamberger, "Sitzungsperiode" (1871), 162; R. v. Bennigsen (NL) SBDR 1 Feb. 1888: 668. In 1888, a pro-government majority voted to extend the legislature period to five years, but unscheduled dissolutions kept the change from taking effect until 1893.

[20] H. Fenske, *Wahlrecht* (1972), 108ff. Between 1884 and 1914, from 1/4 to 1/3 of Commons's seats were often uncontested. W. B. Gwyn, *Democracy* (1962), 29–31; Hermet et al., *Elections*, viii. Calculations for 1871 are my own. I say there were "virtually" no uncontested districts after 1871

for the Catholic Centrum's candidates in Protestant districts, for Protestant candidates in Catholic districts, for Polish candidates in German districts, and for Social Democratic candidates in a wide variety of districts—increasingly the preordained minority party would at least show the flag with a candidate who could hold the victor's tally down. The hopelessness of his prospects did not mean that this "candidate for the count" (*Zählkandidat*) considered the contest only a nominal one.[21]

The political temperature was kept high by the contests for state assemblies that occurred between national elections and which, in spite of their restricted franchises, were inevitably reflectors of many of the issues and much of the heat of the imperial campaigns. And on five occasions—1878, 1887, 1890, 1893, and 1907—the regular rhythms determined by the length of the legislature period were interrupted, as the government, dissatisfied with a Reichstag that balked at passing its legislation, took its case to the people. In sum: beginning in 1870, a German living in Bavaria experienced a national or statewide election every two years; in Prussia, every twenty-one months; in Saxony, every fifteen months.[22] Granted, many people were undoubtedly little affected by an exercise that, however egalitarian, could only punctuate quotidian experience. But some towns and even regions became so politicized that their historians have independently described them as existing, even in nonelection years, within a "permanent election campaign."[23]

Does it matter? Skepticism about the significance of these contests need not be confined to those caught in a teleology ending in 1933. The limitations on the scope of the Reichstag, notably in foreign policy; the important powers reserved to the (less democratic) member states; the prerogatives of the crown, the army, and the bureaucracy; the traditional German deference to authority: these are known to every student of comparative politics. Given this context, both liberal contemporaries and later historians have been uneasy about ascribing too much significance to a suffrage whose "bonapartist" purpose they have seen through. For others, the suffrage has denoted simply the emergence of a "political mass market," a phrase coined at a time when the connotations of

---

because the victories of W. Wehrenpfennig in the 70s, of L. Windthorst in 1884 and 1890, and of Count J. v. Mirbach in 1887, while lopsided, were not unanimous. Mirbach, for example, got more than 10,000 votes in 7 Gumb., while 69 votes went to the Kaiser, 31 to an unnamed LL, and 69 to "others." There may have been a few similar cases of which I am unaware. In the Prussian LT, on the other hand, roughly 40% of all seats were uncontested. T. Kühne, "Elezioni" (1993), 68.

[21] Thus Field Marshal Helmut v. Moltke felt it necessary to explain his refusal to allow his name to be put up against the Z's undefeatable Windthorst by citing his commitment to Memel-Heydekrug. "Aus der Provinz," Lingen, clipping (probably the *Lingen'sches Wochenblatt*) from 30 Jan. 1887. SAO Dep. 62b.

[22] Calculated from G. A. Ritter/M. Niehuss, *Arbeitsbuch* (1980), 140, 155, 172. On the spillovers between elections at various levels: Suval, *Politics* (1985), 28f, 237f, 240; T. Kühne, *Dreiklassenwahlrecht* (1994), 225–28, 230.

[23] H.-W. Steil, *Wahlen* (1961), 109f; R. Kaiser, *Strömungen* (1963), 292; Kühne, *Dreiklassenwahlrecht*, 547; J. Sperber, *Voters* (1997), 167.

both "market" and "mass" were more pejorative than they are today.[24] The success of Germany's political parties was often owed, we are told, to "demagogy"—which is most definitely not the same as democracy.[25] A whole literature has accepted the premise of Germany's baleful "unsimultaneity"—industrial precocity coupled with "tardy" political development; while the declining fortunes of German liberalism (equated with the fortunes of the liberal parties) and even the continued strength of authoritarian institutions have been connected to a premature introduction of the mass franchise.[26] One sometimes gets the impression that manhood suffrage was yet one more barrier to the development of democracy in Germany.[27]

More common, however, has been the conviction that the suffrage was irrelevant because the Reichstag was only a fig leaf for absolutism, in Karl Liebknecht's famous phrase.[28] Historians who believe that, have understandably been less curious about the fig leaf than what they suspected was underneath. In my own view, the relegation of the Reichstag to "parliamentary trappings" is misleading.[29] As a legislature, the Reichstag was powerful. It could always defeat government bills—and did. And contrary to an old canard that is still current,[30] it could indeed initiate legislation, as a look at Article 23 of the Constitution as well as at the history of national legislation from the Jesuit Law in 1872 to the Lex Bassermann-Erzberger of 1913 easily demonstrates.[31] Nevertheless, it is true that the legislature neither chose the government nor could depose it. It enjoyed no organic connection to the executive, whose function was to serve the crown, a task constitutionally "incompatible," as the phrase went, with a seat and vote in parliament, whose function was to represent the people—although ministers could and did speak in the Reichstag at will. The German system, like the American, was based on a separation of powers—or as

---

[24] Coined by H. Rosenberg, *Depression* (1976), 137, the term reflected the distrust of democracy when exercised by Germans that was common—understandably—among Rosenberg's contemporaries. It has now become embedded in German historiography. P. Steinbach invokes the concept, even while he defends the significance of elections against such critics as Claus Offe. *Zähmung* (1990) 1: 55f.

[25] D. Blackbourn, *Class* (1980), 12, 60, 119, 140, 153, 157, 181, 196, 211, 226, 229f, 236–41; idem, "The Politics of Demagogy in Imperial Germany," in idem, *Populists and Patricians. Essays in Modern German History* (London, 1987), 217–45.

[26] D. S. White, *Party* (1976), 201–10; W. J. Mommsen, "Compromise" (1995), 37.

[27] E.g., P. Molt writes of its "negative influences" and "reactionary features" in *Reichstag* (1963), 330; similarly Eckhart Kehr, "Zur Genesis der Königlich Preußischen Reserveoffiziers," in *Der Primat der Innenpolitik*, by idem, edited by H.-U. Wehler (Berlin, 1965), 53–86; 57. An exception: Suval, *Politics*, 10.

[28] Quoted in Carr, *History*, 120. V. Berghahn, *Germany* (1993), 25f, quotes approvingly Liebknecht *père*'s characterization of the political system as "a princely insurance company against democracy."

[29] The phrase is from Mommsen, who is of two minds, but likens Germany's system to tsarist Russia. "Compromise," 37.

[30] E.g., Berghahn, *Germany*, 21; Sperber, *Voters*, 2.

[31] Schuster, *Verfassungen* (1992), 145. Such bills were designated *Initiativanträge*.

Germans called it: "dualism." Unlike its American counterpart, however, Germany's executive was not elected. And when the executive branch floats free of any institutional connection to the voting public, how can elections enforce that responsiveness to the popular will to which representative government classically aspires?

Underlying much of the dismissal of the German franchise has been an assumption that real democracy consists of sovereign parliaments funneling the wishes of elected majorities into policy outputs. Yet this assumption is based on the so-called Westminster model that, among industrial societies, existed in its pure form only in New Zealand—which itself altered it in November 1993.[32] In practice, a variety of quite ordinary institutional arrangements have worked just as effectively as Prussian-German "crypto-absolutism" to deny elected majorities the exercise of undiluted sovereignty. These include written constitutions that bind the hands of a majority, supreme courts appointed (not elected) for life that overrule them, federalism in which majorities in one body cancel majorities in another, and multiparty systems that require compromises that could never win a majority on a referendum, to name only a few. Since elections do not offer unambiguous policy choices, even voters on the winning side can rarely be assured of the policy "outcomes" they desire. Other historians may be as surprised as I to learn that "in fact there is a vigorous debate among political scientists about whether elections in democracies make any real difference to the substance of public policy."[33] This is not a debate my book will engage; my point is only that it seems clear that no special unreality can be claimed for the elections in Imperial Germany.

Those who doubt, however, that in the absence of parliamentary government, German elections had anything to do with power should ask themselves why the parties and especially the government put so much energy into winning them? Why, in the decade before the war, were Social Democrats crowding the streets of Berlin to demand this same Reichstag franchise for Prussia's *state* parliament—whose majority, after all, also lacked the authority to choose the executive?

We might also ask what, even on the most minimal interpretation, do popular elections do? Not the least of an election's functions is to legitimate the political system that makes the election itself possible. Elections do this in part through the folderol associated with them—the speeches, the rallies, the leaflets, the public attention generally: rituals that some have likened, in the expense in time, money, and pomp, to medieval coronations. Elections also legiti-

---

[32] Robert W. Jackman, "Elections and the Democratic Class Struggle," *World Politics* 29 (Oct. 1986): 123–46; esp. 132f, and 145; more generally, W. Kaltefleiter and P. Nißen, *Wahlforschung* (1980); A. Lijphart, *Democracies* (1984), 1–20; D. Nohlen, *Wahlrecht* (1986).

[33] A brilliant summary of just what elections do and do not do in democracies: M. Harrop and W. L. Miller, *Elections* (1987), 244–69; quote on 252; and of what they do and do not do in non-democratic settings: Guy Hermet, "State-Controlled Elections: A Framework," in *Elections Without Choice*, edited by G. Hermet et al. (New York, 1978), 1–18; esp. 13–16.

mate the system by enlisting the active participation of the political nation. Knowing this, governments go to considerable lengths to secure high turnouts. With heavy participation, even contests that are lost by the group in power help to legitimate the procedures, the political community, and the boundaries of the state. Thus the massive Catholic boycott of the 1983 referendum in Northern Ireland on whether to remain in the United Kingdom more than matched the significance of the 99 percent yes-vote of the remaining electorate.[34] Conversely, German Catholics, in flooding to the polls to defeat Bismarck's government during the Kulturkampf of the 1870s, affirmed the constitution he had given Germany and began their own integration into an empire whose boundaries, by excluding Austria, had turned them into a permanent minority. Later on, Social Democrats, in the very act of piling up oppositional tallies in contest after contest, were bestowing legitimacy on the Reichstag they claimed to scorn.

This story is well known to historians under the rubric "negative integration."[35] But the cunning of history works in more than one direction. While imperial elections undoubtedly legitimated the institutions of the empire—quite contrary to the intentions of millions of voters who voiced not approval but dissent with their ballots—these same elections also legitimated the opposition. For it is the unique achievement of competitive elections, as we shall see in chapter 9, that they build into the very mechanism that legitimizes the state the message that opposition too is legitimate, that "there is more than one side to every political issue." In this way, elections help support and sustain a plural polity.[36]

But this ironic tale of unintended consequences is not, of course, the whole story of what popular elections "do." At least as important for a polity as the existence of rituals of legitimation is the form those rituals take. Coronations are rituals that embody the unity of a society at a spectacular and transcendent level. In traditional cultures—England before the First Reform Bill, for example—elections often proceeded in a similarly acclamative mode, as a celebration of the community that was to be represented. When German villages chose their notables to go to Frankfurt in 1848, with no campaigning necessary, we see something of the same thing. But election rituals cease to resemble coronation rituals precisely as they become "democratic"—that is, not just popular, but competitive. Then elections make visible the divisions within the polity, thematize them—and reinforce them. Here is what so distressed our schoolmaster, Franz Pieczonka. Competitive elections are, to filch William James's memorable phrase, the "moral equivalent" of civil war. They express a society's inevitable hostilities, even as they begin to channel them into nonviolent paths. In so doing, they need not refer to anything beyond themselves; that is, they may be, at least in part, a "game." But they are a zero-sum game. They are about

[34] Harrop/Miller, *Elections*, 259.

[35] Guenther Roth, *The Social Democrats in Imperial Germany: A Study in Working Class Isolation and National Integration* (Totowa, N.J., 1963); cf. also Przeworski, "Social Democracy as a Historical Phenomenon," in idem, *Capitalism and Social Democracy* (Cambridge, 1985), 17.

[36] Harrop/Miller, *Elections*, 261.

winning and losing: that is, about power. When we ponder the meaning of elections for participants, we should always keep this in mind.

SOURCES FOR THIS STUDY

*"Literaturkenntnis schützt vor Neuentdeckungen."** No one is more conscious of the truth of Hermann Heimpel's *mot* than I. There is virtually no work on any aspect of the Kaiserreich that could not contribute something to our understanding of Germany's transition to democracy, and a lifetime would not be enough to do justice to all of them. This project has been able to build upon a wealth of existing scholarship: on the histories of parties and interest groups; on longitudinal analyses of elections—in towns, in districts, in regions, and in press coverage; on case studies of particular campaigns; on the social and economic variables behind voting behavior. Even so, I believe that my work departs from that of my colleagues in several important ways.

First, with the exception of statistical studies, relatively little election scholarship attempts to encompass the entire political spectrum or to take in the German Empire, temporally and geographically, as a whole.[37] Second, no study of this scope that I know so consciously locates its story in the world of contemporary "franchise regimes."[38] For this reason I hope it may interest political scientists, historical sociologists, and legal scholars, as well as those historians whose specialty lies outside Germany. Comparative history is never pursued as often as our colleagues in the social sciences would like—not least because historians are rarely able to isolate all of the variables necessary to produce the conclusiveness we all desire.[39] I cannot claim to be a comparative historian in any rigorous sense, but I do recognize a strong familial resemblance in the aspirations, activities, and political institutions of what we have come to know as "the West." The fact that ordinary historians are unable to be systematic should not bar us from being every bit as alert to these family resemblances as were our subjects themselves.[40] Throughout this study it is

* "Bibliographical knowledge protects one from making new discoveries."

[37] Two distinguished exceptions are K. Rohe's superb *Wahlen* (1992), whose temporal scope is even broader than mine, and J. Sperber's *Voters*, which synthesizes the results of ecological regressions with a mastery of the literature. An excellent work that I would like to think is most like my own, Kühne's *Dreiklassenwahlrecht*, although full of insights about national politics, treats the very different Prussian franchise, and concentrates on the Wilhelmine period.

[38] A notable exception is E. Bendikat, *Wahlkämpfe* (1988), which pursues comparative history more systematically than I, but for a five-year period. Suval's *Politics* is also attentive to comparisons, but barely touches the Bismarckian era and focuses on only three of Germany's 397 districts.

[39] "The bridge between historical observations and general theory is the substitution of variables for proper names of social systems in the course of comparative research." A. Przeworski and H. Teune, *The Logic of Comparative Social Inquiry* (New York, 1970): 17–30; 25, quoted in S. Bartolini and P. Mair, *Identity* (1990), 129n. 1.

[40] E.g., the British *Report on the Practice Prevailing in Certain European Countries in Contests for Election to Representative Legislative Assemblies. . . .* (1881). Hereafter cited as Granville Sur-

my hope that the reader will be made aware of these parallels—and of the differences.[41]

Third, my account exploits a body of material that is usually overlooked in election scholarship. These are the election scrutinies (*Wahlprüfungen*): the petitions charging misconduct, the depositions of witnesses taken in response, and the deliberations of Reichstag committees charged with evaluating them.[42] They add a significant dimension to the picture provided by government files, the press, memoirs, and the commentary of legal scholars (to which the letters and postcards of voters like Pieczonka provide a plebeian obbligato); and they have proven especially valuable for the Reich's first two decades, when other sources are less full. The testimonies in these scrutinies are diffuse, full of incoherencies, mixed together with the whole who-struck-John of life itself. They resist topical organization at the same time that their very concreteness tempts us to a certainty historians are rarely granted. It is a temptation I have tried to resist. For the humble are also partisans, and even when they are not, we need to be aware that their witness has often been extracted under circumstances likely to reward the disingenuous and punish the candid.[43] Nevertheless for all their difficulties, the scrutinies are our best source for how elections were actually experienced. They provide the acid that can pick out those homely figures—farmers and brewers, miners and mayors, constables and priests—that are otherwise invisible in the electoral landscape. The practices of these men, we shall see, were often no less authoritarian than the opinions of Franz Pieczonka and Alexander von Below. They introduce us to electoral democracy with a human face—warts and all.

THE PLAN OF THIS BOOK

Several decades ago the political scientist Dankwart Rustow, frustrated by his discipline's preoccupation with what makes democracies survive, began to refocus attention on how traditional or authoritarian societies make the transit to

---

vey Nr. 1. The report was updated for at least two consecutive years, and sent to AA; Gordon, AA to Bötticher, 16 Aug., 17 Sept. 1881, 33 May 1882, BAB-L R1501/14451, Bl. 44–59, 61–63, 99–109v.

[41] I am aware that my pragmatism about comparisons would not satisfy such rigorists as Stanley Lieberson, "Small N's and Big Conclusions: An Examination of the Reasoning in Comparative Studies Based on a Small Number of Cases," *Social Forces* 70/2 (Dec. 1991): 307–20.

[42] Notable exceptions to the neglect of the *Wahlprüfungen* are Pollmann, *Parlamentarismus*; B. Fairbairn, "Authority vs. Democracy" (1990) and *Democracy* (1997); and Kühne, *Dreiklassenwahlrecht*, many of whose discoveries for LT elections in Prussia might justifiably be applied to RT elections for the whole empire. Suval's treatment of the scrutinies was perfunctory, since his premise was that the elections were not only honest, but free. *Politics*, 4, 11, 40–42, 51, 244. Misconduct is less apt to be overlooked in works that analyze the elections of particular regions. One of the best is H. Hiery's *Reichstagswahlen* (1986), which takes the step of problematizing freedom and coercion.

[43] On some occasions the culture of election protests encouraged false witness: e.g., 3 Danzig, AnlDR (1882/83, 5/II, Bd. 5) DS 80: 338–49. While ordinary citizens were usually put under oath, the RT often felt it insulting to require an oath from an accused official. 14 Württ. (Ulm) AnlDR (1881/82, 5/I, Bd. 2) DS 113: 422, 2 Saxe-Weimar, AnlDR (1893/94, 9/II, Bd.2) DS 165: 910.

democracy in the first place. His influential essay marked an important shift away from functionalist analyses of economic and social structures and toward putting history (and contingency) back into the picture. Though described by supporters as a "theory," what Rustow offered his colleagues was not a formula enabling prediction, but the merest outline of a narrative, a roomy plot summary, beguiling in its simplicity, that turns out to describe our own story remarkably well.[44] It requires as its starting point neither an egalitarian social structure nor democratic attitudes (tolerance, civility, agreement on procedures, a consensus on fundamentals), since a civic culture, he argued, is an effect, rather than a cause, of democracy. Rustow's narrative consisted of four parts: one precondition and three "phases." (1) The precondition is a state whose boundaries the majority of the people accept. (2) The engine that pushes a country down a path that *may* lead to democracy is a "hot family feud": a protracted, inconclusive conflict between two or more well-entrenched forces, neither of which is able to defeat the other, over an issue that has "profound meaning" to both. It is no hindrance that at least one (and maybe both) of these sides are not democrats (if they were, there would be no incentive to develop procedures for dealing with conflict), nor that the struggle produces stalemate. It is the intensity and persistence of the conflict or conflicts that promote the tactical compromises, the horse-trading, the reluctantly tolerated procedural expedients so crucial to the practice of democracy.[45] (3) At some point, however (and here is the element of contingency), political leaders must consciously decide to accept the existence of diversity and to "institutionalize some crucial aspect of democratic procedure"—although whether they do so wholesale (as happened in Sweden in 1907) or on the installment plan (as in Britain, over the course of centuries) is a matter of indifference. Neither does it matter that the struggle continues after such decisions are made. In democracies, procedures regulate, but do not end, the fight. (4) Finally, there is the all-important "habituation" to open political conflict that makes the hard decisions of the leadership grudgingly palatable to followers. People who would much rather have won outright become practiced at living with unwelcome compromises, and competition rewards those who support the procedures that make competition possible—producing what Rustow calls a "Darwinian selectivity in favor of convinced democrats."[46]

The Rustowian narrative, which I came upon after completing this manuscript, helps put Germany's story into perspective. It turns some of the very features that have led us to dismiss the imperial period as at best irrelevant to later democrats, at worst, a heavy burden, on their head: the fact that German electoral politics began within the framework of a very well policed state; the existence of intractable struggles over culture and class; the empire's "chronic

---

[44] Narrative is my term. Rustow calls it a "dynamic" or "genetic" model, and refers to "phases." M. S. Fish terms it a "path-dependent" theory. "Crisis" (1996), quote: 145; see also 141–45, 159.

[45] "Transitions," quotes: 342, 355.

[46] Ibid., 358. For problems of consent that democratic elections do *not* solve: R. Rose, "Choice" (1978), 196–212.

crisis" (in the view of some) in the nineties, its "stalemate" (in the view of others) thereafter. These features are not, nota bene, transformed into evidence that the Kaiserreich was a democracy. It was not. But instead of being seen as roadblocks, they can be recognized as signposts marking an (always reversible) journey. In the work that follows I shall on occasion refer back to the Rustowian narrative, since its central story—that people *learn* democracy only by practicing—is my own.

Rustow opened his own argument by claiming that "history . . . is far too important a topic to be left just to historians."[47] I heartily agree, but would add: and politics is too important to be left to political scientists. In recent years the theoretical literature on democratization has tended to divide, if I may oversimplify a bit, between what has been called the "new institutionalism" and approaches that put the spotlight on culture, mentality, experience.[48] In the latter, causality flows, at least implicitly, from society to politics, and institutions are little more than the arena in which politics takes place. For institutionalists, on the other hand, the rules of the game are active agents in effecting political outcomes, especially when, as proponents have recently stressed, they provide incentives for actors to abide by them.[49] The following study can contribute to the institutionalist-culturalist debate, not only by giving the "social scientific mind," as Clifford Geertz has called it, "bodied stuff on which to feed,"[50] but also by situating both components, institutions and culture, in time, and showing more precisely how they interact.

My study is divided into three parts. Part One, "The Framework" (chapters 1–3) outlines the legal, international, and local contexts in which German voting took place. Part Two, "Fields of Force" (chapters 4–7), analyzes the coercive pressures that were brought to bear upon a voter's choice. Part Three, "Degrees of Freedom" (chapters 8–11) examines the ways in which these local webs of power were perforated by other forces, including those from below. In broadest terms, Parts One and Two are concerned with the Old, and Part Three, with the New; but political Germany's most visible novelty, mobilization, makes its first appearance in chapter 4, while the analysis in chapter 6 (on rural

[47] "Transitions," 347.

[48] There are, of course, many ways of slicing this theoretical cake, and some might substitute "social" for "cultural," as more inclusive. The stimulating essay by J. G. March and J. P. Olsen, "Institutionalism" (1984), 738, 741, for example, develops quite complex categories and puts "culture" in all of them. Clearer, because it divides the variables into conflict structures and institutions: Kaltefleiter/Nißen, *Wahlforschung*, 27–29. German political science, which earlier emphasized institutionalist components, has recently discovered culture. See T. Kühne, "Wahlrecht-Wahlverhalten-Wahlkultur" (1993), a magisterial survey of the historical and social scientific literature, which refers (482) to this "paradigm change." R. D. Putnam, in his discussions of "social capital," has given the Tocquevillian cultural argument its most influential recent embodiment. *Making* (1993); idem, "Bowling," 65–78.

[49] Here as elsewhere, I am indebted to numerous conversations with M. Kreuzer, whose *Institutions* (2000) demonstrates these ideas with more rigor and detail, and who introduced me to Rustow and to A. Przeworski's influential *Democracy* (1991), with its game-theoretical perspective.

[50] Geertz, "Thick Description: Toward an Interpretative Theory of Culture," in *The Interpretation of Cultures* (New York, 1973), 3–30; esp. 23.

east Elbia) presents a picture of authority, unsoftened by signs of solidarity, that lasted as long as the empire itself.

Within these broad headings, each chapter is topical and each (with few exceptions) covers the entire chronology of the Reich. Chapters 4 and 5, on the Catholic clergy, introduce us to what was in fact the empire's first "hot family feud": the "battle for culture." Here we see the complex connections between anxieties over the franchise, Kulturkampf legislation, and mass mobilization. We also examine the by-no-means democratic clergy, and the reciprocal relationship between representations of the priest and those of the "people" enfranchised by the new law. Chapters 6 and 7, on bread lords, look first at the changing power (real and imagined) of the "Junker," and then at other kinds of employers. In spotlighting the extraordinary lengths to which bread lords in town and country would go in order to control the votes of their dependents, regardless of any effect on national outcomes, we become aware of their perception of the franchise as something whose very existence diminished their previously seamless authority. We can also see why the possibility of voting was seized by subordinates with such fervor, as if the mere act of casting a ballot were itself an emancipation.

But emancipation—the overcoming of deference and the construction of dissent—is not the whole story, or else practicing democracy would be simply a whiggish version of one of the more usual *Sonderweg* narratives. Although as an account of elections, our center of gravity naturally lies in the constituencies, and while I do not pretend to tackle the complicated question of regime, no adequate account of developing democratic practices can avoid a look at the strategies and responses of power holders at the national level. Consequently, in chapter 8 we move briefly away from the precincts and into Berlin, where Rustow's "conscious decision" took place. This decision was embodied, first, in the deputies' decade-long struggle to guarantee the secrecy of the ballot, and second, in the government's reluctant collaboration with them in 1903. Forced by the Reichstag, the government's reversal suggests that a shift in the balance of power between the executive and legislative branch was beginning to take place. It suggests too that the function of elections was expanding: from emancipation to arbitration. Both developments presuppose, however, that enough freedom already existed in the constituencies to have created the Reichstag's clamorous majorities in the first place.

In the succeeding chapters I try to locate just where these degrees of freedom lay. They lay in the structural conditions of the late empire (discussed in the rest of chapter 8), especially in economic opportunities and increasing material security. These provided the necessary but by no means sufficient conditions for the voter's dissent. A degree of freedom also lay, as we shall see in chapters 9 and 10, in shared cultural norms—especially an ingrained legalism—that dissenters repeatedly invoked; as well as in those very traditional weapons of the community, such as ostracism and boycott, upon which modern parties could build. By chapter 11 we are entirely in the "modern" world, looking at the power of organization and money in political campaigns. The need for funds proved to be a major spur to party development, yet it raised questions—as it does today—about who and what was actually being empowered when an electorate becomes so large that only those disposing of tremendous resources can reach it.

The state, whose self-confidence and legitimacy was both the guarantor of the public peace on which competitive elections always depend, and in Germany the main obstacle to moving to a fully parliamentary regime, appears in the background throughout these chapters. Of all forms of election misconduct, the contemporary consensus was broadest in condemning electioneering on the part of its officials.[51] The possibilities and limits of state influence are treated systematically, however, only as part of the Conclusion (chapter 12). The absence of a fuller treatment may be a shortcoming—not least because it wrongly implies that the only important changes were those from below and that the transformation of substructures obviated significant alterations in the powerful superstructures of the state. But others have taken up this theme, and as Dale van Kley has written in another context: enough is enough.

This book will not attempt to trace and explain the patterns of election victory and defeat—who voted for whom and why. For these questions we already have a considerable literature, much of it statistical.[52] My aim, rather, is to examine how Germans experienced their new franchise, to understand what practicing electoral politics in a democratic key meant in the half century preceding Germany's first parliamentary government.[53]

The discussion will unfold slowly. One of my objects in telling so many stories is not only to convey the quotidian experience of electoral politics (Rustow's "habituation"), but also to convince the reader that here were attitudes and behavior common across regions, across decades, across political parties: ways of responding that we can justifiably call, not just Prussian or Saxon or Bavarian, but German. At the same time, it will become clear that the reference group for Germans, and not only those constitutional lawyers, bureaucrats, and Reichstag deputies most continually occupied with politics, was their fellow Europeans. Far from thinking that they constituted some historical anomaly, some exceptional case, Germans measured their own legality against

---

[51] A consensus that continues in the FRG today: B.-D. Olschewski, *Wahlprüfungen* (1970); A. v. Heyl, *Wahlfreiheit* (1975).

[52] E.g., Monika Wölk, *Der preußische Volksschulabsolvent als Reichstagswähler 1871–1912. Ein Beitrag zur Historischen Wahlforschung in Deutschland* (Berlin, 1980); M. Neugebauer-Wölk, *Wählergenerationen* (1987); Horst Nöcker, *Wählerentscheidung unter Demokratischem und Klassenwahlrecht. Eine vergleichende Statistik der Reichstags- und Landtags-Wahlergebnisse in Preussen 1903 nebst Angaben zu Wirtschafts- und Sozialstruktur nach Vergleichsgebieten* (Berlin, 1987); idem, *Der Preussische Reichstagswähler in Kaiserreich und Republik. Analyse-Interpretation-Dokumentation. Ein historisch-statistischer Beitrag zum Kontinuitätsproblem eines epochenübergreifenden Wählerverhaltens* (Berlin, 1987); J. Schmädeke, *Wählerbewegung* (1995); J. R. Winkler, *Sozialstruktur* (1995); Sperber, *Voters* (1997).

[53] "Elections before democracy" in other countries: E. Posada-Carbó, ed., *Elections* (1996).

developments outside their borders; they judged the norms and practices of their countrymen with an eye to the decent opinion of mankind.[54]

I have avoided defining democracy, for I feel that here, at least, Nietzsche got it right: "All concepts that sum up an entire process semiotically elude definition; definable is only that which has no history."[55] The problem is not only democracy's multiplicity of referents: to social classes and social structures, to constitutions and procedures, to attitudes and norms. The problem is also that, with its powerfully normative penumbra, democracy belongs to a class that the philosopher W. B. Gallie once identified as "essentially contested concepts," concepts whose definition and usage will always be subject to disputes that are both genuine and fundamentally unresolvable.[56] No contemporary would have described the Kaiserreich as a democracy; but men could, and did, describe some of its practices and attitudes as democratic, and many of its politicians (usually pejoratively) as democrats.[57] In the idiom of the nineteenth century, "democratic" often meant simply plebeian, and "democracy," plebeian enfranchisement.

Are there connections between plebeian enfranchisement and our own, modern democracy? Although the whole thrust of this work suggests that there are, I am aware that "modern" is a concept as treacherous as "democracy" itself. E. L. Jones has warned historians of the Industrial Revolution against their tendency toward "a mild form of anachronism," in which the modern economy is the *explanandum*, but the *explanans* (e.g., canals and cotton) usually leads to an "implicit terminus" around 1907 rather than to the electronics, plastics, and hypermarkets of today.[58] The reverse warning should apply to political historians. We must continually remind ourselves that the modern democracy to which imperial German practice might be compared is not that of the late twentieth, but the late nineteenth, century. And *that* democracy is no more like the democracy of our own time and (American) place—with its weak parties, low turnouts, freelance consultants, and millionaire candidates—than the "modern" smokestack is like the computer chip.

In the study that follows we shall find some things that do remind us of our

---

[54] E.g., Windthorst studied the English election reports, thankful that "the means of persuasion [used in England] do not yet obtain [here]." SBDR 28 Mar. 1871: 26. Bunsen blamed France's practice of official candidates for the Second Empire's fate. SBDR 29 Mar. 1871: 43. The German govt. was interested in foreign election modes and mores: Report of Prussian envoy on the Belgian debate on universal suffrage, 6 July 1883, in Akten Belgien; and Report of AA of 24 Aug. 1883 on the British Parliament's reports, in Akten England: BAB-L R1501/14451, Bl. 186f.

[55] *Zur Geneologie der Moral* in *Sämtliche Werke. Kritische Studienausgabe* (Munich, 1988) 5: 317.

[56] "Essentially Contested Concepts," *Proceedings of the Aristotelian Society*, New Series, 56 (1955–56): 167–98, esp. 171f; on democracy: 183–87.

[57] Fairbairn's title, *Democracy in the Undemocratic State* (1997), brilliantly captures this difficulty.

[58] *Growth Recurring. Economic Change in World History* (Oxford and New York, 1988), 180.

own kind of democracy: dirty tricks, certainly, and the longing for a politics, or at least a public life, beyond conflict. But we shall also find things that don't: rapid mobilization and mass participation—though unevenly across the population; strong parties with considerable grassroots vitality, but with curiously disposable candidates.[59] Although the picture includes harbingers of the Weimar Republic's later weaknesses, it includes relatively few signs of the violence, radicalism, and charismatic forms of leadership that would bring, in the early 1930s, parliamentary democracy down.

More generally, we shall see Germans rapidly transforming a segmentary, authoritarian, and communal culture that professed to abhor partisanship of any kind into a nationalized, participatory, public culture, one in which partisan loyalties organized expectations and structured much of public life. We shall see how they created institutions, such as the "discussion speaker," that both stimulated and channeled conflict in the political *Alltag*. We shall see how a "legalistic culture," as one scholar has described it,[60] bore fruit in genuinely competitive elections—which some consider the root and others the defining feature of democracy.[61]

In the late 1880s, an American radical remarked that he had "always been in favor of the idea that the workers should go to the ballot box—even if it only be for practice, as they do in Germany. . . ."[62] The man was invoking, of course, the first of the several meanings of "practice": "to work at repeatedly, so as to become proficient."[63] Practicing democracy, like practicing the piano, involves inevitable, repeated failure. Unlike those practicing the piano, however, beginners at democracy have no tutors who can impart preexisting knowledge nor even a prescribed piece to play. Democracy is no single melody, but a mix of possible conventions and rules. The story of Germans *practicing* at democracy will sound whiggish to some readers and outrageous to others—used as we are to the Central European narrative that begins in authority and coercion and culminates, not in democracy, but in dictatorship and collapse. What about caesarism, bonapartism, manipulation, demagogy, the subaltern-mentality, and all those other forces repeatedly invoked as so many pathologies in the German body politic? In the following chapters we shall certainly catch glimpses of the usual suspects, if we do not exactly round them up. But at the outset let us recall that such phenomena are not themselves the negations of democracy, but among its many possible children—children no less natural for being unwanted. Like Liberalism and like Socialism, Democracy in practice has more than its share of ambiguities, ambiguities that its champions may dismiss as

[59] By the 1880s a larger proportion of the Düsseldorf's electorate belonged to a political party than in the 1980s. N. Schloßmacher, *Düsseldorf* (1985), 253.

[60] T. Poguntke, "Parties in a Legalistic Culture" (1997), 185–215. Contrast A. Hall, "Means" (1974).

[61] D. Nohlen, *Wahlrecht*, 18.

[62] Dr. Ernst Schmidt, chairman of the Anarchists' Defense Committee after the Haymarket riots. Quoted from *Sozialdemokrat*, 25 July 1886, by R. C. Sun, "Martyrdom" (1986), 59.

[63] *Webster's Ninth New Collegiate Dictionary* (1985).

mere exceptions "in practice," but ones to which its contemporary critics were never blind.

Practice, contrary to what we tell our children, does not make perfect. Democracy knows no virtuosi. I acknowledge that Imperial Germany—like prewar England, America, and France—did not enjoy full democracy (although each did not for different, and interesting, reasons). But if we do not ask democracy to be responsible for too much, we can recognize that Bismarck's democratic franchise, however improbable its Minerva-like birth, did not preclude democratization, but encouraged it. Democracy in practice, like any skill, could improve only *with* practice.

The Morphology of Election Misconduct:
International Comparisons

> The incidental . . . counts for nothing, when it is purely incidental,
> when there's nothing in it. But when something's in it, then it is
> essential, because it always reveals the human element.
>
> —*Theodor Fontane*

AN ESSENTIAL requisite of the election's dual ability to legitimate both the
regime and its opposition is the confidence of participants in what Americans
called purity and the French, *sincérité*: genuine competition and an honest
count. Laws in themselves are no guarantors of an election's honesty, safety,
and especially its freedom. The first two of these elements, as we shall see later
in this chapter, Germans enjoyed. They were fortunate legacies bequeathed to
the developing constitutional state from its bureaucratic-absolutist past. The
third, the ability to vote freely, was hard-won over the course of half a century.
This struggle for free elections—in which autonomy for the individual and
liberty for oppositional groups were as apt to conflict as they were to reinforce
each other—is the meta-narrative of our story. In this chapter we shall take a
bird's-eye view of electoral "impurity"—and the procedures contemporaries de-
vised to deal with it. Such a perspective, and the comparisons it allows us to
make, can tell us much about the assumptions underlying German political life.

THE MAGNITUDE OF MISCONDUCT

The assumption that voting is "sincere" is an occupational requirement for
quantitative historians, who must derive generalizations about voters' choices
from outcome statistics.[1] Consequently, the volume of German challenges, and
the degree to which they occupied the legislators, may come as some surprise.
During the first fifty-seven sittings of its first session, the Reichstag dealt with
no fewer than fifty-eight protests.[2] By 1876, the process of evaluating the chal-

---

[1] A point brilliantly argued by P. H. Argersinger, "Perspectives" (1985/6), 670–71. In German, in
which the term for election is "choice" (*Wahl*), the very notion of "unfree elections" is an oxy-
moron, as Dieter Nohlen has pointed out. Cited in Heyl, *Wahlfreiheit*, 15. Also Olschewski, *Wahlprüfung*, 28.

[2] My count. I am treating petitions and *Beschwerde* (complaints) as a single category and will use

lenges had become such a burden to its committee system that it established a standing parliamentary Election Commission (*Wahlprüfungs-Kommission*: literally, Election Validation Commission) to handle the job. But the caseload continued to increase, and even this body, working almost full time, found it impossible to bring closure to all of the charges outstanding. When the fifth legislative period came to an end in December 1884, and it was time to hold new elections, twenty seats from 1881 were still undecided.[3]

A report in the prestigious *Annalen des Deutschen Reichs* revealed that as of the 1887 election, more than 60 percent of the empire's 397 constituencies had been the subject of formal complaint.[4] Every region, urban and rural, was represented, except for the Upper Palatinate and Münster and its environs—anomalies that suggest not so much voting freedom as the absence of significant competition in these most solidly Catholic of political landscapes.[5] Many severely compromised victories escaped annulment for reasons having little to do with the justice of the complaint. Challenges arriving after the filing deadline or suffering other technical shortcomings were dismissed. Deputies whose elections had been impeached remained voting members of parliament until formally unseated, and it was not unknown for the beneficiary of alleged wrongdoing to work to delay the deciding vote—or to cast it himself. Most frequently, legislators found themselves unable to put a number on the votes that malfeasance had tainted, a fatal difficulty for a Reichstag that, with occasional exceptions, took a mathematical rather than a holistic approach to evaluating the validity of election returns. If after subtracting the disallowed votes, the winner's majority still stood, the election was confirmed, no matter how egregious the behavior of the victor or his supporters. For all these reasons, the number of elections finally overturned bore no relationship to the number of challenges whose charges were found to have merit. Of the 108 elections between 1871 and 1887 that were "impeached" (*beanstandet*)—that is, their validation withheld pending an investigation—only twenty-eight were declared invalid. This was about 8 percent of those petitioned. But the *Annalen* estimated that about 42 percent would have been overturned had not the process dragged out so long that the death of the victor, his preemptive resignation, or the end of the legislative period intervened first.[6] These figures would have looked even worse had

---

the terms interchangeably with the terms "protest" and "challenge," although *Beschwerde* is a technical term for a complaint that even if valid, would not necessarily result in overthrowing an election.

[3] H. Marquardsen (NL) SBDR 10 Dec. 1884: 266. Slightly lower figures: G. Leser, *Untersuchungen* (1908), 57.

[4] T. Prengel, "Beiträge" (1892), 4, 20. There are some discrepancies in Prengel's data, as well as some between his data and my own counts, but they concern details, and do not invalidate the general picture.

[5] My counts. They differ from Prengel's in 1874 and 1877 by two challenges—but in a different direction each time.

[6] The 28 invalidated elections included an unspecified number whose illegalities were so obvious that the intervening step of impeachment was skipped. Prengel, "Beiträge," 19f. Although P. includes the date 1890 in his title, his calculations cover only the first 7 legislature periods.

the *Annalen* included the election of February 1890. One of the victories challenged was that of the young Landrat, Theobald von Bethmann Hollweg, Imperial Germany's future—and last peacetime—chancellor, thus ending after four months his parliamentary career.[7]

Since no franchise regime has been spared complaints about election propriety, it is important to put these numbers in perspective. The Reichstag received fifty-six petitions in 1881, eighty-one in 1884, recorded a slight fall-off in 1887, and then received seventy-three in 1890. In the United States, in contrast, the number of petitions submitted after each congressional election in the nineteenth century's last three decades averaged thirteen.[8] Indeed, only 452 of the roughly 16,000 contests for the House of Representatives during its entire first 128 years of existence were the object of postelection challenges. This was only twenty-five more complaints than were sent to the imperial Reichstag during its first sixteen years.[9]

As for Britain, in the six general elections following the Great Reform Bill of 1832 fewer than 10 percent of all victories were petitioned and fewer than 5 percent, formally investigated—and this in an era widely considered to have been corruption's golden age. Since not all of the House of Commons's 657 seats were actually contested in every election, these figures probably underestimate the British propensity toward misconduct. Even so, the contrast with the Reichstag, where postelection challenges during its first seven legislative periods never fell below 12 percent and sometimes ranged to more than 20 percent of the seats, is striking. Moreover, charges against English elections were declining (falling from thirty-three petitions in 1880, resulting in twelve annulments, to a single annulment in 1895), while German elections appeared to be getting worse.[10] In 1898 the Election Commission took stock. Its lengthy report, published separately in booklet form, suggested that three decades after the inauguration of manhood suffrage, misconduct was still flourishing. Between 1893 and 1898 one out of every thirty Reichstag elections was overturned.[11]

Like the weather, everybody talked about election misconduct, but no one did anything about it. At least, not until the reforms of 1903. But even so, the

[7] G. Wollstein, *Bethmann Hollweg* (1995), 23. In 1890 only AL, Upper Bavaria, Berlin, and Oppeln Regency escaped protest—but Oppeln had ceased to be seriously contested.

[8] My figures, which differ marginally in two elections from Prengel's ("Beiträge," 7f, 55, 57, 62–76), which are sometimes inconsistent. U.S. count is also mine, based on C. H. Rowell, *Digest* (1901). The U.S. had 398 congressional districts in 1910; Germany had 397.

[9] My count, based on Prengel, "Beiträge," esp. 6, includes *Hauptwahlen*, runoffs, and *Ersatzwahlen*, but omits *Nachwahlen* (by-elections), for which statistics were unavailable. U.S. challenges: H. W. Allen and K. W. Allen, "Fraud" (1981), 178. The number of U.S. representatives has increased, of course, over time. Only four times in two centuries has a U.S. senatorial election been overturned. M. Garber and A. Frank, *Elections* (1990) 1: 13.

[10] Figures calculated from Seymour, *Reform*, 189f; see also 191–94, 395; and Gash, *Politics*, 133. Seymour, 387, thinks that after the reforms of 1868 and 1883 the scrutiny became more honest. Cf. H. J. Hanham. *Elections*, 263; J. R. Howe, "Corruption in British Elections in the Early Twentieth Century," *Midland History* V (1979–80): 63–77.

[11] Fairbairn, "Authority," 816.

1912 general election—the empire's last—was decried as the worst in history.[12] More than 20 percent of the victories were challenged, although the Social Democratic Party, the most vigorous plaintiff, had directed its affiliates to dispute only those seats they thought they could win themselves if the election were held again. Twelve victories were thrown out almost immediately; and in 1914, after two years of investigation, the fate of twenty-eight victors, including such liberal luminaries as Ernst Bassermann and Friedrich Naumann, was still undecided.[13]

In trying to uncover trends, or even the real magnitude of misconduct, the historian of elections suffers the same disability as the historian of sexual behavior, popular unrest, or crime: since the existence of the thing being counted—unlike, say, a birth, a land purchase, or a home run—is a matter of definition, the numbers wobble.[14] Moreover, one can never distinguish changes in the incidence of an activity from changes in the rigor with which it was reported. Even so, these investigations do more than simply generate material about the electoral *Alltag*. Viewed collectively, they illuminate at least three important features of popular politics in the German Empire. First, the types of behavior Germans protested—and the types they did not—show us where the electoral shoe pinched: what practices were taken for granted, and what aroused anger. Second, the empire's provisions for handling protests reveal its valorization of public functions. This valorization contrasted sharply with Anglo-Saxon attitudes (whose notions of private interest extended even into political life), but it would stand oppositional parties in good stead. Third, the numbers, intensity, and continuity of Germany's election protests suggest the protest exercised a function within electoral politics independent of whether or not a particular seat was won or lost. They are initial signs of that legalism—that persnickety attention to rules—that we shall find to be characteristic of the era, and one of the dependent voter's greatest weapons. Subsequent chapters will elaborate on these themes. But here is a good place to take stock of each of them in international perspective.

TYPES OF MISCONDUCT

Although legal definitions of election misconduct were all but identical across countries, what was not identical was the public's response to violations. The low number of election invalidations in the United States, for example, may not reflect greater honesty so much as greater tolerance for corruption.[15] Indigna-

---

[12] J. Bertram, *Wahlen* (1964), 129–38.

[13] Untitled article, *VossZ* (13 May 1914); untitled article, *Staatsbürger Ztg* 112 (14 May 1918), BAB-L R1501/14653/1, unpaginated; "Reichstagsschluß und Wahl-Prüfungen," in the *Berliner Neueste Nachrichten* (23 May 1914). Instructions to the SPD, confidential report of Polizei-Präsident v. Jagow to MdI, Berlin, 7 Feb. 1912, BAB-L R1501/14645, Bl. 203.

[14] Contrast Seymour, *Reform*, 189f, 193, with Gash, *Politics*, 133. As for German figures, my count, Prengel's, and Leser's occasionally differ.

[15] Argersinger, "Perspectives," 682f.

tion, on the other hand, may be a measure of the friction between cultural norms and political practices. To appreciate the significance of German complaints about election misconduct, then, we must examine not only their incidence, but look at what Germans were—and were not—complaining *about*.

Every country gets the election misconduct it deserves—or wants. The British voter seems traditionally to have considered his franchise in the same light as the local operator of a commercial chain considers his franchise today: as a license to sell something. Anthony Trollope was hardly exaggerating when he depicted a voter's disgust at a candidate who promised electoral purity: "the idea of purity of election at Percycross made him feel very sick. . . . There was to him something absolutely mean and ignoble in the idea of a man coming forward to represent a borough in Parliament without paying the regular fees."[16] Bribery, the offense most reported, most legislated against, and most responsible for the expense of elections was so embedded in British election culture that it could be considered, in the words of one candidate, "part of the constitutional system." "Treating" might mean funding an open tap for as long as six weeks before the election. The Corrupt and Illegal Practices Act of 1883 was thus a kind of sumptuary law.[17] Germany presented a very different picture. Here too, of course, every election produced scattered examples of "treating." Cotters in the east Elbian Herrschaft Pnuwno were given a half bushel of dried peas for voting Conservative. Voters in the Rhenish village of Rodenkirchen who accepted "loyal" ballots were handed a sausage from a large hamper at the door of the polls.[18] A dram of schnapps at the beginning of our period and much larger quantities of *"Freibier"* at the end were common, although not always considered respectable, features of German elections. Nevertheless, I know of only three contests in the entire imperial period in which corruption in the form of treating or bribery was even rumored to have affected the outcome of the election—and in two of them the rumors seem untrustworthy, given that the losing party did not bother to file a complaint.[19] Whatever the incidence of these little reciprocities, it is clear that German voters were not considered venal even by parties hoping to overturn an election, nor did enough money change hands

[16] Trollope quoted in Briggs, *People*, 104. Cf. Seymour, *Reform*, 167n. 4.

[17] Quote from Seymour, *Reform*, 409, 445; similarly, Gwyn, *Democracy*, esp. 64–75, 83–92; L. E. Fredman, *Ballot* (1968), 3. The French considered England the classic land of election bribery. France's *code pénal* commented in its motivation to Article 113: "We leave to the English the scandalous privilege of courting the suffrages of their fellow citizens for money and by dint of expenditures; French honor spurns such means!" Quoted in B. Freudenthal, *Wahlbestechungen* (1896), 37.

[18] 5 Marienwerder (Schwetz), AnlDR (1877, 3/I, Bd. III) DS 106: 351; Nieper SBDR 12 Mar. 1878: 481; 2 Cologne 1887, BAB-L R1501/14664, Bl. 36–41.

[19] The exception was 1 Königsberg in 1907, where 50–60,000 marks were allegedly spent in a NL campaign: AnlDR (1907/09, 12/I, Bd. 16) DS 445: 2465–2506; ibid., Bd. 21, DS 825: 4926–5018. The other two cases were mentioned in a RT debate: 7 Gumb., where a wealthy banker was said to have spent between 50,000 and 100,000 Marks in 1881 to displace Frh. Mirbach (K) on behalf of a LL; and the Königsberg campaign of 1887, where the same Maecenas reputedly spent similar amounts for a Kartell candidate. Mirbach, Dr. Meyer (Halle), Dr. Hegel SBDR 6 Mar. 1888: 1307, 1709.

to give Reichstag deputies, unlike their British counterparts, any stake in regulating it. Bribery simply did not play a role in what Germans thought was wrong with their political process.[20]

If serious bribery was missing in Germany, even more conspicuous was the absence of the violence that so marred Italian, Spanish, Greek, Irish, and American campaigns during the same period.[21] Only a handful of Germans ever lost their lives at election time. In 1871 a voter in Hörde suffered a heart attack as police forced back a crowd chasing a fleeing partisan; two were killed during the height of the Kulturkampf in a tavern brawl in the Hessian Odenwald triggered by a Protestant mayor's failure to include six Catholics on the voting rolls. In March 1891 a crowd in Hanau stoned a rally held by the antisemite agitator Otto Böckel, violence that was quickly quashed, however, by the Prussian army.[22] There may have been a few more such cases. But unlike their Italian and Spanish counterparts, the fallen were the victims of overexcited voters, not of the state. And such casualties could hardly compare with elections in Philadelphia where, in some wards, according to a U.S. marshal in 1881, "scarcely an election goes by without somebody getting killed"; or in Cincinnati, where an election was considered quiet when only eight people lost their lives. Even the most critical journalist in Germany would never have dreamt of asserting, as one midwestern newspaper did in 1884, that nearly everywhere in the country voting was "an arduous task attended by . . . personal danger."[23] One might argue that this kind of violence was merely the nineteenth-century equivalent of soccer hooliganism: supporters of one team may "have at" supporters of another, but political meaning—and impact—is nonexistent. Yet in some polities during our period violence occurred so massively, systematically, and one-sidedly as to kill the very competition that is the heart of an election's meaning. Violence ruled in Louisiana in 1869, where more than two hundred freemen were murdered in a single district and no fewer than two thousand Republicans were slain or injured in another. As late as 1895 a "reign of terror" existed at election time.[24] It was violence, after all, or the threat of it, that kept the American South under one-party rule until 1965. Imperial Germany was well policed. And although scholarship in recent decades has destroyed the picture of Germans as incapable of collective violence, compared

---

[20] Freudenthal, *Wahlbestechungen*, gives no information about the incidence of bribery and no evidence that it was significant.

[21] A major expense during Greek elections was the cost of soldiers to maintain order. *Further Reports on the Practice Prevailing in Certain European Countries in Contests for Election to Representative Legislative Assemblies. . . .* (1882). BAB-L R1501/14451, Bl. 102. In the 1930s brawls in New York got so out of hand that police were required at the polls—an expense that by 1991 was costing the city nearly a million dollars. "Police at the Polls," editorial, *New York Times*, Nov. 1991. In Germany violence or threats of violence were "very seldom." G. Gurwitsch, *Schutz* (1910), 48.

[22] *GA* Nr. 17, 21 Jan. 1871: 97; Nr. 33, 8 Feb. 1874: 186. R. Levy, *Downfall* (1975), 68.

[23] Argersinger, "Perspectives," 684.

[24] Rowell, *Digest*, 1869: 232f, 241f, 246, 519, 526–29.

to Italy, Spain, Ireland, and the United States, Germany was an extraordinarily law-abiding society.

Finally, there is the question of fraud. In Ireland, multiple voting was considered "an integral part of . . . electoral life."[25] In Philadelphia, before the reform of the registration law in 1906, natives joked that all the signers of the Declaration of Independence were still voting. In the New York elections of 1910, total fraudulent—and prevented—votes roughly equaled genuine ones. Pittsburgh, Chicago, Louisville, and San Francisco were also notorious.[26] As late as 1984, nearly 50,000 invalid votes were cast in an Indiana congressional race: 21 percent of the total.[27] In contrast, known cases of fraud in Germany were all but invisible to the naked bureaucratic eye. Every election had its zealous panel chairmen who slipped an extra ballot or two into the urn, its ineligible voter who tried to palm himself off as someone he wasn't. I counted thirty-six allegations of such misconduct after the first election of 1871. But even if all of the charges were true, they would have affected a total of only 1,301 out of almost 4 million votes. Each allegation was investigated by the respective state and prosecuted if evidence warranted. Penalties could go as high as two months in jail.[28] There were four convictions for election fraud in 1902, the first year that the empire's statisticians bothered to record it separately from the (relatively few) cases of bribery and physical coercion. After the general election of 1903, the convictions rose to fifty-four, but even in 1912, following an election in which well over twelve million men voted, the numbers had not risen significantly beyond the meager figures of 1871: forty-three prosecutions for fraud and thirty-three convictions.[29] Of course when voters are fearful of revealing to investigators how they voted, small-time fraud is difficult to prove. These figures must under-represent the incidence. But by definition, frauds so small-time

[25] K. T. Hoppen, *Elections* (1984), 6; also 218.

[26] J. P. Harris, *Registration* (1929), 6, 350–77; idem, *Election* (1934) 1: 315–82; Seymour and Frary, *World* (1918) 1: 261; Argersinger, "Perspectives," 669–87, esp. 672, 677f; Philip E. Converse, "Change in the American Electorate," in *The Human Meaning of Social Change*, edited by A. Campbell and P. E. Converse (New York, 1972), 263–301; and idem, "Comment on Burnham's Theory and Voting Research," *APSR* 68 (Sept. 1974): 1024–27; P. J. Ethington, *City* (1994), 76, 120, 133, 140, 150f, 167. At one time, Converse had estimated the extent of fraudulent voting in the U.S. at between 30% and 75%. Dissenting: the Allens, "Fraud" (1981), 169, who also dispute Harris's assertion that 134,000 names had been illegally purged from the Philadelphia rolls in 1906; William E. Gienapp, "'Politics Seem to Enter into Everything': Political Culture in the North, 1840–1860," in *Essays on American Antebellum Politics, 1840–1860*, edited by S. E. Maizlish and J. J. Kushma (Arlington, Texas, 1982), 14–69, esp. 23–27.

[27] Garber/Frank, *Elections* 1: 14–16.

[28] Royal Landgericht Dresden, 16 Apr. 1912, BAB-L R1501/14461, Bl. 108f. Bavaria's more lenient penalties ranged from five to eight days. BAB-L R1501/14461, Bl. 102–6.

[29] Election fraud, covered by § 108 of the penal code, appears from 1902 to 1912 in *Statistik des Deutschen Reichs*, vols. 155, 162f, 169f, 176f, 185, 193, 228f, 237, 247, 257, 267. These statistics undercount the numbers of ineligibles (foreigners, poor-relief recipients, bankrupts, the retarded) who voted, as a thorough reading of the WPK reports reveals. A summary of responses of all the federated states to an imperial query about fraud in 1912: BAB-L R1501/14461, Bl. 114–19, 197–200.

can have played little role in either the process or the outcome of elections. The historian looking for meaning will not find it here. Gross ballot box stuffing, so common in new democracies, from urban America then to developing countries now, was unknown in the German Empire.[30]

These three offenses—bribery, physical force, and the falsification of results—are the classic forms of election misconduct. They were proscribed in the French penal code in paragraphs that were subsequently taken over by its German imitators. And these three offenses were the crimes against free elections most discussed by Germany's constitutional scholars.[31] Yet bribery, violence, and fraud were not central features of German election controversies— which suggests that they were condemned not only by the penal code, but by bureaucratic norms and popular mores as well. Their absence is probably owing to traditions long fostered and enforced by the state; such norms and mores provided the level playing field within which free and competitive elections might become a genuine possibility.

Significantly missing from the imperial penal code, however, was precisely that transgression charged again and again in German election petitions. This was "influence": the insinuation of persons or groups into the voting process in ways that falsified the citizen's choice.[32] The frequency of this charge (which was often the real point behind protests against many lesser, apparently technical, infractions), like the infrequency of all the others, suggests something important about Imperial Germany's prevailing value system—about its political culture.

"Influencing" the voter was what German election misconduct was all about. It was also, however—as contemporaries were not slow to point out—what elections themselves were all about. The very "influence" that some Germans deemed corrupt was what others thought was the nature of the drama they were enacting. "Election freedom consists in influencing elections," the venerable Conservative Ludwig von Gerlach proclaimed. Paul Laband, a leading constitutional scholar, considered influencing elections an "inalienable human right." "The whole signature of this [election] law," insisted Friedrich von Behr, a Free Conservative deputy for Greifswald, "is exert yourself [*strenge dich an*], exercise your influence as well as you can" so that the voters will elect the Reichstag of your choice. The existence of the secret ballot presupposed, Behr said, a

---

[30] Rumors were reported in the *Mindener Ztg* (29 Jun. 1903) and quoted in P. Hahne, "Reichstagswahl" (1970): 130. But the absence of any election petition in this litigious culture is conclusive evidence against them.

[31] Freudenthal, *Wahlbestechungen*, 1, for example, mentions only these three; Drenkmann, "Wahlvergehen" (1869): 168–79. For the French situation on "Contrainte (faits de pression)," "Inclinée (corruption)," and "Trompée (manoeuvres frauduleuses proprement dites)," see Charnay, *Le Suffrage* and idem, *Les scrutins* (1964).

[32] R. v. Mohl: no other complaint was raised more frequently. "Erörterungen" (1874), 528–663, esp. 571; nearly 40 years later "influence" was designated as the electoral process's main problem by M. E. Mayer, "Bekämpfung" (1910), 21; while Gurwitsch, *Schutz*, 48, put it more specifically as intimidation by employers. *Pression* by the government seems to have been the most common charge against French elections. Charnay, *Les scrutins*, esp. 101.

voter mature enough to decide whether or not to allow himself to be "influenced by these efforts."[33] These were arguments heard over and over again.

Yet Germans could be excused for questioning the solidity of both of Behr's
premises—the secret ballot and the mature voter. Legally, voting for the
Reichstag, unlike most state elections in Germany, was indeed secret. But in
many precincts, as we shall see in chapter 3, this secrecy was at best notional.
Doubts existed about the maturity of the voter as well. In Chicago, a saying had
it, the graveyards voted. In Germany, it was the living voter who was likened to
a corpse, for his allegedly cadaver-like submission to his masters. When power
in a society is distributed very unequally, as it was in Germany, "influence" can
be a nice word for intimidation; "maturity," for an autonomy that all of the
voter's other relationships denied.

Nevertheless—and here is the puzzle at the center of the story of the continuous massive complaints about election misconduct—the results of German
elections by no means support a picture of voters in the clutches of the powerful. The share of seats belonging to those parties whose election the government actively promoted began with 56.5 percent in 1871, a paltry figure when
one remembers that the day before the election had been given over to bell-
ringing, hymn-singing, and torchlight parades celebrating the arrival of peace
after the government's hugely successful war with France.[34] As election followed election, Bismarck's fundamental misreading of the dynamism he had
built into the German political system became harder and harder to deny. The
mandates going to parties stamped with the government's seal of approval diminished almost continuously, sinking to a dismal 25 percent in the last election
before the war—a remarkable figure considering all that has been written about
the effectiveness of authoritarian institutions in Germany.[35] Measured by its results, election misconduct, at least on behalf of conservative forces, was a signal failure.

We shall discuss in chapters 8 through 12 why the race did not always go to
the swift nor the battle to the strong. For now, let us raise the question why,
since intimidation and pressure did not, at least on a national scale, have the
desired effect, the charges of misconduct did not decline. For this question
leads us to our second point—and into the heart of the ambiguous relationship
between precept and practice in imperial elections.

---

[33] Gerlach quoted in "Wahlurnen," VossZ (3 Apr. 1913), BAB-L R1501/14476; Laband: *Das
Staatsrecht des Deutschen Reiches*, 4 Bde. (Tübingen and Leipzig, 1901) 1: 310f, and esp. n. 7;
F.K. v. Behr (FK) SBDR 17 Apr. 1871: 240.

[34] The *GA* and the *HZtg* on Mar. 3–5, 1871 were filled with notices about peace festivities. Did
Bis. time the exchange of ratification agreements on 2 Mar. to coincide with the elections?

[35] These figures are only a rough guide, since the power of the government might not coincide
with "power" on the precinct level. *Pace* Huber, *Verfassungsgeschichte* 3: 878, who puts opposition
deputies at only 57.2% in 1881 and 61.1% in 1912. I include the Z and LLs, since although they
sometimes voted for government proposals on an ad hoc basis, the government never worked for
their election. That a government sometimes drew on the support of the Z and the Richter-ites was
a sign not of its "success" in manipulating elections, but of its movement in the very direction that
Bis. had introduced universal suffrage to avoid—the parliamentary basis for governmental power.

REICHSTAG PROCEDURES AND THE CULTURE OF COMPLAINT

In no country has democratization been the automatic result of franchise extensions. As Charles Seymour, a young political scientist (and future president of
Yale), noted in his pioneering study in 1915, democracy has always also been
dependent on a series of small measures.[36] Apparently minor regulations, often
invisible to the historian, may be central to how contemporaries experienced
what they were doing. Nowhere is the importance of the apparently incidental
clearer than in the procedures for validating elections. Viewed from a sufficiently grand level of abstraction, these procedures were the same throughout
the western world. Representative bodies everywhere insisted on their own authority to decide on the legitimacy of their members: the House of Commons,
since 1586; the American Congress, since its inception in 1788; the French
parliament, beginning with the Revolution. That same legislative prerogative
had been written into the constitutions of Baden (1818), Württemberg (1819),
Hessen (1820), and the Frankfurt Assembly (1849), to give just the first German examples.[37] Article 27 of the Imperial Constitution bestowed similar and
sole authority on the Reichstag.[38] But if we look beyond these gross mor-
phological regularities, we see procedural differences that insured that the
meaning of an election challenge would vary significantly.

In Britain, for example, election challenges were treated as a private conflict.
In 1842, Lord John Russell proposed to establish a board of election commissioners paid by the state. But Sir Robert Peel objected, "We must take care that
we do not throw upon the public the charge of investigating matters of personal
rather than public concern." Whether or not election honesty was conceived as
a matter of personal or of public concern made a difference. British plaintiffs
were forced to come to London, witnesses in tow, to pursue their case, which
made justice a punishingly expensive undertaking. Daniel O'Connell estimated
that he spent between £1,000 and £1,500 to defend his seat against petitioners—but his challenger spent five times as much. In 1860 the average cost
of petitioning a British election was estimated at £2,500. Even after the Election
Petitions Act of 1868 transferred the investigation of elections from the House
of Commons to a tribunal of professional judges, thus allowing testimony to be
taken locally, the costs were daunting. Though witnesses no longer had to
travel, lawyers did, and Britain's special breed of "election lawyers" agreed
among themselves not to serve for less than £200 a brief and 50 guineas a day.
And now parliament required of anyone who wished to petition an election a
deposit of £1,000, a figure set deliberately high to discourage frivolous protests.

---

[36] Seymour, *Reform*, 3–5, 523f. Cf. Nohlen, *Wahlrecht*, 115.

[37] H. Zoepfl, *Grundsätze* ([1863], 1975) 2: 331n. 2; Leser, *Untersuchungen*, 13. A similar authority lodged in the *Ständestaat* of the old German Reich: Olschewski, *Wahlprüfung*, 56–60.

[38] Which maintained it until the Weimar Constitution provided for a court to handle election
protests, made up of deputies and members from the *Reichsverwaltungsgericht*. In the FRG, the BR
has authority, but appeals can be made from the Bundestag to the Supreme Court. Schuster, *Verfassungen*, 175; Olschewski, *Wahlprüfung*, 17, 23 and n. 28.

At that time £1,000 was equal to about 20,000 German marks, a tremendous sum. But the bill might climb five times as high during the course of an investigation.[39] Costs such as these—of petition and of defense—were not the least of the reasons why British election challenges remained rare—and why the House of Commons remained a *very* wealthy man's club.[40] Britain was not alone in leaving the fate of a public good—an untainted election—in private hands. As recently as 1978, when the loser in a Virginia senatorial race could raise only $27,000 of the $80,000 bond required to initiate a recount, he was forced to concede the election—although the winner's margin of victory was only three-tenths of 1 percent.[41]

Not so in Imperial Germany. Here the Kaiser's jurists defined elections as a public function, and the citizen during the act of voting became a "state functionary." From this it followed that the "sincerity" of elections was a matter of state, not the private concern of a losing candidate.[42] The costs of an investigation—postage, travel, and particularly lost wages and other witness fees—were borne by the state in which the election took place. After the turn of the century, as expenses mounted, the state governments tried (unsuccessfully) to get the financial burden shifted to the Reich. But at no time did the Reichstag or the governments ever consider the Anglo-American solution of discouraging protesters by requiring them to make a deposit or post a bond.[43] Moreover, *any* German had standing. That is, he or she could submit a complaint within ten days after the announcement of the election results and be assured of a hearing by the Reichstag. In 1892, after years of controversy, the Reichstag majority restricted this generous provision to citizens qualified to vote within the district being challenged; but the change made no appreciable difference in the number of challenges.[44]

When parliament has the authority to invalidate elections, a possibility always exists that the majority will use that authority to achieve what it could not accomplish on the hustings. Such was the case in France in 1877–78, when Republicans in the Chamber of Deputies threw out 77 elections in one year,

---

[39] Gash, *Politics*, 133f; Gwyn, *Democracy*, 83–92 (quote); also Leser, *Untersuchungen*, 100, 109 and Seymour, *Reform*, 416, 452f. By the first election after the 1883 Reform, however, total electoral expenditure had been cut by three-quarters. O'Leary, *Elimination*, 229, 231. The prewar exchange rate was 20 marks to £1 sterling. Alan S. Milward and S. B. Saul, *The Development of the Economies of Continental Europe, 1850–1914* (London, 1977), 16. Thanks to Jan de Vries for this information.

[40] Even after 1868, "election judges were required to try as a private lawsuit between petitioner and respondent what was really a quasi-criminal proceeding in which the constituency in particular and the public generally were interested." O'Leary, *Elimination*, esp. 47.

[41] Garber/Frank, *Elections* 1: 47f.

[42] E.g., Gurwitsch, *Schutz*, 3f, also 20. Gurwitsch based his views on G. Jellinek, *System der subjektiven öffentlichen Rechte* (Tübingen, 1905), 139, 147, 159–61, 186ff.

[43] Bavarian SM to RdI, 24 Oct. 1910, BAB-L R1501/14645, Bl. 88; Prussian Justice Minister to BH, 19 July 1910. Before responding, BH sent a circular to the state governments, asking their views. BAB-L R1501/14645, Bl. 123–127v.

[44] [E. M. v. Köller], *Ungiltigkeit* (n.d., 1897), 25n. 3. Leser, *Untersuchungen*, 69–72. Women occasionally protested elections, but rarely alone.

effectively driving the Right from political life.[45] Although Germany's Election Commission was never immune to partisanship, its multiparty membership insured that invalidations would always be the exception. The significance of the petition process did not lie in the number of overturned elections—seventy-eight for the whole imperial period—but in the veritable culture of challenge that the ease of lodging a complaint encouraged, and the spotlight it focused on alleged miscreants. The petitions, testimonies, and attendant debates attracted enormous attention. The records of the Krefeld election of 1871 were in such demand that one Liberal deputy claimed that he had spent an entire day chasing around after them. The protocols of the Danzig (Gdansk) election of 1881 were so embarrassing for the government that someone apparently swiped them from the Reichstag's offices. The scrutinies allowed Germans continually to measure themselves against what they believed was appropriate behavior for modern Europeans—and to conclude that they fell short.[46] And even after the deputies themselves had become jaded about misconduct charges, the public's interest remained intense.[47]

We shall explore the use of the protest mechanism in creating space for political parties in chapter 9. For now, it is enough to point out that, at the very least, the election scrutiny offered citizens a forum from which to criticize the practices of those who stood over them. Even when the tainted votes were too few to affect an election's outcome, the result of a scrutiny might nonetheless be a *Rüge*, a formal reprimand, requested by the Reichstag and conveyed by the chancellor to an official who had gone beyond the letter of what was allowed.[48] More important, however, than the sweet psychic pleasures of slapping the hand of authority, the election scrutiny became an engine for forming public opinion and mobilizing support for new legislation—as the debates over the election influence of the Catholic clergy would show. The Social Democrats' 1893 account of their party's activities devoted forty pages to the decisions of the Election Commission. Ten of them gave detailed instructions on how to put

---

[45] Charnay, *Les scrutins*, 84, 117–19. Charnay does not give the number of seats in the chamber, but I counted 531. Between 1906 and 1939—that is, after the Republic was secured—there were only 22 invalidations. G. A. Lefèvre-Pontalis, *Élections* (1902), 13; also 14, 19f, in contrast to Germany: 132.

[46] Wehrenpfennig SBDR 22 Apr. 1871: 322; H. Dohrn (NL) SBDR 16 June 1882: 541–43; H. Ewald (W) SBDR 10 Apr. 1874: 708; Bunsen (NL) on 12 Han. (Göttingen) SBDR 29 Mar. 1871: 41.

[47] Why else would T. Wacker have published a small book on the validation decisions of one legislature period? Wacker, *Rechte* (1890).

[48] The administration laid great stress on the fact that technically the RT itself could not censure an official, but only report the facts to the chancellor and request him to bring the matter to the attention, and if necessary, censure, of the state government involved. But the vehemence with which RdI's blue pencils underlined this provision on newspaper articles explaining the RT's validation procedures indicates that the distinction was by no means obvious to the public or the RT. Unlike the RT, the Prussian LT claimed the power, through Art. 82 of the constitution, to direct the Prussian investigative authorities, rather than go through the Minister President. "Das Wahl-Prüfungsrecht des Reichstags," *Berliner Börsenzeitung* 17 Sept. 1903, clipping with underlines and annotations in BAB-L R1501/14702, Bl.63.

together an election protest, concluding with the Reichstag's address and the recommendation that a copy of any protest be sent to the SPD delegation. The scrutiny was seen as an instrument of political education, a means of turning democracy in theory into democracy in practice. In the last analysis, we can agree with a young law candidate in 1908 who, reviewing the record of forty years, concluded that "the number of election challenges and complaints is a function of the sense of fairness of those who raise them."[49] He might have added: and a measure of the significance the German population invested in the Reichstag as the organ of their own representation. Here was the key to the protests' enormous numbers. It is no wonder that the petitions kept coming.

[49] *Thätigkeit* (1893); Leser, *Untersuchungen*, 57 (quote).

CHAPTER THREE

Open Secrets

A worker was asked by his wife after his first experience at the polls for whom he had given his vote. "How would I know?" was the reproachful reply, "I cast the ballot they put in my hand without looking at it; it is, after all, a *secret* ballot . . ."

—*Story making the rounds in Görlitz (1874)*

Parochialitäten sind keine Herrschaftsfreie Idylle.

Karl Rohe (1981)

WHEN Vincenz Speckbacker arrived at the schoolhouse in Sachrang, ballot in hand, on election morning in 1871, and found the place empty, he complained bitterly that he had lost the entire day coming to the polls and hadn't been allowed to vote. The teacher Johannes Eberle (although only twenty-four, already an important person in the village) had locked up the schoolhouse and repaired to the tavern, where his colleagues on the panel of overseers were already in convention. In spite of mutterings of discontent, only when a sufficient number of voters had collected in the tavern—or, some said, only when it pleased Eberle—would the teacher take troops of them over to the schoolhouse to put their ballots in the urn. Although law required a minimum of three overseers to be present at the polls at all times, none of the teacher's colleagues made the trip.

Unlike Farmer Speckbacker and a few others, however, most of these Upper Bavarian villagers seemed happy enough to spend election day at the tavern, regardless of whether and when they were allowed to vote. The atmosphere grew boisterous, as the energetic Eberle "worked over" the patrons to get them to support his own candidate, the Superintendent of the Postal Stables, Pachmayr—a National Liberal. The teacher used his brief forays into the schoolhouse to rifle through the ballot box, keeping a running score, which he conveyed to all interested parties at periodic intervals. The pro-Pachmayr crowd used their man's early lead to put pressure on the others to jump on the bandwagon. Whenever a new patron crossed the threshold, the innkeeper Elisabeth Neumayer would shout out, "Vote only for Pachmayr, so far Obermayr has only twelve votes."

Young Eberle interpreted his discretionary powers as overseer broadly, as was clear from his handling of two soldiers, Georg Pasigner and Johannes Angerer, who had been turned away from the polls that morning, the first because he was underage, the second because he was not on the voting list. The two made their dissatisfactions known throughout a day of steady drinking and loud complaining. They were joined by Benno Oberhorner, a yeoman whose name was also missing from the list. "So I betook myself to the tavern and raised Cain about not being allowed to vote," he reported. Later that afternoon Teacher Eberle approached the soldiers, gave them Liberal ballots, and indicated that as several voters had not shown up, they could vote in their place. As for Oberhorner, while answering a call of nature, he ran into a border patrolman who gave him a ballot also filled out with the name of the Liberal candidate. Try again, the patrolman suggested, you will certainly be let in this time. So the three presented themselves at the urn, and indeed their ballots were accepted without demur.

When questioned later, the chairman of Sachrang's election panel, Mayor Anton Daxer, a middle-aged farmer, conceded the irregularities. In addition to admitting ineligibles, he had unfortunately turned away a number of perfectly eligible voters—because he had "always been of the view" that only homeowners were allowed to vote. "I see now that I made mistakes in this election and let the teacher count for too much," he concluded ruefully. "I just thought that the teacher would understand the matter better than I."[1] Daxer was not the only village mayor whose diffidence about forms and procedures put him effectively in the hands of the schoolmaster.

The following chapter will look at elections "up close and personal": at the men selected to oversee the voting, at what was at stake in the choice of a polling place. If, as some contemporaries believed, thinking hierarchically was every German's second nature, then thinking communally may have been his first. And as we chart the fortunes of the movement to guarantee greater privacy in voting, we will probe the ambiguous relationship between public politics and private choices.

THE OVERSEERS OF DEMOCRACY

Free elections depend on finding solutions to a massive staffing problem. In Germany of 1871, roughly 50,000 separate panels were needed to oversee the voting: to verify the voters against a list of eligible residents, to count the ballots, to insure the honesty of the process. Who would these men be? Precisely this issue had provided the most heat when the suffrage was discussed in the Constituent Reichstag, whose members rejected the government's proposal that civil servants be on every panel. The integrity of the people's

---

[1] 7 Oberbayern, AnlDR (1871, 1/II, Bd. 2) DS 38: 90–93. Eberle quote on p. 92. Dr. Buhl SBDR 4 Apr. 1871: 186. §85 of the penal code on election fraud did not cover votes that were alleged proxies. Drenkmann, "Wahlvergehen," 175.

OPEN SECRETS

choice, they were convinced, demanded that the people themselves administer their elections.[2]

In the event, a compromise was reached. The selection of the chairman of each panel and of his deputy would lie with the "appropriate authorities" in each of the empire's member states. Typically, these would be the city council or Bürgermeister in the towns; in rural areas, the Landrat (or his non-Prussian equivalent): the government's chief representative in the counties and the hinge connecting state and local administration. The power to appoint the chairman was an important one, as conflicts over such jurisdictions showed.[3] The chairman himself named a recording secretary and between three and six associates. The sole legal qualification for a position on the panel, however, was that a man not be directly employed by the state (i.e., an *unmittelbarer Staatsbeamte*).[4]

The simplicity of the qualification was belied by the ambiguities of German officialdom. Prefects (*Regierungspräsidenten*) and Landräte and their immediate subordinates—district councilors (*Regierungsräte*), constables, and tax collectors—were obviously civil servants and thus excluded. Did the same hold true for forest wardens, postal clerks, and hospital administrators? What about the commandant of the volunteer fire department?[5] What of men who, in addition to their regular professions, had been entrusted with keeping the local register of births, deaths, and marriages?[6] Given the federal character of the German Empire, the answer varied from state to state. Each occupation had to be decided on separately, something that usually happened only when an election was challenged. The status of the three figures most widely available as panel members—the teacher, the pastor, and especially the village headman (*Vorsteher*)—was especially murky.[7] Unlike their urban counterparts, rural mayors and headmen often owed their office not to election but to appointment by the provincial governor, and though technically local (i.e., not royal) offi-

[2] Prof. R. Siegfried to G. Bendix, 15 June 1908, BAB-L R1501/14474: Bl. 167f; see also R. Gneist (NL) SBDR 26 Apr. 1871: 411. By 1908 the RdI estimated the number of polling places for *Prussia* at 60–80,000. Hatschek, *Kommentar*, 170f.

[3] BAB-L R1501/14451, Bl. 133–145v, 149–149v, 154–57, 170–79, 184–184v; Fenske, "Landrat" (1979), 445f.

[4] §9 of the 1869 Election Law (Wahlgesetz), §10 of the 1870 Voting Regulations (Wahlreglement). Hereafter, these two documents will be referred to collectively as the election code. A minimum of three panel members had to be present at all times during the election, and the chairman and the recording secretary were not to be absent simultaneously.

[5] H. v. Friesen (K) SBDR 10 Jan. 1889: 371. Various definitions of "unmittelbares Staatsamt" are listed in an advisory brochure for the Conservative party produced anonymously by Deputy E. M. v. Köller, LR of Kamin: *Ungiltigkeit*, 29f. Also: *Reichstags-Wahlgesetz* (1907), 71–76.

[6] Yes, decided the majority of the WPK, amidst great controversy: 3 Marienwerder, AnlDR (1884/85, 6/I, Bd. 6) DS 273: 1176–78. Postal agents: AnlDR (1890/91, 8/I, Bd. 3) DS 258: 1913; but cf. Hatschek, *Kommentar*, 179.

[7] Complaints about the composition of the panels, citing this or that occupation, are too numerous to list. By 1897 some clarity was emerging: [Köller], *Ungiltigkeit*, 29n. 1. As late as 1912, Protestant pastors sat on election panels, although the practice was, according to the current RT, illegitimate. 4 Potsdam, AnlDR (1912/14, 13/I, Bd. 22) DS 1435: 2945. Mayors had, by then, ceased to arouse objections.

cials, they stood within the state's chain of command.[8] Their technical position within the state's administrative structure was, of course, not really the issue. Dependency was. But as we shall see, dependence and independence proved to be much clearer categories in Berlin, where the Reichstag debated the panels' composition, than in polling places across Germany.

The Prussian government, in making its case for civil servants as election overseers, had predicted that without them the search for qualified personnel would find many rural precincts in "some embarrassment."[9] Critics suspected that the government itself worked to ensure that this prophecy would be fulfilled. In Angerburg-Lötzen, some twenty miles from the Russian border, local Progressives charged that their Landrat had deliberately chosen known drunkards, who "stagger around in the dirt in public streets," to chair their overseers. Their assessment of Angerburg's Landrat—that he was seeking politically reliable panelists—may have been accurate, but many of the same difficulties beset districts whose overseers were of a different political persuasion.[10] Complaints from every political party about the "cultural level" of the overseers were staples of the election challenge.

Whatever the qualities of this or that individual, the brewers and tavernkeepers, the forest wardens and farmers who typically made up rural election panels lacked the experience, the habits, and the inclination necessary to master the niceties of the election code. The neglect of the swearing-in ceremony was the least sign of their nonchalance. Some chairmen appointed associates who were underage. Some delegated authority for long stretches of time to their friends. The overseers' casual way with the voting regulations seemed fruitless to punish (for strict enforcement would have meant throwing out nearly every election) and hopeless to amend (for the deputies were convinced that new regulations, even if radically simplified, would only "introduce greater confusion").[11] Thus the keeping of a duplicate list of voters, the procedures for counting and preserving the ballots, and a whole variety of forms carefully designed to insure accurate and honest returns were found by the Reichstag to be hardly worth discussing when an election was challenged, since they were ignored "almost universally." In the war between the sophistication of the regulations and the ingenuousness (and sometimes disingenuousness) of the human material administering them, the regulations got the worst of it every time.[12]

Far more serious than the irregularities that grew out of the overseers' weaknesses, however, were those that grew out of their strengths. For all the complaints about the unlettered and the uncouth, most of Germany's overseers, rural as well as urban, were not the dregs of society, but men of respect. In the larger

[8] K. Müller, *Strömungen* (1963), 223f; Kühne, *Dreiklassenwahlrecht*, 64.

[9] Hatschek, *Kommentar*, 170f.

[10] Protest 5 Gumb. Richter SBDR 27 Apr. 1871: 432–42, quote: 432. 4 Oppeln, AnlDR (1871, 1/I, Bd. 3) DS 63: 140f.

[11] AnlDR (1877, 3/I, Bd. 3) DS 64: 265f.

[12] Becker SBDR 27 Mar. 1871: 20; Haerle, 13 Mar. 1879: 387; Hermes 6 Mar. 1888: 1317. Similarly in England: Seymour, *Reform*, 362; Hanham, *Elections*, 399f; Vernon, *Politics*, 101f.

towns, where city fathers appointed the chairmen, they were overwhelmingly men who already held high municipal office. And their assistants were distinguished by prosperity and expertise. Typically they were factory owners, builders, and gymnasial teachers of some standing. In the countryside, along with headmen and innkeepers, panelists were often estate-owners or their stewards. But in every community, large and small, urban and rural, they were the big men: those with employment to offer, credit to extend, land to work, favors to bestow, the men to whom their neighbors naturally deferred.[13] And the chief characteristic of the big man was his habit of command, a rough-and-ready authority that—unlike the competencies bestowed on the "direct civil servant"—was neither legitimated nor limited by any particular office or set of rules. As the chairman in a precinct near Northeim, a brewer, growled out to citizens who were about to hand his son a ballot, "Na, that's none of his affair. . . . In my village, I'm the one who gives the orders."[14]

High-handedness was not confined to the patriarch instructing his son. Although voting was supposed to take place from 10 A.M. until 6 P.M. (and after 1903, until 7), some polls did not open until well into the afternoon. (It was, after all, the Feast of St. Kunegunde, the chairman of Höfen's panel reasoned; the people of his precinct would be spending the morning traveling to Bamberg to attend mass.)[15] Sometimes the explanation was less innocent, as when Chairman von Petzinger, an estate-owner in Alt-Gurren and a Progressive, delayed the election until 4 P.M., thereby ensuring that the Conservative-leaning farming population, whose annual fair opened the next morning in a neighboring regency, would have to leave the village before voting.[16] Some overseers forgot— or neglected—to hold an election at all.[17]

Complaints were legion that overseers refused to accept unwelcome ballots, giving excuses that were exhausted only by their own imaginations. Sometimes it was because the ballot was dirty. Sometimes the voter was asked his name or age and when the answer did not precisely jibe with what was inscribed in the voting list, he was turned away.[18] Since voters, though often uncertain about

[13] *GA* Nr. 4, 6 Jan. 1871: 26. "Men of respect": W. Kulemann, *Erinnerungen* (1911), 25.

[14] 11 Han., SBDR 28 Mar. 1871: 25f. Similar conditions obtained in the U.S., on into the 20th century, where a report for the Brookings Institution described local election judges as "a law unto themselves." Harris, *Administration*, 8.

[15] 5 Oberfr., AnlDR (1871, 1/I, Bd. 3) DS 27: 82. French similarities up to WWI: Seymour/Frary, *World* 1: 374, 378.

[16] 5 Gumb., AnlDR (1881, 5/II, Bd. 6) DS 283: 1040. Sometimes manipulation involved keeping polls open *late*: Protest of C. R. Meister et al., Parchim, 9 Mar. 1887, BAB-L R1501/14662, Bl. 26; 2 Saxe-Weimar AnlDR (1893/94, 9/II, Bd. 2) DS 165: 910.

[17] 8 Marienwerder: Haerle SBDR 13 Mar. 1879: 387. In Rotenburg a liberal chairman failed to inform an entire precinct—notoriously Guelf in its sympathies—of the date of the election, thus depriving Guelfs of about 300 votes. 17 Han., AnlDR (1882/3, 5/II, Bd. 6) DS 242: 926. Cf. Pastor Schöbel of Quosnitz, in 5 Breslau, SBDR 29 Mar. 1871: 46.

[18] Dirty Ballots: 11 Han., SBDR 28 Mar. 1871: 25–26; 6 Trier, AnlDR (1882/83, 5/II, Bd. 6) DS 323: 1325; 5 Arns., AnlDR (1885/86, 6/II, Bd. 5) DS 181: 902; intentional misunderstanding of names on voting list: Protest of Liberal Election Committee on 1 Erfurt, 12 Mar. 1887, BAB-L R1501/14664, Bl. 12–29. Switches: 2 Breslau, AnlDR (1912/14, 13/I, Bd. 22) DS 1432: 2931, 2934.

their age, were quite clear as to their own name, these incidents were usually accompanied by altercations—as in little Endrejen in East Prussia, when Teacher Jesset, a Conservative, turned away his seventy-year-old father-in-law, an active Progressive.[19] Some chairmen simply announced to their village that they would only accept ballots for a particular candidate.[20] Others preferred to wait until counting the ballots to exercise their discretionary powers. And not only in rural precincts. In 1878, when a timid Social Democratic voter, endeavoring to forestall any objections, wrote Wilhelm Hasenclever's name in pen next to his printed name (for who could know whether the one or the other way of proceeding might be deemed insufficient?), his Berlin panel, Progressives to a man, threw the ballot out. The grounds for invalidation? The election code specified that a ballot should contain no more than one name. The Berlin overseers were no less cavalier with Conservative ballots. A supporter of Court Preacher Adolf Stoecker had rashly written "I vote for" in front of Stoecker's name—and out it went.[21]

Voting lists provided another window of opportunity for imperious locals. Although the law required that lists of eligible voters be laid out in each precinct for eight days "for every man's inspection," in many places the law was simply ignored. As late as 1887, voters in Thorn-Kulm requesting a look were told by the big man in charge that "he didn't allow snuffling around in election records." Since the slightest non-correspondence between a voter's name and that on the list might provide an excuse for exclusion, such high-handedness had material consequences, especially for Polish voters, who could almost count on their names being misspelled.[22] On the other hand, overseers might also *add* names to the list of eligible voters on election day. In Tilsit, close to the Russian border, a chairman inscribed the names of nearly sixty voters whom the mayor had previously turned away as either underage or having lost their civil rights through criminal convictions. Against his colleagues' objections, the chairman simply claimed that "he had the right."[23]

---

[19] Protest of Kaufmann Louis Rohrmoser in Tilsit and Gen., AnlDR (1881, 4/IV, Bd 4) DS 103: 606f. A Pole was told to come back at five in order for the (German-speaking) chairman to assure himself that he was "really 42 years old." 2 Bromberg, AnlDR (1881, 4/IV, Bd. 4) DS 105: 633. Rickert SBDR 10 Jan. 1889: 358. Protest of C. R. Meister et al., ibid.

[20] 2 Han., AnlDR (1884, 6/I, Bd. 5) DS 148: 538; 10 Breslau, SBDR 11 Jan, 1889: 382.

[21] AnlDR (1880, 4/III, Bd. 4), DS 94: 666f. A panel in Wernigerode threw out a ballot for LR Meyer (K) on the grounds that it lacked a first name—although Meyer was a well-known LR in one of the three counties making up the district. 8 Magdeburg, AnlDR (1881/82, 5/I, Bd. 2) DS 91: 335.

[22] Quote: von Donimirski, Gutsbesitzer auf Lysomice, and E. Czerniewicz, Bauunternehmer in Podgorz, 4 Marienwerder, 12 Mar. 1887, BAB-L R1501/14665, Bl. 82–86; v. Koscielski SBDR 7 Mar. 1888: 1358 and AnlDR (1887/88, 7/II, Bd. 4) DS 153: 661–66. Names: BAB-L R1501/14461, Bl. 165f; 5 Arns, AnlDR (1882/83, 5/II, Bd. 6) DS 292: 1081; 3. Han.: H. Ramme [Kamme?] to Forest- and Domane Inspector R. Clauditz, Lingen, 20 Feb. 1890, SAO Dep. 62b, 2379; 23 Saxony in 1869, 3 Bromberg in 1881: Leser, *Untersuchungen*, 19–22. As late as 1912 workers in Sacrau were told that anyone inspecting the voting list would be required to write down for whom he was voting. 3 Breslau, AnlDR (1912/14, 13/I, Bd. 22) DS 1433: 2939.

[23] Protest of the Kaufmann L. Rohrmoser et al., on 1 Gumb., AnlDR (1881, 4/IV, Bd. 4) DS 103: 600–608; quote on 600.

Possession of the lists meant mastery of the turnout. In Freiburg im Breisgau in 1877, and throughout Berlin in 1881, panels of overseers took advantage of their knowledge of who had voted and who had not to send out messengers to fetch the (desired) truants. And in small towns and villages everywhere, election chairmen would appear outside the polls at regular intervals, read off a list of missing voters and dispatch the village steward, wearing his official cap and equipped with the ballots of the chairman's own political persuasion, to fetch them, whether they wanted to come or not—something quantitative historians might keep in mind before drawing too many conclusions from changes in turnout. As contests might be decided by a handful of votes (nine in Freiburg in 1877 and in the First Berlin district in 1912), these interventions could make a difference.[24] Once the polls closed, the panel might be equally cavalier in their handling of ballots. More than one chairman, instead of publicly counting and recording them, as the law required, locked the urn in which ballots were kept in his desk, or even took it home.[25]

Depending on locality and circumstance, election overseers might or might not be seen to embody the state; but they always embodied the local structure of authority. These were structures that, except in the largest cities, rarely had to accommodate, much less withstand, a direct challenge. The continuous, unbroken nature of local systems of authority can be seen in the survival of what we would call proxy voting. A master might vote for his journeymen, a priest for his parishioners, a father for his son, one brother for another. Except for the rare cases in which wives and children brought in the ballots of their husbands and fathers, proxy voting was almost always a reflection—and affirmation—of the social hierarchy.[26] It was also, however, an affirmation of the power of the big men at the very top of that hierarchy, since as overseers theirs was the decision

---

[24] E.g., 1 and 2 Berlin, AnlDR (1881/82, 5/I, Bd. 2) DS 44: 117–22; Protest of Max Count v. Kageneck et al., on 5 Baden (Freiburg), AnlDR (1877, 3/I, Bd. 3) DS 191: 538–42 and AnlDR (1878, 3/II, Bd. 3) DS 124: 973–75 (F. Specht/P. Schwabe, *Reichstagswahlen* [1908], 252, on 5 Baden, is clearly in error); W. Schmalz, Schreiner, Protest on 8 Kassel, 1890, BAB-L R1501/14668, Bl. 211–24; 7 Frankfurt, AnlDR (1882/83, 5/II, Bd. 5) DS 162: 548; 6 Potsdam, AnlDR (1884/85, 6/I, Bd. 6) DS 248: 1105f; 2 Bromberg, AnlDR (1881, 4/IV, Bd. 4) DS 105: 633; 20 Saxony, AnlDR (1884/85, 6/I, Bd. 6) DS 247: 1103; 16 Saxony (Leipzig Land) in 1887: Rickert SBDR 10 Jan. 1889: 358. Similar examples: 5 Hessen, in 1887, AnlDR (1887/8, 7/II, Bd. 4) DS 155: 673–75, and from Prussian LT elections: Kühne, *Dreiklassenwahlrecht*, 118. Skepticism about the difference made by *Scheppers*: Suval, *Politics*, 4, 36, 244.

[25] 5 Wiesbaden, AnlDR (1877, 3/I, Bd 3) DS 34: 222; 1 Gumb., AnlDR (1881, 4/IV, Bd. 4) DS 103: 604, 607; 2 Bromberg, AnlDR (1881, 4/IV, Bd. 4) DS 105: 630f, 633.

[26] AnlDR (1871, 1/II, Bd. 2) DS 38: 90. Brothers: 5 Baden: Klügmann SBDR 6 Apr. 1878: 780; fathers: 1 Kassel, AnlDR (1881/82, 5/II, Bd. 5) DS 184: 624; sons: 7 Gumb. AnlDR (1912/14, 13/I, Bd. 23) DS 1586: 3428; wives, children: 4 Oppeln, AnlDR (1876, 2/III, Bd. 3) DS 111: 813; 5 Baden, SBDR 6 Apr. 1878: 780; 3 Kassel, AnlDR (1881/82, 5/II, Bd. 5) DS 161: 545–46; 3 Saxony, AnlDR (1881, 5/II, Bd. 5) DS 174: 611; 2 Danzig, AnlDR (1905/6, 11/I, Bd. 3): DS 412: 2407; 1 Königsberg, AnlDR (1907/9, 12/I, Bd. 16) DS 445: 2465 (Katherina Narraisch submitted a RT protest because she was turned away!); Waldeck, AnlDR (1907/9, 12/I, Bd. 20) DS 736: 4627, and [Köller], *Ungiltigkeit*, 32; pastors: 4 Oppeln, AnlDR (1871 1/II, Bd. 2) DS 63: 140; mayors: BAB-L R1501/14705, Bl. 18–28. Other proxies, 1 Minden, AnlDR (1878, 3/II, Bd. 3) DS 99: 835f; 9 Han., AnlDR (1890/91, 8/I, Bd. 1) DS 95: 641.

to enforce or to wink at the regulation prohibiting voting on behalf of someone else.[27]

Or first to wink and then to enforce. Rural bread lords who arrived with a fistful of ballots on behalf of their hired hands or their neighbors might find them accepted or not, depending on the number of people who had already voted. At the end of the day, if the ballot tally did not square with the voting list, these same ballots—or perhaps someone else's, closer to the top of the pile—might be pulled out again.[28]

Doubtless sometimes proxy ballots did reflect the absent voter's real choice.[29] Often, however, the man who gave his proxy to someone expressed the attitude toward voting that we saw in Sachrang, where the soldiers Passigner and Angerer and the yeoman Benno Oberhorner had been insistent on their right to vote, but unconcerned about which ballot they cast.[30] Even today, political scientists tell us, "observers of the processes of decision making regularly discern features that are hard to relate to an outcome-oriented conception of collective choice. . . . Potential participants seem to care as much for the right to participate as the fact of participation."[31] Not yet an act of decision, a declaration that "I am not as other men, my choice is my own," in the early years of the empire, voting was—for such citizens—a ritual of inclusion, confirmation that "I am a full member of the community, present at its deliberations." Such attitudes explain the insouciance with which voters who had given up a day to come to the polls might nevertheless be willing to cast a ballot of someone else's choosing, and the readiness of others, who could not come, to have a ballot, any ballot, cast *for* them. Such "proxies," registering varying levels of voter choice, would be tolerable only so long as parliament itself was not yet seen as a body that *decides*: that is, before parties had succeeded in redefining community and thus representation antagonistically, making the Reichstag the scorekeeper of Germany's competing group identities. Once that happened—and it was a point reached in some places (as we shall see in the next chapter) very early—voting would become a ritual not of inclusion but of differentiation.

In urban precincts, of course, proxy voting was less innocent right from the start. When police officials in Freiburg im Breisgau went around to the houses of the sick in 1877, promising to deliver their ballots to the polls, they were clearly trying to "make" the election. The Freiburg overseers may not have connived at this maneuver. But the shut-in who, however reluctantly, gave his

[27] 5 Oberfr., AnlDR (1871, 1/II, Bd. 3) DS 27: 82. Proxy voting did not disappear: 2 Danzig and Waldeck (cited above), Saxe-Meiningen, AnlDR (1907/09, 12/I, Bd. 19) DS 625: 4233–34; many cases in 2 Breslau, AnlDR (1912/14, 13/I, Bd. 22) DS 1432: 2925, 2929, 2931f.

[28] MdI Meckl.-Schw. to Gutsherrschaft zu Kleefeld, 18 June 1891, BAB-L R1501/14662, Bl. 50; 1 Minden, AnlDR (1877, 3/I, Bd. 3) DS 187: 522.

[29] E.g, 7 Oberb., AnlDR (1871, 1/II, Bd. 2) DS 38: 90.

[30] Similarly, in Dillingen in 1903: BAB-L R1501/14705, Bl. 18–28; 9 Breslau, Protest of Feb. 1887, BAB-L R1501/14665, Bl. 71–75 and also SBDR 6 Mar. 1888: 1817; T. Müller, *Geschichte* ([1925], 1972), 198.

[31] March/Olsen, "Institutionalism," 741.

ballot to the policeman, must have assumed their complicity.[32] At the extreme was an election in Altona, a populous suburb of Hamburg, where workingmen arriving at polls were simply told by the overseers, their social superiors: "You've voted."[33] Where the boundaries of precinct were not those of community, and where habits of deference could no longer be counted on, a brazen display of power sometimes filled the void.

The choice of a polling place could reinforce an overseer's power, as we saw in the Sachrang election with which our chapter opened. Though as recording secretary, Johannes Eberle was officially subordinate to the chairman of his panel, the young teacher considered the school his "house" and acted on it. Used to deference from country people, over whose children he held the rod and who relied on his help in filling out forms or pursuing legal matters, the teacher enjoyed considerable local authority. Not surprisingly, when the parson and the schoolmaster were at odds, the choice of "his" schoolhouse as polling place faced strenuous objections; a near-riot broke out in neighboring Riedering between a veteran pastor and a rookie schoolteacher over the issue.[34] But parsons were not the only ones to see an unfair advantage in locating the polls in the school. In 1878, when voters in the village of Stumbragirren, near the Progressive's stronghold Tilsit, arrived at the schoolhouse carrying Progressive ballots, they were disconcerted to observe their teacher, a Conservative and chairman of their election panel, ostentatiously drawing up a list of tax brackets, a broad hint that voting behavior might have consequences for their school assessments. Did the teacher have authority over their assessment? No; but his Landrat, who appointed school inspectors and was known to be a vigorous proponent of the Conservative cause, certainly did.[35] Fearing a "partisan tax screw," some voters fled "the teacher's polling place." Others, "in order not to incense" the man, followed him into his private chambers, where an exchange of ballots took place. By the end of the day, the schoolhouse floor was littered with discarded Progressive ballots. A protest was lodged. If it were ever going to be possible for "every German to step up to the urn without such goings on," expostulated one angry voter, then "it would be desirable for the polling place to vanish from the school, where only compulsion rules." His suggestion? The home of the mayor.[36]

All parties were alive to the territorial advantage, as heated jurisdictional

---

[32] 5 Baden, AnlDR (1877, 3/I, Bd. 3) DS 191: 538, 540 and (1878, 3/II, Bd. 3) DS 124: 973–75. A similar case occured in 2 Merseburg, when the *Gemeindediener* collected liberal ballots, leading voters to believe that they were thereby casting them "officially," when in reality he destroyed them. SBDR 5 Feb. 1885: 1101.

[33] 8 S-H, AnlDR (1871, 1/I, Bd. 3) DS 28: 84.

[34] 7 Oberb., AnlDR (1871, 1/II, Bd. 2) DS 38: 85–101, esp. 96. Cf. Teacher Schwanbeck, 4 Meckl. (1879, 4/II, Bd. 5) DS 166: 1351.

[35] On Tilsit-Niederung's "effective and reliable" Landräte: "Wahlaussichten für die Provinz Ostpreußen": GStA PK I. HA, Rep. 89/210, Bl. 211. Koblenz RP and IM Puttkamer in 1881 on connection between LR, school inspectors, and the election role of teachers: "Wie Bismarck" 1/5: 10, 12f. LR's role in taxes: P.-C. Witt, "Landrat" (1973).

[36] 1 Gumb., AnlDR (1881, 4/IV, Bd. 4) DS 103: 607f.

disputes over who got to select the polling place showed.[37] But as with the choice of panels, alternatives were limited. In rural areas the choice was often between some big man's shop, factory, or home—locales that invited confusion between personal and public authority.[38] Even in a respectable-sized city of 50,000, not only schools, hospitals, and city council chambers, but also hotels and restaurants might serve. In Munich, already a metropolis of several hundred thousand in the 1870s, complaints arose that elections were held almost exclusively in beer halls. The Reichstag had a laugh at Munich's expense—but the convenience of the tavern made it a common choice in northern as well as southern Germany.[39]

Convenience was the argument that Veen's panel chairman—an innkeeper—gave to voters when they discovered that he had moved the election to his place. When interrogated, he conceded that he "had held the election in my house, on my own authority [*Machtvollkommenheit*]. In earlier elections I had done the same, and indeed, for the double reason that schoolchildren shouldn't be running around outside the whole day and [at my place] the election panel could provision themselves more conveniently with drink and victuals." A structure at once residential (for its proprietor), commercial (for its patrons), and public (for civic and other groups renting space for their functions), the choice of the *Gasthaus* contributed to the fluidity of election boundaries. It was not uncommon for overseers to drift off to an adjacent alcove for a hand of cards, to linger in the tap-room "to warm up a bit."[40] Voters would do the same. In moving the election to his own establishment, the publican-chairman had a sharp eye out for his own advantage. But advantages might be political as well as commercial. Well might Polish voters complain of having to vote in "German" restaurants filled with German customers and campaigners.[41] As tavern sociability sorted itself out on ethnic, religious, class, and—increasingly as time went on—political lines, a public house was often less "public," in the usual sense, than a commercially run clubhouse for a political party.

Inevitably, the proximity of so many ballot boxes to so many taprooms encouraged "treating," often by the overseers themselves. Treating sometimes

[37] Three-year bruhaha in Tilsit: BAB-L R1501/14451, Bl. 133–45v, 149–49v, 154–57, 170–79, 184–84v; and AnlDR (1882/83, 5/II, Bd. 6) DS 293: 1082–84.

[38] 4 Oppeln, AnlDR (1876, 2/IV, Bd. 3) DS 111: 811, 817–25; factories: Torgelow (2 Stettin), AnlDR (1882/83, 5/II, Bd. 6) DS 200: 715; 3 Breslau, AnlDR (1894/95, 9/III, Bd. 2) DS 220: 942–46. Elections were still being held in the homes of chairmen in 1912, with predictable abuses. 2 Breslau, AnlDR (1912/14, 13/I, Bd. 22) DS 1432: 2932.

[39] Munich, SBDR 24 Mar. 1871: 13; Freiburg a. O., SBDR 17 Apr. 1871: 245; Görlitz: *GA* Nr. 4, 6 Jan. 1871: 26; Werne (5 Arns.) in 1884, AnlDR (1884/85, 6/I, Bd. 7) DS 320: 1771; Chemnitz, SBDR 10 Feb. 1888: 826f.

[40] 7 Düsseldorf, AnlDR (1872, 1/II, Bd. 2) DS 10: 16–18; SBDR 31 Mar. 1871: 77ff. More card-playing: AnlDR (1890/91, 8/I, Bd. 3) DS 246: 1873. Other cases of moving polls: 5 Baden, SBDR 6 Apr. 1878: 780; 8 Hessen, AnlDR (1912/13, 13/I, Bd. 16) DS 350: 292.

[41] 3 Marienwerder, AnlDR (1898/1900, 10/I, Bd. 4) DS 507: 2661–62. Political high-handedness of publican: Weaver Wm. Stephan et al., protest against 11 Breslau, 10 Mar. 1887, BAB-L R1501/14664, Bl. 69–76.

looked very much like bribery—as it did in Boronow, where the chairman announced several days before the election that voters might exchange Centrum ballots for those of the (Free Conservative) Duke of Ujest, after which they could get a chit allowing them to refresh themselves to the tune of 1 1/2 silver groschen. Accused of buying votes, the chairman claimed that he was only trying to remedy the district's record of low turnouts—an argument frequently heard after British elections. But unlike Britain, such gratuities—small beer indeed—were the gift of freelancers, almost never part of a party's, much less a candidate's, campaign efforts. Though the Reichstag might not accept a chairman's story about turnout, anyone suggesting that treating had tainted the votes of those treated was immediately met with the winning party's all-purpose dismissal: "we have, after all, a secret ballot!"[42]

THE "VEIL OF SECRECY"

That voting was secret and that secrecy was "the decisive guarantee of free elections" in the empire are premises shared by a number of distinguished general histories of German politics.[43] The violation of secrecy, however, was axiomatic for contemporaries of every political party. It was common knowledge, the liberal Joseph Völk observed in 1871, that in most districts a secret vote did not exist. Three years later, the constitutional scholar Robert von Mohl denounced current practices as a "mockery of the secrecy demanded by law." The Socialist Wilhelm Hasselmann agreed: "For the poor man, there is no secret ballot."[44] Year after year, on through 1912, violations of secrecy were both charged and proven.[45]

The problem began with the ballots. The governments had initially intended to distribute official ballots, and indeed at the time of the first election to the

---

[42] Behr SBDR 17 Apr. 1871: 240. Also v. Lenthe (W) and (on Boronow election, in 4 Oppeln) S. Albrecht (NL), ibid., 29 Mar. and 5 Apr. 1871: 44 and 182. Treating: 5 Baden (Freiburg), AnlDR (1887, 3/I, Bd. 3) DS 191: 538–42 and AnlDR (1877, 3/II, Bd. 3) DS 124: 973–75; 1 Gumb., AnlDR (1881, 4/IV, Bd. 4) DS 103: 604, 607f.

[43] E.g., Huber, *Verfassungsgeschichte* 3: 863 (quote); Suval, *Politics*, 4, 48, 50; Kühne, *Dreiklassenwahlrecht*, 129. Local studies tell a different story.

[44] Völk SBDR 1 May 1871: 515; Mohl, "Erörterungen," 596; Hasselmann SBDR 11 Apr. 1874: 717f. In fact, secrecy was not written into the election laws of either the two Mecklenburgs, nor of the three little Saxonies (Weimar, Coburg-Gotha, Altenburg). Pollmann, *Parlamentarismus*, 92n. 133.

[45] Justizrat Dr. Joh. Junck, Leipzig, to Geheimrat Jungheim, 21 Sept. 1912, BAB-L R101/3346, Bl. 297–298v. In 1907: 17 Han., 5 Kassel, 3 Erfurt, Waldeck-Pyrmont, 2 Frankfurt, all in AnlDr (1907/9, 12/I, Bd. 20), DS 702: 4471f, 4477–79; DS 705: 4489–91; DS 706: 4500–4502; DS 736: 4631; DS 765: 4665, respectively. In 1912: 8 Hessen, AnlDR (1912/13, 13/I, Bd. 16) DS 350: 291f; 5 Merseberg, AnlDR (1912/13, 13/I, Bd. 19) DS 840: 1138; 2 Breslau and 5 Königsberg, AnlDR (1912/14, 13/I, Bd. 22) DS 1432: 2928f, 2931, 2934; and DS 1401: 2900–2901, respectively; 7 Gumb., AnlDR (1912/14, 13/I, Bd. 23) DS 1586: 3396, 3398, 3402, 3418; 8 Breslau, AnlDR (1912/14, 13/I, Bd. 23) DS 1638: 3571f; 1 Meckl.-Schw.: Stadthagen (SD) SBDR 21 May 1912: 2212. Also Leser, *Untersuchungen*, 93n. 2.

North German Reichstag, in 1867, the authorities in the Mecklenburgs, Saxe-Coburg, Saxe-Altenburg, and both principalities of Reuß had gone so far as to have ballots printed up. But Prussia's bureaucrats feared that voters, inconvenienced by long waits in line to receive them, might go home without voting: not a happy prospect for a chancellor who was gambling on the conservative propensities of a mass electorate. Or they might become unruly, a prospect that no German government, vigilant guardians of public order, could abide. In the end it was decided to make each voter responsible for bringing his own ballot.[46] In practice, ballots were supplied by the parties.

Especially in rural precincts and small towns, a national party's contact men were likely to be the very worthies the governments needed to take on the unpaid office of election overseer.[47] As political neutrality was not (any more than in the United States) a requirement for the job, it was not unusual for the chairman of an election panel to distribute ballots for his favorite before and even during the election. Though inside the polling place ballot distribution was illegal, even if a panel were fastidious (and many were not) boundaries were so fluid that the restriction was easy to circumvent—as when an overseer in Krassow told voters appearing empty-handed to get ballots from his wife in the kitchen.[48]

Ballot distribution was part of a continuous process of monitoring (*kontrollieren*) that election overseers felt only too justified in undertaking. In some places, ballots were marked on the outside, and the chairman of the panel conscientiously (though illegally) recorded in his register how each man voted.[49] In others, the voting table was furnished with two election urns, one for each candidate.[50] Often ballots were laid out in front of the urn, and the voter was asked which one he wanted. On estates in Mecklenburg, in industrial Chemnitz, and in villages nearly everywhere, some chairmen simply opened the ballots and looked inside.[51]

Certainly many of the same overseers who felt entitled to know how a man voted felt equally authorized to change it. The stories of chairmen who opened

[46] Pollmann, *Parlamentarismus*, 87, 87n. 108, 88nn. 114f.

[47] On the difficulty of getting men to serve gratis: BAB-L R1501/14461, Bl. 220.

[48] 7 Oppeln, SBDR 5 Apr. 1871: 181. In the U.S. the principle of bipartisanship led to the appointment of election judges by the parties themselves. Harris, *Administration*, 8.

[49] 2 Braunschweig, SBDR 7 Jan. 1875: 873; 5 Marienwerder, AnlDR (1877, 3/I, Bd. 3) DS 106: 351, and SBDR 12 Mar. 1878: 481; 1 Kassel, AnlDR (1881, 5/II, Bd. 5) DS 184: 623; 5 Potsdam, AnlDR (1894/95, 9/III, Bd. 2) DS 243: 1013–15.

[50] 2 Stettin, AnlDR (1882/83, 5/II, Bd. 6) DS 200: 715; 6 AL, AnlDR (1894/95, 9/III, Bd. 2) DS 267: 1140–44; 8 Breslau, AnlDR (1912/14, 13/I, Bd. 23) DS 1638: 3572.

[51] Gut Dargelütz (3 Meckl.-Schw.): BAB-L R 1501/14662, Bl. 26 and SBDR 10 Feb. 1888: 820; 6 Mar. 1888: 1298; 3 Köslin, AnlDR (1884/85, 6/I, Bd. 6) DS 242: 1091; 13 Saxony, AnlDR (1887/88, 7/II, Bd. 4) DS 212: 905; 16 Saxony (Chemnitz), SBDR 10 Feb. 1888: 824, 825, 826; 1 Anhalt, AnlDR (1884/85, 6/I, Bd. 5) DS: 135: 511; 17 Han., AnlDR (1882/83, 5/II, Bd. 6) DS 242: 927; 3 Breslau, AnlDR (1882/83, 5/II, Bd. 6) DS 300: 1095; Lübeck, AnlDR (1893/94, 9/II, Bd.2) DS 131: 789f; 10 Frankfurt, AnlDR (1894/95, 9/III, Bd. 2) DS 195: 884–88; 2 Breslau, AnlDR (1894/95, 9/III, Bd. 2) DS 220: 942–46 and DS 336: 1371–77; 4 Merseburg, AnlDR (1894/95, 9/III, Bd. 2) DS 242: 1004–12; 3 Marienwerder, AnlDR (1898/1900, 10/I, Bd. 4) DS 507: 2663.

the ballot, read it aloud, and then had a member of the panel give the voter another, were legion.[52] "We can't use that ballot," the chairman in Conzell, Lower Bavaria, told voters in 1874 who presented National Liberal ones; "go on over there to his Reverence" (pointing to the priest hovering in the back of the room) "and fetch another." In Rothenburg-Hoyerswerda, Lower Silesia, an overseer took the ballot from Grüsche, the gardener's son, saying, "I just know this one isn't right" and handed him a Conservative ballot. Almost identical words were used a decade and half later in Groß Munzel in Hanover.[53] So long as there was no intent to deceive, who could call these switches "fraud?"[54] Some voters resisted, crying, "That's vile!" and tearing their ballots in their efforts to hang on to them. But the very refusal of this or that farmhand to be intimidated was then used by the winning party to argue that intimidation could have had no consequences.[55]

Opening the ballots, even handing them out in the polls, was often unnecessary for learning a voter's choice. Though regulations required white, unmarked slips of paper, folded so that the candidate's name was covered, the governments took no role in ensuring standardization.[56] Every ballot was presumed innocent until proven guilty. In practice, enforcement of even these minimal regulations was left to the discretion of the agents who distributed the ballots and to the overseers who could rule them invalid. The result was a free-for-all, as anyone wishing to monitor the votes of those beholden to them simply ensured that distinctive ballots were distributed.[57] The Gumbinnen Landrat who announced at a Conservative rally that their man's ballots would be easy to make out because they'd be printed on thick gray paper and smaller than the others was unusual only for not mincing words. Other tints included lemon yellow, violet, red, and ultramarine blue. Two Protest Party men in Alsace-Lorraine decorated their ballots with little pictures of swallows—flying westward.[58]

[52] 5 Breslau, SBDR 29 Mar. 1871: 46; 7 Oberb., SBDR 5 Apr. 1871: 186 and AnlDR (1871, 1/II, Bd. 2) DS 38: 91–94; 4 Königsberg and 2 Breslau in AnlDR (1894/95, 9/III, Bd. 2) DS 333: 1361–67 and DS 336: 1371–77, respectively.

[53] 2 Niederbayern, SBDR 11 Apr. 1874: 716; 10 Liegnitz, AnlDR (1874, 2/I, Bd. 3) DS 61: 238; Groß Munzel: Fr. Sievers, Kleinhändler (SD), Protest (9 Han.), 12 Mar. 1887, BAB-L R1501/14664, Bl. 77–87.

[54] Drenkmann, "Wahlvergehen," 175.

[55] SBDR 29 Mar. 1871: 46; 22 Saxony, AnlDR (1881, 5/II, Bd. 5) DS 193: 689, quote, 691.

[56] § 10 of the *Reichstags-Wahlgesetz*; § 15, paragraph 3 of the *Reglement* in *Reichstags-Wahlrecht* (1903), 11. No infraction was assumed just because one party manufactured its ballots differently from another. *Thätigkeit*, 161f; [Köller], *Ungiltigkeit*, 36.

[57] W. Löwe (F) SBDR 21 Jan. 1875: 1181. E.g., 7 Oberb., AnlDR (1871, 1/II, Bd. 2) DS 38: 94; 1 Arns., 6 Düsseldorf, 2 Magdeburg, 6 Arns., (Dortmund): in AnlDR (1894/95, 9/III, Bd. 2) DS 188: 870–72; DS 301: 1255f; DS 335: 1369–71; DS 354: 1489f, 1494.

[58] LR: 5 Gumb. (where officials were still in jail for previous election violations), AnlDR (1871, 1/II, Bd. 2) DS 80: 197; Richter SBDR 27 Apr. 1871: 432; colors: Meckl.-Strelitz AnlDr (1881/82, 5/I, Bd. 2) DS 32: 98f; A. Traeger (FVp) SBDR 11 Feb. 1888: 844; 6 Trier, AnlDR (1882/83, 5/II, Bd. 6) DS 323: 1325; Hiery, *Reichstagswahlen*, 417. Similarly in U.S.: Fredman, *Ballot*, 21; Harris, *Administration*, 151f.

An obvious solution to a dependent voter's dilemma was to accept the ballot desired by his betters, cross out the printed name, and pencil in his own choice.[59] But election panels delighted in ruling these ballots invalid, and for a long time the Reichstag's own position depended on the vagaries of its momentary composition.[60] So more reliable ruses were necessary. Centrum workers in Bochum spent the night before the 1881 election cutting the edges off their ballots, in order to make them conform to the tiny squares the mine owners were distributing.[61] That same year Munich Social Democrats mass-mailed ballots to working-class addresses, along with the following warning (addressed politely to "Your Well-Born"):

> At the polling place you may *not* count on their accepting the enclosed ballot! Should your situation force you to cast a ballot that bears the precise stamp of another party, without that party agreeing with your views, then you should obtain in one of the larger stationery stores a sheet of the corresponding paper and cut it out in the size of the ballot forced on you. On this slip write for yourself, or get one of your relatives to write, the name of our candidate in a legible hand. Then fold this ballot together precisely according to the model intended for you and put it without any further danger in the urn.[62]

A trip to the stationers did not always suffice. In one rural district, Liberals were stymied when two days before the election Conservatives passed out ballots made of handmade, deckle-edged paper such as could normally be found, they feared, only in archives. Their candidate was saved when a Liberal industrialist raced off to Berlin and searched every antique bookshop in town until he found identical parchment-like paper for his own party's ballots.[63]

As those wishing to monitor dependent voters were forced to make their ballots increasingly complicated (by 1903, Conservatives were issuing ballots in the form of straws, pyramids, and even bows), they were met with ever greater ingenuity on the part of those wishing to disguise their choice.[64] When the polls closed in the Ruhr town of Haspe and the panel (National Liberals all) shook out the urn, they were pleased to see the anticipated heap of triangular

---

[59] 70 LLs in 6 Arns., SBDR 13 Feb. 1886: 1061; 160 SDs in Chemnitz, SBDR 10 Feb. 1888: 824. 96 Z and 8 SD voters in 6 Trier, AnlDR (1891, 8/I, Bd. 3) DS 346: 2211, 2216.

[60] W. Schmalz, joiner, on 8 Kassel, 1890, BAB-L R1501/14668: 211–24; 2 Aachen in 1878: P.H.H. Lepper, *Strömungen* (1968) 2: 533; Lib. Protest in 1 Erfurt, 12 Mar. 1887, BAB-L R1501/14464, Bl. 12–29; 8 Hessen, AnlDR (1912/13, 13/I, Bd. 16) DS 350: 282, 290. RT tolerance: 9 Frankfurt, SBDR 19 Feb. 1888: 830, and Wacker, *Rechte*, 10f, 13.

[61] AnlDR (1882–83, 5/II, Bd. 6) DS 292: 1079; J. Bachem, SBHA 3 Mar. 1882: 627. Similar attempts by Socialists: Hasselmann SBDR 11 Apr. 1874: 718. Workers in 11 Breslau were afraid to attempt such subterfuges: AnlDR (1881–82, 5/I, Bd. 2) DS 104: 354f.

[62] AnlDR (1882/83 5/IV, Bd. 4) DS 123: 987. Cf. Steinwärder's SAP: H. Kutz-Bauer, *Arbeiterschaft* (1988), 119n. 26.

[63] F. H. Schröter (LV) SBDR 9 Dec. 1881: 292.

[64] 11 Breslau, AnlDR (1881/2, 5/I, Bd. 2) DS 104: 354; 1 Köslin: *FrankZ*, Nr. 60, 1 Mar. 1903, BAB-L R1501/14456, Bl. 3. LL solutions: SBDR 13 May 1887: 591–600, esp. 592f.

ballots tumble out. Shock came when they read off the names inside: not the Barmen indigo merchant Ernst von Eynern, but the radical journalist Eugen Richter. To pull off such an eleventh-hour switch was the dream of every party. But when the owners of a coke-smelting plant in Linden discovered that on *their* triangles voters had crossed through the National Liberal and written in the Centrum candidate, they charged ballot-tampering.[65] Wary partisans learned to hold back until the last minute before manufacturing their ballots, in order to ensure that they were sufficiently distinctive to allow easy monitoring—or, alternatively, sufficiently similar to escape it. In 1887 security in Saarbrücken was so tight that the chairman of the Kartell's Election Committee did not inform his colleagues until forty-eight hours before the election where their ballots could be picked up. Agents were to "distribute them personally . . . , [and] only on election day itself," he insisted, "so that the form and the paper remain unknown and can no longer be imitated by the other side."[66] An even greater precaution was the "General Staff Plan" developed by some Liberal groups for a *series* of distinctive ballots to succeed one another over the course of a day's voting.[67]

Voters came to expect dirty tricks. None was more common than the circulation of ballots that appeared to be for one man, but—because of a different first name or some other "error" (such as Adolf for Adolph)—actually designated another. Voters would cast these ballots in good faith, only to have them ruled invalid or credited to some nonexistent candidate.[68] Although craft was typically the weapon of the weak, the prize for cunning went to Eisleben's Free Conservatives, who played on the voters' fear of such a trick as a way to monitor the voting. Handbills posted at the polls warned voters to look carefully at their ballots, for some of those bearing the name of (the Free Conservative) Dr. Otto Arendt were fraudulent and would be invalidated. The purpose? Those voters who did *not* pull out their ballots to check were obviously not carrying Arendt ballots.[69] The Right's perennial complaint against the Reichstag's "secret" ballot was that it invited hypocrisy. In its semisecret state, however, what the Reichstag ballot did most to encourage was resourcefulness.

---

[65] Traeger SBDR 11 Feb. 1888: 844. 5 Arns. AnlDR (1882/83, 5/II, Bd. 6) DS 292: 1078f; 1080.

[66] Rickert SBDR 14 Jan. 1890: 1014. Protest on Schwarzberg-Sondershausen, 27 Dec. 1881, BAB-L R101/3342, Bl. 309–12. Saarbrücken in 1902 by-election: J. Bellot, *Hundert Jahre* (1954), 210.

[67] J. Lenzmann SBDR 15 Feb. 1886: 1061.

[68] NLs issued ballots for the well-known *August* Reichensperger (Z) in Krefeld, when his brother *Peter* was the candidate. SBDR 22 Apr. 1871: 318. In Essen, opponents of Forcade de Biaix were said to have tricked 50 voters with ballots for "Fromage de Brie." *GA*, Nr. 30, 5 Feb. 1874: 173. NL accusations against SDs: 13 Saxony, AnlDR (1887/88, 7/II, Bd. 4) DS 212: 907; Adolf for Adolph: 23 Saxony in 1869, 3 Bromberg in 1881: Leser, *Untersuchungen*, 19–22. Gurwitsch, *Schutz*, 42–44. Such actions were criminal in France, Italy, Spain, and Portugal. Granville Survey Nr. 1, BAB-L R1501/14451, Bl. 56–59. But see Charnay, *Les scrutins*, 101.

[69] 5 Merseburg, AnlDR (1912/14, 13/I, Bd. 19) DS 840: 1136–39, esp. 1137. Posters at the polls were in any case technically illegal.

Now and then some honest election agent would try to get his competitors to agree to standardize their ballots. Such a treaty was worked out in Elberfeld in the eighties and eventually in Bochum and Mülheim, to mutual satisfaction. The legal scholar Georg Meyer claimed to have negotiated similar agreements that had worked for years.[70] When Chaplain Georg Dasbach challenged Baron Karl von Stumm in the Saar to join him in issuing standardized ballots, however, Stumm flatly declined. More commonly, the party with the most local economic power agreed and then double-crossed the other—for example, by producing ballots with missing corners and (when that was hastily imitated) folding them in a five-cornered "bishop's cap."[71]

Given the broad requirement that ballots be on white, unmarked paper, the propriety of these variations was always open to challenge. And the elaborate codes some overseers occasionally set up to link each ballot with its voter were clearly illegal.[72] But even when the letter of the law was strictly followed, the voter's privacy might be breached. Unlike Holland, Belgium, Luxemburg, and England, voting regulations in Germany required that the chairman of the election panel, not the voter himself, put the ballot in the urn, a provision dictated by the governments' anxiety lest some citizen arrive with additional ballots up his sleeve, and by its fear of "tumult" should unruly subjects come close enough to snatch a ballot out.[73] Once he got his hands on it, the chairman had wide latitude in deciding whether the ballot met regulations. An art developed by which practiced chairmen could determine how a man voted. He might make a sharp dent with his thumbnail in the corner of a ballot.[74] He might "candle" a ballot, holding it up to the light so that the name could be read through the paper.[75] Should a candled ballot be invalidated because its secrecy had been violated? To do so would deprive the innocent citizen of his vote in order to punish an overseer who had exceeded his authority; it would be an emphatic statement that the preservation of secrecy was the responsibility— indeed the duty—of the citizen, not a restraint on the state.

[70] Meyer, *Wahlrecht*, 565. Meyer was NL deputy for Jena, 1881–90. Mülheim: Müller, *Strömungen*, 369.

[71] 1 Anhalt (1884/85, 6/I, Bd. 5), DS 135: 509–10 (WPK: "a purely private matter"); 5 Arns. (1884/85, 6/I, Bd. 7) DS 320: 1771; agreements in Elberfeld and Bochum: G. Stötzel (Z) and E. Klein (NL) SBDR 11 Feb. 1888: 840, 845. Asking deputies from all parties to sign a statement requesting all local election committees to make similar agreements: Rickert SBDR 15 Jan. 1890: 1014. Stumm: Bellot, *Hundert Jahre*, 184.

[72] 9 Potsdam (1884/85, 6/I, Bd. 5) DS 74: 247f.

[73] R. Siegfried, "Wahlurne" (1906), 754.

[74] Rickert SBDR 14 Jan. 1890: 1013; Delors (Els) SBDR 21 Apr. 1903: 8925f.

[75] 2 Hessen, 1867; 22 Saxony and 4 Oppeln, 1871; 10 Liegnitz, AnlDR (1874, 2/I, Bd. 3) DS 61: 238; 5 Marienwerder, AnlDR (1877, 3/I, Bd. 3), DS 106: 351; 5 Gumb., AnlDR (1881, 5/II, Bd. 6) DS 283: 1038–40; 3 Köslin and 6 Potsdam, both in AnlDR (1884/85, 6/I Bd. 6) DS 242: 1091 and DS 248: 1105; 2 Merseburg, SBDR 5 Feb. 1885: 1101; Lib. protest on 1 Erfurt, 12 Mar. 1887, BAB-L R1501/14664, Bl. 12–29; 10 Frankfurt, 5 Arns., 4 Königsberg, 2 Breslau, AnlDR (1894/95, 9/III, Bd. 2) DS 195: 884–88; DS 318: 1319–23, DS 333: 1361–67, DS 336: 1371–77, respectively. 7 Gumb., AnlDR (1912/14, 13/I, Bd. 23) 1586: 3442.

To insist on a ballot on which the candidate's name would remain indiscernible under all conceivable circumstances was, some pronounced, the counsel of perfection. Yet effective safeguards for privacy were not beyond the mind of nineteenth-century man to devise. A uniform, officially printed ballot, distributed at the polls, and marked in secret had been introduced in Canada as early as 1856. It had spread rapidly through the Antipodes (where, as the "Australian ballot," it acquired its permanent name), appeared in Louisville, Kentucky, in 1888, and within a few years had been adopted throughout the United States— hardly polities with strong cultural impulses toward standardization. In Portugal and Belgium the Australian ballot had become de rigueur by 1881. Belgium had also enacted severe penalties for secrecy violations and developed a regulation ballot box—with double sets of locks and keys.[76] In this march of progress, France and Germany were the major holdouts.[77]

The toleration of so much multiformity in Imperial Germany had to rest on a broad, if tacit, political consensus. Certainly the Prussian government—which demanded detailed reports on "Election Prospects" from each of its Landräte— gave no sign over the years of a diminishing desire for the fullest possible information on the voting habits of the King's subjects—although its representatives soon learned to be somewhat less candid than our Gumbinnen Landrat in announcing it.[78] But "probably no party," conceded the Progressive Wilhelm Löwe, "could be entirely acquitted of having once, at some time or another, attempted to monitor the balloting." Even Social Democrats had an interest in penetrating the "veil of electoral secrecy," as it was called.[79]

Nevertheless the tacit consensus ensuring that the veil of secrecy remained diaphanous was an unstable one, gaping holes being easier to overlook in the precincts than to defend on the Reichstag floor. Already in 1869 the National Liberal Anton Ludwig Sombart moved to require official ballot envelopes. Though supported by a number of Progressives and even by such prominent

[76] Harris, *Administration*, 18, 152–99; Kousser, however, has plausibly described the introduction of the Australian ballot in the U.S. as an effort to *restrict* suffrage, by making voting impossible for illiterates (the poor generally and African-Americans and the foreign-born specifically). *Shaping*, chap. 2, and "Suffrage," 1249. The continent: Granville Survey Nr. 1, BAB-L R1501/14451, Bl. 52, Bl. 57; [R. Siegfried], "Wahl," *Meyer's Konversationslexikon* 19 (1898/99), BAB-L R101/3344, Bl. 258.

[77] Lefèvre-Pontalis, *Élections*, vii, 17–19; Seymour/Frary, *World* 1: 379f. R. Siegfried to the gov't.: 11 Nov. 1893, BAB-L R101/3344, Bl. 15f.

[78] "Wahlaussichten für die Provinz . . . " as well as Manteuffel's report on AL to Wm. I, 30 Oct. 1881, GStA PK I. HA, Rep. 89/210, Bl. 202–47, inclusive; "Tätigkeit der Geistlichen und Beamten bei der Reichstagswahlbewegung (Geheim)," RR v. Horn to OP in Coblenz, 24 Feb. 1907, LHAK 408/8806 (hereafter: Horn Report); more generally: H. v. Gerlach, *Erlebnisse* (1919), 43f. Reporting to the Kaiser personally: GStA PK I. HA, Rep. 89/211, Bl. 30–38v, 75–80v, 143–45v, 167b–167c, 182–86; GStA PK I. HA, Rep. 89/210, unpaginated.

[79] Löwe SBDR 21 Jan. 1875: 1181. Charges against 8 Saxony, AnlDR (1871, 1/I, Bd. 3) DS 30: 87; but see 1 Oberb. (Munich I), 13 June 1881, AnlDR (1882/83, 5/IV, Bd. 4) DS 123: 981–89, esp. 984. "Veil of electoral secrecy": Gerstner (F) SBDR 5 Apr. 1871: 172; and J. Knorr, "Statistik der Wahlen zum ersten deutschen Reichstag" (1872), col. 341.

Liberal colleagues as Rudolf von Bennigsen the motion failed. In 1875 Joseph Völk, a liberal Augsburg lawyer, submitted a new version of Sombart's motion. This time the National Liberals temporized, preferring to wait for a recommendation from the Election Commission, which had just been created.[80] When the Social Democrats followed with similar envelope motions in 1877–78, they found that seven (and in northern Germany, eleven) years of practice had now established a strong presumption in favor of the status quo.[81] Indeed, the Württemberg Landtag, which had prescribed official ballot envelopes to protect its voters' privacy in state elections since 1868, repealed its envelope law in 1883.[82]

Although Social Democrats, Left Liberals, and Centrum men continued to submit motions to protect the ballot, only in 1894—more than a quarter of a century after the idea was first introduced—did the Reichstag finally mandate an official envelope.[83] But like any legal change, this needed the approval of the Bundesrat, the Prussian-dominated council of federated governments—a body that preferred the devil it knew to the devil it didn't know. When the Dutch government, investigating alternatives to its own election law, inquired of the Empire's Office of Domestic Affairs (*Reichsamt des Innern*) whether Germany's requirement that each voter procure his own ballot had produced any difficulties in the proper administration of elections, Vice-Chancellor Karl von Bötticher responded with a complacent negative. Complaints about violations of secrecy had been plentiful, he conceded, but the overwhelming majority had been disproved upon investigation. He acknowledged that a motion had been submitted to the Reichstag to introduce envelopes, but saw no cause for the federated governments to respond to it. Now that the Reichstag had ruled that a ballot was valid even after the name printed on it had been crossed out and a new one written in, everything necessary for the voter's independence had been insured.[84]

Only in 1903, as we shall see in chapter 8, was the Bundesrat willing to support a version of Sombart's envelope, along with the requirement of some sort of booth or alcove in which to vote. The Right, lacking the votes to defeat it, attempted to kill the measure with ridicule, repeatedly likening the voting

[80] Pollmann, *Parlamentarismus*, 326n. 88. Kircher, Parisius, Gneist SBDR 21 Jan. 1875: 1174, 1178f. Sombert estimated the costs in 1869 at 3,000 Thaler; Parisius in 1876, between 5,000 and 10,000 Thaler. On Völk's motion, W. Frankenburger (F) SBDR 10 Apr. 1878: 871. The WPK recommended envelopes: AnlDR (1876, 2/IV, Bd. 3) DS 111: 816. Rickert SBDR 15 Jan. 1890: 1013.

[81] Antrag Blos and Most, AnlDR (1878, 3/II, Bd. 3) DS 66: 550; Blos SBDR 10 Apr. 1878: 870. Against: F. Dernberg (NL) SBDR 10 Apr. 1878: 872.

[82] BAB-L R1501/14456, Bl. 125. On repeal: BAB-L R1501/14453, Bl. 250; G. Struckmann (NL) SBDR 15 Jan. 1890: 1016f.

[83] Hatschek, *Kommentar*, 324–27. Virtually the same bills, submitted by Rickert (F) and Gröber (Z), reprinted as "Anträge Rickert, bzw. Antrag Gröber und Gen.": in *Reichstags-Wahlrecht*, 32–35. Finally, a resolution by the WPK gave the proposal the wording in which, in session after session, in 1894, 1896, and 1899, it would pass with great majorities, with only K dissent. The history of the proposal in a secret memo recommending adoption: Count A. Posadowsky, 25 Nov. 1902, BAB-L R 1501/14455, Bl. 127–31.

[84] Marschall de Bieberstein to Bötticher, 14 Oct. 1891; Bötticher to Marschall, 14 Nov. 1891, BAB-L R1501/14454, Bl. 108–15.

booth to a horror chamber, a confession box, and most continually and with greatest effect, to a toilet, punning archly on the "closet law" and speculating about what might be done if a voter chose to stay there all day. How would it appear if the chancellor, for example, arrived at the polls and had to be told, "Your excellency must wait, the privy [*geheimer Ort*] is still occupied"? When a Social Democrat responded sarcastically by doubting whether the booth would "provide such an attractive space, that it would offer so many pleasures," the idea was picked up throughout the press and soon found predictable permutations in the humor magazines.[85]

THE ISOLATION CELL

Man walks into shed labelled "voting closet," holding a ballot for a Centrum candidate. "A ballot, a ballot!"

He emerges, fastening his suspenders, sighing "Sooooo!"

Meaning: A Centrum ballot makes good toilet paper.
Figure 1. O. Gulbransson, "Die Isolierzell," *Simplicissimus* VIII (n.d., 1903–4): Extra-Nummer: Reichstagswahl, 10.

[85] The term "*Örtchen*" was a euphemism for toilet—itself, of course, a euphemism. Himburg SBDR 21 Apr. 1903: 8911; Blos, ibid., 8912. The RT President's attempt to explain that the term

The association between the poll booths and privies offered an opportunity for partisan mockery that few could resist.

THE MISUNDERSTOOD VOTING BOOTH

Priest: "Seppenbauer, let's drink one for the Centrum!"
Farmer: "OK by me!

Priest: "And always with the Centrum, right Seppenbauer? Have another pint."

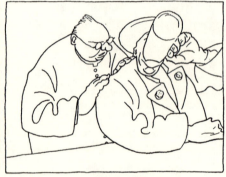

"For Throne and Altar, right Seppenbauer? Just one more pint!"

"And don't forget, Seppenbauer, and now come along!"

Even without the scatological associations insisted upon by professional satirists and conservative polemicists, the voting booth found little favor among the more old-fashioned of the Liberals. Georg Meyer, a jurist with an unrivaled knowledge of suffrage laws thoughout the world and well aware of the terms in which the debate in his own country was being cast, added his voice to the

"Closet Law" was a translation from Australian terminology and therefore not a form of ridicule only provoked greater laughter. Ibid., 8923; "Deutsches Reich. Die Wahlfälschungen," *Vorwärts*, 22 Jan. 1903, BAB-L R1501/14455, Bl. 158. Bülow, distancing himself from a measure his govt. was sponsoring, perhaps to mollify the Right took to referring to the Rickert bill as the *Klosett-Gesetz* and the isolation cell as the "privy." BT, Nr. 134, 14 Mar. 1903. BAB-L R1501/14456, Bl. 38; "Die gestrige Rede des Reichskanzlers," *KrZ*, 21 Jan. 1903, BAB-L R1501/14455, Bl. 156. "Angstkammer:" Müller (FK) SBDR 15 Jan. 1890: 1022; ridicule: Rickert, ibid., 1012, 1015. "Beichtstuhl," Geck SBDR 21 Apr. 1903: 8921.

"OK now, go on in Seppenbauer, and hit it right!"   "Yes–what–is–that–then?"

Figure 2 (*Continued*)

Meaning: The peasant is incapable of understanding the vote, but he does understand how to thwart his pastor.
Fig 2. O. Gulbransson, "Die mißverstandene Wahlkabine," *Simplicissimus* XVI 2/40 (1 Jan. 1912): 705.

chorus declaring that "the voter who . . . needed an opaque envelope and an isolation space" was "indeed an almost comical figure, the entire contrivance, almost an ironic commentary on our modern public life."[86]

The introduction of the ballot envelope in 1903 did not produce satisfaction even among its supporters. Although in some places it clearly contributed to freer elections, voters also complained, as we shall see in chapter 8, that when chairmen used small ballot boxes, the bulky envelopes preserved the order of voting so well that it was child's play to keep track of who voted for whom. Experts in European election processes claimed that the ballot envelope had actually worsened the chances for secrecy.[87] What was needed, it was now clear, was a standardized container, one that would automatically mix the ballots upon opening. From all over Europe, academics, inventors, and businessmen with an eye to profits began to compete to design the perfect ballot box.[88] But the impe-

[86] Although these words were written before the debate in 1903 (Meyer died in 1900), Meyer had followed a decade of polemic over the issue and was convinced of the irresistibility of these safeguards, which enjoyed "an uncommon popularity." *Wahlrecht*, 563.
[87] Predicted: Hodenberg (W) SBDR 21 Apr. 1903: 8921. Siegfried, "Wahllurne," 735; Leser, *Untersuchungen*, 92.
[88] BAB-L R1501/14474, Bl. 107, 164, 167f 200f, 206, 214–22, 263–65, 268, 272, 321–23, 330, 335, 338, 342; BAB-L R1501/14696, Bl. 40–41; "Ein lobenswerter Landrat," *Die Hilfe* 13/3 (20 Jan. 1907): 33. The imperial govt. had been approached with a proposal for a voting machine as early as 1890: BAB-L R1501/14693, Bl. 216–27.

rial government steadfastly refused to put itself behind any of the inventions. Only in 1913, after the empire's last election and the same year that France finally introduced the envelope and voting booth, did the chancellor's office require the "urn" to conform to any minimum specifications.[89] In the meantime, violations of secrecy had continued, universally acknowledged and only partially diminished.

The existence of dwarf precincts had always done much to encourage resignation about the possibility of preserving secrecy. Although the norm for election districts was set in 1869 at 100,000 residents, the election code stipulated that each separate community (*Gemeinde*) should normally form its own precinct, with an outside limit of 3,500 souls. Inside limits were nonexistent. When sparsely populated regions followed these provisions, the result might look like Dörnfeld, in Schwarzburg-Rudolstadt, which in 1871 consisted of four voters: a farmer, his stable boy, his fodder boy, and his hired man—too few even to field a panel of overseers.[90] Except in cities over 20,000, nearly half of Germany's precincts in 1874 contained no more than 100 voters. In precincts with only a handful of voters, or where the estate owner chaired the panel, or where the vote was unanimous, no envelope would provide secrecy. In communities like these, "everyone knew very well how each one has voted, and anyone who doesn't know can easily find out."[91]

Dwarf precincts did not disappear. In fact, Robert von Puttkamer, Prussian Minister of Interior throughout most of the eighties, encouraged the division of rural precincts into even smaller units. In the nineties, when Vice-Chancellor Bötticher was pooh-poohing complaints about secrecy by declaring that violations were limited to small precincts, he implied that these were exceptional.[92] But as late as 1905, 57,286 villages across the land comprised fewer than five hundred people—women and children as well as men.[93] One provision of Heinrich Rickert's secrecy motion would have established a minimum precinct population—originally 400, but eventually whittled down to 125 persons. But even this was too many for the imperial government which, when it finally agreed to envelopes and booths in 1903, pointedly ignored the Rickert motion's modest provision for a minimum precinct size.[94] Thus in many precincts it remained a

---

[89] C. v. Schorlemer, M. of Agriculture, to Delbrück, 26 Dec. 1912, BAB-L R1501/14476, unpaginated; "Die Wahlurnen. Staatssekretär Delbrück und Minister von Dallwitz," *VossZ*, 3 Apr. 1913, "Reichstagswahlurnen," *KrZ*, 3 Apr. 1913, BAB-L R1501/14476. For views that the 1912 election was the worst: Bertram, *Wahlen*, 129–38.

[90] SBDR 24 May 1871: 913. Similarly, in 4 Marienwerder, SBDR 28 Mar. 1871: 29; in 3 Mecklenburg, SBDR 6 Mar. 1888: 1310.

[91] Frankenburger SBDR 10 Apr. 1878: 872; Pollmann, *Parlamentarismus*, 91.

[92] Puttkamer to RPen in Kreisordnungsprovinzen & den Hohenzollernschen Ländern, 7 Sept. 1884, BAB-L R1501/14642, Bl. 9; "Wie Bismarck" 1/5: 9. Bötticher to Marschall, 14 Nov. 1891, BAB-L R1501/14454, Bl. 108–15.

[93] Compiled from the *Statistisches Jahrbuch* (1908), 6. BAB-L R1501/14456, Bl. 127v.

[94] §6 of the "Gesetzes-Antrag betreffend Abänderung des Wahlgesetzes . . . " (Gröber-Rickert bill) in *Reichstags-Wahlrecht*, 32; §7 of the Wahlreglement, as revised in the chancellor's Bekannt-

relatively easy matter for big men to keep track of the voting behavior, if not of all of Germany's citizens, then at least of their own subordinates—which they did. One can imagine the feelings with which a postman, policeman, or railway conductor in the Second Trier opened his newspaper the day after the furious "Hottentot" election of 1907 and learned that his precinct's vote for the Centrum had been unanimous. Such a postman knew (and knew that his superior would know) that either through abstention or dissent, he had failed to meet his "voting obligation." Unanimity, or even a smaller pro-government vote than the number of government employees in his precinct, left him no place to hide.[95]

Clearly, where populations were thin and transportation poor, to insist that precincts be formed across several communities (a solution envisioned in the 1870 Voting Regulations) would have put the polls so far apart as to deny many voters the possibility of exercising their franchise at all.[96] Yet practical difficulties did not tell the whole story. As early as 1878 it was suggested that anonymity could be encouraged without harm to the voters' convenience by simply *counting* the ballots of several precincts at a central location.[97] In Britain such a provision was enacted in 1872—and continues today, long after the need has disappeared. But no comparable measures were taken in Germany. In Mecklenburg-Schwerin, for example, as late as 1912, seventy-five precincts contained twenty-five or fewer eligible voters.[98]

PRIVATE CHOICES, PUBLIC LIFE

In the end, of course, it was not the size of the precincts nor the infirmities of the ballot papers that accounts for the ease with which the citizens of the Reich were able to watch each other vote. Like the snickers that accompanied the introduction of the voting booth, the weakness in Germany's secrecy provisions reflected the ambivalence of many of these citizens about the very privacy that the ballot was meant to guarantee.

The secrecy of the ballot was in tension with the public nature of the election, another premise of voting freedom and one that was (at least in the minds of the legislators) psychologically superordinate. The wording of the 1869 Imperial

machung of 28 Apr. 1903 in *Reichstags-Wahlgesetz*, 12. The government promised to tackle the problem administratively.
[95] Horn Report, 24 Feb. 1907, LHAK 408/8806, letter carriers: "Wie Bismarck" 1/5: 14.
[96] The electors (*Wahlmänner*) of Prussia's LT deputies sometimes traveled almost sixty miles to get to the polls: "Wahl-Eifer," *Preußisches Wochenblatt* 5 (5 Jan. 1856): 363–69.
[97] Frankenburger SBDR 10 Apr. 1878: 872. The Weimar Republic made it illegal to announce the results of elections on the precinct level. Even so an American who made a study of the working of the Weimar election law—a study that is a paean to the German bureaucracy for its honesty and efficiency—reported that safeguards for secrecy were inadequate. These otherwise meticulous *Bürger*, he conceded, did not seem to mind. J. K. Pollock, *Administration* (1934), 33.
[98] Gwyn, *Democracy*, 91–92; Siegfried, "Wahlurne," 758n. 1; Stadthagen (SD) SBDR 21 May 1912: 2212; and in 4 Potsdam AnlDR (1912/14, 13/I, Bd. 22) DS 1435: 2944.

Election Law stated clearly that "the election process, as well as the determination of the election results, is public." The privacy of the voting act, on the other hand, although explicit in § 20 of the constitution, remained only implicit in the Imperial Election Law, in its requirement that ballot papers be folded and that they contain no outward mark. It took a quarter of a century for the Reichstag to feel it necessary to pass an amendment stating clearly that "the election is secret."[99]

Tellingly, the same paragraph that prohibited outward marks on the ballot also forbade the voter to sign it. In enacting this provision, the deputies were deliberately rejecting a practice then enshrined in the Bavaria's election law, which positively required such signatures.[100] Signed ballots, they knew, which made the voter's choice known to those counting the ballots while keeping it secret from his fellows, delivered the voter much more effectively into the hands of those who stood over him than oral voting could ever have done.[101] To leave one's choice secret, however, often went against deferential impulses that would not be denied. Newspapers felt it necessary to instruct their readers that it was "absolutely impermissible" to sign their ballots. But it took some time to convince the voter that the anonymous ballot was not his to take or leave. In 1881 Carl Geissler, a mechanic in the Upper Lausitz, hired a scribe in order to write to Bismarck personally, announcing, with much fanfare, his intent to vote for the chancellor's son Wilhelm—a pointless gesture since Bill Bismarck was not a candidate.[102] Rural voters still held out unfolded ballots to their chairman and asked if they were correct. Liberal jurists might argue that "the secret vote is not a subjective right of the individual, which the latter is allowed to forego," and eventually the Reichstag ruled invalid any ballot that had not been folded. But not even all deputies agreed with this stringent view. And as late as 1912 some voters were still signing their ballots.[103]

Ambivalence about secret voting had underlain the very first discussions about political participation, not only in Germany but throughout Europe. British resistance, before 1872, to George Grote's annual amendments proposing a secret ballot was widely publicized. Lord John Russell had declared "all modern parliamentary history . . . a continuous and successful struggle for public-

---

[99] §9 of the *Reichstags-Wahlgesetz*, 5; also in Huber, ed., *Dokumente* 2: 243–45; constitution of NDB: 231; §11a of the Rickert-Gröber motion: in *Reichstags-Wahlrecht*, 32–47.

[100] Ritter/Niehuss, *Arbeitsbuch*, 152. Bavaria amended the law only in 1881. Some voters signed their ballots, however, to safeguard them from a panel they distrusted: 6 Gumb. AnlDR (1875, 2/III, Bd. 4) DS 82: 838.

[101] The Frankfurt Assembly's Constitutional Commission had included its provision for oral voting in the same paragraph in which they had prohibited state or local officials from sitting on election panels—and indeed as part of the same argument. Oral voting was a guarantee that election results would not be manipulated by agents of the government; that they would, on the contrary, represent "public" opinion.

[102] Geissler to the DKA, 26 Oct, 1881, BAB-L R1501/14693, Bl. 88; *GA* Nr. 46, 23 Feb. 1871: 380; *GA* Nr. 51, 1 Mar. 1871: 423; cf. "Auf zur Wahl!" *KV*, 28 July 1878.

[103] E.g., 5 Königsberg (DS 1401: 2896) and 2 Breslau (DS 1432: 2929), both in AnlDR (1912/14, 13/I, Bd. 22); 7 Gumb., AnlDR (1912/14, 13/I, Bd. 23) DS 1586: 3397f; attaching their addresses: 4 Potsdam, AnlDR (1912/14, 13/I, Bd. 22) DS 1435: 2945. Quote: Hatschek, *Kommentar*, 188–89; cf. also Kircher SBDR 21 Jan. 1875: 1174.

ity. . . ." The young William E. Gladstone had gone so far as to blame the secret ballot for the fall of the Roman republic.[104] German lawmakers and public-spirited citizens generally were familiar with these arguments, and when the Constitutional Commission of the Frankfurt National Assembly reported overwhelmingly in favor of oral voting in 1849, it had cited British theory and British practice on behalf of its decision.[105] Practical arguments in the 1840s had pointed in the same direction. In an age before political parties had begun effectively to structure the electorate, secret voting seemed to court two dangers. The first was that individuals, in their mutual isolation, would scatter their votes among so many candidates as to deprive the winner, whose total count might be tiny and whose margin of victory, accidental, of any legitimacy. The second danger followed naturally from trying to avoid (or, some would say, to exploit) the first. Some men, it was feared, would surely conspire behind the scenes to pool their votes, an arrangement that, given the fragmentation of opinion so long as others were voting "blind," would automatically privilege the "particular interests" of such a cabal over the collective interests of the district.

More important than the fear of the faction, or of the underhand manipulations of state officials, however, was an understanding of *res publica*, of public life, that was incompatible with any kind of secrecy. As recent historians have emphasized, the very concept of a German nation had developed in tandem with the notion of a "public" and a "public sphere," concepts invested with great emotional resonance in a region where only recently a multitude of princely courts, ambiguously straddling private and public worlds, had been the main locus of political power. In 1848 Frankfurt's Constitutional Commission had felt that it was precisely public voting that would enable "the predominant view of a district" to find expression. The phrasing was important. It was the opinion of the constituency, not the individual, that the Commission assumed should be heard; public opinion, not private *opinions*, formed the building blocks of a truly national representation of which the Reichstag was to be the crown. If the nation were to "achieve an independent and energetic character," the Commission had argued, "then all acts of political significance must be exposed to the winds of public opinion. Precisely this offers a counterweight to improper influences from one side or the other." Implicit in the Commission's argument was a belief that public voting had an important pedagogical function. Why else did the Commission see the "publicity of the voting act" as "the most important part of all" of the new franchise? Why else, but because "here alone lies the guarantee that the voting act will attain its proper goal: . . . accustoming the nation to a truly public life. . . ."[106]

Such arguments for open voting were most plausible where the voter could

[104] Among major British figures, only Disraeli seems initially to have supported the secret ballot. Seymour, *Reform*, 209, 214, 431.

[105] Hatschek, *Kommentar*, 180. Rohe, however, emphasizes the long tradition of secret voting prescribed in both the municipal ordinance of Nov. 1808 and the election regulations for provincial LTe. *Wahlen*, 35.

[106] Quoted in Hatschek, *Kommentar*, 80, 167f, 181; Meyer concurs: *Wahlrecht*, 562.

be conceived as a steward for the interests of the unenfranchised—as was the case in Britain. With universal suffrage, however, each citizen could represent himself. Perhaps for this reason, in 1849 the plenum of the Frankfurt Assembly rejected the reasoning of the Constitutional Commission and took the revolutionary step of enacting the secret ballot. When in 1866 the Prussian government resurrected the franchise of the Frankfurt National Assembly, it therefore had a choice between two Frankfurt precedents: the Commission's and the plenum's. Uncertain which was most likely to work in its favor, the government's draft left the secrecy of the ballot implicit.[107] First Peter Reichensperger, a leading spokesmen for Catholic interests, then the National Liberal Hugo Fries, offered constitutional amendments that stipulated secret voting.[108] Even so, principled opposition to the ballot was forcefully expressed by Reichensperger's fellow Catholic and future colleague in the Centrum, the Hanoverian Ludwig Windthorst, who invoked hallowed English precedent and the arguments of John Stuart Mill on behalf of open voting.[109] In the end, neither the Conservatives nor the government felt sure enough of whom secrecy might benefit to oppose it, while the majority gave the motion not so much support as a limp acquiescence.

The Conservatives' uncertainty as to where their advantage lay was never entirely dispelled. In the sixties Hans von Kleist-Retzow and Karl Strosser had argued in favor of a secret ballot, being convinced—with some justice—that Progressive victories in the Prussian Landtag had been owed to economic pressures on the voters exerted by liberal employers. Their arguments continued to find analogs in later decades. In the early eighties, a voter with clear Christian Social (Stoeckerite) views wrote the chancellor pleading for the introduction of the secret ballot in Prussian state elections as the only way to protect the laboring poor from intimidation by Social Democrats, Progressives, and Catholic priests. Still later, a number of Conservatives supported a similar demand for Saxon elections.[110] On the other hand, in 1888 newspapers were reporting rumors that the imperial administration was planning to get rid of the legal requirement for secret balloting in Reichstag elections. In fact, it had already asked for an opinion from Professor Paul Laband, a leading constitutional scholar, about whether such a change would be possible without Reichstag approval. The uproar on the part of the Centrum and Left Liberals was so great,

---

[107] Von Roon's memorandum to the SM, 27 May 1866, tentatively suggested secret ballots as a way to produce *Conservative* LT majorities. BAB-L R43/685, Bl. 21–25. Pollmann, *Parlamentarismus*, 75f and 77n. 53.

[108] Fries: SBNRT, 1867: 414, discussed in Hatschek, *Kommentar*, 182, and Pollmann, *Parlamentarismus*, 84n. 95, 85, 188n. 204, 225nn. 139, 142.

[109] SBDR 18 Apr. 1871: 328. Windthorst soon changed his mind.

[110] Memorandum (unsigned) to Bis., 5 Jan. 1885, BAB-L R43/685, Bl. 185–188v; Saxon SM Memorandum on the Electoral Law, 31 Dec. 1903, quoted in [H.] D[elbrück], "Preußische Wahlreform" (1907), 191; Below, *Wahlrecht*, 155f, 156n. 129, 167; Pollmann, *Parlamentarismus*, 85n. 96, 171n. 110. Liberal disillusion with open voting in LT elections: Kühne, *Dreiklassenwahlrecht*, 115.

however, that spokesmen of the "Kartell" (pro-government) parties and then the government itself were forced to deny any such intention.[111]

For all its insubstantiality in shielding the voter, the "secret" ballot erected a powerful barrier against overturning an election in which someone in authority—election overseer, employer, official, local big man—was suspected of interposing himself between the ballot box and the popular will. It was easy to see that a voter, caught between rival forces in a village, might give promises before the election and, in the face of intimidating queries from their masters, secular and spiritual, make claims afterward that hardly tallied with the precincts' totals. Such discrepancies made it easy for the losing party to cry fraud, but the only way the allegation could be proven would have been to interrogate the voter under oath—putting the vulnerable in "a very peculiar situation." The Reichstag therefore usually refused to investigate charges of ballot snatching and switching, arguing that inquiries that depended on interrogation would "penetrate the veil of the secret vote."[112]

A deputy's concern for the veil of secrecy very much depended, of course, on whose ox, behind the veil, was being gored. Since fraud allegations rarely concerned more than a handful of votes, the Reichstag's reluctance to penetrate that veil in its postelection interrogations was probably of small material consequence for the success or failure of an election challenge. Where the veil's existence really mattered was in defending victories against charges that votes had been extorted by pressures of various kinds: "influence." Whatever threats might be proven, the ballot's putative secrecy cut the connection between an outside power and the conscience of the voter. "We have, after all, a secret ballot!" was, as we have seen, a ready-made rebuttal disarming nearly every attack.[113] The power of the ballot was invoked not only by supporters of the government—Conservatives, Free Conservatives, and National Liberals—but also by Guelfs, Centrum, and Progressives. "We must assume," insisted the Progressive Saxon landowner C. G. Riedel, "that the secret ballot protects the voter from every interference with his franchise. In a word, the system of secret voting stands in contradiction to the assumption of any really effective suborning of elections."[114]

---

[111] Windthorst, Bamberger, Bötticher (Govt.), Bennigsen, O. H. v. Helldorf-Bedra (K) SBDR 1 Feb., 3 Feb. 1888: 657, 661, 663, 666, 693f, 696, 698; Meyer (Jena, NL), Windthorst 9 Feb. 1888: 784, 798.

[112] Quoted: Albrecht SBDR 5 Apr. 1871: 183 and Gerstner SBDR 5 Apr. 1871: 172. For a long time the courts had no similar qualms. M. v. Seydel, *Commentar* (1897), 194f. But the RT commission on the new penal code argued in 1910 that "no witness may be asked about facts from which one could conclude for whom he . . . had cast a secret vote." W. Dreyer, "Beweisaufnahmen in Reichstags-Wahlprüfungssachen durch preußische Amtsgerichte," *Juristische Wochenschrift* 41/12 (1912): 623–38; 626. But see: Delbrück to SS in RJA, 10 Mar. 1910. BAB-L R1501/14459, Bl. 345.

[113] Kanngiesser SBDR 27 Apr. 1871: 428; AnlDR (1871, 1/II, Bd 2) DS 106: 271f. Quoted: Behr SBDR 17 Apr. 1871: 240.

[114] Riedel quoted by v. Lenthe SBDR 17 Apr. 1871: 241, and also 29 Mar. 1871: 44. Similar positions: K. Wilmanns (K) SBDR 17 Apr. 1871: 245; Windthorst 18 Apr. 1871: 328.

Near the conclusion of the first statistical study of an imperial election, Julius Knorr issued a modest disclaimer on behalf of his matter-of-fact new science. "Between the first element of our statistics, the list of voters, and the final outcome of the entire process, namely . . . the person elected . . . , is spread the veil of the secret election, a mysterium that no human eye . . . can penetrate."[115] To anyone reading the challenges these elections produced, Knorr's humility seems oddly misplaced. The only "mysterium" about the "veil of secrecy" was how it was now transparent, now opaque. Transparent, it allowed Germany's thousands of communities, and the big men at their apex, to marshal the social forces that were their strength. Opaque, it concealed these social forces from the censure of the public's gaze. And for a long time both government and deputies, one must conclude, preferred to keep it that way.

CONCLUSION: VOTING CORRECTLY

On its face, Germany's new election code was completely subversive of the quotidian traditional order. Into a world of hierarchy, the franchise decreed men equal for a day. Into the subtle interplay of local power and unwritten custom, it inserted a universal, written law and mandated its display in every polling station in the country. Into the face-to-face community, where boundaries were fluid and most secrets were open ones, it introduced one private act of will: voting.

These revolutionary innovations—decreeing equality, assuming independence—appeared to establish Democracy on paper. They set up a series of expectations not only about voting, but about voting correctly. And yet, as we have seen and will continue to see in the chapters to come, these published safeguards to ensure voting correctly ran up against other, habitual expectations regarding what correct voting meant. Fitting these extraordinary stipulations into the habits and assumptions of their workaday lives was how Germans began practicing politics in a democratic key.

Liberals in all parties had rejoiced at their success in excluding "direct civil servants" from election panels, and scholars have agreed in seeing in that victory "a certain loosening of the seamless relations of authority."[116] Some of the immediate results of the new procedures do suggest that, as early as 1867, in at least some places, space had been established for dissenting forces. The King's own brother, Prince Albrecht, running in the most rural district in East Prussia, where the Hohenzollern name should have meant a great deal, garnered only a 55 percent majority in 1867; four years later, a Progressive candidate defeated him. Bismarck's candidacy in 1867 in rural Jerichow (Prussian Saxony) met

---

[115] Knorr, "Statistik," col. 341.
[116] Pollmann, *Parlamentarismus*, 326.

with opposition from more than a third of the constituents. He did not submit his fate to the voters' approval again.[117]

One must be wary, however, of reading a lackluster polling for the government and its allies as triumphs of the little man. If one believed only the arguments raging in the constituent Reichstag, one would think that it was the state that posed the greatest threat to a citizen's ability to vote freely. Most deputies knew better. In the chapters to come we shall examine the threats posed by other authorities: that of the priest, of the landowner, of bosses of every sort. But even these potentates did not always have the last word. The voting individual in nineteenth-century Germany moved within a web of constraints whose filiations were as apt to be communal as they were royal, bureaucratic, economic, or even sacramental. And within this communal web, the banishment of the civil servant from the election panel may, in some instances, have removed a dissenter's only protection.

Even the local big man, with more to offer and more to withhold than the so-called "direct civil servant," usually dominated his community by being a part of it. It was the community itself, through its self-appointed spokesmen, that often exerted the real influence. Thus when the innkeeper Elisabeth Neumayer shouted out in little Sachrang, "Vote only for Pachmayr, so far Obermayr has only twelve votes," she was appealing to the villagers' desire to be on the winning side—that is, the side of the other villagers. In Riedering, like Sachrang a village in Upper Bavaria, communal opinion supported Obermayr instead of Pachmayr. When the timber dealer Martin Peer fled the Riedering schoolroom without voting, after someone had called out, "Here comes another Pachmayr!" (and his pro-Obermayr brothers had begun to descend on him), he was succumbing to the power of the community, not the *Obrigkeitsstaat*.[118]

That the greater threat to the voter's independence might come not from the state but from the pressures of communal expectations is also suggested by the persistence in towns and villages of unanimous voting—a practice growing out of traditions of acclamation reaching back into the Middle Ages, when an election's purpose was not to choose between competitors but to symbolize the community's collective will and thus to legitimize a petition to the authorities. As precinct-level statistics survive only haphazardly, our information is limited to what crops up in local studies and election challenges. Nevertheless, it is revealing that eight towns in County Montjoie, on the western border of the Rhineland, turned in unanimous votes in 1871. In the Grand Duchy of Hessen, unanimous votes, at least for small towns that were religiously homogeneous, were unremarkable. Eighty towns in the Bensheim-Erbach district alone voted unanimously in 1874, seventy-seven in 1877, and eighty-eight in 1878. In 1881 fifty-nine of Meppen-Lingen's 104 villages and small towns, in the Emsland, did the same. So did, three years later, seventy rural communities in a Köslin

---

[117] Until he had left the chancellorship. Jerichow statistics: Philipps, *Reichstags-Wahlen* (1883), 60.

[118] Authoritarian state; top-down state. 7 Oberb; An1DR (1871, 1/III, Bd. 2) DS 38: 97–99.

district in Outer Pomerania.[119] As late as 1903, a panel in West Prussia blithely filled out their form without even opening the eighty-eight ballot envelopes, reckoning all of them to the Polish candidate—because their precinct always voted Polish.[120]

Similar communal expectations are revealed in the frequent complaints about "electoral geometry." Such allegations roughly paralleled charges about "gerrymandering" in America. Superficially they referred to the same process: the use of government power (in the U.S., the power of incumbency) to draw constituency boundaries in ways that favored some electoral outcomes and prevented others. But the differences are as revealing as the similarities. In gerrymandering, the comical shape of the district signaled the attempt to marginalize (or, as the Germans called it, "majoritize") one's opponents (identifiable by some common demographic characteristic, such as religion, race, occupation, income) by running the boundary of the district through them. Thus a group with considerable strength if its ballots were totaled together might find its votes split between two or more districts. The "trick" in gerrymandering grew out of simple arithmetic: *division* of a group and *subtraction* of part from the total. In Imperial Germany, however, while the term "electoral geometry" also referred to self-serving boundary-making, its target was often not the district, but the precinct. Under these circumstances the "trick" in electoral geometry was not the arithmetical swamping of a voting group, as in the U.S., since the sum of all the precincts was in any case totaled to produce the district-wide winner, but its *social* majoritization, done by dividing its voters during the act of voting itself, and forcing those who might have predominated within a single precinct (Catholics, Poles, metalworkers, for example) to cast their ballots under the eyes of another community.[121] In executing this maneuver, the boundary-makers were acknowledging that effective power was exerted less by commanding than by watching. That those affected invariably cried foul points to why the Reichstag took so long to press for a genuinely secret ballot. Each community (and the parties and powers allied with them) wanted to claim the power of watching for themselves.[122]

---

[119] County Montjoie (1 Aachen): Lepper, *Strömungen* 1: 296; Hessen: White, *Party*, 31f; even into the nineties: Thomas Klein, *Die Hessen als Reichstagswähler. Tabellenwerk zur politischen Landesgeschichte 1867–1933. Bd. 1: Provinz Hessen-Nassau und Waldeck-Pyrmont 1867–1918* (Marburg, 1989); Meppen-Lingen: *Lingensches Wochenblatt*, 2 Nov. 1881, SAO Dep. 62b; 3 Köslin, AnlDR (1884/85, 6/I, Bd. 6): DS 242: 1090–92. Excellent on acclamation: Marcus Kreuzer, "Democratization and Party Development: Elections, Political Organization and Democratic Consolidation in Interwar France and Germany" (Ph.D. diss., Columbia University, 1995), chap. 1.

[120] When they then discovered *one* vote for the Antisemite, and changed it to cover their tracks, they went to jail. BAB-L R1501/14703, Bl. 258–69.

[121] Donimirski (P) SBDR 10 Apr. 1874: 710; *Der Kocherbote* (Gaildorf, Württ.), Nr. 93, 6 Aug. 1878, BAB-L R1501/14693, Bl. 62; *Hannoverscher Kourier* of 4 Oct. 1881 in BAB-L R1501/14451, Bl. 64; 5 Marienwerder: AnlDR (1894/95, 9/III, Bd. 1) DS 166: 806f. For American-style gerrymandering: memoranda of the Ministers of Agriculture and of Finance, 28 Oct. 1867, as well as that of Bis., 23 Dec. 1864, BAB-L R 43/685, Bl. 2–12v.

[122] References to the origins of the term "Wahlkreisgeometrie" in the 1869 Bavarian elections, in

To change these expectations demanded a great deal both of the Reichstag and of the voters. It required first of all changes in habitual ways of imagining community, and thus identity.[123] Some individuals, whether from unusual integrity or sheer orneryness, leapt at the chance to make this change. But before most voters would be able to resist the pull of local gravity, it was necessary to introduce from the outside an alternative field of force. In permitting such an introduction, the *rules* of Democracy, as written down in black and white—the 1869 Election Law and 1870 Voting Regulations—proved of considerable importance, as we shall see in chapter 9.

In the end, the solution to communal pressures turned out to be not more individualism, but more organization. And ironically one of the greatest mechanisms of change turned out to be the peculiar German ballot. *Not* the ideal and purely notional *secret* ballot, for reasons that we have seen; but the real, privately printed and distributed ballot, the very mechanism that all but insured that voters' choices would lie open to public scrutiny. For the distribution of ballots in Germany proved beyond the financial and organizational capacities of hard-working villagers to manage. Outsiders had to make up the deficit. In this, the ballot was like the complicated voter registration requirement introduced in Britain in 1832, a requirement that "unexpectedly provided the greatest single stimulus to the organization of the electorate for party purposes."[124] Although the private distribution of ballots in Germany had originated in the government's desire for efficiency, ineluctably it pulled the regional and national political party, its associations and agents, into the village. Moreover, since the freedom to distribute ballots was surrounded by rigid legal protections that were unknown for the more familiar benchmarks of speech, press, and assembly, these ballots—too large, too small; too yellow, gray, violet, or transparent; with all the frailties that accident and design could devise—provided outsiders with opportunities to organize regionally and canvass locally. These opportunities are scarcely imaginable had the provision of ballots been left in government hands.

The political party could not protect the privacy that the ballot lacked. But, as we shall see in chapters 8 and 9, it did provide a new, national, and in that sense, artificial locus of identification and support that was not necessarily coterminous with the "natural" community at home. Such ruptures in the communal web did not by themselves create space for the individual. But competition

---

which the IM who drew up the precincts was himself the liberal candidate (and victor) against the Z in a district nearly 70% Catholic: SBDR 18 Apr. 1871: 257–66. *HZtg*, 2nd Beilage to Nr. 92, 20 Apr. 1871; [J. E. Jörg], "Das deutsche Reich von der Schattenseite im Reichstag" (1872), 763–75; 852–68. Complaints about precinct boundaries: 6 Gumb., AnlDR (1875, 2/III, Bd. 4) DS 82: 839; 7 Marienwerder, AnlDR (1890/92, 8/I, Bd. 4) DS 481: 2776–78; Schloßmacher, *Düsseldorf*, 53, 70. The fact that people voted communally was used to argue that they would find the required use of a voting booth irritating. Struckmann (NL) SBDR 15 Jan. 1890: 1017.

[123] My phrase is borrowed of course from the title of Benedict Anderson's book, *Imagined Communities. Reflections on the Origin and Spread of Nationalism* (London, 1983).

[124] Britain: Gash, *Politics*, xiii, 117f; Hanham, Elections, 399–404; Seymour, *Reform*, 104; also 122, 126f, 132.

between communities, national and local, began a process of reshaping authority and legitimacy. It soon led to elections that, while often far from "free," were nevertheless competitive. And competitive elections are today rightly considered one of the defining hallmarks of Democracy.[125]

To add paradox to paradox, this new development, the emergence of a nationwide system of mass parties, was first set in motion by the most "traditional" authority around, one whose self-definition was neither political nor national, and certainly not democratic, but local and international, spiritual and hierarchical: the Catholic priesthood—to which we shall now turn.

---

[125] D. Nohlen, *Wahlrecht*, 18, quoting Verba et al., *Participation* (1978), 4. (I could not find on p. 4 or anywhere else in Verba et al. the line Nohlen quoted, but it is consonent with their views.) Similarly: S. P. Huntington, "Meaning" (1989), 16.

PART TWO

Fields of Force

CHAPTER FOUR

Black Magic I: The First Mobilization

> Clericalism proved a great initiator to democratic politics and the
> opportunities for mass control intrinsic to democratic politics made
> the fortune of clericalism.
>
> —*P. M. Jones, on 19th-century France (1985)*

ON THE EVE of the 1871 election Hans Heinrich XI, the Prince of Pleß, summoned his gendarmerie, his pit foremen, his hundred-odd forest wardens, and
the county constabulary to Pleß Castle and told them to work for the reelection
of his neighbor, the Duke of Ratibor. With a mixture of prospects (a paved road,
a connecting rail-line, infusions to the widows' fund) and threats (an end to
wood gathering, a five-Thaler police fine, the unspecified displeasure of the
princely administration), the prince's men worked the constituency. The constables rode back and forth through the hamlets, beating their drums. "Tomorrow
is the Reichstag election (tharrump!)," they cried, "Elect the Duke of Ratibor,
for he is a good Catholic."[1]

The prince was a major industrialist, the largest landowner in Silesia (with
nearly 99,000 acres in County Pleß alone), and the fourth richest man—after
Krupp, Rothschild, and Count Henckel von Donnersmarck—in Prussia.[2] The
object of his solicitude, and the incumbent of the district of Pleß-Rybnik, was
Viktor Moritz Karl, Duke of Ratibor and Prince of Corvey, a member of the
Prussian House of Lords, a general in the cavalry, and, as *Standesherr* of one of
the oldest families in Germany, the social equal of its kings. The elder brother
of Prince Chlodwig zu Hohenlohe-Schillingsfürst (recently Minister President
of Bavaria and later chancellor of the empire), the duke had earned Bismarck's
gratitude in 1866 by helping to found the Free Conservative Union, a party
aimed at rallying aristocratic support behind Prussia's controversial leader. His
own estates encompassed over 82,000 acres, including fifty villages in County
Rybnik.[3] Between the two of them, the prince and the duke owned most of the

---

[1] AnlDR (1871, 1/I, Bd. 2) DS 69: 169; T. Schröder-Lippstadt (Z) SBDR 22 Nov. 1871: 434; *GA*
Nr. 74, 28 Mar. 1871: 626.

[2] As of 1902: R. Martin, *Jahrbuch des Vermögens und Einkommens der Millionäre in Preussen*
(Berlin, 1910) 2: 26–33. Later, however, Martin put Pleß second only to Krupp. R. Martin, *Machthaber* (1910), 226.

[3] On the duke: H. Rust, *Reichskanzler* (1897); H. Jaeger, *Unternehmer* (1967), 17n. 30; Hirth,
ed., *Parlaments-Almanach* (1877), 214; and B. Haunfelder and K. E. Pollmann, *Reichstag* (1989),
452; Joseph Partsch, *Schlesien. Eine Landeskunde für das deutsche Volk* (Breslau, 1911), 8.

election district. Silesia's magnates were accustomed to dictating elections.[4] And yet in 1871 the winner in this remote corner of the empire was not the Duke of Ratibor, but an obscure Catholic chaplain named Müller, running for the Centrum. Clear proof that something was rotten in Pleß-Rybnik was the fact that the Rev. Eduard Müller was a man "whose merits," as Eduard Lasker put it, "may be extraordinarily great, only the world knows little of them, and still less the constituency in which he has been elected." Chaplain Müller, a Berlin resident, had not even appeared in the district.[5]

Pleß-Rybnik had an additional peculiarity that made it especially stony soil for new political growth. It was in 1871 the most populous constituency in Germany. Although the standard of 100,000 residents per district laid down in the Imperial Election Law of 1869 had already been exceeded in a number of metropolitan areas, only Pleß-Rybnik had a population that topped the norm by more than 50,000. But—and here was another oddity—Pleß-Rybnik was also thoroughly rural. Of the district's five towns, the largest, Nikolai, had a population of 5,775.[6] Roads were few and communication difficult. Some of its hamlets were so tiny and remote that even the cartographers of Moltke's General Staff, authoritative on matters of imperial geography, had missed them. Not surprisingly, they were forgotten in the assignment of voting precincts.[7] An infrastructure around which to base a campaign—an extensive press, journeymen's clubs, even ad hoc party organizations—simply did not exist.[8] Heavily populated, but thinly settled: how could word of a newcomer penetrate these fastnesses? How could this district be "worked," except by a candidate like the duke, whom the voters already knew through long local association? Who would hand out his ballots? And how could voters have been persuaded to vote against the candidate of men on whom they were so dependent? How indeed, except through the craft of the Catholic clergy, operating on a benighted population?

That the Pleß-Rybnik election was no fluke was demonstrated by an equally startling victory on the other side of Germany, in the Rhenish city of Krefeld. There August Reichensperger, another outsider also running for the Catholic

<hr />

[4] Also: Weber, *Polen* (1913), 22; Alfons Perlick, *Oberschlesische Berg- und Hüttenleute* (Kitzingen, Main, 1953), 55–57; Schröder-Lippstadt SBDR 22 Nov. 1871: 433; P. Mazura, *Entwicklung* (1925), 54, 59–61, and 61n. 4.

[5] Lasker twice referred to the incumbent's being "pushed out" of "his" district. SBDR 5 Apr. 1871: 174. Bis. repeated the phrase: SBHA, 30 Jan. 1872. O. v. Bismarck, *Werke* (1929) 11: 227. Reichensperger referred to Müller as "chaplain" although technically his title was "mission vicar." Both terms indicate that Müller had never advanced to the point of being put in charge of a parish.

[6] 156,416. Statistics on size of districts are in Knorr, "Statistik," cols. 316–18. Nikolai: Phillips, *Reichstags-Wahlen* (1883), 52.

[7] AnlDR (1871, 1/I, Bd. 2) DS 69: 168.

[8] Mazura, *Entwicklung*, 61. See also 56, 58, 67, 83, 87. Subscriptions to *Katolik* have been put at 1,200 in 1871 and 2,180 in Oct. 1870. Ibid., 81n. 6; Trzeciakowski, *Kulturkampf* (1990), 27. There were five journeymen's associations in the entire *province*, although Trzeciakowski, 28, puts a casino in Pleß "soon" after 1867. Statistics: Dr. [Jakob] Marx, *General-Statistik der katholischen Vereine Deutschlands* (Trier, 1871), 26–31.

Centrum, unseated another well-heeled incumbent and native son, Ludwig Friedrich Seyffardt, a spokesman for the business elite in an industrial district whose prevailing sentiment, measured by previous elections, was overwhelmingly Liberal. Like the Free Conservative upset in Pleß-Rybnik, the Liberal debacle in Krefeld symbolized more than a change in parties. Seyffardt belonged to the small circle of Protestant families who had controlled industry and local politics in Catholic Krefeld for a century. Helped by plutocratic municipal and state franchises, unblushing gerrymandering, and a level of chicanery that made the city, in the words of Julius Bachem, the "locus classicus of National Liberal election pressure," the coterie's dominance would continue for another decade. But in national elections, thanks to the new franchise, it had reached its end.[9]

The debates over these two upsets were reported on the front pages of newspapers throughout the country and came up in the Reichstag again and again over the course of the year. Yet they were only the most glaring examples of victories that—far more than the routine violations of secrecy and voter choice that we saw in the last chapter—raised an alarm about the very possibility of free elections in Germany. Although Catholics were a minority in the new Germany, the influence of their clergy, in the view of much of public opinion in 1871, was *the* sin against the free election. Complaints against Catholic priests exceeded complaints against employers by ten to one and even surpassed charges against government officials, traditionally the villains in election protests, by almost five to three. These charges challenged the legitimacy, not of this or that election, but of Germany's second largest party. Thus Julius Knorr, whom we met in the last chapter as the statistician of Germany's first national election, introduced his analysis with the following disclaimer:

> Those 437,790 votes to which the Centrum delegation owes its existence in the Reichstag are in truth counterfeit in the estimation of all honest people; for no man knows . . . how many of the timid have refrained from proclaiming their German hearts because someone has scared them [by insisting] . . . : "Surely you won't vote against your Lord and Savior!"[10]

Liberal-minded men might have hoped that empowering the people with the vote would encourage a fundamental critique of the authority of this most hierarchical of churches. But as the discussion of these challenged victories proceeded, its terms quickly shifted: from a critique of Catholic priests, to misgivings about the people being enfranchised, to skepticism about the franchise itself. Although in the end only three Centrum mandates were thrown out, these initial controversies over "clerical influence" were a powerful force behind Germany's emerging Kulturkampf, a struggle that would sculpt Germany's po-

---

[9] L. F. Seyffardt, *Erinnerungen* (1900), 50–59; Bachem quoted in Kühne, *Dreiklassenwahlrecht*, 98; gerrymandering, 97–102; H. Croon, "Stadtvertretungen in Krefeld und Bochum" (1958), 289–306.

[10] Knorr, "Statistik," col. 290. Actually, the Z's vote was over 724,000. Calculation of numbers and percentages of protests based on clerical influence are my own.

litical cleavages, and stamp German views about democracy, until the end of the empire.

THE CLERGY AND ELECTIONS BEFORE 1871

Who was society's teacher, its children's tutor, the guarantor of its marital unions, the guardian and interpreter of its values? These and similar questions underlay some of the most continuous and bitter conflicts structuring political debate from Central Europe to the Americas until well into the twentieth century. Inadequately summarized under the rubric "relations between Church and the State" (in German, expressed in the awkward-to-translate adjective *"kirchenpolitisch"*), this motley knot of issues is familiar to our own day as "culture politics." The movement of political debate over the course of the nineteenth century out of the chancelleries and into the constituencies, far from settling such disputes, amplified them. Even where elections did not revolve directly or deeply around religious issues per se, religion often provided the language with which other antagonisms were articulated, the symbols that organized cultural identity. In this, Germany was not unique. As far away as Illinois, Indiana, and Iowa, where Church and State were formally separate, "religion was the fundamental source of political conflict. . . . [It] shaped the issues and the rhetoric of politics, and played the critical role in determining the party alignments of the voters. . . ." In France, it was a truism that political fault lines followed religious observance. "If you went to mass, you couldn't really be a Republican. If you were a Republican, you fought against priests, nuns, superstition."[11] A historian of English elections goes so far as to state that "religion was itself a species of politics." A historian of Irish elections makes exactly the same claim, in exactly the same words.[12]

Politics, which distributes power, and religion, which provides meaning for communities, inevitably came together as extensions of the suffrage gave communities access to power and the means of affirming their own meanings against those of others. It was just as inevitable that the clergy, as a vocal nexus between the world of meaning and the world of power, would play a prominent role. Thus the emergence of the parish priest as a political force, though felt by many contemporaries to be a sign of backwardness, occurred precisely when, as an Austrian liberal noticed with surprise, politics had begun to move "into freer paths."[13] The phenomenon is remarkably similar across national—and denominational—boundaries. During Victorian elections, "no other occupation was so

---

[11] Quotes: R. J. Jensen, *Winning* (1971), 58–59 (cf. also, viii, xii, 57); E. Weber, *Peasants* (1976), 359. Similar faultlines in Colombia: E. Posada-Carbó, "The Limits of Power" (1997), esp. 269–72, and M. Deas, "Role" (1996).

[12] Gash, *Politics*, 175; Hoppen, *Elections*, 37. Similarly, George Kitson Clark, *The Making of Victorian England* (London, 1962), 162. But see: Vernon, *Politics*, 178–80.

[13] T. Pachmann, "Clerikal-Vertretung" (1862): 106–20, quote on 106.

partisan, so militant, so unfloating, as the Dissenting ministers."[14] The charges of "gross clerical intimidation, servile obedience to the priests on the part of the illiterate voters, clergymen canvassing . . . in their parishes or acting as . . . agents in the polling booths," though lodged by *United Ireland* in 1892, could just as easily have come from the procurator-general of Besançon in 1869, or the *Norddeutsche Allgemeine* at the height of the Kulturkampf.[15]

In fact, the clergy seem to have been more audacious outside Germany. The Bishop of Meath himself placed the name of Michael Davitt into nomination in 1892, urged his congregation to come to Davitt's rally armed with sticks, and had a pastoral letter read out at all masses in his diocese predicting divine retribution for "the dying Parnellite."[16] In Wales, Baptist preachers threatened not only ostracism and denial of the sacrament, but seemed to encourage violence and arson against the "Iscariots" who voted Tory. In France, the clergy showed just as little inclination to look over their shoulder. In Brittany, a candidate held rallies in church and bestowed benedictions on his assembled supporters. As in Ireland, here too the clergy (sometimes) resorted to criminal behavior. As late as 1928 seminarians in Les Basses-Pyrénées were sentenced to correctional institutions for having voted more than once.[17] These unblushing traditions of French clericalism may account for the fact that the most egregious clerical electioneering in the German Empire occurred in the former French provinces of Alsace and Lorraine, the "classic land of election-making."[18] Although during the Kulturkampf one indignant priest in Württemberg drew a revolver at a rally and shot into the crowd, Germany's clergy were rarely accused of breaking the law.[19] But while clerical partisanship took more restrained paths than in other lands, the uproar it aroused here was greater and had more lasting consequences—for legislation, for mobilization, for voting allegiances, and ultimately, for democracy.

Why was the outcry greater in Germany? Only in Germany did people experience simultaneously two revolutionary, but not necessarily reinforcing, redefinitions of the political nation: the collapse of a "federated polity" into a truncated, but "unified" nation-state and the expansion of participation through manhood suffrage. In the view of nationalists, the Church, like some evil fairy

[14] J. Vincent, *Pollbooks* (1968), 18 (quote); Gash, *Politics*, 176; Hanham, *Elections*, 15.

[15] Quoted in C. J. Woods, "Election" (1980), 306; Besançon: J.-P. Charnay, "L'église" (1962), 295. An exception seems to be (surprisingly) Austria where Boyer describes the clergy as becoming active only well after the turn of the century. J. W. Boyer, *Culture* (1995), 300, 302f, 310–12, 328.

[16] Irish priests also participated fully in the most common *secular* election crimes: treating, bribery, inciting to riot, instigating multiple voting. Woods, "Election," 300; J. H. Whyte, "Influence" (1960), 245, 247, 306; Hoppen, *Elections*, 245, 245n. 5, 246. Clerical influence accounted for 6 invalidations between 1852 and 1881.

[17] M. Cragoe, "Conscience" (1995), 154, 162, 164; Charnay, "L'église," 269, 272, 295; idem, *Les scrutins*, 82, 84, 89, 92, 92n. 63, 94f, 97f.

[18] Quote: Delsor SBDR 21 Apr. 1903: 8925f; cf. also H. Bodewig, *Wahlbeeinflussungen* (1909), 125; Hiery, *Reichstagswahlen*, 320, 420f.

[19] Where they were, prosecution—and publicity—was swift: *GA* Nr. 164, 16 July 1871: 1476. Revolver: *GA* Nr. 12, 15 Jan. 1874: 68.

godmother, had materialized at the baptism of the newborn nation-state—the first election contest—in order to bequeath to it a future cursed with continued division. Thus they imputed to the clergy what was the inevitable result (and perhaps even the glory) of electoral politics itself. We shall take the rest of this chapter to explore these themes.

Clerical politicking in Germany, as in the rest of the western world, rose (and fell) with extensions (and contractions) of the franchise. The *annus mirabilis* of 1848 saw the clergy's first appearance in politics. Often the only ones in the village to have heard of any of the candidates, men of the cloth, Protestant as well as Catholic, were sometimes chosen as delegates to the electoral colleges; and a number of them—including three Catholic bishops—served as deputies to the Frankfurt Assembly. Both the president and vice president of Baden's revolutionary lower house were priests.[20] But in 1849 the Frankfurt Assembly was dismissed, suffrage restrictions were reintroduced in the German states, and the clerical presence shrank with the electorate.[21] Although the election activity of the clergy (Protestant as well as Catholic) varied with the community, now it was only one of several more or less official impulses on behalf of whomever the government had decided to support. Voters with independent ideas—not a rare occurrence once restrictive suffrages again favored men of property— would ignore them.[22] As for the Catholic bishops, the political direction they had felt empowered to give during the confusing hurly-burly of revolution now proved the exception rather than the rule.[23] Even when elected bodies thwarted the Church's agenda, their response was not to endorse particular candidates, but, like the Protestant high consistory, to issue anodyne pastorals (which they refrained from publishing) admonishing the faithful to participate vigorously in elections and to pray for outcomes pleasing to God. If these pronouncements

---

[20] L. Rosenbaum, *Beruf* (1923), 63. Konrad Repgen, "Klerus und Politik 1848: Die Kölner Geistlichen im Politischen Leben des Revolutionsjahres—als Beitrag zu einer 'Parteigeschichte von Unten,'" in *Aus Geschichte und Landeskunde,* edited by F. Petri and K. Repgen (Bonn, 1960), 133–65; idem, *Märzbewegung und Maiwahlen des Revolutionsjahres 1848* (Bonn, 1960); J. Sperber, *Radicals* (1991), 177; K. Bachem, *Vorgeschichte* (1927) 2: 260, 265; W. Graf, *Beeinflussungsversuche* (1971), 196, 198. In Trier the Catholic clergy had no unified position: Hansjürgen Schierbaum, *Die politischen Wahlen in den Eifel- und Moselkreisen des Regierungsbezirks Trier 1849–1867* (Düsseldorf, 1960), 21, 25, 44. Thränhardt, *Wahlen* (1973), 46n. 34, sees little political difference between the confessions in Bavaria in 1848–49, although Catholics were more democratic.

[21] My account summarizes the regional varieties of clerical behavior, ca. 1849–69: J. Becker, *Staat* (1973), 134f, 134n. 18; H. W. Smith, *Nationalism* (1995), 107; Bellot, *Hundert Jahre*, 32, 37, 78; K. Weinandy, *Wahlen* (1956), 110f, and 110n. 1, 128, 146, 150f, 280; O. Röttges, *Wahlen* (1965), 131, 159, 187, 235, 284, 319; P. Schmidt, *Wahlen* (1971), 73, 77, 82, 87, 101, 120, 175; Mazura, *Entwicklung*, 28f; H. Neubach, "Geistliche" (1968): 251–78; Bachem, *Vorgeschichte* 2: 103.

[22] J. N. Sepp to J. E. Jörg, 20 Apr. 1863, in Jörg, *Briefwechsel* (1988), 224f.

[23] Even after 1852, when a specifically Catholic party (the first "Centrum") established itself in Prussia. S. N. Kalyvas, *Rise* (1996), 174–81, looking at six nations, argues that the hierarchy was positively hostile to Catholic partisan organization. On the hierarchy: Graf, *Beeinflussungsversuche*, 70–175 (esp. 158), 260–65, 292–94; Schmidt, *Wahlen*, 181, 183.

had a ritual ring, it was because their Graces were only too aware that they lived in a Confederation with *two* major confessions; in states where liberal opinion (and conservative bureaucrats) was allergic to signs of episcopal encroachments; and under governments that were simultaneously jealous of their own sovereignty, greedy for the Church's active help, and nervous about any clerical move that might rouse religious passions. The clergy, especially the Catholic clergy, was being watched—and their bishops knew it.

The circumspection of the German Catholic hierarchy in the two decades prior to 1871 was in conspicuous contrast to the assertiveness of the Holy See. Italian liberalism's challenge to the existence of the papal state had spurred Pius IX to a *Flucht nach vorn*, defending his political sovereignty in central Italy by laying claim to a role for the Church in civic life everywhere. The "Syllabus of the Principle Errors of Our Time" (1864), which condemned liberal demands for the separation of Church and State, was only the most sensational sign of the defensive triumphalism ascendant in Vatican circles.[24] But the brassy flourishes of ultramontane political theory, noted with disgust and alarm by Protestants and Liberals, found little echo among German Catholics. Although some hotspurs in the Catholic press called on their priests to take an active part in elections, one of the most significant developments in the 1860s was the degree to which the very idea of a political role for the Church was becoming problematized in discussions within the clergy itself.[25] In 1863, a leading church historian, Fr. Franz Josef Hergenröther of Würzburg, joined the debate with a definitive and balanced survey of the international situation. His conclusion, for which he cited authorities ranging from the liberal canon lawyer Johann Friedrich Ritter von Schulte to the conservative publicist Georg Phillips—German Catholics on opposite sides of the Infallibility question and soon to be on opposite sides of political questions as well—suggests a broad consensus within the mainstream of German Catholic letters, clerical and lay, liberal and ultramontane. There was "today no actual Catholic politics; on the contrary, there is only a politics of individual Catholics."[26]

[24] Although the errors most emphasized in the syllabus were religious indifferentism, unorthodoxy, erastianism, and state control of education, public opinion immediately fixed on Error 15 ("Every man is free to embrace and profess that religion which, guided by the light of reason, he shall consider true") and Error 55 ("The Church ought to be separated from the State, and the State from the Church"). *Dogmatic Canons and Decrees* (New York, 1912).

[25] In the Austrian press: Pachmann, "Clerikal-Vertretung," 106–20, soon reprinted in the daily press; Geo. Clericus, "Die Theilnahme des Klerus an der Gemeinde- und Volksvertretung," *Archiv für katholisches Kirchenrecht, mit besonderer Rücksicht auf Oesterreich und Deutschland* 10 (N. F. 14) Mainz, 1863: 75–93. Hotspurs: Graf, *Beeinflussungsversuche*, 183.

[26] Hergenröther, "Ueber die Betheiligung des Klerus an politischen Fragen," *Archiv für katholisches Kirchenrecht* 15 (N.F. 9. Bd.) (1866), 67–84; quotes from 68f, 71. The article first appeared in the *Bamberger Pastoralblatt* in 1863. Such a reading of Catholic political theory was considerably "ahead" of clerical practice in other Western countries. The Vatican adopted it, in the encyclical *Libertae*, only in 1888. Graf, *Beeinflussungsversuche*, 103. The Protestant clergy also debated this question. "Ob und wieweit sich der Geistliche bei den bevorstehenden Wahlen zu betheiligen habe? Ein Synodal-Vortrag" *Evangelische Kirchen-Zeitung* 68 (1861): cols. 897–906; "Die Kirche und die Wahlaufrufe," *Deutsche Evangelische Kirchenzeitung* 2 (1888): 425f.

Minimalism in theory became quietism in practice as the war between Prussia and the German Confederation in 1866, and the Confederation's quick defeat, left churchmen who had intervened decisively in 1848 paralyzed in the face of this very different revolution. In the ensuing elections, some bishops instructed their clergy to stay out; others waffled; still others did nothing at all.[27] In Prussia, the scattering of priests who had held seats since the late 1850s was reduced in 1866–67 to two.[28] The Catholic delegation, in existence since 1852, disappeared.

Yet in less than a decade this situation was reversed. The politic reserve of the hierarchy; the uncoordinated, largely individualistic interventions of the lower clergy; the emerging consensus that there was no such thing as an "actual Catholic politics, but rather only a politics of individual Catholics"—all were transformed into their opposite: the shared understanding from rural rectory to episcopal *Residenz* that the safety of the Church depended on election outcomes and that only someone who supported a particular party with word and deed was a "true Catholic." The taboo on open campaigning fell. "Priests came to see politics as . . . inseparable from the religious order they wished to preserve," as Helmut Walser Smith has noted. Elections became an extension of religious life.[29] Unlike most changes in mentalité, this one can be given a precise date. The reversal began in south Germany with the democratic Zollparlament elections of 1868 and spread to Prussia during Landtag and Reichstag elections in winter of 1870–71. By 1874 it was complete. The new understanding of politics would endure in its main lines until the end of democratic elections in March 1933.[30] In many parts of Germany it resumed again in 1945. The result was a phenomenon known, especially to its opponents, as "political Catholicism."

GERMAN NATIONALISM AND THE CLERICAL MYSTIQUE

Contrary to what critics claimed, the Church's reversal was not a consequence of the victory of the infallibist party at the First Vatican Council in 1870, but of the momentous redistribution of power throughout Europe over the last decade: especially in the wake of wars that had led to the defeats of two great empires,

[27] The variety between regions, and also between Prussian LT elections in 1866 and the two sets of RT elections in 1867, makes generalization difficult, but points to disarray: Eduard Müller, "Darf der Seelsorger Politik treiben?" *MK* Nrs. 3 and 4, 16 and 23 Jan. 1869: 17–20; Pollmann, *Parlamentarismus*, 105n. 64; Mazura, *Entwicklung*, 52–55; L. Trzeciakowski, *Kulturkampf* (1990), 32; Weinandy, *Wahlen*, 253; P. Möllers, *Strömungen* (1955), 68f, 83; Klaus Müller, "Das Rheinland als Gegenstand der historischen Wahlsoziologie," in *Annalen des historischen Vereins des Niederrhein* 167 (1965): 124–42; 136; Becker, *Staat*, 210; J. Sperber, *Catholicism* (1984), 169f.

[28] Rosenbaum, *Beruf*, 29, 63.

[29] Smith, *Nationalism*, 108.

[30] My argument about the reversal in the clergy's basic political assumptions does not deny that a transformation of Catholic sensibility, in a more ultramontane and "clerical" direction, had been underway for some time. Sperber, *Catholicism*.

the toppling of the thousand-year-old papal state, and Pius IX's declaring himself a "prisoner" in the Vatican. For Germans, the sense of "world history turning a corner" was climaxed by the disappearance of the old Confederation and the birth of a Prussian-dominated nation-state.[31] Riding shotgun on these developments was a growing anti-Catholic discourse that was the dark doppelgänger of a nationalism suddenly made loud and popular with success. Not least because the Catholic population had suddenly dropped from rough equality with Protestants under the old German Confederation to a minority of 36 percent in Bismarck's new creation, the latter was trumpeted, by its greatest enthusiasts, as the "*Protestant* empire." The term invoked an implicit contrast with its alleged predecessor and mirror opposite, the old medieval empire: Catholic instead of Protestant, divided instead of united, its national greatness sacrificed to divisions deliberately fostered by the pope—a contrast given visual embodiment in Hermann Wislicenus's painting, *Resurrection of the German Reich.*[32] In the national narrative that was now being touted as Germany's collective memory, Prussia's victory at Königgrätz was a corrective replay of the Thirty Years' War of the seventeenth century, this time with defeat for the "Catholic" and victory for the "German" side. Within that same narrative, the Roman Church was figured as villain, the author of centuries of weakness; and the autonomy that the Prussian crown had constitutionally guaranteed to both churches as recently as 1850 now looked like a dangerous concession to a perennial foe.[33] In this atmosphere, proposals that in a different context might have seemed merely secularizing (to reform the marriage law, to transfer school supervision from church to state, even to regulate the clergy) could now be described as "national"—a move that cast the shadow of disloyalty on anyone opposing them.

In the midst of this nationalist rush, the new democratic suffrage increased the Church's vulnerability at the same time that it suggested the remedy: popular political action. In late 1870 prominent lay Catholics moved to resurrect the old Centrum Party, the defunct champion of Prussian Catholicism, on a national basis. The bishops rallied. And in many districts throughout Catholic Germany the parish clergy—usually with a wary eye on the election code—quoted from the secularizing proposals being bruited in the press, drew the new party to the faithful's attention, and reminded their congregations who they were. When the

[31] T. Mommsen in 1866, quoted in James J. Sheehan, "Zukünftige Vergangenheit. Das deutsche Geschichtsbild in den neunziger Jahren," in G. Korff, M. Roth, eds., *Das historische Museum. Labor, Schaubühne, Identitätsfabrik* (Frankfurt a.M., 1990), 277–86; 277.

[32] *Wiedererstehung des Deutschen Reiches* (1880–82), reproduced in F. Gross, *Jesus* (1989), 48f, fig. 49c.

[33] E.g., references to the "history and the memories of our people" in a petition against the Jesuits signed by 4,900 citizens of Breslau, published in "6th Report of the Petitions Committee concerning the petitions for and against a General Ban of the Jesuit Order in Germany," AnlDR (1872, 1/III, Bd. 3) DS 64: 261–83; 261f (hereafter: "6th Report"). The RT debates that ensued on 15 May and 14 and 19 June 1872 are reprinted (verbatim for liberals and most conservatives, but with only brief summaries for Catholic deputies!) in "Die Jesuiten-Petitionen im Reichstag" and "Das Verbot des Jesuitenordens," *Annalen des deutschen Reiches* (1872), cols. 1121–70 and 1172–1234.

ballots were counted in 1871 the Centrum, and its particularist allies, had managed to capture almost a third of the Catholic electorate.[34]

One should not exaggerate these results. Although Catholic turnout exceeded that of Protestants (62 to 43 percent), even one-third of the Catholic electorate voting for the "clericals" meant that two-thirds did *not* vote Centrum—as opponents were quick to point out. The Centrum, moreover, commanded the allegiance of only fifty-six of the Reichstag's Catholic members.[35] But the very absence of overwhelming Catholic support for the Centrum helped put righteousness behind the indignation of those coreligionists still sitting on the benches of other parties. How dare the Centrum's supporters claim the name "Catholic" for themselves? If the idea of "party" was still suspect in some circles, the idea of a party that was a Church was scandalous. The liberal *Augsburger Allgemeine Zeitung* referred to the Centrum as "a poisonous fungus, feeding on our viscera, night and day relentlessly continuing its destructive work."[36] The liberal *Görlitzer Anzeiger* foresaw "French conditions" if "political" Catholicism took hold. The ultramontanes, it feared, would make alliances with Feudalism on the one hand and Communism on the other. In the hands of priests, "universal suffrage would very soon become not a means for the extension of freedom but a means of repressing all freedom. . . ."[37] In the *Anzeiger's* comment we see many of the elements of the contemporary liberal picture of the Church: its foreignness, its easy terms with both backwardness and radicalism, and the affinity, under its aegis, between plebeian enfranchisement and threats to free elections.

It is important to remember that what was controversial in the elections of 1871, as in subsequent years, was the influence of the *Catholic* clergy. The Protestant pastor's partisanship was, of course, also well documented. He too spoke at rallies and even preached election sermons.[38] He too distributed propaganda for this or that candidate (usually, but not always, a Conservative) and

---

[34] Sperber, *Voters*, 35; idem, *Catholicism*, 255n. 3. In Düsseldorf by 1871 the campaign consisted entirely of pro- and anti-Catholic slogans. Schloßmacher, *Düsseldorf*, 200f. On church support for Z candidates, see e.g.: Bellot, *Hundert Jahre*, 126; in Posnania, Bishop Ledóchowski urged Catholics to vote for the Koło Polskie. R. Blanke, *Poland* (1981), 26. In some districts, however, clergy continued to support Ks. L. Müller, *Kampf* (1929), 196. W. Claggett et al., "Leadership" (1982), suggests (654) that about 1/10 of all Protestants voted for the Z in 1871, although no Protestants supported it subsequently.

[35] *HZtg* 3rd Beilage to Nr. 92, 20 Apr. 1871; *GA* Nr. 92, 20 Apr. 1871. Turnout: Sperber, *Voters*, 163.

[36] Quoted in Ludwig Ficker and Otto Hellinghaus, *Der Kulturkampf in Münster* (Münster, 1928), 48f. Resentment of the Z by non-Z Catholics: [Jörg], "Das deutsche Reich" I: 763–75; II: 852–68, esp. I: 769; Lasker and Fr. v. Schauß (the latter a Catholic NL) SBDR 5 Apr. 1871: 175 and 180, respectively; L. Fischer, the Catholic Mayor of Augsburg (Liberale Reichspartei) and Bishop v. Ketteler, both quoted in Ketteler, "Centrums-Fraction" (1872), in *Werke* (1977) 4: 48n. 11.

[37] *GA* Nr. 4, 25 Feb. 1871: 391.

[38] R. Schraps (Sax. VP) on Saxony: SBDR 17 Apr. 1871: 246; Windthorst on Thuringia: SBDR 22 Apr. 1871: 328. Also 17 Han., AnlDR (1881, 4/IV, Bd. 4) DS 104: 625; 3 Saxony, AnlDR (1881, 5/II, Bd. 5) DS 174: 611, 613; 5 Arns., AnlDR (1882/83, 5/II, Bd. 6) DS 292: 1081f; 1 Anhalt, AnlDR (1884/85, 6/I, Bd. 5) DS 135: 510; Möllers, *Strömungen*, 89; Bertram, *Wahlen*, 195f.

sometimes sent leaflets and ballots home with the children from his confirmation classes. He too could be seen hanging about the polls, offering ballots to his parishioners and even, on occasion, demanding that they exchange the ones they had brought for the ones he supplied.[39] And sometimes he was guilty of behavior rarely heard in connection with his Catholic counterparts: treating or bribing workers, and using his position on an election panel to keep the polls open after closing time until those he had bribed showed up.[40] This activity was of course also objectionable to the people who criticized the Catholic priest (Centrum deputies, conversely, made a point of *never* objecting to a Protestant parson's political activity—even as they made sure that it never went unnoticed).[41] But—and here is the rub—critics of the Protestant clergy complained of their *behavior*, rarely of their *"influence."* Although now and then a Social Democrat might suggest that the violation of election freedom was the same regardless of denomination, the Protestant clergy's influence never became an issue, and only once, in 1877, was an election thrown out because (in part) of what Lutheran pastors had done.[42] The influence of the Catholic clergy, on the other hand, became a central theme in the discussion of German democracy.

It is difficult in the late twentieth century to recapture the horrified fascination in which the liberal nineteenth century held the Catholic Church.[43] International in an era of growing nationalism, hierarchical in a world where traditional hierarchies were being challenged, infallible when the educated believed that truth was the monopoly of science and the sophisticated denied that it existed at all: the perversity with which the Church turned its back on the Modern World only increased the wonder at its continued survival. How did it do it?[44] Surely by playing on the credulity of the ignorant. Sacramental power and superstitious magic did not look all that different to Germany's secular minds—and perhaps not to all of its religious minds either.[45] Folklorists reported that at times of misfortune even Protestants might request a priest to intercede for them in curing a sickness, finding a cow, banishing a ghost.[46] Clearly anyone who could

[39] 5 Han., AnlDR (1879, 4/II, Bd. 6) DS 228: 1520–22; 3 Danzig, AnlDR (1882/83, 5/II, Bd. 5) DS 80: 338–49, esp. 348; 1 Merseburg, AnlDR (1881/2, 5/I, Bd. 2) DS 44: 169–72, esp. 171, and DS 160: 542; "Ungültigkeit der Wahlen zur Stadtverordnetenversammlung" (1902): 277.

[40] 3 Meckl., BAB-L R 1501/14462, Bl. 25v; Freudenthal, *Wahlbestechungen*, 49n. 4; Gröber (Z) SBDR 26 Feb. 1908: 3424; 7 Gumb., AnlDR (1912/14, 13/I, Bd. 23) DS 1586: 3420. A Catholic Dean was also accused of bribing voters. 6 Posen AnlDR (1912/13, 13/I, Bd. 17) DS 491: 546.

[41] E.g., Windthorst SBDR 22 Apr. 1871: 328, argued that the same standard should be used for both confessions, not that the Protestant clergy's activities were illegitimate.

[42] 1 Minden, AnlDR (1877, 3/I, Bd. 3) DS 187: 515–26, and SBDR 2 Apr. 1878: 677–82. SD criticism of Protestant clergy: C. Severing, *Lebensweg* (1950) 1: 27.

[43] Characteristic: Bamberger, "Sitzungsperiode," 167.

[44] The best explanation so far (but for *Protestant* clergy!): Cragoe, "Conscience."

[45] D. Blackbourn, *Marpingen* (1993); Anderson, "Piety and Politics: Recent Work on German Catholicism," *Journal of Modern History* (Dec. 1991): 681–716; esp. 695–705.

[46] Adolf Wüttke, *Der deutsche Volksaberglaube der Gegenwart* (Berlin, 2nd ed., 1869), 139f;

change wine into blood was someone that no Catholic voter would want to cross. Chaplain Müller, the unexpected victor in Pleß-Rybnik, commented wryly that his skeptical era's faith in the clergy's omnipotence had become a "new kind of superstition."[47]

The priest had an aura. Thanks to celibacy, he had always belonged to what Ernest Gellner has termed a "gelded elite," one set deliberately apart from the society it led. Shaven and shorn at a time when facial hair was the signature of manly propriety, and the full beard, a sign of "freedom," even a "democratic sensibility," the priest was bound to seem epicene, reactionary, even "French."[48] Even as the Protestant pastor was fast becoming indistinguishable from secular urban professionals, his Catholic counterpart continued to go about in his long black *soutane*. The French term, like the style itself, cropped up in County Cork as in the Rhineland. It marked its wearer as a uniformed soldier in a disciplined, cosmopolitan army. As Heinrich von Sybel told his students, "What we're dealing with here is a militarily organized corporation that disposes of more than 30,000 agents in Germany sworn to strict obedience."[49]

The military image owed far more to the reputation of the Jesuits—the "Company of Jesus," spiritual soldiers living under martial discipline and sworn to obedience to a Roman "general"—than it did to the workaday reality, pastoral and electoral, of the secular clergy. In the nationalist imagination, however, it was the Jesuit—militant, clerical, ultramontane—not the parish priest, who embodied the church. The Jesuit was "a power before whom cardinals and bishops trembled." It was he, they believed, who actually governed the dioceses and ran the seminaries. He was the Church's real "agitational and organizational soul."[50] German Jesuits in fact numbered a mere 211 of the more than 17,000

Richard Andree, "Katholische Überbleibsel beim evangelischen Volke," *Zeitschrift des Vereins für Volkskunde* 21 (1911): 113–25, esp. 114; Karl Olbrich, "Der katholische Geistliche im Volksglauben," *Mitteilungen der schlesischen Gesellschaft für Volkskunde* (Breslau) 30 (1929): 90–105, 130. I am grateful to Millie Zinck for these references.

[47] *MK* Nr. 18, 6 May 1871: 142. See the otherwise sensible F. Naumann, "Das Zentrum," (1907), 114f.

[48] Ernest Gellner, *Nations and Nationalism* (Ithaca, 1983), 14–16. Cf. Prof. Thalhofer's articles for the *Augsburger Pastoralblatt* (1863), reprinted that year as "Über den Bart der Geistlichen," *Archiv für katholisches Kirchenrecht* 10/4 (N. F., Bd. 14) (1863): 85ff; Joh. Werner, "Bart der Geistlichen," *Die Religion in Geschichte und Gegenwart* (Tübingen, 1909) 1: cols. 922–24. See the portraits in Haunfelder/Pollmann, eds., *Reichstag*, where clean-shaven laymen born after 1826 are almost nonexistent.

[49] H. v. Sybel, "Politik" (1880), 450. Sartorial developments: Christoph Weber, *Aufklärung und Orthodoxie am Mittelrhein 1820–1850* (Munich, 1973), 184; W. K. Blessing, *Staat und Kirche* (1982), 39, 133.

[50] "The entire system" is "under the direction of the Society of Jesus." Gneist SBDR 19 June 1872, in "Verbot," cols. 1220–22. J. v. Lütz made the equation of clergy and Jesuit explicit: H. v. Mallinckrodt (Z) SBDR 28 Nov. 1871, reprinted in Hubert Schumacher, *Parlamentarische Denkwürdigkeiten. Eine Beleuchtung wichtiger Zeitfragen durch Aussprache der Centrumsredner im Preußischen Abgeordnetenhause und Deutschen Reichstage* (Essen, 1877), 114; Sybel, "Politik," 450. "Jesuiten-Petitionen," cols. 1158, 1165; "Jesuitenpetitionen," *Grenzboten* 49/4 (1890), 398.

priests in Germany.[51] Most Catholics had never seen one. But by 1870 other representations of churchmen—as pastoral shepherd, as friar, as monk—had largely disappeared. The very bishops were "jesuitical."[52] Even the deputies of the Centrum, most of them laymen and fathers of families, were depicted in cartoons in the broad black hat with the curled rim of the Jesuit.[53] On the image of the Jesuit, mysterious and powerful, hung a whole web of evil associations that were extended on credit to the entire Catholic clergy.[54] It was a vision heavy with consequence—as we shall soon see.

And the reality? Two of 1871's most fully documented elections, one in Riedering in Upper Bavaria and another in Oberhaid in Upper Franconia, allow us to look into the "empire in the village" at very close range. The almost identical structure of the process, in precincts more than a hundred miles apart, suggests a pattern that was probably fairly common in rural Germany. In both, the recommendations of veteran pastors standing outside the polling place met with outspoken contradiction by teacher and mayor, respectively. In both, the pastors later insisted upon their "conversational tone" in bringing up their candidate, and on their desire to act not unilaterally, but jointly with other local notables, preferably in a supporting role. In both, the teacher and/or mayor, fresh from distributing Liberal ballots, had tried to muzzle the priest, taking his stand on the "rules." In both, the face-off culminated in a riotous defense of the priest by the voters. The subsequent tally could be read as plebiscites in favor of clerical influence. Was this superstitious magic—or even "social control?" The pastor did supervise the schools (but that hadn't stopped the teacher from confronting him in Riedering). He could dispense and deny marriages and burials and impugn a villager's respectability (but a mayor had economic favors and penalties within his gift). The existence of a minority vote in both of these religiously homogeneous precincts, where the ballot certainly did not insure secrecy, demonstrates that it was still thinkable for a Catholic to resist the recommendation of his priest.[55] Village autocrat, he no doubt often was. But those processions of voters moving from communion rail to ballot box, about which Germans heard so much in 1871 and later, were less likely to be marching than meandering; and "*der Herr*" (as the pastor was referred to, in those locales without its own aristocratic family), was more likely to resemble a

---

[51] Total priests: my estimate. Königliches Statistisches Bureau, *Jahrbuch für die Amtliche Statistik des Preussischen Staates* (Berlin, 1883) V: 356–37. O. Blaschke, "Kolonialisierung" (1996) gives statistics for the turn of the century.

[52] "Zur Reichstagswahl," *GA* Nr. 4, 6 Jan. 1874: 21.

[53] Examples in *Wespen, Berliner Figaro,* and *Ulk,* reprinted in Eduard Hüsgen, *Ludwig Windthorst* (Cologne, 1907), 407, 412, 421; in *Zentrums-Album* (1912), 132, 144, 157, 272.

[54] Accusations that "ultramontanes" practiced "Jesuit-morality: the end justifies the means:" *MK* Nr. 13, 30 Mar. 1872: 103; Schloßmacher, *Düsseldorf,* 198; in novels: G. Hirschmann, *Kulturkampf* (1978), 222n. 285.

[55] Nevertheless both elections were thrown out. Catholic indignation at the RT's slippery criteria in election scrutinies: [Jörg], "Das Deutsche Reich" I: 769–71. Riedering (7 Oberb.) in AnlDR (1871, 1/II, Bd. 2) DS 38: 90–101; Oberhaid (5 Oberfr.) in AnlDR (1871, 1/I, Bd. 3) DS 27: 80–83; SBDR 17 Apr. 1871: 228–43; quote on 238. Details: Anderson, "Voter" (1993), 1448–74.

sheepdog than a field marshal. Much of the priest's success in this first imperial election was owed to the simple fact that he cared who won, and they did not.[56]

INVENTING THE PEOPLE

The power of the priest, the frailty of the people: the equation had international currency.[57] The inevitable consequence of fear of the priest was distrust for democracy.[58] And the converse was also true. That is, fear of priests was a politically acceptable expression for more fundamental misgivings about the people that Germany's leaders had so recklessly enfranchised. Few spokesmen for educated opinion were quite so blunt as Heinrich von Treitschke, who in 1871 described universal suffrage as "an invaluable weapon of the Jesuits, which grants such an unfair superiority to the powers of custom and stupidity." But threaded through the charges of clerical electioneering in 1871 were complaints about the competence of those casting the ballots. In Gleiwitz, an official in the Landrat's office, credibly accused of having threatened Catholic voters with economic penalties if they failed to support the Free Conservative candidate, excused himself by referring to the campaigns of the clergy and, in the same breath, the illiteracy of the rural population.[59] On the other side of Germany, the Liberal Wilhelm Wehrenpfennig, in a debate on the Centrum's victory in Bamberg, a district 83 percent Catholic, delivered a lengthy disquisition on the qualities of its population:

> A wise man once said that sensible people in Germany are very sensible, but the dumb in Germany are very dumb indeed. I don't want to apply this saying to any particular election district [laughter], but in principle, gentlemen, you will concede that it is a dumbness that is very dumb, when any man assumes that his vote for this or that candidate could send him to heaven or hell. But . . . the fact is, unfortunately, that thousands and hundreds of thousands do believe that; and when a clergyman, as runs through so many election protests, abuses this ignorance . . . then I say that we . . . have to do something . . . if we don't want free elections to cease for one-third of the population of Germany.[60]

For their low cultural level, the people themselves were not to blame. Professor von Sybel, another National Liberal, later explained to his Bonn students

[56] "Herr": Blessing, *Staat*, 96; Bodewig, *Wahlbeeinflussungen*, 143, 148; Graf, *Beeinflussungsversuche*, 183.

[57] Anderson, "Limits" (1995), 647–50.

[58] In Italy, decades of agitation to extend the suffrage were countered (until 1912) with the argument that it would put the fate of the country in the hands of the clericals. Women's suffrage, though proposed in 1904, was defeated, presumably with the same argument that defeated it in France until 1946: that women would vote with their priests. Seymour/Frary, *World* 2: 89.

[59] Kreissekretär Fock in 4 Oppeln, AnlDR (1871, 1/II, Bd. 2) DS 63: 142. Treitschke: Winfried Becker, "Liberale Kulturkampf-Positionen und politischer Katholizismus," in O. Pflanze, ed., *Innenpolitische Probleme des Bismarck-Reiches* (Munich, 1983), 69.

[60] SBDR 17 Apr. 1871: 237; protest read 5 Apr. 1871: 190. Similarly: *GA* Nr. 28, 3 Feb. 1874; *MK* Nr. 16, 22 Apr. 1871: 115; Lepper, *Strömungen* 1: 305, 327; Möllers, *Strömungen*, 218.

why it was necessary to move against the Catholic church by pointing to the performance of Catholic gymnasia ever since Prussia's constitution of 1850 had given the Church autonomy in its own affairs:

> After twelve years of experience, I could state in 1874 with documented certainty that a quarter of the students they [the Catholic schools] send to us cannot write grammatically correct German and perhaps three-quarters cannot without difficulty read an easy Greek or Latin author. Is it going too far to express the opinion that while we are perhaps not yet living in Spanish conditions, the clerical system has done its all to bring us to such a point?[61]

The professors were not the only ones convinced that universal suffrage rewarded the Catholic church for centuries of successful obscurantism ("*Verdummung*" was the more vivid German term). A Free Conservative election proclamation stated flatly that the ultramontane party naturally strove to "make the *Volk* stupid."[62] Liberals in Konstanz noted that the "Romelings . . . here are not exactly distinguished by their culture. . . ." In Düsseldorf a protest against a Centrum victory averred that "stupid-looking people almost always vote clerical." Correspondingly, those who lost to the Centrum claimed for themselves, in the words of the Liberal campaign in Cologne, the "greatest part of the educated and patriotic portions of the population."[63]

The clergy, in the view of its detractors, used a variety of techniques to manipulate the thick-witted, including instruments that had served them so well in the Middle Ages. "Anathema," a Krefeld protest argued in 1871, hurled by the Archbishop of Cologne against "all who did not blindly vote for his candidate," had tainted elections in the Rhineland. It was later conceded that the archbishop's rather moderate instructions to his clergy to stress the importance of the elections and to refrain from behavior unbecoming the dignity of a priest was not exactly the same thing as an "anathema."[64] But the subtleties of ecclesiology did not interest liberal deputies, nor, they were sure, had they interested the voter. The fact that the archbishop's statement had appeared in the newspapers, where the voter could see its difference from an "anathema," did not signify—because "newspapers are not as a rule read by the people, especially

---

[61] Sybel, "Politik," 439; Kaiser, *Strömungen*, 298f. The association between Protestantism and *Bildung*, Catholicism and (un-German) ignorance, had been liberal commonplaces since the fifties. D. Langewiesche, *Liberalismus* (1988), 68f.

[62] *MK* Nr. 13, 30 Mar. 1872: 103. Cf. *Gegenwart* quoted in *BK* (1883): 25; Blackbourn, *Marpingen*, 282–87, 291.

[63] Gert Zang, "Die Bedeutung der Auseinandersetzung um die Stiftungsverwaltung in Konstanz (1830–1870) für die ökonomische und gesellschaftliche Entwicklung der lokalen Gesellschaft. Ein Beitrag zur Analyse der materiellen Hintergründe des Kulturkampfes," in *Die Provinzialisierung einer Region. Zur Entstehung der bürgerlichen Gesellschaft in der Provinz*, edited by idem (Frankfurt a. M., 1978), 307–73; 315; Schloßmacher, *Düsseldorf*, 204–6; C. H. Kanngiesser SBDR 22 Apr. 1871: 320; Bock, 317. On NLs loss of Krefeld's LT seats: "there's no remedy against intellectual backwardness." Seyffardt, *Erinnerungen*, 422.

[64] Reyscher SBDR 18 Apr. 1871: 269.

when . . . the greatest part of the population consists of Catholics and poor weavers to boot."

In fact, it was not the alleged devices of the medieval church so much as modern techniques of campaigning that were most alarming. Endorsements had been the earliest form of campaigning in Germany, still very much part of a world in which political cues were given by notables. Typically appearing as brief, dignified announcements in the local newspaper, with maybe a dozen signatures recommending a candidate to their "friends," before 1871 they had often been—and in some regions still were—the only sign that a campaign was taking place. But two enterprising priests going door to door in Krefeld had transformed the very nature of the endorsement by collecting 4,000 signatures—practically a third of the electorate—for the Centrum candidate! No one could believe that 4,000 people were civic luminaries, worthies whose very name on an *Inserat* would sway their fellows. And if the personal influence of these voters was nil, what then could be the purpose of collecting their names? Only to *legally bind* the signers to vote for the Centrum candidate, it was argued, and thus to lock up the election, weeks before the polling actually took place, and under conditions in which the secrecy guaranteed by the ballot could not obtain. If this insidious tactic were to take hold, the most important principles of the Election Law would become a "chimera." When Centrum deputies showed that Krefelders had signed, not a commitment to vote, but the membership list of the local Centrum campaign committee, they were greeted with sarcasm. Campaign committees were traditionally the preserve of a town's best and its brightest. All one had to do was look at the *handwriting* on these endorsements to see that these were not people "who are accustomed to pose as members of any election committee!"[65]

The losers in Krefeld (styling themselves "The Friends of Humanity") had been quick to recognize the transformative power of the signature campaign. But by focusing on the legal obligation allegedly contracted by these signatures, they had misunderstood its operative mechanism. It was not as notaries but as canvassers that the two fathers had sewn up the Krefeld vote. Catholics had been captured not because they had been duped into signing a document they believed to be legally binding, but because they had been *asked* for their support. The busy clerics had discovered the most basic gospel of the political campaign: Ask and Ye Shall Receive.

The gift of a signature was a small one, even smaller than the "Catholic rent" that Daniel O'Connell had demanded of the Irish peasantry in the campaign for Catholic emancipation in the 1820s. But by turning the onlooker into an agent, it served the same purpose. Giving established a relationship, in Krefeld's case between the Catholic voter and the Centrum candidate, making the latter "his"

---

[65] R. v. Keudell, Kanngiesser, and Bock SBDR 22 Apr. 1871: 319f, 327; Reyscher SBDR 18 Apr. 1871: 270. Turnout in the Krefeld election was 80%. Also: Röttges, *Wahlen*, 63f. Dismissal of the "quality" of signatures on Z petitions was standard practice. Möllers, *Strömungen*, 210. It is a common "good government" assumption that tyranny results whenever people make pledges about and receive promises for their votes: cf. Seymour, *Reform*, 434.

candidate. Until now, election convention had cast constituents (in the form of a committee of notables, typically under such names as "Trustees of Liberal Voters") as supplicants, entreating their *candidate* to make the sacrifice of accepting public office. Mass politics reversed this relationship. The Catholic clergy were not magicians; only quick off the mark at perceiving how things would now be done. Their success in the early seventies goes far toward confirming the "organizational hypothesis" of Giovanni Sartori, who argues that political identities are not the automatic reflection of structural (class, religious, racial, etc.) cleavages, but rather that the cleavages themselves, insofar as they become relevant politically, are products of the political system—and especially of those conscious organizers who happen to arrive on the scene first.[66]

The full mobilization of the clergy—and the full potential for Catholic organization—would not be entirely accomplished until the controversy over the Jesuit law in 1872. But meanwhile, in expressing their outrage against these stolen elections, the members of the Reichstag majority failed to see the trap they were setting for themselves. Every attack on the clergy became, either explicitly or implicitly, an attack on the Catholic voter—a man at least potentially their own constituent. The Centrum lost no time in exploiting the mistake. Windthorst made a point of returning to the sneer about the handwriting on the Krefeld Centrum's membership list: "If my honored colleague . . . spent more time among the people, and especially among rural people, he would find that there are many quite capable people who know very well what they want . . . , although they are not in the position to write in a chancellery hand." Waving a Liberal election proclamation that had decorated the city's advertising pillars, the Centrum leader noted sarcastically that these 116 Liberal signatures had escaped the handwriting test, since they were printed, "and *print* is of course always better than *longhand*." Speaking on behalf of all Rhenish Catholics, the Cologne Centrum organization made certain that everyone was aware of what their detractors' charges amounted to: a series of "remarkable, entirely unmotivated attacks on universal suffrage."[67]

These themes—clever priest, uncouth parishioner—had an extraordinary persistence. When voters in Mainz elected Canon Christoph Moufang in 1874, the losers responded by draping mourning crepe over the town's statues of Gutenberg and Schiller—a "fitting demonstration," one newspaper commented, against the defeat of "the enlightened and intelligent part of the population."[68] As late as 1903, election commentary sometimes sounded as if Jan Huss, Giordano Bruno, and Galileo, rather than the navy and the tariff, had been the issues

[66] G. Sartori, "Sociology" (1969), 65–100. My account does not do justice to the subtlety of Sartori's argument.
[67] Quoted by Kanngiesser SBDR 22 Apr. 1871: 320. Windthorst, ibid.: 328f, and, on similar charges about the Rosenheim and the Mörs-Rees elections, SBDR 5 Apr. 1871: 189f.
[68] "Deutsches Reich," *GA* Nr. 26, 31 Jan. 1874: 144. The Liberal *KölnZ* accused the Z of turning "a cold and alien eye on everything that German thinkers, scientists, inventors, poets, artists have dreamed." If it succeeded, Germany would "depart from the circle of competing civilized nations and sink to the level of the Roman peoples." "Jesuitenpetitionen," 396.

facing the voters. Even the Social Democrats, at their party congress that same year, proclaimed that the Centrum's battle cry, "The people's religion must be upheld," really meant "The people must be kept dumb."[69]

The image of the stupid Centrum voter would become a favorite with cartoonists. In "A Father's Pride and Joy," J. B. Engl depicted a fat burgher introducing his son, an obvious simpleton, barely able to stand up, to his priest as "a new voter for our party."[70] *Litany*, by Eduard Thöny, portrays a winding procession of farmers, depicted as cripples, apparently on their way to a pilgrimage church. Their prayer is not to God, but to the "Holy Party," whom they apostrophize as "Protector of the retarded. . . . Harbor for the feeble-minded. . . ."[71] In other representations the voter is portrayed as a child and a puppet, while being given the qualities of a sheep.

The dynamic worked in both directions, however. In defending their elections against the charges of clerical influence, the Centrum's deputies found themselves pushed into a championship of the ordinary voter and his franchise for which little in their political past could have prepared them. These men—lawyers and judges, aristocrats and priests—were socially scarcely distinguishable from the notables who led the other non-Socialist parties, except of course in being "decided" Catholics. They were not democrats in our own sense of the term, and it is not my intention to suggest that any egalitarian idealism lay behind their taking up the banner of universal suffrage.[72] But pragmatism was hardly unique to the Centrum. As Edmund Morgan has rightly pointed out, "We assume too easily that popular sovereignty was the product of popular demand, a rising of the many against the few. It was not. It was a question of some of the few enlisting the many against the rest of the few."[73] At first the Centrum's advocacy was confined to defending the common sense of the common man against his cultured despisers. Before long, however, the logic of their conflict with the liberal parties had pushed them to "inventing" (to borrow Morgan's term) "the people," a *Volk* whose homespun virtues reversed the values of the liberal caricature, one whose merits qualified them for the responsibility of the franchise—and, of course, legitimated their choices.[74]

---

[69] Quote: Bachem, *Vorgeschichte* 6: 187, 188f. Cf. "Siegesallee of Catholic Progress," a cartoon depicting statues of Huss, Giordano Bruno, and various others tied to stakes. *Zentrums-Album* (1912), 213.

[70] "Vaterfreuden," *Simplicissimus* VIII/11 (n.d., 1903–4): 86.

[71] "Bittgang," *Simplicissimus* XV/11 (13 June 1910): 174.

[72] I must have expressed myself poorly if Kühne, *Dreiklassenwahlrecht*, 398n. 10, believes that I ever thought otherwise.

[73] *Inventing* (1988), 169. What Morgan calls a "fiction," D. C. Moore terms a Sorelian myth. *Politics* (1976), 420. In Germany, such fictions were perpetrated (and probably believed) only about one's own party—which made them somewhat less benign.

[74] Contrasting the honest man and his cultured despisers: *Essener Volkszeitung* (Z), 1870: 256, quoted in Möllers, *Strömungen*, 173. Chaplain E. Müller's reference to "vox populi, vox Dei": Rust, *Reichskanzler* (1897), 616–20; Pastor Adolf Wehrle, entering "the broadest democratic highway," put the people's will over the prince's, according to police informants. Amtsvorstand Konstanz to MdI, 20 June 1893. GLA 236/14901. Wehrle's own view of campaigning: *Erinnerungen eines Reichstagskandidaten für das Centrum aus dem Drang-Zwang-Qual-Wahl-Jahre 1887* (Konstanz, n.d. [1887]).

About the Beyond, in the know
Is every good shepherd of the soul.
He points out the path to Heaven's Bliss
For every agriculturist.

Strung along, one by one,
Every single Catholic comes,
And so no lambkin strays or dozes,
The shepherd is there, counting noses.

Through the urn
One after another,
(To be used as needed)
Go the voting fodder.

And after they've all been taken in
—Kiddies, it's home you go again.

Fig. 3. Source: O. Gulbransson, "Das Stimmvieh," *Simplicissimus*, Extra- Nummer: Reichs-tagswahl VIII (n.D., 1903–4): 8.

The partisan advantages for the Centrum of democratic representation were not just rhetorical. Catholics not only stood below Protestants and Jews educationally, as their opponents never tired of implying; economically they were also inferior by a considerable distance. This gap meant that even in regions where their demographic dominance was overwhelming, the various kinds of property qualifications attached to state and municipal franchises neutralized their voting power. The disparity was especially glaring in the Rhineland, where economic and religious cleavages tended to reinforce each other. In Essen's Landtag elections of 1870, for example, the first two classes, voting Liberal and representing 8 percent of the eligible voters, overruled the third class which, voting Centrum, represented 92 percent. If the Reichstag franchise were introduced on the local and state levels, the Centrum could drive Krefeld's Ludwig Friedrich Seyffardt and his Liberal colleagues not only out of the national parliament, but also from the state assemblies and city halls that remained their bastions, often until the end of the empire. Trier's Centrum recognized their opportunity almost immediately; only two years after the first election, its election proclamation demanded the Reichstag franchise for the Prussian Landtag. In the same election, Rhenish Liberals *dropped* this same demand.[75]

In 1873, the Centrum followed through with a bill in the Prussian Landtag to substitute manhood suffrage for the three-class voting system. It was the first such assault on this powerful bastion of privilege, and made at a propitious time: when the combined Landtag seats of the two Conservative parties numbered only 65 out of 433. Windthorst, the Centrum's unofficial leader, ran up against some internal resistance to the reform—although mostly from an "auxiliary member" (*Hospitant*) of the delegation, the Old Conservative, Ludwig von Gerlach. But he was convinced of the advantage of the move. "The motion for universal suffrage," Windthorst explained to Edmund Jörg "is [illegible], but I consider it right, and [it] must be repeated everywhere—in Bavaria, Württemberg, Baden. I also consider it indicated for Austria and Italy."[76] The liberal majority, much embarrassed, tabled his motion.

Between 1876 and 1878 Edmund Jörg and August Schels responded to Windthorst's suggestion by submitting bills and interpellations to the Bavarian Landtag aimed at introducing direct balloting in Bavarian state elections.[77] As for Prussia, by 1876 the demand to implement the Reichstag franchise in state elections had become part of the program of the Centrum's first all-regional campaign committee, established for the Rhine province.[78] Any chance for suc-

[75] Essen: Möllers, *Strömungen*, 175. Trier proclamation: Steil, *Wahlen*, 129, 158.

[76] LW to EJ, 2 Dec. 1873, in Jörg, *Briefwechsel*, 403. As early as 1871 LW and Ketteler had raised objections to the three-class voting system. SBDR 2 Nov. 1871: 103; Anderson, *Windthorst* (1981), 183–86.

[77] By the 1880s, and esp. the 90s, however, when its disadvantage for their own party became apparent, conservatives within the Bavarian Z, dominant until 1899, lost whatever enthusiasm they may once have had for introducing direct elections, joining Liberals in defeating similar SD bills—which were supported by the Z left. K. Möckl, *Prinzregentenzeit* (1972), 496–99, 514–17.

[78] SBHA 26 Nov. 1873: 94–99. In Baden the Catholic VP had introduced a motion to grant

cess, if it ever existed, was a momentary one. That very year the Conservatives began to regain their strength; by 1879 the two conservative parties controlled 161 seats in the Prussian Landtag; and as their numbers continued to rise and liberal numbers fell, the Centrum's advocacy of the Reichstag franchise for Prussian state elections became moot.[79] But the party also turned its attention to Prussia's municipal franchise. After taunts that the Centrum's poor success in municipal elections had proved that the much-vaunted "people" it claimed to represent were in fact only "small farmers, artisans, and day laborers," plus a few aristocrats, the party sponsored a bill to replace the plutocratic municipal franchise with a democratic suffrage, and thus to reveal that precisely this despised constituency was "*the* people." When the reform was defeated, along with a similar proposal by the Progressives, the Centrum tried a variety of other tacks to broaden the municipal suffrage—even sponsoring a motion to enfranchise financially independent businesswomen.[80]

THE LEGISLATORS RESPOND: 1871–76

The same logic connecting clergy and voters that pushed the Centrum's leadership into "inventing the people," and to a precocious championship of the Reichstag franchise, fueled doubts about manhood suffrage among the Church's critics. The very first arguments in what would eventually become a wholesale attack on the imperial franchise were marshaled in the early 1870s, on behalf of a move to disenfranchise the Catholic clergy. No anticlerical supposed that subtracting the votes of priests would significantly diminish the strength of political Catholicism. Nor would prohibiting them from accepting seats, which was now also suggested, end their influence.[81] But the election code guaranteed to the *voter* a bundle of civic privileges that went beyond simply casting a ballot: notably the right to attend rallies and join "election" associations. When anticlericals realized, however, that they would have to disenfranchise the Protestant clergy as well if they were to avoid the charge of religious persecution, they dropped the idea. Ultimately, admitted the Liberal constitutional scholar Robert von Mohl, who had supported disenfranchisement, the only solution to

---

deputies travel allowences and a per diem as early as 1869; the Z, on 10 Dec. 1873. Becker, *Staat*, 231, 262–65.

[79] After 1903 the Z's passion for the reform was rightly considered "platonic." It was not until Jan. 1907 that it submitted another *Initiativantrag* to replace the three-class voting system with the RT franchise. H. Heitzer, *Volksverein* (1979), 126–38; Kühne, *Dreiklassenwahlrecht*, 420–52; H. v. Gerlach, *Geschichte* (1908), 188–203.

[80] NL taunts quoted in Rust, *Reichskanzler* (1897), 656. W. Virnich, *Fraction* (1876), 90–100; female suffrage: 96f. Since numerous Rhenish towns had raised their census from 6 to 18M, in 1886 J. Bachem introduced a bill to set the minimum tax payment necessary for the communal franchise universally at 6M, which would have transformed local governments. It was defeated by NLs. SBHA, 6 May 1886: 1940.

[81] Bis.'s original constitutional draft had excluded the clergy from parliament along with other public servants. C. v. Lachner, *Grundzüge* (1908), 37.

clerical influence would be to replace the entire imperial voting system with a suffrage that excluded *all* "harmful individual classes of the population." The franchise should be limited to those with positive competence in public affairs.[82]

Thus began the Liberals' retreat from their tentative acceptance of manhood suffrage. Treitschke, who in 1869 had advocated extending the Reichstag franchise to Prussian state elections, was only the first and most conspicuous defector. More quietly, Friedrich Kapp, Heinrich von Gagern, John Prince Smith, Rudolf Haym, and Robert von Mohl—Liberals all—joined him.[83] Making campaign hay out of National Liberalism's faltering enthusiasm for the Reichstag franchise, the Catholic clergy now began to style themselves as watchdogs of democracy. Here is Chaplain Schlechter in Bochum during the 1893 election campaign:

> Robbers, thieves, burglars—when they come, then one protects oneself. The National Liberal Party intends to repeal universal suffrage and introduce the [three-] class franchise in its place. Therefore I say once again: guard yourselves against robbers, thieves, and burglars! When the burglar comes, then one shoots him down, grabs him, and brings him to the police. . . .[84]

Few Liberals, in fact, desired to take on the onus of being the party that limited popular rights. Far better to keep the party's position ambiguous and leave the dirty work to the government.[85] In the meantime, the same end could be accomplished via the Reichstag's authority to invalidate elections. The potential for reversing the clerical tide was a real one—as a glance across the border reveals. For within that same decade, France's Republican majority consciously employed the Chamber's authority to nullify elections as an instrument of policy. Its most spectacular intervention occurred in 1877, when it impeached the elections of more than 130 clerical or legitimist deputies, throwing out 77 of them. A contemporary political scientist deemed the nullifications of 1885 "veritable parliamentary *coups d'état*." The result of this wholesale breaking of elections was profoundly demoralizing for the constituencies deprived of their choices. By the nineties their "clericalism" had disappeared and voting returns in the target areas were solidly Republican—although the views of the constituents had hardly changed. The historian of the Massif Central explains the transformation of the political landscape: "What was the point of following the *curé* to the polls if the resultant victory of the conservative candidate was likely to be set aside on the flimsiest of pretexts?"[86]

---

[82] Von Mohl, "Erörterungen," 528–663, esp. 547–51. In 1876 the Electoral Commission of the Bavarian LT also called for disenfranchisement of the Catholic clergy and, when that appeared incapable of a majority, clergy of all denominations. Bodewig, *Wahlbeeinflussungen*, 183, and v. Lachner, *Grundzüge*, 36, differ on the degree of support the motion found.

[83] Sheehan, *Liberalism* (1977), 155f. Local discussions criticizing the RT franchise: K. Tenfelde, *Sozialgeschichte* (1981), 498n. 47.

[84] 5 Arns., AnlDR (1894/95, 9/III, Bd. 2) DS 318: 1322f.

[85] Kühne, *Dreiklassenwahlrecht*, 400; W. Gagel, *Wahlrechtsfrage* (1958), 73–78.

[86] Quoted: Lefèvre-Pontalis, *Élections*, 13 and Jones, *Politics* (1985), 300, 303. Charnay argues

In Germany, flimsy pretexts were defeated by Reichstag scruples. The case of Pleß-Rybnik, when the majority (basing its calculations "more on ethical than on arithmetical grounds") was willing to override the choice of thousands of voters because three pastors had spoken about the election in church, proved the exception. Although robust anticlericals argued that even one partisan sermon could "penetrate" a whole district, and that the only way to teach the clergy to stay out of politics was for the Reichstag to make use of its "House Rights" to render their politicking counterproductive, the argument convinced fewer and fewer deputies.[87] A Conservative deputy warned that such a broad definition of "taint" could put every election at the mercy of any cleric who wanted to overturn it. Suddenly visions of clever priests recommending unloved Liberals from their pulpits in order to *force* the Reichstag to throw out Liberal victories danced before the deputies' eyes.[88] Even more important was a growing awareness—led by that stickler for procedure, Eduard Lasker—that the German parliament was establishing precedents that it would have to live with for a long time.[89] Eventually the only procedure that seemed intellectually defensible was one that subtracted specific votes from the specific precinct in which an impropriety had taken place. Such an insistence on arithmetical over "ethical" considerations, however, made the invalidation mechanism useless for combating clerical influence in precisely those districts where it was most likely to have occurred: places with huge Centrum margins, like Münster, Essen, Koblenz, and Trier. In the minds of the deputies, the price for such self-denial was a heavy one; but we can see that it helped preserve the long-term credibility of a parliament whose cleavages were considerably more complicated than those in its French counterpart.[90]

---

that while clerical influence was harshly punished, holistic evaluations were never adopted. "L'église," 265–67, 295f.

[87] Bamberger, "Sitzungsperiode," 165. Holistic evaluations: Kanngiesser and Lasker SBDR 22 Apr. 1871: 320, 326. Wehrenpfennig and Duncker suggested manipulating the subtraction in a way that might produce easier invalidations: ibid., 322, 325. Kardorff and Duncker: SBDR 5 Apr. 1871: 173; arithmetic invalidations: *HZtg* Nr. 92, 3rd Beilage, 20 Apr. 1871; criticism of unfair validation practices: *MK*, Nr. 18, 6 May 1871: 141f; [Jörg], "Das deutsche Reich" II: 767–71.

[88] M. v. Blanckenburg (K) ibid., 22 Apr. 1871: 325. As late as 1912, an analogous warning against holistic evaluations was used by the WPK to justify its procedures: 1 Meckl.-Schw., (1912/13, 13/I, Bd. 17) DS 478: 512. The danger was no chimera: in 1904 two SD victories were overturned because state influence on behalf of another candidate caused the entire election to be thrown out! A. Stadthagen (SD) SBDR 9 Dec. 1912: 2690.

[89] Here Lasker erred. In the matter of election validations, the chamber was fully sovereign. No court could correct it, and it was not required to follow its own precedents. Schels (Z) SBDR 17 Apr. 1871, 234.

[90] Ad hoc support for holistic evaluations never disappeared entirely. The SDs and the Z demanded holistic criteria in mining regions, when employer intimidation was systematic (6 Trier, AnlDR (1884, 5/IV, Bd. 4) DS 103: 793–99, esp. 798); SDs, in districts in which their rallies had been shut down (1 Hessen, AnlDR (1884/85, 6/I, Bd. 5) DS 124: 477f). LLs also saw patterns: Rickert SBDR 6 Mar. 1888: 1298, 1303; Traeger 10 Jan. 1889: 369. Poles insisted that the proven misconduct of panels in some precincts tainted the entire district: v. Koscielski, 4 Marienwerder, SBDR 7 Mar. 1888: 1358; Rickert agreed: 1360. When a County School Inspector spoke and wrote to the 171 teachers subordinate to him, even the Z demanded that the RT not insist on "mathmatical proofs" as to how many individuals let themselves be swayed. A. Gröber SBDR 14 Jan. 1890: 995.

The alternative to co-opting the invalidation mechanism, however, proved to be legislating directly against the clergy. Already by December 1871 the Centrum's opponents had amended the penal code by adding the so-called "Pulpit Paragraph," which punished political speech uttered in the course of spiritual duties with up to two years in prison.[91] In nothing were liberal Germans so European as in this effort to control the political activity of Catholic priests. Always eager to invoke the practice of the civilized world, Reichstag legislators pointed out that Belgium, Spain, Portugal, and Italy had passed similar regulations (even as they admitted that such measures were unheard of in Britain and North America). The model for the Pulpit Paragraph in fact came from France's *code pénal*. Precedents were also cited from the legislation of the individual German states, beginning in 1813. Unfortunately for this line of argument, Prussia had been moving in the opposite—Anglo-American—direction and by 1851 had eliminated all references to abuses of religion from its penal code. Since it was Prussian law that provided the template for the North German Confederation and empire, the supporters of the Pulpit Paragraph, in departing from this freer Prussian model, found themselves in some embarrassment. Though a few claimed that the definition of Papal Infallibility, promulgated by the Vatican Council in July 1870, had transformed the legal situation, this argument hardly explained why restrictions on clerical speech that had not seemed necessary in January of 1871, when Bavaria had been incorporated within the jurisdiction of the penal code, should become so pressing only eleven months later.

The legislators tried to square the circle of free speech for citizens and criminalized speech for priests by anchoring the Pulpit Paragraph in a distinction between the clergy's personal and his sacerdotal activity. Heavy weather was made with the argument that the priest was a public official. But since only a few of the German states included the Catholic clergy among their civil servants, the category proved useless for national legislation.[92] Eventually they turned to the church building. Since it enjoyed special protections from the state, the state needed supervisory rights over what took place inside. The deputies supplemented this argument with a doctrine that we might call "equal time." At an election rally, where it could be rebutted, clerical speech should be subject to no special restrictions. But inside church walls, with the pastor speak-

---

[91] P. Reichensperger and A. Schels (Z) had dared opponents to enact such legislation: SBDR 5 Apr. 1871: 173 and 17 Apr. 1871: 234, respectively. Demanding a Pulpit Law: Duncker and Kardorff SBDR 5 Apr. 1871: 173; by Behr and Fischer, 17 Apr.: 240–42; by Reyscher, 18 Apr.: 270; by Günther, 22 Apr.: 318–21; *GA* Nr. 97, 26 Apr. 1871: 383; mocked in the Catholic *MK* Nr. 16, 22 Apr. 1871: 128. Criminal prosecution on the Swiss model was suggested in the *GA* Nr. 164, 16 July 1871: 1475; Nr. 173, 27 July 1871: 1552. On the Pulpit Paragraph: Becker, *Staat*, 72–75; Huber, *Verfassungsgeschichte* 4: 701.

[92] "Die Grundsätze des Reichstags des Norddeutschen Bundes und des deutschen Reichstags hinsichtlich der amtlichen Wahlbeeinflußungen" (hereafter: Poschinger Report), 11 Feb. 1879, BAB-L R1501/14450, Bl. 158; O. Elble, *Kanzelparagraph* (1908), 15, 23f; E. R. Bierling, "Sind die Beamten des evangelischen Kirchenregiments in Preussen als Staatsbeamte anzusehen?" *Archiv für Öffentliches Recht* 7 (1892): 212–24.

ing six feet above contradiction, listeners had a right to be protected from words they were not free to counter without being (allegedly) liable to arrest for disturbing the peace.[93]

When we look at the culture of the election rally, in chapter 9, we shall see how this concept of free speech—that it existed only when the right to rebut was simultaneously protected—played itself out in practice. For now, it suffices to say that the formal distinction between a private and/or public space, where speech was free, and a specially protected—and therefore off limits—House of God, though frequently invoked, satisfied few. Lasker, for one, felt compelled to offer additional reasons for overriding a priest's civil rights. Not only the location, but the condition of the listener justified the restriction. The German people knew "very well that a person in a state of religious contemplation is of course far more susceptible to very many impressions than, for example, when he's in a beer parlor." But no argument could disguise the fact that ultimately it was neither location nor listener so much as the identity of the speaker that was at issue.[94] Who could believe (as liberals claimed to) that just because he stood outside his church rather than before the altar the priest was speaking only as a fellow citizen, indeed as another fallible, sinful creature? The beardless face and black vestments, outward and visible signs of a supernatural vocation that accompanied the priest wherever he went, subverted the distinction between private and public persona around which so much of the debate on legitimate election activity revolved. For all their efforts to the contrary, the Pulpit Paragraph's restrictions on clerical speech—which was expanded in 1876 to cover writing—slipped through the legal meshes the deputies were trying to weave and revealed its true identity as a piece of exceptional legislation, defining not an action but a person as being outside the protection of the law.

The desire to control the clergy's electioneering was the motive not only behind the Pulpit Paragraph, but also of Prussia's School Supervision Law of spring 1872, which withdrew school inspection from the clergy (in practice, only from the Catholic clergy). Although commonly viewed as a stage in secularization's *longue durée*, the law has been rightly described as "primarily" an "educational corrective to universal suffrage." Its immediate target, however, was not future generations of children, but the current generation of parsons, who were perceived, often correctly, as using teachers as their election agents. It was this political connection that provided the decisive argument for those deputies who might otherwise have shown little interest in the modernization of elementary education.[95] The desire to combat clerical election influence was

[93] Invoked in 7 Düsseldorf in 1871, AnlDR (1871, 1/II, Bd. 2) DS 10: 16–18, and by Müller-Meiningen, who claimed that contradictors risked arrest under §§166 and 167 of the penal code. Debate on 6 Posen, SBDR 21 May 1912: 2218.

[94] Lasker SBDR 5 Apr. 1871: 175. Contemporaries were clear about the Pulpit Paragraphs electoral function: "Ein Galgen für Geistliche," *MK* Nr. 48, 2 Dec. 1871; v. Mohl, "Erörterungen," 571–79; J. Friedrich, *Wahlrecht* (1906), 11; Cohn, "Schutz" (1907–8): 578–82; 580; Elble, *Kanzelparagraph*, 9–12, 39.

[95] Quoted: Neugebauer-Wölk, *Wählergenerationen*, 59. SBHA: Bethusy-Huc (FK) 9 Feb. 1872:

also one of the impulses behind Prussia's Ecclesiastical Penalties Law of 13 May 1873, and similar legislation in Baden, Hessen, and Saxony making it a criminal offense to issue a public excommunication or to threaten religious penalties in order to affect a person's vote.[96]

One cannot isolate any of these measures from the broader liberal assault on the Catholic church that would soon encompass every point at which Catholic religious life touched the life of the State: an assault its proponents trumpeted as an epochal "Battle for Culture" (Kulturkumpf). But the culture wars themselves, for all they owed to a collision of radical anticlericalism with ultramontane triumphalism, a collision that was international in scope, cannot be divorced from the atmosphere of excited uncertainty that accompanied the introduction of Germany's democratic franchise.[97] To that extent, the Kulturkampf was preeminently a political, not a cultural, struggle. To liberals, nationalists, and even many conservatives, it was during elections that the Church's power became most visible and most threatening. And since success in the cultural battle depended, they believed, on legislation and thus on parliamentary majorities, not surprisingly elections became the arena for "cultural"—that is, for identity—politics. What anticlericals did not realize was that once identity, rather than this or that "policy," had become the stake in the electoral game, the clergy would hold all the trumps.

Jesuit Phobia and the Mobilization of the Priests

The convergence of the nationalists' cultural fears with election anxieties reached its climax with the hysteria over the Jesuits. Feeling against the order had been building for a decade, fueled by reports of its efforts on behalf of the infallibist party in the Vatican and by the rise of a "Protestant" narrative of Germany's national past. For if 1866 were a replay of the Thirty Years' War, then the Society of Jesus, as the embodiment of a Counter-Reformation that had then managed to hold its own, must now be sent packing. Manifestations of hatred toward the order were everywhere. A liberal Augsburg newspaper claimed to have discovered that since the founding of the society, the age at death of Europe's crowned heads had fallen precipitously (a mortality statistic, one Catholic newspaper noted dryly, "remarkable in the history of medicine,

---

712; cf. also Handjery 1 May 1871: 511; Bunsen 8 Nov. 1871: 141; v. Winter 22 Nov. 1871: 429. Anderson, "Kulturkampf" (1986), 102–4; M. L. Anderson and K. Barkin, "Myth" (1982), 647–86.

[96] Lachner, *Grundzüge*, 15, 47n. 1; [R.] v. Campe, "Wahlbeeinflussung" (1912): 6–10.

[97] The Hubers anachronistically describe the 1871 Pulpit Paragraph as a response to *resistance* to the Kulturkampf. E.-R. and W. Huber, *Staat und Kirche im 19. und 20. Jahrhundert. Dokumente zur Geschichte des deutschen Staatskirchenrechts* 2 vols. (Berlin, 1976) 2: 528; Huber, *Verfassungsgeschichte* 4: 701. Before the government had proposed any legislation, Belgium's *Echo du Parlament* commented that the "battle against ultramontanism" was proceeding in Germany with "the energy for which the Prussians are famous." *GA* Nr. 176, 30 July 1871: 1575. According to the Grand Duke of Baden the elections spurred Bismarck's decision to take up the anti-clerical cry: Becker, *Staat*, 305n. 17. The most recent account of the Kulturkampf: R. J. Ross, *Failure* (1998).

and proof of the progress of German science").[98] Popular novels advertised the order's depravity, booking conspiracies, wars, even papacide to the Jesuit account. Caricatures of the Jesuit, strikingly at variance with an otherwise realistic style, appeared in the works of academic painters.[99] The satirist Wilhelm Busch's vulpine *Pater Filuzius* became a best-seller. Among more openly political cartoonists, the Jesuit was also a favorite target. He was the snake in the Garden of Eden.[100] He was the termite in the tree of Germania, which Bismarck was called upon to "exterminate." One *Kladderadatsch* cartoon depicted the sulfurous odor of these hard-faced men forcing even the devil to hold his nose.[101]

Not surprisingly, drastic images suggested drastic remedies. Beginning in the autumn of 1871, petitions began to arrive in the Reichstag demanding that the deputies rid the country of the Society of Jesus, which was "infecting" German Catholicism. Although at first spontaneous, by the spring of 1872 National Liberals in the Protestant Association had turned diffuse anxiety into a well-organized campaign.[102] Huge rallies to gather signatures for expulsion petitions were held from one end of Protestant Germany to the other.

The petitions to expel the Jesuits were not among vox populi's finer moments. Nearly five thousand citizens of Breslau claimed that a Jesuit "must, whether he wants to or not, act unpatriotically, inhumanly, ruthlessly, without regard to conscience." Under the protection of Germany's laws, the Jesuits were enveloping the fatherland in their "meshes" and, Breslauers argued (switching metaphors), they were "sapping the innermost foundations of German *Volkstum*." The charge, from petitioners in ten Rhenish cities, that Jesuits were undermining the very existence of the Reich was echoed by more than a thousand citizens of Magdeburg, in apocalyptic language that soon became characteristic of *völkisch* nationalism. Petitioners from Brandenburg were the most violent, one calling on the government to employ the law against wolves to combat this vermin. (The language of infection would soon be applied to the Church's charitable institutions as well, which were compared to "phylloxera, Colorado bee-

---

[98] *MK* Nr. 50, 16 Dec. 1871: 397. Hostility to the Jesuits was taken for granted in the non-Catholic press: cf. "Der deutsche Episcopat und das Concil," *Die Post* (Berlin), Nr. 487, 23 Sept. 1869: 1; "Deutsches Reich," in *GA* Nr. 148, 28 June 1871: 1335; Nr. 172, 26 July 1871: 1546, and Nr. 226, 27 Sept. 1871: 2013.

[99] Even the *GA* remarked critically on the "grotesque caricature" in Gustav Spangenberg's *Founding of the Jesuit Order in Rome in 1540*. "In der Kunst-Ausstellung. II," *GA* Nr. 179, 3 Aug. 1871: 1604; Gross, *Jesus*, 56f. Gross's viewpoint is that of 19th-century liberals. Negative associations were not confined to imperial Germany. The second meaning for Jesuit given in *Webster's Ninth New Collegiate Dictionary* is "one given to intrigue or equivocation."

[100] Harald Just, "Wilhelm Busch und die Katholiken: Kulturkampfstimmung im Bismarck-Reich." *Geschichte in Wissenschaft und Unterricht* 25 (1974): 65–78; novels: Hirschmann, *Kulturkampf*, 140–52. *Der neue Sündenfall*, 1870/71 cartoon in *Zentrums-Album* (1912), 3.

[101] *Termite:* "*Radical, nicht palliativ*" (1872), in Wilhelm Scholz, *Bismarck Album des Kladderadatsch, 1840–1890* (Berlin, 1893), 69; sulfurous Jesuits: *Petition an den Reichstag* (1872), in Kladderadatsch, *Zentrums-Album* (1912), 19.

[102] "*Infiziert*" appears in petitions from Cologne, Marburg, Mühlheim, Uerdingen, Boppard, Schleiden, and Witten bei Bochum, reprinted in "6th Report," 262. The role of the Protestantenverein: Bachem, *Vorgeschichte* 3: 252f.

tle and other enemies of the Reich.") Every civilized state, supplicants from Brandenburg and Leipzig insisted, had at one time or another expelled the Jesuits—a point felt to be conclusive proof of the objectivity of the charges against them.[103]

These were images and arguments that would become, *mutatis mutandis*, chillingly familiar in the 1920s and 30s. But unlike the Jews, the Catholic minority was not numerically insignificant. Alerted by Centrum deputies, the Catholic public assembled in cities from every corner of Germany—Osnabrück and Bremen in the north; Essen, Duisburg, Krefeld, Barmen, Düsseldorf, Cologne, and Koblenz in the west; Mainz, Freiburg, Würzburg, Eichstätt, and Munich in the south; Erfurt and Dresden in the center; and Breslau, Lissa, Schrimm, and Braunsberg in the east—to hear speakers read aloud what their countrymen were saying about the Jesuits, about their pastors, and about themselves. And those who heard themselves so described responded with indignation. Workers' and journeymen's associations, noblemen and noblewomen, pastors and cathedral chapters, brotherhoods, choirs, sodalities, and especially villages and parishes, came to the order's defense, producing in autumn and winter of 1871–72 more than ten times as many petitions in defense of the Jesuits as those attacking them.[104] The list of these thousands of sponsoring groups covered more than eight double-column pages of very small print. Their efforts were reinforced by a simultaneous campaign, aimed at the Prussian Landtag, protesting the new School Inspection Law. The latter, resulting in more than 19,000 petitions, bearing more than 326,000 signatures, was Central Europe's most vigorous petition drive since 1848.[105] Even more than the elections the previous year, these petition campaigns brought ordinary voters—Protestant and Catholic—into purposeful contact with their elected leaders, intensifying their sense of connection to the legislative process.

Let us recall that in March 1871 two-thirds of the Catholic electorate had not voted for the Centrum. Some of the constituencies that had—like Sachrang, Riedering, and Oberhaid in Bavaria—did so for reasons that can scarcely be called political or even religious. Even the Catholic press had been far from uniform in urging voters to action in the first election. Chaplain Eduard Müller's pugnacious *Märkisches Kirchenblatt*, never one to shy away from political

[103] Breslau petition in "6th Report," 261; Rhenish petitions: ibid., 262, 263; every civilized state: Breslau and Leipzig petitions, ibid., 263; wolf law: Karl Schlez of Brandenburg, cited in "14th Report of the Petitions Committee," AnlDR (1872, 1/III, Bd. 3) DS 141: 608–11, esp. 608f. Phylloxera, etc., a liberal academic quoted in J. H. Kissling, *Geschichte* (1911) 3: 58, and in Blackbourn, "Progress" (1987), 149. Apocalyptic language was not limited to the Protestant side. The GA was replete with quotations from the *Vaterland* (Munich) that, in addition to sounding malicious and extremist, seem to have reflected prophecies of wars between North and South. GA Nr. 33, 8 Feb. 1874: 186.

[104] "6th Report," 263. Not every priest supported the Jesuits, but those who vocally did not, such as Chaplain Mosler, the leader of Essen's Christian Workers' Association, lost their political influence almost immediately. Möllers, *Strömungen*, 194.

[105] Marjorie Lamberti, *State, Society and the Elementary School in Imperial Germany* (New York and Oxford 1989), esp. 43f.

issues, had barely mentioned the refounding of a Catholic party in December 1870, had consigned the Centrum's election proclamation to a back page, and had otherwise ignored the existence of the first election.[106] But already in the first weeks after the election, when press reports on challenged Centrum victories began to appear in the constituencies, the mood started to change. The reciprocal dynamic in the winter of 1871–72 of rally, petition, counterrally, counterpetition was the first truly nationwide experience, since 1848–49, for Germans both Catholic and Protestant, in mass politics. Here was mobilization. Unlike 1848, they were mobilized against each other.

The opponents of the Centrum were shaken by this outpouring—but not dismayed. The very fact that hundreds of thousands of Catholics had organized "under a uniform leadership" proved the ubiquity of Jesuit power. Catholic opinion was dismissed as artificial, the very numbers of their petitions telling against them, since "even the stones have spoken."[107] An examination of the petitions' place of origin strongly supports the liberals' suspicion that the clergy had been indispensable in conjuring these stones to speak. The distribution was by no means exactly coterminous with Catholic populations in Germany. Except for Silesia, Catholics east of the Elbe were represented only nominally: a result, in all likelihood, not only of the dispersion of the population, and all that meant for political organization, but of the relative scarcity of priests in the east. In Bavaria, petitions flowed in from large towns, which repaid skillful organization; but from small and middle-sized towns they were conspicuously few and far between. *Rural* Bavaria, on the other hand, where a pastor could canvass a hamlet in an afternoon and where there were few other notables to challenge him, was strongly overrepresented.[108] Westfalia, where priests were thick on the ground, was likewise heavily overrepresented. Indeed, the First Münster district sent in three times as many petitions as the entire state of Baden, a region with more than nine times the number of Catholics—but with a severe shortage of priests.[109] Thus the petition campaign was strong where the Catholic clergy were strong: another argument for Sartori's "organizational hypothesis." Since the clergy as a whole were being depicted as Jesuits, their initial response can be seen as an act of self-defense. But once they were mobilized, the Reichstag had their attention.

The geographical distribution of clerical power may itself have been a reflection of another, less tangible, indeed somewhat mysterious factor, which for lack of a better name we shall have to call tradition. For in addition to rural

[106] "Norddeutschland," *MK* Nr. 3, 21 Jan. 1871: 23f.

[107] Quotes: Gneist, "Verbot," col. 1223; Wagener, "Jesuiten-Petitionen," col. 1147.

[108] The overwhelming majority of Bavarian towns over 2,000 were unrepresented, and the overwhelming number of petitions, running into the hundreds, were from locales under 5,000, indeed under 1,000. On the ratio of priests to population, see my "Limits," 647–70; esp. 651–56; Blaschke, "Kolonialisierung," 107.

[109] My calculations. On the Baden clergy, who enjoyed less autonomy than their Prussian counterparts: Barbara Richter, "Der Priestermangel in der Erzdiözese Freiburg um 1850. Ursachen und Lösungsversuche durch Pastoralvertretung aus der Diözese Rottenburg," *Freiburgerer Diözesan-Archiv* 108 (1988), 429–47; I. Götz v. Olenhusen, "Ultramontanisierung" (1991), 64–66.

Bavaria, two regions seem to have participated with unusual intensity in the petition campaign. The area in Hessen around the city of Mainz was one. The second, crossing several political and administrative boundaries, was a contiguous chain of election districts running along Germany's western border: beginning with the southwestern corner of Oldenburg in the north, running through the Emsland in what was, before 1866, Hanoverian Westfalia, continuing through the regency of Münster, down the westernmost Rhineland from Kleve-Jülich, and ending in the Mosel valley. Here was the *Pfaffengasse*, Germany's black stripe, corresponding to long-gone ecclesiastical states that had studded the Holy Roman Empire's western boundaries until 1803. This chain of election districts, so prominent in the petition campaign, would become the real bastions of political Catholicism, bastions whose remnants would last well into Konrad Adenauer's and Helmut Kohl's Federal Republic.[110]

Only one Catholic region sent no petitions at all: the so-called Reichsland, the annexed French provinces of Alsace and Lorraine. Demographically these provinces were characterized by precisely those indicators that otherwise correlated with high participation. They were well supplied with priests; their population density, facilitating communication, was among the highest in Germany; and the overwhelming majority of this population was concentrated in villages of 2,000 people or fewer, precisely where pastors were most likely to have things their own way. If the petition movement had reflected only the interests of the clergy, this region should have been well represented. But the absence of voices from the Reichsland points to the second crucial component of the petition campaign: the presence of someone to "receive" the petitions in Berlin. For the *initiative* for the petitions seems to have come not from the countryside, but from the Centrum's parliamentary delegation, perhaps because, with seats on the Petitions Committee, these men were made daily aware, as no parish priest could be, of the dangerous momentum of the anti-Jesuit campaign. Alsace-Lorraine, where elections were not held until 1874, lacked Reichstag representation. And without the leadership afforded by politically interested deputies, their clergy (who would in any case resist unified political organization for a generation) remained silent.[111]

The visible evidence of the Catholic clergy's ability to "make the stones speak" fueled the anticlericals' sense of crisis. This was a battle, liberals were convinced, that had been *"forced upon us."* The German Empire "now found itself in a state of war with the Jesuit Order," described as "the most urgent, the most burning, the most immediate danger to the German Empire." The situation was proclaimed "an emergency in the true sense of the word." Expulsion was the only answer. The 1864 Syllabus of Errors, which someone took the trouble

---

[110] The connection between Catholic *voting* strongholds and the old ecclesiastical states is made by J. Henke in "Hochburgen," (1990), 348–73. In 1907 RR v. Horn noted that that part of the Trier regency that had once belonged to the Electorate of Trier was still entirely under the influence of the clergy. Horn Report, LHAK 403/8806.

[111] The individualist, localist stance of AL clergy persisted even after the region rejoined France in 1919. Hiery, *Reichstagswahlen*, 92–96.

to distribute on the Reichstag floor, provided the proof text against which all doubtful points of law or policy might be settled. And those who objected to the outlawing of people by category were met with reassuring references to the German national character. Gneist admitted that after Jesuit congregations had settled in Germany for twenty years "a conscientious legislator cannot just say: in twenty-four hours after the publication of this law it is criminal *to be a Jesuit. . . .* We do not issue such laws, precisely because we are *Germans*, because we are one of the few nations with real respect and veneration for conscientious conviction."[112]

Three days later, however, the Reichstag did pass such a law, with Professor Gneist in the lead. It was time for the healthy "German *Volksgeist* to throw off this serpent," he now announced, because "self-help," in the form of political associations and the popular press, could no longer be trusted to drive the Jesuit from political life. That was a task that only the state itself could accomplish. Of the tiny handful of National Liberals who shrank from supporting the German Empire's first explicit piece of exceptional legislation, it is surely significant that prominent among them were Eduard Lasker and Ludwig Bamberger: Jews.[113]

Hysteria about the Jesuits was of course not limited to Germany. In France too, where the order was expelled a few years later, it entailed all the classic elements of a conspiracy theory.[114] But in Germany, where Jesuits made up fewer than one-twelfth the numbers they did in France, the phobia's connection with any kind of reality was weaker, while its links to foundational myths of national identity were considerably stronger. For just as Königgrätz had, in the eyes of many nationalists, reversed the decision of the Thirty Years' War militarily, the Jesuit Law was to reverse it culturally. The violence of the anti-Jesuit rhetoric was the product of an unstable mix of euphoria and hysteria, precipitated by national unification, the excitement of universal suffrage, and the prospect of the final and decisive victory in what was now perceived as a struggle for the national soul. The "Protestant" roll-back had begun.[115]

---

[112] Quotes, in order, from "Verbot": F. Meyer (Thorn), col. 1191; Wagener cols. 1178 and 1180; from "Jesuiten-Petitionen": Hohenlohe-Schillingsfürst, col. 1158; from "Verbot," Gneist, col. 1196. Excellent on liberals and the Kulturkampf: Langewiesche, *Liberalismus,* 180–87.

[113] As the Z's historian, K. Bachem, writing at the end of the Weimar Republic, pointedly emphasized: *Vorgeschichte* 3: 254. Gneist in "Verbot," col. 1225. Blackbourn erroneously substitutes Bennigsen for Bamberger: *Marpingen,* 29n. 88.

[114] Geoffrey Cubitt, *The Jesuit myth: conspiracy theory and politics in nineteenth-century France* (Oxford and New York, 1993); Ralph Gibson, *A Social History of French Catholicism, 1789–1914* (London and New York, 1989), 109, 111.

[115] The "war" was seen as the ultimate test of the new nation: "This German people, this people full of faith, full of loyalty, full of decency and morality, which today is embarking on the struggle against the Jesuits, *this people who has conquered Paris will also overcome the Jesuits and the Vatican!*" Dove (NL), in "Verbot," col. 1215. Illuminating on the resistance, decades later, to allowing the Jesuits to return: Smith, *Nationalism,* 104f, 122–27. It took three years of real war, entering its last phase in 1917, for Protestants to feel strong enough to live with the Jesuits.

We have seen that the debate on anti-Jesuit legislation effected Germany's first mobilization—preeminently of the Catholic clergy. But since the Jesuits themselves were a minimal presence, the legislation had no discernible effect on Centrum victories. The other legislative remedies proved equally ineffective in bringing the politicking priest to heel. By outlawing the Grand (i.e., public) Excommunication, the various Ecclesiastical Penalties Laws had attempted to prevent the clergy from imposing social ostracism on those who had voted against the Centrum. But at the village level excommunication was always public, since everyone could see who was missing at the communion rail on Easter Sunday; and ostracism, every local knew, would be decided by the village, not the priest.[116] Prussia's School Supervision Law likewise proved a damp squib. Although school inspection was withdrawn from most Catholic pastors after 1872, teachers continued in many places to act as the pastor's political adjutants; school children continued to be given Centrum ballots and leaflets to take home with them and continued to be enlisted to rip up the election proclamations of the Centrum's opponents.[117] The "eternal rivalry" between schoolmaster and priest, each trying "to master and pastor" the other, as Theodor Fontane put it, all but disappeared in Catholic villages—rendered mute not only by the persistence of relationships once grounded in superiority and dependency, but also now by the solidarity enforced by a mobilizing community.[118] Where a teacher had other ideas, he was usually no more a match for the pastor after 1872 than he had been before.[119] The situation did not change for several decades.[120]

As for the Pulpit Paragraph, the state initially put considerable effort into its enforcement, demanding extensive accounts from the mayors on how they were setting up their surveillances. Police officials and other "suitable persons" were stationed in an "inconspicuous manner" in the churches. But not always inconspicuous enough. "The clergy in general are very careful," the Lord Mayor of Düsseldorf reported, not to offer grounds for prosecution. Even in 1871, pastors had been dimly aware of the distinction between activity backed by the authority of their office, which they perceived would be considered illegitimate, and the free expression of opinion, to which they, as well as anyone, had a civic right. The Pulpit Paragraph increased such circumspection. Now a preacher

---

[116] Rust, *Reichskanzler* (1897), 61.

[117] Horn Report, LHAK 403/8806: 13; 2 Arns., AnlDR (1907/9, 12/I, Bd. 19) DS 636: 4305; Hiery, *Reichstagswahlen*, 418; Bodewig, *Wahlbeeinflussungenn*, 38.

[118] T. Fontane, *Stechlin* ([1898] Munich, n.d.), 57. On the "frères ennemis" in France, cf. Weber, *Peasants*, 362f. There were, of course, plenty of exceptions: K. Kammer, *Kulturkampfpriester* (1926), 102f, and Schloßmacher, *Düsseldorf*, 151, report teachers denouncing priests to the authorities. And in the confessionally mixed district of Gummersbach-Waldbröl, teachers were the principle (LT) campaigners for Wm. Hollenberg (NL), himself (Protestant) pastor in Waldbröl and county school inspector—a professional relationship that could considerably inhibit teachers at election time. Müller, *Strömungen*, 174f, 215f, 235.

[119] Poschinger Report, BAB-L R1501/14450, Bl. 185–185v.

[120] Differences in Württemberg after the turn of the century: Blackbourn, *Class*, 128, 137.

might break off his sermon if he thought he was being spied upon.[121] And the police met a wall of hostile witnesses. The parishioners had slept through the sermon; they had not understood it. As a villager in County Bitburg replied to an examining magistrate who demanded to know why he could no longer recall what the pastor had said: "I want to tell you something, Your Worship. Many a fine lord walks out of the Trier cathedral and has no idea what the gentleman has preached, so you can hardly hold it against a dumb farmer if, half a year later, he no longer remembers a sermon."[122]

At the same time, the clergy used the existence of informers (however theoretical) to make propaganda. Here is a chaplain in the Saar—in 1912.

> Some days ago I received an anonymous note bidding me not to give any kind of election speech today, the last Sunday before the election, because a gentlemen would be in the church who would pay close attention and monitor it. To this gentlemen I remark that 1) I give no election speeches in the church because they do not belong here; 2) I do not abuse the pulpit for such things; and 3) [turning to the congregation] ye've long known what ye've got to do![123]

In truth the Pulpit Paragraph proved so ineffectual that by 1874 Robert von Mohl was suggesting that it be sharpened and expanded to cover other areas of the priest's election activity. By then, however, the Kulturkampf was in full swing, with laws enough on clerical education and appointment to keep the Catholic clergy under continual threat of arrest without the help of the Pulpit Paragraph. Nothing more was heard of Mohl's proposal. Yet while convictions based on the Paragraph were few, in 1906, when the Commission reviewing the penal code suggested dropping it, its iconic significance for the liberals proved too great. So the Pulpit Paragraph remained on the books until 1953.[124] But, as we shall see in chapter 5, it did nothing to stem the clerical tide at election time.

CAESURA

"Religion is in danger!" the election slogan so ludicrous to Centrum critics in 1870–71, was verified in the eyes of Catholic voters by the anticlerical legislation with which the liberal Reichstag responded to the Centrum's first victories. And the controversies over whether or not to throw out these allegedly tainted mandates increased the sense of menace on both sides. The replay of the invali-

---

[121] E.g. 7 Oppeln, AnlDR (1871, 1/II, Bd. 2) DS 69: 165–67. Quotes: Schloßmacher, *Düsseldorf*, 150f. The only region where the Pulpit Paragraph appears to have been vigorously enforced, even in the 1870s, was Hohenzollern. A. Rösch, "Kulturkampf" (1915), 1–128.

[122] Quoted in Kammer, *Kulturkampfpriester*, 110.

[123] *KölnZ* Nr. 38, 12 Jan. 1912, in Anlage 17 on 5 Trier, AnlDR (1912/14 13/I, Bd. 23) DS 1639: 3605.

[124] Between 1894 and 1904 only four priests were convicted. Huber, *Verfassungsgeschichte* 4: 701. Von Mohl: "Erörterungen," 577f.

dated Pleß-Rybnik election was a harbinger of what was to come.[125] While it is questionable whether Chaplain Müller owed his initial success to clerical intervention (twenty-seven of the thirty Catholic pastors in the district had supported the Duke of Ratibor), once his election was thrown out, the new contest, held in spring 1872, produced a very different campaign. Party organization moved into this formerly barren province, rallies were held, newspapers published appeals, and the clergy—some clearly pressured by confrères as well as by parishioners—came out in full force on behalf of the Centrum.[126] The intensity of the national debate raised the stakes locally; voters began to think of their choices "politically": that is, less in terms of private advantage and more in terms of group identity. And as the symbolic weight of the election increased, it ceased to be a choice between rival notables, but rather, organizationally and ideologically, between two political parties.

Catholic mobilization was not limited to districts where previous Centrum victories had been overturned. In Düsseldorf a government official reported in December 1872 that hardly a week went by without a large Catholic meeting being staged somewhere to organize in defense of Catholic interests.[127] Düsseldorf was not typical, but neither was it unique. In the 1874 national elections, Catholic turnouts soared. In districts where they were dominant but not overwhelming, participation averaged 78.7 percent. But tight competition was not the whole explanation. Even in districts where the Catholic majority was so large as to make the Centrum's victory a foregone conclusion, turnouts averaged more than 70 percent, rates the empire as a whole would not reach until 1903. The proportion of eligible voters casting a ballot for Centrum candidates increased 80 percent since 1871, "a percentage increase," as Jonathan Sperber has pointed out, "equivalent to the Social Democrats' great leap forward between 1887 and 1890." More than 77 percent of the Catholic electorate voted for the Centrum in 1874, an increase of 61 percent over 1871.[128]

---

[125] *MK* Nr. 13, 1 Apr. 1871: 112. Carl Wrazidlo, pastor of Lendzin (voting population: 387), suddenly finding himself a celebrity for having "influenced" Müller's triumph, read out to his flock the RT report in which he had been so "maliciously slandered" and collected signatures to restore his good name. It was not lost on Wrazidlo that the reporter for the accusing subcommittee was the same R. Gneist who in 1869 had sponsored the LT motion to close Catholic cloisters. Gneist SBDR 24 May 1871: 913. AnlDR (1871, 1/I, Bd. 2) DS 69: 165f.

[126] 1871 campaign: SBDR 18 Apr. 1871: 252–56; 22 Nov. 1871: 428–42; 7 Oppeln, AnlDR (1871, 1/I, Bd. 2) DS 69: 161–69; Müller, "Organ der Aktionspartei," *BK* (1883): 82f. 7 Oppeln was not the only Silesian district in which some of the clergy had continued to support K and FK candidates. Müller, *Kampf*, 196; glimpses of 1872's rerun in ibid., 174–75n. 4, 249f; Rust, *Reichskanzler*, 616–26; Mazura, *Entwicklung*, 79, 90; Bismarck SBHA, 31 Jan., 9 Feb., and 10 Feb. 1872: 565f, 700f, 722; *MK* Nr. 6, 19 Feb. 1872: 46, and *MK* Nr. 13, 30 Mar. 1872: 103.

[127] Sperber, *Catholicism*, 210.

[128] Sperber, *Voters*, 80. In analogous Protestant districts (i.e., Protestants dominant but with less than 75%) turnouts averaged only 50.3%. My calculations, derived from Ritter/Niehuss, *Arbeitsbuch*, 99f. A direct comparison of Catholic turnouts of 56.8% in 1871 with 70.7% 1874, given the change in "N" from 87 to 97 (because of the accession of 15 AL districts in 1874), may be misleading. I am aware of the "ecological fallacy" of deducing the voting behavior of individuals from the demographic characteristics of election districts, but it is unlikely that Protestants with

The result was a tectonic shift in Germany's political landscape.[129] As far back as the 1830s, German public life had been organized into two camps: those who supported their government versus those who criticized it; roughly speaking, Right versus Left. Beginning with the elections to the Prussian Landtag in late 1870, this constellation had begun to give way. By the second national election, in 1874, the political spectrum had been reconfigured to make room for a third grouping: the Centrum, joined by the regionally based protest parties—the Bavarian Patriots, the Poles, and the "clericals" of Alsace-Lorraine, all Catholic, and usually accompanied by Protestant Hanoverians (Guelfs) and Danes. All of these parties—the "losers," as Sperber has dubbed them, in "the wars of national unification"—represented constituencies who preferred to collaborate with the other minorities, regardless of ethnicity or religion, than with either of the "winners," liberal or conservative.[130] Conversely, in any district where any of these dissenters stood a chance of winning, the *soi disant* "national parties," Left and Right, would join hands in a politics of national concentration (*Sammlungspolitik*).[131] Thus even deeper than the three-group constellation was a more fundamental divide: two political nations whose voters were defined by their opponents as beyond the pale. Contemporary polemic figured the opponents of the "national" parties as "enemies of the empire" (*Reichsfeinde*). Modern political science maps them as the "periphery" against the "center." The simplest labels—for all the exceptions one might make for specific individuals, locales, or contests—is simply Protestant and Catholic, descriptions referring eventually less to religious denomination than to political identity.[132]

---

fewer than 25% of the votes could have produced district-wide turnouts of 70%. Confirming evidence from a close analysis of one LT district: Kühne, *Dreiklassenwahlrecht*, 195, 198. Catholics voting Z: Schauff, *Wahlverhalten* ([1928] 1975), 174. Schauff's figure is probably too low, but I was unable to understand the comparable statistic in Sperber, *Voters*, Table 4.3 on p. 168. Earlier Sperber had given a Z figure for 1874 as high as 97% of all Catholics voting in selected northwestern constituencies. *Catholicism*, 256.

[129] Contrast M. Rainer Lepsius, who argued that voting in the empire was a more or less automatic expression of four social-moral milieux that, with the exception of Social Democracy, had existed before 1871 (and industrialization). Lepsius, "Parteisystem und Sozialstruktur: zum Problem der Demokratisierung der deutschen Gesellschaft," in *Wirtschaft, Geschichte und Wirtschaftsgeschichte. Festschrift zum 65. Geburtstag von Friedrich Lütge*, edited by W. Abel et al. (Stuttgart, 1966), 371–93. I criticized this argument in *Windthorst*, 192–98, as has Thränhardt, *Wahlen* (1973), 100; Kühne, "Wahlrecht-Wahlverhalten-Wahlkultur," 508–13; Sperber, *Voters*, 3f, 282–84, and Rohe, *Wahlen*, esp. chap. 2 and 81–83.

[130] Sperber, *Voters*, esp. 188.

[131] Möllers, *Strömungen*, 171; Anderson/Barkin, "Myth," 679. The fullest and most complex analysis of the caesura in the party system is Rohe, *Wahlen*. Critical of Rohe's resulting three-camp analysis, as not doing justice to the continuing Left-Right division in the Protestant East: Kühne, "Wahlrecht-Wahlverhalten-Wahlkultur," 521f. I find unpersuasive K.'s dismissal of the 1907 Hottentot election, where LLs allied with conservatives in a single "national camp," as "exceptional," since Rohe's argument seems designed to explain not, perhaps, every political *Alltag*, but rather the power of the national card, when it was played, as in 1907, to trump economic and constitutional issues.

[132] Thus in 1907 a campaigning cleric disputed the government's claim that it had appointed "Catholics" to the highest positions as "false . . . since the *Oberpräsident* is, admittedly, Catholic, but *leider Gottes*, national." Horn Report, Kreis Bernkastel, LHAK 403/8806: 6.

Although based on preexisting cultural differences, in their depth and extent these fault lines were genuinely new. As Karl Rohe has shown, they delimited what was, in spite of the familiar names of liberal, conservative, and even Centrum, a new party system.[133] The Catholic camp was not merely the expression of higher turnouts from a previously unmobilized plebeian constituency, although in Prussia that was much of the story. (The proportion of eligible Catholic voters in Prussia supporting the Centrum doubled between 1871 and 1874—from 23 to 45 percent of the Catholic vote, while the proportion supporting liberal parties remained the same: 11 percent.) But the Centrum vote also represented a genuine *re*-alignment for some. By 1874, the once-Conservative Catholic nobility of Silesia and Westfalia had gone over to the "clerical" camp.[134] Catholic industrialists, at first supporters of the Free Conservatives or National Liberals, also began to cross over to the Centrum, while the *Bürgertum* of the Rhineland, which had once provided a reservoir of liberal-radical voters, began to do the same, although in some towns the process was not complete until after the turn of the century.[135] Outside Prussia, Catholic support for liberal parties plummeted, as the ferment of imperial election campaigns nationalized denominational allegiances even where the local situation bore no reflection of Kulturkampf antagonisms—as the luckless campaign manager for an unsuccessful "national" candidate in Württemberg complained in 1878. In Baden and Hessen, although the process took longer and was less complete, voting at the precinct level exhibited the same cleavage.[136]

Once the reconfiguration had taken place, the new constellation enjoyed extraordinary perdurance. The year 1874 marked a level of election success below which the Centrum never sank (and subsequent elections brought it, on occasion, as many as fifteen additional mandates). Thank to the regional concentration of the Catholic population, of the ninety-one constituencies the Catholic

[133] Replacing many earlier discussions: Rohe, *Wahlen*, esp. 63, 65, 71f. In some districts, such as Olpe-Meschede-Arnsberg in a by-election; in Baden, where the culture wars had begun in the sixties; and in Bavaria, where Zollparlament elections had raised questions of national identity, this new bipolarism was already evident by 1867. The cultural divide behind the political cleavage: Sperber, *Catholicism* and Smith, *Nationalism*.

[134] Rust, *Reichskanzler*, 621f. Figures: Sperber, *Voters*, 168.

[135] Some, of course, remained with the Liberal bourgeoisie. For Cologne, see Thomas Mergel, *Zwischen Klasse und Konfession. Katholisches Bürgertum im Rheinland 1794–1914* (Göttingen, 1994); for Frankfurt, Ralf Roth, "Katholisches Bürgertum in Frankfurt am Main 1800–1914. Zwischen Emanzipation und Kulturkampf," *Archiv für mittelrheinische Kirchengeschichte* 46 (1994): 207–46, and idem, *Stadt* (1996); for Bavaria, Langewiesche, *Liberalismus*, 356n. 90. Rohe suggests, tentatively and against Sperber, *Catholicism*, that the Z, not the NLs, were the heir to the Rhineland's liberal tradition. *Wahlen*, 82f. Outside Prussia: Sperber, *Voters*, 168f. Sometimes this realignment occurred only with the change in generations. Müller shows that the Z's gains against liberals in the Rhineland continued long after the Kulturkampf had waned, reinforcing the picture of a caesura that took a generation to complete. *Strömungen*, 180, 221f, 395.

[136] Oberamtspfleger Haaf to Herbert Bismarck, Gaildorf, 6 Aug. 1878, BAB-L R 1501/14693, Bl. 58–61. Although D. Blackbourn, *Class*, dates the confessionalization of Württemberg state politics only with the economic changes in the 1890s, W. Schulte, *Struktur* (1970), 75, 130f, puts it in the Kulturkampf, while noting that because of the failure of the Z to offer candidacies in every election, it was not complete until 1907. J. Schofer, *Erinnerungen* (1922), 61. On Bavaria: Thränhardt, *Wahlen* (1973), 63.

party took in 1874, seventy-three were *never* lost. Seventy-three safe seats in a Reichstag of 397 was an enormous advantage; there were only thirty-one others, and these were distributed among several parties, with the Koło Polskie (Polish Party), which usually voted with the Centrum, getting the lion's share— thirteen. Although as the Kulturkampf wound down, Catholic turnouts would decline, the proportion of Catholics voting for the "national" parties declined even faster.

Because of the strong Catholic presence in some industrial regions, the restructuring of 1870–74 helped retard the emergence of a third camp, Social Democracy, by nearly two decades. It has been estimated that between 1874 and 1881 from 97 to 99 percent of all Rhenish Catholics who voted supported the Centrum. Identity politics kept not only Catholics but also Protestants away from Socialism. On the basis of a worker's religion alone, railroad officials in Bochum knew to which of their employees it was safe to issue passes on election day: Protestant workers could be counted on to vote National Liberal.[137] Thus after having made remarkable progress between 1867 and 1870, the Socialist movement in the Ruhr collapsed in the face of the realignment. Protestant Duisburg and Catholic Essen now became showcases for the conflict between "national" (usually liberal) and Catholic camps, respectively. "Not to put too fine a point on it," writes Karl Rohe, "before it could be a victim of the Socialist Law, . . . [the socialist movement] was already victim of political Catholicism and of the two-camp formation that its rise created."[138] Even in the nineties, after Social Democracy had begun to push some liberal voters over to the right and captured a considerable part of the others for itself, the confessional marker signaling German political allegiances endured. Having survived the upheavals of industrialization, it would persist even after the collapse of the empire. It overrode the crises of hyperinflation in the 1920s and depression in the 1930s. As late as 1994, it remained the most important predictor of voting behavior in the Federal Republic.[139]

[137] WPK on 5 Arns., SBDR 20 Apr. 1885: 1771. Safe seats: Kühne, *Dreiklassenwahlrecht*, 243; Z vote, turnouts, and "national" votes: Sperber, *Catholicism*, 254–255n5, and 265, table 6.2; Sperber, *Voters*, 188.

[138] Rohe, *Wahlen*, 85f; idem, "Alignments" (1990), 107–44; 110f; idem, "Konfession" (1981), 109–26; idem, "Katholiken, Protestanten und Sozialdemokraten im Ruhrgebiet vor 1914. Voraussetzungen und Grundlagen 'konfessionellen' und 'klassenbewußten' Wählens in einer Industrieregion," in his *Vom Revier zum Ruhrgebiet. Wahlen. Parteien. Politische Kultur* (Essen, 1986), 43–60; Möllers, *Strömungen*, 90f, 187, 231–33; J. D. Hunley, "The working classes, religion and social democracy in the Düsseldorf area, 1867–78," *Societas* 4/2 (Spring 1974): 131–49; Tenfelde, *Sozialgeschichte*, 464–562, esp. 471f, 554f, 557f, 565, 576.

[139] Rohe, *Elections* (1990), vii; cf. also his "Introduction" (1990), 3; Jürgen W. Falter, "The Social Bases of Political Cleavages in the Weimar Republic, 1919–1933," in *Elections, Mass Politics, and Social Change in Modern Germany. New Perspectives*, edited by L. E. Jones and J. N. Retallack (Washington, D.C., 1992), 371–97; idem, *Hitlers Wähler* (1991), 350. This is not to deny that in some places, e.g., in Dortmund from 1893 on, class and ethnic-national identities weakened the confessional marker. H. Graf, *Entwicklung* (1958), 27.

CHAPTER FIVE

Black Magic II: Keeping the Faith

> Our hearts are true black and they'll never turn white, for they are color-fast."
>
> —*Mayener Volkszeitung (Catholic) (1887)*

POLITICAL SCIENTISTS refer to the "freezing" of a country's party system after an initial, or important, election as if this were a normal phenomenon. But they have offered surprisingly little explanation for why voters should experience only a single historical moment of choice. To say that constituencies, once wooed and won, are no longer "available" to subsequent suitors begs the question. To argue that party identity passes from parent to child at an early age, that any individual election is a composite of past elections, is only to sketch the outline of a possible answer.[1] Undoubtedly incumbency, for a party as for individuals, does enjoy competitive advantages that help to perpetuate itself, but these advantages cannot have been overwhelming in Germany in the 1870s and 1880s, when party organizations were still fragmentary and the costs of campaigning were still relatively low.[2]

Much of the responsibility for ensuring that the alignment of 1871–74 would freeze surely goes to the Kulturkampf, and to those culture warriors who almost immediately went from trying to control the campaign activity of priests to

[1] "Freezing": Seymour Martin Lipset and Stein Rokkan. "Cleavage Structures, Party Systems, and Voter Alignments: An Introduction" in idem, *Cleavage Structures, Party Systems, and Voter Alignments: Cross-National Perspectives* (New York, 1967), 1–64; esp. 3, 50, 54; Stein Rokkan, "Concept" (1977), 563–70. The canonical status of this concept among political scientists is demonstrated, inter alia, by Sartori, "Sociology," 90; S. Verba et al., *Participation*, 13; Kalyvas, *Rise*, 115, and implied by M. S. Fish, *Democracy* (1995), 79. An analogous emphasis on a formative "critical experience": M. Shefter, "Party" (1977): 403–51. Reassessment of the freezing hypothesis: Bartolini/Mair, *Identity*. Composite of elections: B. B. Berelson, P. M. Lazerfeld, W. N. McPhee, *Voting* (Chicago, 1954), 315. Family transmission: Pomper, *Elections*, 71. On "party identification theory": W. Phillips Shively, "Party Identification, Party Choice, and Voting Stability: The Weimar Case," APSR 64/4 (Dec. 1972), 1203–25. Rohe is good at reconciling the notion of a particular point in time in which an entire party system is born with the recognition that continuity of cleavage structures is not automatic, but has to be continually cultivated. *Wahlen*, esp. 10, 13, 30.

[2] "Realigning" terminology grew out of discussions of V. O. Key's theory of critical elections. Jerome M. Clubb, William H. Flanigan, and Nancy H. Zingale, *Partisan Realignment: Voters, Parties, and Government in American History* (Beverly Hills, 1980); Richard L. McCormick, "The Realignment Synthesis in American History," *JIH* 13 (Summer 1982): 85–105; Allan J. Lichtman, "The end of realignment theory? Toward a new research program for American political history," *Historical Methods* 15/4 (Fall 1982): 170–88.

trying to "nationalize" the next generation of clergy, through the so-called May Laws regulating their training and appointment, and then through punitive measures to compel their compliance. The effort was perceived, and not only by its opponents, as aiming at nothing less than the forcible assimilation of the Catholic Church and its adherents to the values and norms of the empire's Protestant majority. And since any cultural struggle is, as the Kulturkampf's proponents knew, ultimately a struggle about identity, the demands of self-respect led Catholics—young and old, male and female, cleric and lay, big men and small—to cleave to their priests and defy this legislation. Escalation and resistance were then ritually reenacted in election campaigns, as voting itself, especially for Catholics, took over much of the struggle. The democratic franchise, having triggered much of the anxiety that encouraged Kulturkampf legislation, now ensured that the boundaries delimiting the cultural fronts were constantly patrolled and that election campaigns would propel the animosities of the empire's founding decade into the future. By providing a "universal symbolic language," the voting act reduced a confusing multiplicity of issues "to a single choice— the reds against the whites, left against right," as Jacques Julliard has put it, referring to France. In our case the operative dichotomy was Left *and* Right— against Black.[3]

But how did people come to take up that new language? Getting Catholics to respond to cultural threat and offended dignity with disciplined *voting* required a massive work of translation. That was the work of the "chaplainocracy."

"Chaplainocracy"

Wherever Kulturkampf legislation was enforced, Catholics of all stripes were brought into an adversarial relationship to the state. Not only bishops and pastors, but Catholic mayors, Landräte, and police commissioners who failed to keep step with what the laws now demanded lost their jobs. Laity as well as clergy went to jail, hauled off in what they mockingly dubbed "culture wagons."[4] The sharing of martyrdom created solidarity, but with contradictory consequences for the structure of authority within Catholic Germany. On the one hand, the moral stature and popularity of the persecuted clergy rose to unprecedented heights. On the other hand, persecution increasingly removed that clergy from its traditional bridgeheads of power. As more and more bishops and priests were hunted down, jailed, and exiled, the initiative in resisting the Kulturkampf passed from the sees and the rectories to an *elected* leadership: the political party. Thousands might line the streets in homage to a martyred cleric (a drama that both venerated and venerating played for maximum effect); a Reichstag deputy might be so moved at the sight of the incarcerated bishop that

[3] "Political History in the 1980s: Reflections on Its Present and Future," *JIH* 12 (1981): 29–44; quote: 37f.

[4] Kammer, *Kulturkampfpriester*, 38, 45, 49, 76, 89, 94, 118, 122f; Sperber, *Catholicism*, 229–33; purges: Anderson/Barkin, "Myth," 657–65; R. J. Ross, "Enforcing" (1984), 456–82.

he involuntarily sank to his knees—something that, the Centrum's August Reichensperger vowed, until now he had never done before any man. But symbolic self-abasements could scarcely mask the fact that a transfer of leadership within the Catholic community was taking place. A fundamental consequence of the Kulturkampf was to privilege the political decisions of the Catholic party over those of prelates, and to habituate the laity to looking toward their *party* leadership for direction. But—and here is what made the issue of whether or not the Centrum was a "clerical" party such an impossible one for either contemporaries or historians to resolve—the transfer of authority to the party gave those clergy who were not exiled or on the lam an enormous incentive to involve themselves in that party in every way possible. Which they did.[5] This produced the "chaplainocracy."

Here Germany does seem unique. Although the intertwining of religious with political issues was a universal feature of electoral politics during the development of western democratic institutions, automatically giving the clergy a leading role, nowhere else in Europe or America did clerical influence become so widespread, so continuous, so coordinated, and so effective as in Catholic Germany. Nowhere else was it institutionalized in a powerful party.[6] Although only a few priests—Canon Christoph Moufang and Bishop Wilhelm Emanuel von Ketteler of Mainz come to mind—were prominent Reichstag figures, no fewer than 91 of the Centrum's 483 deputies during the course of the empire were clergymen.[7] In the eastern provinces of Silesia, West Prussia, and Posnania, the Centrum and the Koło Polskie would have been hard put even to find sufficient candidates had they not been able to call on their priests.[8] The supply was even more exiguous in Alsace-Lorraine, where sentiment for boycotting the German elections was so strong that Canon Moufang had to press the Bishop of Strasbourg to take the initiative, with the result that, of the ten Alsatian deputies in 1874 of the "Catholic" persuasion, seven were priests and two of these were bishops.[9]

The clergy's real political weight, however, lay outside parliament, in the accordion-like organizational infrastructure they enjoyed by virtue of their vo-

[5] Reichensperger, in Ä. Ditscheid, *Matthias Eberhard* (1900), 100, 104–6; Anderson, "Kulturkampf," 109–15.

[6] In Ireland the clergy dispersed their efforts among competing parties, and were effective only when powerful laymen (O'Connell, Parnell) were able to subordinate them. K. T. Hoppen, "Priests" (1996), 117–38. Brilliant on why French clericals alone in Catholic Europe did *not* organize their own party: Kalyvas, *Rise*, 114–66.

[7] R. Morsey, "Der politische Katholizismus 1890–1933," in *Der soziale und politische Katholizismus. Entwicklungslinien in Deutschland 1803–1963*, edited by A. Rauscher (Munich and Vienna, 1981) 1: 110–64; 119. I identify 14 priests among Z deputies during the RT's first LP, some elected in by-elections. Even in 1906, 20% of the RT fraction (excluding P and Els) were clergy and 11% as late as 1912. Suval, *Politics*, 69f. Similarly for the LT in Bavaria and Baden: Bodewig, *Wahlbeeinflussungen*, 12.

[8] Neubach, "Geistliche," 251 ff, 265, 276.

[9] Josef Götten, *Christoph Moufang. Theologe und Politiker. 1817–1890. Eine biographische Darstellung* (Mainz, 1969), 194; Graf, *Beeinflussungsversuche*, 195; Hiery, *Reichstagswahlen*, 139–42.

cation. Some, barely known to the wider public, became political "insiders," conduits funneling information and advice on an almost daily basis between the parliamentary party in Berlin and selected members of the hierarchy, some in the Vatican.[10] Others became organizers—of such semipolitical clubs as cooperatives, trade unions, legal aid societies, and the "People's Association for Catholic Germany" (*Volksverein für das katholische Deutschland*), a multipurpose organization aimed at adult education, but unofficially a major support for the Centrum and especially its Left wing. By 1913 nearly 70 percent of all the parishes in the Archdiocese of Freiburg were equipped with a branch of the *Volksverein*, and each branch was either largely or entirely under clerical direction.[11] Some priests were journalists. Not just major Centrum publications, but the entire Sunday press and most of the local "cheese sheets" in Catholic regions were written, managed, and edited in the spare time of some overworked priest. And dynamos like Pastor Theodor Wacker of Baden and Chaplain Georg Friedrich Dasbach of Trier managed to combine in one person the offices of popular tribune, labor leader, journalist, publishing entrepreneur, and regional party boss.[12]

Priests forged the connecting links between the various levels of electoral politics. Sometimes this network was explicit. As early as the 1871 election the "diaconates" of the diocese of Trier, each encompassing from nine to twenty-two parishes, had become de facto party wards, composed of precincts (the ecclesiastical term was "definitions") of several parishes each. Trier's diocesan paper, *Eucharius*, published a detailed plan showing how ward-bosses and precinct captains (parsons all!) could produce the desired election results.[13] In areas where formal organization did not appear until later, or where the laity took the initiative, the clergy were still the indispensable brokers of the political process, and not just during the actual campaign. In Baden pastors were the chief recipients of "inquiries and assignments from the district and central party leadership, leaflets and election newsletters to be distributed, requests for funding these and other campaign activities."[14] Priests were also automatic members (called "born members") of district nominating committees, where they nearly always made up the largest single group. As such they frequently served as

---

[10] As the papers of Alexander Reuß and Bishop Michael Korum, 108/817 make clear. BAT 105/1490–1660 and BAT 108/817.

[11] H. Lepper, "Cronenberg" (1968), 57–148, and idem, ed., *Katholizismus* (1977). On the *Volksverein*, which numbered 805,000 members by 1914: Heitzer, *Volksverein*, esp. 124–26, 148–59, 161, and G. Klein, Volksverein (1996), 37–92; Götz v. Olenhusen, "Ultramontanisierung," 59.

[12] Also Adolf Franz, editor of the *SVZ*, and Paul Majunke, who edited the Berlin *Germania*, and whose press agency, *Korrespondenz für Zentrumsblätter*, supplied stories to the entire local Catholic press. When *Swiastun Górnosaski* was founded in Piekary in January 1868, its editor was a cleric ("whose command of Polish was slight"), its board of editors comprised 3 priests and a suffragan bishop, and 300 of its 500 subscribers were priests. Trzeciakowski, *Kulturkampf*, 26. Good on clergy's dominance of Catholic literature: Blaschke, "Kolonialisierung," 118–35.

[13] Steil, *Wahlen*, 97f. The equation of deaconates and *Definitionen* with precincts and wards is my own gloss.

[14] Heinrich Köhler, in C.H.E. Zangerl, "Courting" (1977), 227f.

buffers between warring economic factions. Since their own interests were above all in winning, they had a strong stake in forcing the factions to accept compromises.[15] Even in constituencies where the Centrum's parliamentary delegation played the deciding role in choosing the candidate, the Berlin leaders would still consult first with the parish clergy. If local demography meant that the Centrum had no chance of winning, the crucial question became whether they should put up their own man anyway—a symbolic "candidate for the count" (*Zählkandidat*), whose totals would at least reveal the party's strength— or throw their support behind another party. Local laymen, it was felt, could not be trusted to decide these issues. More vulnerable to government pressure and more susceptible to government promises than the clergy, they were apt to make the kind of muddy compromises that risked losing the militant loyalty of the voters on which the party's long-term power ultimately rested.[16]

Inevitably these *Hochwürden*, especially where lay notables were few, exercised authority not only by virtue of their social or sacerdotal position but by amassing specifically *political* power, including a kind of patronage. *Their* decision to sponsor him for elective office could turn a clodhopper into a notable— a transfiguration hilariously, but not entirely inaccurately, depicted in the "correspondence" of the immortal Jozef Filser, Ludwig Thoma's fictional peasant who suddenly found himself traveling first class to Munich's "barliament" to take up the burdens of "governing."[17] The clergy's sponsorship was even more important for local political office than for the state and national legislatures. Catholic mayors and councilmen, who operated as ex officio members of local Centrum campaign committees, found that if they wanted to keep their positions and the economic perks that went with them, they had better stick close to their clerical patrons. As one nobleman noted ruefully to another, a man whose aspirations for a Reichstag candidacy had been frustrated by the Würzburg Centrum's nominating committee: local Catholic leaders only were what they were through the clergy; the withdrawal of clerical support would mean their fall.[18]

Did all this make the Centrum a "clerical" party? On issues of *national* policy, even national religious policy, these men took their marching orders from

---

[15] K. Müller, "Zentrumspartei und agrarische Bewegung" (1964), 850; Müller, *Strömungen*, 84, 353, 358, 361, 363, 371; for LT elections: Kühne, *Dreiklassenwahlrecht*, 104, 348. Of the 70 signatures on the Election Proclamation of Josef Lingens for Siegburg in 1898, 44 were priests. The protest of the Kraus Society: "Memorandum to the Bishops of Germany on the Political Agitation of the Clergy," *DZJ* Nr. 11, 17 Mar. 1907. Exceptions include the Essen Z which was dominated by the laity and run for many years by the businessman Mathias Wiese—though his great rival was a chaplain, Joh. Laaf, who headed the Christian Social Workers' Movement. Möllers, *Strömungen*, 263.

[16] Windthorst to unnamed priest, 25 Oct., 29 Oct. 1876; 5 Oct., 9 Oct. 1879; priest to W., 30 Aug. 1882; Wm. v. Schorlemer-Vehr to Ziner, 13 Aug. 1889: BAK Kleine Erwerbung Nr. 596; Chaplain Kurtz to Baron Fechenbach, 28 Feb. 1882, BAK Nachlaß Fechenbach. The travails of an Oberwesterwald LR in negotiating with the pastor over Catholic support: Kühne, *Dreiklassenwahlrecht*, 232f.

[17] *Briefwechsel eines bayerischen Landtagsabgeordneten (Filzerbriefe)*, 2 Bde. (Munich, 1909–12). The clergy's decisive power when the local party was split: Monshausen, *Wahlen* (1969), 329.

[18] Von Schauensee to v. Fechenbach, 18 Oct. 1884, BAK Nachlaß Fechenbach.

the leadership of a democratically elected party—a remarkable phenomenon in a religious culture that defined the clergy, in theology textbooks, as "the Church," the laity only as "in" the Church.[19] In *state* politics, on the other hand, the record is more complicated. In German-speaking Prussia, and perhaps even in Württemberg and Hessen, policy decisions also remained largely in lay hands. In Bavaria, however, from the nineties on, and in Baden from the very beginning, the party's leadership was clerical.

But the priest remained a key figure even when the decisions were taken by others, and even in places like Marburg, where Catholics made up such a small percentage of the population that a Centrum victory was unthinkable. The Left Liberal journalist Hellmut von Gerlach related how he sought the Centrum's support in Marburg in 1903, in a close runoff against a Conservative. Richard Müller, Centrum deputy for nearby Fulda, who stood on the Left of his party, obligingly put through the necessary resolution on Gerlach's behalf. But Müller instructed Gerlach "not to hold any rallies in Catholic villages, but only to visit the pastors." Gerlach tells the story to demonstrate the power of the priest; yet just as revealing is how the Centrum's lay leadership used the clergy as a funnel for their own political decisions—thereby denying Gerlach any independent access to their constituency. Since the German election system required an absolute majority for victory, as long as priest and lay politico cooperated to prevent outsiders from leading them into temptation, the strategic value of these several thousand voters, less than 13 percent of the Marburg electorate, would always remain high.[20]

The role of the priest was of course different in the economically depressed hamlets of the Eifel than in metropolises like Cologne; in the south than in the north; in religiously or ethnically homogeneous districts than in those with mixed populations. But in the eyes of the ordinary small-town Catholic, the priest *was* the Centrum Party. Germany's strict laws of assembly (*Versammlungsgesetze*) conspired to push the priest to the fore. Every public meeting had to be registered in advance with the police and, in most states, the sponsor was required to reside in the community in which the meeting was to be held. In those small towns and villages where the Centrum's supporters were economically dependent on big men who were Conservatives or Liberals, the pastor was often the only Centrum adherent who dared put his name down as sponsor of the event.[21] Campaign rallies thus depended on him. (Conversely, for a priest to refuse to sponsor a rally when requested was to expose himself as a traitor before his confrères and his congregation.) Not only was the pastor or his assistant the indispensable chairman of the election rally (and voters could pick up their admission tickets at the rectory), often he or his chaplain was its main speaker. Rallies were frequently held on Sunday afternoons, and it was

[19] Contrast France: Charnay, "L'église," 297.

[20] H. v. Gerlach, *Rechts* (1937), 173–74. Schulte, *Struktur*, 120–25, lends support to my supposition.

[21] Sponsors of rallies by all oppositional parties faced intimidation: cf. F protest on 20 Saxony, AnlDR (1884/85, 6/I, Bd. 6) DS 247: 1102f.

not unusual, at election time, for a regional paper to list thirty or more villages at which Centrum rallies would be held "immediately after the principal divine service. Place to be announced there."[22] One could hardly be surprised when a parson, still riding high after a long afternoon of campaigning, inadvertently began his evening sermon with *"Meine Herren!"*[23]

The line between political and pastoral duties blurred when the parson took up the cudgels for the Catholic press. The popular image of the parson as a Mrs. Grundy, keeping a sharp eye out for any signs that the households under his care were receiving subscriptions to the "bad" press (and making life miserable for those that did), was as prevalent at the end of the empire as at the beginning and was undoubtedly based on fact. Along with the countless small intrusions in the lives of their parishioners to which pastors felt entitled, the attempt to control the flow of political information was conceived as a natural extension of his traditional responsibility for their moral health.[24] But as the Kulturkampf turned even the moral realm into a political one, the clergy's relationship to the press was "modernized." Needy editors urged parish priests not only to raise funds for their papers, but to invest their own money in the Catholic press—which one out of every six Würzburg clergymen did. Where a paper's financial backing depended so clearly on the clergy's enthusiasm, its editor's independence was limited. "From the moment he begins to pursue his own policies," a contemporary remarked, "his position is untenable." Though technically a private enterprise, the Catholic/Centrum press was also, as the editor of the *Fränkisches Volksblatt* tried to argue, "a kind of diocesan institution." It was, in fact, a trade organ for a professional clerical lobby.[25] The *Kölnische Volkszeitung*, run by the Bachem family, was an exception.

One of the pastor's most important political tasks was to serve as the local subscription agent of the Catholic press. The modernization of the communications infrastructure, far from weakening religious identification, as has been claimed for France, in fact quickened it. As early as September 1871 (i.e., six months after the first national election), the *Donau-Zeitung* launched its subscription drive with the slogan, "Don't become Lutheran, stay Catholic."[26] Every quarter, as renewal time came around, pastors would preach the necessity

[22] Zangerl, "Courting," 227f; Bodewig, *Wahlbeeinflussungen*, 146; *Saarbrücker Volkszeitung* Nr. 288, 16 Dec. 1911, and *KölnZ* Nr. 38, 12 Jan. 1912: 5 Trier, AnlDR (1912/14, 13/I, Bd. 23) DS 1639: 3604f; also Müller, *Strömungen*, 196.

[23] "Religion und Politik," *DNJ* 3/47 (1911): 556–61, quote on 557.

[24] Smith, *Nationalism*, 80–84.

[25] Von Schauensee to Fechenbach, 18 Oct. 1884, BAK Nachlaß Fechenbach; Zangerl, "Courting," 223, 226; Bodewig, *Wahlbeeinflussungen*, 145. Being funded by the diocese, as some of these papers were, did not guarantee agreement with the bishop. *SVZ* 16 Oct. 1888, 21 Oct. 1888; Gossler to Bis., 22 Oct. 1888. US NA/AA/LT. The call of the Fulda Bishop's Conference in 1874 to establish committees in every diocese to oversee the content of the Catholic press aroused thinly disguised indignation among the (often clerical) editors, who were prickly about maintaining their independence. H. J. Reiber, *Tagespresse* (1930), 120–25; Ditscheid, *Matthias Eberhard*, 24. Comprehensive: Michael Schmolke, *Die schlechte Presse. Katholiken und Publizistik zwischen 'Katholik' und 'Publik'* (Münster, 1971).

[26] *GA* No. 221, 21 Sept. 1871: 1969. *MK* Nr. 2, 9 Jan. 1869: 11 argued that Catholics should avoid the "political" press altogether.

of a Catholic paper in every home, proclaiming that it was "nothing less than the baptismal certificate of the twentieth-century Catholic" and the "entrance ticket to the heavenly kingdom."[27] Their efforts were helped incalculably by the slings and arrows of mainstream journalism, which heaped contempt on Catholics every day.[28] In 1871, 15 million Catholics had been served by 126 newspapers. Within the next decade, the number of Catholic papers doubled.[29] Soon the Catholic press outstripped its rivals in density and circulation.

The relentless pressure to increase circulations eventually put the local and Sunday Catholic press in competition with the Centrum's regional organs, threatening to dry up the latter's subscriptions. This problem led to Pastor Theodore Wacker's notorious "election ukase" to all the Catholic rectories in Baden, right before the hotly contested state elections in 1905. After detailing the ways (from special meetings to door-to-door canvassing) in which he expected Baden's parsons to extract subscriptions for "your party" from every last straggler, he also demanded that "the appropriate stimulus" be applied to those stalwarts in every community who would agree ("if . . . urged to do so from the right side") to take two papers.[30] It took little imagination to see how the freedom of the voter might be compromised by this hard sell. When a subscription to the party newspaper became a badge of religious commitment, pinned on by the parish priest and "worn" six days a week, the protections of the "secret" ballot hardly mattered—especially when its secrets were as open as they were in most of Germany.

The most important of all the parish clergy's tasks was to make sure that the Centrum's ballots got distributed. The party's dependence on them for this task, though it varied locally, was always high. A table constructed in the eighties for Bentheim-Meppen-Lingen, one of the "blackest" election districts in Germany, reveals that more than 67 percent of the contact men responsible for ballot distribution were priests. Even in Baden, at the other end of the scale as far as Catholics' solidarity with the Centrum was concerned, an investigation ordered by the grand duke in the early nineties revealed that of the 800-odd parishes in the state, 160 pastors were, contrary to the desires of their government, working for the Centrum. Priests distributed ballots through their communion classes if possible; by standing at the door of the polling place if necessary.[31] Pastor

[27] Quoted in Bodewig, *Wahlbeeinflussungen*, 62f.

[28] [Jörg], "Das deutsche Reich" II: 767; Kissling, *Geschichte* 2: 299; Graf, *Beeinflussungsversuche*, 184; Josef Lange, *Die Stellung der überregionalen katholischen deutschen Tagespresse zum Kulturkampf in Preußen (1871–1878.)* (Diss. Regensburg, 1974), 35.

[29] H[einrich] Keiter, *Handbuch der katholischen Presse* (Essen-Ruhr, 3rd ed., 1908). Only in Württemberg, Baden, and esp. AL, where legal disabilities were unusually severe, did the Catholic press show only moderate growth (Hiery, *Reichstagswahlen*, 139, 143; Reiber, *Tagespresse*, 4, 135–37, 139), although in Berlin circulations declined after the Kulturkampf: Jürgen Michael Schulz, "Katholische Kirchenpresse in Berlin," in K. Elm and H.-D. Loock, *Seelsorge und Diakonie in Berlin. Beiträge zum Verhältnis von Kirche und Großstadt im 19. und beginnenden 20. Jahrhundert* (Berlin and New York, 1990), 427–50.

[30] Bodewig, *Wahlbeeinflussungen*, 70–73; "Der katholische Geistliche auf der politischen Arena" *DNJ* 1/8 (1909): 90–94; 90f; Zangerl, "Courting," 226.

[31] "Vertrauensmänner," Oct. 1884, SAO Dep. 62–b; H.-J. Hombach, *Reichstags- und Land-*

Gotherr of Eschbach rousted the farmers out their beds at 4 A.M. on election day
to give them Centrum ballots before they departed for work. Pastor Schäfer in
Liptingen went out into the fields, pressed a ballot into a tardy peasant's hand,
and watched his horse and plow for him while he went off to the polls.[32] In a
letter to the *Kölnische Volkszeitung* another rural pastor passed on a tip to his
fellow clerics. "Approximately twenty voters from my little hamlet have for
some time lived in the industrial region. It was easy for me to inquire after their
addresses. I will send each an exhortation to vote for the Centrum in the runoffs." This kind of networking, he suggested, could be done "generally and
systematically." As late as 1912, the following handwritten note was sent out to
voters in Posnanian parishes:

> Dear Herr X X,
>
> I take the liberty of reminding you of the great obligation which you as a *Catholic*
> have to fulfill on next Monday.
>
> With friendly greetings,
>
> Your obedient servant,
>
> Dean Klamt.[33]

"Obligation," as it appeared in Sunday sermons and in reminders like these,
meant voting, and indeed voting "according to your conscience"—a formula
beloved by the clergy for the nod it made in the direction of the voter's freedom, at the very moment of reminding him what "conscience" for every good
Catholic required. In 1907 even the Pope admonished German Catholics to
"vote your conscience." In an era when politics were conceived, in the words of
Gladstone, as "morality writ large," these references to conscience could have
only one meaning—and lest anyone miss it, the clergy simultaneously warned
that voters were "responsible" to God for their political decisions.[34] Similar
reminders of their civic duty appeared on election handbills to which the pastor's name, followed by that of the vestry (*Kirchenvorstand*), would be appended.[35] Although given the thousands of pulpits and thousands of Sundays, I
cannot be certain, rarely it seems (Bavaria and Silesia in the 1870s, and the
Trier regency at various times, were exceptions) was the term "mortal sin"
(which might have brought down the Election Commission) explicitly used for
failure to vote. Theological terminology—with its implied religious penalties—
was always an embarrassment for the laymen in the Centrum's national leadership, many of whom were more than a little ambivalent about the clerical com-

---

tagswahlen (1963), 201; Smith, *Nationalism*, 52–54; Hiery, *Reichstagswahlen*, 418. This was not
unusual by Irish standards: Hoppen, *Elections*, 247f.

[32] Amtsvorstand Staufen to MdI, Baden, 1 July 1893, GLA 236/14901, 4/a; Bodewig, *Wahlbeeinflussungen*, 89, 109. 10 AL, SBDR 16 Nov. 1906: 3691–3726; details: Hiery, *Reichstagswahlen*, 420f.

[33] 6 Posen AnlDR (1912/13, 13/I, Bd. 17): DS 491: 548; Bodewig, *Wahlbeeinflussungen*, 143.

[34] "Responsible to God": Ketteler, *Mainzer Journal* 1871, Nr. 49: 1. The papal note of 1907
referred to the Spanish elections, but was read by Pastor Roth to his congregation in County Prüm
on 20 Jan. 1907. Horn Report, LHAK 403/8806: 15.

[35] Bodewig, *Wahlbeeinflussungen*, 141.

pany they were obliged to keep. And the clergy themselves were usually willing, within broad outlines, to employ the euphemisms that propriety required. The bishops too, unlike their French counterparts, took care to avoid the word "sin" in connection with elections, preferring instead to emphasize the "voting obligation." But the weight of this "obligation" was clear in 1919, when polling fell for the first time on a Sunday: the Archbishop of Cologne declared that the voting obligation took precedence over the Sabbath obligation.[36]

Because it was visible to everyone, because it was essentially a particular—if peculiar—form of party infrastructure, the work of the "chaplainocracy," as contemporaries dubbed it, could not be *ipso facto* grounds for invalidating an election.[37] Election "influence," if it meant anything, had to refer to violations of the voter's freedom, not through the clergy's performance of a political task, but through the explicit or implicit use of its spiritual office to exercise political pressure. But pressure was hard to prove. It was considered bad form by the Church itself for a priest to name anyone from the pulpit, whether for praise or for blame, and not only candidates for public office.[38] Which is not to say that it never occurred.[39] But although injunctions to vote were usually expressed in careful generalities, the absence of any explicit endorsement was obliterated by the fact that these injunctions were repeatedly quoted in the Centrum's own party press. The prudery with which the clergy draped their partisanship in the universal and individualist language of conscience, transparent veils at best, was intended to disarm charges of mixing politics with religion.[40] The prayers at mass before the elections in the 1870s for a good outcome gave way in the eighties to the practice of dedicating the so-called general prayer at the end of the mass to "an important matter"; to calling for rosaries to be said "so that the up-coming very important day will proceed favorably"; to celebrating mass on election day with the special intention of a "result pleasing to God." Nuns were more outspoken, instructing their schoolchildren to say paternosters for a *Centrum* victory and distributing ballots during mass from the high altar.[41]

---

[36] Accusation that a priest termed voting against the Z a "mortal sin" and not voting, a "triple sin": 6 Trier, AnlDR (1882/83, 5/II, Bd. 6) DS 323: 1329; "Gottesdienst?" *KZ*, Nr. 27, 9 Jan. 1912, in Anlage 7, 5 Trier, AnlDR (1912/14, 13/I, Bd. 23) DS 1639: 3605. Graf, *Beeinflussungsversuche*, 166 (voting obligation), 172f (absence of language of "sin"), "Todsünde," 183; similar cases, 172f, in the 1920s (pro-BVP), the 1930s (anti-NSDAP), the 40s and 60s (anti-KPD and SPD). Charnay, *Les scrutins*, 73n. 21. But cf. Blackbourn, *Class*, 169; Bodewig, *Wahlbeeinflussungen*, 160.

[37] "Chaplainocracy": J. Most (SD) SBDR 10 Apr. 1878: 875; Max Weber, "Parlament" ([1918] 1958), 309, 313.

[38] Ketteler, "Die Centrums-Fraction." 24. Govt. agents reported that almost the entire clergy in County Prüm waged the 1907 election campaign "with all means," including the pulpit, but "more or less cautiously." Horn Report, LHAK 403/8806: 3. Cf. however, Monshausen, *Wahlen*, 343.

[39] Hombach, *Reichstags- und Landtagswahlen*, 210; A. Kelly, ed., *Worker* (1987), 177; 6 Trier, AnlDR (1882/83, 5/II, Bd. 6) DS 323: 1329.

[40] E.g., "Katholischer Wähler," *Katholischer Volksbote* Nr. 29, 21 July 1878. Such veils were obstacles to prosecution: v. Campe, "Wahlbeeinflussung," 36.

[41] SM Turban to Grand Duke Friedrich, 31 Mar. 1887, GLA 60/494: 2. Prayers: Steil, *Wahlen*, 121. Nuns: 4 Oppeln, AnlDR (1912/13, 13/I, Bd. 19) DS 798: 1096; Bodewig, *Wahlbeeinflussungen*, 149.

The proliferation of political duties meant a drastic transformation of the clergy's own self-image. Gone were the days when a priest would feel able to argue, as Professor Hergenröther had in the sixties, that there was no such thing as "Catholic politics." The chapel that grateful friends presented to Pastor Theodor Wacker for his parsonage garden in Zähringen in 1894 was emblematic of the change. The chapel was divided by a curtain. On one side of the curtain was the choir niche, with a picture of the Immaculate Conception. On the other side, where he could read the newspapers, draft his articles and brochures, and confer with party colleagues, was—in the ingenuous words of Wacker's chief deputy—"a workspace for the politician on hot summer days."[42]

The clergy's role in elections and Centrum politics did not diminish over time. In fact, as the waning of the culture wars in the nineties began to reduce communal pressures for conformity and the Catholic nobility began to shift to the conservative parties, the clergy's relative weight within the Centrum grew. The movement of Germany's populations into the cities depleted the Centrum's lay cadres in the smaller towns and countryside that formed the electoral base of the party; it made the party, especially in southern Germany, even more dependent on its network of black-clad organizers. In Bavaria, the clergy acquired a weight in electoral and parliamentary politics that would have been inconceivable in the 1860s. In Hessen, the clergy reached the apogee of its influence within the party in the Weimar Republic—after the Centrum's own hold over the allegiance of the Catholic population had itself considerably loosened.[43] Even in places where ethnic and economic issues divided the Catholic vote, as in Upper Silesia in the early twentieth century, when the Polish National Democratic challengers finally wrested five seats from the Centrum in 1907, three of the *new* party's victors were priests.[44] The slurs of the Centrum's opponents—the cartoons of *Simplicissimus* depicting cassocks swirling like bats and swarming like mice, the references of opponents to clergy as "maggots crawling out of living bodies"—these should not, in their hatefulness, mislead us. The critics were at least correct in perceiving the degree to which, at the grass roots level, these black-clad figures *were* the Centrum Party.[45]

---

[42] Schofer, *Erinnerungen*, 72.

[43] On Bavaria: Thränhardt, *Wahlen* (1973), 81f, 87; Hessen: H. G. Ruppel and B. Groß, eds., *Hessische Abgeordnete 1820–1933. Biographische Nachweise für die Landstände des Großherzogtums Hessen* . . . (Darmstadt, 1980). No priests served in the Hessen LT until after WWI, although given the significance of Ketteler until 1877 and Moufang until 1890 in Z affairs, the lay composition of the Hessen fraction should not be given too much weight. After WWII, Domkapitular Geo. Lenhart, chair of the Z in the Hessen LT during the Weimar Republic, remarked in his memoirs that he could not imagine a modern Z "without a clerical advisory board." Graf considers the actual heydey of "Centrum prelates" to have come only after WWI. *Beeinflussungsversuche*, 197. J. Becker, "Ende" (1968), 353–58, 361f, explains why.

[44] I. Schwidetzky, *Wahlbewegung* (1934), 78f.

[45] "Maggots": T. Held (NL), 1907. He later amended his remarks to say that the Protestant Guelfs seemed "as happy among the Catholic clergy as maggots in bacon." Quoted in M. Erzberger, *Bilder* (1907), 21, 24, 26. Mice: "Der deutsche Michel," *Simplicissimus* VIII/1 (n.d., 1903–4), title page; "Der Schwarzseher," ibid., XI/2, Nr. 27, 1 Oct. 1906, title page.

AUTHORITY AND DISSENT

The economy and efficiency of this clerical network insured that the military images of the seventies would continue to be associated with the Centrum long after the Jesuits had been driven from the land. In the eyes of opponents, parsonages, deaconates, and episcopal sees were "simply military command posts" for the Centrum. Devotional sodalities were "auxiliary troops." The "People's Association for Catholic Germany," founded in 1890 and staffed largely by priests, was "heavy cavalry during the election campaigns," remaining "under arms and in drill" even in nonelection years.[46] Theodor Wacker, the young cleric who revitalized the Baden party in the 1880s, was deemed its "Supreme War Lord," the "field marshal of elections," who ran his campaigns by "*Kommando*," issuing "election ukases" to confrères who became his field commanders. The meetings of the Congress of Catholic Associations (*Katholikentag*), held annually in September, were "fall maneuvers." Catholic voters became an army. A reporter in the Saar compared "the black regiment of bunk- and boardinghouse people storming the polls" to "Tartars."[47] Such, in the eyes of its opponents, still trying to negotiate the transition from committees of notables to mass politics, was the electoral juggernaut that was the Centrum.

Did clericalism in politics encourage an authoritarian political culture? The Church's own teachings about the structure of legitimate authority, which can be documented from any seminary handbook or lexicon of theology, might seem to support this conclusion. So strict was the ultramontane conception of hierarchy that the very idea that legitimate suggestions might flow upward, even within the clerical caste itself, had been condemned by the pope as "mad fantasy."[48] In 1906 a papal encyclical affirmed that "the majority has no other right than to allow themselves to be led and to follow their shepherds like a docile fleet."[49] Language such as this was impossible to harmonize with the independence ("maturity," in the contemporary idiom) that *all* of Germany's political parties agreed was essential for a voting public.

Yet when one moves from lexica and encyclicals to practice, particularly electoral practice, the "mad fantasies" that those at the bottom had a legitimate

[46] Bodewig, *Wahlbeeinflussungen*, 9, 13, 69.

[47] "Eine Tatarennachricht," *Saar-Post* Nr. 15, 19 Jan. 1912, Anlage 19, on 5 Trier, AnlDR (1912/14, 13/I, Bd. 23) DS 1639: 3606.

[48] Graf, *Beeinflussungsversuche*, 157f; Christoph Weber, "Ultramontanismus als katholischer Fundamentalismus," in *Deutscher Katholizismus im Umbruch zur Moderne*, edited by W. Loth (Stuttgart), 1991, 20–45. In 1906 the Archbishop of Salzburg created a sensation with an encyclical that claimed that God had given the priest "even power over Himself." Bodewig, *Wahlbeeinflussungen*, 43.

[49] *Vehementer nos* (1906). As late as 1960 the *Osservatore Romano* asserted that "every Catholic in every area of his life must conform his private and public behavior to the . . . instructions of the hierarchy." Only in 1966 did the German Church, via the bishops of North-Rhine-Westfalia, affirm that no one may any longer claim ecclesiastical authority for another in the ordering of earthly matters—which must be the Catholic equivalent of the SPD's Godesberg Declaration. Quotes in Graf, *Beeinflussungsversuche*, 159, 161f, 271.

say in clerical politics kept reappearing. The priests themselves proved more than willing to break the chain of command when the instructions from their superiors offended their *party* loyalties. Massive disregard of the professed wishes of the pope himself occurred in 1887. In order to do Bismarck a favor, Leo XIII told the Centrum to support the government's military bill, which required a seven-year budget (*Septennat*). When the Centrum, which was on record as favoring *annual* budgets, twice refused, Leo leaked his instructions to Bismarck, and allowed the chancellor to publish them for election purposes. This open conflict between pontiff and party caused enormous scandal. But the clergy, beginning with the Bishops of Cologne, Osnabrück, and Trier, decided for the party. And those few prelates who (for political reasons of their own) did side with Rome, found their instructions ignored by their diocesan priests— in spite of their demands for "loyal, childlike attachment" to the intentions of the Holy Father.[50] Asked by a heckler at a rally in Münstertal what he would do if his bishop, Johann Baptist Orbin, sent his clergy the same election instructions as (the Bismarckian) Bishop Klein, Pastor Bauer shouted back, "Then I would still vote no!" His vicar became so passionate on the subject that the police had to threaten to dissolve the rally. Throughout the archdiocese of Freiburg, even in districts where a loyal Centrum man had no hope of winning, the lower clergy showed their colors by repeatedly supporting Democrats or the *Freisinnigen* (Left Liberals) rather than the National Liberal whom the pontiff was said to favor. Here is Pastor Dieterle in Dogern: "In worldly matters the pope was just as much a sinner as humans [*sic*!] are." Pastor Eble in Minseln had only sarcasm for a heckler who threw up to him Leo XIII's instructions to support the Septennat: "Now all of a sudden the pope is infallible!" In Achern, Pastor Bronner was reported as declaring that "the current pope" (!) was "by no means as beloved by him as he is by the 'gentlemen' and their ilk." More privately (though not privately enough, apparently, for he was arrested afterwards for violating §166 of the imperial penal code, outlawing insults in public to the institutions or uses of a church) Vicar Vögtle opined in a tavern in Ballrichten: "The pope is an old grandmother. Old grandmothers have many wishes that can't be fulfilled—I can prove that to you out of the catechism!"[51]

Defiance of papal wishes occurred again in 1893, also regarding a military bill. These were only the most spectacular occasions when electoral politics subverted ecclesiastical hierarchy. In lesser cases it happened over and over again.[52] Government officials were shocked to learn of a runoff election between a Conservative and a Social Democrat in which the rector of a parish supported the Conservative, his chaplain, the Social Democrat. In County Bitburg, where Chaplain Georg Friedrich Dasbach was a hero to farmers and

---

[50] Quote: Graf, *Beeinflussungsversuche*, 272. My *Windthorst*, 335–58, has an account of the notorious "Septennat Election" of 1887. Ultimately, however, the Z abstained on the bill.

[51] SM Turban reporting to Grand Duke Friedrich, 31 Mar. 1887, GLA 60/494. The report mentions 40 priests by name—a testimony to the diligence of Baden's political police.

[52] E.g., Müller, *Strömungen*, 309f. Also in the Weimar Republic, for the Z to accept *political* directives from the episcopate or Vatican was unthinkable: Becker, "Ende," 358.

workers, "the bishop himself"—a pastor proclaimed in 1907—"if he were to come here and put himself up against Dasbach, wouldn't get a single vote."[53] It is worth remarking that when Max Weber reflected on political Catholicism he referred not to the "hierarchy" but to the "*chaplain*-ocracy." The term is revealing. It was not a term anyone used for Ireland or for France. Here too, the German experience was unique.[54]

But the fact that under the pressures of electoral politics chaplains might defy pastors, pastors ignore bishops, and bishops cleave to party over pope does not prove that, at the very bottom of the chain of command, for the layman and voter, the same freedom to overturn degree prevailed. If Pastor Thröne's confident remark in a tavern in Rosenberg that the pope "can't mix into political things; the farmer will listen to the pastor first" supports skepticism about the *hierarchy's* political authority, it should make us equally careful about jumping to conclusions about the voter's independence.[55] Here the evidence is more ambiguous. Not every Catholic liked a politicking priest, and mayors in particular, even of tiny hamlets, might feel strong enough publicly to oppose him—especially when they thought they were expressing the wishes of the state.[56] But most objections to clerical campaigning were likely to be silent—as in the case of a rural voter who protested his pastor's too-political sermons (which seem to have been very wide ranging indeed) with a comment written at the bottom of his (liberal) ballot:

"Gambetta.
Rochefort.
Raspail.
The Pope.
Garibaldi & the
Pastor of Büchelberg.
Of these six, one is worth about as much as another."[57]

Germany presents us with few instances comparable to Ireland, where the conspicuous campaigning of the clergy was met with equally conspicuous examples of Catholic defiance. Irish election mobs smashed rectory windows and roughed up pastors on the hustings, crying, "Mind your own business," "No priest in politics," and—tellingly—"Hurrah for Bismarck!" They staged dramatic walkouts from church. They rose in their pews to denounce the election

---

[53] Amtsvorstand Ettlingen to MdI, 25 June 1893, GLA 236/14901: 9/a; Horn Report, LHAK 403/8806: 4v.

[54] Although in Ireland, too, the parish priest provided an indispensable organizational network. Whyte, "Influence," 249–51.

[55] Thröne quoted in SM Turban to Grand Duke Friedrich, 31 Mar. 1887, GLA 60/494.

[56] 5 Oberfr. AnlDR (1871, 1/I, Bd. 1) DS 27: 80–83; SBDR 17 Apr. 1871: 228–43; cf. my "Voter," 1451f.

[57] *GA* Nr. 62, 14 Mar. 1871: 521. The Marquis de Henri Rochefort (1830–1913) was a radical French playwright, journalist, and Communard. François Vincent Raspail (1794–1878) was a French scientist, revolutionary, and anti-Jesuit polemicist.

advice being offered from the altar. When the seventy-five-year-old bishop of Meath attacked Parnell's supporters in a sermon in his cathedral, a worshipper shouted out, "You are a liar!"[58]

We see little of these spontaneous outbursts in Germany. Catholic voters had been known to defend their hearths against the intrusions of door-to-door clerical canvassers, as when a Trier businessman forcibly removed the young Chaplain Dasbach from his premises. But such instances were legendary precisely because they were startling.[59] Catholic objections to clerical importunities, when they occurred at all, were likely to be silent; or, if not silent, then collective and well organized. In Liptingen an unpopular pastor who had conducted a one-man campaign in 1906 to end his village's long tradition of National Liberal voting ran up against such a wall of resistance that he appears to have come close to a nervous breakdown, losing control of himself in the middle of a sermon. When he then denied communion to a woman whose husband distributed the liberal newspaper, the village revolted. A group of 150 Catholic men, close to Liptingen's entire voting population, signed a declaration announcing their resolve to avoid Pastor Schäfer's "outrages" by not entering the church so long as "this gentleman officiated; alternatively we will bring in a pastor with different beliefs"—that is, an Old Catholic. But Baden, where this protest occurred, was exceptional in the tenacity with which the tradition of Liberal voting within certain Catholic populations resisted the advances of the clergy-sponsored Centrum.[60] And I've found no resistance, even in Baden, to priestly politicking by members of the congregation *within* a church: no fists shaken, no cries of outrage, no huffy walkouts.[61] Outside Baden, we have to scour the landscape for open signs of Catholic anger at clerical electioneering, at least before the twentieth century.[62]

Was this silence because, as the liberal argument for the Pulpit Paragraph

[58] Quoted in Hoppen, *Elections*, 240–42; Woods, "Election," 300f; Whyte, "Influence," 247–49. Whyte argues—as does Conor Cruise O'Brien, *Parnell and His Party* (Oxford, 1957), 43—that the clergy were under more constraint from voters than the voters were from the priests. But see ibid., 27n. 3, 129, 215ff.

[59] "Der katholische Geistliche auf der politischen Arena," 93.

[60] Conversely, Catholics punished unpopular clerics by voting against the Z. Amtsvorstand Bonndorf to MdI, 30 June 1893, GLA 236/14901; Bodewig, *Wahlbeeinflussungen*, 89. On Baden's pockets of Old Catholicism and hostility to the Z: Oded Heilbronner, "Die Besonderheit des katholischen Bürgertums im ländlichen Süddeutschland," *Blätter für deutsche Landesgeschichte* 131 (1995): 225–59. Also Monshausen, *Wahlen*, 341.

[61] Unless one counts the walkout on Domvikar Dr. Beck of Trier, protesting his *anti-Z* behavior!—an action that got one state employee fired. Rust, *Reichskanzler* (1897), 719f.

[62] The silence on disruptions by Bodewig, *Wahlbeeinflussungen*, and Elble, *Kanzelparagraph*, who otherwise scrape the bottom of the barrel for evidence against the clergy, seems conclusive. Smith found between 1870 and 1914 only 8 cases of disruption reported in all of Baden and Württemberg—denomination unspecified. *Nationalism*, 101. So strong was identification with the Z in some places that the pastor himself, if he backed another candidate, was subjected to the irritated disapproval of his parishioners. Graf, *Beeinflussungsversuche*, 189f. Liberal newspapers published letters complaining about the priest's sermon—but they were anonymous. "Gottesdienst?" *KZ*, Nr. 27, 9 Jan. 1912, in Anlage 7, 5 Trier, AnlDR (1912/14, 13/I, Bd. 23) DS 1639: 3605.

implied, holy *spaces* enjoyed special protections? Perhaps. Special protection hardly seems to have been necessary, however, given general cultural attitudes in which the right to be undisturbed on one's own property (*Hausfrieden*) went, even in taverns and assembly halls, (largely) unchallenged by the public and, on the rare occasions when trouble appeared, was strictly enforced by the secular arm. Take the case of a teacher in Meßkirch, who felt that a sermon attacking liberalism contained an allusion to him personally. Far from crying out, he simply contacted the public prosecutor.[63] Could the willingness of parish dissenters to report politically obnoxious pastors to the authorities be a sign that the "judicialization" of conflict, posited by Winfried Schulze for the eighteenth century, continued into imperial Germany? Recent work on the clergy in Baden suggests that this may well have been the case.[64]

But when all is said and done we cannot ignore the possibility that in the face of pastors who behaved like party agents, the silence of German congregations, in such marked contrast to the unruly Irish, also meant consent—although consent of a non-individualistic, communal sort. For just as important as the clergy's social, sacerdotal, and organizational advantages, was the priest's ability to define the community in ways more plausible than those given to the other notables—mayors, teachers, Landräte, employers—who was his main competition.[65] One sermon that was used to throw out a Centrum election began by announcing, *"You are a significant Catholic congregation,* and no one will hold it against you if, as such, you should give your votes to a Catholic man." Voters apparently conceived themselves as "Catholic men," who did things in "Catholic ways."[66] Julius Knorr, whom we heard above, was no doubt correct in suspecting that such an identity conflicted with "proclaiming their German hearts." "Catholic" here meant not only a profession of faith, but also

[63] Amtsvorstand Meßkirch to the Baden MdI, 17 July 1893, GLA 236/14901: 1/h; Bodewig, *Wahlbeeinflussungen,* 89. A somewhat similar case in AL: "Momentbild aus der Zentrumsagitation," *DNJ* 2/2 (1910), 21. Ireland: Whyte, "Influence," 247. In Germany we have only the most scattered evidence of open resistance to politiking priests. E.g., *GA* Nr. 6, 8 Jan. 1874: 33. For the travails of the FK priest Franz Künzer, see Leonhard Müller, "Zur Geschichte der Freikonservativen und Reichspartei," *Schlesische Freikonservative "Partei-Korrespondenz,"* (1914) 1: Nrs. 11 (28 Feb.) through 17 (31 May) and 19 (30 June) through 21 (31 June).

[64] Götz v. Olenhusen, "Ultramontanisierung," esp. 60–63. Schulze's *"Verrechtlichung"* concept has appeared most fully in "Peasant Resistance and Politicization in Eighteenth-Century Germany," paper delivered at the American Historical Association, Dec. 1987. See also: idem, "Der Ungehorsam des Gemeinen Mannes. Ziele und Formen des Widerstands in der deutschen Geschichte vom 16. bis zum 18. Jahrhundert," in *Trierer Beiträge. Aus Forschung und Lehre an der Universität Trier* 19 (Feb. 1988): 3–14. William W. Hagen has also drawn attention to the use of the court system by 18th-century peasants and farmworkers in "The Junkers' Faithless Servants: Peasant Insubordination and the Breakdown of Serfdom in Brandenburg-Prussia, 1763–1811," in *The German Peasantry: Conflict and Community in Rural Society from the Eighteenth Century to the Present,* edited by R. J. Evans and W. R. Lee (London, 1985), 71–102.

[65] Ketteler, in "Centrums-Fraction," 110, commented sarcastically on the readiness of Berlin deputies to define to whom Pless-Rybnik belonged. Similarly: Fr. Müller in *MK* Nr. 6, 19 Feb. 1872: 46.

[66] Quotes: Oppeln, AnlDr (1871, 1/I, Bd. 2) DS 69: 164; "Catholic ways:" Württ. petition, quoted in Smith, *Nationalism,* 48.

a membership in a community, and one whose claims were more exigent than those of the "German" community as defined by liberals, nationalists, and the government.

Election appeals invoked loyalty at least as much as they did piety. Among the sins included in the *Prayer and Instruction Book for the Catholic Men's World* were "Reading only liberal papers and always wanting to be the government's 'good boy.'" The person committing these sins demonstrated his lack of solidarity and "on election day would be a weathercock and a traitor."[67] One Saarland pastor responded to the news that four miners in his congregation had allowed the mining company to press them into distributing National Liberal ballots by banishing the banners of the miners' club from the church. But he invited the transgressors to come to his office and apologize: "Then in their name he would ask the parish for its forgiveness." Note that it was the parish— as much as God—who was presumed to be offended. Here was real power— but rather different from that conjured up by visions of dark confessionals and threats of damnation.[68]

The clergy behaved that way because they could usually count on support.[69] However discreetly the priest might comport himself, his bookkeeper, his bell ringer, his vestry men, and his grave digger, any or all of whom might be sitting on the election panel, felt little compunction against telling a dissenter that if he continued along Liberal (or Conservative, or Social Democratic) paths, then he was no longer a "Catholic man." When a voter in a Mosel pub sounded off against the Centrum, the party stalwart at the next table could be counted on to call over to him: "Sure! And we all know *you* have lost your faith!"[70]

It was precisely this element of genuine "horizontal" reinforcement—and its extension in wider networks of association and opinion reaching beyond the parish—that reveals the essential and characteristic difference between the voting legions of the clerically staffed Centrum and the outwardly similar troops of needy-and-greedy voters in vertically organized, "clientelist" structures in Iberia, Latin America, and Africa.[71] Both structures depend on a democratic franchise, and in both the voting decision is located somewhere between coercion and consent. But in classic clientelism, political connection is based on

[67] Dr. Anton Keller, Pfarrer in Gottenhein bei Freiburg, *Das Gebet- und Belehrungsbuch für die Katholischen Männerwelt* (Kevelaer, 1902), quoted in Bodewig, *Wahlbeeinflussungen*, 92.

[68] Another pastor, however, allegedly threatened that those NL ballots would one day burn in their hands! 6 Trier, AnlDR (1882/83, 5/II, Bd. 6) DS 323: 1329.

[69] When an Aachen worker criticized the clerical president of his sodality for a Z speech, he waited until he was surrounded by members of his own insurgent Christian Social Party. Lepper, ed., *Katholizismus*, 215; similarly, 224.

[70] Bodewig, *Wahlbeeinflussungen*, 141, 143. Clubs had the power of "excommunication" by simply arguing: "he's no longer even a Catholic." GA Nr. 188, 13 Aug. 1871: 1682. The Z Election Proclamation for 13 Württ. in 1878 assumed that "all" would be Z voters and the only difficulty would be in bringing the lazy to the polls. "Wählet! Wählet! Wählet! alle Moritz Mohl," BAB-L R1501/14693, Bl. 65.

[71] Excellent discussion of clientelism in Rouquié, "Controls" (1978), 19–35, esp. 22–27.

individualistic and circumscribed mutual exchanges of a very material sort, while in the Centrum, voters were being integrated into a national system of opinion-based politics.

Little wonder that the generation of Catholic liberals born before 1840 was not replenished. Protestant Liberals along the Rhine and Mosel complained that even when they found Catholics who shared their views, they would not run for office, fearing that their neighbors would say "he has no religion" and that they would be boycotted by the entire population. In a land where religious homogeneity within small communities was the rule (and as late as 1907, 122 of the Reichstag's 397 electoral districts were made up of populations with religious homogeneity greater than 95 percent) the social penalties for dissident behavior could be severe.[72] When Catholics were watching Catholics, the terrors of the confessional, which played such a large role in liberal polemic, were hardly necessary.

SOLIDARITY: THE MILIEU, CATHOLIC WOMEN, AND "BALLOT CATHOLICS"

The kinds of pressures for conformity that existed spontaneously in the village were replicated artificially in urban areas in an extensive associational network that gave any priest who wanted to weigh in politically an inestimable advantage over notables of rival persuasions. Marian Congregations, Rosary and Corpus Christi Brotherhoods, prayer societies, Heart of Mary and Ludwig Mission Associations: Catholic club life, especially in northwestern Germany, was socially even more inclusive than the electoral constituency, since it encompassed not only all sorts and conditions of men, but women as well. And presiding over each of these clubs, vetting its speakers, shaping its agendas, was a priest. The police counted 139 Catholic associations in the Cologne area in the early seventies, Trier had even more, and in the Düsseldorf regency their numbers reached 389. In the Westfalian part of the diocese of Paderborn, 46 percent of the Catholic population, of all ages, belonged to at least one such Catholic club, and in some areas the numbers reached two-thirds.

In the historical literature this web of religious practices, feast (and fast) days, social clubs, and, eventually, business and political organizations has come to be known as the "milieu," with inevitably narrow connotations. Its own publicists were pleased to call it "Catholic Germany," a counterworld that might be only a subset of any given geographically defined region, but was also, with its trans-local connections, as broad as the nation itself. Thus did the

---

[72] Generationational breakdowns show that between 1867 and 1917, of 569 NLs in the RT, only 51 were Catholic, and of these, 36 were born before 1840 and had begun their careers before the great re-confessionalization. The few districts in which Catholics could still be elected as liberals were Munich, Bonn, Düsseldorf, isolated spots in Hessen and the Bavarian Palatinate, Baden south of Freiburg, and in the area along the Swiss border. Of the 122 confessionally homogeneous election districts, however, 96 were Protestant. Smith, *Nationalism*, 34f, 96.

Catholic cause in Germany escape the identification with a single class that so crippled Catholic politics in France and Spain.[73]

This Catholic *"Vereinskosmos,"* as Josef Mooser has dubbed it, established a safe zone that was all the more welcome after 1866; that is, after representatives of the "national" culture felt increasingly free to speak of Catholics as intruders in their own country. The baroque articulation of every aspect of daily life in "Catholic" terms, to the point where shoppers were encouraged to go in search of "Catholic coffee" and "Catholic beer," was easy to mock. The milieu's own answer was "We jolly well better look for Catholic beer, especially now when . . . we're scarcely allowed to raise a glass anywhere in a public locale without anti-Catholicism being sp[it] into it."[74] The pattern of this finely meshed grid appeared devotional when viewed from one angle, but with only a slight shift in perspective, the same pattern might resolve itself as social, or, with yet another half-turn, as political. Before the founding of the empire the knots in this multistranded web had been common participation in the sacraments. After 1871 these knots were made tighter by rituals of solidarity (especially in celebrations of a priest's release from prison) and rituals of opposition, via electoral politics.

Solidarity was not equality. *"Das katholische Deutschland"* was egalitarian only at the communion rail—and at the voting urn.[75] Its components were hierarchical and they were distinct, with different functions assigned to clergy and laity, male and female, and every conceivable *Stand.*[76] There was no promiscuous mixing, for each was expected to take pride in his or her own estate. The nobility joined the mass demonstrations paying homage to their persecuted

[73] See Franz Borkenau's sharp contrast between Germany's "social" and Spain's very unsocial Catholicism in *Spanish Cockpit* (London, 1937), 9f. The concept "milieu," which has sparked an enormous literature, has become so contested and refined as to be almost unusable, unless one insists on a minimalist, ordinary-language meaning, which is the only way I shall use it here. See chap. 4, n. 129.

[74] E. Müller, "Dann laß ich fünf Fuß tiefer Graben," *BK* (1883): 3. On the milieu: Smith, *Nationalism*, esp. 79–113; J. Mooser, "Das katholische Vereinswesen" (1991), 452, 455; and its creation: Sperber, *Catholicism*, 39–98. Although it existed well before the Kulturkampf, before 1871, as Rohe points out, the milieu was by no means always politically revelant. *Wahlen*, 54.

[75] Efforts of workers and artisans to find equality not only at the urn but at the stage of nominating Z candidates were resisted by bourgeois leaders for as long as they could get away with it—which meant until their more humble coreligionists succeeded in mobilizing their own voting power against them. The career of Aachen's Eduard Cronenberg demonstrates that relations between the conservative and radical wings of the clergy, as well as between radical Catholic voters and the bourgeois Z leadership, could be *denkbar schlecht.* Since Cronenberg eventually spent two years in prison for sodomy and financial malfeasance, of which the latter charge was certainly justified, the skepticism of his opponents, whose refusal to nominate him for the RT helped precipitate a split within Aachen Catholicism, may have been based on the kind of personal knowledge that necessarily eludes the historian, who must draw her conclusions largely from Cronenberg's printed programs (which are progressive indeed), and from his speeches and letters (which do not inspire confidence). Cf. Lepper, "Cronenberg," esp. 62–64, and idem, ed., *Katholizismus.*

[76] Excellent on social conflicts within political Catholicism: W. Loth, *Katholiken* (1984); idem, "Soziale Bewegungen im Katholizismus des Kaiserreichs," GG 17 (1991): 279–310, and Kühne, *Dreiklassenwahlrecht*, 341–49.

bishops, but they marched in separate delegations under their own banners, and they contributed to the Catholic cause through their own organizations, such as the Knights of Malta.[77] The university graduate, as a member of the Görres Society for the Cultivation of Scholarship (established in 1876), found his pen enlisted on Catholic Germany's behalf—but could continue to glory in belonging to the *Bildungsbürgertum*. Worker and journeyman took part in activities appropriate to the cultures of their trades, indeed under certain circumstances might even find their social radicalism encouraged, all while remaining within the "fold" of their black-clad shepherd. The participation of women—maid and married—within this Catholic public sphere insured that they too would eventually be assigned a political role, a practice that socialized them into Centrum politics long before they had the vote and prepared the way for their massive support for the Centrum, in 1919 and beyond, once they did.[78] Clerical leadership encouraged these separate self-understandings. But along with differentiation, Catholic culture, and therefore its political culture, set an equally high valuation on solidarity, on a mutual dependence that encompassed not only the living but the dead.[79] The Centrum's election clubs were not called "Freedom," much less "Equality"; instead they sported names like "Concordia" and "Harmonia."

The power of this language of solidarity, which maintained differences but harmonized latent (and not-so-latent) social hostilities, did not depend upon theology, the universality of the salvation message. Nor did it demand the reactivation of medieval corporativist ideology, although a corporativist haze still hovered over the habits and language of late-nineteenth-century Catholics, particularly when, like Father Franz Hitze and Freiherr Karl von Löwenstein, they developed a theoretical as well as a practical interest in the "social question."[80] Rather, the solidarist vision took its vitality from the democratic suffrage which, in the atmosphere of the Kulturkampf and interpreted organizationally by the chaplainocracy, brought all Catholics, *as* Catholics, together on election day, in their own kind of political corporate communion. The Emsland's *Katholischer Volksbote* apostrophized those "farmers blessed with a team: equalize the differences between the estates, and if necessary hitch up your wagons and drive the old and weak to the election urn. The deed will be its own reward."[81]

Such solidarity enforced high turnouts, often independent of any credible competition. In 1903 in the Upper Bavarian village of Hollenbach, 172 of its 175 eligible voters cast ballots for the Centrum. Of the remaining three, one

---

[77] Christian Stamm, *Dr. Conrad Martin Bishof von Paderborn. Ein biographischer Versuch* (Paderborn, 1892), 369; Rust, *Reichskanzler* (1897), 621f, 826.

[78] In some districts, up to 70% of the Z vote came from women. Bachem, *Vorgeschichte* 8: 271.

[79] A point brilliantly made by H. McLeod, "Frömmigkeit" (1988), 152. These separate self-understandings, however, led after the turn of the century to counterproductive organizational rivalry between the *Katholischer Frauenbund* and the *Volksverein*. Heitzer, *Volksverein*, 35f, and Klein, *Volksverein*, 94f.

[80] Hitze's preference for an occupational parliament: Blackbourn, *Class*, 126f, and 127n. 31; corporativism opposed by the Z mainstream: Anderson, *Windthorst*, 312–14.

[81] "Katholischer Wähler," *Katholischer Volksbote*, no. 29, 21 July 1878.

was too ill to be moved. In the city of Ingolstadt, even centagenarians were not allowed to remain at home. Poles in 1912 in Lautenburg, a little town in the West Prussian county of Strasburg, were reminded by Dean Klatt that "the purpose of the runoff elections has already been discussed. It has already been stated that all—blind and lame, cripples and retired—have to appear. In the last election, forty-two Poles were missing." In some parts of Catholic Germany support for the Centrum reached levels that exceeded participation in Easter communion. But even more remarkable was the party discipline that allowed Centrum leaders to "deliver" constituencies unanimously in the runoff to parties that had viciously attacked them in the main election—in return for promises of similar help elsewhere.[82] It was this discipline that accounted, at least in part, for the drop in Centrum totals in 1912, as Centrum leaders "gave" some of their voters to Conservative candidates on the first ballot.[83]

Since Catholics as a community felt under attack, women, as members of the community, were expected to join the defense. Women and girls were active in the resistance to the Kulturkampf, thronging cathedral squares in demonstrations, collecting signatures on statements of solidarity, holding sit-down strikes, and at one point requiring the intervention of the army—when they guarded the school in Upper Silesia's Laura Hütte to protect religion classes held by "unauthorized" priests, and when they stormed the school in nearby Königshütte to remove their children from classes conducted by an Old Catholic apostate. Some wrote newspaper articles, paid fines, even went to jail.[84] Chaplain Eduard Müller in his *Märkisches Kirchenblatt* responded to the Pulpit Law by calling on each parish to establish a "Civil Liberties Association" to protect the clergy

---

[82]Fairbairn, *Democracy*, 185; Smith, *Nationalism*, 92f; Suval, *Politics*, 116, 207, 224. Nationally, however, Catholic turnouts dropped after the Kulturkampf and, as the SPD mobilized its constituency, Protestant turnouts exceeded them.

[83]The widespread impression, beginning with Schauff's *Wahlverhalten*, that support for the Z was declining after 1900, has been disputed by Zangerl ("Courting," 229–32, 238) and by Sperber (review of Blackbourn's *Class* in *New German Critique* 26 [Spring–Summer 1982]: 206–8, and in *Voters*, 82) as a statistical illusion. The Z's control of the Catholic vote allowed it, as a "donor party," to determine the outcome of elections even in districts it did not contest, and these "donations" were especially heavy in 1912. If one takes 1907 rather than 1912 as one's point of comparison, however, then the picture (as in Langewiesche's *Liberalismus*, 133) that given a growing population, the Z's increase in voters (only 38% between 1874 and 1912) constituted a decline, must be modified. Between 1874 (the Z's "best" year in terms of percentage of the vote) and 1907, population grew 48%, but the numbers voting for the Z grew 51%. (Extrapolated from G. Hohorst et al., *Arbeitsbuch* [1978] 2: 27f.) Local examples: Thomas Mergel, "Christlicher Konservatismus in der Provinz: Politischer Katholizismus in Ostwestfalen 1887–1912," in *Unter Pickelhaube und Zylinder: Das östliche Westfalen im Zeitalter des Wilhelmismus 1881 bis 1914*, edited by J. Meynert et al. (Bielefeld, 1991), 283–301; esp. 287–90, 296; B. Liebert, *Wahlen* (1988), 163 (on 1887), 176f (on 1890); Schulte, *Struktur*, 120–25.

[84] Ditscheid, *Matthias Eberhard*, 94; Kammer, *Kulturkampfpriester*, 45, 121, 143; Rust, *Reichskanzler*, 684; along with some of the rioting mothers, Emilia Miarka, wife of Karol Miarka, was arrested for an article she wrote in the *SVZ* after his arrest: Trzeciakowski, *Kulturkampf*, 93, 148. Similarly in County Pless: K. Franzke, *Industriearbeiter* (1936), 117.

against false denunciations. Every time their pastor spoke in public in an official capacity, three reliable members of his congregation, "male or female,"
should be present as witnesses to what he said. Müller was happy to publish
negative comments on the candidacy of his rival in Pless-Rybnik, the Free
Conservative Duke of Ratibor, as *women's* opinions. Almost as much as the
sturdy farmer, "the Catholic woman" became a useful political fiction into
whose mouths commentary was put whenever a Centrum author or speaker
wished to interject the voice of healthy common sense, or indeed, the voice of
the community as a whole.[85]

From cultural defense to election activity was an invisible step. Women took
the initiative in arranging for Centrum speakers to come to their towns before
elections.[86] They themselves were legally barred from attending many such
events, and indeed from any explicitly political club or gathering. Their very
presence—as liberal and Social Democratic women were also finding out—
gave local police a welcome excuse to shut down the assembly or even dissolve
the organization. But "lecture evenings" on such obviously political topics as
the school question drew female audiences in the hundreds in Catholic cities; in
Breslau as early as 1867. Traces of a female presence in political assemblies
can be found in Düsseldorf in the seventies, and the local Centrum began inviting women (occasionally and, one assumes, cautiously) to their meetings in
1884.[87] In 1908 the Imperial Law of Associations granted women the right to
appear at political meetings throughout the empire—the Centrum having been
one of the parties sponsoring the reform.[88] A burst of female election activity
was the result. In 1912 the *Berliner Tageblatt*, despairing over liberal election
prospects in Krefeld, complained that "the [Catholic] women have been mobilized for agitation in the home. The Centrum held three rallies for women
here on January 9th alone."[89]

After its motion to enfranchise businesswomen in municipal elections in
1876, however, the party did not take up the issue of female suffrage again.
Catholic women's organizations, like most of the nonsocialist German women's
movement, did not push for the vote, even in the decade before the war, when
the question of female suffrage was becoming for Catholics, as in Socialist,

[85] *MK* Nr. 48, 2 Dec. 1871: 380; 382.

[86] Windthorst to Heyl, Han., 14 [illeg.] Aug. 1880, in private hands. Thanks to Dr. Josef Hamacher of Haselünne for a copy.

[87] Mazura, *Entwicklung*, 62; ladies' night: Trzeciakowski, *Kulturkampf*, 155; Steil, *Wahlen*, 117.
Schloßmacher, *Düsseldorf*, 32, 56. In Aachen, Cronenberg (Christian Social) accused the Z's Constantia of using wives to keep their husbands' support. Lepper, ed., *Katholizismus*, 214.

[88] Antrag von Hompesch u. Gen., 29 Nov. 1905, AnlDr (1905/6, 11/II, Bd. 2) DS 43: 1608–9; the
LL motion, ibid., DS 52: 1613. Stöcker's progressive position: J.-C. Kaiser, "Politisierung" (1993),
266–69.

[89] *BT* 2. Beiblatt, Nr. 14, 9 Jan. 1912. The SPD also appealed to wives: v. Saldern, *Wege* (1984),
197; the complaints of a Herr Maxden (apparently from Central Silesia) to Bülow, n.d. (filed 8 July
1903), BAB-L R1501/14696, Bl. 22f.

liberal, and even Conservative women's circles, a political issue.[90] But while accepting the premise that ballots were to be cast by men, the Catholic milieu insisted that politics concerned everyone. Already in 1876 the *Schlesische Volkszeitung* appealed for women's help in the upcoming Prussian Landtag elections, a practice that eventually spread to Catholic newspapers everywhere. It became routine at the annual *Katholikentage* for leaders to exhort women to "weigh in with your influence in this struggle," especially with help getting out the vote: "under all circumstances Catholic women must take pains that no National Liberal is elected."[91] Before the last election, the journal for the Catholic Workingwomen's Association covered the campaign extensively, with no fewer than six articles stressing the significance of elections, analyzing the political parties, and discussing the Catholic woman's role.[92]

What *was* the role of the un-enfranchised Catholic woman? The old assumption that the franchise was a trusteeship, to be exercised on behalf of (and under the eyes of) the whole community,[93] seems to have lived on in Catholic suggestions that the household was somehow (through its husband and father) voting collectively. The degree to which a Catholic man's vote actually did reflect his household's common opinion is impossible to discover and must have varied considerably.[94] The Centrum's opponents, at any rate, were convinced that women were decisive, citing incidents such as occurred during the heated 1884 Centrum-Conservative race in the Eleventh Breslau district, when a Catholic daughter threw herself around the neck of her prominent father as he departed for the polls, and in tears pleaded with him not to vote for the Conservative candidate.[95]

Not surprisingly, therefore, one of the earliest topoi in protests charging clerical influence was that the priest, especially as confessor, enlisted women to impose upon their husbands, brothers, sons, and fathers. The clergy's "pliable auxiliary," "welcome accomplices," and "marionettes" at election time were

[90] An exception: the convert Elisabeth Gnauck-Kühne. Lucia Scherzberg, "Die katholische Frauenbewegung im Kaiserreich," in *Deutscher Katholizismus im Umbruch zur Moderne*, edited by W. Loth (Stuttgart, 1991), 143–63. Chaplain Müller suggested female suffrage in 1871. *MK* 2 Dec. 1871, Nr. 48: 382.

[91] Windthorst at the 1884 Amberg Katholikentag, quoted in Bodewig, *Wahlbeeinflussungen*, 65. Mazura, *Entwicklung*, 101; Hiery, *Reichstagswahlen*, 419.

[92] I owe this information to Douglas J. Cremer's article "The Limits of Maternalism: Gender Ideology and the South German Catholic Workingwomen's Associations," *Catholic Historical Review* 88 (2002) and his "Cross" (1993). The Z's close association with Catholic women was in sharp contrast to the Christian Socials in Austria. Boyer, *Culture*, 445.

[93] As Gash, *Politics*, 177 puts it so well; cf. also Sperber, *Radicals*, 176; F. O' Gorman, "Rituals" (1992), 79–115.

[94] The good offices of Prince Karl of Arenburg-Meppen on behalf of Windthorst in 1878 seem to have reflected the interest of the "Frau Duchess." Karl of Arenburg to [Forstinspektor R.] Clauditz, Marienbad, [July] 5 [1878], SAO Dep. 62–b, 2379. Thanks to Dr. Josef Hamacher for supplying me copies.

[95] Köller SBDR 5 Feb. 1885: 1102. Fhr. v. Buol-Berenberg's opposition to government blamed on his wife, "born a Savigny": v. Eisendecher to Bismarck, Karlsruhe, 10 Feb. 1887, BAB-L R1501/14642, 155f.

always "the weak sex," by whom otherwise upright men, in their longing for family peace, could be ruled.[96] "Two-thirds of those who vote clerical are voting on behalf of females [*Weiber*]," who were thus participants in an "indirect universal suffrage," a newspaper close to the government complained in 1874.[97] The claim would be echoed in popular literature, cartoons, and repeated by political scientists abroad.[98] Since a common justification for the exclusion of women from voting was that, as wives, their interests were already virtually represented by their husbands, the possibility that these wives might actually wish to bring their interests to bear on their husbands' choice should not have seemed subversive. But just as partisan imperatives pushed the Centrum's propagandists into exalting the political perspicuity of women, the same logic drew anticlericals into a discourse with misogynist undertones. Bochum Liberals figured Catholic women as driving "their husbands to the polling place with their rolling pins." In the government press Centrum voters were described as "henpecked wimps" (*Frauenpantoffel[n]*).[99]

If the Centrum's women were viragos, wielding rolling pins, they were also sexual manipulators, and reason enough not to allow local self-government into the Rhineland, Bismarck concluded in a conversation with Krefeld's Ludwig Friedrich Seyffardt. What the priests could not do directly, through the confessional, he said, they did indirectly, through "Mother Eve."[100] By the turn of the century, the theme that confessors were exhorting women to deny sexual favors to their husbands unless he voted for their candidate, so prominent in France in the eighties and nineties, was taken up by Germany's anticlericals. When Würzburg's *Christian Pilgrim* wrote in 1903 that "a woman can effect a lot. On election day it is important that she use the natural gifts given to her by her

---

[96] *DZJ* Nr. 38, 22 Sept. 1907; Bodewig, *Wahlbeeinflussungen*, 64f, 142; Schloßmacher, *Düsseldorf*, 206. G. Meyer, in *Wahlrecht*, 455f, cites fear of strengthening the power of the Catholic clergy as a reason to resist enfranchising women, but refers only to Italy. Connecting anticlericalism with misogyny: Blackbourn, "Progress," 143–67: 149f; idem, *Marpingen*, 288–95; McLeod, "Frömmigkeit."

[97] *Norddeutsche Allgemeine Ztg* Nr. 7, 9 Jan. 1874, quoted in Steinbach, *Zähmung* 2: 392n. 69.

[98] "Before the Election" depicts a fat priest admonishing an even fatter woman to "take care that your husband votes *kirchentreu*, Frau Niederhuber, otherwise it's all over with eternal bliss." Response (in untranslatable dialect): "Ach, that's all we need! All that money for the Peter's penny, the church window, and masses for the soul—up the chimney!" *Simplicissimus* VIII/6 (n.d., 1903–4): 46. Thus the ludicrous notion that one could lose one's soul by a vote was shown to be plausible in a religion in which materialistic superstitions were already rife. The theme of reciprocity: "Vor der Landtagswahl," in ibid., XVI 2/42 (15 Jan. 1912): 747, in which a kerchiefed woman of the people is told "Nanndl, you may now risk a mortal sin, I've just got 300 days indulgence for my ballot"; and "Zentrumspredigt," ibid., XVI 2/46 (12 Feb. 1912): 815. Foreign political scientists: Seymour/Frary, *World* 2: 28.

[99] Quotes: 5 Arns. (Bochum), AnlDR (1882/83, 5/II, Bd. 6) DS 292: 1075f; Steinbach, *Zähmung* 2: 392n. 69, respectively. Cf. also Meyer-Jena (NL) SBDR 13 Feb. 1886: 1060; and v. Mohl "Kritische Erörterungen," 571. Ks made a similar point: e.g., Graf C. v. Behr-Behrenhoff (FK) SBDR 13 Feb. 1886: 1053.

[100] Seyffardt, *Erinnerungen*, 165. The "Eve" motive could also, however, be used by a priest when an election went wrong. Stanlislaus Stephen, *Der Beuthener Prozeß im Lichte der Wahrheit* (Königshütte, 1904), quoted in Bodewig, *Wahlbeeinflussungen*, 129f.

creator for the good of the people, the state, and the church," it opened the door to hostile innuendo. The anticlerical hotspur Ernst Müller, deputy for Meiningen, drew snickers when he brought the Reichstag's attention to the clergy's instruction to women "to use their natural advantages above all at election time (great merriment from the Left, disquiet from the Centrum). You know that I have quite concrete things in mind . . . (merriment)." Had the *Christian Pilgrim*'s reference to "natural gifts" really advocated sexual extortion? *Honi soi qui mal y pense.* Quite unlike France, this charge in Germany was never, so far as I can tell, made explicitly, even by Müller-Meiningen. Anticlericals were forced to grasp at other straws—such as the report that Pastor Böhmer had suggested at a Centrum rally in December 1906 that wives should not *feed* their husbands until they had dispensed their voting obligations—a peculiarly German understanding, perhaps, of conjugal duties.[101]

When female employees in Aachen during the elections of 1907 expressed their horror to their bosses over the possibility that their district might return a Protestant or a Liberal, the outrage of the Centrum's opponents knew no bounds. Here was clear evidence of the nefarious influence of the clergy! For how else could these women have arrived at such a silly opinion?[102] Like earlier associations between the power of the priest and the dumbness of the people, the alleged weakness of the female sex was itself proof that clerical machinations had corrupted the voters' choice—and that the proper structure of authority (in the family, in the workplace) had been subverted. The improbability that the importunities of employees (and female employees at that) would affect the votes of their bosses—black magic indeed!—suggests the real offense in Aachen was that these women had expressed political opinions at all.

In 1903, *Monika*, a magazine for Catholic women, featured an article on the Reichstag elections that suggests that Catholics themselves saw the principal site of women's political activity neither in the bed, nor in the kitchen, much less on the shop floor—but on their knees.

> "'What business of ours are these elections?' *Monika* readers will ask.—'We women aren't concerned with politics!' There is a manner of participating in politics, however, that even the most modest, simple woman can, yes even should, practice—and it is this: pray for our Centrum! . . .
>
> Enemies who otherwise hate each other have united in order to take as many Reichstag seats from the Centrum as possible, and unfortunately it is to be feared that if God does not help us, the enemy will win in all too many places.
>
> Therefore Catholic women, on to prayer! We will show the world that trust in God and piety still exist even in the century of Enlightenment. If every dear reader hears *one* holy mass for the victory of the Centrum, then that will be an incalculable num-

---

[101] Bodewig, *Wahlbeeinflussungen*, 64f, 147 (quotes); see also 53, 59f, 88, 142, 147. Bruno Paul's cartoon "Das Brotkörbchen" depicted a female speaker suggesting a similar political tactic to a meeting of feminists. *Simplicissimus* II/35, 1887: 272. France: Weber, *Peasants*, 365n; Charnay, "L'église," 289, 294.

[102] Bodewig, *Wahlbeeinflussungen*, 142.

ber! And in each of these holy masses, Christ sacrifices himself through the hands of the priest to the heavenly father also for the victory of His Church. . . . Let us add, if we want to be zealous, a daily rosary to it, and through his much-loved Son and his most blessed Mother, God will help us to victory!"

A Liberal read the *Monika* article aloud in the Bavarian diet, commenting (to jeers of approval) that it was "so beautiful that only a pastor could have written it," and expressing pity for anyone whose face did not blush in shame at this "completely despicable abuse" of religion. The justice of this condemnation has been accepted as obvious by a modern historian, who considered these pieces bordering on blasphemy. The same might be said of Matthias Erzberger's six commandments for the Reichstag election, published in 1912 in the illustrated monthly, *The Christian Maiden* (*Jungfrau*), in which he assured his readers that "taking the sacrament on January 12 and praying for a good election will give our Catholic maidens a pretty strong influence on the overall result of the election."[103]

But the question of blasphemy puts another light on the question of clerical influence. Who was being "influenced" by the readers of *Monika* and the *Christian Maiden*, the electorate or the Almighty? Unlike the denial of the sacraments by a priest or the withdrawal of sexual favors by his feminine instruments, both of which anticlericals would have liked to have been able to demonstrate but almost never could, the force of women's prayers—unless of course one believed that elections were amenable to divine intervention—lacked the necessary coercive element. By their very fury over propaganda such as *Monika*'s, the anticlericals testified to a reading of the issues that confirmed the very anxieties that found expression in the Centrum vote. The Catholic *religious* community could cease to see the Centrum as a necessary resource only when the prayers of Catholics ceased to be of concern to German legislative bodies. As in so much of the debate over clerical politicking, the term "influence," like the more modern term "mobilization," elided the crucial distinction between pressure and persuasion.

From the beginning the Centrum had claimed that it was not a "confessional" party, emphasizing that it would welcome Protestants as well as Catholics into its ranks and insisting on the rights of all three of Germany's religious communities. But the very features about Centrum culture that domesticated high politics for the Catholic voter—the language of its appeals, the forms taken by its propaganda, the presence of those black-clad figures on every podium—all but guaranteed that Protestants and Jews would stay away. What could non-Catholics possibly make of the Nördlingen election announcement that described the Centrum's candidate, a priest, as "the Lord's anointed, God's representative on earth, Dr. Weißenhagen"? Corporate communion was celebrated for the Cen-

---

[103] "Die Reichstagswahlen," *Monika*, Nr. 21, 23 May 1903: 251; Graf (the modern historian), *Beeinflussungsversuche*, 214–16. Quote excerpted in Bodewig, *Wahlbeeinflussungen*, 65. Erzberger article as well as a similar *Monika* article, quoted in Bertram, *Wahlen*, 194f.

trum's Landtag delegation in Berlin every Saturday. Centrum rallies were listed in local Catholic newspapers under "church announcements," right after the four Sunday masses. A church schedule for June 16, 1903, proclaimed: "6:30 Confession, 7:00 Procession, High Mass, and Sacred Heart Meditation. From 10 to 19:00 Reichstag election."[104] When Bishop Ketteler resigned his seat in 1872, entrusting it to a Protestant lawyer by the name of Schulz, was it an accident that the bishop's *Mainzer Journal* left its readers with the impression that Ludwig Schulz was a Catholic? Two could play this game of denominational deception, of course, but rarely with equal success. In 1887, when Leo XIII's election intervention was making headlines, the Free Conservatives in Lingen attempted to cut into the support of the Centrum's incumbent and Leo's most prominent counterweight, Ludwig Windthorst, by posting huge signs at the railroad works, the town's largest employer, mendaciously describing their own man as also a Catholic, who had been warmly recommended by the Holy Father. "The sudden conversion of *Obergerichtsrat* Hänschen will certainly be a joy to W[indthorst]," a local Centrum pol remarked wryly. "Hänschen probably doesn't even know himself yet that he has converted in Lingen." The writer then suggested that the Centrum could wreak havoc with their opponent's Protestant base by seeing that the blessed event got the broad publicity it deserved.[105]

Religious and political language were regularly confounded. A list of cautionary instructions published in Baden about how to avoid the "brutal election influence" of government officials was entitled "Ten Commandments for Voters." The *Prayer and Instruction Book for the Catholic Men's World*, written by a pastor and published with the archdiocesan imprimatur, included a chapter entitled "How do you vote?"—leading detractors to dub it the "Election Prayer Book." Various election or worker "catechisms" might ask the question, "For whom should the worker give his vote at elections?" followed by the predictable answer.[106] For opponents, such "catechisms" were clear evidence that the Catholic clergy and its party "mixed religion and politics," which they certainly did; and proved their charge that the Catholic voter was not free, which is far less certain.

Particular indignation was caused by an article entitled "The Ballot" that appeared in the *Seraphischer Kinderfreund* (loosely, the *Guardian Angel*), a periodical for Catholic children. The article included the following admonition:

---

[104] *MK* Nr. 3, 21 Jan. 1871: 24; Quotes: Bodewig, *Wahlbeeinflussungen*, 144; Hahne, "Reichstagswahl," 126.

[105] Hlarer [? illeg.], Z Vertrauensmann, to Forstmeister [R.] Clauditz, L[ingen], 21 Feb. 1887, SAO Dep. 62b, 2379. Dr. Josef Hamacher, who kindly supplied me with this document, suggests that "Henschen," not "Hänschen," was the person meant. Similar trick by SDs in Mülheim, 1890: Müller, *Strömungen*, 287. The more normal pattern, used successfully by FKs in 5 Wiesbaden, 1884, was to allege the conversion of a liberal opponent, or the promised conversion of his children, to convict him of a dirty deal with Windthorst in exchange for Catholic votes. SBDR 9 Apr. 1886: 2005, 2007, 2008. Also: Erzberger, *Bilder*, 38f.

[106] Schofer, *Erinnerungen*, 16; Bodewig, *Wahlbeeinflussungen*, 82, 92f; Bertram, *Wahlen*, 195.

The ballot counts for just as much as you do. . . . It has rested on your breast, your eye has watched it and, to make a long matter short, it is a part of your sense of self, of your personality. Not your ballot, but you yourself, in a spiritual sense, will lie there in the election urn. Without you, the election is not complete; without you, something will be lacking in the respective furnishings of the state, the community, in the Church. Things cannot improve completely if you do not cast your vote. Oh, much, much depends upon your ballot! . . .

Thus far, the article reads like a lesson in good citizenship; a sentimental, somewhat exalted, but sensitive effort to convince the child and future voter that it is his ballot that will one day connect him personally to the political world—defined as state, community, and (!) church—and even give him some power over it: precisely what any effort to socialize children into the practice of democracy must do. But then the civics lesson is given its peculiarly Catholic dimension.

On your ballot stands the Christian name of your candidate, the name of a saint, of a holy patron. Do you think it is a matter of indifference to the saint and to our Lord God whether or not you vote? Do you think that your ballot is too petty for God the Almighty to concern himself with? The Lord God, who does not shrink from counting the hairs on your head . . . will also not grudge the effort of counting ballots, and one day He will demand of you, "Give me an accounting of your stewardship."

The liberal writer who reprinted this article, with its allusion to Christ's parable of the talents, intended to demonstrate that the machinations of the Catholic clergy did not stop even at the nursery door. "No name, no party is mentioned," he concedes in a footnote, "but still the party politics is so clear." The failure to mention the Centrum may have been a disingenuous omission, a sign of willing the effects of religious partisanship without appearing to will its cause. But it also reveals that party identity, for Catholics, was taken for granted. Only the magnitude of the voting decision needed working. Into the sacred and communal rituals that mediated the Catholic's relationship to the larger world, voting had now been incorporated as a major, indeed defining element. Voting was not just a civic, or even a moral, but a religious act. Such was "ballot Catholicism," as Centrum opponents derisively labeled Catholic political culture.[107] Ultimately the voter was encouraged to identify, not with a candidate—a mere mortal, who might change from one election to another—but with the *ballot* itself, an outward and visible sign both of his membership in a community, and of his share of power over the political process.

AFTER 1900: THE SPECTRE OF CLERICAL INFLUENCE RETURNS

During the Kulturkampf, and even in the decade after agreements between Berlin and Rome marked its formal conclusion in 1887, public opinion seems to

---

[107] Graf, *Beeinflussungsversuche*, 166. Quotes: Bodewig, *Wahlbeeinflussungen*, 12, 64.

have accepted, however unhappily, Centrum victories as indeed representative of "the real demand of the Catholic people." After 1874 serious challenges aimed at overturning Centrum victories all but dried up, and legal scholars ceased to include "clerical influence" in their discussions of the threats to free elections.[108] The SPD's report to its constituents in 1893 did remind them that if a clergyman campaigned during the "so-called divine service," they could cite that fact in their protest; but unlike the other forms of illegal influence the report covered, no examples from recent elections were described. In 1898, when the Reichstag's Election Commission took stock of the most frequent complaints against elections, clerical influence was conspicuous by its absence from the committee's list.[109]

And then, at the turn of the century, simmering indignation at Catholic clergy's political role suddenly boiled over again, and the issue acquired a salience in public discussion that rivaled that of the early 1870s. Some states ordered local officials to document the public utterance of every pastor under their jurisdiction during state and national elections.[110] Constitutional scholars reopened the question of the clergy's political equality: whether its members should have the right to give speeches, to hold elective office, even to vote.[111] A high-ranking Liberal judge claimed to have culled forty-nine solid cases of recent election influence by Catholic priests, although a "far greater number" had been mentioned in the press and parliamentary literature.[112] The Reichstag's dismissal of most of the complaints in 1903 (the Centrum's voting bloc of 100-plus deputies providing a powerful barrier against nullification) only stimulated the public outcry.[113] During the raucous "Hottentot" elections of 1907, the gov-

---

[108] E.g., silent: K. M., "Schutz" (1885), 157–59. Between 1874 and 1882 only two challenges to Z victories (2 Lower Bavaria in 1874, Bochum in 1881) included charges of clerical influence—and they were unsuccessful. Occasional charges lodged later were halfhearted and hardly taken seriously by RT committees. 10 Posen, AnlDR (1884/85, 6/I, Bd. 5) DS 44: 145; 2 Kassell, SBDR 5 Feb. 1885: 684; Köller (on 11 Breslau), 5 Feb. 1885: 1102. The 1890 election, which was followed by the largest number of challenges, proportionally, thus far, produced *no* protests against Z victories from the regions that had dominated complaints in the seventies—Upper Silesia and Upper Bavaria—nor any from AL. A short debate in the RT in 1892 concluded that clerical influence was immaterial. SBDR 18 Mar. 1892: 4841f. Although an investigation of the practice of state parliaments would exceed the scope of this study, in 1875 the Prussian LT did overturn three Z victories for clerical influence. Rösch, "Kulturkampf," 110–22; Virnich, *Fraction*, 18, 37f.

[109] Reprinted in *Reichstags-Wahlgesetz*, 77–86. SPD: *Thätigkeit*, 155f.

[110] The Baden government initiated a "razzia" against its 1,300 clergy; in the Rhineland, the governor undertook a county-by-county, rectory-by-rectory, surveillance during the 1907 campaign. Horn Report, LHAK 403/8806; Schofer, *Erinnerungen*, 90. Everling (NL) SBDR 6 May 1908: 5194.

[111] At the end of the century Meyer had surveyed the practice in various countries of excluding officials, including clergy, from elective office. His silence on Germany suggests that little had been heard of the issue before his death in February 1900. Meyer, *Wahlrecht*, 487f.

[112] v. Campe, "Wahlbeeinflussung," 6. Campe was also, however, a member of the central committee of the Protestant League and a RT deputy. Smith, *Nationalism*, 136.

[113] The RT considered the following charges irrelevant (all citations are from AnlDR unless SBDR is listed): distributing ballots: 1 Bromberg (1899, 10/I, Bd. 2) DS 212: 1591; 10 AL (1905/6, 11/II, Bd. 6) DS 483: 4733–42, esp. 4739; 3 Allenstein (1912/14, 13/I, Bd. 20) DS 1061: 1972; 4

ernment mobilized this indignation on its own behalf, and postelection challenges kept the issue alive.[114] At the state and local level, parliaments, prosecutors, and local officials proved more willing to crack down on Catholic priests. In Baden and Württemberg, efforts were made to interpret the existing laws against government election influence to include influence by the clergy.[115]

The Protestant League (Evangelischer Bund), which had been launched in 1886, as the government was abandoning the Kulturkampf, in order to continue the culture wars at the guerrilla level of public opinion, now took a new lease on life. Companion organizations bubbled up as well: the Gustavus Adolphus Association; the Pan-German "Los-von-Rom" movement; the Anti-Ultramontane Election Coalition; the Anti-Ultramontane Imperial Federation; the Giordano Bruno Bund (of Ernst Haeckel's Monist Society); the Goethe Bund of the Free Thinkers (with its journal *Free Speech*); and the Academic Bismarck Bund, a student organization (with its paper, *Trusty Eckard*). Among disaffected Catholic intellectuals, the Kraus Society with its weekly, *The Twentieth Century: The Organ of German Modernists*, edited by a former priest and secretly subsidized by Bavarian court circles, beat the same drum.[116]

More telling than either the rash of election challenges or the new anti-"ultramontane" ginger groups were the demands—three decades after the Pulpit Paragraph, the expulsion of the Jesuits, and the Ecclesiastical Penalties Law—for new penal legislation.[117] After the 1907 national elections, in which the

---

Oppeln (1912/13, 13/I, Bd. 19) DS 798: 1096; collecting signatures: 6 Trier (1903/4, 11/I, Bd. 3) DS 411: 2400; speaking at rallies: 10 AL (1905/6, 11/II, Bd. 6) DS 483: 4737. It considered the following relevant: ringing church bells before the polls opened: 10 AL: SBDR 16 Nov. 1906: 3593ff; 2 Arns.: SBDR, 26 Feb. 1908: 3421ff; 8 AL: SBDR 6 May 1908: 5179 ff; 6 Posen: SBDR, 21 May 1912: 2217 ff; 2 Trier (1912/13, 13/I, Bd. 17) DS 379: 322; collecting voters in sacristy: 3 Oppeln (1912/14, 13/I, Bd. 22) DS 1436: 2954–65; threatening denial of absolution: 4 Oppeln, AnlDR (1903/04, 11/I, Bd. 2) DS 228: 989.

[114] E.g., from AnlDR: 15 AL (1907/09, 12/I, Bd. 19) DS 638: 4314; 2 Arns. (1907/09, 12/I, Bd. 19) DS 636: 4303–9; Munich (1 Oberb.) (1907/09, 12/I, Bd. 20) DS 737: 4633–36; 4 Oppeln (1912/13, 13/I, Bd. 19) DS 798: 1094, 1096–98.

[115] An Alsatian Bezirkstag, upheld by a court in Colmar, applied RT decisions invalidating elections for *Beamten* influence to the clergy in 1906; the Württ. LT in 1908 established guidelines for similar invalidations. Schofer, *Erinnerungen*, 90; Leser, *Untersuchungen*, 91n. 2; Mayer, "Bekämpfung," 22; cited approvingly by Müller-Meiningen SBDR 21 May 1912: 2218f; Bodewig, *Wahlbeeinflussungen*, 72, 94–99, 116f. Bodewig's work, which recounts proven and *dis*proven charges with equal diligence (87f), is itself an example of the contemporary hysteria.

[116] Internal evidence suggests that most of the contributors, and therefore perhaps most of the Kraus Society's membership, were disaffected South German priests. A more clearly right-wing Catholic group, with a similar goal, was the *Deutsche Vereinigung*, founded in 1907–8. Horst Gründer, "Rechtskatholizismus im Kaiserreich und in der Weimarer Republik," *Westfälische Zeitschrift* 134 (1984): 107–55; N. Schloßmacher, "Antiultramontanismus" (1991), 167–71; Möckl, *Prinzregentenzeit*, 118f, 512, 538.

[117] E.g., Cohn, "Schutz," 581; v. Campe, "Wahlbeeinflussung," 6–10; 36–38; Mayer, "Bekämpfung," 22f; *BT* 2 Mar. 1913, BAB-L R1501/14653. In the RT the Left submitted a motion to extend §339 of the imperial penal code, which ordered prison terms of up to 5 years for the abuse of official power to influence elections, to the clergy, reopening the definitional questions of the 1870s. SBDR 16 Nov. 1906: 3696 B; the Württemberg LT discussed a similar motion on 15 June

Centrum did very well despite scurrilous government attacks, Bethmann Hollweg, then Prussia's Minister of the Interior, raised the possibility with Chancellor Bernhard von Bülow of inserting a paragraph in the Prussian Penal Code to
criminalize the use of religious threats or penalties in elections.[118] Tougher in-
carnations of the Imperial Pulpit Paragraph were proposed in individual states.
Although civil servants, such as Landräte or mayors, could run in the district in
which they officiated, Baden and Württemberg had already denied that right to
members of the clergy.[119] In Bavaria the Conservative Count Ernst von Moy,
scion of a distinguished Catholic family, resurrected in 1904 a thirty-year-old
Progressive motion to disenfranchise the clergy (of all denominations) altogether. Here, as in most other questions, German discourse was full of legitimating precedents from other "civilized countries." Moy himself claimed to
find them in Spain, Italy, Belgium, Luxembourg, Switzerland, Great Britain,
and unspecified parts of the United States. In fact no other state had disenfranchised the clergy, although they had excluded some types of clergy from
holding parliamentary office.[120]

The intense new public scrutiny, government surveillance, and prosecutions
turned up some delicious scandals, the messiest of which was the 1903 campaign in industrial Kattowitz (Kattowice)-Zabrze, where candidates from two
Catholic parties competed for the same electorate, neither shrinking from religious appeals. When the young Polish National Democrat Albert (Wojciech)
Korfanty, a former miner and now editor of a National Democratic paper, defeated the longtime Centrum incumbent, his supporters had masses sung in
celebration—not in Kattowitz-Zabrze, to be sure, but a few miles across the
Austrian border in Cracow. But it was revelations about the pro-Centrum clergy
that raised the most eyebrows. Before the election the very "governmental"
Prince-Bishop of Breslau, Cardinal Georg Kopp, had admonished his diocesans
that "your priests would have the right and the obligation to deny . . . the
blessings and graces of the Church" to anyone who allowed National Democratic publications into their home.[121] Centrum clergy had referred to Albert
Korfanty and his party as "snot-nosed brats"—and worse. After the National

---

1907. Other imperial laws that were proposed to extend to the clergy were §§106, 107, 167, and
253. Bodewig, *Wahlbeeinflussungen*, 48, 95, 100.

[118] BH to Bülow, 9 Mar. 1907, BAB-L R1501/14645, Bl. 51.

[119] Lachner, *Grundzüge*, 48f; Bodewig, *Wahlbeeinflussungen*, 149; Elble, *Kanzelparagraph*, 40f,
43, 62.

[120] Ernst Graf v. Moy, *Das Wahlrecht der Geistlichen* (Munich, 1905); Franz Heiner, "Ausschluß
der Geistlichen von den politischen Wahlen (Antrag des Grafen von Moy in der I. bayerischen
Kammer)," *Archiv für katholisches Kirchenrecht* 48 (3. Folge, 8. Bd) (1904): 107–17; *DZJ* 23 Jan.
1904, Nr. 4, and 12 Feb. 1905, Nr. 7; Friedrich, *Wahlrecht*. Cf. Thöny's cartoon, "An Opponent of
the Lex Moy," *Beiblatt des Simplicissimus* VIII/45 (2 Feb. 1904), n.p. Baden: Schofer, *Erinnerungen*, 89f.

[121] Quoted in Schwidetzky, *Wahlbewegung*, 62. On the failure of the Silesian Z to do justice to
Polish demands for representation: A. H. Leugers-Scherzberg, *Porsch* (1990), esp. 76–80, 120f,
128; the breakup of the Catholic camp in Silesian LT elections: Kühne, *Dreiklassenwahlrecht*, 298f,
303 and 303n. 56.

Democrat's victory, one furious pastor had allegedly exploded from his pulpit: "I curse the entire Polish Catholic people in Upper Silesia." Others had punished their parishioners by going on strike: refusing to preach, to celebrate High Mass, or to hold religion classes for children whose fathers had supported the National Democrats. The most spectacular of these religious penalties was the Centrum clergy's refusal to marry the twenty-eight-year-old Korfanty. In what became an international *cause célèbre*, involving testimonials of theology professors and the intervention of the Vatican, the future vice president of the Polish Republic was finally allowed a church wedding—but in Cracow, not in Germany. Korfanty's paper wasted no time retailing these stories, and Cardinal Kopp responded with a class action libel suit on behalf of his Silesian clergy. But the revelations about clerical political intervention that emerged in the course of the trial proved to be even more damaging to Breslau's prince-bishop than those in Korfanty's newspapers. As tension mounted, Kopp suddenly sent a telegram offering to withdraw his suit—and to pay court costs. The *Schadenfreude* of the Centrum's opponents knew no bounds. Who could doubt the cardinal's fear that a continuation of the trial would have uncovered even worse scandals?[122]

Upper Silesia may well have been, as Centrum spokesmen were quick to insist, "a world unto itself," not typical of the rest of Catholic Germany. The overwhelming number of charges against the clergy elsewhere were for activities that had been grudgingly tolerated for years. Even the worst offenses (like the case of the dim-witted Pastor Gaisert of Gündelwangen who, panic-stricken in the face of a postelection investigation, tried to get a parishioner to perjure himself on his behalf) resulted more from embarrassed cover-ups of obvious Centrum campaigning than from violations of the voter's freedom.[123]

What then is the explanation for the renewed uproar over the Catholic clergy? Four clear trends are discernible: anxieties provoked by a new round of democratization; the successful integration of Alsace-Lorraine into the Reich; the fraying of Catholic solidarity as secular issues—economic but especially "national" issues—became more prominent; and the unprecedented power wielded by the Centrum's Reichstag delegation.

1. The new campaign against "clerical influence" was connected, as was the original outburst in 1871, with **anxieties about democratization**—as the striking overlap between those regions where the clergy's campaigning stirred the greatest controversy and those states that had reformed their election laws after the turn of the century makes clear. Beginning in Baden in 1904, followed by Württemberg in 1905, and culminating in Bavaria in 1906, constitutional changes were transforming the political systems in these southern states. Until now, although their franchises had been almost as inclusive as the Reichstag's,

---

[122] Bachem, *Vorgeschichte* 6: 189–91; Bodewig, *Wahlbeeinflussungen*, 54, 127–32 (quotes); *DA* 22/15 (10 Apr. 1904): 233f.

[123] Hatschek, *Kommentar*, 204–6, lists many examples of dismissed charges. In 1912 the WPK on 6 Posen tied, 7–7. AnlDR (1912/13, 13/I, vol. 17) DS 491: 541–49; SBDR 21 May 1912: 2217–21. Bodewig, *Wahlbeeinflussungen*, 75–84; quote: 133.

indirect balloting and gerrymandering had privileged liberal and governmental parties. Now all three southern states enjoyed direct manhood suffrage; Bavaria and Württemberg also redistricted, and the former introduced the Australian ballot, the latter, proportional representation.[124] Unlike the national democratic watershed of 1867–71, however, this new democratic breakthrough in the south was not a gift from above, but the fruit of a decade of agitation, in which for much of the time (Württemberg after 1897 is the exception), the lower clergy had played a vociferous role. The reforms' most immediate impact was on participation. Once voter choices were no longer muffled by indirect two-tier balloting and gerrymandered districts, turnout in state elections soared.[125] Given party systems that were already structured around religio-cultural conflicts, a sharpening of religious rhetoric on all sides was an almost inevitable by-product of the mobilization process. And although it is not clear whether it was the electoral reforms themselves, or the mobilization that preceded and followed them, that increased the Centrum's representation in these state parliaments, the liberal-governmental connubium that had long ruled the south was clearly threatened.[126] Liberals feared, as *Simplicissimus*'s cartoons made clear, that once the "people" were in the saddle, the Centrum was going to ride. Baden politicians pointed the way for Bülow's "Bloc" of 1907 when, beginning in 1905, all the parties from National Liberals *through* the SPD, and with the government's tacit blessing, immediately formed an anti-Centrum *Sammlung*: the "Grand Alliance" (*Großblock*). Then they proceeded to annul Centrum victories.[127]

It was within the context of this second round of democratization that renewed clero-phobia must be seen. Count Moy submitted his bill to disenfranchise the clergy at a time when even the Bavarian government was offering proposals for franchise reform. Few observers believed that the Count, an intellectual lightweight, had dreamed up this exceptional legislation on his own. Since the Centrum had enough seats to prevent its passage, the significance of his bill lay not in what it could practically accomplish, but in the spotlight it turned on the Catholic clergy's massive presence in elected bodies—roughly 20

---

[124] K. H. Pohl, *Arbeiterbewegung* (1992), 465–509, esp. 467–72. Bavarian towns, where liberals found their strongest support, continued to be protected by reserving 28 seats for them. Seymour/ Frary, *World* 2: 32; Huber, *Verfassungsgeschichte* 4: 395f, 411–18; Schofer, *Erinnerungen*, 60, 62– 66, 82, 84f.

[125] In Bavaria it was climbing in any case: from 39.5 in 1899 to 51.1 in 1905. Now it shot up from 51.1 to 72.9—an increase of more than 70%. My calculations, extrapolating from Ritter/ Niehuss, *Arbeitsbuch*, 157. The SPD got only 15.3% of the vote in 1899, the Z, 48.2%. Over the next decade, the SPD's share rose, the Z's fell, ending at 19.5% and 40.9%, respectively. Ibid., 160. Möckl, *Prinzregentenzeit*, 486–90, 497–500, 502f, 508.

[126] Results varied. In Württemberg, Z, SPD, and K/BB benefited, NLs and VP lost; in Baden the SPD gained much, the Z, some; in Bavaria, the Z actually lost relative to the last pre-reform (but post-mobilization) election. The Bavarian changes benefited the Z's Right wing. Möckl, *Prinzregentenzeit*, 509–12, 516–19, 541n. 257; Blackbourn, *Class*, 122–25, 130n. 46.

[127] Ernst Lehmann, "Die badischen Landtagswahlen," *Die Hilfe* 15/38 (19 Sept. 1909): 595f; Schofer, *Erinnerungen*, 88–90; Carl H. E. Zangerl, "Opening" (1974), and idem, "Courting," 223– 26; Blackbourn, *Class*, 168. Cartoon (among many): "Die Württembergischen Wahlen," *Simplicissimus* XI 2/41 (7 Jan. 1907): 654.

percent of the Centrum's deputies to the Bavarian and Imperial parliaments.[128] In the early seventies Sybel had predicted, "The more democratic the spirit of the age, the more powerful will be the [clerical] party that disposes of one and a half million voters with military efficiency." Thirty years later liberal nationalists like Friedrich Naumann were still wary of priestly power "in a democratic age."[129] Like the Austrian legislators who tried to attach riders criminalizing clerical abuses to the Reichsrat's franchise reform in 1906, Moy's backers—the government and (some hinted) even some Catholic bishops—were preparing for the democratization they now saw as unstoppable with a shot across the bow to the Centrum clergy, whom they blamed for bringing it about.[130] Not surprisingly, in early 1907, when the Centrum's clergy and party were again under massive attack, the Centrum responded by resurrecting its bill to replace Prussia's three-class voting system with the Reichstag franchise.[131]

2. In **Alsace-Lorraine**, not franchise changes, but another process related to democratization was taking place: **integration and mobilization**. Although the most Catholic *Land* in Germany, turnouts there had remained far behind that of German coreligionists—except during the exceptional "plebiscites for France" in 1874 and 1887 (the latter fueled by rumors that General Georges Boulanger was about to reclaim the lost provinces). During these first decades, religious fault lines had been rendered invisible by an alliance between clericals resisting the German Kulturkampf and "Gambettist" notables protesting the annexation. Indeed the nomination of the Bishop of Metz for a Lorraine candidacy had been spearheaded by a Republican and a Jew, the Metz banker Edouard Gordchauz. In the 1890s, however, Alsatians who had been born in the empire, and were now undemonstratively identifying with it, became increasingly open to the kind of systematic organizing their fathers had ignored.[132] At the same time, the Alsatian press continued to report extensively on French events—at a time when the Dreyfus Affair, the face-off between Church and Republic, and the ultimate victory of the Left dominated the news. The anticlerical crusade with which the French Left celebrated its triumph in the Dreyfus Affair, culminating after the turn of the century in the suppression of Catholic schools and the

---

[128] Rosenbaum, *Beruf*, 23, 29, 33, 62f. Von Lachner conceded that such a "limitation of rights, cutting so deeply into the political principles of a democratic people" required more justification than in Moy's bill. *Grundzüge*, 39, 49f, 54.

[129] Sybel, "Politik," 452; Naumann, "Das Zentrum," 114f.

[130] One supporter of the measure, probably himself a priest, thought that the bishops would welcome the freer hand the Moy bill would give them, "once the clerical Herr Deputies, who have so often exercised downright terrorism over many an Ordinariat, have disappeared from the picture." "Das Wahlrecht der Geistlichen" *DZJ* 5/7 (1905): 70–72; Pastor Tremel, "Wahlrecht der Geistlichen-Gedanken zum Antrag Moy," *Augsburger Abendzeitung* Nrs. 46, 47, 48 (15, 16, 17 Feb. 1904).

[131] The F's similar bill included redistricting—assumed to be dangerous to the Z's rural constituencies. Loth, *Katholiken*, 124f; Kühne, *Dreiklassenwahlrecht*, 495f.

[132] Low turnouts: E. Manteuffel to King, 3 Nov. 1884, 5 Mar. 1887, GStA PK I. HA, Rep. 89/211, Bl. 33; 75–81v. Hiery, *Reichstagswahlen*, 146 (Dupont's candidacy), 235, 269, 282, 284, 306f, 311, 317–19, 320, 324, 334, 419–21, 432f; turnouts: 160f, 247 (table), 321.

expulsion of religious orders, both encouraged the further integration of Alsace-Lorraine into the empire and overshadowed—as the Kulturkampf had for *German* Catholics in the seventies—the accompanying mobilization. Once again Liberalism (and its allies, Socialists, Protestants, and Jews) and Catholicism squared off, as each convicted the other of sins committed on the other side of the Franco-German border. Both the Centrum and the liberals (until 1903; and then the Social Democrats) were the beneficiaries, civility the loser, in this process. Especially in Colmar, Hagenau-Weißenburg, Saargemünd, and the Strasbourg countryside, the Centrum became increasingly conspicuous, vociferous—and obnoxious.[133] In some towns and villages, rallies degenerated into fights. Antisemitic slurs were hurled at the liberal anticlerical candidate Daniel Blumenthal, and stones at the windows of Jewish shopkeepers. Young clerical hotspurs were held responsible (often justifiably) for these outbursts—and for the Centrum's election victories. By 1903, turnouts in the region were reaching unprecedented (and never repeated) heights. One Alsatian district, with 93.2 percent participation, set the existing record for the Reich. Attempts to throw out Centrum mandates because of the "influence" of the clergy reached a climax that same year.[134]

3. The re-problematizing of clerical election influence occurred also because **Catholic solidarity was fraying at the edges**. As the Kulturkampf faded into memory, the politics of "Catholic Germany" was no longer so obviously coterminous with the religious culture of Germany's Catholics. As early as 1887, the Centrum had begun to lose some supporters, especially among the Rhenish nobility, when for the first time the party fought an election entirely on a secular issue—opposition to Bismarck's Septennat. For the press, Pope Leo XIII's implicit repudiation of the Centrum when intervening on behalf of Bismarck's military bill was a "man bites dog" story if there ever was one, and certainly the most spectacular example of *attempted* clerical influence in Germany's history. But since the injured party—the Centrum—was the very one most interested in keeping the issue of clerical influence quiet, the papal intervention produced no postelection complaints that might have kept the issue alive. Nevertheless, the 1887 election exposed the vulnerability at the heart of political Catholicism: the more important the purely political agenda of the Catholic deputies became, the greater the arena of potential disagreement among those who made up their constituents. And the greater the area of disagreement, the more the party instrumentalized its clergy, in order to enforce or at least project

---

[133] Hiery, *Reichstagswahlen*, 283, 302, 318f, 321, 323, 325f, 328, 330, 433; earlier antisemitic rhetoric: 216; Sperber, *Voters*, 128.

[134] 10 AL in 1903 (26 charges of abuse of the pulpit and 29 of the confessional): AnlDR (1905/06, 11/II, Bd. 4) DS 483: 4733–42; SBDR 16 Nov. 1906: 3691–3726; 10 AL and 15 AL in 1907: AnlDR (1907/09, 12/I, Bd. 29) DS 638: 4314. On antisemitism in the Z and its constituency: Blackbourn, "Catholics, the Centre Party and Anti-Semitism," in idem, *Populists and Patricians. Essays in Modern Germany History* (London, 1987), 168–87; H. W. Smith, "Alltag" (1993), 280–304, idem, "Religion" (1994), 283–314; idem, "Discourse" (1994), 315–28; O. Blaschke, "Herrschaft" (1991).

the message of Catholic unity. Not surprisingly, then, the clergy became the targets of *intra*-Catholic disagreements. In the late eighties and early nineties, disgruntled Catholic aristocrats had sniped at priests for aiding the triumph of a hated new "democracy" (read: middle-class leadership) in the Centrum.[135] Populist insurgents too—workers in the seventies, artisans in the eighties, farmers in the nineties—included the clergy prominently among their opponents.[136] Lumped now with the Left, now with the Right, when solidarity was breaking down, the clergy could be all things to all men.

When discontent with the Centrum's policies grew out of material interests, disagreement could (although with difficulty) be contained. And when conflicts arose over the relative weight of different interest groups within the party, the weight of community had helped to muffle criticism—and to isolate the critics.[137] But "national" issues, which put the definition of community itself into question, were more corrosive. When the Wilhelmine government, to the cheers numerous noisy pressure groups, began loudly to push imperialism abroad and more intensive "German" goals at home, nationality and nationalism took on a salience greater than at any time since 1866–74. Suddenly the pressures for conformity within quite disparate real Catholic communities opened up fissures within the imagined Catholic community—the "Catholic Germany" that imagined itself anew every time it went to the polls.[138] And because the clergy now became active on both sides of the process—of reimagining the "old" Catholic community and of imagining it in new, more "national" ways—outsiders got an earful.

The imperfect fit between the "Catholic Germany" of Centrum discourse and the real-existing Catholic communities in the empire was most obvious on the nationality frontiers. If the integration of Alsace-Lorraine into the nation was increasing the salience of clerical influence in the west, the disintegration of political Catholicism into its ethnic components was raising the issue in the east—as we have seen in the case of the Korfanty election of 1903. The Centrum's refusal to comply with the Polish Central Election Committee's demand in 1904 to cease contesting any seats in eastern Pomerania, West Prussia, Pos-

---

[135] E.g., Fürst Karl Isenburg-Birstein, *Ist die heutige Zentrumsfraktion des deutschen Reichstags noch die wirkliche Vertreterin des katholischen Volkes*? (n.p., 1893), 3.

[136] *Politisches A-B-C Büchlein. Ein nützliches Lesen für den bayerischen Bürger und Bauersmann. Von einem Centrumsmann* (Augsburg, 1898), a collection of election flyers, suggests the salience of anticlericalism among Catholic farmers by many of its headings: "What's the position of the leaders of the Peasant League on priests?" "Does the clergy seek its own advantage?" "The [salary] amelioration of the clergy from 1894 and 1898?" Also Ian Farr, "From Anti-Catholicism to Anticlericalism: Catholic Politics and the Peasantry in Bavaria, 1860–1900," *European Studies Review* 13 (1983): 249–69; Möllers, *Strömungen*, 300; Bachem, *Vorgeschichte* 5: 278; Müller, "Zentrumspartei," 850.

[137] Although it became more difficult as time went on. Loth, *Katholiken*.

[138] Blanke, *Poland*; G. Eley, *Reshaping* (1980); Smith, *Nationalism*, 144–46, 185–205. Discord in the Z: R. J. Ross, *Tower* (1976); M. L. Anderson, "Inter-denominationalism, Clericalism, Pluralism: The *Zentrumsstreit* and the Dilemma of Catholicism in Wilhelmine Germany." *CEH* 21/4 (1990): 350–78.

nania, Ermland, and Upper Silesia brought a simmering conflict to a boil. And in Upper Silesia, the stubborn resistance of the Centrum's regional "German" leadership to offering candidacies to ethnic "Silesians" provided an opening through which radical Polish nationalism burst in 1903. Even in such strongholds as Pleß-Rybnik, where as recently as 1892 the Centrum had garnered 99 percent of the vote, the party went into a free-fall, plummeting to 10.5 percent by 1907.[139] In an obvious attempt to assert the priority of the religious community over political divisions, the Centrum defended itself by deliberately putting up priests as candidates in as many districts as possible. (Just as in 1928, when lay leaders on the party's *left* believed that the danger of a split was so great that only a cleric as head—Msgr. Ludwig Kaas, in the event—could hold the party together.) The Polish National Democrats responded with clerical candidacies of their own.[140] With priests manning the front lines on both sides of the political divide, the first casualties could only be the reputation of the clergy, as Germans witnessed the same blizzard of charges and countercharges about the misuse of religious office that had followed analogous Silesian upsets in 1871 and 1874. As in the seventies, a striking feature of these controversies was the fact that churchmen provided testimony for both sides. With the dissolution of the single imagined community, the *omertà* that had shielded the clergy's practices for so long disappeared.[141]

Disunity among Catholics was also the theme in Württemberg, Bavaria, and especially in Baden. Here, where the Centrum had only recently made inroads into long-standing liberal bastions, those priests who identified themselves with the liberal cause railed against the politicking of their Centrum colleagues. About what it was that separated them from the Centrum, the dissenters were as vague as they were emphatic; but "national," rather than social, economic, or political issues, were clearly paramount.[142] As one of them exclaimed, he was tired of being told over and over again at every Catholic gathering, "what 'we' are, how strong 'we' have become, and what all 'we' are going to demand from

[139] Schwidetsky, *Wahlbewegung* (1934), 81, gives the date for the high tally as 1893, but she must mean the by-election of 1892, since otherwise her figures do not jibe with Specht/Schwabe, *Reichstagswahlen*, 88. On the new rivalry between the Z and the parties of ethnic minorities in general: Sperber, *Voters*, 92f.

[140] Neubach, "Geistliche," 251–78; Schwidetzky, *Wahlbewegung*, 55, 60, 78f. Becker, "Ende," 354–58, 361, puts Kaas's election in the context of the Z's post-1918 structural crisis, but his argument also holds, mutatis mutandis, for the prewar Z.

[141] Spiritual intimidation charged 95 times in 6 Oppeln: AnlDR (1903, 11/I, Bd. 3) DS 402: 2301–3. Also 4 Oppeln, AnlDR (1912/13, 13/I, Bd. 19) DS 798: 1098. [Heinrich Krückemeyer], "Die polnische Bewegung in Oberschlesien," *Historisch-Politische Blätter* 132/2 (1903): 713–33 blamed the success of the NDs largely on *Katolik*. Failure of efforts to heal the breach: Leugners-Scherzberg, *Porsch* (1990), 100–107; W. W. Hagen, *Germans* (1980), 237, 364n. 21. For the 1908 LT elections, the leadership of the two parties reached a no-competition agreement. Kühne, *Dreiklassenwahlrecht*, 227.

[142] Esp. the articles in *DZJ* and its successor, *DNJ*. Their nationalism is most apparent in Fr. Sch., "Die Religion meiner Kindheit" 2/41 (9 Oct. 1910): 483–86, and "Religion und Politik," 559f; [O. Sickenberger], "Katholikentag" (1905), 412. Response: Georgius, "Darf ein katholischer Geistlicher liberaler Parteimann sein?" (1909): 389–96.

the '*Herr* State.' "[143] Soi-disant "progressive Catholics" could not understand why they had to acquiesce in a "we" that carped at the government, spoke disrespectfully of the state, gave succor to Germany's "enemies" (Poles and "Frenchies")—and forced on them an exclusion from the "we" to which they felt they really belonged: the national (and nationalist) "we" of a modern, prosperous, twentieth-century Germany.

And so in article after anonymous article, dissenting priests in the south reported to a not-very-surprised public the inside story of the petty oppressions, quotidian venalities, the all-too-human scandals that arose when men of the cloth interposed themselves between the citizen and the ballot box.[144] In 1905, under the aegis of the Kraus Society, they submitted a proposal to condemn clerical electioneering at the annual *Katholikentag*. Congress organizers, with their close ties to the Centrum, made sure the motion never reached the floor. In 1907 the dissenters made similar representations in an open (i.e., published) letter to the bishops.[145] The fact, however, that these same men loudly supported a Catholic pastor who, against the wishes of his bishop, chose to run for parliament as a National Liberal, and that in 1912 they published an election proclamation of their own, revealed that it was not really clerical electioneering per se that they hated, but only "ultramontane"—that is, Centrum—electioneering.[146]

Such dissenters remained a tiny minority within the clergy. They never achieved their goal: to "liberate" the "Catholic people," and ultimately the Fatherland, from the Centrum's black-cassocked electoral armies. But they did show that the ties of community were loosening. And they gave the public plenty to talk about.[147]

4. The rhetoric of the attacks on clerical influence as well as the changing representations of the clergy themselves point to a fourth strand in the renewed

---

[143] [Sickenberger], "Katholikentag," 411.

[144] E.g., "Der katholische Geistliche auf der politischen Arena," 90–94; "Momentbild," 21; "Ein Stimmungsbildchen aus dem 'nicht-konfessionellen' Zentrum" *DNJ* 3/24 (11 Jun. 1911), 283f. Less explicit but in a similar vein: "Das Wahlrecht der Geistlichen," 70–72; D. E. K., "Geistliche Wahlbeeinflussung" *DNJ* 1/40 (3 Oct. 1909): 479; D. V. C. "Das Zentrum in Lothringen," *DNJ* 1/22 (30 May 1909): 263; idem, "Die Krisis im Zentrum," *DNJ* 1/33 (15 Aug. 1909): 387–89; idem, "Religiöses Bekenntnis und Parteizugehörigkeit" *DNJ* 1/40 (3 Oct. 1909): 478; "Religion und Politik," 556–60. *DNJ* warmly recommended Bodewig's *Wahlbeeinflussungen* to its readers.

[145] [Sickenberger], "Zum Katholikentag," 409–14; open letter to the bishops in *DZJ* VII/11 (17 Mar. 1907). Schloßmacher, "Antiultramontanismus," 173, 176f.

[146] The same Pastor Tremel who got in trouble with the Bishop of Bamberg for addressing the (very anticlerical) Young Liberals, was an advocate of the Lex Moy, insisting that political activity on the part of the clergy "alienates the affections of the educated classes in particular." He then endorsed the LT candidacy of his colleague, Pastor Grandinger, running as a NL. Tremel, "Wahlrecht der Geistlichen. Gedanken zum Antrag Moy," *Augsburger Abendzeitung* Nr. 46, 15 Feb. 1904, and Nr. 48, 17 Feb. 1904; *Augsburger Abendzeitung* Nr. 138, 19 May 1907. On the Tremel and Grandinger affairs: Georgius, "Geistlicher," 389–96; Kessler, "Kann ein überzeugter Katholik und insbesondere ein Priester dem Liberalismus anhängen?" (Landau, 1909).

[147] Quote: Schloßmacher, "Antiultramontanismus," 180. "Was ist das Zentrum? Eine präsumptive Antwort von einem katholischen Arzt," *DNJ* 1/50 (12 Dec. 1909): 589f, expressly stated "reproduction allowed," suggesting that it was intended for use by other parties for election purposes.

clero-phobia: **resentment at Centrum power**. For the new attacks reversed the terms of the early seventies. No longer was the Catholic party vilified because it represented a lobby for a powerful and mysterious clergy. Rather, the clergy was attacked because it lobbied for a powerful and—to some—still mysterious party.

> The specter of the Centrum penetrates every situation. It works clandestinely at the courts of the sovereigns, it spins its web around the Conservatives and, to some extent, the National Liberals; it bewitches the Social Democrats. All roads lead to Rome. Always, in all the controversies among the rest of the people, Rome always calls the shots, because it has adherents everywhere. Even among the Social Democrats, it has silent allies. . . .

Thus Friedrich Naumann in 1907.[148] Rome—that is, the Catholic clergy—was here a synecdoche for the Centrum.

Not everyone was as spooked as Naumann, but the Centrum was intensely resented, and unlike the Jesuits, its power was not mythological. From the mid-90s on, the party had been extending its dominance to a number of state legislatures, notably Bavaria's, where it now held an advantage of eighty seats over its nearest competitor. In the Reichstag, except for the three-year rule of the "Kartell" between February 1887 and March 1890, it was the largest party from 1881 until 1912, often leading other delegations by margins of forty seats or more.[149] After 1898, it lay in the Centrum's hand to "make" either a Left or a Right majority. No bill had a hope of passage without it. Watching Peter Spahn cast the deciding vote on every item in the list of the Tariff Commission, Adolf Wermuth turned to his neighbor and said, "If I were not Chief of the Imperial Office of Domestic Affairs (*Reichsamt des Innern*), I'd want to be the leader of the Centrum."[150]

It is resentment against the power of this "cattle-trading party" that quivers behind the image of the priest in contemporary satire and caricature. The slender, smooth-shaven, epicene figure of the 1860s and 1870s now appeared with a belly and a bristly five o'clock shadow. The exotic had become familiar; the uncanny, merely canny; the lean and hungry Jesuit, the porcine parish priest.[151] Once feared as dangerous, he was now merely hated as corrupt. The transformation of the clergy's image from plotter to pig was a strong clue that the real fault lay not in the parsons but in the party.[152]

[148] "Zentrum" (1907), 114f.

[149] The Z usually disposed of an additional 30–40 votes from regional parties (W, P, Els). Ritter/Niehuss, *Arbeitsbuch*, 39–42. By 1906 it had become the largest party in the the Württemberg LT; by 1912, the dominant force in Baden politics.

[150] Martin, *Machthaber*, 394. It was "the black serpent, squeezing Germany . . . with its poisonous body." *Saar- und Blieszeitung*, quoted in Erzberger, *Bilder*, 8.

[151] *Simplicissimus* cartoons: "Die Wahlschlacht" VIII (n.d., 1903–4) Extra-Nummer Reichstagswahl: 2–3; "Zentrum ist Trumpf" XIV 1/3 (19 Apr. 1909): 39; "Die Württembergischen Wahlen" XI 2/41 (7 Jan. 1907): 654;

[152] From *Simplicissimus*: the cleric as pig: "Neue Deutsche Spielkarten" VIII/42 (12 Jan. 1904); the bishop as shepherd not of sheep but of swine: "Alles fürs Zentrum" XIV/10 (7 June 1909); cf. *Zentrums-Album* (1912), 201, 213, 239, 243, 254–56, 258f, 268, 273, 276, 286. Erzberger, *Bilder*,

Negative clerical images were always nastiest where distrust of the voter was greatest, and the domestication of the image of the priest corresponded to analogous changes in the representations of the Catholic *Volk*. Voters who had once been dismissed as "dumb" were still figured as half-witted, as marionettes, as children. But they were no longer imagined as threatening, given to mob violence, actual or potential criminals. Now they were sly but venal rustics.[153] The suggestion that the Centrum was a cynical commerce between grasping voters and jobbing clerics echoed traditional Lutheran criticisms of Rome as reducing salvation to a set of materialistic calculations. That a Catholic electorate should think that God would issue heavenly penalties for their votes was no more implausible, according to this line of thinking, than the multiple other bargains brokered by the Church between the superstitious and the Almighty.[154] Purchasing an indulgence, voting for the Centrum: what were these but other-worldly and this-worldly variants on the same theme? Although rooted in images going back centuries, the picture had resonance precisely because of the success of the Centrum—figured as a fat, pig-like, wheeler-dealer priest—in securing grain tariffs and in brokering hoof-and-mouth legislation, bans on margarine, and a wide range of other economic packages desired by its constituents.[155] As a fictional child put it in a satirical "School Essay" on elections, "When you want to go to heaven and don't want to allow any pigs to get in here, that's called the Centrum."[156]

The party had been just tolerable so long as Bismarck, embodying the might

21, 24, 26. In *Kladderadatsch* the images were darker: e.g., the Z was depicted in 1904 as Charybdis, in Jesuit hat, about to devour the tiny German Michel (Scylla was the SPD). Reprinted in *Zentrums-Album* (1912), 233.

[153] The association between the Catholic masses and criminality: Rust, *Reichskanzler*, 685–87, 696. Still contemptuous but less threatening representations as halfwitted in *Simplicissimus*: "Vaterfreuden," VIII/11 (n.d., 1903–4): 86; "Nach Einberufung des bayerischen Landtags," VIII/27 (29 Sept. 1903), n.p.; "Erprobte Zentrumswähler," XI 2/43 (21 Jan. 1907): 688; "Reichstagswahlen in Bayern" and "Der Zentrumswähler auf dem Heimweg" XI 2/52 (15 Mar. 1907): 699, 704, respectively; "Wahlbefähigung" XII 1/15 (8 Jul. 1907): 232; "Bittgang" XV/11 (13 June 1910): 174.

[154] In *Simplicissimus*: "Vor der Wahl," VIII/6 (n.d., 1903–4): 46; L. Thoma, "Wählt Zentrum!" VIII (n.d., 1903–4) Extranummer: Reichstagswahl: 7; "Himmelsstrafen" XI 2/48 (25 Feb. 1907): 779; "Bittgang" XV/11 (13 June 1910): 174; "Probates Mittel" XVI 2/40 (1 Jan. 1912): 710; "Vor der Landtagswahlen" XVI 2/42 (15 Jan. 1912): 747; "Zentrumspredigt" XVI 2/46 (12 Feb. 1912): 815. The image of the "money-changers in the temple" and "soul-merchants" were traditional religious topoi that were now applied to those of political "cattle-trading" and "backstairs" deals. Proclamation of Evangelischer Bund, in Erzberger, *Bilder*, 9. The overlap between popular and legal culture can be seen when a legal scholar cites the actions of the parish priest in Ludwig Thoma's 1906 anticlerical novel *Andreas Vost* to argue for the criminalization of dirty tricks. Mayer, "Bekämpfung," 23.

[155] Blackbourn, *Class* (1980), esp. 50n. 90. The Christian Farmers Associations, a Catholic agricultural lobby close to the Z, with 348,000 members in 1907, topped the membership of the Farmers League (BdL) at 290,000. David W. Hendon, "German Catholics and the Agrarian League, 1893–1914," *GSR* 4 (1981): 427–45; esp. 435. SD propaganda also sounded the materialism theme, likening the "blackskirted" labor leaders of the Volksverein to "pimps." Quoted by Sachse (SD) SBDR 10 May 1912: 1829.

[156] "Die Wahl. Ein Schulaufsatz," *Simplicissimus*, VIII (n.d., 1903–4): Extranummer Reichstagswahl: 9.

of the imperial government, had been there to balance—and denounce—it. But signs that the government was flattering it, even seeking its favor, were insupportable to those whose German identity was bound up with a national narrative celebrating victory over Rome. Luther's pamphlets attacking the Church were quoted with the comment that "these words, written nearly 400 years ago, correspond line for line precisely to our situation today." Chancellor Bülow's apparent dependence on the Centrum raised the specter of that "clerical shadow government of yore," installed through a combination of "back stairs duplicity and intrigue and the most brutal power politics"—that is, through decisions to bestow or withhold its 100-odd Reichstag votes. When, having brought his tariff safely into port, Bülow announced that he would now support allowing the Jesuits back into Germany, the fury of liberals and conservatives knew no bounds.[157] Bülow was not slow to see his opportunity. Dissolving parliament at the end of 1906, he waged an election campaign in early 1907 against Centrum power—and those other "enemies of the Reich," the Social Democrats.[158] The exalted popular response—from a saturnalia of Kulturkampf rhetoric to the boycott of Catholic shops in Bielefeld, Gütersloh, Duisberg, and Hanau-Gelnhausen—vindicated Bülow's political instinct. It was the third time (the others were in 1887 and 1893) that a German government had dissolved the Reichstag in order to have at the Centrum.

And yet the *policies* this party advocated were not, by and large, the source of outrage. None of its secular demands were beyond the pale for a wide swath of political opinion, and its many points of contact with both Right and Left agendas supported the party's claim to being truly "centrist." Even its ecclesiastical demands were by now important mainly as points of principle—campaign shibboleths for rallying the faithful—as was clear in 1899, when the party made reform of the Rhenish election law, rather than return of the Jesuits, its price for supporting the Mittelland canal.[159] But for those outside the Centrum's milieu, the very fact that their government depended on such a party for the passage of national legislation was galling. Unlike the other major parties, the Centrum knew from the outset that it was condemned to remain a "part" and could never proffer even a prospective claim to represent the "whole" of the nation.[160] Thus it was not just a party among parties, but the very embodiment *of* party, the *Ding an sich*. For a "power-hungry minority," whose constituency proclaimed its special identity every time it cast its ballots, to have a veto

[157] Good on Bülow's mishandling of this: K. A. Lerman, *Chancellor* (1990), 80–82, 104f. *Saar- und Blieszeitung* (Feb. 1907), quoted in Erzberger, *Bilder*, 8f.

[158] W. Becker, "Kulturkampf" (1986), 59–84, esp. 78n. 3, demonstrates that the Z, not the SPD, was the primary target; G. D. Crothers, *Elections* (1941), 95–102. Stimulating on the integrative function of confessional polemic, but more convincing for the Protestant than the Catholic side: August-Hermann Leugers, "Latente Kulturkampfstimmung im Wilhelminischen Kaiserreich. Konfessionelle Polemik als konfessions- und innenpolitisches Kampfmittel," in *Die Verschränkung von Innen-, Konfessions- und Kolonialpolitik im Deutschen Reich vor 1914*, edited by J. Horstmann (Paderborn, 1987), 13–37.

[159] Blackbourn, *Class*, 30; Zangerl "Courting," 234.

[160] Socialist analogies: Przeworski/Sprague, *Stones*, 29–40.

over the decisions of the majority was the tail wagging the dog. The bitter humor of the anticlerical cartoon depended upon a shared sense of the illegitimacy, and therefore the absurdity, of Centrum power.[161] And the more the Centrum acted like a genuine secular political party—wheeling and dealing, making legislative trade-offs, concluding election pacts now with Social Democrats, now with Conservatives—the more it made other Germans acutely aware of the dependence of their ship of state on the vicissitudes of party politics. If willingness to put up with partisan conflict is a prerequisite for parliamentary government, then the public's renewed preoccupation with the chaplainocracy after the turn of the century was a sign that many Germans were still ambivalent about such government, and some were longing to emancipate themselves from "party" altogether.[162]

CONCLUSIONS: CLERICAL INFLUENCE AND DEMOCRACY

Controversy over clerical election influence never ended. In 1912 opponents believed the misuse of the pulpit was "spreading ever further."[163] When an appellate court established in Alsace-Lorraine to adjudicate challenges to provincial elections departed from recent Reichstag precedents and threw out six elections because the clergy had allegedly limited the voter's freedom, the ensuing headlines gave a new and partisan boost to long-standing multi-partisan efforts to replace the Reichstag's cumbersome Election Commission with an independent court.[164]

From the beginning, efforts to invalidate "clerical" elections assumed that the priest's control over the sacraments, particularly that of penance, rendered Catholic voters helpless. In 1907 efforts were made to establish an "Imperial League Against the Confession Box" to press for a law against auricular confession.[165] Educated Centrum supporters, schooled in the official Church's sophisticated

[161] "Germania": *Simplicissimus*: XI 1/12 (18 June 1906): 200; "Bei der Stichwahl" ibid., XI 2/46 (25 Feb. 1907): 783.

[162] Pastor Graudinger (NL) revealed the connection between hatred of the Z and a hatred of "party" per se when he ended an attack on clerical electioneering by exclaiming, "How beautiful it would be if in parliaments the decision in important questions of culture did not always depend upon party considerations." Bodewig, *Wahlbeeinflussungen*, 8.

[163] "Wahlreden von der Kanzel," *BT* Nr. 14, 2. Beiblatt, 9 Jan. 1912.

[164] Geh. Justizrat Diefenbach, "Der reichsländliche Gerichtshof zur Prüfung der Gültigkeit von Wahlen," *BT* 5 Mar. 1914, Morgenblatt, BAB-L R1501/14653; Dr. v. Zahn for Geh. ORR Dr. Schulze, "Aufzeichnung über Wahlprüfungen," 17 June 1912, BAB-L R1501/14653 (23 pages). Spahn, chairman of the WPK and a Z leader, criticized the Colmar decisions, an act that shocked since Spahn was himself a judge. SBDR 5 Apr. 1913: 4494 ff. The SPD also opposed the NL motion to replace the WPK with a court, as diminishing the authority of the RT. The SPD was less concerned about clerical influence, perhaps, as Blackbourn suggests, because they were less vulnerable in the face of democratization. *Class*, 169. Such a court was established in the Weimar Republic.

[165] Erzberger, *Bilder*, 34f. The confessional was a potent symbol in all Protestant countries. Hanham, *Elections*, 305.

distinctions between various kinds of authority, had long insisted that such accusations misunderstood the very nature of this sacrament. "Any peasant can take his catechism and see for himself that it is *nonsense* to deny absolution because one has voted for or against the wish of the pastor. . . ."[166] Referring to their own experiences, they dismissed as "scarcely conceivable" the possibility that a priest might abuse his sacramental authority by asking unwanted questions about a penitent's vote.[167]

But the degrees of freedom that technically existed for the Catholic faithful had never been ones that the parish priest himself was eager to stress. When outsiders heard stories of a pastor's hinting darkly to his congregation that his help would be more useful on their deathbeds than that of the Liberal or Conservative Bürgermeister's, they could be excused for ignoring the finer points of Catholic theology.[168] Thwarting every hope of eradicating the problem, however, was the fact that the sacrament of confession, like voting itself, was secret.[169] Thus precisely to the degree that a pastor's powers of absolution were effective as political devices, they escaped the jurisdiction of the Catholic voter's would-be protectors. For any attempt to eliminate the abuse of the confessional through legislation confronted a paradox. Those voters who felt inwardly bound by the priest's admonitions were least likely to object to them, certainly not publicly and perhaps not even privately. And if voters voluntarily accepted this external authority, to what degree could that authority still be considered "external?" Yet if it were not external, what business had the Election Commission, state legislation, or public opinion to say it nay? Judges and legislators were powerless to devise meshes fine enough to capture a quarry that was not political, but psychological, enforced less by a specific set of ecclesiastical penalties than by a culture.

In the world of political theory, a free election takes place when a party persuades a voter to support a candidate; an unfree election, when someone coerces him. Within the Catholic milieu, however, whether in its constructed urban filiations or in its more "natural" village manifestations, the distinction between the persuasion of a voter and the mobilization of a community, be-

---

[166] Schröder-Lippstadt SBDR 22 Nov. 1871: 440 (quote); Virnich, *Fraction*, 43; Catholic members of the WPK: 5 Arns. (Bochum), AnlDR (1882/83, 5/II, Bd. 6) DS 292: 1076.

[167] "Scarcely conceivable," *KVZ* 21 Nov. 1906. The same paper, however, had conceded after the Beuthen trial that such a thing must have happened in Upper Silesia. Bodewig, *Wahlbeeinflussungen*, 60. Cf. Hiery, *Reichstagswahlen*, 419. The Bishops' Conference of 1913 concluded that election behavior could only be discussed in the confessional when the penitent himself raised the issue or when his antichurch éngagement had become public knowledge. Graf, *Beeinflussungsversuche*, 173.

[168] E.g., Amtsvorstand Meßkirch to MdI, 17 July 1893, GLA 236/14901: 1/h; Horn Report, LHAK 403/8806: 14/b.

[169] Legal difficulties: Mayer, "Bekämpfung," 27. The closest outsiders could usually come to proof of the misuse of absolution were the hints in the published *Beichtspiegeln*, the formulaic examinations of conscience the Church officially recommended to penitents. As late as 1957 they included such questions as "Have I given my vote in elections to opponents of my faith?" Graf, *Beeinflussungsversuche*, 178.

tween the mobilization of a community and the coercion of an individual, became as elusive as the distinction between the sacred and the profane.[170] That the milieu itself had the power to defy the authority of the confessional was demonstrated by the more than 20,000 Polish-speaking Silesians who voted for Albert Korfanty in Kattowitz-Zabrze in 1903.[171] But, as we shall see in chapter 10, the freedom of a community does not necessarily translate into freedom for its individuals. Ultimately it was not clerical coercion but mobilization that destroyed election competition in Catholic communities and that offended outsiders' sense of fair play; the real grievance was located not in the confessional box inherited from the Middle Ages, but in the very modern politics of identity.

Although both sides of the argument were ever ready to cite examples and precedents from other "civilized nations," Germany was by now locked in a debate that, in its intensity, was hardly recognizable in the rest of the North Atlantic world.[172] In the United States, though religion continued to organize and give meaning to political conflict, and preachers exercised considerable political leadership, religious affiliations were so plural and rules on free speech so deeply embedded in the national culture that clerical influence was no more salient an issue in America than stuffing ballot boxes (for analogous reasons of national culture) was in Germany. In Ireland, where the Church's weight in society was more comparable to Germany, a number of election invalidations finally led to the inclusion of clerical influence among the offenses covered by the Corrupt Practices Act of 1884. The Irish priest never hesitated to throw his religious weight around at election time, especially in the two decades from 1852 through 1872. But the public responded with recrimination, not demands for exceptional legislation, and even after the clergy's last hurrah, the defeat of Parnell in 1892, losers on both sides of the Irish Sea ultimately recognized that it was Irish opinion, not clerical opinion, that had defeated them. In England, as late as 1909, the election intervention of an Anglican bishop was an embarrassment to the Church, but certainly not an issue for the state. And in France, as we have seen, a spectacular series of invalidations for clerical influence in the 1870s and 1880s had wiped out the clerical "option" in the Third Republic.[173] The issues in the French conflict were in any case not sociocultural, but primarily institutional, and by the beginning of the new century they were being settled in a different arena.

Institutional conflicts can be ended, not least because (as French Republicans had demonstrated in 1905, with the separation of church and state) one side can

---

[170] I am indebted to Marcus Kreuzer for pointing out the distinction between persuasion and mobilization. Graf, *Beeinflussungsversuche*, 159f, reveals that even the bishops tried to elicit obedience to their instructions by demonstrating their value through arguments.

[171] Calculations based on the 1905 by-election that followed invalidation. Specht/Schwabe, *Reichstagswahlen*, Nachtrag: 23.

[172] Though not in Latin America. Posada-Carbó, "Limits"; Deas, "Role," 164–72.

[173] D.V.C., "Geistlichkeit und Politik," *DNJ* 1/51 (19 Dec. 1909): 611f; Whyte, "Influence," 244, 247, 252; Jones, *Politics*, 300, 303; Charnay, "L'église," 267–69, 289n. 109. The issue remained alive in Puerto Rico as late as the 1960s.

win. In Germany, however, the institutional rivalry between Roman Church and nation-state had from the first been complicated by tensions between minority and majority populations; that is, between cultures. Insistence on some clear sign of cultural assimilation as the price for legitimating their representation was the message behind the Protestant majority's outrage at clerical politicking just as surely as a vote for their clergy's party embodied the Catholic minority's rejection of that demand. Under these circumstances, the debate over whether the chaplainocracy was violating the voters' freedom could never come to closure, because in the minds of those who took the affirmative in this debate, it was really their *own* national freedom, the freedom of the Protestant majority to be assured of a legislature that would think in ways they considered *German*, that, with every Centrum victory, was being violated.

The continued salience of "clerical influence" in election challenges should not be read univocally as a sign of German political "backwardness." By becoming agents of a political party, the Catholic clergy had acquired a "modern," practical usefulness to their congregations enjoyed by few of their clerical counterparts in other countries. In the process, what Dankwart Rustow has elsewhere called "habituation" also took place. For this same clergy acquired a pragmatic, but nonetheless real, commitment to democratic elections, parliamentary procedures, and party politics—commitments in which they schooled their flock, by their practice as much as by their preaching.[174] Not surprisingly, in the spring of 1907, when the clergy and party were again under the greatest attack, the Centrum responded by resubmitting the bill it had first introduced in 1873: to replace Prussia's three-class voting system with the Reichstag's democratic franchise.

But the very success of the clergy's party as a vehicle for the minority's desire for cultural validation, a success that ensured the continuance of the "hot family feud" that Rustow considers a prerequisite for any "transition to democracy" and one that legitimated democratic forms of conflict for most of the Catholic population, undermined the legitimacy of these forms among many of the Protestant majority. By embedding ancient religious differences in modern party conflict, the very existence of the Centrum made the reconciliation of a significant number of Germans to party and parliamentary conflict unusually difficult. One should not be surprised, therefore, that efforts to invalidate elections allegedly tainted by "clerical influence" showed so little regard for freedom of speech as the foundation upon which all free elections depends. Nor that such challenges implicitly denied that Catholic voters were mature enough to make genuine choices. But the consequences were nonetheless heavy ones. Edmund Morgan has suggested that the political fiction of a wise and independent yeomanry was essential to the ability of the British parliament (and later, the American colonies) to wrest sovereignty from the Crown. If "inventing" a common people with qualities sturdy enough to entrust them with power (even if at first only fictionally) is indeed a necessary precondition for insistence

---

[174] Martin, *Machthaber*, 399; similar conclusions: Posada-Carbó: "Limits of Power," 272.

on parliamentary sovereignty, then the fateful topoi of manipulative priest and childlike people elaborated during Germany's decades-long culture wars worked in the opposite direction. And it helps explain why so many quite modern citizens tolerated a less-than-parliamentary monarchy so willingly, so long.

Bread Lords I: Junkers

If I eat someone's bread, I sing his song.

—German Proverb

"BREAD LORD": the German word for employer carried a penumbra of connotations that extended beyond relationships in the field or on the shop floor.[1] It evoked a world where power and authority came bundled, where the economic, the political, and the moral were three legs of the same social tripod. Distances within hierarchies varied with the workplace: from the familial intimacy of the small shop, where the journeyman labored alongside his master and even ate at his table (but below the salt) to the unbridgeable divisions of caste on the estates in the flatland.[2] But everywhere employers assumed responsibility for the deportment of those whom they employed and demanded deference from them. By the second half of the nineteenth century, the term bread lord was only just beginning to be superseded by its modern variant: *Arbeitgeber*, "the giver of work." (Neither term, which emphasizes the worker's dependency on others for employment, exists in English, where the activist "bread-winner," meaning the one who supports a family, has been in use since the 1820s.) Most, although by no means all, bread lords had shed their claims to a say over their employees' religion, their marriages, and even (more gradually) over other aspects of social and domestic life now deemed to be private.[3] The worker's

[1] Proverb quoted by LR of Bochem, in 1887 election: SBDR 11 Feb. 1888: 840. The phrase was repeated endlessly: cf. Chief Marine Engineer Dede to workers at the imperial shipyard at Danzig, quoted: SBDR 2 Dec. 1882: 587; mayor to crop farmer, 6 Trier, AnlDR (1884, 5/IV, Bd. 4) DS 103: 794; A. Strosser (K), SBHA, 19 May 1909: 6026–29. In addition to "bread lord," contemporaries used "Lohnherrn." "Arbeitslohn," in H. Wagener, ed., *Staats- und Gesellschafts-Lexikon* (Berlin, 1859) 2: 489.

[2] "Tripod" is Mack Walker's term: *Towns* (1971). W. Keil, *Erlebnisse* (1947) 1: 74–77; Hainer Plaul, "Grundzüge der Entwicklung von Lebensweise und Kultur der einheimischen Landarbeiterschaft in den Dörfern der Magdeburger Börde unter den Bedingungen der Herausbildung und Konsolidierung des Kapitalismus der freien Konkurrenz in der Landwirtschaft," in *Bauer und Landarbeiter im Kapitalismus in der Magdeburger Börde*, edited by H.-J. Rach and B. Weissel (Berlin [East], 1982), 79–115; esp. 101. How the economic order gradually precipitated out from that of the "house," which had once exercised the functions of the school and other public tasks, is a theme of J. Kocka, *Arbeitsverhältnisse* (1990); hierarchy: 156, 159. Kocka rightly warns against assuming that just because a worker slept and ate with them that he was treated as a part of the family. Families were of course also hierarchical.

[3] Jaeger, *Unternehmer*, 99, 270f; Bellot, *Hundert Jahre*, 107n. 7; W. Manchester, *Arms* (1968), 178; E. G. Spencer, *Management* (1984), 76.

public life, however, including the clubs he joined, the papers he read, and especially his vote, was still widely regarded as within the purview of the one who "gave" a man his work, the "lord of his wage and bread."[4]

This enduring world of *Herrschaft*—the real world—bore no resemblance to the fictive universe of the franchise. An electorate, however restricted, is a temporary republic; its one law, equality. At its borders, all baggage is checked and each of its denizens issued the coin of the realm, the vote, in a single denomination. Extending the boundaries of the republic from the few to the many inevitably inflates this currency, a prospect the original citizenry can be expected to oppose. But far more subversive than inflation are the opportunities any significant extension of the boundaries creates for smuggling in the relationships of the real world. In the hands of dependent voters, so ran a classic European and American argument, the coin of the republic would never be freely spent, but would merely augment the purchasing power of those who stood over them. To admit dependents into the voting republic trespassed against the rights of the other residents, on whose radical, if artificial, equality the very act of voting was predicated.[5] So, at any rate, the theory. A deputy to the Frankfurt Assembly put it more simply. "The aristocracy should not be given the means of ruling via the masses."[6]

Yet these familiar objections to widening a restricted franchise were barely voiced in 1867, when Bismarck proposed a national voting law that contained none of the limitations, categorical and tax-based, found in the electoral institutions of every German member state. An amendment to exclude voters with no hearth of their own, which would have denied the franchise to live-in servants and stable hands, was rejected without debate. Those who might have feared the consequences of manhood suffrage for their own power seem to have counted on precisely such dependency relationships to guarantee outcomes to their liking. The old forty-eighter Hermann Schulze-Delitzsch framed his appeal for a secret ballot by reminding the deputies of the "great and justified influence" of the bread lord. "The person who has a significant social position," he assured them, "a great landowner, for example, a great employer in the business world, a factory owner, will exercise such an influence in every kind of election."[7] It was the same argument that Disraeli—and indeed James Mill—had used to parry English objections to a broader suffrage. "It is possible for a man who is possessed of this power [derived from property]," Mill wrote, "to exercise it in such a manner as to become the object of affection and reverence, not only to all those who come within the sphere of his virtues, but, by sympathy with

---

[4] See, e.g., G. Birk, "Entwicklung" (1982), 175f.

[5] Classic arguments: J. Morgan Kousser, "Suffrage," in *Encyclopedia of American Political History*, vol. 3, edited by Jack Greene (New York, 1984), 1236–58; here, 1236, 1241; Cowling, *1867*, 49f; in California: Ethington, *City*, 205, 253f.

[6] Fr. Scheller, in Gagel, *Wahlrechtsfrage*, 9. Similarly: Hamerow, "Origins," 106, 108; Meyer, *Wahlrecht*, 182; Morgan, *Inventing*, 169.

[7] Quote: Below, *Wahlrecht*, 75; Meyer, *Wahlrecht*, 240.

them, of all those to whom the knowledge of his character is diffused. The wishes of such a man become a motive to his fellow creatures."

Disraeli and Mill were not suggesting, however, that subordinate classes simply took their politics from a higher class, but only that voters within definable communities naturally adopted the opinions of their acknowledged leaders.[8] And perhaps it was this kind of intra-communal diffusion of sympathy that Schulze-Delitzsch, founder of the cooperative movement and a believer in social harmony, meant by the influence of great employers, rather than the exercise of authority across the class line. But we may doubt whether a distinction as subtle as this one had much meaning to an audience schooled in the social realities of Central Europe. When in Germany conservatives of all stripes invoked the existence of definable communities, it was to justify their own embargo on any challenge to "legitimate and natural authorities" that might be imported from the outside. "Only where they [already] occupied common territory was it permissible for authorities to compete [with each other]," insisted a Conservative deputy.[9]

The absence of conservative objections to manhood suffrage in 1867 would later provide a constant reference point to defenders of the bread lords whenever voters complained of pressure at election time. The silence of the founding fathers in the face of such a radical proposal, the Right argued, was conclusive evidence that they assumed the election influence of the "natural authorities" to be self-evident.[10] In the social landscape, of course, as in the physical, "nature" is always on the side of the strong. The attribution of "natural" to the authority of bread lords and others was little more than society's grunt of assent to power.[11] Perhaps more convincing than the silence of conservatives during the Constituent Reichstag's deliberations was the fact that the Election Law made no provision, as French, Spanish, and Belgian law did, and as Germany's law does today, for polling to be held on Sunday. Did weekday elections give employers a right to deny their workers time off to vote? While bosses tried it and constitutional theorists justified it, the legislators usually declared the prohibition out of bounds.[12] But the interest of employers was more typically expressed in requiring their workers to vote than in preventing them. Weekday elections—

---

[8] D[avid] C[resap], "Political Morality in Mid-Nineteenth Century England: Concepts, Norms, Violations," *VS* 13 (1969): 5–36; 9, Mill quoted on 11; Disraeli, in Cowling, *1867*, 53.

[9] B. v. Puttkamer-Plauth (K) SBDR 13 Feb. 1886: 1049, also 1048. Cf. Helldorf SBDR 10 Dec. 1885: 277; Kulemann, *Erinnerungen*, 25–27.

[10] C. A. Munckel (FVp), quoted by P. v. Reinbaben SBDR 11 Jan. 1889: 395, Munckel SBDR 13 Feb. 1886: 1048, 1067. Agreement: Hamerow, "Origins," 105.

[11] Threats to dismiss men for voting a certain way were "in itself natural [*an sich naturgemäß*] and indeed precisely a correlate of the free and secret voting right." K. Thile (FK), 7 Oct. 1878, quoted in Poschinger Report, BAB-L R1501/14450, Bl. 164v. Also Helldorf SBDR 13 Feb. 1886: 1072; Reinbaben SBDR 11 Jan. 1889: 384f.

[12] 17 Han., AnlDR (1882/83, 5/II, Bd. 6) DS 242: 927; Lübeck, AnlDR (1893/94, 9/II, Bd. 2) DS 131: 791; 3 Marienwerder, AnlDR (1898/1900, 10/I, Bd. 4) DS 507: 2660. Employer's right to refuse to release workers to vote: P. Laband, *Das Staatsrecht des Deutschen Reiches*, 4 Bde. (Tübingen, 5th ed. 1911–14) 2: 332.

maintained against Social Democratic motions throughout the entire life of the Empire—advantaged employers by ensuring that the act of voting would take place within the world of work.[13]

How correctly conservative supporters of manhood suffrage had assessed the "natural" order of things can be seen by the easy jokes—retailed in the press as news items—about the behavior of the bread lord at election time:

> A farmer in Alt-Chemnitz received three ballots, one for a National Liberal, and two for a Social Democrat. When asked what he had done with so many, he replied: "Well, I kept the National Liberal ballot for myself, the other two I gave to my men. The Socialist is good enough for them."

And from Berlin, a stronghold of wealthy Progressives, came the yarn about a factory foreman who learned that his boss's coachman was about to vote for the Socialist fire-eater Wilhelm Hasenclever. The foreman hastened to inform the errant driver that someone had made a proper fool of him, and gave him a Progressive ballot instead. On returning from the polls the dutiful coachman reported that he had indeed voted Progressive; but then added slyly that he had really put one over on a colleague, the coachman for *Kommerzienrat* N. N., by persuading *him* to cast the Hasenclever ballot![14]

The paper that published these "election stories" left its readers to reflect on their various lessons. On their face, the tales illustrated the tutelage that employers freely assumed over employees. Yet in both stories the assertion of authority has been undercut by stupidity: the employer's in the tale from Alt-Chemnitz, the employee's, in the one from Berlin. The latter story, moreover, operated on a second level. In resorting to guile instead of command in getting the coachman to take the Progressive ballot, the foreman implicitly conceded that the coachman's vote was his own. It is this conceded freedom that allows the tables to be turned when the foolish coachman "tricks" his peer, the other coachman, and thus, inadvertently, his master—thereby revealing the subversive possibilities inherent in the new franchise, which could both reinforce and undermine the economic pecking order. The currency of jokes such as these in the early years of the empire marked a particular stage in the democratization of political rights in Germany. Tricks are, after all, the weapons of the weak. Once an electorate is truly politicized, such behavior is no longer a laughing matter. Once it is truly empowered, the point of these stories dissolves, and they cease to be told.

Empowerment, however, will be conspicuously absent in the following chapter, on Germany's rural bread lords. Traditional relationships of authority, which in

---

[13] Until legislation passed in May 1890, however, even Sunday might be a workday. The government's view and foreign comparisons: Referent Landrichter Dr. Schulze, "Sonntag als Wahltag," n.d. (post-1908, and from its placement, ca. 1911), BAB-L R1501/14460, Bl. 166f.

[14] "Vermischtes," *GA* Nr. 17, 21 Jan. 1874: 97; "Vermischtes. Folgende Wahlhistorie," *GA* Nr. 21, 25 Jan. 1874.

Catholic areas were transformed by the politics of identity into communal obligations, which in some industrializing areas (as we shall see in chapter 9) were resisted and rejected, were in the Protestant flatland simply transposed *onto* the act of voting. Challenges from below would appear in the 1890s: on behalf of antisemitism, of agricultural protection, and of Social Democracy. But these challenges barely shook the powers that were, much less dislodged them. Nevertheless, although we can find little reason in rural east Elbia to revise the familiar picture of Germans entering the twentieth century with little experience in the articulation of dissent, the organization of diverse interests, the practices of civility in difference, and in competition in a free political marketplace, the flatland does belong to our story of German political development. For the new electoral politics, though they failed to enhance the power of rural dependents, did radically rearrange the relations *among* those traditionally exercising authority—that is, between the landed elite and the government.

THE LORDS OF HUMANKIND

It was a truth universally acknowledged, that a man or woman in possession of a sizable piece of land must never be in want of election influence. On country estates across the north German plain, especially in the old Prussian provinces of East and West Prussia, of Pomerania and Brandenburg, as well as in Silesia and provincial Saxony, in Holstein, and throughout the duchies of Mecklenburg, polling day followed a set pattern. The overseer would summon the workers to the servants' room. There he (or his master or mistress) might or might not make a short statement; might (or might not) offer buttered bread and brandy; but would certainly distribute ballots. Then, whether the polling took place in the adjacent overseer's room or off the premises entirely, the manor's influence would be felt. Election panels would be manned by the estate's agents, its owner often at their head. They would feel no compunction about looking into a folded ballot.[15] Nor would a mistress of the manor flinch from interposing her authority between the election code and the act of voting.[16]

The "permanent campaign" we saw in so many Catholic regions did not exist in the Protestant flatland. The election statements of rural bread lords, when they made them at all, are a fair measure of the intensity of political debate.

[15] 3 Meckl.: BAB-L R1501/14662, Bl. 26; villages throughout 7 Frankfurt, AnlDR (1881/82, 5/II, Bd. 5) DS 162: 551–53; 2 Bromberg, AnlDR (1881, 4/IV, Bd. 4) DS 105: 630f, 633; 1 Köslin, AnlDR (1893/94, 9/II, Bd. 2) DS 149: 882; testimony of Frau Rittergutsbesitzer Lessing zu Prust, 5 Marienwerder, AnlDR (1895/97, 9/IV, Bd. II) DS 195: 1263f. Also *Hofgängerleben* (1896), in Kelly, ed., *Worker*, 218.

[16] 1 Minden, AnlDR (1878, 3/II, Bd. 3) DS 99: 833; 13 Saxony, AnlDR (1887/88, 7/II, Bd. 4) DS 212: 905, 1 Köslin: *FrankZ*, 60 (1 Mar. 1903), 5. Morgenblatt, BAB-LR1501/14456, Bl. 3; the Duchy of Lauenberg in S-H: Gerlach, *Erlebnisse*, 45. Estate owners, bosses in general, and their agents "voted" their underage, foreign, or otherwise ineligible employees: Protest against 9 Breslau, Feb. 1887, BAB-L R1501/14665, Bl. 71–75; 2 Breslau, AnlDR (1912/14, 13/I, Bd. 22) DS 1432: 2926, 2931.

They hardly qualify as speeches. Here is Mecklenburg's Baron le Fort, chairman of his election panel, speaking in front of the schoolhouse in Boeck, just before the polling:

> He for his person would vote for Count von Plessen of Ivenack and he wished that the remaining voters would do so as well. Whoever intended to vote this way could make use of the ballots laid out in the polling place. Whoever wanted to vote differently, however, could go home and write out a ballot for himself.

The absence of arguments on behalf of the Baron's choice was not accidental. What bread lord could wish, by starting political hares, to stimulate reflections among his dependents about the nature of the civic duty they were being called upon to perform? As it turned out, all of those present availed themselves of Le Fort's ballots.[17] Here was the democratic franchise working precisely as Bismarck had foreseen it, as Disraeli had foreseen it, as Radicals like John Bright and Karl Twesten, with heavier hearts, had foreseen it.[18]

Can we interpret rural election returns as the action of "deference communities," as has been famously asserted for mid-Victorian England?[19] When economic power was veiled with the decent draperies of condescension, as it was by Baron le Fort, compliance might look a lot like deference. But condescension was compulsion with a human face. Compulsion with the veils off seems to have been the norm, with election chairmen and estate owners bellowing at the men who appeared at the polls with the wrong ballots—like Herr Demuth, in the village of Leichnam (!) in Royal Saxony:

> Thou't all jackasses! Ye needn't come to work any more! Tell the people in the village that I shall have only *Reich* [a local estate owner and a Conservative], otherwise thou'lt get no more work! Only the ballots lying there shall ye take.[20]

Where voting had existed for centuries and people knew what to do, as in England, authority hardly felt the need for such hectoring. But in rural Germany, even plutocratic state elections were of recent vintage. Perhaps for that reason, little in the electoral politics of the flatland was left to habit or to chance.

We must not suppose that the choleric Herr Demuth of Leichnam or the irate lord of Buchenhaben, in northern Schleswig, who ran after canvassers and grabbed their ballots, felt any embarrassment about their badgering and ballot-snatching. Power, as Napoleon noted, is never ridiculous. When a scrupulous panel member mentioned to his election chairman, Herr von Loos, that it was

---

[17] 4 Meckl., AnlDR (1879, 4/II, Bd. 5) DS 166: 1350.

[18] Gagel, *Wahlrechtsfrage*, 31, 40f; Hamerow, "Origins," 109, 111, 117; cf. Cowling, *1867*, 58.

[19] Moore, *Politics*; Nossiter, *Influence*, 47f; Hanham, *Elections*, 18f.

[20] 3 Saxony AnlDR, (1881, 5/II, Bd. 5) DS 174: 613f. Similarly: AnlDR (1882/83, 5/II, Bd. 6) DS 300: 1095–98 (3 Breslau); (1893/94, 9/II, Bd. 11) DS 149: 882 (1 Köslin); DS 217: 1142–48 (Schwarzburg-Rudolfstadt); (1894/95, 9/III, Bd. 1) DS 166: 804f (5 Marienwerder); (1894/95, 9/III, Bd. 2) DS 186: 865–68 (4 Köslin); DS 230: 960f (1 Stralsund); DS 278: 1212–18 (3 Posen); DS 303: 1257–59 (4 Meckl.-Schw.); DS 333: 1361–67 (4 Königsberg); DS 342: 1428 (4 Kassel).

against the law to tear up the ballots that he didn't like, the gentleman shrugged: "*Ach was, das kann uns nichts schaden.*"[21] Far from risking any loss of caste, such "energetic, German-to-the-core" interventions to protect one's own were openly recommended by those organs of public opinion that articulated the squirearchy's interest.[22] The *Deutsches Adelsblatt*, the voice of Prussian High Toryism, urged its readers in 1890 to dispatch political interlopers from the towns with threshing flails—"in good old German fashion."[23] It suggested enlisting village elders to organize a watch that could instantly signal the presence of any outsider and stop him at the first cottage. Postmen should be prevented from delivering newspapers and ballots from the outside, and political material that escaped the embargo should be systematically destroyed.[24] The *Adelsblatt* was preaching to the converted. Not just the gentry but farmers as well, especially in the early nineties, organized their men into cudgel crews, plied them with strong drink, and used them to drive political invaders out of their villages.[25]

The social distance separating the powerful from the powerless by no means required physical distance. On the contrary. A landowner who valued good order, economically and politically, wanted his bunkhouse—although it united the worst features, visual and olfactory, of the slum and the barnyard—hard by his manor. Combining a dormitory for farm servants with separate quarters for overseers and artisans, the bunkhouse provided the squire with an additional instrument of control. When Hellmut von Gerlach's aunt, a former lady-in-waiting at court, suggested that her brother's vista might be improved by screening the *Gesindehaus* with a row of fir trees, old Gerlach snorted that the only way to keep his farmhands and their women on the straight and narrow was to let them know that they were under constant surveillance. "This way at least no one can come into the bunkhouse without my seeing him." That the price of authority was eternal vigilance had been demonstrated one election day when the squire's presence had been required in Berlin. He returned to find that the polling had gone badly. "Our hands seem to have voted Radical. The lads are too dumb. The minute you turn your back, they fall in with some big mouth. But let that be a lesson to me. Never go missing on election day again!"

---

[21] "Whatever. It can't do us any harm." 3 Breslau, AnlDR (1882/83, 5/II, Bd. 6) DS 300: 1098. Protest of the Worker Election Committee in Flensburg (2 S-H), 10 Mar. 1887, BAB-L R1501/14664, Bl. 1–8; Schmidt SBDR 27 Apr. 1887: 414–16.

[22] *DA* 8/39 (28 Sept. 1890): 652.

[23] "Das moderne Heidenthum," ibid.; "Good old German fashion": *DA* 8/41 (12 Oct. 1890): 687.

[24] Anon., "Organisierte Abwehrmaßregeln," ibid. Only occasionally were less coercive measures mentioned for winning the rural population: *DA* 9/36 (6 Sept. 1891): 622; *DA* 9/39 (27 Sept. 1891): 678f; *DA* 9/40 (4 Oct. 1891): 695–97; *DA* 9/41 (11 Oct. 1891): 716f. An irate readership could be relied upon to point out that these other methods were too expensive: Fhr. v. Durant (Eingesandt), *DA* 9/38 (20 Sept. 1891): 657f.

[25] H. Hesselbarth, *Sozialdemokraten* (1968), 39, 139; K. Saul, "Kampf" (1975), 179, refers to "bloody clashes," but points out that the courts, unlike the provincial administration, were unwilling to tolerate such measures.

The same solicitude led others to simply move the polls from the designated polling place to their own *Herrenhäuser*.[26]

The very principle of the secret ballot was a thorn in the side for gentlemen of the old school, who believed that for "the worker to hide his real stance towards the employer by a ballot" was a clear "breach of faith" (*Treubruch*—a word that also means felony). Since proven violations of secrecy were among the few offenses that the Reichstag's Election Commission could be counted on to judge harshly, by the late eighties Conservatives were pressuring the government to amend the constitution so as (in the words of one spokesman) "to protect the little man as much as possible from the danger of casting a vote contrary to his stated convictions."[27] In the absence of any immediate prospect for such a reform, Conservative landowners did not hesitate to protect the little man themselves.[28]

Not every bread lord was as unblushing as Baron von Richthofen-Brechelshof, who took out advertisements in the local paper informing workers in Faulbrück of his intention to dismiss anyone who voted wrong.[29] But that dismissal for political disloyalty was considered well within his rights, at least within his own reference group, is seen by an editorial in the *Deutsche Post*, an illustrated Conservative weekly, which recommended that rural employers follow the industrialists' example by banding together to ensure that no man dismissed for political deviancy on one estate be allowed to earn his bread on another.[30] A bread lord's claim was felt, by some, to extend even after an employee had left his master's service. When a young Protestant pastor was so ill-advised as to run as a Free Conservative candidate for Wohlau-Guhrau-Steinau, the leader of the provincial Conservative Party scotched the candidacy with an announcement in the Wohlau County Gazette declaring it an impertinence for someone who had once, as house tutor, been in his employ (*in Lohn und Brot*) to make so free as to oppose his will.[31] "You know whose bread you eat!" was usually all that was needed to keep dependents in line.[32]

The east Elbian gentry's authority over employees was buttressed by their local administrative power: over taxes, schools, poor law, and often the Pro-

[26] Gerlach, *Rechts*, 22, 32. Gerlach had grown up in County Wohlau, 1 Breslau. Cf. 2 Bromberg, AnlDR (1881, 4/IV, Bd. 3) DS 105: 628, 630f.

[27] Rauchhaupt SBHA 6 Dec. 1883, quoted by Rickert SBDR 7 Feb. 1888: 744. On IM Puttkamer's alleged approach to Prof. Laband for an opinion on eliminating the secrecy provision: Windthorst, Bamberger, Bötticher (Govt.), Bennigsen, Helldorf, Dr. Meyer (Jena) SBDR 1 Feb., 3 Feb. 9 Feb. 1888: 657, 661, 663, 666, 693f, 696, 698, 784, 798.

[28] E.g., in Liebertwolkwitz, Probstheida, Görnitz, Gerichshain, Cröbern, and Großstädteln: 13 Saxony, AnlDR (1887/88, 7/II, Bd. 4) DS 212: 904–6.

[29] 11 Breslau, AnlDR (1881/82, 5/I, Bd. 2) DS 104: 353–56. On this and subsequent elections in the district: Leugers-Scherzberg, *Porsch*, 29f.

[30] Quoted approvingly in *DA* 8/41 (12 Oct. 1890): 687f.

[31] Gerlach, *Rechts*, 32, gives "Seydlitz," but this must be a misprint for Otto Th. v. Seydewitz. Of the many examples of rural Polish workers evicted and fired by German bread lords: 5 Marienwerder, AnlDR (1894/95, 9/III, Bd. 1) DS 166: 802–5; Hagen, *Germans*, 370n. 87.

[32] Ortsvorsteher Carl Wommer to Nikel Brill, crop farmer and village factotum in Ronnenberg, 6 Trier, AnlDR (1884, 5/IV, Bd. 4) DS 103: 794.

testant parish church. Exempted from the Prussian Communal Regulation (*Gemeindeordnung*) of 1853, many estates constituted special administrative units (*Gutsbezirke*) whose police and judicial authority remained in the hands of their owners. The arrangement left much of the rural population outside the protections of communal self-government: 36 percent in Pomerania, 28 percent in Posnania, 20 percent of rural Prussia as a whole. Although a new Rural Communal Regulation (*Landgemeindeordnung*) in 1891 allowed for the incorporation of the estates into the jurisdiction of neighboring villages, which themselves enjoyed a modest measure of self-government, such incorporation had to be approved by the county's executive committee (*Kreisausschuss*). Dominated by estate owners, the committees resisted the process. By 1914, only 641 of Prussia's 15,612 *Gutsbezirke* had lost their jurisdictional autonomy. And even the rural communes still stood under the authority of the *Amtsvorsteher*, a kind of Lord Lieutenant, elected by the gentry-dominated County Estates (*Kreistag*), invariably a member of the gentry himself, and, after the 1870s, almost always a Conservative. This was the man to whom village mayor and village teacher had to answer; to whom innkeepers owed their dance licenses.[33] The interweaving of the gentry's economic with its administrative power paid election dividends. For example, after ransacking every house on his own estate for Social Democratic ballots, the landlord in Neukirchen issued, in his capacity as *Amtsvorsteher*, an *official* ban on any further ballot distribution. When one intrepid soul threatened to publish his action in the newspaper for all the world to see, the squire retorted "Do me the honor!" He knew that he would find the ready support of the only people whose approval he valued. And because the office of *Amtsvorsteher* was unpaid, whatever election influence he exercised was considered "private" and thus not subject to the Reichstag's hostility toward "official" influence.[34]

Beyond those who, from shepherds to Protestant parsons, lived directly under the gentry's authority, were ranged concentric circles of neighbors in the estate owner's orbit, men for whom, on the outer margins at least, "client" rather than "dependent" is a better term. Even a quite substantial farmer might still need the tenancy of a pond here, a meadow there—all in the estate owner's gift—if he were to sustain his prosperity.[35] And the fortunes of *all* rural producers, from the prosperous few to the indigent many, whose economic marginality is scarcely even suggested by our word "crofter," were dependent on *Waldstreu*—

---

[33] Traeger SBDR 13 Feb 1886: 1052. T. Kühne, "Liberalen" (1995), 281. Molt, *Reichstag*, 119; Saul, "Kampf," 180f, 180n. 73. Huber, *Verfassungsgeschichte* 4: 362 considers the reform, in light of the very low property qualification for communal elections (*Gemeindevertretung*), democratizing.

[34] 7 Merseburg, SBDR 10 Feb. 1888: 831.

[35] Messenger going house to house threatening loss of tenancy: LL Protest in 1 Erfurt, 12 Mar. 1887, BAB-L R1501/14464, Bl. 12–29; threat of eviction: 4 Oppeln, 5 Apr. 1871: 182; 1 Köslin AnlDR (18 93/94, 9/II, Bd. 2) DS 149: 883; 5 Marienwerder, AnlDR (1894/95, 9/III, Bd. 1) DS 166: 803–5.

EAST ELBIA

"There was *one* liberal vote cast. From now
on, the schoolmaster gets no more potatoes."

Fig. 4. E. Thöny, *Simplicissimus*
XVI 2 Nr. 40: 715.

a term for everything that might be found on the forest floor. *Waldstreu* provided humus, kindling, frost cover for root crops, fodder, and—for those who
could never have afforded straw—litter for barn or stable. Access to *Waldstreu*
was the key to successful husbandry, and it was controlled by the estate owner,
either personally or through his entrée with state forest officials. In every election, threats to deny *Waldstreu* were the gentry's stock in trade. To measure the
power of the rural elite, a Centrum deputy argued, one must count not only
their own workers, "but also the—otherwise independent—farmers," for whom
this resource was "required with the same exigency as *das liebe Brod.*" By

threatening to withhold *Waldstreu*, a "coterie of great landowners can keep the election completely in their own hands."[36]

In the eastern reaches of Prussia, the gentry's sway might extend even into neighboring market towns. Thus in Medzibor, Festenberg, Juliusburg, and Bernstadt, shopkeepers who were "denounced" as liberals found that conservative landowners not only withdrew their custom, but, as creditors, demanded immediate payment on outstanding bills, instead of waiting until the customary first day of the year. In the early eighties the entire liberal election committee of Bernstadt (population 4,000) formally resigned, citing business reasons. No Bernstadter dared rent a hall to liberal speakers—and even if they had, the departing committeemen averred, no one would have dared step forward to register the event with the local authorities or to open the meeting. The upshot of such pressure was that a district that had just voted Progressive, found itself, when the victor accepted a mandate elsewhere, immediately and forcibly returned to the Free Conservative camp.[37]

The openness with which the eastern gentry used the press, both to demand obedience from subordinates and to communicate techniques for insuring it, argues for a robust consensus about voting norms within the landed elite. But we should be wary about identifying these norms with "political culture." If "culture" means anything, then it refers to disciplines that are internalized, to expectations pervasive enough to remain implicit. If culture is the medium in which political creatures swim, then it must be shared, perhaps not by all participants, but at least in principle across class lines. But the resolve of old Gerlach never to be absent on another election day, the house searches and ballot-snatchings of his compeers, and the extraordinary lengths to which all of them went to ensure that their ballots could be "read" from the outside suggest how little the lords of the flatland were prepared to trust those inner, "natural," relationships between master and man to nature—or to culture—alone. We should remember these maneuvers whenever contemporaneous voting patterns across the English channel tempt us to imagine elections in the flatland as the outgrowth of "affirming communities."[38]

In particular regions, of course, the hand of the landowner lay especially heavy. The "Counts' Corner" (*Grafenecke*), a thinly populated peninsula jutting off the east coast of Schleswig-Holstein, presents an especially blatant example

[36] Schröder-Lippstadt SBDR 21 Jan. 1875: 1175. Threats of loss of *Waldstreu* are too frequent to list.

[37] 3 Breslau, AnlDR (1882/83, 5/II, Bd. 6) DS 300: 1096f. Other examples of credit withdrawn: 5 Marienwerder, AnlDR (1894/95, 9/III, Bd. 1) DS 166: 801.

[38] 11 Breslau, AnlDR (1881/82, 5/I, Bd. 2) DS 104: 354; 7 Frankfurt, AnlDR (1881, 5/II, Bd. 5) DS 162: 551–53; 2 Bromberg, AnlDR (1881, 4/IV, Bd. 4) DS 105: 631, 633; protest of the Worker Election Committee in Flensburg (2nd S-H), 10 Mar. 1887, BAB-L R1501/14664, Bl. 1–8; Schmidt SBDR 27 Apr. 1887: 414–16. Suval's discussion of rural voting sometimes seems to distinguish between "obedience," "deference," and "affirming community" as successive points along a scale of freedom; elsewhere, he conflates them. *Politics*, esp. 101f, 106. For all its ambiguity, his picture definitely implies that at some unspecified point, those who voted K did so because they wanted to. A similar view: Nossiter, *Influence*, 198.

of grandee power. How little the Rantzaus, Reventlows, Bülows, Ahlefeldts, Holsteins, and other great families who resided here feared the onset of mass politics can be inferred from the fact that during the first two elections they left the field free for Progressives and Social Democrats to fight over. But 1874 proved to be the Left's last hurrah in the *Grafenecke*. Suddenly the aristocracy decided to claim control. Count von Holstein-Waterneversdorff won big in 1877. By 1878 the Left, which had commanded 14,000 voters in 1874, had been reduced to 805 Social Democrats and 76 Progressives. Shutting down Leftist opinion was child's play in a district that, as late as 1905, could not boast a single town of 5,000 and where most villages lay within the boundaries of someone's estate. The pothouse was a hamlet's only vulnerable point, and word went out that no innkeeper was to rent space to Count Holstein's opponents.[39] On his own broad acres the Count left his taverns untenanted, preferring to forfeit income rather than provide an occasion for his people to come into unsupervised contact with outside ideas—and with each other. As late as 1893 the success of the rural quarantine could be read off the election returns for the villages of Futterkamp, Rantzau, Neuhaus, and Kletkampf. Count Holstein got 795 votes; his opponent got three.

Holstein held the Counts' Corner until his death in 1897. Friedrich Naumann, the charismatic Protestant pastor who had recently founded the National Social Party on a platform of imperialism abroad and social reform at home, thought he detected an opportunity in the ensuing by-election. Naumann persuaded Adolf Damaschke, the well-known proponent of land reform who published a paper in nearby Kiel, that he was a natural for the rural constituency. Yet in all of the *Grafenecke*, a district of nearly 100,000, Damaschke's *Bodenreform* and Naumann's *Hilfe* shared seven subscribers between them: a good index of the new party's prospects. Although they had originally hoped to bring their campaign to each of the district's 182 precincts, National Social canvassers were barred from appearing anywhere except in its very few freeholder hamlets and market towns. There, their speeches were disrupted by the agents of the estates. Although Damaschke's intrepid campaigner Hellmut von Gerlach claimed to have discerned the noses of the rural proletariat pressed against the dark windows of the halls where he was able to speak, none of the curious dared come inside. The Conservative candidate, a squire so deaf that his managers decided to keep him away from his constituents altogether, won effortlessly.[40]

Conservatives made no bones about their technique. Ernst von Köller, Conservative deputy and Landrat (and, in the mid-nineties, a notably pugnacious—and short-lived—Minister of the Interior), published a brief legal handbook that

---

[39] Pothouses generally: *Deutsche Post* Nr. 40, 5 Oct. 1890, quoted in *DA* 8/41 (12 Oct. 1890): 687f. Also *DA* 9/32 (9 Aug. 1891): 549–51; *DA* 9/33 (16 Aug. 1891): 566f. The latter quotes an SD publication's "Suggestions on Rural Agitation" that fully recognized the difficulty of penetrating the villages. Rohe, *Wahlen*, 87f, 90, runs through possible explanations for the Left's successes in rural Holstein in the early 70s without, however, finding a generally applicable answer.

[40] Precinct figures: Gerlach, *Rechts*, 156.

became a Bible for colleagues wishing both to win and to avoid post-victory invalidations. The *Kleine Köller*, as it was called, warned that it was illegal to hinder the distribution of ballots in any way, but, in a telling footnote, reminded landowners that "obviously" no one could trespass on another's property against the will of its owner. A word to the wise is sufficient. Where the Doberman and Great Dane could enforce a landowner's love of privacy, every estate became a "forbidden city" to canvassers.[41] Without space in a public house, or parish priests as distributing agents, opponents of the bread lord simply could not get their ballots into the voters' hands.

Skepticism about "community," affirming or otherwise, in the rural northeast finds its strongest justification in Silesia. Worried observers remarked on the indifference of the Silesian aristocracy to customary responsibilities and relationships. The web of mutual obligations that had once knit rural society together was here, as the young Max Weber complained in 1892, already "a ruin." Yet more modern relationships were spurned. Weber claimed that elsewhere an industrialist or businessman, no matter how rich, would know better than to omit the "Mister" in addressing officials who worked for him and would not fail to address his workers with the polite form of "you" (*Sie*). In Silesia, however, a noble landholder "can scarcely bring the word 'Mister' across his lips . . . , and addresses his coachman, servant, etc., even when they are married . . . with '*du*'—while insisting on 'your worship' for himself."[42] Weber overestimated the spread of more polite forms in the flatland outside Silesia; but he was not off the mark about their absence within the province. And estate officials, in German-speaking Protestant Lower and Central Silesia as well as Polish-speaking Catholic Upper Silesia, were rarely nice about the methods they used to produce election results. Burly forest wardens stationed themselves at the polls, grabbed the hapless citizen, and searched him for offending ballots. His pockets turned inside out, the bread lord's ballot thrust into his hand, ordered to keep his hands high above his head, the voter was then shoved or kicked up to the voting table. By this time he was often—as Johann Warzecha testified—so intimidated that he acted "as if unconscious" and meekly handed the chairman the ballot that had been forced upon him. When a somewhat higher social standing precluded such rough treatment—or when the voter was more physically prepossessing than Warzecha—Silesia's bullies employed other options: rigging the count or even canceling the election. One chairman, apparently convinced that the whole hamlet promised his bread lord no good, announced to all comers:

[41] [Köller], *Ungiltigkeit*, 10n. 2. References were made to it as early as the late 1880s. Hermes SBDR 11 Jan. 1889: 382. On Köller as IM, T. Nipperdey, *Geschichte* (1992) 2: 710, 714. On the 1898 campaign and the "forbidden city": Gerlach, *Rechts*, 156f, 161.

[42] Weber, *Verhältnisse* (1892), 494, 633. Also 635f for an hypothesis about the economic bases differentiating political loyalties in the East.

Today is no election, I am not voting, and thou'lt also not vote, and [pointing to two voters who had just come in] both of ye shall stand there at the door and tell that to anyone else who comes.[43]

The Hohenlohe clan was notorious for making Upper Silesian elections in this way. The Duke of Ratibor (a Hohenlohe-Schillingsfürst), whose upset in Pless-Rybnik was mentioned in chapter 4, was only the mildest offender—which may account for his seemingly miraculous defeat. The mandate of the Duke of Ujest (Fürst zu Hohenlohe-Oehringen) in Groß Strehlitz-Kosel was thrown out in 1875 for practices that had already been amply documented when he had "won" the seat in neighboring Lublinitz-Tost-Gleiwitz in the previous election.[44] Prinz Karl von Koschintin (a Hohenlohe-Ingelfingen) forestalled a similar invalidation only by resigning his seat in Lublinitz-Tost-Gleiwitz in 1876—on the last day of the session.[45] Erbprinz Christian Krafft zu Hohenlohe-Oehringen likewise relinquished his seat in Kreuzburg-Rosenberg in 1881, after the Election Commission finally arrived at an invalidation recommendation. But until then the Hereditary Prince, unimpeded by the scandal of his election, had voted in the Reichstag for nearly three years.

Against voters who ignored their wishes, the agents of the Hohenlohes employed all the usual means by which a landlord could make life hard for his dependents. They withdrew the small offices (such as supervision of the town clock) that enabled a man to extend a tiny income. They terminated gleaning and grazing privileges. They called in outstanding debts, raised taxes, canceled tenancies. They evicted. In the case of the Prince of Pless—exacting revenge for the defeat of the Duke of Ratibor—whole villages were cut off from poor relief.[46] What distinguished the "Hohenlohe" elections in Upper Silesia from the countless other cases of proven intimidation by rural bread lords, and what eventually made their victories vulnerable to invalidation, was the visible complicity of government officials (from Landrat to gendarme), along with the high levels of criminal behavior—violence, open fraud, brazen dishonesty—em-

[43] Five protests in 1 Oppeln, AnlDR (1880, 4/III, Bd. 4) DS 179: 920–23. Also SBDR 21 Jan. 1875: 1175; AnlDR (1876, 2/IV, Bd. 3) DS 111: 812. Similarly in 7 villages in 3 Breslau, AnlDR (1882/83, 5/II, Bd. 6) DS 300: 1097.

[44] 3 Oppeln, AnlDR (1874/75, 2/II, Bd. 4) DS 176: 1122–37; Parisius et al. motion of 19 Jan. 1875, Nr. 204 and Lingens et al. motion of 20 Jan. 1875, Nr. 206: 1264; SBDR 21 Jan. 1875: 1153–71 (invalidation); AnlDR (1875/6, 2/III, Bd. 3) DS 195: 722; AnlDR (1876, 2/IV, Bd. 3) DS 72: 665; SBDR 26 Dec. 1876: 844f. Mazura, *Entwicklung*, 99f, 107.

[45] 4 Oppeln, SBDR 5 Apr. 1871: 182–86; AnlDR (1871 1/II, Bd. 2) DS 63: 139–45; 4 Oppeln, AnlDR (1874/75, 2/II, Bd. 4) DS 149: 1105–13; Kircher-Gneist motion of 20 Jan. 1875, AnlDR (1874/75, 2/II, Bd. 4) DS 207: 1265; SBDR 21 Jan. 1875: 1171–83; 4 Dec. 1875: 422–42; AnlDR (1875/76, 2/III, Bd. 3) DS 64: 242f; AnlDR (1876, 2/IV, Bd. 3) DS 111: 809–25; SBDR 21 Dec. 1876: 998. Prinz Hohenlohe's letter "laying down" his mandate on the last day of the session in order to spare the RT "in the last hour . . . a time-consuming debate" was greeted with laughter. Ballestrem asked how one could "lay down" a mandate that one had never legitimately possessed.

[46] Letter of 1 Apr. 1871 from the Pleß Central Administration (Schloß Pleß) read by Schröder-Lippstadt SBDR 22 Nov. 1871: 434f.

ployed by flunkies on their behalf.[47] These strong-arm practices produced victories, but also endless controversy. Eventually the Hohenlohes wearied of defending their ill-gotten gains against the postelection challenges of their lesser neighbors. And thanks to the Kulturkampf, the Centrum was able to organize these smaller Catholic farmers, who were after all bread lords themselves, to withstand the threats of the grandees, eventually carrying these districts even in state elections held under the three-class voting system.[48] One by one the Hohenlohes vacated the field.

The exception was Christian Krafft, Erbprinz Hohenlohe-Oehringen. After a preemptive resignation in 1881 when his election was about to be invalidated, he recovered his seat in 1883 and held it uninterrupted until January 1912, when he handed it over to a fellow Conservative landowner. Christian Krafft's unbroken string of post-1883 successes is explained by the presence in his district of a large Protestant minority of 40 percent—the only concentration of Protestants in Upper Silesia. Such a constituency needed no special persuasion to vote for a fellow Protestant against any Centrum challenger. With this ace in the hole the Erbprinz was in a strong position to make some kind of an arrangement with Catholic good society. This he must have done between 1881 and 1883, apparently in a complicated trade-off in which Conservatives and Centrum divided the district's two Landtag seats between them (pushing out the hitherto dominant, anticlerical Free Conservatives), and Christian Krafft was given the Reichstag spot. For after a decade of hotly contesting (and protesting) the Erbprinz's victories, once coming within five votes of taking the seat, Hohenlohe's Catholic neighbors suddenly handed him the by-election of 1883 and thereafter ceased to put up candidates against him. The ensuing cross-denominational consensus among the district's elites was broad enough to obviate the need for openly illegal measures. Competition—and the protests against Christian Krafft's victories in Kreuzburg-Rosenberg—dried up.[49]

"AFFIRMATIVE VOTING" AND BRITISH COMPARISONS

Recently Stanley Suval, in a justly praised piece of revisionism, turned a kindly light on elections in the east Elbian flatland. "There can be no question," Suval

---

[47] On 1 Oppeln: SBDR 5 Apr. 1871: 171–80; SBDR 11 Apr. 1874: 732–35; AnlDR (1880, 4/III, Bd. 4) DS 179: 918–23. On 4 Oppeln: SBDR 5 Apr. 1871: 183, and 8 Nov. 1871: 139. Elsewhere in Silesia it was the government that sought grandee support, but did not always get it: Puttkamer to Breslau OP, 8 Oct. 1881 on need for the Schaffgotsch interest in 8 Liegnitz: quoted in "Wie Bismarck," 1/5: 9.

[48] After detailing bread lord intimidation against Z voters, Mazura adds: "In order for dependent clericals not to face the danger of disciplinary action, in the LT elections of 1876 the hired men of ultramontane farmers were in many places designated the electors (*Wahlmänner*), whereas in 1870 predominantly clergy and teachers were elected to it." This tactic can, of course, be read two ways. *Entwicklung*, 100–101n. 18.

[49] 1 Oppeln: Specht/Schwabe, *Reichstagswahlen*, 84, and Nachtrag, 23; T. Kühne, *Handbuch* (1993), 344–46.

conceded, "that a few eastern voters were like those long-sought-after Prussian battalions obediently trooping to the polls." And Suval also quoted a Conservative contemporary to the effect that " 'natural social differences found their robust political expression in the rich old-fashioned syntax of relationships based on obedience.' " But neither of these statements captured for Suval the basic reality of Eastern elections. Rather, at some never specified point during the course of the empire, those "followers" who had once cast Conservative ballots as a matter of obedience gave way to "affirming communities." That is, they became voters tied together by a "combination of interest group and sub-cultural needs." High agricultural prices were of course the chief interest these voters shared—and by the late 1890s organizations such as the Farmers' League had helped to transform "the style of east Elbian politics from the expectation of deference to serious and consistent political campaigning." But even interest group politics never predominated "over the congeries of symbols and relationships that determined political actions in the German east." "Congeries of symbols and relationships" is a slippery phrase. Suval illustrated what he meant by quoting Robert Frank's description of an ideal-typical Conservative meeting in rural Brandenburg, presided over by the inevitable *Herr Major*, whose invocations of ruling house and native soil evoked loyalties to an order simultaneously familiar and timeless; an order that, even more than high agricultural prices, Conservatives were sworn to preserve. "It was only one small step," Suval concluded, "from such behavior to affirmative voting."[50]

Although the edges of the concept are soft, "affirmative voting," if it is to have superseded obedience, must be voluntary.[51] Frank himself supported this inference by stating that "the majority of the rural population saw in the Conservatives people like themselves."[52] But who were the constituents attending Frank's ideal-typical Conservative meeting? Frank called them middle-sized and small farmers (*Bauern*). We might also include those elements of rural Brandenburg society that old Dubslav von Stechlin, Theodor Fontane's fictional

---

[50] Suval, *Politics*, 101–6; also depicting freely voting East Elbians: Below, *Wahlrecht*, 154n. 126.

[51] In fact, Suval waffles so much that the question is ultimately never joined. He begins by conceding that "rural voters in the east were essentially deferential followers" (*Politics*, 102), but then dismisses the notion that the strength of the K vote could have been caused by "intimidation" as "doubtful" (105), while his description of rural voters as affirming communities implies a strong voluntary element. In the end he makes his case not against contemporary liberals (who had denied that K tallies in the east had been produced freely), but against Hans Rosenberg's concept of "pseudo-democratization," a straw man that he easily knocks down: "As long as one considered the democratic model of voting as the only reasonable outcome [Rosenberg's mistake], then undoubtedly the use of mass electoral manipulation for anti-democratic ends becomes a 'travesty' "; but contemporary East Elbians did not consider it so (103). Thus after asking a question about how rural votes were produced (was it by deference, obedience, intimidation—or by affirmative voting?), Suval answers it by referring to what these votes were *for* ("anti-democratic ends"). His conclusion—that the fact that these ends were antidemocratic does not mean that the vote was manipulated—is quite logical; but it leaves us not one whit closer to an answer to the question of whether these votes themselves were a "travesty": that is, unfreely given. Contrast T. Nipperdey, *Organisation* (1961), 241ff.

[52] Frank, *Brandenburger* (1933), 174–77.

representative of all that was best in Prussia's landowning class, gathered around his table on special occasions: the Protestant pastor, the game keeper, the steward (*Rentmeister*), and the owner of the lumber mill. Each of these men had a clear place in the local hierarchy and all, except perhaps the mill owner, would stand in relationships of varying degrees of dependence on the land-owner. But the Suval-Frank argument, by eliding the types and gradations of dependence in rural society, offers a temporal explanation for a phenomenon that was really social. Progress along a scale from coerced to deferential, and from deferential to affirmative voting was not a transformation that once-depen-dent citizens experienced as they were emancipated across time, but a trick of observation, made when the historian, perhaps inadvertently, shifts social cate-gories. Intimidation and obedience are easy to dismiss as exceptional, as Suval does, if we are talking about the transactions between Dubslav von Stechlin and the men sitting, or eligible to sit, around his table—agents, game keepers, mid-dle-sized farmers and businessmen; for outside of Upper Silesia and perhaps rural Holstein, blatant coercion had rarely been part of the social equation con-necting such men with the lord of the manor and with each other.[53] But what about the masses of voters lower down the social scale?

With few exceptions, the need to marshal the votes of the little men did not lead the big men to soften their "feudal" tone. Here, right before the 1912 election, is Ulrich Prinz Schönburg-Waldenburg, lord of Guteborn in Ruhland and chairman of the Farmers' League for the county of Hoyerswerda, summon-ing his neighbors—in the local sharpshooters' club, gymnastics society, volun-teer fire department, glee club, and veterans association—to a meeting under his chairmanship in Ruhland's alehouse on January 6, at which the Landrat (and Conservative candidate) would speak:

> I daresay I may expect you all to appear in full strength, and to give testimony to your sentiment for the Herr Landrat on 1.6 as well as on 1.12 [election day]. I would take *personal offense* if you betrayed me on the sixth or the twelfth of January. I have after all *taken pains* to stand on a friendly footing with Ruhlanders and assume that I may now demand *this quid pro quo for the good of the Fatherland.*

We are told by spokesmen for the Ruhland sharpshooters that they rejected this "attempt at moral extortion."[54] Perhaps they did. But even men as small as these had never made up those "Prussian battalions obediently trooping to the polls" of which contemporaries complained and whose existence Suval all but denies. Even the members of little Ruhland's various clubs and associations were never "the majority of the rural population."[55] Rather, each of these men

[53] Indirect evidence: "Wahlaussichten für die Provinz Ostpreußen:" reports on the necessity of keeping the "great mass of the smaller landowners," who had turned away from "democracy" in 1878 after the attempt on the King, under the K colors. GStA PK I. HA, Rep. 89/210, Bl. 211.

[54] "Aus der Reichstagswahlbewegung. Der abgeblitzte 'gnädige Herr,'" *Handels-Ztg des Berliner Tageblatts* 2 (2 Jan. 1912) (Abend), 2. Beiblatt.

[55] Frank's words: *Brandenburger*, 174. Frank's study, based on newspapers, is confined almost exclusively to reporting the statistical results of each election in each Brandenburg district. His

(and the "affirmative voters" at Frank-Suval's ideal-typical Conservative meeting) would himself have been bread lord over laborers and stable jacks—many of whom slept in the stalls of the animals they cared for and whose presence was scarcely desired to swell the crowd at the political gatherings of the *Herr Major*.[56] The smallest full-time farmer had his *Hofgänger*: hired hands no less dependent than those teams of laborers who toiled directly for the more substantial Junker.[57] Servants (*Gesinde*), laborers (*Tagelöhner, Einleger, Heuerlinge, Hofgänger, Wanderarbeiter*) with or without contracts, and cotters (*Anbauer, Brinksitzer, Büdner, Drescher, Eigenkäthner, Gärtner, Gütler, Häusler, Instleute, Kätner, Körbler, Köther, Kossäten, Söldner*) unable to support themselves on their own tiny plots: these were the voters who formed the silent majority in the countryside. It is impossible for an English-speaking historian to capture the variations of economic viability and dependency expressed in these terms. Even the great agricultural historian Georg Knapp, as Edgar Melton recently noted, "who devoted his scholarly life to studying the rural population of east Elbian Germany, confessed that he had never discovered exactly what a cottager was."[58] Yet it was with conscripts such as these that the voting battalions east of the River Elbe—but not only there—were stamped out of the ground.[59]

The ideal-typical (or perhaps just idealized) picture of rural "affirmers" also assumes the absence of dissenting voices—easy enough to do when, as was often the case, the landowners and their agents silenced them. They silenced them not only by barring ballotteers from their own estates and villages and by shutting down the few public buildings (as we have seen in the Counts' Corner); but also by occupying the public spaces in such force that they could drive the others out. In tiny Ossa (Royal Saxony), where a candidate for the *Freisinnige Volkspartei* was scheduled to speak at the tavern at 7 P.M., Colonel von

---

views on what motivated voters appear only on his final three pages, and he never says on what evidence they are based. Frank says that high turnouts indicate little absenteeism due to intimidation. In fact in 1898 the P demonstrated that estate owners had refused to inform workers of the day and place of the election (as was their legal obligation), refused to allow them time off to vote, and threatened and dismissed those who failed to vote for the NL candidate. The WPK repeatedly voted to invalidate that election, but the NLs were able to prevent a plenum vote for five years. 3 Marienwerder, AnlDR (1898/1900, 10/I, Bd. 4) DS 507: 2660, 2663; SBDR 14 Mar. 1903: 8665f.

[56] E.g., Dienstknecht H. Fuchs in 9 Breslau: SBDR 6 Mar. 1888: 1317; H. Steins in Esbeck (9 Han.): AnlDR (1890/91, 8/I, Bd. 1) DS 95: 641.

[57] "Otto," and Franz Rehbein, *Das Leben eines Landarbeiters* (Jena, 1911), excerpted in Kelly, ed., *Worker*, 205–29; 188–203; J. A. Perkins, "Worker" (1984); Hesselbarth, *Sozialdemokraten*, 53–65.

[58] Excellent on various kinds of labor: Kocka, *Arbeitsverhältnisse*, 149–53; and on what was a "large and highly stratified continuum": Edgar Melton, "*Gutsherrschaft* in East Elbian Germany and Livonia, 1500–1800: A Critique of the Model," *CEH* 21/4 (Dec. 1988): 315–49; 340; Wehler, *Gesellschaftsgeschichte* (1995) 3: 772; agricultural wage earners made up 1/7 of the population of the Empire, by far the largest single group of wage earners. H.-P. Ullmann, *Interessenverbände* (1988), 72.

[59] On Berkersheim in 8 Kassel: [Knabe] [sign. missing here, but is in a subsequent postcard] to Daßbach, Praunheim, 15 Mar. 1890, BAB-L R1501/14668: Bl. 215f.

Bastineller arrived a half hour early, flanked by seventy of his own sharecroppers and farm servants, by members of the village councils whom his impromptu circular had alerted, and by his fellow landowners and their retinues. He immediately got this crowd to elect him chair of the meeting, and then moved that they deny the floor to anyone from outside the district and limit even the candidate himself to forty-five minutes. When the candidate, a schoolteacher, asked to speak against the motion, the Colonel barked, "Don't interrupt me!" and called for the question, which immediately passed. Recognizing what was planned—Colonel von Bastineller had reserved the room for himself for the slot beginning 7:30—the teacher left the hall that he had paid for to his opponents. The Colonel then denounced the *Freisinniger*'s manners—and turned the floor over to the Conservative incumbent, who had just arrived.[60]

If Robert Frank's belief that "the majority of the rural population saw in the Conservatives men like themselves" reflected the elite's own sentimental understanding of its role in landed society, Stanley Suval's adoption of it owes a good deal to the picture of the reciprocal complaisance and deference so often attributed to election culture in Victorian England. English rural society does offer an illuminating vantage point from which to look at the German flatland, but the contrasts are as revealing as the similarities. First of all, the calibrations measuring English landed grandeur were set on an altogether different scale. Statisticians put the threshold for the top category of landownership in England at 10,000 acres; in Prussia the corresponding threshold was 275 acres.[61] True, Upper Silesia, with its grandees, approached English conditions, with close to 46 percent of the arable held by fifty-four owners (and over 26 percent by only seven, each of whom possessed more than 20,000 hectares; i.e., 49,400 acres). But the largest of these, with 197,600 acres, was not a Junker at all, but the state. Outside Upper Silesia, however, a typical Junker rarely owned more than three or four hundred acres—a domain that would not even qualify as an "estate" in Britain, whose sixth and lowest category of estate spanned holdings from 6,000 acres down to 3,000 acres. A typical Junker's holdings were in fact not much bigger than the average Kansas or Nebraska farmer. (Although his more humble neighbors in the Mark Brandenburg referred proudly to old Dubslav von Stechlin's "palace" [*Schloß*], to objective eyes, Fontane tells us, the manor was "an old box and nothing more.")[62] Rural inequality in Germany was certainly very great, not only in Upper Silesia, but in Posnania (dominated by the Polish aristocracy), Pomerania, and the two Mecklenburgs, where 1 percent

---

[60] 14 Saxony, AnlDR (1885/86, 6/II, Bd. 5) DS 117: 569, 571.

[61] Or even lower: 100 hectares (247 acres): "great estates," Frank, *Brandenburger*, 109; "rural elites": S. Baranowski, *Sanctity* (1995), 189n. 18; more than 100 acres: "latifundia," Perkins, "Worker," 20. Wehler, however, sets it at 600 morgen (360–540 acres). *Gesellschaftsgeschichte* 3: 175, 811. Silesia: Weber, *Polen*, 21.

[62] Fontane, *Stechlin*, 7, 9. Anyone who doubts Fontane's view of the relatively modest living arrangements of many (though not all) Prussian Junkers need only look at the pictures in A. Gräfin Eulenburg and H. Engels, *Ostpreussische Gutshäuser in Polen. Gegenwart und Erinnerung* (Munich, 1992).

of the landowners held 44, 51, and 65 percent of the territory, respectively. But even they hardly matched the broad acres of the British aristocracy. In 1874 80 percent of the entire British land mass, encompassing a population of well over thirty million, was owned by 7,000 individuals.[63]

Differences in scale such as these suggest two consequences for the power of the roughly 85,000 members of the north German squirearchy at election time.[64]

1. With dependents typically numbering in the scores rather than in the hundreds, the ability of the German landlord to track the political behavior of each of his "people" was considerably greater than that of his British counterpart, even before the introduction of Britain's genuinely secret ballot in 1872.[65] His opportunities for surveillance were enhanced, moreover, by the requirement that polling precincts correspond, whenever possible, to existing, "organic" communities. In thinly populated parts of the northern flatland, this meant that precincts, as we have seen, might be coterminous with the boundaries of a single estate.

2. But if commanding the votes of dependents was easier in Germany than in Britain, cashing them into controlling political stock was much more difficult. Not only were holdings so much smaller, election districts were so much larger. Although British constituencies consisting of only 600–700 voters were no longer plentiful after the Reform Bill of 1832, they were still possible. Norman Gash has estimated that at least forty-two persisted in England and Wales in which a single patron possessed enough "interest" to determine single-handedly the outcome of the election. H. J. Hanham has argued that even after the 1867 Reform Act, at least forty such boroughs remained. Even in December 1885, the Redistribution Bill set the bottom limit for the population of a borough constituency at 15,000. In Germany 100,000 souls was the legal norm for an election district. Although some were considerably smaller (and many, vastly larger), the smallest in 1885 still encompassed 35,372 people (with 7,788 registered voters); while the average population of even a rural constituency that same year was 107,073.[66] With numbers like these and with voting taking place simultaneously in as many as 200 polling precincts, control of an entire district

[63] In England in the mid-seventies, 55% of the country consisted of estates of more than 1,000 acres. In order to encompass 55% of Germany's land mass, we would have to include farms as small as 50 acres. D. Barkin, "Germany" (1987), 200–211, esp. 203f; idem, "Study" (1970), 373–404, esp. 376 (the Kansas-Nebraska comparison). David Spring, ed., *European Landed Elites in the Nineteenth Century* (Baltimore, 1977), intro., 2–5; F.M.L. Thompson, *English Landed Society* (London, 1963), esp. tables on 32, 114f, 118. Wehler, *Gesellschaftsgeschichte* 3: 803–16, table on 827, although primarily concerned with the nobility, is very good on great landownership in general.

[64] And ca. 20,000 families in 1880. Wehler, *Gesellschaftsgeschichte* 3: 811.

[65] I say this while recognizing the fact that British estates were not actually *farmed* as a whole, but leased out in parcels to substantial tenant farmers, who themselves employed agricultural laborers. Until 1884 it was these tenants, not their laborers, who comprised the majority of the county constituency. But high incomes did not make them politically any less dependent. D[avid] C[resap] Moore, "The Other Face of Reform," *VS* 5 (1961): 7–34, and idem, "Concession or Cure: The Sociological Premises of the First Reform Act," *HJ* 9/1 (1966): 30–59.

[66] Gash, *Politics*, 25, 203–38, and appendix D; Hanham, *Elections*, 18f, 19n. 1, 44f, 409–12; Seymour, *Reform*, 433, 507.

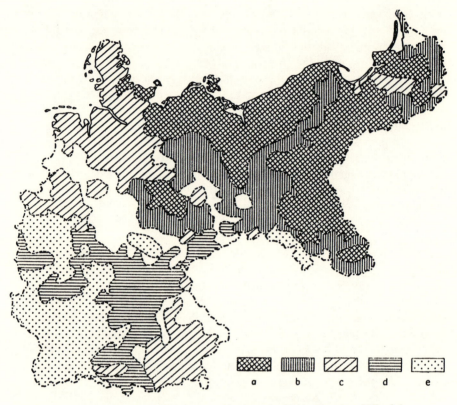

a. Areas where great estates over 100 hectares predominate (make up more than 40% of the land).
b. Areas where great estates (over 100 hectares) are strong (20 to 40% of the land).
c. Areas where farms of 20–100 hectares predominate (more than 40% of the land).
d. Areas in which farms between 5–20 hectares predominate (more than 50% of the land).
e. Areas in which farms of fewer than 5 hectares predominate (more than 20% of the land).

Fig. 5. The size of land holdings in the German Empire. Source: Hellmut Hesselbarth, *Revolutionäre Sozialdemokraten* (Berlin, 1968), 244.

by one or even two or three "interests" was impossible.[67] An examination of voting returns across Germany for the life of the empire suggests that out of all 397 districts only one even looked like what the British called a "close constituency," that is, the preserve of a single family.[68]

[67] Rural average: V. Lidtke, *Party* (1966), 259; smallest: "Die Ungleichheit der Wahlkreise," pts. I, II, *BrZ*, 23 and 25 Mar. 1885, BAB-L R1501/14451, Bl. 301, 303. Upper Silesia, whose scale and pattern of ownership might have made an exception, for confessional and ethnic reasons did not.
[68] 5 Frankfurt was held by the v. Waldow und Reitzensteins from 1867 until 1903, except for 11 years when apparently no family member was available. Count Conrad Holstein-Waterneversstorff sat for 6 Holstein from 1877 until his death in 1897; Christian Krafft, Erbprinz (later Fürst zu) Hohenlohe-Oehringen, sat for 1 Oppeln from 1880 through 1912 except for 1881–82, when the Z

Fragmentation of landowning power did nothing to increase the freedom of the individual voter. But it positively required the efforts of some force from beyond the estate if the desires of its owner were to become politically effective. The services of the government, or, failing that, of a political party, however loosely organized, were indispensable: not to herd the voters to the polls (for that, rural overseers were quite sufficient), but to act as broker in each rural district among the numerous families and interests that made up good society. Otherwise the landlords' efforts would be dissipated among a multitude of competing candidates, and they would be no match for their opponents, for whom the towns provided coherence and a natural base. For a time, during the 1850s, the Prussian Ministry of Interior's energy on behalf of the Conservative cause, performing the services not only of procuring agreeable candidates, but of printing and distributing their ballots, had obscured this truism from those most in need of perceiving it. It was a mistake they would come to regret.[69]

JUNKERS AND THE STATE

Never was the dependence of conservative landowners upon intervention from beyond their estates so glaringly apparent as in the early seventies, when they found themselves in opposition to the whole direction of their government's policies. It was not the democratic franchise, but the government's shift in allies that threatened their political power. Bismarck's cooperation with the liberals opened up fissures within Prussia's conservative elite that multiplied with each new step. Every measure—in the Kulturkampf, whose repercussions for the Protestant Church they feared; in the reorganization of county government (*Kreisordnung*), which the government had rammed through Prussia's upper house by creating new peers—forced them to declare themselves for or against Bismarck, for or against each other.[70] Hostilities between the chancellor and the Conservative Party reached their height in February 1876, when Bismarck's attempt to destroy the *Kreuz-Zeitung*, the journalistic stronghold of the Conservative ultras, provoked a "declaration" of defiance signed by hundreds of blue-blooded readers.

Bismarck had introduced manhood suffrage in order to increase the power of his government in elections. It is one of the ironies of history that it was only against the Conservatives that this government—impotent against the Centrum, hamstrung, as we shall see in chapter 9, against Social Democracy—proved truly effective. But against the Right that power was lethal, as the elections of

---

held the seat. G. Hirth, ed., *Parlaments-Almanach* (1887), 232; *Parlaments-Almanach* (1898), 278. Even the considerable number of "nepotistic survivals" in LT elections were more a consequence of the difficulty of finding willing candidates than of proprietary districts. Kühne, *Dreiklassenwahlrecht*, 306–8, 331.

[69] H. Fischer, "Konservatismus" (1983), 120f.

[70] Good on K fracturing: Pflanze, *Bismarck* (1990) 1: 336–38, 422–26; 2: 210–12, 337–45. Best explanation for why the *Kreisordnung* stuck in their craws: Wehler, *Gesellschaftsgeschichte* 3: 813.

1873–74, catastrophic for the Conservatives, made clear to all. From fifty-seven Reichstag seats in 1871, the party plummeted to twenty-two in 1874, even as the size of the Reichstag itself increased from 382 to 397 deputies, with the enfranchisement of Alsace-Lorraine. The Right's collapse was even more dramatic in the 1873 elections to the Prussian Landtag, where their mandates dropped to little more than a quarter of their previous strength. "Old" Conservatives—that is, the most outspoken dissenters from the Bismarckian line—were reduced to six. Of the fifteen Protestant districts in East Prussia, Conservatives won only three seats in the Reichstag elections of 1874; in the Landtag elections they struck out completely in 1873, as they did again in 1876.[71]

What is the explanation for this debacle? The Right's collapse did not mean that rural voters had suddenly become empowered. In the west, where they were marginal anyway, Conservatives were the inevitable losers as notables and voters alike hurried to proclaim their colors in the culture wars—by voting either Centrum or liberal. In the Protestant east, they were victims of Bismarck's announced determination to teach them what came of "overestimating the weight of the aristocracy in Prussia and underestimating the weight of the crown."[72] Contrary to what the chancellor's own self-serving commentary sometimes implied, however, Conservative losses did not demonstrate that the "crown" had enlisted the "royalism" of the voters and turned it against their masters. The Prussian executive had no ability to insert itself between the voter and his bread lord. The government's power lay not in what it could do, but in what it could withhold. For without any overarching structure of communication to coordinate the scores of possible election choices—such as district-wide party organizations would provide in the future and which the government had provided in the past—the landlords' control over their dependents dissipated in countless contradictory directions.

And Bismarck took steps to insure that just this structure of communication and coordination was denied them. In his own staunchly conservative neighborhood of Varzin, the chancellor actually encouraged Liberal forces.[73] But more important than what Bismarck did for Liberals was what his administration did not do for Conservatives. Word went out that the government's friendly offices would no longer be available for Conservative candidates. Immediately before the 1874 election, Bismarck removed the Landräte of Schlawe and Stolp (in the First and Second Köslin Districts) because they had shown themselves too friendly to "Old" Conservatives, and the new Landrat in Schlawe was warned against giving succor to the government's Conservative opponents.[74] The purge,

---

[71] Figures: Ritter/Niehuss, *Arbeitsbuch*, 38, 140 (slightly different for LT in Wehler, *Gesellschaftsgeschichte* 3: 814); Kühne, *Dreiklassenwahlrecht*, 58.

[72] Bis., "Aufzeichnung," Berlin, 5 Feb. 1874, *GW* 6c: 53.

[73] Kühne, *Dreiklassenwahlrecht*, 273. Kühne convincingly attributes the Right's LT losses to a combination of "terroristic" pressures by the F gentry (ibid., 56–58), loss of govt. support as reflected in the drop in the number of LRe serving in the LT from 41 in 1870 to 12 in 1873 (88), and the K's own demonstrative abstentions in response (60).

[74] B.'s note to a deputy of the IM, 15 Aug. 1873, quoted in GW 6c: 39. Also ibid., 14: 839, 843;

while not affecting the Köslin elections, produced a chilling effect elsewhere in the east. The quiet little meetings in the Landrat's chambers, so necessary for hammering out agreement on a common Conservative candidate, were simply not called—or (and here was another consequence of the estrangement) when they were called, the invitations were disregarded.

Conservatism in the early 1870s was much less a party than an affinity: the like-mindedness of country gentlemen. Although the events of 1848 had once spurred these men to prodigies of organizational activity, by the mid-fifties they had reverted to more congenial habits, relying on the infrastructures of government—prefect, Landrat, county secretary, gendarmes, village headmen—to unite local notables, choose candidates, distribute ballots, and in general to mediate their relationship to the broader public. Now they were left with little in the way of organization that could fill the gap left by the government's defection. The consequence of the withdrawal of the Crown's good offices was chaos. Conservatives ran against each other in Landsberg-Soldin, Salzwedel-Gardelegen, Belgard-Schivelbein-Dramburg, and Neustettin. In Labiau-Wehlau, four different Conservatives (a prince, a Landrat, a professor, and an untitled landowner) faced the National Liberal incumbent. In Prenzlau-Angermünde, dominated by large entailed estates, a Conservative was driven out by a Free Conservative.[75] No lifelines were offered. Incumbents close to the government, on whom Conservatives had formerly relied—such as the chancellor's cousin, old Wilhelm von Bismarck in Osterburg-Stendal, and the Landräte of Teltow-Beeskow-Storkow and Landsberg-Soldin—now declared themselves indisposed to run. Liberal candidates were the beneficiaries.[76] In Jerichow, the Conservatives were only able to make a showing at all because someone distributed ballots for the hero of Königsgrätz, Count Helmuth von Moltke: a quixotic gesture since it was well known that the old field marshal would never desert Memel, his "own" district. Normally men like Moltke were put up outside their intended districts only to show the flag (as "candidates for the count") in regions where the "demographics" against their party were hopeless. Jerichow, which had a substantial Conservative constituency, should not have fallen into that category. But with the government backing a candidate from the *Liberale Reichspartei*, only a name with the luster of Moltke's had a hope of compensating for the missing infrastructure that could have decided upon, and then communicated, a common Conservative choice.[77] In Arnswalde-Friedeberg, where Conservatives had split as early as 1871, fifteen voters were so disgusted with

---

Phillips, *Reichstags-Wahlen*, 32; B. Mann, *Handbuch* (1988), on LT elections in the two districts: 540–42; the biographies of local opponents of B.: 145, 151, 423; B.'s letter to the LR in Rügenwalde (in the Schlawe district), cited by Kühne, *Dreiklassenwahlrecht*, 59n.7; cf. also 273n. 19. Conditions did not always allow B. to dispose of unreliable LRe so quickly: Fenske, "Landrat," 441f. The role of the LR in selecting candidates: Gerlach, *Rechts*, 32.

[75] I.e., 2 Frankfurt, 1 Magdeburg, 4 and 5 Köslin, 2 Königsberg, 4 Potsdam. Phillips, *Reichstags-Wahlen*, 1, 20, 24, 33f, 60; Fischer, "Konservatismus," 121; Frank, *Brandenburger*, 90.

[76] I.e., 2 Magdeburg, 10 Potsdam, 2 Frankfurt: Phillips, *Reichstags-Wahlen*, 10, 60; Frank, *Brandenburger*, 120.

[77] I.e., 3 Magdeburg: Phillips, *Reichstags-Wahlen*, 61.

their options—between a Bismarckian Liberal and an equally Bismarckian Conservative—that they wrote in the name of the Kaiser.[78] In Minden-Ravensberg, in the Protestant part of Westfalia, they demonstratively did not vote at all.[79]

Voting tallies do not speak a univocal language, and never less than when relations between the landowning class and the government were in flux. Why was no Conservative candidate willing to stand in 1874 in Ückermünde-Usedom-Wollin or in Randow-Greifenhaben, two eminently conservative constituencies in Stettin?[80] When Baron Otto von Hüllessem-Meerscheidt, Conservative Landrat of Königsberg-County, was unseated in Königsberg-Fischhausen by a National Liberal estate owner of lower rank, did the upset express the sentiments of a gentry that was still liberal—or the hostility of a mightily displeased government? Probably the latter, given the district's Conservative voting record before and after the Liberals' 1874 victory. When the Progressive Leopold von Hoverbeck trounced Gumbinnen's new prefect, Robert von Puttkamer, in rural Sensburg-Ortelsberg, was the latter's defeat the product of local Progressive traditions, of the systematic "terrorism" commonly practiced (said Puttkamer's partisans) by the dominant Progressive elite, or of Conservative anger at the government's new *Kreisordnung*, aimed at robbing them of police powers on their own estates, which the young prefect had been brought in to implement? To individual questions, case studies alone can give us the possibility of positive answers.[81]

One lesson, however, the 1874 elections made clear. An individual landowner's "interest" was politically inconsequential without the help of either a party or the government. By 1876 steps were being taken by Conservatives to overcome both of these deficits. That year they buried their differences by founding a new denomination of the conservative faith, the "*German* Conservative Party." In itself, the new organization left much to be desired. Less a party, in fact, than a skeletal clearinghouse through which the Conservative parliamentary delegation tried to coordinate its reelection campaigns, it was envisioned as having no role independent from the decisions of local power-holders, whose instrument it remained. Although opinions differ on the effectiveness of its organization, as late as 1909 the party proved unable to insist upon the most minimal, and vital, prerogative of any political party: the right to use a by-election in a safe district to give a seat to a party leader who had been defeated in the general elections.[82] Nevertheless, the founding of the "German Conserva-

---

[78] 1 Frankfurt. *GA* Nr. 17, 21 Jan. 1874: 95. Five votes for the Kaiser were cast in 1 Minden in 1877: AnlDR (1877, 3/I, Bd. 3) DS 187: 517.

[79] Kühne, *Dreiklassenwahlrecht*, 60.

[80] Phillips, *Reichstags-Wahlen*, 29f.

[81] 7 Gumb. A. v. Puttkamer reports only on his father's simultaneous (close) victory in the neighboring Oletzko-Lyck and says the *Kreisordnung* was a perfect success. *Puttkamer* (1928), 32f. One of the real puzzles of the 1874 elections are the K successes in 1 and 2 Köslin—whose *LRe* Bis. had removed immediately before the election because they were too friendly to Ks.

[82] Nipperdey, *Organisation*, 352–54, 263f. However, Fischer, "Konservatismus," and Kühne,

tives" marked for conservative country gentlemen an important step toward political security. For the party's central article of faith, from which so long as Bismarck remained in power it did not swerve, was never to go into an election without government support again.[83]

And the government, for its part, responded as early as 1879 by putting its entire apparatus, at least in the eastern reaches of Prussia—from Provincial Governor down to local school and prison inspectors—in the service of Conservative elections. Only the Catholic Church could rival this communications infrastructure; no political party, and certainly no bread lord, urban or rural, disposed of its like. The same move, moreover, that bestowed a political machine on the new Conservative party almost overnight withdrew from the Liberals and Progressives many of the very men—school teachers, public health doctors, county clerks—who had worked for their election (some voluntarily, some not) in the past.

Not all rural bread lords, of course, were Conservatives or Free Conservatives. It is only linguistic convention that reserves the term "Junker" for the Conservative squire, since strictly speaking Junker is a social rather than a political category.[84] This same convention implies that only Conservative elections were won by the "traditional" methods of the bread lord. That was far from the case. In the Hessen countryside, the gentry were National Liberal. In Hanover, landowners were either National Liberals or Guelfs. The former enjoyed unbroken government favor throughout the course of the empire; the latter did their best to turn government harassment into a moral and therefore electoral advantage; but both made free with whatever voting influence could be extracted with economic power. In the frontier province of East Prussia, at least until the late seventies, many country gentlemen cleaved to the Progressive cause. Concentrated in the regency of Gumbinnen and in Second and Third Districts of Königsberg, the Progressive gentry were every bit as willing as their Conservative counterparts in Brandenburg and Pomerania to exact political conformity, both "vertically," from their Masurian and Lithuanian peasants and the small tradesmen within their orbit, and "horizontally," from their fellow landowners, through their control of local government, producer cooperatives, stud competitions, and especially the credit unions upon which indebted agrarians were so utterly dependent. Thomas Kühne has shown how these collective pressures operated to produce Progressive victories in Landtag elections. It is unlikely that elections to the Reichstag were much different. True, the ballot would have

Dreiklassenwahlrecht, esp. 66, 66n. 47, and 75, have shown that the backwardness of K organization has been exaggerated.

[83] Bismarck's relations with Ks: Pflanze, *Bismarck* 2: 340–45. On K organization after 1876 and its dependence on the government: J. N. Retallack, *Notables* (1988), esp. 31f, 55. The government's obligingness once the Ks had come around: Kühne, *Dreiklassenwahlrecht*, 65f.

[84] While Baranowski reserves Junker for families ennobled before 1400, she concedes that it came to be applied to the entire landed class. *Sanctity*, 29, 31, 189 n. 18. I am using it for the German landed gentry, which need not be ennobled.

kept a gentlemen's personal choice from his neighbors' prying eyes—for who would dare rip it from his hand? But as soon as a landowner made use of his interest politically, by enlisting his people—or by failing to enlist them—his preferences became as public as the tallies of his villages. He would then have been subject to all of the disabilities nonconformity might bring.[85]

In West Prussia and especially in Posnania, the Polish *szlachta* disposed of their battalions of rural workers and other dependents with the same ease.[86] Unlike the German Junkers, however, the *szlachta* had no need for the Landrat to provide their staff work. From the moment Landtag elections were introduced in Prussia in 1850, they had established their own hierarchy of committees, at the precinct, county, and election district level, to coordinate candidate selection. This was the system of "electoral authorities" (*władze wyborcze*), whose choice was then certified as the "legal" (i.e., official) candidate for the Polish electorate—obligatory for anyone who adhered to the Polish cause.[87] Thus the *szlachta*'s decisive intervention did not come at the point of balloting, where ethnic solidarity, the Kulturkampf, and exhortations by the Catholic clergy usually sufficed to guarantee voluntary support for the candidate of the Polish "electoral authorities." Rather, the *szlachta*'s real influence came at the point of candidate selection in the precinct meetings. Although these meetings were nominally open, they were run by the gentry—as the younger, more urban, more secular, and more radical National Democrats learned when, after the turn of the century, they made their own bid for leadership of the Polish movement. By simply packing these local nominating meetings with their dependents and laborers, the gentry were able to keep political control in their own hands. The result was a considerable brake on the National Democrats' radicalism, as the newcomers were forced to make concessions to the *szlachta* and the clergy who supported them. For all the National Democrats' youthful dynamism, as late as 1912 the Polish gentry continued to control fourteen of the eighteen seats comprising the Polish Reichstag delegation.[88]

Liberals had wasted no time congratulating themselves in the early seventies on the approaching end to the gentry's privileged position. *"Das Junkertum kann sein Testament machen,"* one Progressive newspaper pronounced.[89] Yet reports of the conservative squirearchy's demise were exaggerated. The 1874 election

---

[85] Liberal strongholds among agrarian classes: Puttkamer, *Puttkamer*, 27; Molt, *Reichstag*, 114f. G. Below (admittedly a K partisan) on Insterburg (3 Gumb.), *Wahlrecht*, 154n. 126. A supporting example: 5 Gumb., AnlDR (1882/83, 5/II, Bd. 6) DS 283: 1034–37, 1040. Kühne, *Dreiklassenwahlrecht*, 56–58, 60. Nor were such pressures confined to the East: 8 Hessen, AnlDR (1912/13, 13/I, Bd. 16) DS 350: 290.

[86] 2 Bromberg, AnlDR (1881, 4/IV, Bd. 4) DS 105: 630f, 633.

[87] Hagen, *Germans*, 114; Trzeciakowski, *Kulturkampf*, 168f, 174. It is, not surprisingly, easier to find evidence of German estate owners oppressing Polish workers than Polish estate owners oppressing Polish workers.

[88] The NDs were all from Posnania. Hagen, *Germans*, 237–39, 367n. 45; power of the clergy, 243f, 248.

[89] "Junkerdom can make out its will." *GA* Nr. 80, 4 Apr. 1871: 678.

marked the low point in Conservative fortunes. By 1878 they had more than doubled the dismal tallies of that black year. Throughout the eighties, although their share of seats fluctuated considerably, they never got less than 15 percent of the national popular vote. In the Prussian Landtag, with its undemocratic three-class voting system, they became the largest delegation in 1879, a position they never lost.[90] Liberal suspicions that the appointment of Robert von Puttkamer to Prussia's Ministry of Interior in 1881 meant that Conservative contrition was about to be rewarded with government electoral aid proved more than justified.[91] Soon it became unnecessary in the east Elbian flatland to distinguish between the wishes of the bread lord, the Landrat, and the local Conservative election committee. And yet: this mutually beneficial *ménage à trois*, while it put paid to the Progressives' chances in the rural east, was hardly a resumption of "traditional"—in the sense of spontaneous and unreflected—political relationships. No one doubted that the Landrat's friendly offices were dependent on the squires' continued good behavior. Even the chancellor's shift from free trade to moderate protection in 1879, although decried as a harbinger of Junker ascendancy, was not done at their behest.[92] Standing in the long shadow of Bismarck, the Conservative resuscitation had a spectral air.

The popularity of Ernst von Wildenbruch's melodrama, *The Quitzows*, which took Berlin by storm in 1888, was a sign of the times. The saga of this violent clan of robber barons, who had once so terrorized the Mark that townsmen dared not venture outside their walls, now provided a pleasurable *frisson* for theater-goers; the Quitzows' suppression by Friedrich of Hohenzollern in 1414, a contemporary morality tale.[93] The "Kartell," that unlovely and unloved corral into which the chancellor had herded, during the 1887 elections, his Conservative sheep along with his National Liberal goats was, after all, a sign of Junker submission no less clear than the Quitzows' smoking castles. When the *Deutsches Adelsblatt* commemorated Bismarck's seventy-third birthday in 1888 with some doggerel that concluded

I am ashamed I hated you,
One can truly only love you[94]

it was yet one more demonstration of how thoroughly the Conservative aristocracy had been brought to heel.

[90] Ritter/Niehuss, *Arbeitsbuch*, 38f, 140. A useful table of K election results by state and (for Prussia) by regency, from Ritter/Niehuss, is in Retallack, *Notables*, 245–49.

[91] Miquel to Cuny, 11 Sept. 1881, in Oncken, *Bennigsen* 2: 473fn. 2; Seyffardt, *Erinnerungen*, 136. On the use of the term "reaction" in 1879: Anderson/Barkin, "Myth," 647–86; Kühne's objections, *Dreiklassenwahlrecht*, 61–63, and 62n. 14.

[92] Karl W. Hardach, *Die Bedeutung wirtschaftlicher Faktoren bei der Wiedereinführung der Eisen- und Getreidezölle in Deutschland 1879* (Berlin, 1967); Anderson, *Windthorst*, 223–37; K. Barkin, "1878–1879. The Second Founding of the Reich, A Perspective," *GSR* 10/2 (1987): 219–35.

[93] Wildenbruch (1845–1909) was the grandson of Prince Louis Frederick Christian of Prussia. I owe details on the Quitzows to Gordon A. Craig.

[94] Constant v. Wurzbach, "An Bismarck," *DA* 6/15 (8 Apr. 1888): 232. Kartell as "fundamental evil": *DA* 11/26 (25 June 1893): 502–4.

How Mighty the Junkers?[95] Competition from the Social
Democrats, the Antisemites, and the Farmers' League

Within the next five years, the public's sense that their national robber barons
had been safely relegated to stage and storybook abruptly disappeared. The
word "Junker," after a long ban from polite society, again became a staple of
adversarial discourse as free traders, urban intellectuals, social reformers, and
Social Democrats seized upon a symbol that offered as much potential political
mileage as "Jesuit" had given an earlier generation of anticlericals.[96] Their success among the broader public was registered even by Dubslav von Stechlin,
when he opined to his dinner companions that "Junkerdom" had so colossally
increased its power in recent years "that sometimes it seems to me as if the
Quitzows of blessed memory are climbing out of their very graves." Like
changes in the image of the priest at the turn of the century, the resurrection of
the "Junker" topos in the nineties registered a shift in the assumptions governing politics, both at the top and at the bottom of the German polity.[97]

Three broad developments lie behind the gentry's becoming targets of renewed opprobrium. **First**, the united front between the government and Conservatives shattered after Bismarck's departure in 1890. Without the Iron Chancellor's iron hand, the government's will was now as fragmented as the gentry's
had once been. And as Bismarck in retirement immediately leant himself to
intrigues against his successor, General Leo von Caprivi, and his New Course,
the result was general confusion.[98] How was a Conservative to demonstrate his
adherence to the "government," when it was increasingly unclear who spoke for
that government? And who *really* represented Conservative interests: The Conservative Party? The group of unorthodox "social reformers" behind former
Court Preacher Adolf Stoecker? The "Frondeur of Friedrichsruh" and men

[95] The phrase is from W. W. Hagen, "How Mighty the Junkers? Peasant Rents and Seigneurial
Profits in Sixteenth-Century Brandenburg," *Past and Present* 108 (1985): 80–116.

[96] No longer "*hoffähig*": *DA* 12/7 (18 Feb. 1894): 123f; cf. Retallack, *Notables*, 65. Use of
"Junker" in 60s and early 70s: *DA* 10/46 (13 Nov. 1892): 918–20. In fact, the word had continued
in polemical use: in 1879, Ludwig v. Pastor, *August Reichensperger 1808–1895* (Freiburg im Br.,
1899) 2: 180; in 1881, White, *Party*, 100; in 1884, [E. Richter], *Neues ABC-Buch für freisinnige
Wähler* (1884), 173f; in 1893, *DA* 11/31 (30 July 1893): 585–87; *DA* 11/38 (17 Sept. 1893): 710f.
Noting a new tone: *DA* 12/18 (6 May 1894): 344–47, and Nr. 19 (13 May 1994): 365–70, which
cited a *Grenzboten* article as saying that it would be just as well for Germany if 10,000 East Elbian
noble landowners disappeared; *DA* 15 (1897): 797–99, 818, 820; the series "Konservative 'Junker'
und liberales 'Bürgerthum,'" *DA* 17 (1899): 247–50, 268–70, 283–86, 299–301, 310–20.

[97] *Stechlin*, 7, 268f. Currents at the top and bottom of society making Junkers vulnerable: Eley,
Reshaping, 252f.

[98] The following numbers of the *DA* testify to the disorientation among Ks when Bis. and the
govt. were at odds: "Sprechsaal," *DA* 8/46 (16 Nov. 1890): 783; Max Schön, 10/32 (21 Aug. 1892):
684f; 10/35 (28 Aug. 1892): 705–7; 10/43 (23 Oct. 1892): 860–62; the three-part series entitled
"Royalist oder Frondeur? (Eingesandt)," 10/44 (30 Oct. 1892): 882–85, 10/45 (6 Nov. 1892): 903–
5, 10/46 (13 Nov. 1892): 922f; "Politische Wetterfahnen," 10/27 (2 July 1893): 523–26. Generally:
Pflanze, *Bismarck* 3: 381–98. K disarray, Retallack, *Notables*, 80ff; Nipperdey, *Organisation*, 256,
260; combined with ministerial "particularism": idem, *Geschichte* 2: 700, 705.

around him?[99] Quarrels within the royal and imperial administration, on the one hand, disarray within the Conservative camp on the other (culminating in an inner-party coup against its leader, Otto von Helldorf-Bedra), inevitably brought unfavorable attention to the class from which government and party both drew. They raised uncomfortable questions about a triangular relationship that all three—government, party, and class—would have preferred to take for granted.

Second, the prestige of the landed aristocracy could only suffer from its association in the public mind with the velleities of William II, a man constantly proffering himself, as the spirit moved, as a caricature now of absolutism, now of feudalism. Monarch since 1888 and intent upon establishing his "personal rule," William II was driven to greet the most conventional occasions with rodomontade.[100] "There is only one master in the Reich, and that is I," he announced to the Rhenish Provincial Estates. Upon visiting Munich he inscribed the phrase "*voluntas regis suprema lex est*"—the will of the King is the supreme law—in the city's guest book (as a "gallantry" to the King of Bavaria), forcing even that staunch monarchist Hans Delbrück, editor of the *Preußische Jahrbücher*, to register the "insult" to public opinion at this royal "declaration of war." And William opened the Brandenburg Provincial Estates with the promise to "smash" his opponents, summoning the assembled country gentlemen to follow their "margrave . . . through thick and thin, wherever he may lead!" The intended target of these outbursts was not the Reichstag, but William II's endlessly troublesome ex-chancellor. Nevertheless, appeals to a vassal's fielty sounded jarringly out of tune with a century moving toward its close. They elicited an anxious demur from the head of the Brotherhood of German Nobles, who noted that however much one might *wish* to follow one's margrave through thick and thin, "passages of this kind, in the constitutional life of our state, which has grown entirely unaccustomed to such experiences, must lead to convulsions and uncertainty in public life."[101]

The bread lords in the flatland had no more to do with William II's grandiose *obiter dicta* than with the nests of intrigues in Berlin and Fredrichsruh. Many, like the spokesman for the Brotherhood of German Nobles, may have heartily

[99] "Frondeur aus Friedrichsruh": Fürchtegott Peinlich [George Friedrich Dasbach?], Registrator im Dienst der geschichtlichen Wahrheit, *Die Wahrheit über Bismarck. Eine Studie über die Geschichte der Friedrichsruher Fronde* (Trier, 1892). Bis.'s reptile press's attacks on the K: ibid., 18f; the unreliability of the east Elbian "Landratspresse" (*Kreisblätter*) in support of the government after 1890: Saul, "Kampf," 189, and 189n. 110.

[100] Generally: Erich Eyck, *Das persönliche Regiment Wilhelms II* (Zurich, 1948); John C. G. Röhl, *Kaiser, Hof und Staat. Wilhelm II. und die deutsche Politik* (Munich, 1987), 119–40; Lamar Cecil, *Wilhelm II* (Chapel Hill, 1989, 1996) 2: 195, 208f, 229–31, 240f, 248, 260–62, 308. As for the question of the *reality* of personal rule, I find convincing the critical arguments of Huber, *Verfassungsgeschichte* 4: 183 and Wehler, *Gesellschaftgeschichte* 3: 1016–20.

[101] Quotes in order: "Die Düsseldorfer Kaiserrede," *DA* IX/19, (10 March 1891): 317f; Munich speech and Delbrück response: "Der König als Führer und Erzieher des Volksthums," DA X/1 (3 Jan 1892): 3. "Die neueste Kaiserrede," IX/9 (1 March 1891): 141f, quoting from a speech given on 5 Mar. 1890; head of the Brotherhood of German Nobles, quoted (disapprovingly) in "Die Düsseldorfer Kaiserrede,"*DA* IX/19 (10 Mar. 1891): 317f.

regretted them, or at least the controversy they excited. But loving their Kaiser for his enemies as they did, and given their commitment to "authority not majority," as their election slogans proclaimed, the gentry inevitably found itself depicted as the embodiments of the "neo-feudalism" that William II's outbursts were thought to exemplify. Unflattering representations did not affect the landed elites' relations with their dependents, nor their ability to harvest this election fodder on voting day. They did, however, turn an unwelcome spotlight on the rural elite, a spotlight that could only have encouraged challengers from below.

These challengers provided the **third** development in the nineties that focused attention on "Junkerdom." All of them were eventually repulsed by the still-powerful landowners. But the challengers did succeed in turning "Junker" into an all-purpose political epithet that yoked together disparate groups and institutions in an all-encompassing symbol of privileged backwardness.[102] It is to their efforts that we shall now turn.

The first to appear on the scene was Social Democracy. Although it was an axiom of rural gentlemen that every election constituted an injury to the "natural authority" necessary in social and working life, little of this injury was visible in the countryside.[103] Social Democracy's spectacular successes in February 1890, when it doubled its popular vote and captured nearly 20 percent of all votes cast, had been just as spectacularly limited to metropolitan or industrialized areas. In districts not blessed with at least one town with a population over 20,000 (either within its boundaries or nearby), Social Democratic tallies had been dismal. In such constituencies the party averaged 735 votes—not per precinct, but per election *district*. The low numbers were a good index of the gentry's continued effectiveness at the polls. In October 1890, one month after the lapsing of the Socialist Law, the Social Democrats, meeting in Halle, resolved to take advantage of the freer climate by redirecting their energies toward the rural electorate. Although the party set its sights on independent farmers in the south and west at least as much as on agricultural laborers in the east, alarmed Conservatives immediately interpreted the Halle resolution as an invasion "into the actual domain of the aristocracy."[104]

The conversion of the flatland, however, proved easier said than done. If "large collectivities," as Giovanni Sartori has suggested, "become class structured only if they are class persuaded," and if persuasion requires "a powerfully organized network of communications," then the Social Democrats suffered crippling disabilities. The union movement that had enabled them to penetrate the mining industry, putting starch in potential voters via civil rights associations (*Schutzvereine*) and support funds, labored under so many legal fetters in

[102] Fairbairn, "Interpreting" (1992), 37; Hesselbarth, *Sozialdemokraten*, 44ff. Authority not majority: Gerlach, *Rechts*, 27; *DA* 8/1 (5 Jan 1890): 7.

[103] Helldorf SBDR 3 Feb. 1888: 699. After being quoted critically by Reichensperger (SBDR 1 Feb. 1888: 675) and Rickert (SBDR 7 Feb. 1888: 743), H. all but retracted his statement, saying he meant only *campaigns*, not the act of voting itself. Ibid., 747.

[104] This phrase appeared already in the 1890 election. Von W. W., *DA* 8/12 (23 Mar. 1890): 192f. See also the articles in the *DA* cited in footnotes 22–24.

the old Prussian provinces that unionizing rural workers proved almost impossible.[105] Club life of even a convivial sort, which might have provided a cover for political activity, operated under severe restrictions—even apart from those imposed by lack of time and physical exhaustion. On the one hand, Prussian laws of 1854 and 1860 forbade agricultural laborers and servants to found clubs themselves. On the other hand, they were sometimes herded by their employers into organizations run by their betters. It was often well into the twentieth century before the Social Democrats succeeded in setting up those innocuous-looking cycling societies, men's choirs, and gymnastic teams that could provide a cover for evangelization—and rarely, even then, did they penetrate rural areas. In the meantime? Comrades from each market town were simply assigned a stretch of countryside to visit, of a Sunday, where they were expected to strike up political conversations with the rural poor. Considering how very few Social Democratic voters, let alone party members, made up the party's base in these little towns, the task of the recruiting agent, even though many appear to have been paid for their work, cannot have been an easy or a pleasant one. Their intended recruits did not need to be directly employed by the Junker to feel his wrath. A barber in Altendorf in Thuringia, who was discovered slipping SPD literature to his customers in 1894, lost his clientele when laborers were forbidden to go to him for their haircuts.[106] The party set high hopes on those whose peripatetic trades—in construction or in farm machinery repair—brought them in contact with the rural population and then removed them from harm's way. But the very mobility that gave these artisans a measure of safety ensured that they would never stay anywhere long enough to establish lasting relationships. Judging from the names that appear in the numerous protests about the mistreatment of Socialist balloteers, most of these party workers, paid and unpaid, appear to have been cobblers—men not dependent on any single bread lord for sustenance—and men who plied their trades in towns of considerable size.[107]

By the century's end, the Social Democratic campaign, which had begun with such an enormous expenditure of enthusiasm and resources, could record a measurable success only where the party already enjoyed strength in nearby towns: that is, in royal Saxony and Thuringia especially, and more generally in a rough ellipse stretching across central Germany from Kassel in the west and Hanover in the north, to Liegnitz in the east and Hof in the south. Even here, Socialist canvassers often met with pugnacious farmers and snarling dogs.[108] The western and eastern rims of the empire, even at the end of the decade, remained all but inviolate. In the west—that is, rural Catholic Germany—regardless of whether holdings were large or small, the Centrum (in the Münsterland, Rhineland, southern Württemberg and Baden, and Lower Franconia) re-

---

[105] Sartori, "Sociology," 85; Saul, "Kampf," 171, 175.

[106] Hesselbarth, *Sozialdemokraten*, 264n. 123; Saul, "Kampf," 172f; Birk, "Entwicklung" (1982), 175–77, 190f; *DA* 26/17 (26 Apr. 1908): 245.

[107] E.g., 4 Saxony AnlDR (1882/83, 5/II, Bd. 6) DS 260: 964–68; *DA* 9/33 (16 Aug. 1891): 566f.

[108] Hesselbarth, *Sozialdemokraten*, 130; Saul, "Kampf," 169, 172–74; White, *Party*, 133.

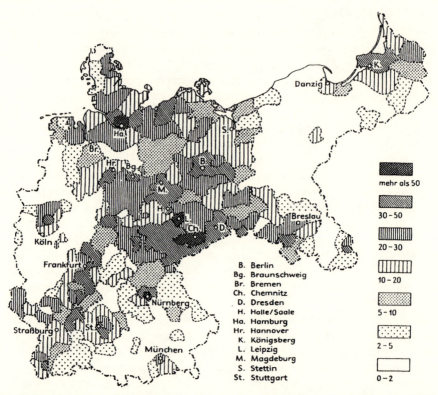

Fig. 6. The distribution of SPD votes in villages with a population under 2,000 in the 1898 Reichstag election, given in percentages. Source: Hellmut Hesselbarth, *Revolutionäre Sozialdemokraten* (Berlin, 1968), 246. [Note to reader: the first darkened square says "more than 50."]

sponded with a countercampaign that more than compensated for the SPD's efforts. The Polish party did the same in the Catholic east: in West Prussia, Posnania, southern East Prussia, and eastern Pomerania. The result was that in these areas the 1898 election registered an actual decline in Socialist strength.[109]

Equally disappointing was the Protestant northeast. The Junkers—whether of German or Polish observance—exercised "strict patronage" to make sure that

[109] An early recognition of the resistance of Catholic areas, even in industrialized regions: R. Blank, "Zusammensetzung" (1905), 510f, 523, 531, 533, although G. A. Ritter has relativized this finding, suggesting that as early as 1893 as many as one-third of those Catholic voters employed in the commercial ("*gewerbliche*") sector were voting Social Democratic. "Strategie" (1978), 324n. 40. SPD victory over the Z in Cologne: R. C. Sun, *Enemy* (1999). SD failure in the regencies of Gumbinnen, Marienwerder, Danzig, and Allenstein cannot be entirely explained by the strength of confessional and ethnic factors. P. Steinbach, "Entwicklung" (1990), 1–35, esp. 15. Also: G. A. Ritter, "*Sozialdemokratie*" (1989), 295–362; Hesselbarth, *Sozialdemokraten*, 248f; v. Saldern, *Wege*, 82. Even when the Z itself briefly lost ground to the BdL and other agrarian pressure groups, the combination of their rival campaigns was deadly for Social Democracy. On the peasant leagues: I. Farr, "Populism" (1978), 136–59.

no innkeeper who knew what was good for him rented a hall to Socialist campaigners. The message was reinforced by the provincial authorities with hints
about what might happen to dance licenses and opening hours, and what might
be found to violate building and health codes, if Socialist speakers appeared.
Open-air meetings as well as those in private residences also fell to their discretionary powers. The SPD was reduced to appending requests for information
about possible meeting halls to the bottom of its leaflets. As late as 1907 there
were thirty-nine election districts in the east where the party could not find a
single tavern that would take their money. Even in 1912, in all of East and West
Prussia they had access to only 110 locales. When one reflects that well over 60
percent of the nearly four million people in these two provinces were dispersed
among communities smaller than 2,000, one gets a sense of the magnitude of
the Social Democrats' task.[110] With the exception of the East Prussian seacoast,
where the cities of Danzig and Königsberg gave them an urban base from
which to fan out, and excluding those districts in Mecklenburg whose proximity
to the greater Hamburg area enabled Socialists to grab second place, the rural
peace in the northeast continued undisturbed. With only one campaign committee, based in Lübeck, to evangelize both Mecklenburgs, with another in Breslau
to handle all of Silesia and Posnania, and another for the entire provinces of
East and West Prussia (and each of these committees limited to a radius acces-
sible by foot or bicycle, that is, to ten or twenty kilometers each Sunday), how
could it have been otherwise?[111]

As frustration stimulated quarreling and controversy among the SPD's different wings, the gentry began to relax.[112] Not until 1903 was Social Democracy
able to make sizable showings anywhere in the rural east, and these votes are
largely attributable to men not employed in agriculture. Few rural workers can
have shown the gumption of Willy Brandt's grandfather, who "accidentally"
knocked over the soup tureen holding the ballots in the overseer's house, thus
denying his Mecklenburg bread lord positive proof of his Social Democratic
vote. Even the gains of 1903 receded in subsequent imperial elections, as those
who had managed to use their ballots as a protest mechanism found a better
outlet by leaving the flatland altogether. The fact that the Central Association of
the Conservative Party, which distributed election pamphlets addressed to urban
workers and craftsmen, issued no analogous leaflets directed to agriculture is
the best possible evidence of Conservative confidence that the mass of eastern
rural voters were still firmly under their command.[113]

---

[110] Bertram, *Wahlen*, 201; Saul, "Kampf," 171–72n. 31, 184; L. E. Schücking, *Reaktion* (1908),
97. Other parties—notably, but not exclusively, the Z in Bavaria—also denied campaign opportunities to competitors in their bailiwicks. Population: G. Hohorst et al., *Arbeitsbuch* 2: 42.

[111] Hesselbarth, *Sozialdemokraten*, 23–8, 33f, 39. The SD's own "Suggestions for Rural Agitation" in *DA* 9/33 (16 Aug. 1891): 566–71. LLs were not better off: R. Breitscheid, "Hinterpom-
mersche Wahleindrücke, *Die Hilfe* 13/8 (24 Feb. 1907): 115–17.

[112] *DA* 12/48 (2 Dec. 1894): 919f.

[113] My own conclusion, deduced from Fairbairn's analysis, *Democracy*, 113f; cf. also 136. Brandt
story: Suval, *Politics*, 50.

As Gerhard A. Ritter has demonstrated, the SPD's campaign for the rural electorate must be termed a failure. Even in 1912, in the last imperial election, 107 of Social Democracy's 110 mandates came from districts where more than 50 percent of the population was engaged in commerce or industry; the remaining three, from districts where at least a relative majority of the population earned their living in these two branches. In east Elbia, on the other hand, the party's share of the vote lay under 10 percent. In none of the 109 solidly agricultural election districts, nor even in the 23 districts where only a relative majority earned their living in the primary sector, were Social Democrats able to win a single mandate.[114] Even after its bicycling circuit riders were supplemented by automobiles and telephones, the east remained *terra inviolita* to the SPD. It was a deficit that the comrades' successors, in the freer conditions of the Weimar Republic, found impossible to make good.[115]

A second challenge to the Conservative gentry's power over rural elections— at least in the eyes of Conservative alarmists—came from the antisemitic populism of men like Otto Böckel and Hermann Ahlwardt, urban academics bent on saving the countryside by leading a fight against "Junkers and Jews." Böckel, a handsome young librarian at the University of Marburg with a degree in folklore, burst onto the political stage in 1887. There was no mistaking the democratic flavor of his campaign. Announcing himself the champion of the little man, Böckel progressed around the Hessen countryside, the red, black, and gold banner of the 1848 revolution attached to his wagon, shaking hands and demanding cheaper litigation, rural credit unions, a progressive income tax, stipends for parliamentary deputies, a genuinely secret ballot, the extension of the democratic Reichstag franchise to state elections—and restrictions on usury, immigration, and the political equality of Jews. A few years later Hermann Ahlwardt, a Berlin educator whose shady bookkeeping had got him fired as a school principal, embarked upon a second career of courting jail terms by writing paranoid tracts and slandering prominent Jews.[116] Like Böckel, Ahlwardt canvassed his rural constituencies directly. Traveling from small farm to small farm in Outer-Pomerania, he asked every proprietor how many morgen of land he had and how many cows. Upon hearing the answer he would turn to his secretary, who drew forth a gigantic notebook, and dictate, "Note that down! Gussow has thirty morgen, five cows, four pigs; must have: sixty morgen,

[114] Ritter, "Strategie," 317, 319. He gives slightly different figures in "Bases" (1990), 38. Saul, "Kampf," 175; Fairbairn, *Democracy*, 137.

[115] Critical analysis of SPD's clumsy efforts in East Elbia: Walther Pahl, "Wahlkampf im Osten," *Das freie Wort. Sozialdemokratisches Diskussionsorgan* 1/13 (29 Dec. 1929): 8–11. Baranowski, *Sanctity* (1995), 38, 40, 66f, 79–81, 100.

[116] Levy, *Downfall*, esp. 43–99; Retallack, *Notables*, 98, 102. Putting the whole thing together: G. Eley, "Anti-semitism" (1993). For a chronology of the various names by which the antisemitic movement went, see Specht/Schwabe, *Reichstagswahlen*, 402. Their 19 pages of different programs (403–22) is a measure of their divisions: the Z's and the SDs' programs take up only 3 and 9 pages, respectively.

twelve cows, ten pigs."[117] Ahlwardt's message: the great estates must be divided. This was a pronouncement that scandalized not only country gentlemen, but even Adolf Stoecker, the father of "social" Jew-baiting, who termed it "naked communism." Antisemitic appeals, once praised by the pious *Kreuz-Zeitung* as the "bridge" over which the masses could pass from the Liberal to the Conservative Party, seemed to be leading to altogether different shores.[118]

Ahlwardt gained national attention in 1893 when he ran in an Outer-Pomeranian district whose county seat, the small market town of Neustettin, had lost its synagogue to arsonists in the spring of 1881, five days after Ernst Henrici (another dismissed Berlin schoolteacher) had delivered a rabble-rousing speech calling for a national "struggle" against the Jews. The following summer, on the heels of another of Henrici's speaking tours, and just as the press was reporting on pogroms in Russia, twenty-one Neustettin shops had been trashed, along with its liberal newspaper and the windows of several hundred local residences. All of them were owned by Jews. Over the course of the summer of 1881, the hooliganism had spread outward from Neustettin in concentric circles, until a military presence put a stop to it. Given this dismal history, it is not surprising that antisemitic agitators in the nineties targeted Neustettin. But they caused a sensation in Conservative circles when they attacked none other than the antisemitic tribune of the people Adolf Stoecker, humiliating the former Court Preacher and breaking up one of his election rallies. Stoecker hadn't been worth the little people's "losing their bread in open voting" in Landtag elections, one speaker averred. "Fight for thy feudals and debt-ridden squires if you want," he dared, "we're fighting for the small office-holder, the craftsman, the suffering farmer. . . ." Ahlwardt's men demanded "a reform movement that . . . for once reaches down smartly into the purses of the rich . . . !"[119]

Thus, like the Social Democrats, antisemitic populists contributed to the prominence of the Junker topos in the nineties. Unlike the Social Democrats, however, they rarely targeted the gentry's own territory for conversion. They made their pitch where small towns and small farms, not noble estates, predominated; where "Junkers" were an evil even more remote than Jews. These were districts that in the past had sent liberal deputies to the Reichstag about as often as Conservatives.[120] The antisemites did best in Hessenland, where farms were

[117] Gerlach, *Rechts*, 30f; Paul W. Massing, *Rehearsal for Destruction* (New York, 1949), 92–97, 240f, 300–305. What constituted a "morgan" varied locally from .6 to 2.1 acres.

[118] "Bridge," and "naked communism": quoted in W. Frank, *Stoecker* (1928), 300, 307f. For a similar view of antisemitism as a stage in the transition of *Mittelständler* from liberalism to conservatism: Schulamit Angel-Volkov, "The Social and Political Function of Late 19th Century Anti-Semitism: The Case of the Small Handicraft Masters," in *Socialgeschichte Heute. Festschrift für Hans Rosenberg zum 70. Geburtstag*, ed. H.-U. Wehler (Göttingen, 1974), 416–31; esp. 419f, and Schulamit Volkov, "Anti-Semitism as a Cultural Code," *LBIY* (1978), 25–46.

[119] *DA* 11/31 (30 July 1893): 585–87. Also *DA* 11/38 (17 Sept. 1893): 710f; *DA* 12/18 (6 May 1894): 344–47, and Nr. 19 (13 May 1994): 365–70; Christhard Hoffmann, "Politische Kultur und Gewalt gegen Minderheiten. Die antisemitischen Ausschreitungen in Pommern und Westpreußen 1881," in *Jahrbuch für Antisemitismusforschung* 3 (1994): 93–120.

[120] Contrast Retallack, *Notables*, 98. Fairbairn's analysis suggests that the antisemites were partic-

small (averaging from five to little more than twelve acres) and where anti-Junker rhetoric was an expression of anti-Prussian *ressentiment*—that is, resentment against someone *else's* Junkers.[121] Two of the Hessen districts they took in 1893 had indeed been held by Conservatives (Marburg and Hersfeld), but five had belonged to liberals (Alsfeld, Bensheim, Gießen, Rinteln, Eschwege), while one (Fritzlar) had always been up for grabs. Of these districts, five were rural and four were urbanized, but in both rural and urban districts production units were small and therefore the numbers of votes any single bread lord could control were limited.[122] Such a social structure invited mobilization efforts from outside. Antisemites also did well in some parts of royal Saxony, and in Berlin-Charlottenburg and Nordhausen (Prussian Saxony) they likewise made their presence noisily known. This was not Junker country. It was the same densely populated, urbanizing (if not always urban) landscape of central Germany where Social Democracy was also growing. The two radical movements were in fact competing for the same constituency: the hard-pressed *Mittelstand*, for whom liberalism's free market evangelium no longer promised any good news.[123]

The only "Junker" strongholds the antisemites captured in the early nineties were Arnswalde-Friedeberg in Brandenburg and, briefly, Neustettin in Outer-Pomerania. These proved to be very much special cases. In Arnswalde-Friedeberg, where population was declining and no towns reached the ten thousand mark; where large estates made up more than half of the arable land in one county and 40 percent of the other, contests in the past had been fought between big and small agriculture: between the gentry-backed Conservatives on the one hand, and liberals of varying sorts on the other.[124] The sudden death in 1892 of the Conservative incumbent (himself the beneficiary of an unexpected by-election when the previous victor, the Left Liberal paladin Max von Forckenbeck, accepted a seat elsewhere), caught the Conservative gentry unprepared. Antisemitic agitators, pouring in from Berlin, were quick off the mark. They

---

ularly successful where turnouts were low and (as shown by the necessity of runoffs) voters were fragmented. *Democracy*, esp. 128f. From Schwarz, *MdR* (1965), and Specht/Schwabe, *Reichstagswahlen*, one sees that from 1871 to 1912 ca. 10 of the Reform Party's districts had been K in previous elections, and ca. 9 had been liberal or otherwise "left," while 2 had shifting political allegiances. Two were from Z districts in Lower Bavaria, as were 2 victories by the sometimes antisemitic Economic Union (Wirtschaftliche Vereinigung).

[121] Excellent here: Levy, *Downfall*, 48, 51–54, 58; White, *Party*, 134–42.

[122] Fairbairn's socioeconomic "Constituency Typology" for each of the 397 election districts is helpful here. *Democracy*, 263–76.

[123] Based upon my own count of electoral districts. For the geography of antisemitic strength in 1893: Levy, *Downfall*, 90, 148; D. Warren, Jr., *Kingdom* (1964), x.

[124] Entailed holdings in Friedeberg reached 15%, 55.5% of them larger than 100 hectares, and 51.5% of them larger than 200 hectares. Even in Arnswalde, where no estates were entailed, estates larger than 100 hectares made up 40% of the holdings, and those over 200 hectares made up 37.5%. Large landholders could thus be a significant force in the district, how significant depending on their own efforts and those of their opponents. Statistics (as of 1895): Frank, *Brandenburger*, 131. Contrast Fairbairn's interesting discussion of "electoral environments," in which Arnswalde-Friedeberg does *not* appear as a Junker stronghold. *Democracy*, 263–76.

found a receptive audience in the liberals' hereditary constituency—small producers reeling under falling agricultural prices. When antisemites faced *Freisinnige* in the runoff, the Conservative gentry had no difficulty choosing which party to support. The Junker establishment and the provincial bureaucracy weighed in on Ahlwardt's behalf. It was only when Conservatives tried to recover the district the subsequent year that Ahlwardt responded with his anti-Junker cry, solidifying the support of the small producers behind him. Thereafter, Ahlwardt and his antisemitic successors proved impossible to dislodge. Although their vote declined in the twentieth century, even in 1912 they were able to come from behind to win a runoff against the Conservative candidate—this time, apparently, with Social Democratic and National Liberal votes. Their last deputy held his seat (as a member of the DNVP) until 1930.[125] But initially, it was the *Freisinnige*'s constituency, not the Junkers', that Ahlwardt had stolen.

As for Neustettin, although antisemitic activity there was no novelty, what led Ahlwardt to think he might take the district, one of the safest Conservative seats in all of Germany, is not clear. Stoecker also ran for the seat, which suggests that the *official* Conservative candidate, a man named von Hertzberg (who in fact outpolled both of these antisemites in the first ballot—the *Hauptwahl*), may have been at least distantly "Jewish" and therefore vulnerable. A Jewish connection seems not to have been disabling among the region's aristocracy. Free Conservatives had earlier run the baptized Rudolf Friedenthal (soon to be a *Staatsminister*); and the district's successful Conservative candidate for the Landtag seat in 1893—against Ahlwardt's colleague, Bernhard Förster— was one Moritz von Oppenfeld, who although Protestant himself may have had Jewish antecedents. It is also not clear that it was Ahlwardt's leveling rhetoric against the "feudals" that was the source of his strength. The Ahlwardt supporters who had broken up Stoecker's rally in 1893 were not locals, but rowdies brought in from Berlin. Already in 1898, Neustettin's Landrat, Bogislav von Bonin-Bahrenbusch, a man far too reactionary to countenance antisemites representing his district, took the election in hand. He easily defeated Bernhard Förster and held the seat against all comers until 1918. It was probably Bonin who, in his capacity as Landrat, later banned Ahlwardt from entering a county in Pomerania.[126]

Thus for all its anti-Junker propaganda, the populist victories cannot be read as challenges to gentry power, much less as signs that the gentry's electoral grip on their dependents was loosening. Those voters who had been free before, mainly small and medium-sized producers, now simply switched their alle-

---

[125] 1 Frankfurt, AnlDR (1912/13, 13/I, Bd. 17) DS 480: 525–33, and SBDR 9 Dec. 1912: 2687– 92; Specht/Schwabe, *Reichstagswahlen*, 38. Levy, *Downfall*, 81f.

[126] Von Hertzfeld: Specht/Schwabe, *Reichstagswahlen*, 53; safe seat and Oppenfeld: Kühne, *Handbuch*, 262–64. Also: Hugo Gotthard Bloth, "Bogislav von Bonin (1842–1929). Antisemiten-Gegner und 'Kanalrebell,'" *Baltische Studien* (N.F.) 57 (1971), 86–94; Bogislav v. Bonin-Bahren-busch, *25 Jahre Landrat. Ein Beitrag zur Neustettiner Kreischronik* (Neustettin, 1924); Mann, *Handbuch* (1988), 76; Levy, *Downfall*, 137.

giance (probably collaring their own little retinues to come with them). Those who had not been free continued to vote as their bread lords wished.

What populist agitators did challenge was the presumption of those "retired majors" in the landowning elite to a God-given right to leadership *within* the antisemitic camp. From the earliest days of Stoecker's "Berlin Movement" the line between opportunist Conservatives and so-called "Genuine" antisemites had been blurred. Of the eighteen deputies initially elected under antisemitic auspices, the Genuines complained, seven had been co-opted by the Conservative Party the minute they arrived in Berlin.[127] Since fifteen deputies were the minimum necessary to claim *Fraktion* status in the Reichstag—indispensable if members wanted to submit motions, serve on committees, or have a reasonable hope of being allowed to speak before the very end of a debate—the loss to the antisemitic cause through crossovers to Conservatism was more than symbolic. Ahlwardt's much-quoted slogan "Against Junkers and Parsons," far from being a plan of campaign for the flatland, much less one directed against the Conservative Party, was in fact a thinly coded attempt to police the movement's boundaries. It was also aimed at wresting leadership within the antisemitic camp from its most prominent, and opportunistic, figures—the "Junker" ex-army officer, Max Liebermann von Sonnenberg, and the "parson," Adolf Stoecker, founders of the German Social and the Christian Social parties, respectively. Tired of being kept in leading strings, infuriated at *these* "feudals" for compromises in their name, the Genuines were determined to be their own spokesmen.

Some aristocrats claimed to be as alarmed by the Böckels and the Ahlwardts as by the Social Democrats. But the "Genuine" antisemites' attacks on "Junkers" only challenged the gentry's control of conservative political *discourse*; it did not imply any plan to suborn their "people."[128] By 1904 at the latest, the Conservatives could be complacent about a movement whose limited successes had occurred, they said, "only temporarily, through accident and special circumstances." Now their "time was long since passed." The antisemites only commanded attention "as at best auxiliary troops for Conservatives."[129]

The third potential challenge to the gentry's control of the flatland came from agrarian populism. Drought, hoof-and-mouth disease, rural indebtedness, and finally the collapse of farm prices in the early nineties had brought crisis to the countryside. Caprivi's trade treaties of 1891–94, which reduced tariffs on imported grain, were blamed, along with those deputies whose votes had allowed them to pass. The same economic desperation that had simmered in regional farmers' movements in the late eighties, that had allowed Left Liberals to snatch two seats in Pomerania from Conservative estate-owners at the turn of

---

[127] *DA* 11/31 (30 July 1893): 586.
[128] K ambivalence toward the antisemites in the pages of the *DA*: 10/47 (20 Nov. 1892): 938; 10/51 (18 Dec. 1892): 1021–23; 11/23 (4 Jun. 1893): 446f; 11/26 (25 Jun. 1893): 502–4; 11/27 (2 Jul. 1893): 522f; 11/28 (9 Jul. 1893): 537–40; 11/31 (30 Jul. 1893): 585–87.
[129] *DA* 22/43 (23 Oct. 1904): 685–87.

the decade, and that had fueled the antisemites' early rural successes, now boiled over. Agrarian rage was given conspicuous and powerful form in February 1893 with the founding of the Farmers' League (*Bund der Landwirte*; hereafter, BdL).[130] Adopting a down-home style, the Farmers' League succeeded in enlisting ordinary Protestant farmers of humble birth (but bread lords themselves) in the protectionist cause. According to the Farmers' own statistics in 1898, they had enrolled 157,000 small and 28,500 middle farmers, compared to a mere 1,500 large landowners. Although we have evidence that in some regions the propensity to join the BdL correlated positively with a farmer's tax share, large landowners after 1900 still constituted less than 1 percent of the growing membership.[131]

For all its angry radicalism, however, the BdL was a movement that united rather than divided rural producers. The landed elite was never forced to beat it, because they were happy to join it. Like the clergy with the Centrum, the gentry were present at the creation. They soon occupied many of the BdL's leadership positions. In regions where the gentry was National Liberal, such as the Grand Duchy of Hessen, the structure of the BdL, for all the organization's official independence, overlapped with that of the National Liberal Party—not always to the latter's comfort, since of the two organizations, the BdL was often the stronger, the more confident, the more independent.[132] Where the rural elite was Conservative, the BdL's managers likewise read like a list of Conservative Party *Prominenten*. But although the Farmers' League's most dramatic impact was in Prussia's "new" provinces, Hanover and Hessen, and polling behavior in the east scarcely changed, the BdL leant the eastern agricultural interest organizational muscle and a populist dynamic that was as welcome as it was new.

The Farmers' League signaled a pressure group of a new kind, one with no intention of confining itself to petitions to the Reichstag or polite delegations to ministries and party congresses. By targeting the election district itself, by collecting and distributing funds to put at the disposal of any candidate, regardless of affiliation, who signed its protectionist program, the BdL hitched the agrarian

---

[130] Retallack also sees the founding of the BdL as a reaction to pressure from below. *Notables*, 102. Similarly, Eley, "Anti-Semitism," which is good on the different nature of League activity, East and West. Also valuable: Barkin, "Study," 378. LL victories in by-elections in 7 Stettin (1888) and 1 Köslin (1890): Kühne, *Dreiklassenwahlrecht*, 366. For the South: Farr, "Populism," 136–59.

[131] Taxes and BdL membership, B. Ehrenfeuchter, *Willensbildung* (1951), 335; cf. also 199. Generally: Retallack, *Notables*, 91–112; and esp. H.-J. Puhle, *Interessenpolitik* (1966); statistics: Dieter Fricke, "Bund der Landwirte (BdL) 1893–1920," in *Die bürgerlichen Parteien in Deutschland. Handbuch der Geschichte der bürgerlichen Parteien und anderer bürgerlicher Interessenorganisationen vom Vormärz bis zum Jahre 1945* (Leipzig, 1968) 1: 129–49, esp. 133. Hesselbarth, *Sozialdemokraten*, 143, 249, notes that it encompassed in 1893 perhaps 5% of all agricultural producers; Ullmann, *Interessenverbände*, 89–94; connections with the ZdI: Molt, *Reichstag*, 205; D. Stegmann, *Erben* (1970), 140–43.

[132] Eley, *Reshaping*, 27f, 154 (arguing that the relationship with the BdL was fatal for the NLs); White, *Party*, 143–45; figures: Molt, *Reichstag*, 287. By 1898, the BdL had become so powerful that by capturing the NL nomination in 6 Trier, the home of the FK Baron Carl v. Stumm, it was able to deny him first place in *Hauptwahl*, driving him into a runoff against the Z. In 1903 the BdL's refusal to support the NLs helped the Z to victory. Bellot, *Hundert Jahre*, 201, 213.

wagon to the electoral process. Its target, however, was not the voter, but the parties; its aim, not to replace, but to control, them. Almost immediately it began to influence the nominations of candidates in rural districts. The Farmers' League kept close tabs on voting records, and a deputy's failure to follow through on his promises meant loss of BdL support in the next election. Like the Centrum and the Social Democrats, the BdL quickly became successful in enforcing the so-called "imperative mandate," the requirement that the deputy vote according to his constituency's instructions. Nothing could be a surer sign that the old politics of notables—men who cherished their independence as a chief qualification for office—was dead. Although the exact number of deputies "belonging" to the Farmers' League is not known, 25 percent of the Reichstag is said to have signed its program by 1893. By 1907 their share was well over a third. This too was a sign of Germans' practicing democracy.

Rural populism barely affected the landed elite's relationship to their social inferiors, but its impact on their relations to their political superiors was dramatic. The BdL's pressure in the constituencies was responsible for turning the Conservatives, at least for the next decade, into what they had never quite been before—a single-mindedly agrarian party.[133] As a result, Conservatives discarded what had been the alpha and omega of the squirearchy's credo for nearly twenty years: unswerving subordination to the wishes of the Prussian-German government. Their silence when agrarians published an attack on a sitting chancellor, in an article whose title pronounced him a cur (*Schweinhund*), signaled the new relationship.[134] Provincial officials who failed to support agrarian candidates might find themselves not only vilified by the Farmers and hounded by its press—but cut by their neighbors. Kurt von Willich, the stiff-necked Landrat of County Birnbaum, was driven to suicide. In the seventies, Bismarck's premise in sponsoring manhood suffrage—that humble voters everywhere would prove as subject to pro-government pressure as those in the east Elbian countryside— had been refuted by the Catholic clergy. Now the assumption underlying that premise—that east Elbians themselves were at the government's disposal—was foundering. The Farmers' League put the government on notice. It would put "a stop to what we have always considered a matter of course, *making elections for the government in our districts.*"[135]

The nineties saw the beginnings of a corresponding reluctance among a new generation of civil servants, now with professional as well as social allegiances, to put the bureaucratic thumb so openly on the Conservative side of the scale at

[133] Molt, *Reichstag*, 112; Nipperdey, *Organisation*, 249. But stressing complexity and diversity, see Fairbairn, *Democracy*, 130–36. Challenges to Puhle's implication (e.g., *Interessenpolitik*, 38– 39) that Junker leadership in the BdL meant the manipulation of smaller farmers began with James C. Hunt, "Peasants, Grain Tariffs, and Meat Quotas: Imperial German Protectionism Reexamined," *CEH* 7/4 (Dec. 1974): 311–31; also Eley, *Reshaping*, 9, 28, 331. The Junkers' own evaluation: *DA* 11/41 (8 Oct. 1893): 769–71.

[134] K. D. Barkin, *Controversy* (1970), 101; F. Hartung, *Geschichte* (1952), 226f.

[135] Quoted in J. Ziekursch, *Geschichte* (1930) 3: 59. Von Willich: Kühne, *Dreiklassenwahlrecht*, 85–88.

election time. Eventually the Minister of Interior let it be known that Landräte were not to accept candidacies.[136] Provincial officials who were already deputies, and who publicly cast their lot with the gentry against the government, might find their own jobs at risk: as eighteen Landräte and two prefects discovered in 1899, after voting in the Prussian Landtag to defeat the government's Mittelland Canal Bill. As the twentieth century dawned, the Prussian cabinet was reshuffled, and the connubium between the Prussian gentry and the German government seemed to have gone the way of all flesh.

But was it divorce—or only an estrangement? Optimists began to claim that the ministers and secretaries of state felt closer to Liberals than to Conservatives. They speculated that the sensible Bethmann Hollweg, Interior Minister and then State Secretary of the *Reichsamt des Innern* since 1905 and chancellor in 1909, might just effect a wholesale replacement of Conservative with National Liberal prefects and Landräte, and "against a National Liberal government apparatus, the Conservatives would no longer have a leg to stand on." Proof lay in the fall of a Conservative bastion—Oletzko-Lyck-Johannesburg— to a Liberal in a 1910 by-election. For the Right, the handwriting was on the wall.[137] But the jubilation was premature. The jubileers seem not to have noticed that even the "Canal" Landräte had been reinstated. After getting a tariff in 1902 that raised grain duties a whopping 40 percent, Conservatives could afford to distance themselves from the BdL's more extreme positions and behave civilly toward the government.[138] In any case, ministerial displeasure rarely survived the trip from Berlin to the counties—as the aftermath to the much ballyhooed Liberal victory in Oletzko-Lyck-Johannesburg made clear. For the gentry immediately prevailed upon their Landrat to divide Lyck's 85 precincts into 132, so that their boundaries would correspond more closely to those of the estates. In 1912 the district was returned with ease to the Conservative column.[139] Whatever the administration's desire for a professional stance truly "above parties," whatever the shift in sympathy of the "overwhelming majority" in the government in a Liberal direction, by now, with Social Democrats controlling one-third of the seats in the Reichstag, the government *needed* the Conservatives.

It also needed the Conservatives because the Kingdom of Prussia, Germany's largest state, had already become increasingly "parliamentized": not, as that

[136] Saul, "Kampf," 196n. 138; Fairbairn, "Authority"; X, "Die Stellung der Beamten im politischen Leben," *Die Hilfe* 15/18 (2 May 1909), 279f. The bureaucracy was losing both the power and the will to intervene decisively in elections: Kühne, *Dreiklassenwahlrecht*, 66, 79–81, 88f, 291, 309f. Contrast: Witt, "Landrat," esp. 214 and 214n. 54.

[137] Quote: Martin, *Machthaber*, 524. Similarly, Naumann quoted in Kühne, *Dreiklassenwahlrecht*, 513f. Cf. also J. N. Retallack, "The Road to Philippi: The Conservative Party and Bethmann Hollweg's 'Politics of the Diagonal,' 1909–14," in *Between Reform, Reaction, and Resistance: Studies in the History of German Conservatism from 1789 to 1945*, edited by L. E. Jones and J. N. Retallack (Providence and Oxford, 1993), 261–98; esp. 277.

[138] But see Eley, *Reshaping*, 239.

[139] "Die kunstvolle Verkleinerung der Wahlbezirke im Kreise Lyck," *BT* XVI/7, 2. Beiblatt (4 Jan. 1912).

term usually implied, by a liberal Landtag majority, but by a conservative one. Well might the ministers wish that Germany were blessed with a modernized Conservative Party on the English model, able to keep up with the times; well might they hope that a timely reform of the Prussian franchise, perhaps by giving plural votes to some members of the middle classes, might force the Conservatives to pay more attention to the desires of the entire electorate.[140] With the two conservative parties in control of roughly half the Landtag's seats, the government found it wise to consult the leader of the Conservatives in advance before submitting any new initiatives in domestic policy. Given Prussia's dominant position in the Reich, no chancellor could afford to alienate them.[141]

Even had the imperial administration been determined to cut Conservatives loose from its Reichstag election help, it is doubtful that the result would have been as punishing as hopeful liberals believed. Developments since 1893 had shifted the balance of power between the ministry and the Conservative gentry. Except for pressure applied to its own 1.2 million employees (sure to be censured in the Reichstag), the government had few means of its own to deliver elections. Whatever Bethmann Hollweg's hopes about "pushing" the Conservatives "forward" into the twentieth century, the gentry no longer needed provincial bureaucrats to coordinate its candidacies, to print its press releases, and to deliver ballots to its estates.[142] The BdL—and a more developed Conservative party structure—did the job. Although Conservatives did lose three seats to liberals in the Gumbinnen regency in 1912, Bethmann Hollweg was no Bismarck. The upheaval of 1874 did not come again.

ALL QUIET ON THE EASTERN FRONT

As late as 1912, the eastern gentry's "effortless dictatorship" of rural elections (Bethmann Hollweg's term) faced few challenges. Good-natured landlords continued to distribute ballots to their dependents along with a handful of pennies, a cigar, or a bundle of firewood, and then, as chairmen of the election panel, watch as these ballots were cast.[143] Ill-tempered landlords (or their inspectors)

---

[140] "Begründung des Eventual-Entwurfes" (Pluralwahlrecht) Oct. 1907, GStA PK I. HA, Rep. 90a, A. VIII. 1. d., Nr. 1/Bd. 10, Bl. 88f.

[141] W. Frauendienst, "Demokratisierung" (1957), 729–33, supported by quotations from Bethmann Hollweg and IM R. v. Sydow; Kühne, *Dreiklassenwahlrecht*, 481, 529f; stopped in 1910: 539. Frauendienst goes too far when he dates Prussia's parliamentization as early as 1892. But my own impressions from reading the cabinet deliberations from 1900 to 1914 supports his more general hypothesis of the "parliamentarization" of Prussia. E.g., SM minutes, 2, 3 Jan. and 15 Oct. 1908, GStA PK I. HA, Rep. 90a, A. VIII. 1. d., Nr. 1/Bd. 9, Bl. 36, 39–39v, 183–185v; SM minutes, 26 Feb., 7 Mar. 1910, ibid., Bd. 11, Bl. 126, 129f.

[142] BH quoted in Wollstein, *Bethmann Hollweg*, 36. Employees in Wehler, *Empire*, 67. Contrast: Schücking, *Reaktion*, esp. 105. Schücking's own role was ambiguous: cf. Kühne, *Dreiklassenwahlrecht*, 79.

[143] In Sellnow, Raakow, Adolfsaue, Friedenau: 1 Frankfurt, AnlDR (1912/1913, 13/I, Bd. 17), DS

continued to demand written promises to vote a certain way, to herd their "people" to the polls, to rip up ballots they did not like and replace them with their own, to rough up opponents' poll watchers, and to pace up and down the line until all the new ballots were cast.[144] Here, in the words of Marie Skerra, is what happened on the Gilgenau estate in County Ortelsberg, a district that had not left the Conservative column in thirty years. "Chief Inspector Klimmek stood . . . the entire day in front of the polling place and threatened to beat up any voter and give him no firewood or food if he didn't vote for [the Conservative candidate] von Bieberstein."

> My husband, the gardener Karl Skerra, is an adherent of the National Liberal Party. When he . . . left the polling place yesterday, cutting across the manor courtyard to get to the garden, Chief Inspector Klimmek . . . yelled to him, 'Thou Social Democrat, the scum from Berlin has turned thy head' (By the designation scum, he meant my son, who is serving in Berlin as a soldier and was home for Christmas). My husband's only answer was: 'I am no Social Democrat.' In that moment, he got such a blow on the chest from Herr Klimmek that he is now seriously bedridden, especially because he was already weak and sick.

Another man was beaten with a stick until he voted Conservative.[145] Forty years of manhood suffrage had not softened the relationship between master and worker in the rural east.

Dissenters had small hope, but they did what they could. One Saxon voter tried to invalidate the ballot he was forced to cast for the antisemitic nationalist General Eduard von Liebert by scribbling this *cri de coeur* under the candidate's name: "Obeying compulsion, not my own desire!" (*Der Not gehorchend, nicht dem eignen Triebe*.)[146] In Schebitz, when the domanial inspector's back was turned, his people told a Social Democratic campaign worker, "We would have liked to have voted for someone besides Heydebrand, but you can see that under these circumstances we can't do what we would so much like to do."[147]

480: 528; in Langendorf: 7 Gumb., AnlDR (1912/14, 13/I, Bd. 23) DS 1586: 3412, 3414; in Lützlow and Seehausen: 4 Potsdam, AnlDR (1912/14, 13/I, Bd. 22) DS 1435: 2950. In 46 precincts in Glogau (in 3 Liegnitz), the chairman of the election panel was an owner of a noble estate. "Wie die Behörden im Wahlkampf arbeiten," *BT* XLI/5 (4 Jan. 1912). Bethmann quoted in Wollstein, *Bethmann Hollweg*, 36.

[144] In Bingerau, Kuschwitz, Wirschkowitz, Powitzko, Schebitz, Esdorf, Kapitz, Paulwitz, and Kawallen: 2 Breslau, AnlDR (1912/14, 13/I, Bd. 22) DS 1432: 2928, 2931–34; in Stücken bei Belzig, Grabow bei Niemegt: 9 Potsdam, AnlDR (1912/13, 13/I, Bd. 19) DS 807: 1109; in Barranowen, Choszewen, Gaynen, Jägerswalde, Prawdowen, Schimonken, Seeheften, Talten: 7 Gumb., AnlDR (1912/14, 13/I, Bd. 23) DS 1586: 3404, 3406, 3422, 3424, 3426, 3428, 3430, 3432, 3436, 3442; in Gramzow, 4 Potsdam, AnlDR (1912/14, 13/I, Bd. 22) DS 1435: 2953; in Rittergut Dammereez, Rittergut Scharbow, Rittergut Barnekow, in Groß-Hundorf, 1 Meckl.-Schw., (1912/13, 13/I, Bd. 17): DS 478: 513f.

[145] 7 Gumb., AnlDR (1912/14, 13/I, Bd. 23) DS 1586: 3392–94.

[146] 14 Saxony, AnlDR (1912/13, 13/I, Bd. 19) DS 718: 926.

[147] 2 Breslau, AnlDR (1912/14, 13/I, Bd. 22) DS 1432: 2932f. Almost the same thing occurred with liberal farm workers in both Salwarscheinen bei Petershagen and in Schirten. In Grunau, Rehfeld, Worienen, Wermten, Partheinen, Klein Steegen, and other villages in the district workers

Although the words were whispered as if someone might care about the voters' real loyalty, the marching columns themselves were the clearest evidence that not loyalty, not community, but obedience, was at stake here. Threats to dismiss nonconformists underlined the message.[148]

The regency of Köslin, with five election districts, offers an instructive, if perhaps extreme, example of the continued grip of the bread lords. Only 8 percent of the Köslin electorate's third class even came to the polls in Landtag elections—a turnout traditionally taken as a measure of the lower classes' alienation from a system that made Conservative success a foregone conclusion.[149] That same lower class, however, swarmed to the polls in Reichstag elections—to give Conservatives in 1907 more than 66 percent of the regency's vote. Indeed, in one district, with nearly 80 percent participation, the Conservative got more than 86 percent of the vote.[150] The dramatically contrasting turnouts in Köslin's Reichstag and Landtag elections, coupled with Conservative landslides under *both* systems, suggests that when the Köslin gentry could rely on an unequal franchise to ensure Conservative outcomes they did; and when they could not, they took appropriate measures. The contrast should also make us wary about drawing too many conclusions about popular attitudes from changes in rural turnouts.[151]

The bread lords' vulnerability lay not in any loosening of their control over their dependents, but in two powerful demographic trends. First was the gradual *sub*urbanization of Germany. The secular decline of Conservative voting strength in the Mark Brandenburg was a reflection of this fact. Although much of the population still resided—and voted—in the rural regencies of Frankfurt and Potsdam, they earned their bread in Frankfurt-on-Oder or in Berlin. The separation of workplace from polling place—especially when the former was in a good-sized city—put many a voter outside his bread lord's reach. In royal Saxony, commuting workers had begun to erase the political differences between urban and rural voting behavior as early as the seventies. In Hessen, the

---

were intimidated by obvious violations of secrecy. 5 Königsberg, AnlDR (1912/14, 13/I, Bd. 22) DS 1401: 2900f, 2903f. The table of village election results in County Wanzleben, provincial Saxony, is instructive: Birk, "Entwicklung," 192.

[148] 2 Breslau, AnlDR (1912/14, 13/I, Bd. 22) DS 1432: 2933. Other threats to dismiss: In Hedersleben: 5 Merseberg, AnlDR (1912/13, 13/I, Bd. 19) DS 840: 1136–39, esp. 1137; in Kerstinowen: 7 Gumb., AnlDR (1912/14, 13/I, Bd. 23) DS 1586: 3410; in Döhlen: 14 Saxony, AnlDR (1912/13, 13/I, Bd. 19) DS 718: 927; in Groß-Ziethen in 4 Potsdam, AnlDR (1912/14, 13/I, Bd. 22) DS 1435: 2951f; on Rittergut Klein-Krankow, and Rittergut Rögnitz, 1 Meckl.-Schw. AnlDR (1912/13, 13/I, Bd. 17) DS 478: 516f.

[149] An intriguing counterargument: Kühne, *Dreiklassenwahlrecht*, 165–203.

[150] 4 Köslin, Specht/Schwabe, *Reichstagswahlen*, Nachtrag, 14; Ritter/Niehuss, *Arbeitsbuch*, 71, 140.

[151] E.g., Worker Stahnke testified that he had been forced by his "Brotherrn" to cast a NL ballot when he hadn't even intended to vote: 3 Marienwerder AnlDR (1898/1900, 10/I, Bd.4) DS 507: 2663. Bertram, *Wahlen*, 206f. But see Kühne, *Dreiklassenwahlrecht*, 290.

process of the suburbanization began in the nineties, with corresponding gains for Social Democrats in previously "rural" districts.[152]

Second, the growth of a high-wage urban job market made it increasingly difficult for the squires to compete for labor. The "flight from the land" provided a neat alibi for Conservative apologists, who were fond of proclaiming that employers were in no position to threaten workers with dismissal: "They count themselves happy when they don't lose their workers." Although no evidence suggests that rural workers were ever able to turn labor shortages to political advantage,[153] nevertheless the urbanization of the job market did indirectly subvert the estate-owners' power on election day. For as better wages—and also, according to the Junkers' own admission, the "drive for freedom"—attracted the sons and daughters of the lower orders away from the countryside, their places were increasingly taken by foreigners.[154] On the eve of the Great War foreign labor had become "the really distinctive feature of Germany's transition from feudalism to capitalism," accounting for nearly a third of the country's agricultural employees.[155] Unprotected by the cushions of custom or contract, these workers were much more pliable economic instruments than natives in the hands of producers bent on increasing productivity through intensification. But since foreigners were ineligible to vote, the Junkers' economic gain came at the price of political loss.[156]

This loss was not yet adequately measured by Reichstag seats. In refusing to redraw election districts to take account of massive population shifts from country to town and from east to west, the imperial government had made it possible for the gentry to elect Conservative deputies even with (relatively) fewer and fewer votes. By 1907 it took a mere 17,700 votes on average to elect a Conservative, while an average of 75,800 votes was required to elect a Social Democrat.[157] In a country where region and party were so closely correlated—

[152] Saxony: Steinbach, "Entwicklung," 16; Hessen: White, *Party*, 133, 173; Magdeburg region, Birk, "Entwicklung," 177, 184. In 1895, 27% of all men employed in the "flatland" worked in industry. Blank, "Zusammensetzung," 531.

[153] One case in Saxony was admitted to be exceptional: *DA* 26/17 (26 Apr. 1908): 246. Below, *Wahlrecht*, 153 (quote); *DA* 26/17 (26 Apr. 1908): 246.

[154] "Drive for freedom": *Deutsche Post* (K), 40 (5 Oct. 1891), cited in *DA* 8/41 (12 Oct. 1890): 687f.

[155] Perkins, "Worker," 24; cf. also K. J. Bade, "'Kulturkampf'" (1983), 121–42, esp. 139; and Christel Heinrich, "Lebensweise und Kultur der in- und ausländischen landwirtschaftlichen Saisonarbeiter von der Mitte des 19. Jahrhunderts bis 1918," in H.-J. Rach and B. Weissel, eds., *Bauer und Landarbeiter im Kapitalismus in der Magdeburger Börde* (Berlin [East], 1982), 117–62; esp. 127f.

[156] Loss: Bertram, *Wahlen*, 217, and so it seems when one compares their share of the popular vote in 1912 to their share in 1907—at least in the regencies of Königsberg, Stettin, Bromberg, and especially Frankfurt and Gumbinnen. Ritter/Niehuss, *Arbeitsbuch*, 67, 70, 72.

[157] Falter, *Wähler*, 131. "Das Reichstag Wahlrecht-ein Pluralwahlrecht," *Vorwärts* 19 (25 Feb. 1911), BAB-L R101/3360: Bl. 7–9, lists the 25 largest districts, with more than 13 million inhabitants, while the 25 smallest had little more than 1,787,000. The case most often cited, Schaumburg-Lippe, where by 1912 one vote was 25 times as valuable as one from Teltow-Charlottenburg, part

and, given the Junkers' control over their people, not accidentally—these inequities became the subject, as we shall see in chapter 10, of mounting complaint, growing louder with each passing year.

Although forty years of manhood suffrage had not shaken the aristocracy's hold on the levers of bureaucratic, diplomatic, military, or local power, they had forced it to play the parliamentary game. While the gentry still hardly needed a party to mobilize its retinues, they did require a delegation in the Reichstag to prevent the worst. By the nineties, the landed elite's own economic livelihood had become a stake in the election competition. After the turn of the century, as pressure to redistrict Reichstag constituencies and end Prussia's three-class voting system mounted, the stakes shifted to the very rules by which this elite maintained its power. Perched at the top of a local pyramid whose base was now composed of noncitizens, the Junker landlord might justifiably wonder how long these inequities, and the Conservative Party that he relied on, could last. The first postwar elections, in which every candidate representing the gentry in East Prussia, Pomerania, Silesia, Saxony, and even Schleswig-Holstein was defeated, gave the answer.[158]

---

of greater Berlin (Huber, *Verfassungsgeschichte* 3: 874) is unrepresentative of the problem, however, because LLs were as apt to win as FKs.

[158] M. Schumacher, "Wahlbewerbungen" (1982), 363.

CHAPTER SEVEN

Bread Lords II: Masters and Industrialists

> I am Krupp, I think for all o' yer.
> I am Krupp, I am your God and Lord.
> I am Krupp, and if ye're not happy here,
> Good! So long! Just jump off board.
>
> —*Parody of Alfred Krupp's proclamations to his workers (1872)*

> The power the giant firms attain over those they employ extends
> even beyond the work situation; it extends to their entire social, reli-
> gious, and political being. Even the shopkeepers who do business
> with the workers can come under the dominion of the managers of
> these firms. Regions are emerging within the Reich where it is not
> the will of the legislator, but that of the owner, that is law.
>
> —*Lujo Brentano (1905)*

> Right hands up!
>
> —*Cry of Bochum foremen to their miners, after exchanging
> their Centrum ballots for National Liberal ones (1887)*

THEIR MASTER'S VOICE

Georg Wollmann was a china painter in the firm of Egmont Tielsch, a porcelain
manufacturer with small establishments in Neu-Altwasser and Neu-Salzbrunn,
rural communities in Central Silesia. Shortly before the 1887 election, the head
painter in Tielsch's factory called Wollmann and the handful of other painters
together and led them into the counting house, where the boss was waiting for
them.[1] According to young Wollmann, the conversation ran as follows:

> Well, so thou'rt Social Democrats!
>   We disputed this, whereupon he declared that "we'd be better off not arguing about
> it, after all we belonged to the Good Times glee club in Neu-Weißstein, which pur-
> sued Social Democratic goals." He demanded that we resign from the club as of today
> and if we didn't, he would sack us.

---

[1] 10 Breslau AnlDR (1889/90, 7/V, Bd. 3) DS 105: 418–25; esp. 418, and Beilage 2 (1887/88,
7/II, Bd. 4) DS 215: 917f.

But Tielsch had more in mind than glee clubs. The demand that his men withdraw from Good Times was only a prelude to a more immediate ultimatum.

> Either each individual one of ye gives me the promise that he will abstain from this election, or I'll sack the lot of ye immediately.

Wollman and his fellows tried to put Tielsch off with equivocations and assurances of loyalty. But they were interrupted by their foreman who forced the question by slowly reading out their names, one by one. In the silence, as their bread lord sat waiting, resistance collapsed, and each of the men gave his word not to vote. Satisfied that he had obtained his object, Herr Tielsch became more conciliatory. Just this time, because this election was so important, he said, he wanted to exert all his influence. "Later thou canst vote for whomever thou willt, only not Socialist."

As Tielsch informed Reichstag investigators,

> The men named had been pointed out to me by a competent authority as belonging to a Social Democratic organization. I have posters in my factory making it known that I will not keep Social Democrats in my employ, but will dismiss them immediately. I confronted the said painters with the reported accusation, and they swore up and down that they were not Social Democrats. I expressed the wish that they then give me proof of their assurances by abstaining from the election on 17 February 1887. This they voluntarily promised to do.[2]

Later on, as the runoff election approached, the manufacturer unbent. Outside of Breslau, Social Democrats were all but invisible in the province and had not even contested Tielsch's district. The election there was between the National Liberal industrialist, Dr. Egmont Websky, prominent locally and soon to become an economic advisor of William II, and Eduard Eberty, well known as the *Freisinnige* son of a Progressive father. Tielsch had earlier warned his men against Eberty, and for the runoff decided that it was safe to allow them to vote.

> I gave a ballot to each of my workers . . . [and] let it be known . . . that as far as I was concerned they were not prevented from participating in the runoff. I myself was absent shortly before the runoff and made no demands at all on my workers to abstain from voting, as the distributing of ballots made clear.

His ballots also made clear, however, for whom his workers were to vote: the National Liberal industrialist Egmont Websky.

So far the liberal manufacturer's behavior during the 1887 election had been scarcely distinguishable from that of the most high-handed Junker on the flatland. Nor was it unheard of for factories deliberately to keep their men working through the lunch hour on election day to prevent them from voting.[3]

Tielsch was mindful of the pieties to which every German employer gave at

---

[2] The practice of extracting promises from workers, sometimes at a tavern along with treats, was common: e.g., Witten: 5 Arns. AnlDR (1882/83, 5/II, Bd. 6) DS 292: 1081. A. Krupp made his workers sign a pledge not to vote SD and soon extracted analogous promises against the Christian Social Verein (Z): Möllers, *Strömungen*, 333n. 3, 336n. 6.

[3] Lübeck AnlDR (1893/94, 9/II, Bd. 2) DS 131: 787–91; 5 Marienwerder AnlDR (1894/95, 9/III, Bd. 1) DS 166: 805; greater Hamburg: Kutz-Bauer, *Arbeiterschaft*, 118n. 23.

least lip service, and the responsibility of a bread lord for the political education of those within his charge was high among them. This responsibility was a natural outgrowth of the traditions of household production, in which both rural lord and urban master stood *in loco parentis* to his dependents, overseeing their behavior in everything from morals to table manners.[4] Among the most progressive-minded, like the Ruhr entrepreneur Friedrich Harkort, election instruction was a central component of what had become a whole range of activities promoting worker self-help and adult education.[5] On the flatland, as we saw, the announcement of the bread lord's own preference at election time was often felt to be education enough. Egmont Tielsch, exacting the fealty that he felt was owed him, but also, as we shall see, endeavoring to enlighten his staff about their own rational self-interest, lay somewhere in between, a not atypical example of the many employers who felt the call to instruction, without relinquishing their right to command.

Shortly before the runoff, Tielsch composed, printed, and posted in both of his factories a proclamation under the headline: "Those with Ears to Hear—Let Him Hear!" Inviting his men to "just look one more time" at the candidates, Tielsch laid out their similarities and differences.

> Herr **Dr. Websky** stands firm behind the constitutional rights of the German people; Herr Eberty does too;
>
> Herr **Dr. Websky** is a decided opponent of the brandy and tobacco monopoly— Herr Eberty is too.

The glaring *difference* between National Liberals and Left Liberals was in social policy: something that, to Tielsch's astonishment, his men seemed to ignore. In the 1880s, a decade in which both tariffs for producers and insurance for workers dominated political debate, the Left Liberals had continued to insist that the state must not interfere with the market on behalf of either side. Their leader, Eugen Richter, had gone so far as to declare that a Social Question did not exist for his party.[6] In contemplating the Left Liberals' rejection of any and all social legislation, Tielsch's exasperation at the perversity of his workforce got the better of him. "Is it not known to ye then," he asked, that the *Freisinnige* Party had voted against Workers' Compensation Insurance? In the next session, Worker's Old Age Insurance would be coming up for deliberation. The National Liberal Websky would be its "benevolent advisor and advocate." The *Freisinnige* Eberty, he pointed out, could be counted on to continue his party's obstruction.

If so far Herr Tielsch had made things easy for himself by appealing to *homo economicus*, he did not flinch from grasping the nettle of the Septennat, the seven-year military budget that provided the central theme of the 1887 cam-

[4] Jürgen Kocka, *Weder Stand noch Klasse. Unterschichten um 1800* (Bonn, 1990), 144–51.

[5] E.g., his *Brief an die Arbeiter* (1849), his *Wahlkatechismus pro 1852 für das Volk* (1852), and his *Arbeiterspiegel* (1874). Sheehan, *Liberalism*, esp. 32. Other employers sometimes modeled their own proclamations on Harkort's. J. Paul, *Krupp* (1987), 228.

[6] Quoted in Wolfgang Pack, *Das Parlamentarische Ringen um das Sozialistengesetz Bismarcks 1878–1890* (Düsseldorf, 1961), 24.

paign. Seven-year budgets were nothing new—Germany's armies had been funded by them since 1874, although controversy had attended the passage of every one. But two new factors made the issue especially explosive in the winter of 1886–87. For the first time the Reichstag was controlled by an oppositional majority, one that included Eberty's *Freisinnige* Party, which had long been on record as opposing any Septennat. Second, reports about the French War Minister, the handsome Georges Boulanger, whose provocative public appearances had earned him the name General *Révanche*, provided genuine cause for alarm.[7] Although the oppositional majority had agreed to "every man and every penny" in the government's current army bill, it had refused to grant the sum for seven years. To commit funds for longer than two full Reichstag-terms, they believed, made a mockery of parliament's power of the purse. Tielsch met these constitutional objections with sarcasm:

> Herr Eberty is **against the Septennat** because his party, in a show of noble modesty, claims not to be able to grant 7×43 Pfennige per head, per year, but declares that it is only authorized to grant 3×43 Pfennige per head, per year, although the Reichstag has already twice legally resolved on 2 such Septennats (in 1874 and 1880).[8]

Tielsch acknowledged that "the opposition parties are trying to make thy hair stand on end with hints about losing universal suffrage, about monopolies, although Prince *Bismarck* has announced to the whole world that these are **lies**." In his men's apparent readiness to believe these prognostications, their employer read a perverse misplacement of confidence. "Does Herr Eberty of Berlin, with his old wives' tales about threats to human rights, carry **more** weight with ye" than Prince Bismarck?

If Tielsch's efforts to bring light into his workers' darkness implicitly accorded them rationality and independence, other passages in the same proclamation revealed the continued hold of more traditional assumptions. The bread lord let them know that he was still keeping tabs on them. Precinct returns from their villages had "delivered the proof" that most of them had "not obeyed" his warning against the *Freisinnige* candidate in the first round of voting. A modern man, the manufacturer obviously knew what the new times required:

> That thou'st a complete right to such behavior may well be, and I am not going to reproach ye for thy vote. . . .

But Tielsch had grown up in a world in which master and man had owed each other more than a discrete fee-for-service, determined by the market. They had been connected instead by a continuous mutual exchange—succor for loyalty (*Treue*), to use the traditional terms—with no tight boundaries limiting the

---

[7] Pflanze, *Bismarck* 3: 228; Hiery, *Reichstagswahlen*, 220, 237.

[8] 10 Breslau AnlDR (1889/90, 7/V, Bd. 3) DS 105: 418 and AnlDR, Beilage 2 (1887/88, 7/II, Bd. 4) DS 215: 917f; Hermes SBDR 11 Jan. 1889: 382; SBDR 14 Jan. 1890: 992–1108. The case was widely followed in the country: Aug. Roese, book printer, to Wm. II, BAB-L R1501/14693, Bl. 245–56.

obligations of either side.[9] Should his men continue to vote Left Liberal, they would break these connections and introduce a market-oriented clarity into their relationship—as his conclusion made clear:

> If circumstances should turn out so unfavorably that, with the current dearth of orders, it becomes necessary to limit production, I will as a consequence determine my own policy according to thine.

They should no longer assume that he would carry them in hard times. "Let it be known to ye as of today, that I will not gladly employ those who work against the noble efforts of our sublime Kaiser to remove social evils through progressive improvement in the condition of the workers. . . ."[10] Modernity, apparently, cut two ways.

Proclamations posted by bread lords at election time were common practice until well into the twentieth century. Egmont Tielsch was unusual only in his willingness to argue, however cursorily and sarcastically, the concrete political issues of the campaign.[11] In Saxony, where Social Democrats had already captured six of its twenty-three constituencies in 1884 and had become the second party in eleven more, the faith of employers in political argument was considerably lower. Much more common were blunt references to the logic of a situation in which losses for the governmental parties could result in economic instability. Here is Preuß and Company, a factory in Leipzig *Land*:

> Each may vote freely, according to his own conviction, but consider the following consequences. If the government party wins, then industry will flourish again, peace will be maintained. If the opposition wins, then we will surely have war, and *immediately after such an election result we will dismiss half of the workers and have to introduce the eight-hour day* [i.e., short hours]. All the other factories will find themselves in the same situation. Therefore, workers, be well warned.

The Election Commission refused to see in Preuß and Company's proclamation a threat. "Anyone," it said, "can prophesy the future."[12]

If some employers attempted to educate their workers and others pronounced on economic rationality, still others responded emotionally to the personal disloyalty they read in contrary voting. Such a figure was Chief Mining Director

---

[9] Otto Brunner, *Land and Lordship. Structures of Governance in Medieval Austria* ([Vienna, 1939], Philadelphia, 1992), 214–24.

[10] I have introduced periods into Tielsch's passage in order to make it easier to follow.

[11] Cf. announcement by the director of the Silesian *Aktien-Gesellschaft* in Mazura, *Entwicklung*, 93. Heinrich Mann has his antihero, Diederich Heßling, owner of a paper factory, supply his latrines with "educational paper," stamped with "state-sustaining" maxims, "whose use was unavoidable." *Der Untertan* (1918), 331f.

[12] P. Singer (SD) on 13 Saxony, SBDR 10 Jan. 1889: 351f. Italics in original. Similar examples: Müller, *Strömungen*, 242. In 9 Saxony, FKs ran the director of the steel works and peppered the newspapers with endorsements they had extracted, with threats and promises, from workers in the plants that he headed. AnlDR (1884/85, 6/I, Bd. 7) DS 328: 1788. In general: v. Vollmar (SD) SBDR 13 Feb. 1886: 1055.

von Detten, a man responsible for production, profits, and the maintenance of good order in the state's mining operations in the Hameln district. Good order in the mines had been overturned almost everywhere *except* Hameln during the Great Miners' Strike of 1889. Beginning in the Ruhr, where 87,000 men had laid down their tools, and then spreading to the Saar, Upper Silesia, and Saxony, the strike had been a public-relations disaster for those mining administrations involved. Von Detten's bailiwick, however, had remained quiet. Located in sleepy Hanover, where election battles were still fought out between triumphalist National Liberals and unreconstructed Guelfs; where middle-sized farms, craft trades, and small-scale industry still dominated economic life, the Hameln *Revier's* experience with radicalism had been confined to what its residents could read in the newspapers.[13] The good behavior of von Detten's miners had been rewarded by the Kaiser, who had singled them out in September for a gracious visit.

But the Chief Mining Director's satisfaction was short-lived. Within six months, a pied piper appeared in Hameln, in the form of a Social Democratic shoemaker by the name of Baerer. In the elections of February 1890, Baerer doubled his party's previous share of the vote and forced the National Liberal incumbent, Ferdinand von Reden, a local landowner, into a runoff. The ballot box had done what the organizers of the Great Strike of '89 had failed to do. It had brought the miners' rebellion into Hameln.

Von Detten responded as a man betrayed. Announcing that "when unknown, self-anointed popular evangelists are imposing themselves upon ye, it is my **Duty not** to look in silence," he posted "A Last Serious Word to All Miners and Pensioners" throughout the thirteen mining villages in the counties of Hameln, Linden, and Springe.

> Be warned, miners. In the **final** moments before the runoffs **have a thought for the consequences** of thy decision for **von Reden** or for **Baerer!!** **Mania** is **short-lived**, **regret, long**!

"A Last Serious Word" rang the changes on timeworn themes. Monarchy, state, property, religion, marriage, family, morality, culture, humanity, peace at home and abroad: each got a mention. But Von Detten had little heart for his duties as political educator. The truly painful meaning of the election lay not in any assault on the eternal verities. "For us mining people on the Deister, a ballot for **Baerer** means **infinitely more** still. For ye and me it means the **End of the Peace** that has existed between us in good times and bad, it means the **Onset of Strife. . . .**" The implicit social contract—fealty for succor—had been broken.

> Each ballot cast for **Baerer** by a miner **tears** the bands of trust between us, **cripples** the hand that is always caring for the miners' welfare, **freezes the heart** that beats so

[13] On Hanover: G. Franz, *Entwicklung* (1951); Ehrenfeuchter, *Willensbildung*; Hans-Georg Aschoff, *Welfische Bewegung und Politischer Katholizismus, 1866–1918. Die Deutschhannoversche Partei und das Zentrum in der Provinz Hannover während des Kaiserreiches* (Düsseldorf, 1987).

warmly for all miners, pensioners, and widows in their every need; it destroys the **quiet, order, unity, and comradeliness** of our crews. . . .

Particularly galling for Von Detten was the revelation, delivered by the election results, that he did not know his own men. He now realized that he was surrounded by "hypocrites, who last September **cheered our Kaiser** and can today serve the sworn **enemy** of the Kaiser, . . . who **today, in the open,** assure me that they are **no** Social Democrats and **tomorrow secretly** come out for **Baerer.**" In a working world acutely conscious of the social meanings of personal pronouns, the proclamation's diction, veering wildly between the matey first person plural ("us mining people on the Deister") and an infuriated, autocratic second person familiar ("ye miners")—that is, between an appeal to solidarity and an assertion of authority—betrayed the manager's difficulty in sorting out whether it was a breech in community or a challenge to hierarchy that the votes for Baerer revealed.[14]

Von Detten prayed to the Almighty "that we shall not **rue the day**." But while expressing confidence in the runoff's outcome ("however much the first election set me thinking"), he made clear that he would not ignore the gauntlet that had been thrown down. "Should **Baerer** emerge from the urns in our mining villages as victor," he announced, "my decision has been made, a decision that duty demands of me!" The men should expect from him "**no cowardly retreat.**"

> **Be warned** at this **last** minute, ye **miners**, thy work, thy wage, thy **pensions**, thy support funds are all at stake if the Social Democrats move in through thy support.

The shoemaker's vote dropped by thirty-two in these villages in the runoff election. But for every miner who was intimidated by their bread lord's "Last Serious Word," probably ten more were angered. The count was very close. The Reichstag ignored evidence that throughout the district laborers at mills, brickworks, and glassworks had been threatened with dismissal if a Social Democrat won. But because numerous small frauds and technical violations were discovered and because von Detten was a *royal* and not a private mining official, the Liberal victory in Hameln-County Linden-Springe was thrown out.[15]

THE UBIQUITY OF EMPLOYER PRESSURE

As these examples show, hierarchy, two decades into the practice of manhood suffrage, remained the basic assumption of working life. It was not confined to agriculture, nor to the backward east, nor indeed to any particular industry or

[14] Workers were quite conscious of the choice of pronouns. Kelly ed., *Worker*, 55. Their significance for class relations was common knowledge. Weber, *Verhältnisse*, 633; and went back as far as 1848. B. Moore, *Injustice* (1978), 160, 267.

[15] "Ein letztes ernstes Wort an *alle* Bergleute und Invaliden," along with examples from other industries in 9 Han. AnlDR (1890/91, 8/I, Bd. 1) DS 95: 641f; also Auer (SD) SBDR 3 Dec 1890: 762f. The SPD republished the report in full in *Thätigkeit*, 156f. Emphasis in original.

region. Paper and glass, coal and iron, craft bench and assembly line: all were governed by the same assumptions—in the shop and at the polls. Concern for hierarchy dictated the actions of Liberal businessmen, such as Tielsch, with his tight-lipped yet "modern" appeals to the voters' rational self-interest, and of aristocrats such as von Detten, tangled up in an attempt to assert mutual identity ("*us* mining people") simultaneous with (second person familiar) social control ("be warned, *ye* miners!"). The chemical industry was among the most modern in Germany. Yet the Baden Aniline and Soda Company of Ludwigshafen, a giant among employers, whose management corresponded to the local leadership of the Liberal Party, was a continual offender against free elections. Its foremen were instructed to inform factory workers that immediate dismissal would be the lot of any man who voted Centrum or Social Democratic against the longtime Liberal incumbent, Dr. Ludwig Groß. The following couplet made the rounds among the concern's 1,600 workers:

> Wer nicht wählt Dr. Groß,
> Der ist morgen arbeitslos!

After the election the firm made good on its threat.[16] The strategies at the disposal of industrial bread lords were no less varied than their agricultural counterparts: the extraction of oral or written promises; threats of dismissal; eviction and foreclosure.[17]

The nature of our sources provide little evidence of condescension in extracting the voting tribute, but it must have been common enough to provoke this warning by National Liberals facing Conservative competition in Central Silesia in 1890:

> Are the elections important? Certainly! Just look! A few days before the election your estate owner or employer, your superior at the office, your bread lord or benefactor will seek out your company; if you are in a public locale, he will motion you over to him as inconspicuously as possible, or if you are with him in his chambers, he will have you come to him in his chair in the most friendly manner—normally he probably has you stand at the door—and will give you a white slip, printed or inscribed with a name, and will say: na, my dear Müller or Schulze, I hope and expect that you shall indeed—normally he says: 'thou willt'—put this slip into the urn on election day. And if you read the slip, then there will stand either the name of your *Land*—or some other kind of *Rat*—or that of the Herr Pastor or some other unknown, often very high, often very insignificant person.

(The local Landrat denounced the Liberal election warning as an assault on the authorities [*Obrigkeit*].)[18]

[16] "Anyone who doesn't vote for Dr. Groß / Will be out of work tomorrow!" 1 Pfalz AnlDR (1881/2, 5/I, Bd. 2) DS 116: 426f. The same thing happened in 1884, when it employed 2,500 workers: Frohme SBDR 1 Apr. 1886: 1818.

[17] Evictions: 5 Arns. (Bochum) AnlDR (1885/86, 6/II, Bd. 5) DS 181: 898, 904; 13 Saxony (Leipzig Land) AnlDR (1887/88, 7/II, Bd. 4) 212: 905f; 3 Breslau AnlDR (1912/14, 13/I, Bd. 22) DS 1433: 2939.

[18] Proclamation on Striegau quoted in SBDR 17 Apr. 1891: 244.

Nevertheless, most snatches of recorded conversation reveal a distance between master and man that did not disappear in even the smallest firms on election day. Here is a friendly conversation in 1881 in a foundry near Ulm:

Foundry Manager Pfeiffer: "Well, tomorrow is the election."

Carpenter Bulling: "So, so."

Foundry Manager Pfeiffer: "Not 'so, so.' Thou'lt vote for Federal Councilor [Regierungs-Rat] Riekert; otherwise thou canst look for work in Heidenheim."[19]

We see a similar situation, with friendliness rapidly becoming authority, in northern Schleswig. As Jürg Jehsen was leaving work for the midday meal, he was invited by his employer, H. C. Petersen, to join him in a stroll to the polls. Jehsen was evasive: "I don't have my ballot with me." On his way home, however, Jehsen acquired a ballot—Social Democratic—and set off to vote. At the polls, Petersen was waiting for him, grabbed his ballot, and on reading it cried out, "So! thou'rt one of *that* kind." "In order not to anger his master and possibly lose his bread," Jehsen reported, he left without voting, hoping to be able to come back in the evening. But Petersen so overwhelmed Jehsen with tasks that afternoon that he was never able to get away. Even so, he was sacked at the end of the week.[20]

Although the bread lord's normal tactic was to discharge dissenters individually *pour encourager les autres*, mass dismissals for contrary voting were far from unknown. Protests to the Reichstag that workers were made to pay with their livelihoods for exercising their civic rights were continual: across decades, across occupations, across regions, and across parties (although most of the complaints came from Social Democrats, Centrum, Poles, and Left Liberals). Some districts were notoriously bad. In Thorn [Torun], a medium-sized town in West Prussia, hundreds of supporters of the Polish Party "lost their bread" after every election. As early as 1874 factory workers complained of being sacked for their votes in the Ninth Hanover, later the bailiwick of Chief Mining Director von Detten.[21] The ill fame of Upper and Central Silesia was not confined to the countryside. In 1876 the Conservative *Schlesische Zeitung* challenged anyone to furnish the names of a Silesian worker who had been punished for his vote. In the course of the next two months, the Centrum's *Schlesische Volks-*

[19] 14 Württ. AnlDR (1881/82, 5/I, Bd. 2) DS 113: 423. Of the many cases of intimidation in small, artisanal establishments: Protest against 9 Potsdam by Hermann Werndeck et al., 10 Mar. 1887, BAB-L R1501/14664, Bl. 64–68.

[20] Protest of Worker Election Committee, Flensburg, 10 Mar. 1887, BAB-L R1505/14664, Bl. 1–8; Schmidt SBDR 21 Apr. 1887: 415. Cf. Carpenter Anton Heilwerk et al., on 9 Potsdam, 10 Mar. 1887, BAB-L R1501/14664, Bl. 64–68.

[21] 9 Han. AnlDR (1874, 2/I, Bd. 3) DS 118: 397–99; SBDR 10 Apr. 1874: 706–12; v. Koscielski, on 4 Marienwerder SBDR 7 Mar. 1888: 1359. Characteristic: the estate owner called out to "us Polish people": "Wait up! Ye eat German bread and don't want to follow me? Wait up! . . . " Pieter Dabkowski (?) to RT, 3 Mar. 1887, BAB-L R1501/14665, Bl. 90. Hatschek's list of 20 cases of employer influence hardly scratches the surface. *Kommentar*, 207. On mass dismissals of Z voters: Windthorst SBDR 15 Jan. 1890: 1022; Gröber SBDR 21 Apr. 1903: 8925; BAB-L R1501/14456, Bl. 134.

zeitung came up with a hundred (with addresses) who had been disciplined or dismissed—a deliberate attempt to provoke a libel action that would allow the paper to demonstrate the injury to the workers' franchise in court.[22] But protests about dismissals and threats of dismissals (as well as evictions) were not confined to particular tarnished regions. They came from every corner of the Reich.

Because of the cooperation of panel chairmen with employers, distance between job and home (and therefore, polling place) was not necessarily a protection—as the factory worker August Eggers discovered. Eggers might reasonably have hoped that since his factory was in Freden, in the Prussian province of Hanover, while he lived and voted a few miles away in little Ammensen, in the Duchy of Braunschweig, the border between two federal states would provide a shield against his employer's demands. But Eggers had drawn attention to himself by protesting when the chairman of his panel unfolded his ballot to see for whom he had voted. When a few days later his foreman gave him his walking papers, Eggers, again mindful of his rights, demanded to see his boss. Director Heise granted the interview and, when the worker asked the reason for his dismissal, was quite unapologetic. "He wanted to say to him quite candidly, it happened because he had voted for Baumgarten [the *Freisinnige* incumbent]." "The Director could not possibly know that," Eggers cried, "since the vote was a secret one." Heise replied that "he knew it quite well and would uphold the dismissal. He couldn't use people who didn't vote the way he wanted."[23] Eggers was not the first or last worker to lose his job because a panel chairman funneled voting information to employers.[24]

The dismissals seem in some cases to have been politically effective. In 1881 the Landrat of Mülheim in the Rhineland attributed the decline in Social Democratic votes in his county to the "circumspection, severity, and energy of the factory owners." The energy may have diminished in some places by the twentieth century, but the severity did not. In 1901, eighteen years of service at the Hohenlohe mine could not protect from dismissal a Silesian worker suspected of canvassing for the Centrum. As the owners saw it, eighteen years of good employment deserved some loyalty![25]

Just as the demands of hierarchy and subordination were not limited to particular sectors of the economy, they were not imposed solely on the humblest classes. Arguing that his duty to abstain from political agitation was offset by his duty to give witness to the truth, the Superintendent of the Protestant

---

[22] Mazura, *Entwicklung*, 100; cf. also 97.

[23] Protest by the Gandersheim (3 Braunschweig) Freisinn Election Committee, 12 Mar. 1887, BAB-L R1501/14657, Bl. 4. The NL winner, Kulemann, *Erinnerungen*, 38f, 149.

[24] 14 Saxony (Borna) AnlDR (1885/86, 6/II, Bd. 5) DS 117: 568, 573; similar cooperation: 3 Marienwerder (1898/1900, 10/I, Bd. 4) DS 507: 2663; or implied cooperation: 10 Breslau AnlDR (1889/90, 7/V, Bd. 3) DS 105: 425; Hermes SBDR 11 Jan. 1889: 382.

[25] Larry Schofer, *The Formation of a Modern Labor Force: Upper Silesia, 1865–1914* (Berkeley and Los Angeles, 1975), 95. Similarly in 1873 in Thorn: Trzeciakowski, *Kulturkampf*, 174. Quote: Müller, *Strömungen*, 158.

Church in Saxe-Coburg, a man whose position was roughly that of a bishop, sent his clerical brethren a letter (marked "confidential") suggesting that they vote for the National Liberal. The churchman's intervention was perceived not as "clerical" influence (religious arguments went unmentioned), but as a classic attempt ("*optima forma*") by a superior to strong-arm his subordinates. One of these clerics was sufficiently offended to leak it to the public. County School Inspector Gregorovius of Waldenburg carefully affixed the word "*privatim*" to the circular he sent to his 171 teachers telling them for whom to vote—which meant, his supporters said, that no "official" influence could be charged against him. But the Left surely provided the correct translation. *Privatim* "only meant, *auf Deutsch*: 'do what I want, and keep your mouth shut about it.' "[26]

It was a Conservative article of faith that in big cities, Left Liberals (Progressives and later *Freisinnige*) imposed their choices on those within their orbit—either in their role as bosses of commercial or financial firms, or as contractors for municipal governments. A painter from Breslau discovered that his credit had been withdrawn by Jewish liberals, who made up a third of the population and half of the city council, because they believed (probably correcting) that the Artisan Protection Association, which he headed, was antisemitic.[27] As late as 1909 Conservatives were claiming that any bank employee who demonstrated his conservative politics on a "practical level" could reckon on a vigorous dressing down by his Left Liberal board of directors. The realization that only a strict enforcement of the secret ballot would allow them to tap many small employees, artisans, and shopkeepers led the antisemitic parties to demand ballot envelopes and to support the secret ballot in Prussian Landtag elections. On occasion, even Conservatives agreed.[28]

Those in white collar occupations rarely faced explicit threats of dismissal, but they too moved in a culture which, from the top down, insisted upon their demonstrating a strong sense of what loyalty to their employer required. Thus Wilhelm von Oechelhäuser, the General Director of the German Continental Gas Company in Dessau, took pains to request permission from his board of directors when he wanted to run as a National Liberal for the Second Anhalt. Beginning in 1881, he renewed the request before each of his reelection campaigns, in 1884, 1887, and 1890—which enabled the company continually to monitor any changes in his or his party's political positions. A refusal to campaign actively on behalf of an employer's choice (or against a candidate he disliked) could have unpleasant consequences even for high-level employees— as Mining Inspector Adams of the Stumm Works in Saarbrücken discovered in

[26] Quotes, in order: Singer SBDR 11 Feb. 1888: 855; *Rechte*, 36–38, 43, 49.

[27] Theodor Rüdiger, writing from Posnania Province, to (the antisemite) Baron Fr. Carl v. Fechenbach, 23 Mar. 1882. BAK Fechenbach Papers. On Elberfeld-Barmen: Unsigned, n.d., probably collected by the OP, "Wahlaussichten für die Rhein Provinz," GStA PK I. HA, Rep. 89/210, Bl. 230v; Behr-Behrenhoff SBDR 10 Dec. 1885: 261.

[28] Below, *Wahlrecht*, 154; antisemitic platforms: Specht/Schwabe, *Reichstagswahlen*, 406, 412, 416.

THE GOOD HEART

"So! Now I'm voting for a Social Democrat! Damn the consequences!"

"Nix, nix, I'm voting Social Democratic."

"Children, Children, your father is voting for a Sozi!!"

"Ach, good morning, my dear Herr Secretary– going to the election too?"
"Jawohl, Herr District Councilor [*Regierungsrat*]."

1901, when a telegram informed him of his disciplinary transfer.[29] As for middle- and lower-level employees, their vulnerability was proved over and over by firings during the Kulturkampf and the peak of antisocialist hysteria.[30]

Political subservience on the part of middle-class employees was a favorite

[29] BAB-L R1501/14456, Bl. 125; Gröber SBDR 21 Apr. 1903: 8909; Jaeger, *Unternehmer*, 101n. 344.

[30] Catholic civil servants during the Kulturkampf: Anderson/Barkin, "Myth," and Catholic mailmen: Sperber, *Catholicism*, 243f; and other postal workers: Singer SBDR 29 Apr. 1907: 1211; government employees with SD inclinations: Möllers, *Strömungen*, 332; village mayors (W supporters): 17 Han. AnlDR (1882/83, 5/II, Bd. 6) DS 242: 928; other local officials: Horn Report, 24 Feb. 1907, LHAK 403/8806, Bl.7v; threats to Seminar Direktor Turowsky of Ragnit (2 Gumb.), "Zwei Fragen an die königliche Staatsregierung," *NL Correspondenz* 49/1 (3 Jan. 1912), BAB-L R1501/14460, Bl. 140.

"Na, we both know what we owe to the state, my dear Herr Secretary!"
"Jawohl, Herr Federal Councilor."

"No, that'd be just too shabby! I'll vote for my National Liberals again."

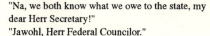

Fig. 7. W. Schulz, *Simplicissimus* XVI/40: 703.

butt for the barbs of humor magazines from *Fliegende Blätter* to *Simplicissimus*.[31] As the above strip suggests, intimidation was hardly necessary to bring the lower employee into line; a word from the right person at the right moment, and habitual deference would kick in. Only physicians and lawyers, whose clients were not employers, seem to have been exempt from the exigencies of "loyal voting." Not for nothing did Germans group them together as "free" professions.

In three branches of the economy—forestry, railways, and heavy industry (coal, iron, and steel)—pressures on voters were especially strong. In all three, the workforce of any given employer was unusually large. All three enjoyed strong traditional ties to the state—and in the railroad industry, these ties were increasing.[32] Even in those mines and forests now in private hands, it was not uncommon for managers to have begun their careers in government service. In all three of these sectors, the ordinary claims of hierarchy were reinforced by an ethos, hammered home through middle-level supervisors, that equated loyalty

---

[31] "Election Day" (*Simplicissimus* III [1898–9]: 91) depicts a little man who sets off to vote, meets first a conservative, agrees with him, ditto with a liberal, ditto with a pastor, ditto with workers—and ends up getting drunk and never voting at all. *Fliegende Blätter* includes cartoons that make a similar point. Cf. Fontane's immortal Herr Schickedanz of the Pluvius Hailstorm Insurance Company: *Stechlin*, 104. The *Essener Blätter* complained before the 1873 Prussian LT election of *Beamten*: "probably most of them will sing the beautiful song, 'Whose bread I eat, his song I sing.'" Möllers, *Strömungen*, 221. On the politics of officials: Rickert SBDR 15 Jan. 1890: 1015.

[32] In 1879 more than a quarter of Prussia's 17,600 kilometers of railway were in state hands. By 1888, Prussia's rail net had increased to 23,700 kilometers, of which 95 percent now belonged to the state. Spencer, *Management*, 26, 31f; Bellot, *Hundert Jahre*, esp. 217f; Huber, *Verfassungsgeschichte* 4: 1064f.

to the employer with patriotism. The way to demonstrate this allegiance was by good voting.

In the forests, few if any of the decencies were observed. The wardens assembled the loggers, gave them ballots, and took them in teams to the polls. Although the loggers' corporate identity may have made the overall pattern of their choices "affirmative," as Stanley Suval has termed it, rather than coerced, the fact that some wardens required their men to walk with their ballots held above their heads suggests that the bosses were not taking any chances. Dismissals for contrary voting were frequent enough to indicate that corporate identity, if it did exist, was far from universal.[33] When the Conservative candidate Julius von Mirbach sent an urgent warning to Bismarck in 1881 that the forest wardens in East Prussia were failing to do their duty, the Minister of Interior Robert von Puttkamer "built a fire" under the Minister of Agriculture to get the situation reversed. Not surprisingly, however, Mirbach's report had been a false alarm. Master Forester Ulrici responded to complaints by assuring the minister that his wardens and head foresters were already passing out Conservative ballots and that he could guarantee the vote of every forest official under him.[34]

As for the railways, they were classic sites of employer intimidation. The Centrum and Progressives had opposed the nationalization of the German railways precisely because it would concentrate this voting power in the hands of a single employer—the government. By 1888 the Prussian state already employed 86,714 railway "officials" and 157,997 "workers"—a total of 244,711 personnel. Railway officials subjected their employees to exacting political surveillance, even in nonelection years.[35] Not only were trade unions forbidden, as they were for all public employees, but as late as 1907 even festivals held by Catholic or labor organizations were off limits to railway personnel. Officials cooperated with private employer associations in requiring their employees too

---

[33] Intimidation, violation of secrecy, dismissals and economic penalties against woodcutters: Weaver Wm. Stephan et al. to RT on 11 Breslau, 10 Mar. 1887, BAB-L R1501/14664, Bl. 69–76; 9 Han. AnlDR (1874, 2/I, Bd. 3) DS 118: 399; 6 Gumb. AnlDR (1875, 2/III, Bd. 4) DS 82: 838f; 8 Kassel AnlDR (1877, 3/I, Bd. 3) DS 68: 269; 13 Han., and 14 Württ. (Ulm), both in AnlDR (1881/82, 5/I, Bd. 2) DS 121: 429 and DS 113: 421–24; 11 Breslau AnlDR (1881/82, 5/I, Bd. 2) DS 104: 353–56; 6 Potsdam AnlDR (1884/85, 6/I, Bd 6) DS 248: 1105; 20 Saxony AnlDR (1884/85, 6/I, Bd. 6) DS 247: 1102; 2 Han. AnlDR (1884/85, 6/I, Bd. 5) DS 148: 534–39; 1 Anhalt AnlDR (1884/85, 6/I, Bd. 5) DS 135: 511; Kröber (VP), on Bavaria, SBDR 29 Nov. 1888: 65; Saul, "Kampf," 185. Ambiguous: 8 Königsberg AnlDR (1879, 4/II, Bd. 6) DS 276: 1631–37; 5 Kassel AnlDR (1907/9, 12/I, Bd. 20) DS 705: 4494; BAB-L R1501/14450: Bl. 195–202v; monitoring: (signature omitted) Protest against 1890 election in 8 Kassel, BAB-L R1501/14468, Bl. 233. Moritz Bromme intentionally stresses his logger father-in-law's traditionalism, but also reveals that the logger thought voting SD was acceptable, if one could get away with it. *Lebensgeschichte* (1905), excerpted in Kelly, ed., *Worker*, 231–51; esp. 235.

[34] Puttkamer to Bis., Ulrici's reply: quoted in "Wie Bismarck" 1/5: 13. Similar efforts by the Gumb. RP: Ibid., 14.

[35] Königliches Preussisches Ministerium der öffentlichen Arbeiten, *Archiv für Eisenbahnwesen* 13 (Berlin, 1890), 438; Müller, *Strömungen*, 132; Blackbourn, *Marpingen*, 80f and n. 126. Cf. Jensen, *Winning*, 53; Ethington, *City*, 205, 253f.

to present on demand work certificates (*Arbeiter Nachweise*), detailing each man's employment record—a system that facilitated political surveillance when groups of employers agreed not to hire anyone whose certificate showed that he had previously been dismissed or had quit.[36] Even a Bahnhof restauranteur who displayed Progressive newspapers on his rack might count on losing his concession.[37]

At election time, those parties enjoying government favor could always count on the help of obliging railway officials, for everything from posting election proclamations in workrooms, to appointing a "trusty" to accompany each column of workers to the polls.[38] Railway workers who for some reason or another were ineligible to vote, would return to the polls again and again, insisting that they had to cast the ballots their superiors had given them. With whips like these, and personnel nearing 350,000 by 1890 and 700,000 by 1910, it is hardly surprising that turnouts in the German Empire were so high.[39] In rail yards throughout Hanover, Silesia, Saxony, and even Bavaria, a worker's vote was less a matter of individual choice or party solidarity than a tax on his employment.[40]

IN THE REALM OF THE CHIMNEY BARONS

The smokestack industries disposed of Germany's highest concentrations of workers—and voters. And since ownership was often overlapping (not all mining companies owned iron and steel plants, but most iron and steel firms owned mines), the chimney barons' control over employment opportunities stretched beyond that of a single trade or even a single industry. One-fifth of all the coal production in the Ruhr by the early twentieth century was controlled by steel

[36] Examples: Altona: Stegmann, *Erben*, 48; Naumann, "Konservative Industriejunker" (1909): 6f; 17 Han. AnlDR (1877, 3/I, Bd. 3) DS 138: 390–92; 5 Arns. (Bochum) AnlDR (1884/85, 6/I, Bd. 7) DS 320: 1769; v. Saldern, *Wege*, 68. Influence by railway officials was also charged in 1 Württ. (Stuttgart) in 1893: MAA, Stuttgart, 21 Aug. 1894, BAB-L R1501/15691, Bl. 8; in 3 Danzig AnlDR (1882/83, 5/II, Bd. 5) DS 80: 348; 3 Marienwerder (1898/1900, 10/I, Bd.4) DS 507: 2662. Official scrutiny into how railworkers voted in 1890 in 2 Koblenz (Neuwied): Monshausen, *Wahlen*, 274. SPD complaints on behalf of employees: SBHA 19 May 1909: 6804–53, esp. 6815.

[37] Mirbach to Bis., Bis. to Puttkamer, 20 Aug. 1881, in "Wie Bismarck" 1/5: 12f.

[38] 3 Saxony AnlDR (1881/82, 5/II, Bd. 5) DS 174: 610f, 614. The SPD, whose economic retaliation provided some counterweight in other branches of the economy in Prussian LT elections, gave up here. Kühne, *Dreiklassenwahlrecht*, 114f.

[39] 6 Potsdam, SBDR 10 Mar. 1885: 1105. *Statistisches Jahrbuch für das Deutsche Reich* (1880), 108–9; (1890), 108f; (1910), 137, 141.

[40] Fr. Sievers, SD Protest against 9 Han., 12 Mar. 1887, BAB-L R1501/14664, Bl. 82; Gottlob Leuge and Workers' Com., Protest against 4 Erfurt, 10 Mar. 1887, BAB-L R1501/14664, Bl. 88–93; H. Ramme [Kamme?] to Forest-and Domane Inspector R. Clauditz (3 Han.), 20 Feb. 1890, SAO Dep 62b, 2379; inspectors of horse railway depots in Berlin: 6 Berlin AnlDR (1880, 4/III, Bd. 4) DS 94: 666–75; 669f, 673; 14 Saxony AnlDR (1885/86, 6/II, Bd. 5) DS 117: 569, 572; 6 Breslau: Singer SBDR 6 Mar. 1888: 1312–14; 10 Breslau: Hermes SBDR 11 Jan. 1889: 382; Kröber (VP), on Bavaria, SBDR 29 Nov. 1888: 65; on Göttingen, where the railway was the largest employer in town: v. Saldern, *Wege*, 129, 183.

firms like the Phoenix Steelworks, the Gutehoffnungshütte, and Krupp (the fifth, eighth, and eleventh largest coal producers, respectively). Heavy industry accounted for 61 percent of all "giant" employers—those employing 1,000 workers or more. As early as 1882 somewhat more than a third of the firms in heavy industry fell into the "giant" category.[41] By the outbreak of the war, Krupp was giving work to more than 70,000; Gutehoffnungshütte, Deutscher Kaiser, and Harpener Bergbau-AG, more than 20,000; the Bochumer Verein, Hibernia, Hoesch, and the Rhenish Steelworks, more than 10,000 workers each. Yet the twenty-odd firms whose modern chimneys dominated the Ruhr skyline were no less determined to extract political obedience from their teeming thousands than the most traditional master artisan concerned with a pair of journeymen sleeping in his hayloft. And not only in the Ruhr. If Left Liberals punned about Windthorst's bailiwick in the Emsland as a political "Muffrika" ("black," backward, and as impenetrable to their progressive gospel as the dark continent itself), they were no less scathing about the electoral sheikdom of Baron Stumm's "Saarabia."[42]

More frequently than in forestry and the railways, the commanding heights of the mining and metal industries were held by men who played a visible role in national, state, and especially local politics, where they were used to having their own way. In Essen, Alfred Krupp was so wealthy that sometimes he alone made up the entire first class in municipal elections. In 1874 and then again in the years between 1886 and 1894 Krupp, followed by his son Friedrich, had the right to name a third of Essen's aldermen personally—a monopoly that continued with only a brief interruption until 1918.[43] Oligopolies were more common, however, than monopolies. Westfalia's Municipal Ordinance allowed any taxpaying "juridical person" to vote in municipal elections. As just such a taxpayer (*und wie!*), the Bochum Association for Mining and Steel Manufacturing (hereafter, the Bochumer Verein) constituted the city's entire first class. The result was that seats as aldermen became for all intents and purposes the property of the Bochumer Verein's directors, "bequeathed" from one generation to the next. Entrepreneurs also dominated Bochum's second class, and even the third class was the preserve of lower levels of management. These same men dominated the local campaign committees of the National Liberal (or, alternatively, Free Conservative) Party in national elections as well—especially as rising campaign costs in the eighties turned Reichstag politics in Ruhr and the Saar into a rich man's game. Thus Louis Baare, the Bochumer Verein's managing director

---

[41] Spencer, *Management*, 21f; H. Kaelble, *Interessenpolitik* (1967), 59.

[42] "Muffrika" is from Gerlach, *Rechts*, 175f. "Saarabien" was coined by Fr. Naumann in 1895, says Bellot, *Hundert Jahre*, 106. Soon it was in general use: "Ein Saarabisches Wahlbild," *Saar-Post* 25 Jan. 1912, AnlDR (1912/14, 13/I, Bd. 23) DS 1639: 3609, 3590; Schwarze (Lippstadt) SBDR 21 May 1912: 2218. L. Brentano, "Arbeitsverhältnis" (1906): 135–50, esp. 141.

[43] Tenfelde, *Sozialgeschichte*, 567. Not all local powerholders were coal and steel magnates: Ziese, owner of the Schichau Shipyards, controlled the first class in Elbing, and named 20 of the 60 aldermen. Jaeger, *Unternehmer*, 87, 87n. 281, 88, 113, 142, 262. In many Rhenish cities, fewer than 1 percent of the entire population was eligible to vote in the first class in 1898.

from 1855 to 1895 and a man with connections to nearly every other important industrial organization in the region, held most of the threads of Bochum's political life in his hand. As deputy to the provincial diet and the Prussian Landtag; as brother-in-law of Bochum's long-standing Reichstag incumbent, Dr. Wilhelm Löwe; as head of Bochum's Election Association and therefore responsible for financing National Liberal campaigns, Baare personally dictated the responses of the district's Liberal candidate to social and economic questions, shouting down spokesmen of the official party and threatening to take the Bochumer Verein's money over to the Free Conservatives if his demands were not met.[44]

The determination of chimney barons like Baare to keep their candidates on the straight and narrow was mirrored by the equally tight control they exercised over their employees. Albert Hoesch himself, of Dortmund's powerful Hoesch Iron and Steelworks, signed the dismissal letter of a worker who had the temerity to campaign for the *Freisinnige* Julius Lenzmann "in spite of our posting a request that officials and workers cast their vote in the Reichstag election for candidate Kleine. . . ." When the worker pleaded to be taken back, Hoesch again responded in person. The plaintiff had "given the clearest evidence" of being a "convinced Lenzmann supporter," Hoesch said, and "our own interest, as well as that of our officials and workers, enjoins us to keep our opponents away from our works. . . ."[45]

Usually, however, the employers' political authority was asserted indirectly, through their supervisors: the *Steiger* (pit foremen) in mining, the *Werkmeister* in metallurgy, men who had themselves been carefully screened for political reliability—that is, hostility to unions, Social Democracy, political Catholicism, and often Left Liberalism. Sometimes positive tokens of political loyalty were demanded as well. In Bochum, twenty-some Catholic mining officials were told to sign an election appeal for Dr. Löwe (and thus, against the Centrum candidate), or leave. (At least two pit foremen chose dismissal.) Many firms, especially the larger ones, saved themselves trouble by making a point of hiring only Protestants for these positions.[46]

Supervisory personnel were in constant personal contact with their workers, whom they knew by name, but from whom they kept the greatest social distance. Although at one time *Steiger* and *Werkmeister* had risen from the ranks, by the nineties they had become a distinct stratum, distinguished by specialized training, forbidden to take part in manual labor, set apart not only by salaries as much as 80 percent higher than the wages of their men, but also by their bourgeois clothes, separate company housing, and leisure organizations. The pub sociability and good-bye presents that might soften British workers' off duty relations with their immediate superiors had no counterpart in Germany. Em-

---

[44] Kulemann, *Erinnerungen*, 155–59; H. Croon, "Stadtvertretungen," 289–306; Mann, *Handbuch* (1988), 51.

[45] Read by Lenzmann SBDR 13 Feb. 1886: 1062.

[46] 5 Arns. AnlDR (1882/83, 5/II, Bd. 6) DS 292: 1079; Bellot, *Hundert Jahre*, 116, 207; Möllers, *Strömungen*, 327; Spencer, *Management*, 84–89.

ployers encouraged social distance by deliberately seeking nonlocals as overseers; they enforced it by fining a worker who forgot to tip his cap to his
foreman, and by their willingness to prosecute in court any signs of insolence.[47]
With virtual autonomy in hiring and firing, in setting wages and even production levels, in distributing tasks and levying fines, *Meister* and *Steiger* were
monarchs in their domains, and they ruthlessly used this authority to exact
voting discipline. A cashiered worker would find it hard to get a job elsewhere.
Even when blacklisting was not a publicized policy, dismissal slips often bore
inconspicuous marks designating political malcontents. In Silesia's Kreuzburg-
Rosenberg district, employers wrote to their counterparts as far away as Russia,
to make sure that their dismissed Polish workers would not be able to find
employment under the Tsar.[48]

Ruthlessness was combined with vigilance. Former policemen were hired as
supers in workers' housing blocks and given the added task of sniffing out
subscribers to objectionable newspapers. They would wait until a man was on
the job and then chat up his wife, casually demanding a piece of newspaper to
light his cigar, or asking if he could see her copy of the *Tremonia* (a Centrum
organ), since he needed to look something up.

The same argus-eyed personnel manned the voting panels in their regions:
not surprisingly, since unlike rural panels, whose chairmen were chosen by the
Landrat, the selection of urban panels was the privilege of the respective municipal governments. Corporate proprietorship over Ruhr elections was vividly
illustrated in 1884 when Bochum's Lord Mayor (who doubled as Landrat for
the *Stadtkreis*) moved the twelfth precinct's polls into the "Steel House," the
Bochumer Verein's own canteen and bunkhouse. It would have been difficult to
imagine any locale in which the chimney barons had greater territorial claims.
Lounging about in an adjacent room were supernumerary crowds of masters, pit
foremen, and engineers, fueled by free alcohol and worked up by National
Liberal organizers, ready to toss out any citizen who distributed dissenting ballots or otherwise showed signs of disloyalty. In Essen, where the boss himself
was a candidate in 1893, a Krupp official told metalworkers at a polling place:
"Here on our own property we have the right to look each man sharply in the
eye and appeal to his conscience, so that he votes for the one from whom he
has received his bread."[49]

In religiously mixed precincts, where the Kulturkampf structured political
identities, pressure on Protestant miners and metalworkers was often not
needed, as they could usually be counted on to vote "national" at least until the

---

[47] R. Biernacki, *Fabrication* (1995), 188–90; His examples, drawn from the textile industry, are *a fortiori* true for heavy industry.

[48] 5 Arns. AnlDR (1884/85, 6/I, Bd. 7) DS 320: 1769. Magdeburg vicinity: Gerlach, *Erlebnisse*, 71; Stumm's Saar: Bellot, *Hundert Jahre*, 147, 159f, 162, 166; Kreuzburg-Rosenberg: P. Majunke (Z) SBDR 2 Dec. 1882: 600.

[49] 5 Arns. (Bochum) An1DR (1884/85, 6/I, Bd. 7) DS 320: 1767–73; Protest of Z Committee of Bochum, 20 Jan. 1891, BAB-L R1501/14668, Bl. 188–97; 6 Arns. (Hörde) AnlDR (1890/91, 8/I, Bd. 3) DS 292: 2052; quote: Paul, *Krupp*, 275.

nineties and sometimes well beyond. Here surveillance might be limited to making sure that they voted—and threatening dismissal to those who did not.[50] Catholics required more effort. Thus at the Burbacher Steel Works in Saarbrücken, Protestants were given standard printed (Liberal) ballots, while Catholics working the night shift were summoned to a meeting by their supervisors, told of a rumor that a Catholic master had been disciplined for a Centrum vote, and then asked to prove that they had the company's interests at heart by *volunteering* to accept distinctive—lithographed—ballots for the Liberal candidate, Ernst Bassermann. As three masters began to distribute the ballots, the leader warned: "Anyone who accepts one of these written [lithographed] ballots has to cast it, lest he bring suspicion on one of his co-workers." Even during the Great War, works officials in Stumm's old district, where his son-in-law and successor at the firm was candidate in a by-election, subjected each ballot to a handwriting inspection.[51]

Miners were an easy target. In some places, foremen simply took away their ladders, leaving masses of suspected dissidents stranded at the bottom of the shaft until the polls closed.[52] Steelworkers, since they normally worked in columns, were easy to keep in formation from shop to polls—although they looked (as one contemporary complained) more like "a prisoner transport than free voters." Those with other jobs, or who worked the night shift, did not escape the pressure. As many as one hundred Polish laborers at a time would be rousted out of company-owned barracks by *Schleppers*, often with the help of a large dog.[53]

Protests were full of testimony about the efforts of supervisors and foremen to track down every last possible dissenter, either to fix his vote or, if that proved impossible, to make sure that he did not vote at all.[54] The bosses' repeated declarations that they wouldn't bother wasting their efforts on Catholic voters has been accepted by some historians.[55] But contemporary complaints about heavy industry's strong-arm tactics were at least as frequent from supporters of the Centrum and Poles as from Protestant Social Democrats and Left

[50] 5 Arns. (Bochum) AnlDR (1887/88, 7/II, Bd. 3) DS 57: 297–303.

[51] "Ein Saarabisches Wahlbild," *Saar-Post* 20 (25 Jan. 1912), in AnlDr (1912/14, 13/I, Bd. 23): DS 1639: 3609. Jaeger, *Unternehmer*, 186n. 98.

[52] 5 Oppeln AnlDR (1879, 4/II, Bd. 4) DS 105: 647f; 5 Wiesbaden, Spahn SBDR 9 Apr. 1886: 2007, and AnlDR (1884/85, 6/I, Bd. 7) DS 304: 1710. Polish miners at the "Pluto" were given double shifts or threatened with dismissal and expulsion to their *Heimat*. 5 Arns. AnlDR (1884/85, 6/I, Bd. 7) DS 320: 1773.

[53] 1878 Bochum election, described in AnlDR (1882/83, 5/II, Bd. 6) DS 292: 1079, 1081; similar reports from Saarbrücken, as late as 1912: 5 Trier AnlDR (1912/14, 13/I, Bd. 23) DS 1639: 3590–92, 3594.

[54] Every last voter: see Johann Jarczewsky's testimony on 5 Arns. AnlDR (1884/85, 6/I, Bd. 7) DS 320: 1777 and AnlDR (1885/86, 6/II, Bd. 5) DS 181: 907f.

[55] E.g., Hans-Otto Hemmer, "Die Bergarbeiterbewegung im Ruhrgebiet unter den Sozialistengesetz," in *Arbeiterbewegung am Rhein und Ruhr*, ed. J. Reulecke (Wuppertal, 1974), 81–109; 99. Tenfelde, *Sozialgeschichte*, 567, makes a similar point, although not all of his data support it. A different view: Elaine Glovka Spencer, "Rulers of the Ruhr: Leadership and Authority in Germany. Big Business before 1914," *Business History* 53/1 (Spring 1979): 40–64.

Liberals. At the "Bunny Run" (*Hasenwinkel*) mine in Dahlhausen, pit foremen fanned out among the Catholic workers, telling them to stay away from the polls. When the machinist Karl Thöne was approached by his chief with this message and told to keep his brother Heinrich away as well, he diplomatically said nothing. His silence apparently roused suspicion, for later in the day yet another foreman appeared in his shop demanding an explicit commitment to remain away. At that Thöne admitted that he wanted to vote. "The supervisor said, one vote won't make any difference, I should therefore stay away from the voting. *If I did, I would do the Herr Head Supervisor a great favor. I wouldn't suffer from it.*" Thöne's brother, also a machinist, met with similar treatment.

The Thöne brothers decided to vote anyway—a calculated risk, but the odds seemed good. In a region where the workforce was notoriously nomadic, they were aware of having spotless records as skilled and respected craftsmen, with more than a decade of employment at the Bunny Run. Moreover, they knew how to play the game. They got themselves ballots that were visibly National Liberal on the outside, and then crossed out Gustav Haarmann's name and wrote in that of Baron Burghard von Schorlemer-Alst, the Centrum candidate— as did two of their relatives who had been subjected to the same dark hints. But when the four men arrived at the polls, they discovered that the doors were closed—a bad sign, because it meant that, contrary to § 9 of the Election Law, the "public" was being excluded. They would have no protective observers from their own camp to monitor what went on. Their forebodings increased when they got inside. "In place of the election panel," Heinrich Thöne reported, "the *Head Supervisor Strohsberg* was functioning as chairman. *The latter felt my ballot from all sides* and did the same with that of my brother and brother-in-law." Even when the ballot itself did not betray the voter, members of election panels carefully kept them in a stack that preserved the order in which they were cast, to be compared later against a list recording the order of voters. Strohsberg must have availed himself of such a strategy, for the next day, Heinrich Thöne reported, the head supervisor "asked me sarcastically, *whether I and the other two considered ourselves to be smarter than he was himself.* I asked him how he meant this. Whereupon he said that by tomorrow, we'd find out."

Probably to his surprise, Heinrich Thöne was not fired. But his pay was docked half a shift because of the time lost voting; he lost his extra job administering the powder magazine, which had brought him an additional fifty to eighty marks a quarter; and everything was done to make things as hard as possible for him and his brother. He decided to look for work elsewhere.[56]

The Thöne brothers were model employees, who had weighed the risks carefully and had concluded—wrongly—that they were safe. August Hundt, a hewer at the Baaker Mulde colliery in the same district, was cut from different cloth. Immediately after the same election he was given two weeks' notice "for

---

[56] 5 Arns. AnlDR (1884/85, 6/I, Bd. 7) DS 320: 1777f.

unexcused absence and troublemaking." The hewer was convinced that "troublemaking" could only refer to an incident shortly before the election, when he had stopped off for a drink with eight of his mates at a tavern on the way home from the pit. As they sat outside, drinking their schnapps, the conversation had turned to the approaching election. "Among other things, we said that the eight of us would all give our votes to Baron von Schorlemer, and in closing I offered a cheer for von Schorlemer, and all the others joined in." The friends then went off in their different directions. But their pit inspector, Richard Schepmann, had also "turned up" at the tavern, Hundt recalled after the election. He must have overheard their talk (of course, Schepmann countered: Hundt was drunk and noisy), for when the men arrived at work the next day, "the eight of us mates were written up on the blackboard, five were fined one and a half marks, three of us (including me) fined three marks for knocking off without leave and for making trouble." The same grounds were given when Hundt got his walking papers—the day after the election.

Had August Hundt been fired for his politics? As it turned out, he *had* quit work early. Since it was payday, he had left the pit two hours into his shift, to collect his wages. Once out, he simply "didn't feel like riding out there [to the coal face] again at such a late hour, since the excavation was already so far along that we would soon cut through." The next day they did indeed cut through, as Hundt's partner, drilling above ground, knocked out the ceiling of Hundt's seam, drenching the hewer with mud and water. Hundt said that he couldn't work in wet clothes and was going home—"to which," he believed, "there could be no objection." Since home was three-quarters of an hour away, however, he had not bothered to come back, and so Shepmann had voided his shift. "We had the usual auditing and deductions from our work—and me and my mate (who is also Catholic) were docked thirty wagons of coal except for the slack coal." A week later, Hundt was sacked. Was this a political penalty, exacted for raising a glass to Schorlemer? The hewer certainly thought so, averring that "after the Reichstag election, Foreman Schepmann made it known to the workers in the pit that it would go hard with the workers from Blankenstein from now on," because of their support for Schorlemer. But one could equally well argue that Hundt was docked and then fired because he had timed his workday by the clock of his own common sense. Even without crediting entirely Schepmann's side of things (and the widespread practice of knocking off work early on payday, like truancy on Blue Mondays and other unofficial holidays, was a constant thorn in management's side), August Hundt's story can be read a number of ways. But whatever the justice of his dismissal, the tale demonstrates how easily the quotidian irritations of the workplace were translated into the language of electoral politics—and vice versa. It also demonstrated the Ruhr workers' conviction that their most casual conversation, if overheard by the wrong person, would be used against them.[57]

---

[57] Ibid., 1776 and 5 Arns. AnlDR (1885/86, 6/II, Bd. 5) DS 181: 906f. J. Lenzmann (F) cited an

Alfred Krupp and the Bottom Line

Of course, in Germany, as in any society, there were always employers who didn't care about elections so long as production quotas were met.[58] In Aachen, a textile town, a Catholic Christian Social movement led by a charismatic priest offering a radical, and rhetorically scurrilous, class analysis of local politics challenged the Catholic oligarchy's dominance of the city, and came within an ace of taking Aachen's seat from the Centrum in 1877; yet that same oligarchy left weavers and factory workers to vote as they chose.[59] Even in Bochum, where blacklisting for bad voting was in force, we hear regret in the tone of an employer who told a job-seeker who, three months after the 1887 election, was still out of work: "Bring me a different dismissal slip [*Abkehrschein*], and I will take you on. With that one, I'm not allowed to employ you."[60] At the extreme were those who identified business with politics and never relented in their efforts to control their workers. Baron von Stumm, whose activities on behalf of the metal industry ranged from snooping in the homes of his workers to serving energetically in the Reichstag himself, is the classic example. Many employers, however, seem neither to have identified the political with the economic so consistently as Stumm, nor to have regularly distinguished them, as seems to have been done at Daimler in Untertürkheim. Like Egmont Tielsch, our porcelain manufacturer, they ignored some elections and intervened coercively in others—an intermittent oppression that may have roused most resistance.[61] Some bread lords may even have encouraged their workers' political autonomy. The Progressive manufacturer Ludwig Löwe of Berlin, who employed hundreds, claimed that his workers were so free that some had taken up a collection right outside his factory to oppose his own election. Our sources are naturally biased against these men; enlightened behavior does not produce election protests. Did solidarity between master and man at the workplace ever spill over into the political sphere, as Patrick Joyce has found among Tory workers in England? The Breslau factory owner Hermann Seidel (with the help of free beer and "love cigars") put together a torchlight parade of more than 12,000 workers on behalf of his district's Conservative candidate in 1887. The

---

iron puddler who was fired after 20 years for offering a toast to him on election night. SBDR 13 Feb. 1886: 1062. On these daily conflicts: Tenfelde, *Sozialgeschichte*, 256, 276, 578f.

[58] E.g., middle-sized farmers in 9 Han.: Ehrenfeuchter, *Willensbildung*, 113; Daimler in Untertürkheim: P. Fridenson, "Herrschaft" (1988), 77f, 87. A factory in Chemnitz tolerated SD graffiti. P. Göhre, *Three Months* (1895), 104. One of W. Keil's employers put up with his activism for two years—until he began to miss work. *Erlebnisse* 1: 121f.

[59] There were no RT challenges against the Z's Aachen victories, and the minutes of the Christian Socials' meetings, devoted to attacks on the Z's Election Club as representatives of the bosses, contain no hint that their opponent's success was owing to pressures on workers. See the superb edition by Lepper, ed., *Katholizismus*, 106–9, 121–23, 125–27, 132–44, 151f, 162f, 167, 172f, 177, 186f, 193–99.

[60] Quoted in Wacker, *Rechte*, 23. Miners in the Wurm and Inde-Revier (2 Aachen), fired for refusing liberal ballots, were rehired a few weeks later. Lepper, *Strömungen* 2: 533.

[61] So argues Moore, *Injustice*, 483; cf. Spencer, *Management*, 63.

fact that he was then the recipient of a royal decoration, however, suggests the rarity of such an event.[62] Certainly developments outside the workplace sometimes produced voting solidarity across class lines, regardless of labor conflicts—most plausibly in Catholic or Polish neighborhoods during the Kulturkampf, but also within the Protestant milieu in places where the Centrum offered a credible challenge.[63] Such harmony of sentiment or even interest across the chasm of authority and dependency, however, we can only infer, for with few exceptions our sources for solidarity are silent. On intimidation and coercion, however, they speak loud and clear.

Nowhere did the war between business rationality, whose laws dictated strict indifference to any demands but those of the bottom line, and the deeply embedded beliefs of German employers in the holistic nature of authority rage more continuously than in the breast of Alfred Krupp of Essen. Although Krupp was a caricature of the captain of industry, a Bounderby who detected turtle soup and caviar behind every move of his employees toward self-determination, the very exaggerations of his behavior help us see more clearly a world that encouraged both anger at the bread lord and, even in the hungry seventies, at least some political independence from him.

Reputedly the richest man in Europe, Krupp initially responded to elections as the *homo economicus* that he was. Far from viewing them as an opportunity to commandeer his workers behind a favored party, he mourned the hour or two that voting lost to production. "It costs thousands . . . and is it worth that much?" he wanted to know. In 1877 rumors that some of his turners and fitters had been taking up collections for the Socialists during their breakfast break brought the Landrat of Essen to his door. The government had noted a suspicious correlation between Socialist votes and Krupp residential blocks ("colonies"). The prefect himself appealed to Krupp for help in scotching Social Democracy among his employees. Aware that his firm had recently secured a large loan from the prefect's brother, the then-president of the Prussian State Bank, Krupp certainly had an interest in being obliging. But he hesitated. "If one wanted to chuck the Social Democrats out," the magnate reasoned, "then all the people would have to be sent away."

But Krupp could not rest content with live and let live. It was perhaps inevitable that a man who pinned up "Rules of Deportment" in his guest rooms at the Villa Hügel (and fired off notes to overnight visitors complaining of infractions) would try to control the behavior, and eventually the politics, of his workforce as well. As labor organizers became increasingly visible in Essen,

---

[62] Löwe SBDR 8 May 1880: 1251; Joyce, *Work, Society and Politics. The culture of the factory in later Victorian England* (Sussex, 1980); Seidel: Müller, *Geschichte*, 352f. The occasional ballot with the name of the FK candidate F. Krupp *written in* suggests the existence of some Krupp supporters among Essen Catholics who were unwilling, because of the censure of family and friends, to use official Krupp ballots. We do not know, however, whether they were workers. Reply . . . of the National Party Election Committee, Anlage B AnlDR (1893/94, 9/II, Bd. 2) DS 214: 1136f.

[63] Rohe, "Konfession," 121, 123; idem, *Wahlen*, 84; Jaeger, *Unternehmer*, 93f.

Krupp's definition of what constituted an unreliable worker expanded. Overriding his managers' misgivings, he put his men under continual surveillance. Stenographers and eventually masters were sent to cover Social Democratic rallies, an expense that caused even the Bürgermeister to shake his head. "Without secret police," Krupp insisted to his more skeptical managers, "we will not get shut of the thing."[64] The men owed him, after all, "their daily bread."[65] Such Jehovahian claims, reinforced as they were by efforts at equally Jehovah-like omniscience, were requited with what one commentator has called "an endless guerrilla war" on the factory floor, as Krupp posted political proclamations, workers tore them down, and Krupp responded by hiring watchmen to guard his "encyclicals" round the clock, without regard to cost.[66]

The year 1877 was the depth in Germany of what was once called the Great Depression. The mining industry laid off an average of 10 percent of its workforce—according to one report, 10,000 men at the beginning of the year. But Krupp's operations were expanding so rapidly that 1,648 ovens, 298 boilers, 294 steam engines, 77 steam hammers, 18 rolling mills, and 1,063 machine tools were kept fully employed. Skilled welders and machinists did not grow on trees; some took years to train. Krupp foremen had at one time gone as far as Russia in search of good workmen. While the old man gave orders to fire troublemakers "no matter how short-handed we might be," indeed to dismiss "any worker who even makes a face that suggests opposition . . . even the most skilled, the best worker or master, without regard to his indispensability"—for all his bluster, Krupp never forgot the central reality that every market, including the labor market, was made up of two participants. Although in the spring of 1877 Krupp dismissed well over a hundred politically suspect workers, Catholics as well as Social Democrats, when faced with the necessity of doing without the skills of a particularly able, but tainted, hand, the canon king flinched.[67]

The worker's name was Freßberger. During the 1877 election campaign, in

[64] Paul, *Krupp*, 226, 238 (quotes); see also 150f, 210f, 216, 224f, 235 (stenographers), 260–63. To IM Puttkamer's request for influence with his workers in 1 Koblenz in 1881, Krupp responded more warmly: "Wie Bismarck" 1/5: 10. Socialist activity in Essen in the late 60s: Möllers, *Strömungen*, 132, 152. Krupp's idiosyncracies: Peter Batty, *The House of Krupp* (London, 1966), 98.

[65] Quoted in Paul, *Krupp*, 32f. Krupp workers received the best wages in Rhineland-Westfalia, esp. before the 20th century: Bajohr, *Krupp* (1988), 46, and table: 47; in general, W. Manchester, *Arms*, 69, 171f, 177.

[66] W. Boelcke, ed., *Krupp* (1956), 38 (quotes). "Ein Wort an die Angehörigen meiner gewerblichen Anlagen," 11 Feb. 1877, quoted without date in Möllers, *Strömungen*, 317f, from W. Berdrow, ed., *Briefe* (1928), 2 vols. I was able to obtain only the English translation of Berdrow, *Krupp* (1930), which excerpts the letter on 340–44. Cf. Paul, *Krupp*, 234. "*Neuester Hirtenbrief*" is the characterization of the *Essener Freie Ztg*. Ibid., 235.

[67] Krupp to the Firm, 24 Feb. 1870, Berdrow, ed., *Krupp*, 248; excerpts quoted in Möllers, *Strömungen*, 151. I have chosen to translate the passages given in Möllers myself, rather than follow the translation in *Krupp Letters*. Also Krupp's letters to his Prokura and to Karl v. Wilmowski, in Boelcke, ed., *Krupp*, 50n. 35, 52n. 36. J. J. Kulczyncki, *Worker* (1994), 49; Tenfelde, *Sozialgeschichte*, 479; Lepper, *Strömungen* 2: 520, Manchester, *Arms*, 105; Paul, *Krupp*, 239–42.

an unguarded (and intoxicated) moment, he had shouted, "The king is a swindler!" Arrested for lèse majesté, he was also immediately discharged. After the man had served his sentence, he asked to be taken back, and the firm relented. Since Krupp was not sentimental, Freßberger must indeed have been indispensable. ("Hardworking, talented," was how management put it.) But rehiring Freßberger appeared to wink at the insult to His Majesty—and Krupp lived on government contracts. Even worse, given the firm's well-publicized policy of employing no one who had run afoul of the law, it risked an intolerable loss of face. The extraordinary lengths to which Alfred Krupp would go to protect his political credibility among his workers were demonstrated by the remarkable journey he made to Berlin a month after the elections to explain the Freßberger situation to the monarch. While Krupp waited in his hotel, his chief executive officer Johannes Pieper arranged an interview with the chief councilor (*Vortragender Rat*) in the Kaiser's Civil Cabinet.

Pieper laid the matter on the table. In order to take the man on again, Herr Krupp would have "to 'pardon' this Freßberger." (The chief councilor's inverted commas around "pardon" are an orthographical raised eyebrow. The very idea of an industrialist taking it upon himself to "pardon" a man for insulting William I! Where was the real lèse majesté?) Pieper wanted to let His Majesty know that Krupp was making this exception in the case of Freßberger only "because of his efficiency and otherwise clean record." It was hoped, also, that "the current flap among working-class circles will be pacified somewhat."

Pieper must have given a similar report of the conversation to his employer, for Krupp immediately perceived that his deputy had failed to insist on the central point of the interview. Consequently at noon, the chief councilor reported,

> Krupp himself appeared and said to me that Dr. Pieper had not fully expressed his intention. It was not simply a question of explaining the matter in case the newspapers get hold of the incident, but rather *only if H. M.* [His Majesty] *issued a pronouncement* to the Herr Geheimrat [i.e., Krupp] that the employment of the worker convicted of lèse majesté appeared desirable, did he intend to take this Freßberger on again, as an exception.[68] (Emphasis added)

Krupp was staying in Berlin at the Hotel Royal until early the following morning; "He requests His Majesty's quick decision."

Unwilling to face his workforce as a master who allowed production requirements to override his absolute authority, or to risk the mockery of the Social Democratic press for backing down because of a "flap among working-class circles," the same man who declared that he always ruthlessly went his own way, asking no one what was right, had journeyed 570 kilometers to ask the eighty-year-old William I to cover for him. If Krupp's own political authority could be represented as submitting to a higher one, the principle of hierarchy

---

[68] Vernehmungsprotokoll des Vortragenden Rats im Zivilkabinett, Anders; and Marginaldekret von v. Wilmowski, Berlin, both 11 Apr. 1877, in Boelcke, ed., *Krupp*, 50f.

and subordination would be preserved, and Krupp would be free to make the economically rational decision of rehiring Freßberger. The King obliged. His councilor conveyed the welcome news that the monarch left Freßberger's reemployment "entirely up to H[err] Krupp's discretion." As far as the All Highest was concerned, "he had nothing against it."[69]

Back in Essen, some workers may have gloated at the news of Krupp having to eat his words. For others, the royally authorized pardon for the lucky Freßberger could only intensify their sense that even the hairs of their heads were numbered—and they departed for the United States and Latin America.[70] But just as Krupp's trip to Berlin demonstrates how jealously employers defended their claim to authority over their workforce's politics, the accommodation with Freßberger reminds us that economic relationships are by their nature bilateral. In our next chapter, when we discuss worker's ability to withstand employee pressure, we will come back to this central fact of economic life. Workers need jobs; but employers—even during a downturn—need workers.

INTERNATIONAL PERSPECTIVES

Germany was not unique in having employers who compelled or restrained the votes of their men. In parts of Spain, a historian of the peninsula reminds us, "a man's job depended on his vote." In France, although the election code punished any threat to employment with up to a year in prison and 2,000 francs fine, in certain industrial towns, brigades of factory workers were also marched to the polls where they were penned up until each had voted. French management style has been described as "essentially more autocratic" and less rule-bound than that of their German counterparts; Daimler, for example, gave a dismissed worker a fortnight's notice in 1910, while at Renault he got an hour to clear out. As for Britain, we have it on good authority that, at least at mid-century, "to do justice to the general electoral situation, it is necessary somehow to contemplate at once the existence, indeed the centrality of force, power, coercion, defeat, in an almost military sense, between different groups. . . ." In the United States, the Missouri State Supreme Court in 1892 deplored "the tyranny of giant corporations and concentrated wealth," which, along with the

---

[69] Ibid. The indirect quote from Krupp about his rugged individualism is from Jaeger, *Unternehmer*, 280. *Geheimrat* was obviously an abbreviation for *Geheimer Kommerzienrat*. On the meaning and distribution of that title: Spencer, *Management*, 38. Contrast Paul's view of the Freßberger pardon as a "goodwill-action" in order to polish the firm's image. *Krupp*, 247.

[70] Möllers, *Strömungen*, 330 n. 36; Paul, *Krupp*, 250f. After a covert and unsuccessful try for the RT himself in 1878, Krupp refused further RT candidacies and declared himself uninterested in his workers' politics: loyalty and domestic morality were his sole concerns. Count Pückler to Krupp, 29 Sept. 1884; Krupp to Pückler, 3 Oct. 1884; Berdrow, ed., *Krupp*, 391–93, esp. 393. Only in 1887 did he again directly engage himself—on behalf of his son.

influence of labor unions and political parties, "make it exceedingly difficult for any save a bold and courageous man to vote an open ticket."[71]

Yet the intervention of Germany's employers in national elections seems of a different order of magnitude than any encountered elsewhere.[72] In France, where voting took place on Sunday, the influence of the *patron* was a specific complaint in only two elections after 1871, and disappeared altogether after 1900.[73] In Spain, at least outside Andalusia, not the employer but the political boss (the *cacique*) was the primary source of election influence, and *caciquismo*, it has been argued, was "true patronage," an exchange of services which, though founded on an acceptance of inequality, entailed "trust and a kind of friendship."[74] In England, employer influence was normally the counterpart of "deference," that peculiarly English term whose deft elision of the distinction between the voluntary and the coerced probably corresponds to an experience equally ambiguous. The secret ballot, introduced in 1872, coupled with the franchise extensions of 1885–86, seems to have curbed the political power of superiors over their dependents. Whatever the influence of employers in the Age of Peel, we hear very little of it by the Age of Gladstone and almost none by the Age of Salisbury.[75]

No one claimed that the ballot protected the sanctity of the vote in the United States, although the degree to which American election practice was corrupt is still a matter of debate, and obviously varied locally. In some regions, notably in the mid-West, national elections were "clean." "If more than fifty mid-westerners lost their jobs for supporting Bryan," Richard Jensen points out, "the Democrats certainly did not know of it."[76] Elsewhere, where honesty could not

---

[71] Spain: E. Malefakis, 98, quoted in C. Dardé, "Fraud" (1996), 201–21; 212. Lefèvre-Pontalis, *Élections*, 12, 17; Charnay, *Le Suffrage*, 241n. 1, 243; Fridenson, "Herrschaft," 81, 82, 84f, and esp. 88; French election code: K.J.A. Mittermaier, "Bestrafung" (1849), 361. Vincent, *Pollbooks*, 24. U.S.: Argersinger, "New Perspectives," 673, 676, 682, quote on 681; Seymour/Frary, *World* 1: 249.

[72] Employer comparisons more favorable to Germany, though he does not discuss elections: Fridenson, "Herrschaft."

[73] At least this is what I deduce from the scattered references in Charnay, who mentions only clerical and government influence in the 74 victories nullified in 1877 on nontechnical grounds. Of the 33 elections between 1881 and 1902 invalidated for influence ("*pression*"), the only ones in which employers are mentioned are 1898 and 1889 (2 and 22 cases, respectively), and the latter conflates clerical and employer influence. *Les scrutins*, esp. 84, 89, 92, 95, 97f, 101. In idem *Le Suffrage*, the space given patronal pressure (239–43) is dwarfed by government, (211–38) and clerical influence (254–76). Seymour and Frary, otherwise very critical of French elections, barely mention employer influence. *World* 1: 368–92.

[74] Dardé, "Fraud," 219n. 34.

[75] Stressing the voluntary or ambiguous: F. O'Gorman, "Culture" (1996), 17–32. Emphatic on the element of control: Gash, *Politics*, 175; Vincent, *Pollbooks*, 10–12, 25; and Seymour, *Reform*, 182f, although later (403), he suggests that the promise of future advantage was as important as fear. Nossiter, *Influence*, by emphasizing the "organic nature" of Victorian society, finds both industrialist control (79, 88, 92, 95, 99) and signs of freedom (197–200, 202). The secret ballot of 1872 both is (80, 203) and is not (91, 95, 104) a turning point; it "did not mark the end of the old . . . but only the end of the beginning of the new. . . ." Seymour/Frary offer little evidence for their view that the problem continued after 1872. *World* 1: 159–61.

[76] Jensen, *Winning*, 35–37, 46f, 50f, 57; quote on 50. Jensen admits the existance of complaints,

be presumed, American voters were still sufficiently independent to require fraud and bribery to subvert the free exercise of their franchise. And where they lacked economic independence—as was the case of freedmen in the south— violence, not employer control, was the instrument of choice.[77] Between 1867 and 1901, I counted only five challenges to United States congressional elections that alleged employer intimidation.[78] In contrast, in every German parliamentary election, but especially from 1881 on, the evidence of massive employer intimidation, appearing in petition after petition to the Election Commission, is overwhelming. In no other country—at least among the "civilized lands" to which Germans liked to compare themselves—was the practice of election intimidation by bread lords felt to be so universal, so unvarnished, and so enduring.

What can be the explanation for a cultural difference as great as this? The contrast between the relative unimportance of employer intimidation in America compared to Germany may have been encouraged by the difference in the party systems. Inherited from England, America's two-party system was powerfully reinforced by election rules that awarded victory to anyone with a plurality, however slender. With runoffs obviated, preelection coalitions among groups with different interests were rewarded, and class divisions tended to be subsumed into two broad, internally heterogeneous, camps. "The ballot box," an American historian proclaims, became the "coffin of class consciousness."[79] In Germany, on the other hand, the legal requirement that the victor have an absolute majority made runoffs inevitable. Experience soon taught political groups to hold on to their separate identities, even in districts where they had no hope of winning, in order to deny the absolute majority to the strongest party, since advantages that eluded a minority in the first ballot (*Hauptwahl*) might still be attained through bargaining away their votes at the time of a runoff. The multiparty system that then ensued—not just at the level of parliament, but eventually replicated in election districts throughout the country— reinforced the initial advantages of separation.[80] When so many interests

---

however, and excludes big-city machine elections from analysis. Ibid., 47, 49. Contrast Allen/Allen, "Fraud," 153–94, with Argersinger, "Perspectives." Even Argersinger's pessimistic assessment puts much more emphasis on fraud, bribery, and violence than on employer intimidation.

[77] Rowell, *Digest*, 227, 232f, 241–46, 258, 275f, 283, 382, 386, 429–31, 449f, 518–20, 526–29, 608.

[78] Ibid., 337, 434, 452, 470f, 490.

[79] Alan Dawley, *Class and Community. Industrial Revolution in Lynn* (Cambridge, MA, 1976), quoted in Richard L. McCormick, *The Party Period and Public Policy. American Politics from the Age of Jackson to the Progressive Era* (New York and Oxford, 1986), 101. Qualified on the discouraging effect of first-past-the-post systems on class parties: G. Sartori, "European Political Parties: The Case of Polarized Pluralism," in J. LaPalombara and M. Weiner, *Political Parties and Political Development* (Princeton, 1966), 171.

[80] Maurice Duverger's argument, in *L'influence des systèmes électoraux sur la vie politique* (Paris, 1950), that systems that require a majority rather than a plurality for victory encourage a multiparty rather than a two-party system, has encountered much debate. E.g., William H. Riker,

remained discrete, it was perhaps inevitable that—wherever an organization existed to "class-persuade" them—the voters' class interests would also be perceived and expressed along, rather than across, party lines. The election urn, to alter the American phrase, proved a cradle for class consciousness. And the relative salience of class at the party level cannot have been unimportant in explaining the different behavior of employers in the two countries.

But if we may explain the universality and perdurance of employer pressure in German elections by referring to a multiparty system that reinforced, rather than a two-party system that helped disguise, class differences, we must still wonder whether such systemic considerations really account for its brazen manifestations. Max Weber, for one, felt that the behavior of German employers had roots that went beyond the economic, beyond even, in any concrete sense, the "political." In a debate in 1905 before the prestigious Social Policy Association (*Verein für Sozialpolitik*), Weber squared off against Alexander Tille, spokesman for the Saar's chimney barons, claiming that when viewed from abroad, German employers made the impression of being concerned less with power than, like parvenus, "above all with the appearance of power. . . ." Indeed, Weber averred,

> Something like this just sticks in the blood of our employers, they cannot get away from the itch to control, they want not simply the power alone, the powerful, factual responsibility, and the power that lies in the management of every great firm, no, they must also be able to document outwardly the subordination of others.

The very idiom of the work rules in German factories—"whoever does this and that will be punished"—what was this, Weber wanted to know, but "cop talk"? These same company regulations could have been formulated differently, "but precisely this tone, this cadence, is what makes up, it seems, their actual psychological charm. . . . Scratch one of these gentlemen [i.e., the bosses], and you get the police."[81]

Weber's picture—although drawn from the workplace, not the polling place, and particularly from the struggle over unionization—gets considerable support from what we know of behavior of employers during elections. Could Director Heise in Braunschweig, Foundry Manager Pfeiffer outside Ulm, Herr Petersen in Schleswig, and other bread lords, north and south, who were so insistent on accounting for the vote of every last dependent really have imagined that the single deviant ballot would affect the composition of the Reichstag in a way not to their liking? Surely not. Indeed, "national" employers in Lingen in 1890 continued to monitor their employees' ballots even though the "national" parties themselves had decided to let the hated Windthorst run unopposed.[82] The

---

"Duverger's Law Revisited," in B. Grofman and A. Lijphart, eds., *Laws* (1986), 19–42 (pro); and Nohlen, *Wahlrecht*, 201–9 (con); a refinement: Sartori, "Influence" (1986), 43–68.

[81] Weber, "Diskussionsreden," 395–97. Also stressing Germany's peculiarity and the power of military norms: Wehler, *Gesellschaftsgeschichte* 3: 725–29. Contrast Fridenson, "Herrschaft," 69–74.

[82] H. Ramme [?] Kpln [= Kaplan] to Clauditz, L[ingen], 20 Feb. 1890, SAO Dep. 62b, 2379.

operative assumption seems to have been Use It, or Lose It: hierarchy must be constantly asserted if it were to be maintained.

What lay behind this stance? Weber himself was quick to refer to "our German traditions," as well as to specifically Prussian habits of command and regimentation that underlay a parlous character formation. A stock explanation; but hardly more flattering was Weber's insistence that a root cause of authoritarianism in the shop was the lack of any real political power exercised by the employer, or any German citizen, in the state. Describing what others have mocked as the "bicyclist" personality, Weber argued that "the more government takes place over his head, . . . all the more does he [the German employer]. . . . need to show to those who are under him that now he has something to say and that the others have to knuckle under." Weber's perception of tone and cadence was acute. (The following year the National Liberals felt compelled to expel from their midst Weber's antagonist in this debate, Alexander Tille, for opining during a strike that "all this prattle about human rights belongs in the rubbish room.") But Weber's own cadences were so very passionate—charging that "this petty bourgeois itch to bully" had "depraved" the character of the German nation, and that these German "canaille" (i.e., the employers) excited the "contempt" of the "entire world"—that some of those in the audience of the sedate Social Policy Association (and not only Herr Tille) may well have concluded that the eminent sociologist had once more gone over the edge.[83]

Weber put his finger on the symptoms, but his diagnosis of the disease, though in line with his views about the character-building properties of parliamentary government, is less convincing. However one assesses the growing powers of the Reichstag within the German Empire (and I would put them higher than Weber), the German bourgeoisie to which many, perhaps most, of these employers belonged hardly lacked political power in the areas that most directly affected their lives—the towns and cities, where a steeply plutocratic franchise and voice voting reserved for them a dominant role. In the Ruhr alone sixteen of the region's thirty-eight leading industrialists served on their respective city councils. A high political profile carried with it, of course, the risk of embarrassment. (In 1910 the multimillionaire August Thyssen quit the Mülheim city council after it approved a canal project that favored the interests of Hugo Stinnes—immensely rich, but not so rich as he—over Thyssen's own firm.) We shouldn't be surprised that many employers preferred working behind the scenes to assuming direct political leadership in order to get what they wanted. But get it, they usually did. Moreover, after having amassed a certain fortune, bread lords could expect to be honored by the state with at least the title "Commercial Councilor," sometimes with the coveted prefix, "Privy." Many of the wealthiest, such as Thyssen, Stinnes, Emil Kirdorf, and Friedrich Krupp, had the satisfaction of turning down patents of nobility.[84]

[83] Weber, "Diskussionsreden," 395, 396. Tille quoted in Bellot, *Hundert Jahre*, 220.
[84] Spencer, *Management*, 33, 38, 61. Some, of course, accepted them: e.g., Cornelius Heyl, the "Krupp" of Worms and leader of Hessian National Liberalism, became Baron Heyl zu Herrnsheim

And when state and industry came into conflict, the employer knew how to wield electoral as well as economic power to achieve his ends. Thus in 1881, when royal mining officials refused to go along with the drastic measures he considered necessary in his fight against Social Democracy, the most powerful employer in the Saar, Karl Ferdinand Stumm, took revenge by refusing to run again as Reichstag candidate in his constituency, throwing the entire pro-government camp in his region into disarray. To show the government what happened when he withheld his influence, Stumm allowed the Centrum to win the first round of the election, forcing the Right's candidate into a runoff. It is probably no coincidence that Stumm was elevated to hereditary membership in Prussia's House of Lords the following year—whereupon his Saar district reverted to its normal Free Conservative/National Liberal election pattern. Having won his showdown with the state, Stumm now extended his authority over it. When provincial administrators expressed an independent opinion, he saw to it that they were given disciplinary transfers (*strafversetzt*); a similar fate befell the two chairmen of Saarbrücken's National Liberal election committee in 1898, when they had dared to seek a candidate (from outside the district, naturally) who might preserve some autonomy vis-à-vis Stumm.[85] Although few employers exercised the authority of "King" Stumm, even fewer would have recognized themselves in Weber's portrait of impotence. Not habits of subservience but the habit of command was behind the autocratic behavior of German employers at election time.

Of course, it was not only in the Kaiserreich that employers were used to command. But in England and America, industrial labor was more likely to be conceived of as a commodity, like any other. "You are no *master* of mine, but only a man who buys my labor for a good deal less than its worth," announced an English rule-maker in the 1840s to his employer. German bread lords, who *were* masters at the workplace, experienced a more powerful "disconnect" between the formal equality set forth in the franchise of 1867 and the holistic and hierarchical norms they had inherited and that continued to pervade other aspects of society: the family, the church, the community, as well as the shop floor. To be sure, these norms no longer went unchallenged. In fact, challenges to the employer's unlimited authority over the workplace, far more than claims on his profits, fueled the most bitter labor conflicts of the late nineteenth and early twentieth century.[86]

Nowhere was the discrepancy between the ways of the microcosm and the rules of macrocosm so great as in Germany. In England, a society acutely conscious of degree, we have seen that suffrage laws, still based on property, car-

---

in 1886. White, *Party*, 129. Refuting the "feudalization thesis": Wehler, *Gesellschaftsgeschichte* 3: 720–26.

[85] Kulemann, *Erinnerungen*, 165—who was the candidate, but was later asked to withdraw. "Wahlaussichten für die Rhine Provinz," GStA PK I. HA, Rep. 89/210, Bl.227–32v; Bellot, *Hundert Jahre*, 157–59.

[86] Spencer, *Management*, 63, 82f, 86–88, 93–97; Moore, *Injustice*, 153, 249. Different workplace cultures: Biernacki, *Fabrication*, 166, 170, 189–92; quote on 193.

ried no message of absolute citizen equality until plural voting was ended in 1949. During much of England's long reign of inequality, contests were not fought, as in Germany, between insiders and outsiders, but between two groups of elites, each flanked by its own voting retinues, for the spoils of a system congenial to both. Support for one or the other was not going to undermine the authority of anyone. The hierarchies themselves had withered in practice long before they were countermanded in 1918 by universal suffrage for men (and most women). In France, although franchise democracy had a longer history than in Germany, national political parties in the German and British sense were nonexistent, and national issues surfaced only intermittently in the campaigns. Contemporary complaints about voter indifference and about the continued ability of prefect and subprefect to "make" elections for the ministry by shrewd allocations of economic patronage suggest that manhood suffrage was hardly seen by those who counted as a challenge to traditional authority. In Spain, where the same suffrage was instituted in 1890, the absence of any previous practice in voting even in local contests made for an electorate whose passivity offered little resistance to their masters' understanding of the fitness of things.[87] As for the United States, where revolutionary mythology and electoral pragmatism combined to legitimate political equality, the democratic franchise was even less disconsonant with quotidian norms. And where the discrepancy between egalitarian ideology and an authoritarian, racist reality did cut deep, as in the South, repression of the exercise of that franchise was swift, violent, and enduring.

Thus only in Germany did universal, equal, direct manhood suffrage come to a population whose customs and attitudes were deeply hierarchical, but one whose local experience—in guilds, clubs, voluntary societies, and municipal *Kirchturmpolitik*—already encouraged considerable political energy.[88] This was

[87] The relative absence of challenges to French elections is said to have been a sign of resignation in the face of the Chamber's undisguised partisanship in deciding disputes. Lefèvre-Pontalis, *Élections*, 13f, 19; absence of parties: 28f. But L.-P., who complained of French indifference, thought German voters were indifferent as well: ibid., 12, 27, 116. On the difficulty of politicizing rural France: Weber, *Peasants*, chap. 15; an acute assessment of the way national politics were reflected in the provinces: Michael Burns, *Rural Society and French Politics: Boulangism and the Dreyfus Affair* (Princeton, 1984); and the ways they were not: Jones, *Politics*. Voter apathy, stemming from inexperience, is Dardé's main explanation for the corruption in prewar Spanish elections. "Fraud," 215.

[88] For early political life, the place to begin is with the remarkable "Prussian *Städteordnung*," reprinted in Vogel et al., *Wahlen*, 316–23; Walker, *Towns* esp. 34–72, 108–42, 307–53, 378–404; T. Nipperdey, "Verein als soziale Struktur in Deutschland im späten 18. Jahrhundert und frühen 19. Jahrhundert," in *Geschichtswissenschaft und Vereinswesen im 19. Jahrhundert: Beiträge zur Geschichte historischer Forschung in Deutschland*, H. Boockmann et al. (Göttingen, 1972), 1–44; Langewiesche, *Liberalismus*, 34–38; Klaus Tenfelde, "Die Entfaltung des Vereinswesens während der industriellen Revolution in Deutschland (1850–1873)," in *Vereinswesen und bürgerliche Gesellschaft in Deutschland*, ed. by O. Dann (Munich, 1984), 55–114; 111. Making a strong argument for continuity across the 1918 divide: Rudy Koshar, *Social Life, Local Politics, and Nazism: Marburg, 1880–1935* (Chapel Hill, 1986), esp. 209–44, and R. Chickering, "Mobilization" (1992), 307–28.

an energy sustained by one of the highest literacy rates in the world and by a rapidly developing communications infrastructure that allowed Germans, even in the small communities where most workers lived, to follow intently what *others* were doing and what was being done to them in districts far from home. Both employers and their dependents shared a conception of the Reichstag as a giant "mirror" of the nation. Neither believed that microcosm and macrocosm could remain discordant for long.[89] It was not the dissolution of relationships of authority that encouraged the growth of civic norms in Imperial Germany, but the growth of civic norms themselves—legitimated by the franchise, buttressed by election protests, and sustained, if all too rarely, by the rulings of the Reichstag—that loosed the ties of dependency. By his tight-lipped insistence on political fealty, the bread lord was revealing more powerfully than he knew just how liberating this franchise could be.

At the same time, the demand of the bread lord to serve *in loco parentis* for his workers at elections was an assault on the dignity of men whom the law itself now declared *mündig*: mature, rational, autonomous. Although later liberals and Progressives would scourge the SPD for its harping on class, for inciting workers against employers and thus preventing the creation of "a great democratic party" that would have threatened the Prussian power structure, it was the employers themselves who, by defining loyalty to the firm in political terms and enforcing it with surveillance, intimidation, and exemplary punishments, insured the plausibility of a class interpretation of politics.[90] The conviction that every election, in and of itself, damaged the authority of the employer was of course a self-fulfilling prophecy. By politicizing the workplace, the bread lords not only heightened the consciousness of class difference, they helped construct that class difference along essentially political lines.[91]

CHANGE THE PENAL CODE? THE RINTELN MOTIONS OF 1886

Throughout the eighties, the voices for suffrage reform that we missed in Germany in the sixties now made themselves heard, as popular movements from all points of the political spectrum demanded remedies against the employers' coercion of the voter. Catholic artisans and small tradesmen held mass meetings and sent petitions to the Reichstag. Stoeckerites in the capital and in their Westfalian strongholds of Minden and Siegen remonstrated, usually in private letters or through their leaders.[92] A Berlin house servant, dismissed for refusing to vote for Eugen Richter, took his master to court. The plucky servant cited § 107 of

[89] As a printer in Swinemünde (now Świnoujście) made so bold as to point out in a letter to the Kaiser shortly after the 1890 election. Aug. Roese, 6 Mar. 1890, BAB-L R1501/14693, Bl. 245–56.

[90] [Hans] D[elbrück], "Der sozialdemokratische Parteitag. Politische Korrespondenz," *Preussisches Jahrbuch* 130 (Oct.–Dec. 1907): 192f.

[91] And—on estates in the East—on ethnic lines. Von Koscielski (P) SBDR 15 Jan. 1890: 1027.

[92] Catholics and Stoeckerites: Kühne, *Dreiklassenwahlrecht*, 409ff; Bellot, *Hundert Jahre* (1954), 167. Dissatisfaction with the limited remedies against secrecy violations: Mendel (F) SBDR 3 Mar. 1881: 131.

the penal code, which outlawed hindering another's vote by violence or threat of violence. But Berlin's judges were strict constructionists as to "violence," and the employer was acquitted.[93] "Respect for the vote of another," a citizen complained in a letter to Bismarck, "unfortunately does not belong to the fundamental precepts of our political codex."[94] One artisan, by no means on the Left, went so far as to demand of the Kaiser that he look through the index of Reichstag deputies; then he would see that the economic pressures of employers had produced a thoroughly unrepresentative parliament. "Almost exclusively they are rich people, who cannot by the farthest stretch of the imagination have an idea of what it means for a worker or an artisan to raise a family of five or more, decently and honorably, on an average annual day wage of 1.50 marks."[95]

What was to be done? For all the complaints of their *Fußvolk* from the humbler classes, nothing could be expected from Conservatives or even National Liberals. Initiatives sponsored by Social Democracy, who counted only twenty-four deputies as late as 1884, were doomed from the outset.[96] The *Freisinnige* Heinrich Rickert promised a Berlin Workingman's Association that his party would submit a bill calling for strict punishment for anyone who influenced an election, a proposal that the popular periodical *Grenzboten*, normally considerably to the right of the *Freisinn*, praised as "quite timely."[97] But Rickert spoke in advance of his party, and nothing more was heard of a *Freisinn* initiative. Eventually, ninety (of the ninety-nine) Centrum deputies sponsored a bill in late 1885 aimed at protecting the voter's freedom from threats to his employment. The measure was drafted by Viktor Rinteln, *Geheimer Oberjustizrat* in Berlin and longtime member of the Reichstag's Election Commission. To § 109 of the penal code, which outlawed the buying and selling of votes, the Rinteln motion proposed adding a sentence punishing any employer or functionary of an employer who fired or threatened with penalties someone in his employ because of the exercise or non-exercise of the franchise.

The skepticism that greeted the Centrum's bill was instantaneous. Wouldn't an amendment to § 107, which outlawed the use of force in elections, have been a better place to attack the problem? Weren't the penalties—no less than three-months in prison and the loss of civil rights and honor—exorbitant?[98] The

---

[93] Berlin's LLs had issued a proclamation reminding supporters of their advantages as apartment owners and employers, noting that "once these matters are fully exploited, our victory cannot fail." Köller SBDR 13 Feb. 1886: 1065f; deplored by an embarrassed Munckel on behalf of his party: ibid., 1067.

[94] Unsigned memorandum to Bis., by a Berliner with Christian Social views (but not Stoecker himself, as a comparison of handwriting reveals), 5 Jan. 1884, BAB-L R43/685, Bl. 185v. The author was arguing for a secret ballot in LT elections but his argument applied to the RT as well.

[95] Aug. Roese to Wm. II, 6 Mar. 1890, BAB-L R1501/14693, Bl. 245–56. Other K complaints: Puttkamer-Plauth SBDR 13 Feb. 1886: 1048.

[96] AnlDR (1878, 3/II, Bd. 3) DS 66: 551.

[97] K. M., "Schutz," 157–59.

[98] AnlDR (1885/86, 6/II, Bd. 4) DS 26: 92f. Early misgivings against such an extension of the concept of force. Drenkmann, "Wahlvergehen," 171. As Rinteln was called away by a family emergency, the task of introducing the motion fell to an unprepared Windthorst, whose lame de-

absence of any similar provision against the election pressures exerted by priests was loudly deplored—a not-so-veiled warning to the bill's Catholic sponsors.[99] No deputy denied the existence and extent of the evil. But the cure was worse than the disease. Conservatives, predictably, were most extreme, claiming that the Rinteln Bill "raped" the employer by potentially involving him in a criminal action every time he needed to reduce his workforce. It would "poison" the relationship between a *Herr* and his *Knecht* ("*Knecht*?" a Social Democrat cried out in feigned amazement). National Liberals were no less hostile. Once they had offered to throw out any election tainted by economic pressures. That had been in 1871, when only four challenges even mentioned employers, and Liberals had been anxious to present some bona fides in their pursuit of the politicking priest.[100] By the second election they had changed their tune. When sixty workers in Kiel lost their jobs for defying an order not to leave the work site before six (when the polls closed), Liberals had agreed with the Reichstag majority in judging it a "private" matter—an interpretation of the Election Law that would dominate the Reichstag's judgments until 1912, when the composition of the chamber swerved decisively to the Left.[101] Left Liberals were divided, but even those who supported the Rinteln Bill were ambivalent.

The distinction between "public" and "private" was crucial here. Deputies in every party but the Conservatives and Free Conservatives were usually ready to throw out votes deemed to have been tainted by the influence of royal officials. It was largely by claiming that the clergy fell under the rubric of public employees that Kulturkämpfer had been able in the 1870s to find majorities willing to cancel "clerical" elections. But the relationship between master and man was governed by private contract: employment was in the *Arbeitgeber's* gift. As the deputies became more familiar with Social Democratic propaganda, opinion hardened. Under what principle could the Reichstag deny a man's right to remove from his payroll a person whose party characterized employers as bloodsuckers, parasites, and thieves, and called for their expropriation?[102] The Centrum and the Social Democrats responded: under the principle of free elections.

It was not only freedom of contract, however, but the moral freedom of each

---

fense suggests that the juristic misgivings expressed by the other parties were shared by some in the Z. The bill was referred by the deputies variously as the Rinteln and as the Windthorst motion.

[99] SBDR 13 Feb. 1886: 1048f. "Exorbitant": Puttkamer-Plauth: 1053; Meyer-Jena: 1060; Behr-Behrenhoff: 1056; Munckel: 1068.

[100] E.g., Miquel SBDR 5 Apr. 1871: 190; Wehrenpfennig 17 Apr. 1871: 237. "Poison": Puttkamer-Plauth SBDR 13 Feb. 1886: 1049; "raped": Behr-Behrenhoff: 1053; cf. also Helldorf: 1072; Meyer-Jena: "After all, the employer has as good a claim to the protection of his interests as the employee," 1069.

[101] SBDR 10 Apr. 1874: 696f. Private matter: 2 Kassel AnlDR (1884/85, 6/I, Bd. 6) DS 165: 684; 7 Merseburg, SBDR 10 Feb. 1888: 831; 3 Danzig (Danzig city) AnlDR (1882/83, 5/II, Bd. 5) DS 80: 338–49; 4 Königsberg AnlDR (1894/95, 9/III, Bd. 2) DS 333: 1361–67.

[102] E.g., Reinbaben SBDR 11 Jan. 1889: 384f. Analogous views: Puttkamer-Plauth and Traeger SBDR 13 Feb. 1886: 1049 and 1062; the NL-leaning H. A. Bueck, quoted by Bebel, SBDR 11 Jan. 1889: 393. The NL press, certain Catholic papers in Bavaria: Möllers, *Strömungen*, 333n. 3. Opposing these arguments: Windthorst and v. Vollmar SBDR 13 Feb. 1886: 1047; 1055–58, respectively.

individual voter to take responsibility for himself that was invoked to justify a hands-off policy. Although on some occasions the majority of the Election Commission had been willing to term threats of dismissal "thoroughly reprehensible, morally," even as it declined to invalidate the votes extorted by such threats,[103] others actually shifted the moral onus from the man who extorted to the man who bent under extortion, since any man of character would refuse.[104] The fact that workers had their ballots torn from their hands, new ones thrust into them, and were forcibly marched to the polls did not signify. As the Landrat Paul von Reinbaben argued: "A grown man does not allow a ballot to be simply 'ripped away' from him."[105]

Deputies professed to believe that voting under employer pressures was "precisely what an election with a universal franchise is, and up until now what it has been everywhere in the world, and in other places for the most part is still worse." As a description of contemporary affairs this was, at best, an exaggeration. Whatever their failures in practice, France, Britain, and Belgium, as well as some of the American states, had criminalized such pressures.[106] Of course criminalization by itself, especially in a society with as high a tolerance for lawlessness as in many regions of the United States, is an unreliable indicator of practice. But in Germany, where regard for the letter of the law was strongly internalized among all classes, one might justifiably ask, if the law itself failed to stigmatize a practice, who could claim that it was really illegitimate?

Conservatives argued that "it is the lot of the economically weak, that they must, in the exercise of their political rights, submit to the influence of the economically stronger." In their hearts, many others agreed.[107] The widespread conviction that an individual's freedom depended upon having the gumption to assert it stands in contrast to a judgment made in an analogous situation by the American Congress. Ruling on the intimidation of former slaves in Louisiana, Congress's equivalent to the Reichstag's Election Commission argued that the circumstances of the voters, "their condition of dependence or independence," were always more important than whether or not physical force had been used, noting that "coercive measures do not operate alike upon all voters. That which

---

[103] 1 Pfalz (Ludwigshafen) AnlDR (1881/82, 5/I, Bd. 2) DS 116: 425–27; a similar judgment on 11 Breslau: AnlDR (1881/82, 5/I, Bd 2) DS 104: 353–56; Meyer-Jena on the Rinteln Motion: SBDR 13 Feb. 1886: 1069.

[104] 6 Berlin AnlDR (1880, 4/III, Bd. 4) DS 94: 666–75, esp. 669f; minority report on 5 Arns. (Bochum) AnlDr (1884/85, 6/I, Bd. 7) DS 320: 1770. The WPK sided with the plaintiff, but the RT did not annul. An analogous response to bullying by workers: R. Schraps (Sax. VP, SD) SBDR 17 Apr. 1871: 246.

[105] Reinbaben SBDR 18 Feb. 1888: 827.

[106] Quoted: Löwe SBDR 11 Apr. 1874: 718. France: fine of 100 francs and from 3 months to a year in prison. Traeger SBDR 13 Feb. 1886: 1051; France and England: Windthorst, ibid., 1070; Mississippi and France: Mittermaier, "Bestrafung," 345, 361. More ambiguous: Charnay, *Le Suffrage*, 243.

[107] E.g., Löwe SBDR 11 Apr. 1874: 718. Quoted: Reinbaben on 10 Breslau SBDR 11 Jan. 1889: 384f. In LT elections, all were aware that the "worst violations" as Kühne puts it, were the work not of K LRe but of LL municipal administrations. "Liberalen," 283.

would have no effect whatever upon one class might, nevertheless, exert an irresistible influence upon another class."

> Nor is it . . . either a logical or a just doctrine that the oppressive acts which will void an election must necessarily be of such a character as to overpower the will of voters of reasonable courage and intelligence. Such a principle as this would, in its practical operations, result in the disfranchisement of the weak and the ignorant electors, who should ever be the object of the law's solicitude. . . .[108]

These fine sentiments did not, as we know, translate into protections for former slaves and their descendants until 1965. Nevertheless, if hypocrisy is the tribute that vice pays to virtue, the striking contrast in tone between the solicitude of the Reconstruction Congress for the "weak and ignorant" and the terse judg- ment of the Reichstag's Election Commission that "the state is not in the posi- tion to guarantee social independence for election purposes to a socially depen- dent voter" does suggest how low the autonomy of that voter ranked on the table of virtues for much of Imperial Germany's political class.[109]

Consequently, the debate on the Rinteln bill was, everyone agreed, an "exe- cution."[110] The *Freisinn* supported it only to the extent of providing enough votes to send it to committee for closer examination. Within three months it was a dead letter. Rinteln's second bill, answering some of the initial objec- tions, proved no more successful.[111] The year 1886 proved the first and last time the Reichstag attempted to legislate directly against employer influence. An early dissolution and new elections in 1887 drastically altered the composition of the legislature. The *Freisinn* was returned at less than half its former strength, far short of what would have been necessary, with the Centrum and eleven Social Democrats, to pass the Rinteln bill, even had they been able to overcome their own philosophical objections.[112] As if recognizing the ambiva- lence of their allies, the Centrum did not resurrect the bill even after the parlia- mentary constellation changed three years later. Nor did redress come in 1910, when the official draft of a new imperial penal code was made public. By tightening the wording of relevant paragraphs, the code made election crimes easier to prosecute. But two of these crimes—fraud and physical coercion— were almost never committed, while the third—bribery—occurred in doses too small to have been of political significance. The intimidation of employees, on

---

[108] Rowell, *Digest* (1901), 527.

[109] The WPK refused to distinguish between the voter's dependence on his employer and his "social dependence" on clubs and peer groups (*Standesgenossen*) that also escaped the state's con- trol. 5 Arns. (Bochum) AnlDR (1884/85, 6/I, Bd. 7) DS 320: 1770.

[110] SBDR 13 Feb. 1886: 1047–75. "*Hinrichtung*": an interjection during the speech of Heine (SD): 1069. Cf. also Hegel SBDR 14 Jan. 1890: 996.

[111] Traeger SBDR 20 May 1886: 2088. Antrag Rintelen und Gen., AnlDR (1886/87, 6/IV, Bd. 2): DS 12: 77.

[112] Rinteln SBDR 10 Jan. 1889: 374. Thereafter when deputies protested employer intimidation, (e.g., Hermes SBDR 11 Jan. 1889: 383), opponents referred them to the "stillborn" Rinteln motion: Reinbaben SBDR 11 Jan. 1889: 384.

the other hand, which was the violation of free elections that occurred most frequently and most effectively, remained free of penalty.[113]

What about the Reichstag's authority to invalidate tainted victories? It provided no more direct help against these pressures than the penal code. Employers who were willing to intimidate their workers were also willing to pressure them into signing statements declaring their bread lords innocent of the charges.[114] Even without post-balloting intimidation, the best one could hope for, as a voter pointed out in a letter to the Kaiser, was an invalidation at the tail end of the session, when it was too late to make a difference.[115] During Bismarck's "Kartell Reichstag" of National Liberals and Conservatives (1887–90), the Election Commission abandoned any pretense of nonpartisanship. After weighing violations of secrecy with punctilio worthy of a better cause, taking years to reach a decision, the Commission presented its findings to the plenum without bothering with a written report, ignoring twenty years of precedent in favor of oral summaries read aloud by a member chosen chiefly, or so it seemed, for his inaudibility. The votes were a foregone conclusion.[116] A discussion about removing validation authority from the Reichstag and entrusting it to an impartial court, which had begun among legal scholars in the mid-eighties, picked up steam.[117] But even after the elections of 1890 cut the strength of the Kartell by nearly half, the rulings of the Election Commission remained en-

---

[113] Mayer, "Bekämpfung," 19; Gurwitsch, *Schutz*, 18, both writing in 1910. Bellot, *Hundert Jahre*, 234; 3 Breslau AnlDR (1912/14, 13/I, Bd. 22) DS 1433: 2939.

[114] E.g., Royal *Grubensteiger* H. Haunschild of Waldenburg submitted to investigators a "Declaration to my Miners" with 76 signatures. 10 Breslau AnlDR (1889/90, 7/V, Bd. 3) DS 105: 418–25, 433.

[115] Aug. Roese to Wm. II, Swinemünde, 6 Mar. 1890, BAB-L R1501/14693, Bl. 245–56.

[116] Although surveillance had been proven, the charge of secrecy violation might be dismissed if plaintiffs failed to say that workers were forced to hold their ballots in the air. Puttkamer-Plauth on 6 Breslau, SBDR 6 Mar. 1888: 1314. The WPK failed to see any meaning in the fact that ballots had been numbered: Reinbaben SBDR 10 Feb. 1888: 827. Miners in Hörde: 6 Arns. (Dortmund) AnlDR (1890/91, 8/I, Bd. 3) DS 292: 2050, 2052–54. The courts were somewhat more protective of secrecy: Rickert, citing Traeger, SBDR 15 Jan. 1890: 1014f. Criticism of the WPK: Rickert SBDR 6 Mar. 1888: 1318, 1321, 1325; Wacker, *Rechte*; Prengel, "Beiträge."

[117] Von Mohl had argued for the extension of parliament's powers in "Über die Untersuchung bestrittener ständischer Wahlen durch die Abgeordneten-Kammern selbst" (1847, 1860). He had reconsidered in 1874, only to conclude (with misgivings) in favor of parliament over court ("Erörterungen"). Every subsequent discussion, to my knowledge, took the opposite position. "Gutachten des Herrn Professor Dr. Georg Jellinek in Wien (1885)," *Gutachten in den Verhandlungen des Neunzehnten Deutschen Juristentages* (Berlin, 1988) 2: 121–34; Heinrich Jaques, *Die Wahlprüfung in den Modernen Staaten und ein Wahlprüfungsgerichtshof für Österreich. Eine Staatsrechtliche Abhandlung* (Vienna, 1885); Max v. Seydel, "Parlamentarische oder richterliche Legitimationsprüfung," *Annalen des Deutschen Reiches* (1889): 273–85; Adolf Rosinski, *Das Recht des Reichstags zur Ungiltigkeitserklärung der Wahlen seiner Mitglieder und die Notwendigkeit der Erneuerung der Wählerlisten. Eine Interpretation des §. 34 des Wahlreglements zum deutschen Reichstag* (Berlin, 1897); Leser, "Untersuchungen"; M. de Jonge "Parlament" (1912), 207–10. Public support for scrutiny by the RT: Counterprotest in 6 Arns. AnlDR (1890/91, 8/I, Bd. 3) DS 292: 2060.

meshed in the same scruples about private rights as before.[118] Only when the
employer was the royal government itself—as at the Danzig shipyards—or
when there had been an egregious violation of secrecy were votes thrown out.[119]

The Conservative Party's handbook, put together in the eighties by a veteran
member of the Election Commission for the purpose of instructing party activists on how to avoid invalidations, and reissued thereafter at regular intervals,
reveals the state of play. Edition after edition listed the cases in which the
Reichstag refused to throw out votes that had been extorted by employer pressures: reassuring evidence to bread lords everywhere that they had nothing to
fear from parliament.[120] Only after Social Democracy's landslide victory in 1912
delivered the Commission into the hands of the SPD and the Centrum did its
rulings cease to treat the employer's control of the votes of his employees as a
"private" matter.[121]

---

[118] The courts, too, asked to decide similar cases in local elections, wrung their hands, although
apparently not so much because of the right of contract as because of the difficulty of proving that
the influence made the numerical difference. [Delius], "Beantwortungen von Anfragen. Arbeitgeber,
Wahlbeeinflussung einer Gemeindewahl durch A," *PVB* 28/12 (22 Dec. 1906), 227; Landesgerichtsrat Dr. Mangler, "Die Anfechtung von Reichstagswahlen," *DN* (15 Feb. 1912), BAB-L
R1501/14653, unpaginated.

[119] Shipyards: 3 Danzig AnlDR (1882/83, 5/II, Bd. 5) DS 80: 338–49; SBDR 16 June 1882: 541–
43 and 2 Dec. 1882: 582–602; tenant farmers on crown domains: Meckl.-Strelitz SBDR 8 May
1880: 1255–63; AnlDR (1880, 4/III, Bd. 4) DS 153: 831–37. See also chap. 12.

[120] [Köller], *Ungiltigkeit*, esp. 18f; Freudenthal, *Wahlbestechungen*, 58–59n. 22; and as late as
1914: Hatschek, *Kommentar*, 206f.

[121] E.g., 5 Trier AnlDR (1912/14, 13/I, Bd. 23) DS 1639: 3589, 3592; on 5 Merseburg AnlDR
(1912/13, 13/I, Bd. 19) DS 840: 1136–39, esp. 1137; on 8 Hessen AnlDR (1912/13, 13/I, Bd. 16)
DS 350: 293.

PART THREE

Degrees of Freedom

Disabling Authority

> Who can deny that the secret ballot is the negation of every authority
> and in effect also the negation of the authority of the crown?
>
> —*Wilhelm von Rauchhaupt, Landrat, 1883*

THE SCHOLARSHIP on German elections has not taken the question of voting freedom very seriously. It typically reports an anecdote or two about intimidation, drawn perhaps from a Social Democratic memoir, and then passes immediately to the analysis of voting patterns—that is, to the results of the election. The swift plunge to the bottom line discounts, implicitly at least, the effectiveness of surveillance, threats, and reprisals in affecting either turnouts or outcome.[1] In contrast, during Parts I and II, I have tried to document the taken-for-grantedness of surveillance and, in the last two chapters, of the bread lord's pressure in its full pervasiveness and severity. Although the employers' interest was not equally strong in every district or in every election, we have no evidence that their desire for control diminished over time. On the contrary, as the country became practiced at voting, their stake in their workforces' election choices grew. Yet the efforts of the powerful to enforce political conformity sit uncomfortably with facts known to every student of German elections: that the unloved Centrum commanded, with the help of its Guelf associates, the largest delegation in the Reichstag from 1881 until 1912, when it was finally surpassed by the even more disfavored Social Democrats; that Social Democracy became Germany's largest vote-getter as early as February 1890 (while the Socialist Law was still in effect), and that in the next quarter century it nearly doubled its vote and probably quadrupled its membership. "No other European socialist party," writes William Guttsman, "with the exception of the Austrian Socialists after 1918, came even near to its achievement."[2] How do we bring together the micro-histories of intimidated, even coerced voting individuals with this macro-political success story?

This chapter is the pivot of our story. We will begin with national politics: starting with changes in public opinion, and moving to the tense relationship between Reichstag and government that culminated in the electoral reform of

---

[1] E.g., Suval, *Politics*, 42; W. L. Guttsman, *Party* (1981), 135. Some exceptions: Ritter, "Strategie," 315; Bellot, *Hundert Jahre*; Bajohr, *Krupp*; Fairbairn, "Authority" (but see 818); and most relevantly, Kühne, *Dreiklassenwahlrecht*, part I.

[2] Guttsman, *Party*, 130f.

1903 protecting the secrecy of the ballot: perhaps the most significant contribution of Germany's elected deputies to their country's democratic development. Neither the parties nor the government knew for certain what the consequences of the reform might be. For all of them, it was a decision "to subject their interests to uncertainty." It is precisely the continuing uncertainty a reform like this builds into the system that constitutes, for institutionalists like Dankwart Rustow and Adam Przeworski, the decisive milestone in the transition to democracy.[3]

But the 1903 reform itself presupposed a steady reformist majority in a Reichstag confident of its powers. And this majority, elected by plebeian voters, still needs to be explained. To uncover the explanation, we will move back out into the country, to look first, in the rest of this chapter, at the structural conditions—notably a rapidly expanding economy—that provided necessary, although not sufficient, space for political freedom.[4] From an economy that was modernizing we will then shift, in chapter 9, to cultural traditions—a highly developed legalism and a sense of the "public" that was implicitly controversial—that allowed parties to exploit and extend that space. In the final chapters we will examine the ways communities and then parties fought to control that space, with weapons that evoked both their communal past and foreshadowed electoral politics' organized, monetarized future.

THE SECRET BALLOT AND THE STRUGGLE FOR REICHSTAG POWER

When the Reichstag showed itself unwilling to protect the voter against private power—either by passing the Rinteln Bills in 1886 or by consistently employing its authority to invalidate coerced victories—those deputies concerned with free elections resumed their earlier efforts to strengthen the secrecy of the ballot.[5] Moves to buttress secrecy, however, meant confronting not only the bread lords, but the imperial government. The latter was acutely conscious that whether or not the secret ballot remained "by and large a theoretical idea" would affect its interests far more nearly than the breadth or narrowness of the franchise.[6] As early as the eighties, when faced with motions aimed at introducing secrecy in Landtag elections, the Prussian government had bullied its way out by threatening to rescind the Reichstag's "secret" ballot.[7] In 1888, as we

[3] Quote: Przeworski, "Problems" (1986), 58.

[4] The concept of "social space," used to explain the ability of subaltern groups to articulate their own agendas, is interestingly developed in Moore's *Injustice*, 482, drawing on the work of A. O. Hirschman, *Exit, Voice, Loyalty* (Cambridge, MA, 1981). Moore's inquiry into the origins of a sense of injustice, as defined by rebellious strikes, is analogous to my inquiry into rebellious voting. But his premise is that while most workers can rebel, only some of them "want" to—and so he asks *why*. My premise, supported by election scrutinies, is that while many voters wanted to dissent, only some of them could—and so I ask *how*.

[5] Acknowledging bitter reality: *Thätigkeit*, 158.

[6] Quote from a chairman of the Election Commission, in Hatschek, *Kommentar*, 324.

[7] Cabinet discussions: 4 Dec. 1883, GStA PK I. HA, Rep. 90a, A.VIII.1.d., Nr. 1/Bd. 5, unpagi-

saw in chapter 3, it went so far as to ask Professor Laband about the constitutionality of eliminating the Reichstag's ballot without Reichstag approval. A number of National Liberals encouraged these soundings by letting it be known that it was only the existence of open voting in the Prussian state elections that made the Reichstag franchise tolerable.[8]

Nevertheless, beginning in 1889 *Freisinn* and Centrum deputies redoubled their efforts to enact safeguards to ensure the integrity of the ballot, coupling the perennial cry for envelopes with a new demand for a voting booth. Secrecy's advocates waxed eloquent about the Australian ballot, about the experiences of England, Norway, Belgium, Massachusetts, and Connecticut, reading lines from the American liberal journal *The Nation* into the Reichstag's minutes.[9] Opponents offered every possible objection, a Liberal reminding the deputies that "even sticking a ballot in an envelope is for many people by no means so simple and easy. Take our workers, whose hands are used to quite different things than dealing with paper. . . ." (To which Windthorst interjected: Are our people less cultured than *Belgians*?[10]) Finally, in 1894, with Bismarck in noisy retirement, the Rickert Bill (as it came to be called, after its most prominent sponsor) found its first majority.[11] The Bundesrat, whose approval was necessary for any legislation, killed it with silence. But the Reichstag passed it again. And again. In various forms, the Rickert Bill was submitted nine times in ten years. Each time the bill passed, its majority grew.[12]

Why, after more than two decades of tolerance for un-secret voting, had the demand for ballot guarantees become so popular now? From below, the desire of voters for political independence had been building since the early eighties— as all those petitions and protests that provided the impetus for the Rinteln Bills of 1886 made clear. By 1889 the ballot envelope had even found its way to the

---

nated; Christoph Tiedemann to Herr Graf (illeg.), 31 Dec. 1883, BAB-L R43/685, Bl. 179–82. The Z motion, which received F votes, was submitted in 1881; the LL Stern and Uhlendorff Motions, in 1883 and 1886, respectively. Gagel, *Wahlrechtsfrage*, 107f, 122. Letter to Bismarck, no visible signature, but Christian Social rhetoric, pleading for the Stern motion: 5 Jan. 1884, BAB-L R43/685, Bl. 183–88.

[8] Windthorst, Bamberger, Bötticher (govt.), Bennigsen, Helldorf, SBDR 1 Feb., 3 Feb. 1888: 657, 661, 663, 666; 693f, 696, 698; Meyer-Jena, Windthorst, 9 Feb. 1888: 784, 798.

[9] International examples: Rickert SBDR 15 Jan 1890: 1018f. Dissatisfaction with secrecy provisions in England: Lionel Helber, Speaker's Office, House of Commons, to R. Siegfried, 27 Apr. 1893, BAB-L R101/3344, B. 17. 735–60; Siegfried, "Wahlurne," 735–60, esp. 754, 758, 758n.

[10] Quotes: Stuckmann, Windthorst SBDR 15 Jan. 1890: 1017, 1022. Apparently, however, when booths were introduced some voters did linger inside, looking for a mailbox! Geck (SD) SBDR 21 Apr. 1903: 8923.

[11] In Oct. 1889 H. Rickert and T. Barth resubmitted an earlier motion calling for a stamped envelope, a private room, and explicitly allowed handwritten ballots: AnlDR (1889/90, 7/V, Bd. 3) DS 26: 54; SBDR 15 Jan. 1890: 1011–29. Two almost identical versions of a bill amended by the Z were resubmitted, under Barth's and Rickert's names, in July 1890. AnlDR (1890/91, 8/I, Bde. 1 and 2) DS 139: 810; DS 140 (misprint says 139): 813. A bill drawn up by A. Gröber (Z) in 1892 was substantially the same, and the two are often referred to as the Rickert-Gröber Antrag.

[12] Comprehensive: Hatschek, *Kommentar*, 324–27. A list of all 9 bills: Meyer, *Wahlrecht*, 554n. 5.

top of the platform of the fledgling German-Social Party of Max Liebermann von Sonnenberg, considered the most conservative of the new antisemitic groups: a telling signal that secrecy was an idea whose time had come.[13] Nevertheless, the preponderance of those delegations that supported reform (Centrum, Left Liberals, and SPD) over those generally counted with the government (National Liberals and conservatives) was no greater in the nineties than it had been between 1881 and 1887. What was new were voices from the educated middle class, those academics and professionals who everywhere play an important role as opinion leaders—and nowhere more than in Germany. Under this pressure, even the Liberal delegation eventually came around.[14]

Two developments help explain the new receptivity of this crucial stratum toward a protected ballot. The first was the outbreak of severe labor conflicts, of which the Great Miners' Strike of 1889 and the Hamburg dock workers strike of 1896–97 were only the most conspicuous. Class struggle pervaded the atmosphere of the nineties as much as cultural struggle had in the seventies, but in ways that kindled sympathy across class lines. The second development was the threat of illegality, and perhaps even of violence, in the form of a government coup (*Staatsstreich*) to revoke the Reichstag franchise. The shadow of this threat lay over the whole decade. Now that it was called into question, the imperial election law became *the* political issue of the nineties, transforming the ballot matter into part of a more general constitutional crisis. Let us look at these two developments.

Industrial conflict not only grabbed headlines; it kept the public spotlight on the issue of dependency. As Germany's most powerful bread lords flouted not only the demands of their subordinates, but the efforts of clergymen, academic reformers, and even the Kaiser to reestablish social harmony, they forfeited much of the public's esteem and goodwill. Emil Kirdorf's arrogant comment that "neither Kaiser nor kings have anything to say inside the works. We alone determine that!" was widely reported, and did the bosses' cause no good.[15] Public opinion, someone once pointed out, is published opinion. And published opinion began to shift dramatically in favor of the weak. Emblematic of the change was a showdown in the Saar in 1896 between a group of Protestant pastors who had attempted to organize a modest workingman's association and the most powerful employer in the region, Karl von Stumm.[16] When the

---

[13] Specht/Schwabe, *Reichstagswahlen*, 406; see also Liebermann's support, SBDR 21 Jan. 1903: 7458.

[14] Kühne detects a Left-ward shift even among NLs in Prussian LT, beginning in 1898. "Liberalen," 302.

[15] Quoted in K.-M. Mallmann/H. Steffens, *Lohn* (1989), 76. Loss of sympathy for bosses: Rudiger vom Bruch, "Streiks und Konfliktregelung im Urteil bürgerlicher Sozialreformer 1872–1914," in *Streik. Zur Geschichte des Arbeitskampfes in Deutschland während der Industrialisierung*, edited by K. Tenfelde and H. Volkmann (Munich, 1981), 257, 262.

[16] Saarbrücker evangelische Pfarrkonferenz, ed., *Stumm-Halberg* (1896), esp. 31–33 (a documentation), and H. Kötzschke, *Brief* (1895), 14f. Pastor Kötzschke was the Christian Social editor of the *Evangelisches Wochenblatt*, which Stumm sued, and was sympathetic to the SPD. The pastors'

choleric baron denounced the clerics as a "cancer," attacked their morals in his newspaper, and instituted proceedings against them in the Royal Consistory, thirty-six of them responded with a declaration excoriating Stumm's political control not only over his own workers, but also over the Saar's innkeepers, shopkeepers ("one stroke of the pen can eliminate all their customers"), and printers, who had been threatened if they published the Pastoral Conference's Sunday paper. Stumm's system of spying and intimidation extended, they said, even to members of city councils and, indirectly, to his fellow employers. The ideology of family so often invoked by the bread lords like Stumm to legitimate their right to act *in loco parentis* in determining the election choices of their employees was rebutted in a leading journal of Protestant opinion: "A family numbering thousands is a nonsense; and where is the single personality who can devote fatherly care to thousands?"[17] For Superintendent Adolf Zillessen the Stumm regime was "a system of brute force that completely disregards the inalienable rights of every other personality." If denunciation by the highest official of the Protestant Church in the region were not enough, a newspaper war broke out between the *Saarbrücker Zeitung* and the *Neue Saarbrücker Zeitung*—the latter founded by the baron precisely to drive the former out of business. The leftward-drifting Pastor Friedrich Naumann, whom Stumm tried to prevent from speaking in the district, and Professor Adolf Wagner, a "national economist" and former Conservative Landtag deputy whose criticisms had provoked Stumm to demand satisfaction, added their own talent for publicity to the fray.[18]

High-profile conflicts such as these were made to order for the Rickert Bill's proponents, who could now cite men of the cloth (and *Protestants!*) as well as celebrity intellectuals in support of their picture of the worker's vulnerability. The controversy cast a garish light on a system that Stumm was trumpeting as a model for employers everywhere. What made the Saar tempest so newsworthy on a national level, however, was the fact that the baron, a man known to have the ear of the Kaiser, stood for a small but conspicuous current of conservative opinion that was pushing, loudly as well as behind the scenes, for a "revolution from above"; that is, for a rollback of "the precious treasure of universal suffrage" itself.

This brings us to the second development that, in addition to labor conflicts, lay behind public opinion's shift in favor of the secret ballot: the government's repeated hints that it was willing to resort to a *Staatsstreich* if the Reichstag

---

work was spurred by fear of the attractive power of the local Catholic organizations led by the irrepressible Chaplain Dasbach.

[17] "Freiherr von Stumm und die Geistlichen an der Saar. Ein offenes Wort zum Frieden," *Deutsch-evangelische Blätter* 21 (1896): 624–39; esp. 627, 629, 635. This anonymous article was commissioned by Willibald Beyschlag; worded so as not to offend Stumm adherents, it nevertheless gave uncompromising support to the pastors.

[18] Saarbrücker evangelische Pfarrkonferenz, ed., *Stumm-Halberg*, 49 (quote), 71f. Confirmation of a spy system that extended to the most intimate private relationships and caused even the middle classes to converse in whispers: Kulemann, *Erinnerungen*, 165, 168f, 173.

were not compliant.[19] When the issue of reform became tied to the integrity of parliament, the public rallied to reform, as we shall see.

Those who advocated rolling back manhood suffrage held influential positions in the Kaiser's entourage, and they could count on support from key individuals in the army, the Prussian cabinet, and heavy industry. Through speeches and gossip, cabinet leaks and plants in favored newspapers (the *Hamburger Nachrichten* liked to present itself as the mouthpiece of the chancellor emeritus, reporting regularly from Friedrichsruh his strictures against the secret ballot; the *Kölnische Zeitung* twice leant itself to threatening stories attributed to the Prussian Finance Minister and onetime Liberal, Johannes Miquel) the impression was cultivated that a Reichstag elected on the basis of manhood suffrage, more than two decades after its inauguration, was still only an experiment—one that had now been determined a failure and might at any moment be ended.[20]

Rumors of a *Staatsstreich* were not new. They had been floated whenever the Reichstag set its face against legislation the government considered vital, such as the military budgets of 1887, 1890, 1898, and 1899. In the eighties, the oppositional parties had thrown the loose talk of a *Staatsstreich* back at the government, demanding a clear answer, so that Bismarck was forced to reaffirm his commitment to the constitution. But the rumors that circulated in the nineties were different. Here a coup was not threatened in order to extort legislation. Rather—so it was rumored—the legislation itself was being proposed in order to provoke the Reichstag's rejection and precipitate a coup.[21] It was a scenario that Bismarck had toyed with in early 1890 and the Kaiser had rejected.[22] But

---

[19] H. v. Oppen, *Reform* (1895), 9, with "nothing against" a *Staatsstreich*, is evidence of the background "noise." "Precious treasure" is Kötzschke's phrase, *Brief*, 71. "Revolution from above," quoted in J.C.G. Röhl, *Germany* (1967), 216; also 277; Ziekursch, *Geschichte* 3: 80; Steinbach, *Zähmung* 2: 416.

[20] Amtsgerichtsrat Schmölder, "Das allgemeine gleiche Wahlrecht," *KölnZ* (15 Oct. 1890), Nr. 286, BAB-L R1501/14453, Bl. 90f. The *KölnZ*'s doubts about the franchise had begun with the 1884 election. Müller, *Strömungen*, 205, 381f. Excellent on disaffection with the franchise among NLs: Gagel, *Wahlrechtsfrage*, esp. 132f.

[21] See the vivid account of Bachem, who was there: *Vorgeschichte* 5: 393f, 407, 413, 461–63; 6: 13–15. The older pattern: C. zu Hohenlohe-Schillingsfürst, then Statthalter and fully aware that he would be precipitating a crisis, had advocated muzzling the press, expelling citizens, and suspending elections in AL until the military bill had passed in 1893: that is, in order to achieve a *particular* RT constellation. He went so far as to include a draft of the proposed decree: H.-S. to Wm. II, Straßburg, 13 May 1893, and H.-S. to [? Eurer Excellenz; probably IM], GStA PK I. HA, Rep. 89/211, Bl. 182–87. The 80s: Anderson, *Windthorst*, 303, 341, 389; Bismarck: Kühne, *Dreiklassenwahlrecht*, 408n. 12.

[22] The controversy over Bis.'s intentions: H. D[elbrück], "Die Auflösung des Reichstags" (1907), 186, argued yes. Meinecke, *HZ* 98: 461f, at first disagreed, but in *HZ* 102: 153f, was less certain. Below, *Wahlrecht*, 169. Hatschek considered it "out of the question" that Bis. could have considered reintroducing a property qualification (*Kommentar*, 7), while Kulemann, *Erinnerungen*, 139f, 142–44, defended Delbrück's view, reporting the fear in parliamentary circles, especially NLs. More recently: John C. G. Röhl, "Staatsstreichplan oder Staatsstreichbereitschaft? Bismarcks Politik in der Entlassungskrise." *HZ* 203 (Dec. 1966): 610–24; Stürmer, "Staatsstreichgedanken im Bismarckreich," *HZ* 209 (1969): 566–15; Nipperdey, *Geschichte* 2: 707f, 713–15. The franchise re-

after the Reichstag proved no more docile for the sovereign than for his chief minister, William II seems to have changed his mind.

Three times during the decade the Kaiser put his weight behind legislation whose immediate target was Social Democracy, but whose ultimate end was provocation. The first was the Sedition Bill (*Umsturzvorlage*), aimed at making it possible to prosecute anyone hostile to the existing order. That a category this vague might someday be stretched to include even scholars and thinkers, like the irritating Professor Wagner or the voluble Pastor Naumann, was not lost on the bill's opponents—nor its supporters, of whom Stumm and his colleagues in heavy industry were the loudest. The second measure, dubbed the "Little Socialist Law," would have amended Prussia's Law of Association in such a way as to put freedom of assembly even more in the discretion of the police. The third was the so-called "Penitentiary Bill" (*Zuchthausvorlage*), prescribing hard labor for anyone who, in organizing and enforcing strikes (or lockouts), used violence, threats, or "insults to honor and reputation." A press campaign on behalf of the Penitentiary Bill was subsidized, at the government's confidential behest, to the tune of 12,000 marks, by the Central Association of German Industrialists.

And the result? The Sedition Bill of 1895 was quashed by the Reichstag at the end of its second reading. The "Little Socialist Law" was defeated in 1897 in the Prussian House of Deputies (whose three-class franchise, ensuring the domination of the Right, might have been presumed to guarantee a better outcome). As for the Penitentiary Bill, it never even reached committee. In November 1899 the Reichstag voted down each paragraph. The vote against the clause prescribing three years of hard time was unanimous, the first unanimous vote in Reichstag history.[23] In the event, none of these defeats for the government precipitated a dissolution, much less a *Staatsstreich*. At the end of a decade of sedition from on high, of psychological warfare as well as open challenge, manhood suffrage remained firmly in place. Why?

Most obviously, the adventurism and illegality implied in such plans were abhorrent to all those who conceived of themselves as sensible men. Here is the reaction of the Prussian cabinet, reported by General von Waldersee, a principal figure in the intrigues, when William II opened his mind to them about a possible *Staatsstreich*: "You should have just seen the faces of the gentlemen; I thought they would sink into the earth." No clear-headed, responsible minister, however dissatisfied with the existing state of affairs, could have been pleased at the idea of discarding legal procedures and turning decision-making powers over to a cabal beholden only to "William the Sudden." Energetic opposition was also expressed by the governments of the federated states, whose coopera-

---

former H. v. Gerlach disingenuously denounced as "a cheeky attempt to mislead public opinion" any suggestions that Bis. ever ceased to hate the three-class system. *Geschichte*, 91.

[23] Röhl, *Germany*, 263; A. Hall, *Scandal* (1977), 171–73. Cf. Hartung's playing down of the Penitentiary Bill in his *Geschichte*, 230, with Bachem's description of the crisis atmosphere throughout the 90s: *Vorgeschichte* 5: 387f; 6: 13–15. As a player in "this RT," as its critics called it, his description has the emotional intensity of autobiography.

tion would have been essential for any such venture. Even the Conservative deputies, when sounded out, opposed a departure from constitutional paths.[24]

It was characteristic of the men who toyed with the idea of a *Staatsstreich* that they both did and did not want this talk to be made public; that they both did, and did not, want it to be taken seriously. Without the talk of *Staatsstreich*, the pressure on the Reichstag to pass the government's legislation would evaporate. But once the talk was acknowledged, its sponsors would be called to account; to specify ways and means; to weigh alternative expedients (of which there were none) for various contingencies—all of which was bound to be deeply embarrassing to those men entrusted with the day-to-day running of affairs of state. Thus the report by the Centrum deputy Richard Müller, a factory owner from Fulda, that a plan had already been drafted to change the Reichstag franchise created a sensation—and triggered an immediate *dementi*. But Müller's colleague, Carl Bachem, reiterated the allegations at an election rally in Krefeld: "From my own knowledge I can even extend Herr Müller's communication. . . . The idea . . . of a *Staatsstreich*, that is, of a *violent* liquidation of the Reichstag franchise, persists. This idea has even been seriously considered by influential ministers." Bachem likened the intriguers to Schiller's Wallenstein, imagining, as they deliberated over whether or not to break the law, that

> In thought, 'tis a monstrous crime;
> Consummated, a deed the poets sing.

He reminded them, however, to bethink what happened to Wallenstein. (A bureaucrat clipped this comment from the newspaper where it appeared and appended the note: "Please show to His Majesty.")[25]

Although the Right immediately charged the Centrum with "election maneuvering," the brouhaha over the rumors forced the ministry, spurred by repeated demands from the All-Highest, to issue a *second* denial of any *Staatsstreich* plans. Anyone could see that the government protested too much—as a furious Count Arthur Posadowsky-Wehner, the Chief of the Imperial Office of Domestic Affairs, recognized. It all made a disastrous impression.[26]

Posadowsky surely recognized the rumors as another example of the Kaiser's penchant for "trying on" personae: now the mantle of Caesar, now the cloak of Wallenstein. Of a piece with the combination of bravado and fecklessness so

[24] Advocates of a *Staatsstreich* apparently included the King of Württemberg, Miquel at various times, Gen. v. Waldersee, Pruss. Minister President Botho v. Eulenberg, IM v. Köller. Opposed: Chancellor Hohenlohe (according to his extremely controversial diary, and contrary to his stance when Statthalter in AL), most of the BR, and apparently the Prussian cabinet. Ziekursch, *Geschichte* 3: 68, 73f, 81–83 (Waldersee quote); Röhl, *Germany*, 220f.

[25] Clipping: *Germania* 26 May 1989, BAB-L R1501/14454, Bl. 150. Fairbairn has a good discussion of the Müller uproar: *Democracy*, 203.

[26] Posadowsky's fury is evident not only in his words, but in the hurried scribble, quite unlike his usual hand, with which he recorded the affair: Posadowsky Memo, 28 May 1898, BAB-L R1501/14454, Bl. 148. Dementi: *Deutscher Reichs-Anzeiger und Königlich Preußischer Staats-Anzeiger*, 11 May Abend 1898, Nr. 111: ibid., Bl. 151.

characteristic of William II's on-again, off-again relationship to affairs of state, the talk of *Staatsstreich* did not constitute any considered agenda, much less any "plan." The circumstance in which a violent breech of the constitution would ever have been attempted is difficult to imagine. The attempt would surely have failed, as insiders like the sober-sided Posadowsky knew. Yet for ten years, members of parliament felt themselves, and the institutions to which they had devoted their lives, under constant threat.

And this brings us back to our story. For it was this atmosphere of pressing yet vague menace that is the second explanation for the growing salience of Rickert's bill to safeguard the secret ballot. The discussion of democracy that in England was inaugurated with the First Reform Bill and that was so conspicuously missing when Bismarck introduced universal suffrage now began in earnest—and never stopped. Social Democrats and Centrum made the defense of the Reichstag franchise the cardinal issue of their 1898 election campaign, vying with each other to see who could be its staunchest champions, turning the government's intimidating rumors into a weapon against it. And they were not alone. So central had the issue become that the editor of the *Dresdner Neueste Nachrichten*, a moderate conservative, wrote to Chancellor Chlodwig Hohenlohe personally, begging him to make an unambiguous declaration in support of the Reichstag franchise—or the government would lose the elections![27]

Massive labor conflict, political tutelage in the factory, threats to the Reichstag franchise: the three were linked in the legislative battles of the nineties. Baron Hans von Hammerstein-Loxten, who headed Prussia's Ministry of Interior from 1901 to 1905, hit the core of the controversy over the Rickert Bill when he noted to his colleagues that although technically the measure only fleshed out a provision in the existing constitution, for its opponents, even when they objected to no specific item, it was a synecdoche for the very electoral system they wished to see replaced—and, once passed, would become an obstacle to their doing so. For its supporters, the bill had the same symbolic and practical significance. Although drawn up to remedy a particular evil, the Rickert Bill became the Reichstag's counterthrust to the Sedition Bill, the Little Socialist Law, the Penitentiary Bill—and to the threat of a *Staatsstreich*. And each time the deputies passed it—in Commission in 1892, then on the Reichstag floor in 1894, 1896, and 1899, and with ever growing majorities, they underlined, for both supporters and opponents, this meaning.[28] By 1899 this technical bill requiring ballot envelopes and voting booths represented the guarantor not just of the democratic franchise, but of the constitutional claims of the Reichstag itself.

---

[27] Otto Fr. Koch to H., 12 June 1898, BAB-L R1501/14694, Bl. 191–92. On the Z: Fairbairn, *Democracy*, 203–5; Kühne, *Dreiklassenwahlrecht*, 455–58.

[28] IM v. Hammerstein-Loxten to Bülow, 18 Jul. 1902, BAB-L R1501/14455, Bl. 59–63. The article on "elections" (*Wahl*) in the popular *Meyers Konversationslexikon* (1898/99) contained a vigorous criticism of the government for failing to confirm the measure. The anonymous author was the Königsberg election expert, Dr. Richard Siegfried. BAB-L R101/3344, Bl. 258f.

At the end of the decade, the Jena jurist Georg Meyer, then completing his 700-page survey of the suffrage laws of twenty-one German states and eighteen sovereign countries, offered his readers a view of what just such "sensible" men as I have described as making a *Staatsstreich* impossible thought of the constitutional situation. A National Liberal, on the conservative wing of his party and no friend of the Rickert Bill, whose implementation he expected to produce more rather than fewer election challenges, Professor Meyer acknowledged that the idea of the secret ballot had become so popular that "no political party that doesn't want to dig its own grave can make its abrogation part of its program. The liquidation of the secret ballot by legal methods is no more possible," he added, significantly, "than the termination of universal suffrage." If *illegal* methods were chosen, however, they would leave in their wake resentment so deep that any advantage would probably be too dearly bought. Writing not only in his capacity as a constitutional lawyer, but (surely) out of his experience as a Liberal deputy, Meyer concluded: "There's nothing for it, therefore, but to make one's peace with the existing situation. Even politicians must under certain circumstances be in the position to practice resignation."[29]

The Jena jurist's pragmatism was widely shared. Similar signs of a shift in elite opinion had already appeared in 1896, when the *upper* as well as the lower house of the Baden Landtag passed a bill analogous to Rickert's—unanimously. Three years later Württemberg's state parliament followed suit.[30] Nevertheless the Bundesrat, under pressure from Prussia, departed that same year from its practice of ignoring the Rickert Bill, and explicitly rejected it.[31] Lest anyone suppose that the octogenarian Chlodwig zu Hohenlohe's replacement by Bernhard von Bülow in late 1900 signaled a change, Bülow announced in January 1902 that he would refuse even to consider the measure.

THE ELECTION CODE REFORMS OF 1903

And yet, precisely one year later, Bülow confounded friend and foe alike by reversing the policy of decades, promising the Reichstag to implement the protections for secrecy it had demanded for so long.[32] Indeed, the bureaucracy immediately began calculating the sums required to supply envelopes in time for the elections scheduled just five months away—140,000 marks would be neces-

[29] Meyer, *Wahlrecht* (1901), 563.

[30] BAB-L R1501/14456, Bl. 125. The experience of these two states were important arguments within the government for experimenting with envelopes and isolation areas. Minutes of SM, 17 Jan. 1903, BAB-L R1501/14455, Bl. 211. Even turbulent Saxony, in imitating Prussia's three-class voting system in 1896, left its own secret ballot intact.

[31] Prussian responsibility: Posadowsky in SM, 17 Jan. 1903, BAB-L R1501/14455, Bl. 212.

[32] Bülow SBDR 20 Jan. 1903: 7431. Amazement: "Ein freisinniger Erfolg," *SaaleZ*, 21 Jan. 1903, BAB-L R1501/14455, Bl. 157; "Sicherung des Wahlgeheimisses," *FrZ*, 29 Jan. 1903. Also "Zum Reichstagswahlrecht," 16 Jan. 1903, and "Der Schutz des Wahlgeheimnisses," 21 Jan. 1903. BAB-L R1501/14455, Bl. 160, 162.

sary for Prussia alone. Bülow ordered double the requisite number, to be prepared for runoffs and emergencies.[33] How do we explain so complete a reversal?

The Rickert Bill had acquired a champion at the highest level of the government: Vice-Chancellor Count Arthur Posadowsky-Wehner, Chief of the Imperial Office of Domestic Affairs. This career bureaucrat was a man whose previous work at the Imperial Treasury had already (in the very disapproving view of his 1935 biographer) provided "evidence that in imperial governmental circles the power of the Reichstag was now seen as a given and inviolable"—largely "because this Reichstag was the product of . . . the constitutionally grounded universal suffrage."[34] To his colleagues in the Prussian cabinet Posadowsky insisted that "ethical as well as political reasons argue for obliging the Reichstag now." The Conservative Party's arguments against the Rickert Bill were not based on "objective grounds," but only on their unwillingness "to relinquish the possibility of influencing voters." This position was impossible, Posadowsky declared, for the government to defend in public: a remarkable, but apparently conclusive, argument. Bülow agreed that "a realistic policy requires satisfying, on the matter at hand, the repeated demand of the great majority of the Reichstag, to which, in addition to all the liberal parties, the Centrum also belongs."[35]

Indeed, the public itself attributed Bülow's change of heart to pressure from the Centrum, which the chancellor was then wooing.[36] The rumor made sense. The bill had been tirelessly pushed by Adolf Gröber, a democratic Swabian whose legal expertise was as formidable as his ascetic piety. It was Gröber who had steered the secrecy bill through committee in 1892, Gröber who had sponsored the analogous bill enacted in Württemberg in 1899—and Gröber who, with three others, ran the Centrum's delegation in the Reichstag. Posadowsky

[33] Studt for IM and Fin. Min. to King, 1 July 1903: GSt A PK 89/212, Bl. 140f; Memo of Chancellor, signed by Posadowski, 27 Mar. 1903, BAB-L R1501/14644, Bl. 42.

[34] M. Schmidt, *Posadowsky* (1935), 29, 30; also 34.

[35] Minutes of Session of the SM, 17 Jan. 1903, BAB-L R1501/14455, Bl. 210–11. A comprehensive history of the Rickert motion: Posadowsky to SM, 25 Nov. 1902 (Geheim), ibid., Bl. 107, 127–31. Six months earlier Bülow had solicited opinions from his colleagues. They recommended that if his desire was to accommodate the RT, it was better to meet the bill's proponents through a "Proclamation" (*Bekanntmachung*) than through a change in the election law, which would open the door to further amendments. Bülow to MdI, [n.d. 13] June 1902; IM Hammerstein-Loxten to Posadowsky, 18 Jul. 1902, BAB-L R1501/14475; IM Hammerstein to B., 18 Jul. 1902; Gutbrod to SSdI (Geheim), 20 Aug. 1902. BAB-L R1501/14455, Bl. 23–25; 59–63, 80. B. then inquired about the experience of states that had enacted similar measures (ibid., Bl. 81, 87, 89) and concluded that accommodating the RT would be "practicable and expedient." B. to MdI, 9 Oct. 1902, ibid., Bl. 97. In the end a Proclamation instituted official envelopes, a private space for voting, and forbade ballot distribution during polling.

[36] "Der 'bereitgestellte Nebenraum,'" *SchlZ* (K), 1 Feb. 1903, citing "Sicherung des Wahl-Geheimnisses," in Richter's *FrZ*, 29 Jan. 1903, BAB-L R1501/14455, Bl. 183. Elsewhere, however, the LLs claimed the credit: "Ein freisinniger Erfolg," *SaaleZ*, 21 Jan. 1903, BAB-L R1501/14455, Bl. 157. Saul, "Kampf," 197n. 142, attributes the change to Bülow's desire to placate liberals after his tariff.

had long argued for a close working relationship between the government and this party that, with its Polish and Hanoverian allies, disposed of more than 120 Reichstag seats, dwarfing its two nearest rivals—the Conservatives and the SPD, who tied for runner-up.

Uncertainty, which plays such a pivotal role in the models of today's "institutionalists," was here the name of the game. Many believed that the Centrum would be the principal beneficiaries of the Rickert Bill—in the Saar, on the Lower Rhine, and in the Grafschaft Mark. But Left Liberals, too, some thought, would gain, at last having a chance to break into those runoff contests in the east that had hitherto been limited to Conservatives and Social Democrats. The SPD, though gaining vis-à-vis employers, might lose its commercial constituents, those voters who had supported the party because of pressure from their customers—a consideration that Centrum spokesmen had played up in their conversations with Bülow.[37] Even some conservative voices admitted a potential advantage in the government's eventual proposal: it established sufficient privacy to cut the voter off from observation by party monitors—which would disadvantage, they thought, the SPD—but left his activity visible to the panel, men sympathetic (the unspoken argument ran) to the forces of order.[38] But all calculations were gambles. Within the cabinet, two ministers, one in favor of the reform, the other against it, agreed that it was "a leap in the dark."[39]

Most Conservatives, however, responded to Bülow's announcement with fury—and threats. Precisely those voters who trusted in the wisdom of their government, they claimed, would no longer be willing to suffer the inconvenience of voting: a remarkable admission. They tried to get the measure watered down, demanding that the use of the voting alcove be voluntary: "No one [should] be forced to visit it." This was a demand Britain's House of Lords had made, with no more success, against the Ballot Act in 1872. Most of all, Conservatives attacked Bülow for deserting Bismarckian paths: for ceasing to view the franchise as a means to an end, as an instrument aimed at the "pragmatic management of affairs of state," and for treating it instead as a question of principle (*Grundsatzfrage*). Privately Conservatives were saying that the reform would cost them thirty seats.[40]

In June 1903 the first general election under the new rules took place. When the votes were counted, the Right claimed that their predictions had proved

[37] W. Schwarze (Z) SBDR 18 Feb. 1903: 7993; earlier: Windthorst SBDR 15 Jan. 1890: 1022. P. Spahn had predicted to Bülow that the SD would win only 10 additional seats (in reality, they immediately got 25). Lerman, *Chancellor*, 83. Calculations: "Sicherung des Wahl-Geheimnisses," *FrZ*, 29 Jan. 1903, BAB-L R1501/14455, B1. 183.

[38] "Zur Sicherung des Wahlgeheimnisses," *Die Post*, 24 Mar. 1903, BAB-L R1501/14456, Bl. 101f.

[39] Hammerstein-Loxten and G. Frh. v. Rheinbaben. Minutes of the SM, 17 Jan. 1903, BAB-L R1501/14455, Bl. 211.

[40] "Der 'bereitgestellte Nebenraum,'" *SchlZ* (1 Feb. 1903), BAB-L R1501/14456, Bl. 195f; "Zur Sicherung des Wahl-Geheimnisses," *FrZ*, 13 Mar. 1903, ibid., Bl. 39. House of Lords: Fredman, *Ballot*, 15.

Fig. 8
The 1898 and 1903 Elections Compared

	1898	*1903*	*Change*
K	56	54	
FK	23	21	
Total Conservatives	79	75	−4
NL	46	51	+5
Total "National"	125	126	+1
LL	49	36	−13
Z	102	100	−2
Total Rickert Bill Sponsors	151	136	−15
SPD	56	81	+25

Source: Compiled from Ritter/Niehuss, *Arbeitsbuch*, 41.

true; the results spoke for themselves.[41] In fact, however, the Conservative delegation lost only two members. Between them, the two conservative parties fell from seventy-nine to seventy-five seats, not nearly so dramatic a loss as in the previous election. Since the National Liberals gained, the total size of the "national" delegation in parliament had actually grown by one. It was the Rickert Bill's sponsors who lost ground: the Centrum, by two seats, and the combined Left Liberals by thirteen—the latter a devastating blow to a grouping that was in any case small. Nevertheless, the election had produced its sensation. For the Social Democrats gained twenty-five new mandates, pushing them at last ahead of the two conservative parties combined and, in terms of votes, ahead of the entire national grouping! It was not the biggest relative jump in the history of the party; their breakthrough election had been in February 1890. But it was one more sign of continuous, unbroken growth, and in absolute terms, their biggest success so far. They had gained nearly a million additional voters and were now noisily trumpeting themselves as a "Party of Three Million." They looked unstoppable.

Angry letters rained down on Bülow, as conservative-minded citizens expressed their sense of betrayal at his hands. "The energies of even the most upright and selfless men have been crippled," one man complained, thanks to these ballot envelopes and alcoves. "The courage to continue the fight for Kaiser and Reich has been completely broken."[42] The most thoughtful postmortem came from the chairman of the National Liberal Central Committee for Annaberg-Schwarzenberg, an alderman who had been involved in the election cam-

[41] Schmieding (NL) in PAH, quoted in "Nationalliberale Wahlrechtsfeinde," *Die Hilfe* 11/21 (28 May 1905): 1.

[42] E.g., Adalbert Dahm, leader of Spandau's "Neuer Wahlverein" (K) to Bülow, 18 June 1903, BAB-L R1501/14695, Bl. 207–9; unsigned postcard from Groß-Lichterfelde to B., n.d. [received 26 June 1903] from a voter of the FrVp, demanding immediate institution of open voting, ibid., Bl. 211; Maxdon [apparently from Silesia] to B., n.d. [filed 8 July 1903], urging him to grant stipends for deputies in exchange for the RT's acceding to oral voting. BAB-L R1501/14696, Bl. 22f.

paign for months, and one whose Saxon district, which until now had enjoyed an unbroken record of "national" representation, had fallen to Social Democracy. He did not deny that the first cause of this catastrophe was the "unfortunate situation in Saxony," but he also noted "the monstrous vacuum in enthusiasm for *imperial* policy and discontent with so many deeds of the new course." (Where is the servility for which the Wilhelmine subject, at least since the publication of Heinrich Mann's novel of that name, is notorious? Not in the letters following the 1903 election!) He did not spare the chancellor. The controversial agricultural tariff should have been introduced a year earlier, so as not to play into the hands of Social Democrats with their slogans of "Bread Usury." He accused Bülow of "kow-towing" to the SPD, and excoriated especially (here spoke the heartland of the Reformation) his decision not to oppose the return of the Jesuits to Germany—a concession that "excited the German folk soul to its deepest core." Last but not least, there was the "so-called 'closet law' [the voting space] which has had such a fatal effect." All of these blunders made it "understandable that the German *Bürgertum* betook itself only very reluctantly to the field of battle." And what did the government do to overcome these handicaps? "No word of encouragement to spur them on sounded from those men whom the nation considers its leaders. Therefore, since the leaders let them down, the foot soldiers had to grasp the initiative. . . . It was a sorry sight to see the German *Bürgertum* left to its own devices in the election campaign." And then came the most radical criticism of all: "I would have liked to have seen your Excellency during the campaign, if for only a couple of hours a day, step down among the people and take their mood. . . ."[43] Such recommendations—that members of the government openly participate in the election by campaigning in public—would become more numerous as time went on.[44]

Of course "campaigning" was precisely what, within existing constitutional arrangements, a German chancellor was not supposed to do. Since the monarch was "above parties," his servants must also be above election campaigns. However moth-eaten this "indispensable fiction" (*Lebenslüge*) of the monarchical state, the government's banishment from electoral politics was, for all but the far Right, the very ark of the covenant.[45] No other kind of influence was so sure to result in a cashiered election as interventions by organs of state.[46]

[43] Gustav Slesina, Stadtrat in Buchholz, Saxony, to Bülow, 27 June 1903, BAB-L R1501/14696, Bl. 14f. Evidence that secrecy provisions *had* made a difference: Bellot, *Hundert Jahre*, 224f.

[44] E.g., Ernst Krieger (pseudonym?), Lt. a.D., to Bülow, Bad-Kreuznach, 5 Jan. 1907, BAB-L R1501/14697, Bl. 105f; Mangler, "Die Anfechtung von Reichstags Wahlen," *DN* (25 Feb. 1912), BAB-L R1501/14653, unpaginated.

[45] Gustav Radbruch, "Die politischen Parteien im System des deutschen Verfassungsrechtes" (1930), 289, quoted in Kühne, *Dreiklassenwahlrecht*, 27. "Representative monarchy": Zoepfl, *Grundsätze* 2: 250, 252, 276f. Because of the conceptual distinction between "governing" and "administering," however, and because the administration was believed to be "responsible" to the people as well as to the crown, there was no similar "incompatibility" between service as a judge or LR and running for parliament—almost always as the choice of a particular party or coalition of parties. However imperceptible these distinctions seem for an American, the RT's acceptance of such eligibility—the Right, because it saw in the LRe, the Liberal Left, because it saw in the judges, its natural personnel—coupled with its vehement warnings that "governmental" or "minis-

Nevertheless, in the *Lex Rickert* (as it was now called) and in the criticisms of their government by angry loyalists, we can discern a major impulse not only behind Bülow's change of "partners" in 1907, when he ran against the Centrum as well as the perennial Socialist enemy, but also behind changes in both practice and theory. Unlike Bismarck's Septennat "plebiscite" victory two decades earlier, which for all the efforts of the *apparat*, from Protestant schoolteacher to night watchman, had probably been owed mainly to the extraordinary pressures of bread lords in the private sector, the plebiscite in 1907 brought the top reaches of the government directly into the campaign. Bülow had taken his nationalist critics' point: never again would the German *Bürgertum* be "left to its own devices." While the chancellor himself did not, even then, "step down among the people," as the Saxon alderman had desired, high-level surrogates—the colonial secretary, Bernhard Dernberg, and his under-secretary, Friedrich von Lindequest—did go directly to the public. Meeting with groups in Berlin, Munich, Stuttgart, Frankfurt, Dresden, Hamburg, and Cologne, they promised a panoply of public works, concessions for investors, and attractive taxation policies—"to the stupefaction of the bureaucrats."[47] At the same time, although the government-as-breadlord was active in this election (as thousands of postal workers learned), the role of the private bread lord in getting out the nationalist vote now proved less important than the work of organizations to which many contributed: the big lobbies, who subsidized the government's campaign; the patriotic societies; and especially, at the grassroots level, the veterans' clubs (*Kriegervereine*), who got out the vote. Among such groups, threats by employers began to be superseded by emotional—that is, *political*—appeals, encouraged and coordinated by the government.[48]

The demand that the chancellor "step down among the people" and actively campaign was a pregnant sign of the erosion of those dualistic assumptions that

---

terial candidacies" had brought down Napoleon III's Empire suggest that—for all the theoretical and practical inconsistencies of the doctrine—many Germans perceived a difference.

[46] Criteria, however, were never consistent: Poschinger's Report, 11 Feb. 1879, BAB-L R1501/14450, Bl. 154–88, concludes in despair of finding any clear principles about what was permissible and impermissible for officials. Contrast the demand that the MdI issue no electoral instructions, nor subsidize the press, nor use the postal service to favor a candidate ("Der Minister des Innern," *Berliner Review* 26/13 [1861]: 431–34) with the jurist's judgment that any government that did not want to abdicate should not have to leave the field to its opponents, so long as it remained within the law: Zoepfl, *Grundsätze* 2: 282–83n. 1, a view cited approvingly by Leser, "Untersuchungen," 76n. 1, and Mangler (member of the Saxon second chamber), "Die Anfechtung von Reichstagswahlen," DN (25 Feb. 1912), BAB-L R1501/14653, unpaginated. Valuable: Pollmann, *Parlamentarismus*, 93–100; Steinbach, *Zähmung* 1: 31; Fischer, "Konservativismus," 119, 126.

[47] Writes G. D. Crothers, thus testifying to the unprecedented character of open promises of patronage. *Elections*, esp. 106f, 164f; D. Fricke, "Imperialismus" (1961), 538–76; Becker, "Kulturkampf," 59–84.

[48] Disappointment with *Beamten*, including postmen, in Horn Report, LHAK 403/8806: 1, 7v. Cf. "Working" (1907) in *Blackwood's Edinburgh Magazine*, 279, which stated that "the ballot is absolutely secret, and no attempt is made to spy upon what they [civil servants] do." Yet postal workers' oppression continued to be a thorn in the side of the SPD and LLs. SBDR 29 Apr. 1907: 1211, and SBDR 28 Mar. 1912: 1086–1101.

had for so long shielded the sovereign from assuming any "responsibility towards a party" (*keine Verbindlichkeit gegen eine Partei*).[49] But if the Right's criticisms of Bülow's conduct in 1903 had spurred this turn of events, the introduction of greater protections for the secret ballot set the stage for its legitimation—by opening the door to a rethinking of election misconduct. As we have seen, demands for pure elections had always run up against a central difficulty: the Reichstag had proved no more able to draw a line between legitimate campaigning and illegitimate influence than a draftsman could draw a line in the sea. Only in the case of *government* activity had the majority proceeded with undivided conscience, stringently invalidating any votes the government might have tried to "influence," confident in the knowledge that, unlike the priest and the employer, whose political rights as citizens must be respected, *the government had no rights in an election campaign at all*. Such was the ineluctable consequence of the ideology of dualism—of a government "above parties."[50] But once the majority of the Reichstag had decided that the way to protect the voter from parson and bread lord was neither by criminalizing those who attempted to influence votes nor by cashiering elections in which such influence took place, but by prescribing procedures protecting the election process itself, it unintentionally shifted the ground on which government interventions had incurred the strictest political penalties. Although the Reichstag would always remain sensitive to charges of government influence (as we shall see in chapter 12), its Election Commission registered the new situation created by the Lex Rickert by announcing that it would cease to automatically invalidate votes merely because some civil servant had involved himself in a campaign—an announcement that encouraged them to involve themselves even more.[51]

The claim to the *right* to influence the voter, after all, had always had two bases: a traditional one, derived from preexisting dependencies within a deferential social order, and a modern one, derived from the right to free speech. As greater safeguards were put in place to protect the voter from the harmful effects of the first, greater leeway could be allowed for the exercise of the latter. Thus the lowly envelope and private space prepared the way for a philosophical shift of great magnitude, one with ramifications not only for the individual voter, the political parties, and the freedom of the election, but for the very foundations of the German state. The reforms of 1903, by obviating the fiction of a government above parties, took a giant step toward legitimizing the breakdown of that constitutional dualism that had isolated the executive from the

---

[49] Zoepfl, *Grundsätze* 2: 252; Bötticher SBDR 2 Dec. 1882: 595.

[50] And an administration conceived as representing *all* the people: "Das Beamtentum der alten Monarchie bildete eine Volks-Repräsentation." Von Roon, "Votum," 27 May 1866, BAB-L R43/685, Bl. 23v-24.

[51] 10 AL AnlDR (1905/06, 11/II, Bd. VI) DS 483: 4741 and U. v. Oertzen (FK) SBDR 16 Nov. 1906: 3698, 3718 (objections: Müller [Meiningen] and Müller [Sagen], ibid., 3696, 3710f, 3720). Similarly: 1 Düsseldorf and 1 Kassel: AnlDR (1907/9, 12/I, Bd. 20) DS 685: 4442f, and DS 705: 4487f. The RT's reverse in 1912, invalidating more than 2,000 votes because 11 officials signed a petition supporting a K candidate, reflected the new power of the SPD: 2 Magdeburg AnlDR (1912/14, 13/I, Bd. 22): DS 1497: 3030–39.

consequences of elections and that kept the Reichstag sealed as a conduit to executive power.[52]

And yet, here as elsewhere, we see that history does not have true joints. The fateful watershed that the Right had seen clearly in 1903, the bend in the road that I believe can be discerned, from the distance of nearly a century, in constitutional assumptions, were both invisible to the Left which, looking in different places, saw quite different things. They continued to see massive violations of the secret ballot.[53] The remaining elections continued to produce the familiar stories: of the big man who "made himself important after the election by saying 'that he knew how every individual voter had voted' ";[54] of bread lords distributing ballots and chairmen marking them; of voters marching to polls and watching each other vote—far fewer in number, certainly, but in substance the same as the empire's first three decades.[55]

What is the explanation for these violations of the voter's now-protected privacy? Unfortunately for German democracy, the erosion of dualism was moving the government, at least in the short run, toward greater dependence on the Right. In the face of Conservative hysteria that contingents of their enemies might camp out in the "private space" and prevent their own forces from voting, the government had wavered, and let the "private space" remain in view of the overseers. Moreover, in small precincts, where providing physical separation would have been too expensive, a side table with a curtain was allowed to suffice. Most important, the dwarf precincts remained. Although the Rickert Bill's demand for a minimum population per precinct had over the years been whittled down from 400 to 125 in order to gain broader support, Bülow declined to include even this minimum in the new reform, promising instead to

[52] Landesgerichtsrat Dr. Mangler argued that for the government to involve itself in elections, now that the WPK had cleared the way with its new standard for invalidation, was a good thing. "Die Anfechtung von Reichstagswahlen," *DN* (25 Feb. 1912), BAB-L R1501/14653, unpaginated.

[53] In 1903 in 38 precincts in 9 Potsdam alone. H. v. Gerlach, "Die sogenannte Wahllurne" (1904/5), 693. "Das Wahlgeheimnis in Hinterpommern," *BT* 22, Mar. 1911, BAB-L R1501/14475, unpaginated. Cf. Seymour, *Reform*, 434, who claimed that after Britain's 1872 Ballot Act "the new power of intimidation" exercized by party agents became "quite as despotic and no less effective than that of the landed and business aristocracy"! The true reformer is never satisfied.

[54] Quoted by Gerlach, "Wahllurne," 693. Cf. also 5 Kassel AnlDR (1907/9, 12/I, Bd. 20) DS 705: 4491. In the same volume: 17 Han., 3 Erfurt, Waldeck-Pyrmont, 2 Frankfurt, ibid., DS 702: 4471f, 4477–79; DS 706: 4500–4502; DS 736: 4631; DS 765: 4665, respectively. Cf. also 2 Saxe-Weimar and 2 Arns., AnlDR (1907/9, 12/1, Bd. 19) DS 572: 3455f and DS 636: 4315, respectively.

[55] AL: Delsor SBDR 21 Apr. 1903: 8925f; 2 Saxe-Meiningen AnlDR (1907/9, 12/I, Bd. 19) DS 625: 4233; 5 Kassel AnlDR (1907/09, 12/I, Bd. 20) DS 705: 4494; 10 Saxony AnlDR (1907/9, 12/I, Bd. 20) DS 800: 4720; 3 Magdeburg AnlDR (1912/13, 13/I, Bd. 19) DS 765: 1062; 9 Potsdam AnlDR (1912/13, 13/I, Bd. 19) DS 807: 1109; in Bingerau, Kuschwitz, Wirschkowitz, Powitzko, Schebitz, Esdorf, Kapitz, Paulwitz, and Kawallen: 2 Breslau AnlDR (1912/14, 13/I, Bd. 22) DS 1432: 2928, 2931–34; 2 Magdeburg AnlDR (1912/14, 13/I, Bd. 22) DS 1497: 3031, 3038f; 5 Königsberg AnlDR (1912/14, 13/I, Bd. 22) DS 1401: 2901, 2903f; 6 Trier in 1912: Bellot, *Hundert Jahre*, 234.

regulate the matter through future instructions to provincial administrators.[56] Without a standardized urn, the skeptics' warning that ballot envelopes would make monitoring the voters even easier came true. For while ballot slips might slosh around in the urn, the bulky envelopes, given a small enough container, could easily be "layered," that is, kept in the order in which they were cast, which would allow any panelist who so desired to keep dual lists—and match the order in which people voted with the order of the ballots. The Reichstag had in fact asked the chancellor to issue instructions for standardized, secure election urns.[57] The anxious might have done better to have remained silent, for the violations occurred precisely as predicted.[58] After the 1903 and 1907 elections 156 protests alleged violations of secrecy. While not all of these allegations were proven, many people, including some in the government, believed that they were but the tip of an iceberg.[59] Yet those Social Democratic poll-watchers who insisted on shaking the urn before the ballots were counted got four months in jail for the crime of unauthorized exercise of a public office.[60]

After 1903 high-profile defenses of the secret ballot by members of the government—like Count Posadowsky's much-quoted statement that "either voting is secret or it is not" and his challenge to those Conservatives who insisted on the "manliness" of open voting to be manly enough to offer a bill to strike the words "secret voting" from the constitution—dried up.[61] Precisely as leadership in imperial legislation was passing increasingly "from the responsible power, the government, to [the imperial] parliament," Bülow was recognizing the importance of its Prussian counterpart.[62] And given the Landtag's importance, the SPD's massive new campaign to introduce the Reichstag election code into Prussian *state* elections put the question of secrecy in an increasingly dangerous

[56] Untitled, *FrankZ* (24 Mar. 1903), BAB-L R1501/14456, Bl. 105.

[57] "Das Klosettgesetz," BT (14 Mar. 1903); "Zur Sicherung des Wahl-Geheimnisses" (13 Mar. 1903); "Nochmals das Klosettgesetz" (13 Mar. 1903), *Deutsche Tageszeitung* (K); "Die Sicherung des Wahl-Geheimnisses," *Vorwärts* (24 Mar. 1903); "Die 'Sicherung' des Wahl-Geheimnisses," *Volkszeitung* (2 Apr. 1903); "Es dämmert endlich," *Deutsche Tageszeitung* (2 Apr. 1903); "Die geschäftliche Behandlung des Klosettgesetzes" (1 Apr. 1903). In the debate on SBDR 21 Apr. 1903: 8909–26, two deputies, Pachnicke (LL) and Baron v. Hodenberg (W) accurately predicted what would happen, giving a detailed description of layering. Even the NLs submitted a motion asking for standardized urns and mixing of envelopes: Antrag Bassermann, Buesing, AnlDR (1905/6, 11/II, Bd. 8) DS 586: 5352f.

[58] Gerlach, "Wahlurne," 693. Cf. 9 S-H (the Counts' Corner) AnlDR (1903/4, 11/I, Bd. 3) DS 373: 2077; "Die Wahlkiste," *Volksstimme* (Berlin), Nr. 304 (July 1906) on 2 Königsberg, BAB-L R1501/14474, Bl. 19; Leser, "Untersuchungen," 92–93 (2 Mittelfranken). The most heavily challenged region was West Prussia. There were no challenges in Baden, Württemberg, or Posnania province, nor in some of the smaller states.

[59] Eg. Geh.RR Dr. Lucas, Minutes of Commissarial Deliberations on Amendments to the Election Regulations, 27 June 1910, BAB-L R1501/14475, unpaginated. Siegfried, who had a business interest in standardized urns: "Wahlurne," esp. 735, 741.

[60] O. Landsberg (SD) SBDR 13 Feb. 1913: 4744, BAB-L R1501/14460, Bl. 423.

[61] Posadowsky SBDR 21 Apr. 1903: 8916. Applauded in Gerlach, "Wahlurne," 693; "Die Wahlurne," *SaaleZ*, 16 Mar. 1911, BAB-L R1501/14475, unpaginated. Attacks on P. from the Right: Schmidt, *Posadowsky*, 148–50 and thereafter.

[62] Quote: Schmidt, *Posadowsky*, 156, whose Reichsamt perspective and whose disapproval of this process add weight to this judgment.

light. The Right's power in the Landtag, as was borne home to the ministers through confidential discussions with Conservative Party leaders, now depended less on Prussia's three-class voting system, on which compromise was possible, than on the open ballot. No government could mount a vigorous defense of the open ballot for Prussia and at the same time take vigorous steps to insure secrecy in the Reich without coming into apparent conflict with itself. Thus Reichstag bills that would have prosecuted any election overseer who betrayed how a man had voted were rejected out of hand. The promised instructions to eliminate or ameliorate dwarf precincts were postponed until November 1911. And the adoption of a standardized, secure urn, over which the ministers brooded and dithered for a decade, had to wait until June 1913; that is, until a year after the empire's last general election.[63]

These delays were a political mistake. Whatever its shortcomings, secrecy had now been established to a degree that insured the opposition's chances of victory. Outside the rural East, the pressure of the bread lord had indeed become a far less prominent feature of the balloting. But without the security in *every* precinct that these final safeguards would provide, the government's greater direct involvement in national campaigns, instead of being accepted philosophically by its opponents as a move toward a more unitary form of government, and thus one more compatible with a parliamentary system, continued to be compromised for another decade.

The Lex Rickert of 1903 was part of that whole movement for genuinely secret voting that swept franchise regimes from Australia to Norway, from Romania to Chile in the half century after 1856.[64] It was the German analog to Britain's Ballot Act of 1872 and to France's belated introduction of envelopes and voting booths in 1914—both of which also initially fell short, in practice, of their advocates' ideal.[65] But the Lex Rickert was of deeper moment than

---

[63] The complexities of the urn question recur throughout the following folders in the BAB-L R 1501: 14459–61, 14474–76, which would be wearisome to cite. Key are: IM Moltke's memo, 8 Jan. 1908, against accepting the Hompesch motion to criminalize violations of secrecy, because it was inconsistent with refusing even to *allow* secrecy in Prussia (BAB-L R1501/14459, Bl. 5; included verbatum in 14474, Bl. 93–93v); IM Moltke to Chancellor BH, 5 Jan. 1910, refusing to go into the question of uniform, self-acting urns because (inter alia), "Precisely at the present moment it seems to me especially little suitable" to open these questions because of their "probable unfavorable feedback [*Rückwirkungen*] on the solution to the franchise question in Prussia." BAB-L R1501/14475, unpaginated. Minutes of Commissarial Deliberations on Amendments to the Voting Regulations, in which Geh.ORR Falkenhayn from the MdI reported: "His chief considers occupying the public so soon again, right after feeling has just calmed down, extremely risky [*höchst bedenklich*]." 27 June 1910, RdM 14475 unpaginated. Even after 1903 at least some in Prussia's cabinet still hoped eventually to repeal the Reichstag's secret ballot, as did some conservative voters.

[64] Here are some of the relevant dates: official ballots with isolation space: Australia 1857, England 1872, Luxemburg 1884, Belgium 1884 and 1894; official envelopes with isolation space: Norway and Romania 1884, Chile 1890, Baden 1896, Württemberg 1899. [Siegfried], "Wahl," BAB-L R101/3344, Bl. 258; Seymour/Frary, *World* 2, esp. the optimistic summary on 315; Weber, *Peasants*, 271.

[65] In England the Lords had insisted on a numbering system to allow scrutiny by the overseers—which passed! Fredman, *Ballot*, 15.

these ballot acts and even the U.S. Voting Rights Act of 1965. Important though the latter were, they guaranteed only the voter's freedom *within* a polity where popular representation itself was no longer at stake. But precisely because the German franchise and the Reichstag that it elected were still at issue, Rickert's Bill, by the time the government conceded its major provisions in 1903, had acquired a significance beyond the dependent voter's struggle for autonomy. It had become a constitutional matter of the first order. Posadowsky's moral argument, insisting on the government's obligation either to enforce the constitution that prescribed secrecy or to try to amend it, was a powerful one in a culture as legalistic as the German bureaucracy's. But even more persuasive than his moral argument had been his political one. In 1903 the governmental parties (both conservatives and National Liberals) commanded only 125 votes in a Reichstag of 397. Even adding the thirteen Antisemites (which on the secrecy issue Bülow could not do), the government's bloc was overwhelmed by the Centrum and the Left Liberals, who with the Centrum's particularist allies disposed of 185 votes—even without drawing on the SPD's fifty-six-vote strength. Posadowsky and Bülow had overcome their ministerial colleagues' extreme aversion to secrecy by referring to the continuous pressure of the Reichstag *majority*, and to the government's need for a positive working relationship with that majority in order to pass the other legislation it desired. Once a *Staatsstreich* had been excluded—and after the Hohenlohe-Miquel era it was, in the words of Thomas Kühne, a "taboo theme"—the government really had no choice.[66]

Yet if we insist on seeing 1903 as an important watershed, not only for democratic practices on the precinct level but also for Germany's constitutional development, we face an obvious question. If it took ballot envelopes and private spaces to protect dissenting voters from the powers that be, how do we explain their ability to elect a Reichstag majority capable of holding the government's feet to the fire and forcing the Rickert reforms in the first place? It is to that question that we shall now turn.

THE GEOGRAPHY OF DISSENT

Unsympathetic contemporaries were wont to explain the willingness of so many voters to behave "uneconomically" at the polls, risking their livelihoods for their convictions, by pointing to a "higher" kind of economic thinking. Self-interest in the present, they argued, was being overridden, at least among those

[66] Kühne, *Dreiklassenwahlrecht*, 36; "taboo theme," 458. My interpretation of these years contrasts in tone, if not in particulars, with Wehler's view that "missing everywhere . . ." in the late empire, "[was] above all the most important thing: the fighting will and the readiness to take risks by a self-conscious, power-hungry parliament in the course of a great conflict for the pinnacle of the governing hierarchy." *Gesellschaftsgeschichte* 3: 1039. To insist that any "great" fight must be for the "pinnacle of the governing hierarchy" implies that sovereignty is always undivided, and misses the "fighting will" and "readiness to take risks" the RT's deputies repeatedly demonstrated.

who supported the main outsider parties, by self-interest regarding the future. Risks were accepted because of a naive conviction in the imminence of utopia (the Social Democrats' *Zukunftsstaat*) on the one hand, or because of an equally naive fear of hell (by Catholics) on the other. But can naive fanaticism (for that is what this explanation implies) have been in sufficient supply to account for the development of Centrum and Social Democracy into mass parties? I doubt it.

A less tendentious explanation has been found in Germany's explosive urbanization. In the crucial decade before the Socialist breakthrough in 1890, the number of cities with populations over 100,000 increased from fifteen to twenty-six. Supported by the anonymity of the metropolis, urban voters could escape both the terrors of employers and the meshes of community. Town air makes free. Metropolises are simply too large for traditional authorities to control.[67]

There is much plausibility to this argument. Support for Social Democracy correlates positively with the size of cities—or, at least, with Protestant cities.[68] Hamburg, Berlin, Breslau, and Kiel were among the early bastions of the SPD. Yet the sheer size of a district's total electorate has not always disabled local power holders who wanted to monitor voting. Socialists proved unable to take Kiel and four of Berlin's six huge districts even once before 1893. We need only reflect on the last municipal elections in the German Democratic Republic, in May 1989, as on those in many metropolises throughout the world today, to find urban mockeries of free elections. Such reflection forces us to recognize the implicit premise required by the urbanization explanation for the Empire's oppositional outcomes: that there were certain kinds of interference which even the powerful rejected as out-of-bounds. Violence against voters (so endemic in turn-of-the-century Madrid and in Reconstruction New Orleans) was one; wholesale removal of names from the voting rolls (as in contemporary Bologna and Padua) was another.[69] No German alderman, however arrogant, would have boasted with New York's William M. (Boss) Tweed, that "the ballots made no result; the counters made the result"; or with his San Francisco counterpart, Chris Buckley, that the favorable returns from his precincts were limited "only by the modesty of the election officials." The absence of violence or even fraud on any measurable scale in Germany is something contemporaries took for granted; yet we should not. The self-imposed, if selective, forbearance of the powerful is a central fact of imperial elections. It points to an ingrained respect for Rules pervasive in German culture, a feature to which we shall return in the next chapter.[70]

[67] Lidtke, *Party*, 179; Guttsman, *Party*, 85–99. Yet these authors do not neglect the small town and small firm bases of German Socialism.

[68] E.g., Steinbach, "Entwicklung," 16. In metropolises of more than 100,000 the SD usually won more than 50% of the vote. Blank, "Zusammensetzung," 507–53, esp. 528; G. A. Ritter, "Bases" (1990), 33.

[69] Rowell, *Digest*, 227f, 232f, 241f, 519. Madrid: Dardé, "Fraud;" Bologne and Padua: Seymour/ Frary, *World* 2: 115.

[70] Quoted in Argersinger, "Perspectives," 678. Chicago was notorious for ballot box stuffing until the 1930s. Harris, *Administration*, 340–60 and idem, *Registration*, 350–62. Note that the Allens,

But even given the culturally determined self-denial of those in authority, the urbanization hypothesis does not take us nearly as far as we need to go. Most Reichstag deputies did not represent metropolises. In 1890, after two decades of unprecedented population growth, nearly 60 percent of Germany's citizens still lived in communities of fewer than 2,000 residents. And although the urban explosion continued unabated, as late as 1905 communities under 5,000 still accommodated slightly more than half of the population.[71] Even in the Weimar Republic, only every fourth worker lived in a large town, and a slim majority—particularly evident in Saxony, Hessen, and Württemberg—lived in communities of fewer than 10,000 residents. The ideal-typical Social Democratic constituency in the 1890s in the Ruhr, Karl Rohe tells us, was not the metropolis but the small mining village.[72] And the Centrum's success in the Catholic countryside was not limited to those areas where the bread lord himself might be a supporter of the party, but extended to regions like Pless-Rybnik, where, in all four elections in the seventies, the largest employer was a powerful and bitter opponent.

The inability of employers and their government allies to stop the march of Social Democracy in the Kingdom of Saxony also suggests that urbanization, at least in the form we imagine it today, may not have been the crucial factor in securing space for electoral freedom. For unlike the rest of the empire, the incidence of Social Democratic voting in royal Saxony remained independent of size of community or distance from metropolitan centers. Saxony had been since the Middle Ages the most densely populated region in Europe; since 1875, the most industrialized region in Germany.[73] In Dresden, Leipzig, and Chemnitz it had three cities with populations over 100,000. Yet throughout the imperial period, at least three-quarters of Saxony's population lived *outside* the Kingdom's big cities. Agriculture, mills, and mining tended to be small scale, while industry, though the leading sector in terms of employment, was dominated by light manufacturing. Employers were not big enough to offer the high

---

"Fraud," 169, dissent from Harris's view that 134,000 names were illegally purged from the Philadelphia voting rolls in 1906. German elites were, of course, no angels. The manipulation of census data to draw tendentious precinct boundaries, esp. in LT elections, was notorious. Kühne, "Liberalen," esp. 283–85. But the magnitude of the difference in degree between Germany and the U.S. really does point to differences in kind. And differences in *kind* is what we are investigating.

[71] Calculated from *Statistisches Jahrbuch für das Deutsche Reich* (1893), 1, with figures from the 1890 census; ibid. (1908), 6; and G. Hohorst et al., comps., *Arbeitsbuch* (1978) 2: 52, the second table.

[72] Weimar: Falter, *Wähler*, 200, 218; ideal-typical: Rohe, "Alignments," 115.

[73] Hohorst et al., comps., *Arbeitsbuch* 2: 61, and 73, table 3. Warren, *Kingdom*, 1f, 5. Steinbach, "Entwicklung," 16. Rohe, *Wahlen*, 85f, speculates that early Socialism did better in less urbanized Saxony than in the large secularized metropolises, because Lassalleanism was an ersatz religion; but adds that in the very early stages of a party, organization itself accounts for more than any cultural factors, a point made more generally by Sartori, "Sociology," 65–100. Prussian Saxony was a much less favorable environment: Thomas Klein, "Reichstagswahlen und -Abgeordnete der Provinz Sachsen und Anhalts 1867–1918. Ein Überblick," in *Zur Geschichte und Volkskunde Mitteldeutschlands. Festschrift für Friedrich von Zahn*, edited by W. Schlesinger (Cologne and Graz, 1968) 1: 65–141.

wages, or company housing and insurance funds, that might have forced a potentially independent worker to think especially hard about his vote.[74] And however determined Saxon employers were to wipe out Social Democracy, their
own antagonistic political allegiances (Progressive, Liberal, Conservative)
worked against the easy networking that made blacklisting a real political
weapon in the solidly National Liberal northwest.[75] A bread lord in Saxony,
however jealous of his authority in political matters, could not assume cooperation from anyone but the state. And the state, even with the best will in the
world, would repress only certain kinds of activity—not the actual act of
voting.

It was precisely this economic topography—dense population but small-scale
enterprise, rather than the giant factory and the metropolis—that limned Germany's most favorable geography for political choice. Such an employment
landscape offered workers too few incentives and too many alternatives for
threats of dismissal to have the force they enjoyed in regions where the employment pie was controlled by fewer chefs, and where the "perks" attendant on
staying in place were considerable.[76] "The free market and the horizontal mobility of economic agents are conditions of competitive elections," a student of
clientelist systems in authoritarian contexts has noted. Saxon election results
reflected precisely this relative social space. Even during the hysteria over the
red menace in 1878, the Socialist vote there continued to rise.[77] By 1903, all but
one of Saxony's twenty-three election districts had fallen to the Social Democrats.[78]

We should be wary of envisioning Marx's proletariat when we look at statistics on German "industry." Much of the work in Saxony was done by artisans
or "put out" to domestic workers. Even in Dresden, a city of almost 400,000 in
1900, 86 percent of its 22,000 industrial enterprises employed no more than five
workers.[79] It was this artisanal milieu of small masters and their dependents that
had provided the seedbed since 1848 of a vigorous culture of plebeian dissent.[80]

---

[74] H. Zwahr, "Arbeiterbewegung" (1987), 448–507. Employer insurance plans in Hessen: White,
Party, 48.

[75] Although Stumm was FK, the disappearance of the FKs in the Saar after his death indicates
that the party's strength in the NL Saar was a function of the baron's powerful personality. Bellot,
Hundert Jahre, 204f.

[76] Solingen (SD from 1881), Hamburg, and Munich (SD from 1890), with similar structural
features, also provided a favorable environment for the SDs. W. Bramann, *Reichstagswahlen*
(1973); Kutz-Bauer, *Arbeiterschaft*; Pohl, *Arbeiterbewegung*, esp. 50f, 63.

[77] As it did, however, in Hamburg and other metropolises. Rohe, *Wahlen*, 90; Guttsman, *Party*,
38; Kutz-Bauer, *Arbeiterschaft*, 13. Quoted: Rouquié, "Controls," 28.

[78] Out of 10 Saxons, seven voted either for the SDs or the antisemites. Warren, *Kingdom*, ix–xi,
1f.

[79] Population: *Statistisches Jahrbuch für das Deutsche Reich* 42 (1903), 14; employment: J. N.
Retallack, "Antisocialism" (1992), 53. In 1882, 50% of Germany's workers were found in shops
employing fewer than 5 employees; even in 1895, the figure was somewhat more than 46%. Lidtke,
Party, 11. A useful critique of the assumption that German "workers" were "proletarians" employed
in huge firms and huge cities. Moore, *Injustice*, 173–84.

[80] Lidtke, *Party*, 183. GDR historiography disputed this widespread description, insisting on the

Indeed, not just in Saxony, but wherever there were craft trades, we find a kind of freemasonry—with its own songs and proverbs, its own neighborhoods and associations to press common interests, its own rituals of introduction (*"Ein fremder Drechsler spricht um Arbeit vor"*) and a network of hostels providing the tramping journeyman with shelter or at least a stipend until he reached his next berth—that offered the plebeian voter some measure of protection and support.[81] In fact, it was not the classic factory proletariat, but the craft trades with strong guild traditions—masons, carpenters, printers, leather workers— that ultimately supplied many of the active members and most of the leadership of the trade unions and the national Social Democratic party, from the cabinet-maker August Bebel on down.[82] The party's gains in the eighties in city council elections, all conducted on the basis of a plutocratic three-class voting system, in Bremen, Braunschweig, Esslingen (Württemberg), Glauchau (Saxony), and Mannheim (Baden) are further evidence of Socialist strength within the artisan class. Bebel once bragged to the Reichstag that all of Germany's urban artisans were Social Democrats. He exaggerated. Similar structures sustained dissenting commitments in hostile local environments among Left Liberal, Antisemitic, and Centrum artisans as well.[83]

And not only sustained—but spread. The far-flung friendships and mutual reciprocities encouraged by the tradition of journeying established ready-made channels for disseminating a new political gospel once a core of apostles had been recruited.[84] And there is some evidence that by the eighties, recruitment was being carried on by some of the bread lords themselves—even by Social

---

"proletarian" as opposed to artisanal, character of the Saxon working class: H. Zwahr, *Zur Konstituierung des Proletariats als Klasse. Strukturuntersuchung über das Leipziger Proletariat während der Industriellen Revolution* ([Berlin, 1978] Munich, 1981). See, however, Lidtke's skeptical review of Zwahr in "The Formation of the Working Class in Germany," *CEH* 13 (1980): 393–400. On working and wage conditions in Saxony: Zwahr, "Arbeiterbewegung," 448–507; Warren, *Kingdom*, 5.

[81] "A turner from afar asks for work." Keil, *Erlebnisse* 1: 49–52, 67, 70, 72f; quote on 73; A. Bebel, *My Life* ([1912], New York, 1973), 43. Hamburg's early Social Democracy may owe less to the city's size than to the fact that it was populated with many small and medium-sized firms employing skilled workers. Kutz-Bauer, *Arbeiterschaft*, 112f.

[82] Insofar as they were not intellectuals. Lidtke, *Party*, 10n. 12; Molt, *Reichstag*, 212, 222, 227, 236; 155f; Kutz-Bauer, *Arbeiterschaft*, 160–62, 213–31, 432–35; Müller, *Geschichte*, 351; W. Blos, *Denkwürdigkeiten* (1914), vol. I.

[83] Lidtke, *Party*, 184; Kutz-Bauer, *Arbeiterschaft*, 125. As early as 1905 Robert Blank had used statistical breakdowns to argue that at least a quarter of the SPD votes had to come from middle class (*"bürgerliche"*) voters. "Zusammensetzung," 507–50, esp. 521n. 1. Max Weber criticized the statistics in the same issue ("Bemerkungen" [1905], 550–53). More recently, G. A. Ritter has rejected Blank's conclusions, in an argument made in 1959 but excerpted in Ritter, "Strategie," 324n. 40. But see Sperber, *Voters*, 64–69; Warren, *Kingdom*, 49. A reporter for *Blackwood's* remarked that the audience at SPD rallies in the large towns "consists of men in easy circumstances," of "easy-going 'bourgeois.'" "Working," 270f.

[84] SDs were accused of equipping laborers coming into Saxony in search of work with "a veritable obligatory pass" distributed by the constituency committees in the various election districts, forcing them to report to the *Vorständen*, where they were told which taverns they could visit and from which shopkeepers they could buy. Fhr. v. Friesen (K) SBDR 10 Jan. 1889: 371.

Democratic employers, and not only in Saxony. Wilhelm Keil, on the tramp as a journeyman carpenter, was introduced to socialism in Cologne by the son of his master. The latter offered him copies of the party's newspaper, and when it proved too sophisticated for the untutored Keil, got the teenager to subscribe to the *Kölner Arbeiterzeitung*, a more popular version of the same. At Keil's next station, in sleepy Koblenz, the master himself turned out to be a Social Democrat. He was, in fact, a leader in the invisible life of the small Koblenz party as well as the local contact man for visiting Socialist organizers. Keil's conversion was easy. The intimacy of artisanal work encouraged conversation, and part of Keil's wages included room and board with the master—a practice that artisan self-help organizations were trying to abolish, not least because of the political dependency it fostered. Mealtime discussions with Keil's Socialist bread lord in fact revolved around politics, "but they were pretty one-sided," the future Social Democratic leader admitted. "For we young journeymen, in our political naiveté, could hardly steer them. We just went along with the opinion of the master."

Keil nowhere says that his Socialist masters pressured him to vote for the party, and it would have been contrary to both doctrine and ethos had they done so. Nevertheless, good relations were no doubt as helped by like-mindedness among Socialist employers and their employees as they were among Conservatives. And if the employer himself commanded respect, he was well positioned to influence the political education of his dependents. The Social Democratic credentials of Keil's master then furnished the young journeyman with an entrée into party circles as far away as Darmstadt and Mannheim.[85]

To summarize: The cover of anonymity provided by big cities; the plural employment opportunities characteristic of the small-scale industrial landscape, especially in the Saxonies; the dispersion of political affiliations—which might include even Social Democratic affiliations—among employers in such a landscape, especially within the artisanal world: all of these features helped provide for some voters the space to dissent either from their bread lords—or *with* their bread lords but from the parties favored by other authorities, especially the government.

ECONOMIC RATIONALITY: A TWO-WAY STREET

As we investigate the willingness of voters to risk their livelihoods, we must keep in mind not only these variations in the geography of power but also the worker's growing opportunities to exploit them. The empire's explosive industrialization was spurred by liberal legislation in the late sixties that for the first time allowed complete freedom of movement (*Freizügigkeit*) between the various German states. And workers' autobiographies suggest that, politics aside, the young changed jobs with breathtaking insouciance, apparently undeterred

---

[85] Keil, *Erlebnisse* 1: 53, 66f, 74, 76, 83, 90. Of SD politics among pit foremen in 1912: Hall, *Scandal*, 92.

by fears of unemployment, even in the hungry 1880s.[86] By the mid-nineties, jeremiahs were decrying the ceaseless movement of people back and forth, in and out of jobs, as a veritable "plague."[87] Thus while angry bread lords could import workers from outside, workers themselves could drain away—as they eventually did from the estates in east Elbia. Given the empire's highly developed transportation infrastructure (with rail tickets for workers offered at cheaper prices), a man whose own neighborhood offered no alternative employment might presume on finding it elsewhere—even if he had been fired for his politics.[88]

Movement was encouraged not only by conjunctural upswings, which in any case did not become nationwide until the nineties. From the first, friendly societies and trade unions had adopted the guild tradition of supplying their members with "travel money" (10 to 15 pfennige per mile). Conceived not only as a means of regulating the local labor market by encouraging the superfluous to go elsewhere and as an act of solidarity with the worker in search of a job, the subsidy was also testimony, among the "Free" Unions (associated with Social Democracy), to their belief that travel in and of itself encouraged political emancipation and the development of class consciousness. Important as early as the 1850s, travel money comprised the largest single expenditure from union support funds, making up nearly one-third of all such outlays in 1893.[89]

The connection between electoral freedom and economic opportunity was especially obvious in Hamburg. There wages and employment were sufficiently strong for Social Democrats to organize mass absenteeism from the workplace on election day, thereby making surveillance by employers immensely more difficult. It is no accident that during the decade when that city-state became the national bastion of Social Democracy, 1877–87, Hamburg's local economy was visibly stronger, and the position of its workers considerably better, than the imperial average.[90]

Since statistics on unemployment were usually not collected by the Imperial government, it is difficult to say who might have been in a stronger bargaining position at any given time and trade.[91] Enormous variations among industries,

[86] Keil, *Erlebnisse* 1: esp. 49–53. Cf. Eugen May, who quit in 1907 because his master wouldn't give him election day off to distribute SD ballots: "Mein Lebenslauf," in Kelly, ed., *Worker*, 380; and "A Barmaid," ibid., 252–68.

[87] Von Oppen, *Reform*, 11. Cf. prefects in the 90s quoted in H. Romeyk, *Wahlen* (1969), 47.

[88] Cheaper tickets for workers: Bade, " 'Kulturkampf,' " 112. Cf. also advertisements aimed at traveling workers: *GA* Nr. 207 (5 Sept. 1871); Nr. 208 (6 Sept. 1871) and Nr. 209 (7 Sept. 1871): 1859, 1863, 1873.

[89] K. Schönhoven, "Selbsthilfe" (1980), 152, 157 (Table 3), 162–67, 174; F. Tennstedt, *Proleten* (1983), 130.

[90] Kutz-Bauer, *Arbeiterschaft*, 118, 127, 140f, 273, 277, 300, 418–21. Perhaps casual labor enabled political independence as well. Cf. Karl Ditt, "Fabrikarbeiter und Handwerker im 19. Jahrhundert in der neueren deutschen Sozialgeschichtsschreibung. Eine Zwischenbilanz," *GG* 20 (1994), 299–320; 308.

[91] "Unfortunately one gropes entirely in the dark if one wants to calculate the number of unemployed," confessed the Christian Social editor of the *Evangelisches Wochenblatt*. Kötzschke, *Brief*,

local and regional differences in the tempo of industrialization, as well as sharp seasonal fluctuations, discourage confident generalizations. Although the German economy crashed in 1873 and remained severely depressed until 1879, and although recovery was not complete until 1896, we cannot assume that employment dried up even during these decades. As we saw in the case of Alfred Krupp and the obstreperous Freßberger, even when falling production encouraged layoffs, an employer might need a particular worker at least as much as the worker needed him. When the historian of Polish migrant labor tells us that the number of people living in the Rhineland and Westfalia who had been born in Silesia, Posnania, and East and West Prussia rose in the 1880s by over 94,000, the inescapable conclusion is that tens of thousands of new jobs were being created, even during the recession. When the percentage of women employed in Hamburg in domestic service dropped from 10 percent of all those employed in 1871 to 4.4 percent in 1895, we are justified in seeing an increase in better paying jobs with freer working conditions.[92]

There is no such thing as a single labor market, and certainly not in a society undergoing rapid industrialization. What we can say is that during the first three decades of the German Empire, economic growth as a whole soared. The Social Democrats' breakthrough election, in February 1890, occurred on the heels of a "boom year." And it is tempting to see the SPD's jump in 1893, when it gained an additional 25 percent more votes (even though turnout as a whole increased by less than 1 percentage point) as a reflection, not only of the end of the Socialist Law, but also of the greater freedom provided by increasingly favorable employment opportunities.[93] From the dependent voter's point of view, it was a matter of extraordinary good fortune that universal suffrage arrived in Germany at the same time as its industrial revolution.

After 1896, the terms of trade became even more favorable for workers. For the prewar years, Kenneth Barkin has calculated that Germany's mean unemployment rate was an astonishing 2.7 percent, nearly 2 percentage points below Britain's. Wages in many major industries crept up in the nineties, and then

---

46. Most of our unemployment statistics were collected by the trade unions, which became significant forces only in the 1890s. Barkin, "Germany," 207; F. Tennstedt, *Sozialgeschichte* (1981), 204. Government statistics for some months in 1895 show unemployment fluctuating between 1.11 and 3.4%. Wehler, *Gesellschaftsgeschichte* 3: 781.

[92] Statistics: Kulczyncki, *Worker*, 51 and Kutz-Bauer, *Arbeiterschaft*, 118. Even during the depths of the depression, Hamburg refutes any notion of universality in unemployment, at the same time that it suggests a discernable connection between SD successes (and losses) and the labor market. Some unemployment was "a normal condition" even in Hamburg (ibid., 68–70, 111, 135–37; but see 139), and the drop in Socialist votes in 1878 may have had at least as much to do with the nadir of the recession as with the stepped-up repression. Ibid., 131f, 134. Now authoritative on the "Great Depression": Wehler, *Gesellschaftsgeschichte* 3: generally: 103–5; wages: 548, 559, 592; unemployment (in some industries 25%): 561, 571; recovery: 569; later cycles: 575, 577. On unemployment in mining: Spencer, *Management*, 41, and Tenfelde, *Sozialgeschichte*, 579. Strong fluctuations among workers in Essen: Möllers, *Strömungen*, 145.

[93] "Boom year": Wehler, *Gesellschaftsgeschichte* 3: 577. Percentages calculated from Ritter/Niehuss, *Arbeitsbuch*, 40.

raced ahead.[94] For all the justified outrage about families going hungry because their breadwinner had voted independently, a worker around 1903 who knew that he was defying his boss might well consider the boom and take his chances. And statistics for the SPD showed that he did.

What was true of the individual was *a fortiori* true of large groups. This is not to discount the severity of mass dismissals. But economic imperatives, as we have seen, worked both ways. An industrial outfit located in a rural village where the vote was unanimous was in a poor position to be politically demanding.[95] No employer, party newspapers assured their readers, could fire everyone. (Junkers were an exception only because they could draw on an apparently limitless supply of foreign workers.) Even strikes, a much more direct challenge to a bread lord's authority than contrary voting, were requited with exemplary rather than universal punishment. Roughly 20,000 Ruhr coal miners laid down their tools in 1890, 1891, and again in 1893. Although every strike produced dismissals, the highest figure was 823 in 1893, a mere fraction (1/24) of the rebel labor force. After the economic recovery moved into full swing, securing adequate manpower became so pressing that managers were willing to hire known strikers, unionists, and insubordinates.[96]

Knowledge that they were a resource that employers needed may have actually spurred some dissatisfied workers to treat their vote as a way of declaring "take this job and shove it." Eighteen miners at the Marianne and Steinbank mines handed in their workbooks (*Abkehrschein*) at election time in 1881— *before* being dismissed: an example that stirred others "tired of election slavery" to do the same.[97] For some contrary souls, the risk of losing their job for the sake of declaring political autonomy was one they were aching to take.[98] Most voters of course hoped to get through an election without making a peep, much less searching for a new livelihood. For many, casting a *blank* ballot was as much protest as they would chance.[99] One ventured a step farther: he took the

---

[94] Employment: Barkin, "Germany," 207; Tennstedt, *Sozialgeschichte*, 204. Further evidence of labor shortages, in agriculture as well as industry: Romeyk, *Wahlen*, 46f, 49f, 55, 57, 60. But see: G. Steinmetz, *Regulating* (1993), 203f. Wages: Barkin, *Controversy*, table on 117.

[95] Workers at the railworks in Meppen-Lingen: [illegible: Hlarer?] to Clauditz, L[ingen], 21 Feb. 1887, and H. Ramme (sp?) Kpln [= Kaplan] to Clauditz, L[ingen], 20 Feb. 1890: SAO, Dep. 62b, 2379.

[96] Spencer, *Management*, 40f, 67. Reassurance from party press: *Rheinisch-Westfälischer Volksfreund* (21 Jul. 1878) and the *Essener VolkZtg* quoted in Paul, *Krupp*, 258.

[97] "Election slavery" is the Centrum's comment. 5 Arns. (Bochum) AnlDR (1882/83, 5/II, Bd. 6) DS 292: 1079f.

[98] Aug. Schubert, Stellenbesitzer, 10 Breslau (1889/90, 7/V, Bd. 3) DS 105: 426. Examples of others who energetically protested what they saw as misconduct on the part of the election panel: 6 Berlin (1880, 4/III, Bd. 4) DS 94: 669; 22 Saxony AnlDR (1881, 5/II, Bd. 5) DS 193: 689; 5 Arns. (Bochum) AnlDR (1885/86, 6/II, Bd. 5) DS 181: 898–900; 14 Saxony AnlDR (1885/86, 6/II, Bd. 5) DS 117: 567–75; Einbeck: Count v. Rittberg SBDR 28 Mar. 1871: 25; 5 Breslau: Becker SBDR 29 Mar. 1871: 46; in Sachrang, Bavaria: SBDR 5 Apr. 1871: 186; 1 Minden (1877, 3/I, Bd. 3) DS 187: 522; 1 Minden AnlDR (1878, 3/II, Bd. 3) DS 99: 833–43.

[99] Voters in Hörde: 6 Arns. AnlDR (1890/91, 8/I, Bd. 3) DS 292: 2050; workers in 1 Berlin in 1881, caught between the antisemite Max Liebermann v. Sonnenberg and the F factory owner,

boss's ballot and, after the candidate's name, wrote "is not the man for me"—and succeeded in getting the unwanted ballot thrown out.[100] I do not want to belittle their risks. It can hardly have been a comfort to know that if they were thrown out of work, the job market was favorable, or that most of their mates would escape their fate. By turning the act of defiance—in voting as in striking—into a game of Russian roulette, even a single dismissal might be enough to produce considerable conformity in the shop, as it was on rural estates.

Not surprisingly, therefore, "sacrifice" became an important part of every party's political vocabulary—used not as an injunction, but as a description of the political process, as it worked itself out every day. Sacrifice (*Opfermut*) was the virtue extolled by a party in its deputies, toiling far from home and (until 1906) without official pay. The word lauded those "candidates for the count," running in hopeless districts so that the faithful might have a chance to show the flag. *Opfermut* commended also the widow's mite of hundreds of small contributors, as we shall see in chapter 11.[101] But the term was used most of all to praise the voters themselves, who might be called upon to make the ultimate sacrifice. The word cast a moral penumbra over every aspect of the political process.

No party preached reckless heroism.[102] For the voter, as for Alfred Krupp, the decision for "economics" over "politics," or vice versa, was rarely made once and for all; it had to be a series of shifting calculations, and the parties knew it. In coping with retaliation against voters, the parties saw their task not only as inculcating *Zivilcourage* (much as they tried to do that), but also as doing everything in their power to lessen the risks and improve the odds.

INSURING THE VOTER

The worker's willingness to take his chances at the polls was encouraged when the parties themselves could supply emergency employment—a difficult task in a polity where even victors disposed of no public patronage. Polish and German Catholics benefited from the clergy's informational network, but all parties depended heavily on advertisements in their affiliated newspapers, asking supporters for information that could connect jobs with seekers—one reason why the more autocratic employers did their best to ban such papers from home and tavern as well as from the shop floor.[103]

Ludwig Löwe. Frank, *Brandenburger*, 60. Cf. 80,000 Israeli Arabs who cast blank ballots in the Knesset election in May 1996.

[100] 14 Saxony AnlDR (1912, 13/I, Bd. 19) DS 718: 926.

[101] It was used by Ks as well as the Left. Adalbert Dahm to Bülow, Spandau, 18 June 1908, BAB-L R1501/14695, Bl. 207f. Some resistance: Kutz-Bauer, *Arbeiterschaft*, 329.

[102] Cf. the advice of Probst Wloszkiewicz in Skalmierzyze to agricultural workers, given (in church) in Polish and in German. 10 Posen AnlDR (1884/85, 6/I, Bd. 5) DS 44: 145.

[103] ZP: Möllers, *Strömungen*, 330f; SD and ZP: Paul, *Krupp*, 243–46, 267f; 5 Arns. (Bochum) AnlDR (1882/83, 5/II, Bd. 6) DS 292: 1081; Kühne (Prussian LT elections): "Elezioni," 60, and

The parties also collected support funds to tide over the victims of retaliation. Essen's Social Democrats managed to take in 1,400 marks in a few months in 1877, receiving donations from as far away as Bavaria and Hamburg. (Essen's mayor then denied the men relief from local poor funds, arguing that their own support committee kept them well provided!) Berliners held auctions and lotteries (a sewing machine dealer donated his wares as the prize) as well as passing the hat, collecting and distributing 9,273 marks to 53 people over an eleven-month period between 1878 and 1879. Catholic support groups were no less active. In the 1901 by-election in Stumm's old district, the Centrum's candidate, the Cologne businessman Eduard Fuchs, set up a fund to support victims of the campaign in advance of the election. Dismissals might also be countered by work stoppages.[104] In hard times, of course, it proved difficult for a party to distinguish between the politically unemployed and those who were simply out of work. Socialist organizers complained that men were appearing in their offices asking for relief who had "never belonged to the party and had to be considered outright opponents"; that is, "arch-Liberals" and even "ultramontanes." Since in the seventies and eighties Social Democrats were already digging deep in their pockets to help those incarcerated or emigrating to America, and Catholics were supporting clergy whose salaries had been stopped, the cushions that Socialist, Centrum, and the Polish Party supporters were nevertheless able to offer those victimized on their behalf seem remarkable.[105]

In weighing economic against political desire, the job itself was not the only weight on the economic side of the voter's scale. Company benefits—housing, pensions, consumer cooperatives, health and life insurance policies—were also considerations. Though designed to ensure a stable workforce, and thus ultimately a sign of the employer's vulnerability, these benefits were also, as Lujo Brentano argued, an instrument of class war, "a weapon that . . . strengthened the superiority of one of the two parties. . . ." All benefit funds, including the ones to which the employer required the worker to contribute, were forfeit once he left the firm. Having a stake in these provisions, therefore, screwed the voter's anxiety "for his dear bread" one notch tighter.[106] The inability of Saxony's many small firms to deploy such weapons was one more reason for their early ineffectuality against Social Democracy.

But the firm was never the only source of security on a rainy day. Germany had a long history of locally regulated, sometimes compulsory, health insurance funds, and by the second half of the century these local funds were spreading.

Dreiklassenwahlrecht, 107, 197. State harassment of the oppositional press worked in tandem with employers. Paul, *Krupp*, 274; M. Czapliński, "Presse" (1990), 20–37; 31–33.

[104] Mazura, *Entwicklung*, 66; Majunke SBDR 2 Dec. 1882: 600; Bellot, *Hundert Jahre*, 206, 214, 216; Kühne, *Dreiklassenwahlrecht*, 107; idem, "Elezioni," 60; E. Ernst, *Polizeispitzeleien* (1911), 40f, 46.

[105] Paul, *Krupp*, 245 (quote); Müller, *Geschichte*; Sperber, *Catholicism*, 246–49.

[106] Brentano, "Arbeitsverhältnis," 142; Möllers, *Strömungen*, 327, 330 (second quote). Workforce stability: Moore, *Injustice*, 268; Cf. also, Manchester, *Arms*, 170–72; v. Saldern, *Wege*, 59f. B. Menne, *Blood* (1938), 178, says that membership in Krupp's funds was compulsory; but as the firm's own election analysis shows (see below) at least by 1903 that was not the case.

By 1870, 550,000 such funds existed in Prussia (with cities having the right to compel employers to contribute); most of Bavaria's towns had also established them; and an estimated two-thirds of all German workers had some coverage. Moreover, guild tradition had accustomed workers to establishing mutual support funds (*freie Hilfskassen*) of their own—and membership in such a fund legally exempted them from joining compulsory municipal schemes, although some workers would enroll in both. By 1860, more than 400,000 people were enrolled in self-help funds in Prussia alone, 40 percent of them factory workers. Though these mutual funds were often so small as to be vulnerable to any major call on their resources, with the rise of trade unions, and especially after the funds became more centralized, their value expanded exponentially. From the first, Socialist, Centrum, and Polish newspapers had urged their readers not to patronize company-run plans but to set up their own.[107] In some cases, the newspapers themselves established insurance schemes. The publishing house of *Katolik*, for example, with its devoted following among Upper Silesians, established a life insurance program for its subscribers. Especially valued by women, the fund not only recruited new readers for the paper, but put starch in the subscriber's resistance to his boss on election day.[108] Although the funds of these friendly societies might be used to cover sickness, old age, strikes, travel, and eventually even unemployment (paying out more than eleven million marks to the unemployed in 1913), most important, for our purposes, was the fact that from the very beginning a small but significant portion, especially of union monies, was given out to the *"Gemaßregelte"*— those subscribers who were being punished by the authorities (private or public) for their political behavior.[109]

The impact of this network of insurance coverage—both self-help and (sometimes) compulsory and municipally regulated local funds—on the freedom of German elections has yet, to my knowledge, to be investigated in detail. What we do see is that by decoupling insurance benefits from the bread lord's favor, by providing emergency relief, and by facilitating geographic mobility, such coverage contributed to the worker's independence.[110] The landmark impe-

[107] Steinmetz, *Regulating*, 125f; Hartmut Zwahr, "Ausbeutung und gesellschaftliche Stellung des Fabrik- und Manufakturproletariats am Ende der Industriellen Revolution im Spiegel Leipziger Fabrikordnungen," in *Kultur und Lebensweise des Proletariats. Kulturhistorisch-volkskundliche Studien und Materialien*, edited by W. Jocobeit and U. Mohrmann (Berlin, 1973), 85–136; 100; Müller, *Geschichte*, 82f; Paul, *Krupp*, 167, 259f; G. A. Ritter, *Welfare* (1983), 77.

[108] Czapliński, "Presse," 31. As in the British labor movement, scandal and bankruptcy dogged these friendly societies, with their amateur bookkeepers and the lack of legal regulation. Examples from Catholic worker associations: H. Lepper, "Cronenberg," 57–148, esp. 100, 145, and more generally: Lepper, ed., *Katholizismus*; Ernst Thrasolt, *Eduard Müller. Der Berliner Missionsvikar. Ein Beitrag zur Geschichte des Katholizismus in Berlin, der Mark Brandenburg und Pommern* (Berlin, 1953), 205–8; from Social Democracy or funds close to them: Keil, *Erlebnisse* 1: 96; Bellot, *Hundert Jahre*, 186.

[109] Schönhoven, "Selbsthilfe," 156f, 174, 179, 180, 190; Tennstedt, *Sozialgeschichte*, 112f, 133, 232f; idem, Tennstedt, *Proleten*, 164, 220f, 302, 328f; Ritter, *Welfare*, 80f.

[110] Contrast Steinmetz, *Regulating*, 125 who argues that "eligibility for social insurance required

rial legislation of 1883 and 1889, establishing sickness and old-age insurance nationwide for certain kinds of industries, and putting all existing schemes—those of municipalities and communities (*Ortskrankenkassen* and *Gemein-dekrankenkassen*) as well as the *Freie Hilfskassen* run by workers—under state regulation, completed the edifice. Moreover, the umbrella of state-regulated insurance allowed the Socialists' own programs to survive, with slight name changes, during the era of the Socialist Law. As one-third of the funds in the state-regulated insurance plans came from the contributions of employers, the latter controlled one-third of the boards administering local funds. But two-thirds of these boards, thanks to the new legislation, were elected by the insured wage earners (including, after 1891, women wage earners). Union members and even Social Democrats soon held the majority of the seats. They used their (salaried!) positions on these state-regulated boards to dispense financial support for workers who had been disciplined or dismissed for political reasons—and at no cost to their own organizations.[111]

Finally, all of these insurance organizations together—communal, municipal, party, and worker-sponsored—amounted to an enormous job-creation project. Into the positions administering the funds flooded precisely those workers who had been fired and blacklisted for their political activity. Even an unskilled laborer could man the counters of the local insurance office, helping other workers fill out their forms or make their claims. ("And are you the deceased himself?" one conscientious functionary was reputed to have asked a client reporting a death.) At higher levels, the insurance bureaucracy provided its own "second *Bildungsweg*" for young, talented, and politically ambitious workers. This process of integrating political and trade-union activists into the social policy bureaucracy has been likened, for its unexpected, long-run political importance, to the introduction of manhood suffrage itself. Such blue-collar bureaucrats became the "non-commissioned officers of Social Democracy."[112]

The system of state-regulated funds had many deficiencies—not least their lack of provision for unemployment. But after the turn of the century, as Social Democrats began to sit on more and more city councils, a number of municipalities adopted a Belgian-inspired program of subsidizing the labor unions' own unemployment relief funds. By mid-1914, twenty-two cities contributed

---

that workers remain stably employed and make steady payments. . . . a powerful incentive against irregularities . . . from union activism and other forms of insubordination that risked firing and blacklisting, to blue Mondays."

[111] Good on all of this: Ritter, *Welfare*, 74–80; Schönhoven, "Selbsthilfe," 154, and 154n. 17. Sometimes, however, protesters alleged that local officials threatened withdrawing their (state) accident or old age insurance if they voted wrong. E.g., in 1912: 8 Hessen AnlDR (1912/13, 13/I, Bd. 16) DS 350: 290; 7 Gumb. AnlDR (1912/14, 13/I, Bd. 23) DS 1586: 3412; 14 Saxony AnlDR (1912/13, 13/I, Bd. 19) DS 718: 927. Criticism of insurance by SD: Tennstedt, *Proleten*, 289, 316, 322. But see also ibid., 323f, 326, 412, 424, 432, 436, 446, 486. Emphasizing the disempowering features of the insurance: Steinmetz, *Regulating*, 124–31.

[112] Quote: Tennstedt, *Sozialgeschichte*, 172, 180f, 233. These non-coms were sometimes resented by workers unable to live in such "sweet idleness." Bernhard Gehle (Munich) to Bülow, 4 Jan. 1907 BAB-L R1501/14697, Bl. 91–92v.

(usually 50 percent) to union unemployment insurance programs.[113] Other deficiencies in the state-regulated funds spurred the development of so-called "*Volksversicherung*," that is, privately owned and administered insurance for low-income clients. By 1910 one out of every nine Germans owned such a "*Volks*" insurance policy. In some regions the numbers were even higher: 50 percent of the Social Democrats and 64.7 percent of the trade-union members in Waldenburg (a district where intimidation of voters was at its worst) held such policies in 1913, according to an investigation carried out (nota bene) by the local SPD *election* club.

The "genuinely power-political" significance of the lowly insurance policy was recognized even by ordinary voters. One conservative soul recommended that any new Socialist Law be aimed at the SPD's insurance funds (*Cassenbestände*). Both Conservative agrarians and radicals within the SPD feared funds that might be administered independent of their control. Only after years of battling the SPD's leadership, which assumed that the advantages of establishing the party's own *Volks*-insurance would go to the Reform wing, were the unions finally able, in 1912, to establish a *Volksfürsorge* stock company, replacing the older sickness, old age, and burial societies.[114] Immediately conservatives suspected that the *Volksfürsorge* would seek to enroll agricultural laborers—and in so doing, bring Social Democracy to the countryside. The General *Landschaftsdirektor* of East Prussia and chairman of its regional life insurance fund, Wolfgang Kapp, who would later gain notoriety for his role in the ill-starred Kapp Putsch of 1920, appealed to the imperial government to forbid it! Significantly, Bethmann Hollweg, circumventing Kapp's supporters in the Prussian cabinet, deflected the request. Instead, the government put its authority behind the use of objective juridical, as opposed to political, criteria in approving insurance societies. As it turned out, events vindicated the predictions of the doomsayers on both Left and Right. The unions' *Volksfürsorge* did indeed encourage the economically dependent voter's political autonomy—as the Conservatives had predicted. But it also, as Socialist radicals feared, sped his integration into German society.[115]

Telling evidence of the role of independent insurance funds in helping to break the bread lord's control over the ballot box is provided by the contrasting outcomes of the 1903 elections in Essen and the Sixth Trier in the Saar. Both constituencies had recently lost their commanding industrialist. The Sixth Trier's Baron von Stumm had died in 1901. Friedrich Krupp, son of the canon king, had been hounded to suicide the following year, after the relentless exposures of his homosexuality by the Italian, Centrum, and especially the Social

[113] Steinmetz, *Regulating*, 202–13.

[114] A. Jädicke, Dresden-Plauen, to Bülow, 8 Jan. 1907, BAB-L R1501/14697, Bl. 118f. "Genuinely power-political," and much of my analysis, is from H. Trischler's excellent "Sozialreform" (1994), 618–33; quote: 624. The radicalization of workers *not* integrated into the union's insurance system is demonstrated in the otherwise reformist Munich SPD. Pohl, *Arbeiterbewegung*, 520.

[115] Trischler, "Sozialreform," 623, 625, 627–30.

Democratic presses.[116] In 1903, Social Democrats in Stumm's district captured a mere 170 of the 34,363 votes cast; in Krupp's stronghold, 22,773 Social Democratic voters appeared overnight.[117]

Essen was electrified. The Krupp management, stung by press reports that it was their workers who had supplied the new Socialist votes, launched an investigation. The result, a report that ran to nine pages of tiny print, was perhaps the first attempt at "electoral sociology" in German history.[118] The investigators' operating assumption was that, in a district roughly 60 percent Catholic, no Protestant worker would have voted for the Centrum and almost no Catholics would have voted for the "national" standard-bearer, a Protestant *pastor* (chosen, undoubtedly, to reestablish the national camp's moral image after the Krupp scandal). The National Liberals' own postelection investigation, by comparing the Protestant church's tax rolls with precinct lists recording who had voted, concluded that turnout among eligible Protestants in Essen proper had reached an amazing 94 percent.[119] After making calculations based on religion, employment, residential patterns, and population turnover since the last election in 1898, as well as changes in turnout at the precinct level, Krupp statisticians reluctantly admitted that it was conceivable, in their worst-case scenario, that somewhat more than one-quarter of Krupp's 17,000 eligible workers had voted Social Democrat.

Who or what was to blame? Exogenous insurance funds! That, at least, was management's conclusion. The largest of these funds was the Hamburg Universal Sickness and Death Benefit Fund for Metalworkers—a major, and now nationwide, Social Democratic institution. The 25 plus percent that was the firm's estimate of *Kruppianer* who might have voted Socialist was conspicuously identical, they pointed out, with the number of recent newcomers who had

[116] Menne, *Blood*, 208–14; Hall, *Scandal*, 178; v. Saldern, *Wege*, 67, 127. The SPD was also the guardian of heterosexual morality, forcing the resignation of the Z leader Julius Bachem in 1891 by exposing a paternity suit against him. Müller, *Strömungen*, 269.

[117] Although no SPD votes are listed in Essen for the previous election (1898) in Specht/Schwabe, *Reichstagswahlen*, this was because the (demonstrative) 4,429 votes cast for Ludwig Schröder, a leader of the Great Miner's Strike of 1889, were automatically invalid because Schröder had been convicted in the infamous Essen perjury trial and was ineligible. A preview of the 1903 RT elections had occurred in April, when the Free Unions narrowly outpolled the Christian Trade Unions for the first time in elections to the local industrial court (*Gewerbegericht*). "Ein Mene Tekel für die Reichstagswahlen," *Die Zeit* 2/28 (9 Apr. 1903): 33f. Although the Free Unions were commonly thought to be Socialist, W. Düwell, head of Essen's SPD, complained in 1902 that of its 2,500 members, only 362 belonged to the party. Bajohr, *Krupp*, 36. On the political significance of the *Gewerbegerichte*: Tennstedt, *Sozialgeschichte*, 199–210.

[118] "Die Kruppsche Arbeiterschaft und die Reichstagswahlen in Essen" (hereafter Krupp Report), BAB-L R1501/14696, Bl. 56–60. It is interesting to compare this document with the analysis of the SD constituency published two years later by Blank, "Zusammensetzung." A copy of the report was sent to Wm. II by Krupp's widow, Margarethe, on 29 Oct. 1903.

[119] Every citizen who earned more than 900 marks a year paid church taxes, and even SDs rarely withdrew from these rolls. Vernon Lidtke, "Social Class and Secularisation in Imperial Germany. The Working Classes," *Yearbook of the Leo Baeck Institute* 25 (1980): 21–40. Of these men, 78% had voted for Pastor Klingemann, which left 2,954 Protestant voters unaccounted for. They must have voted either Z (highly unlikely) or SPD. Krupp Report, BAB-L R1501/14696, Bl. 56–60.

chosen not to belong to the company's own insurance scheme. The argument demonstrated the link, at least in the Krupp official mind, between insurance and political conformity.[120]

The report also demonstrated that although the Essen family enterprise had become a corporation with Alfred's death in 1887, some things had not changed: neither the firm's desire to control the politics of its employees nor— oddly enough—its own almost apolitical parochialism. Even in the twentieth century, votes of *Kruppianer* seem to have concerned the firm only as a measure of its own authority. The actual results of the election, in terms of who got sent to the Reichstag, barely mattered. We can see this in what the firm described as its "worst-case" scenario: the possibility that 25 percent of its workforce had voted Social Democratic on the first ballot (*Hauptwahl*). But the very worst case, from the standpoint of *outcomes*, was what happened in the runoff—an election Krupp statisticians chose to ignore, because, they claimed disingenuously, "factors that didn't exist in the first election" (presumably the elimination of the "national" candidate) may have influenced its outcome. In the runoff, the Centrum picked up fewer than 4,000 new supporters, while the Social Democratic vote soared from 28 to 46 percent of the Essen electorate: a landslide of 10,000 additional votes. It hardly needed the refinements of Krupp statisticians to divine where *these* votes had come from. But the obvious conclusion, that about half of the obedient supporters of the "national" party in the first ballot had now thrown their votes behind Social Democracy, went unmentioned. Once the firm-backed candidate had been eliminated, how employees disposed of their votes—and who won the election—was a matter of indifference.[121]

If the Krupp firm's preoccupation with authority rather than with results provided an element of continuity between the era of canon king and the twentieth century, the methodology employed in its report revealed that a new political epoch had indeed dawned. Emblematic of the changes since Alfred's death was the fact that the 1903 report was entirely statistical. Not a single *Kruppianer* was interviewed; even those foremen whose political opinions were known to

---

[120] Cf. Heinz Reif, who argues that the use of welfare benefits for political purposes at Krupp began only after 1900: "'Ein seltener Kreis von Freunden.' Arbeitsprozesse und Erfahrungen bei Krupp 1840–1914" (1986), 541–91, cited in Bajohr, *Krupp*, 53.

[121] D. Fricke writes that on 29 Oct. 1903 the chairman of Krupp's board, Max Rötger, sent Bülow a 9-page printed report on the results of their own internal investigation into the SPD avalanche. Fricke "Imperialismus," 539. Fricke cites the document as Reichskanzlei Nr. 1792 fol. 93–99. This seems to be another copy, or perhaps an earlier *Signature*, of the same document that I saw in BAB-L R1501/14696, Bl. 56–60. Yet while Krupp "terror methods" were precisely what I was looking for, the document I saw contained nothing that would warrant the following characterization by Fricke: "The terror methods of monopoly capital entrepreneur-absolutism were propagated here and recommended for the struggle against the entire German working class"; so perhaps it is a different document. I have also seen no evidence that the report was prompted by the Imperial government. Excerpts from the Krupp report, or at least the version located in the archives of the Geh. Civil Cabinet, GStA PK I. HA, Rep. 89, have been printed in Boelcke, ed., *Krupp*, 117–20. The latter is the version to which Jaeger, *Unternehmer*, 92n. 300, refers.

be reliable seem not to have been queried about the politics of their subordinates. The report refers to no observations, no overheard conversations, none of the snooping that had been taken for granted under the old man. The sharp reduction in personal contact between the labor force and the men supervising them was part of a general move in German industry, in which the replacement of family ownership with corporate structures found its counterpart in the growing impersonality of supervision in general.[122] But how long could one expect the same rituals of political devotion from workers whose stern but personal Jehovah had now been replaced by a Deism of the slide rule?

[122] Spencer, *Management*, 88f.

CHAPTER NINE

Going by the Rules

> Whoever makes use of his legal right injures no one, and anyone who feels injured because of it is usually in the wrong.
>
> —*German proverb*

THE QUESTION of free elections has two aspects. The first concerns the individual and the degree to which he is able to cast his ballot as he chooses. It asks about the voting act itself. But freedom of choice requires the freedom to inform oneself about these choices, and the freedom to try to persuade others to join in support of that choice. Hence a second aspect of free elections concerns the campaign and often, the party. Since one of the main protections of the individual may be the party, the two aspects are intimately connected. Since individuals may sometimes feel as coerced by a party as by a bread lord or big man, the connections work in several directions. Although analytical clarity gains from considering separately these two requirements of electoral freedom—space for the individual and space for the campaign—the issues inevitably bleed into each other. Both are necessary to explain the successes of parties that were detested and harassed by the powerful. And the viability of parties is both a prerequisite for, and proves the existence of, genuine competitive elections—often described as the hallmark of democracy.[1]

So far we have looked at Germany's larger material structures—geographic and economic—in our search for the degrees of freedom within which voters moved. But another kind of structural parameter, a cultural one, proved at least as significant in establishing a zone of liberty during elections, even in regions where neither economy nor party could offer much support. Edward Thompson has written eloquently of the "sub-political" traditions that gave English plebeians the grit to assert their interests and call them rights. One such tradition Thompson located in the "robust and rowdy" riot, legitimized in the popular consciousness by unwritten laws about a moral economy; another, he found in the Bible-based, often millenarian, dissidence of dissent.[2] Neither of these traditions played a role in Germany: Protestantism in Central Europe lacked the fissiparous vitality of English nonconformity; and Imperial Germany (which, unlike Georgian England, was well and thoroughly policed) proved a hostile environment for the unruly of any sort. Yet Germans disposed of their own sub-

---

[1] Nohlen, *Wahlrecht*, esp. 18.
[2] E[dward] P. Thompson, *The Making of the English Working Class* (London, 1963), 59, 63–67.

political tradition, apparently the opposite of England's "rowdy" one, yet no less useful in providing a "purchase" for political dissent. This was a tradition of respect for Rules.

Germans consider themselves a legalistic tribe, insistent to a fault upon being in the right (*Rechthaberei*)—with right being defined, often as not, by the prescripts of some law, ordinance, or permit.[3] Certainly foreigners who have lived in the country for any length of time share this perception. Citizens of the Reich took pride in belonging to a *Rechtsstaat*. At a minimum, the word described a state governed according to fixed procedures that could be universally applied, binding the ruler as well as the ruled. Yet the word *Recht* denotes not only positive law, but also justice and right. This verbal identification of rules and regulations with justice (and vice versa) encouraged a fruitful ambiguity, and suggested that a rule's authority derived not only from its legal source (crown, parliament, God, etc.) but also, and perhaps even more powerfully, from the universality of its application. A willingness to "judicialize" conflict, which depends upon just such confidence in the universality of rules, has been traced in the German lands at least as far back as the eighteenth century.[4] Of course rules in Germany—like the Bible in England—were often transgressed in practice. But like the Bible invoked by English dissenters, the transcendent value of rules was something all levels of German society publicly and privately acknowledged. In Germany as in England, the strength of such a cultural tradition gave a powerful advantage—and enormous moral energy—to whomever could claim it for themselves.

The conviction that rules must be obeyed, sometimes cited as a fatal weakness in their political character, making Germans vulnerable to any established authority, could thus also have subversive consequences, for it established a logically consistent basis for resisting authority as well. Although union leaders and Social Democrats waxed sarcastic about German legality, the sarcasm was that of a neglected lover. Even the scornful became adept at making Germany's intricate web of rules and regulations work for them. Fat party "handbooks" instructed loyalists on the laws of speech and assembly, led them through the procedures to follow should they be arrested, told them how to put together an election protest.[5] A laborer in Flensburg voiced what would become a constant

---

[3] Poguntke, in his discussion of contemporary Germany in "Parties in a Legalistic Culture," gives no argument for the "legalistic culture's" existence: a taken-for-grantedness that is itself powerful evidence for my assertion.

[4] Schulze, "Resistance"; Peter Blickle, *Bäuerlicher Widerstand und feudale Herrschaft in der frühen Neuzeit* (Stuttgart/Bad Cannstatt, 1980).

[5] The Bavarian SPD's handbook (Landesvorstand der Sozialdemokratie Bayerns, *Handbuch für Sozialdemokratische Gemeindewähler* [Munich, 1908]), which includes a questionnaire by which members were to gather local statistics, is noteworthy for its objectivity and educational seriousness. The SPD also went so far as to publish a booklet defining the most important foreign phrases that had become part of the educated person's political lexicon. Other handbooks: *Konservatives Handbuch* (Berlin, 1892); *Ratgeber für Konservative im Deutschen Reich* (Leipzig, 1903); Paul Hirsch, ed., *Der preussische Landtag. Handbuch für sozialdemokratische Landtagswähler* (Berlin, 1903); Vorstand der Sozialdemokratischen Partei, *Handbuch für sozialdemokratische Wähler. Der*

election refrain: "The law is there in order to be followed, and even a single infraction against it suffices to make its effect or purpose illusory. . . ."[6] Whatever the Left's millenarian hopes for the *Zukunftsstaat*, it was on the *Rechtsstaat* that it put its money.

RULES OF THE GAME

How did this faith in the force of rules play itself out? First of all, voters conned the election codes, which the law required be displayed in each polling place. Great advantage was taken of § 9 of the Voting Law, which provided that proceedings be public. As early as 1871 Catholic priests were invoking § 9 to put polling places under surveillance, ready to protect their interests by reporting the slightest technical infraction or sign of "influence." By 1874 Poles in Thorn had set up a relay system, so that whenever one of their own partisans left the polling place, two others appeared in his stead.[7] In Berlin and Saxony, Socialists were also, by the mid-seventies, taking up their positions.

If the meaning of laws were transparent, societies would have no need of lawyers; if rules were self-acting, no need for courts. Germany's rules and laws were no exception in being open to interpretation. Thus we see, on the one hand, a gendarme in Hanover, confiscating ballots that named the legitimist (Guelf) candidate, but sheepishly returning them shortly thereafter, explaining that he had just learned from his superior officer that *this* was a *free* election. On the other hand, an agent for the Progressives who insisted on equal treatment among poll watchers in Kant's Königsberg, because "they all stood under the same laws and every one had to respect them," found himself thrown out by a policeman exclaiming "Ach! What law! It's only a matter here of what is decent and in order!"[8] Concern for what was "decent and in order" led some chairmen to forbid the taking of notes; others to chase poll watchers away with fire hoses; others, unable to master the activists, to shut the polls down altogether.[9]

Those in authority had every intention of intimidating, and no law could prevent them if none were fearless enough to invoke the law. Whatever the

---

Reichstag. 1907–1911 (Berlin, 1911); *Handbuch der Deutsch-Konservativen Partei* (Berlin 4th ed., 1911). By 1912 only the Z had not produced such a handbook. L. Bergsträsser, "Geschichte" (1912), 248.

[6] H. Mahlke et al., Protest of Worker Election Committee of Flensburg, 27 Apr. 1887, BAB-L R1501/14664, Bl. 8. Arndt (FK): "Our legal system is acknowledged everywhere, as anyone who has ever lived abroad knows." SBDR 13 Feb. 1913: 4744, clipped and filed in BAB-L R1501/14460, Bl. 441; v. Saldern, *Wege*, 69f; Mallmann/Steffens, *Lohn*, 78f. Contrast Witt, "Landrat," esp. 218.

[7] AnlDR (1871, 1/II, Bd. 2) DS 38: 94f, 98f; A. v. Donimirsky on 4 Marienwerder: SBDR 10 Apr. 1874: 710.

[8] Gendarme: Graf v. Rittberg SBDR 28 Mar. 1871: 25; 3 Königsberg (1879, 4/II, Bd. 6) DS 232: 1526f (quote); also 17 Han. AnlDR (1877, 3/I, Bd. 3) DS 138: 392. Cf. Hall, "Means."

[9] O. Reimer (Lassallean) and v. Donimirski (P) SBDR 10 Apr. 1874: 696, 710; 8 Kassel AnlDR (1877, 3/I, Bd. 3) DS 68: 270.

regulations said, in practice every right had to be fought for, on the ground, by voters and partisans themselves. A poll watcher needed grit to stand up to bullies—those on the panel as well as the self-appointed or privately employed (i.e., other poll watchers hanging about). Scuffles could break out if a poll watcher tried to collect samples of an employers' distinctive ballots in order to buttress a postelection challenge. The laborer Ernst Girod, accosted by both a gendarme and an estate owner, the latter waving his cane and yelling, "You snotty kid, you have absolutely no business here!" retorted with a *sang froid* that only a knowledge of the rules could give: "I have the same right to stand here as you."[10]

Both sides were aware that these confrontations might result in an election's invalidation, and many big men were convinced that their antagonists were trying to provoke them into ill-considered exercises of authority—an insight that did not prevent them from rising to the provocation. Volumes of protests convey the same election-day picture: hundreds of skinny, insistent little men, fanning out all over Germany, election law in hand, pointing to paragraphs, demanding their rights, being frog-marched to the door, often as not thrown down the stairs—but repeating their demands undeterred, returning with a court order, and ultimately exciting sympathy rather than contempt from onlookers.[11] They came from every party, but Polish and Socialist poll watchers suffered the worst treatment, often being jailed for weeks on the flimsiest of excuses. No wonder that in some, perhaps most, election districts poll watchers were paid by their parties for their pains.[12] The SPD usually fetched theirs from far away, so as to relieve economically vulnerable locals from the burden of confrontation. Characteristically the man would present a printed slip to the panel, which described him as authorized by his party to observe the election (and spared him from having to search for words of his own under trying circumstances). Like as not he would be met with the argument that only those eligible to vote in that particular *precinct* were ever "authorized" inside its polling place. He would then be forced to cast about—usually in the tavern—for some local whom he could pay to observe and report back to him.[13] Many of the emissaries

---

[10] 7 Gumb. AnlDR (1912/14, 13/I, Bd. 23) DS 1586: 3428, 3430. Rowdies employed by K: 19 Saxony AnlDR (1884/85, 6/I, Bd. 7) 327: 1785.

[11] Examples from 1877 to 1912, ranging from the regencies of Marienwerder, Gumbinnen, Köslin, Stralsund, Magdeburg, Merseburg, Erfurt, Schleswig-Holstein, Leipzig countryside, Minden, and Kassel to the cities of Flensburg, Harburg, Hörde, Lübeck, and Munich, are too numerous to cite. E.g., the puny Aug. Schmidt, tobacco worker, 8 Magdeburg AnlDR (1881/82, 5/I, Bd. 2) DS 91: 333–36; similarly, in Dorstfeld: Heinrich Boecker, shopkeeper, 6 Arns., AnlDR (1894/95, 29/III, Bd. 2) DS 354: 1495; note-taking: RP d'Haussonville to MdI, Köslin, 4 Aug. 1892, BAB-L R1501/14668, Bl. 42; Worker Party member [signature missing] to Daßbach (SD), Praunheim, 15 Mar. 1890 on 8 Kassel BAB-L R1501/14668: Bl. 215f.

[12] Reimer and Donimirski SBDR 10 Apr. 1874: 696, 710. A paid K pollwatcher, threatened by Liberals: 7 Gumb. AnlDR (1912/14, 13/I, Bd. 23) DS 1586: 3438, 3440.

[13] 1 Württ. AnlDR (1894/95, 9/III, Bd. 2) DS 268: 1144–54 in BAB-L R1501/14691 unpaginated. Also Reimer SBDR 10 Apr. 1874: 697; LR of Penneberg, in 17 Han. SBDR 13 May 1878: 485.

who took on these chores were too young to vote themselves, and some no doubt were looking for trouble. Perhaps also a poll watcher had an interest, as a court once ruled, in "showing his power position [*Machtstellung*] as the envoy of Social Democracy." But officially the SPD instructed its branches to avoid these problems by sending "only completely reliable, calm, and sober men," at least twenty-five years old (voting age), and with identification to prove it.[14]

Most of the altercations ostensibly revolved around who, according to § 9, constituted the "public." As early as 1869, spokesmen for the imperial government had described as "axiomatic" the admission of *any* eligible voter to any polling place.[15] Such was the logic of a nonterritorially based, *national* parliament, whose every deputy was constitutionally bound to represent not only his own constituents but the "people as a whole." But it took two decades before the Reichstag would consistently define the "public" that § 9 authorized to observe the polling this broadly. Then in the early 1890s the deputies, supported by the Berlin Supreme Court, ruled that every eligible voter, regardless of where he was registered, was admissible as a poll watcher anywhere in Germany. The subsequent spate of Reichstag-ordered "rectifications" and "censures" (*Rügen*) of local and county officials who had tried to keep back the army of unwelcome sentries increased accordingly.[16] In 1892 the Reichstag's criterion was reinforced by ministerial decree.[17] Eventually election overseers were denied the authority even to require that someone desiring entry as poll watcher first prove that he was an eligible voter, a German citizen, or even an adult. Wilhelm Hasenclever had once demanded to know "why, if elections are to be public, if every human being really can be on hand there, should he then still have to produce a [document of] legitimation? One can see that he is a human being simply by looking at his face." Hasenclever had at last been vindicated. Although the designation "human being" obviously still did not include women and children, who were *visibly* ineligible to vote, it did put the burden of proof on the chairman to show why an otherwise plausible person should not be admitted. And even when tight space justified restrictions on the number of observers, no applicant could be excluded on the basis of his party affiliation

[14] *Thätigkeit*, 136f; RP v. Heydebrand u. d. Lasa to IM Herrfurth, on 9 Königsberg (Allenstein), 6 Oct. 1890, BAB-L R1501/14666, Bl. 34f.

[15] SBNDR, 13 May 1869: 978; Hatschek, *Kommentar*, 172. Ironically, in Prussian LT elections, where voting was oral, everyone but eligible voters were to be excluded from the polling place—on the grounds that the proceedings were not public! IM to SM (in Vertretung, Herrfurth), 13 Aug. 1884; Maybeck, Votum, 19 Aug. 1884; Bötticher, Votum . . . , 1 Sept. 1884; Bronsart v. Schellendorff, Votum, 13 Sept. 1884; Fin. Min. (Vertretung), 17 Sept. 1884; Gossler, 3 Oct. 1884, GStA PK I. HA, Rep. 90a, A.VIII.1.d., Nr. 1/Bd. 5.

[16] Strafsenat . . . , 3 Nov. 1890, BAB-L R101/3343, Bl. 176–180v; SBDR 18 Mar. 1892: 4841; AnlDR (1890/92, 8/I, Bd. 2) DS 169: 1224, DS 184: 1382; (1890/92, 8/I, Bd. 6) DS 707: 3858. Memo from 13 Jun. [1892] BAB-L R1501/14668: Bl. 11; AnlDR (1894, 9/II, Bd. 2) DS 217: 1147; SBDR 1 May 1900: 5174; Hatschek, *Kommentar*, 172, 174.

[17] Ministerial Erlaß of 18. July 1892, cited as a warning in [Köller], *Ungiltigkeit*, 28. Enforcement can be traced in Mem. of 13 June 1892, and in Hanic (of the MdI) to the Chancellor, 11 July 1892, BAB-L R1501/14668, Bl. 11, 14.

without jeopardizing the validity of the whole contest. Although even in the empire's last election, some poll watchers were still being thrown out, the consequences for the respective elections' validity were severe.[18]

The movement toward guarding election purity through party-appointed poll watchers was an international one. Nevertheless, Germany was in advance of both Belgium, which allowed no party representatives, only voters, to observe the voting, and Hungary, which allowed delegates of a party, but not voters themselves.[19] Although they were not as advantaged as the Americans, who were admitted inside the guardrail surrounding the panel, German poll watchers enjoyed more privileges than their British counterparts, who were forced, whatever the weather, to stand outdoors. The way was being prepared for the Weimar Republic, where "party checkers" were given officially designated space inside the polls, a sign not just of the legitimacy, but of the hegemony, of "party" in German political life.[20]

The scrutiny of a poll watcher always raised the possibility of a postelection challenge. And here German law, in making the accuracy of elections a *public* matter, protected and paid for by the state, rather than (as in Anglo-American norms) the concern merely of the loser, to be investigated out of his own pocket, had consequences. Parties were quick to make use of the protest mechanism. Along the Ruhr and Rhine, newspaper announcements preceded every election, asking voters to report to their party immediately if they discovered "anything at all untoward."[21] Quickly there developed a culture of complaint. At first plebeian challengers framed their protests too loosely, without names and dates, and found them almost invariably rejected for insufficient evidence. But they soon learned from their mistakes.[22] Of course not all protesters were plebeian. Those willing to use pressure to influence a vote did not shrink from using pressure to get signatures for election protests of their own. After the obscure Eduard Müller defeated the Duke of Ratibor, his neighbor, the Prince of Pless, was determined to get to the bottom of it. It was the prince's police investigation into Sunday sermons that had triggered the controversies in 1871 over

---

[18] Hasenclever SBDR 13 May 1878: 487. A. Heine (SD) SBDR 13 Jun. 1890: 319; P. Spahn (Z) 1 May 1890: 5177f; AnlDR (1897/98, 9/V, Bd. 3) DS 286: 2368; AnlDR (1907/09, 12/I, Bd. 14) DS 253: 1267f; *Thätigkeit*, 144–48, esp. 145; Hatschek, *Kommentar*, 172–74.

[19] Granville Survey Nr. 1 (Apr. 1881), BAB-L R1501/14451, Bl. 46–49.

[20] Hatschek, *Kommentar*, 174. England and (Weimar) Germany compared: Pollock, *Administration*, 34; America: Seymour/Frary, *World* 1: 256. Scuffle between Z and NL pollwatchers: "Ein Saarabisches Wahlbild," *Saar-Post* Nr. 20, 25 Jan. 1912, in AnlDR (1912/14, 13/I, Bd. 23) DS 1639: 3609.

[21] Mining Director E. Kleine (NL) SBDR 11 Feb. 1888: 845 (quote); *Mülheimer Anzeiger* (Z) 17 (30 Sept. 1879): in Müller, *Strömungen*, 126f; Z handbill reprinted in Nettmann, "Witten in den Reichstagswahlen" (1972), 253; examples in *Volksboten* 16/25 Feb. 1888: Tenfelde, *Sozialgeschichte*, 567n. 358; the Socialist proclamation in 1878: Steinbach, *Zähmung* 2: 683.

[22] Insufficiencies in SD Protest on 2 Düsseldorf (Elberfeld-Barmen) AnlDR (1882/83, 5/II, Bd. 6) DS 263: 970; 13 pages of detailed, largely statistical information in Protest of Karl Schön in Heilbronn (SD) vs. 3 Württ., 9 Mar. 1887: BAB-L R1501/14691 unpaginated.

clerical influence, led to the overthrow of the Pleß-Rybnik election, and became, as we have seen, one of the catalysts for the Pulpit Paragraph. But later a penitent village headman, Freeholder Pudelko, confessed that his testimony against his pastor had been squeezed out of him (*"ausgequetscht"*)—a proceeding that he described as an "Inquisition by the Prince Pless Secret Election-Police" (*"Fürstliche Plessische Geheim Wahlpolizei-Inquisition"*). More subtle was the technique used by Berlin Progressives who inveigled the wives and daughters of workers to sign a petition against the election of Hasenclever, by showing them voting lists from which their men's names had been accidentally left off. The men themselves then signed the Socialists' counterpetition, vowing that, *had* they been admitted to the polls, they surely *would* have voted for Hasenclever. Which of the two sets of signatures had been extorted by the greatest pressure was anybody's guess.[23] But it is impossible to dismiss all protests as products of pressure rather than conviction. For we have cases like that of the stalwart voter of Baden's Gutach who, when his precinct was reported as having unanimously returned a National Liberal, was prepared to swear that he, at least, had voted Centrum—thus making public his deviance from all 160 of his neighbors.[24]

The SPD's handbooks devoted pages to the art of putting together an accurate and respectable challenge. Quite responsibly, the party tried to lead its constituents away from preoccupation with purely formal infractions ("details"), which, it said, "overburdened" the Election Commission and made its business "uncommonly more difficult," but which changed few results.[25] In practice, however, local activists were sticklers for the letter of the law, not hesitating to challenge even a ballot on which a voter had crossed out the SPD candidate's name and written in someone else's, especially when the latter's name lacked an identifying occupation, a title, or a first name. When their loss was a close one, Socialists went through the voting lists with a fine-tooth comb, insisting on the exclusion of anyone who had *ever* undergone bankruptcy proceedings; anyone with *any* mental or psychological disability; *any* youth even a month underage (although their own platform called for lowering the voting age to eighteen); *every* suspected foreigner (however long he might have resided in Germany) who could not produce citizenship papers in perfect order. The party of Social Democracy did not scruple to interpret "poor relief" as broadly as possible in order to demand that every recipient of any form of public assistance, even including schoolbooks for his children, be struck from the rolls. No

---

[23] Pudelko quoted by T. Schröder (Z) SBDR 22 Nov. 1871: 434. On 6 Berlin AnlDR (1877, 3/I, Bd. 3) DS 93: 322, 324. Other wives allegedly pressured to put down their three crosses: testimony of Johann Seidel et al., 9 Königsberg, Sept. 1890, BAB-L R1501/14666, Bl. 25–33. Fear of reprisals for protest: 9 Han. AnlDR (1874, 2/I, Bd. 3) DS 118: 399.

[24] 5 Baden AnlDR (1878, 3/II, Bd. 3) DS 124: 973–75; WPK report passed without discussion: SBDR 2 May 1877: 990.

[25] *Thätigkeit*, 134–45, quotes: 135; Vorstand der Sozialdemokratischen Partei, *Handbuch für Sozialdemokratische Wähler* (1911), 751–58; instructional brochures exposing their opponents' dirty tricks: Müller, *Geschichte*, 155.

matter that the effect of their exclusions was plainly undemocratic. By eliminating voters, the size of the absolute majority would be reduced, the likelihood the election would be thrown out for a minor infraction, increased. In 1912, for example, the SPD brought down their most famous opponent, General Eduard von Liebert, chairman of the "Imperial League Against Social Democracy," by getting so many names of poor voters struck from his district's lists that the general, seeing the handwriting on the wall, resigned in anticipation of the impeachment that surely awaited him.[26]

The efficacy of such legalism did not depend upon the Reichstag's overturning every election credibly charged with impropriety. As we have seen, the deputies took a philosophical view of formal infractions; as one member put it, if they threw out every election in which there were problems, there wouldn't be any deputies left.[27] As in every parliament with the prerogative of election oversight, standards changed with shifts in its own political composition. Even when the personnel on the Election Commission remained stable, each case was so circumstantial that in any given instance the outcome was unpredictable—as one high imperial official concluded despairingly at the end of his sixty-four-page analysis of a decade of Reichstag election rulings.[28] Nor did his opponents' knowledge of the possibility of protest guarantee a voter's freedom. A lengthy survey of the Election Commission's decisions at the close of the century revealed little change in the manner and frequency of undue influence and other blemishes during the three decades since the introduction of the franchise.[29]

Yet if its *direct* influence on the composition of the Reichstag was small, the protest mechanism was not useless. It informed the public of abuses of power. It provided a forum for the articulation of oppositional interpretations of the law. Most important, the stipulation that the Reichstag itself validate each election and review every single alleged infraction, although the despair of jurists, gave dignity not only to the complaints, but to the plaintiffs. Moreover, the process of soliciting and then pursuing complaints solidified the personal connection between the voter and the party of his choice, especially important when preexisting social networks were slight. Thus when Adam Schaub, master woodworker, reported his dismissal for voting Socialist to an SPD agent in 1890, he didn't expect his protest to overturn the victory or to get his job back. But he did want, Schaub said, his party to "make the matter quite clear and make a beautiful poem out of it and let it appear in the newspaper, and send a

---

[26] 14 Saxony AnlDR (1912, 13/I, Bd. 19) DS 718: 924f, 928–30; counterprotest of Eduard v. Flottwell, Kapitan a. D.: 932–34. On Liebert: Chickering, *We Men* (1984), 85, 128, 182n. 149, 221, 244; Marilyn Sheven Coetzee, *The German Army League. Popular Nationalism in Wilhelmine Germany* (New York, 1990), 96f. Other SD protests against poor relief recipients: 16 Saxony: SBDR 10 Jan. 1889: 373; 1 Berlin AnlDR (1912/13, 13/I, Bd. 17) DS 450: 415.

[27] SBDR 11 Apr. 1874: 718; see also E. Banks (F) SBDR 10 Apr. 1874: 691.

[28] Poschinger Report, Feb. 1879, BAB-L R1501/14450.

[29] Bericht der Wahlprüfungskommission über die Ergebnisse der Wahlprüfungen in der neunten Legislaturperiode von 1893 bis 1898, in *Reichstags-Wahlgesetz*, 77–86.

few of the papers to me so that I can distribute them, *so that society is ashamed of itself.*"[30] (Emphasis added.)

When society is capable of being "ashamed of itself," the postelection challenge becomes a political and organizational weapon in its own right. Even parties that had come in a poor third could force an investigation.[31] The ensuing publicity would then become the opening salvo of its next election campaign, aimed at mobilizing voters, organizing workers, and educating citizens.[32] When charging employer pressure, the election challenge constituted war by other means. The SPD's very first victory in the Arnsberg regency, the heart of the Ruhr, occurred in the wake of a storm of damaging publicity over the behavior of National Liberal employers during the two preceding contests, publicity that had led to the invalidation of one and the victor's resignation in the other.[33]

A protesting party also hoped that by publicizing election outrages—and the accompanying poems and stories so dear to their supporters' hearts—they might provoke a libel action on the part of the offender. In 1903, for example, a chief figure in the Saar mining industry, Geheimrat Ewald Hilger, filed suit against Ludwig Lehnen, editor of the Centrum's *Neunkirchener Zeitung*. The result was a veritable show trial on bread lord intimidation. Every election since 1890 in which Saar miners and metalworkers had been pressured by their employers was now rehashed in public—with witnesses under oath. When the state mining budget came up for a vote in the Prussian House of Deputies, the election testimony was dragged out again, provoking a two-day debate. Although the court declined to hold Hilger responsible for the actions of his predecessors or subordinates, it accepted as proven the massive spying, denunciations, and intimidation waged by the industry. No sooner was the Hilger-Lehnen trial finished than a second libel trial commenced, this time by the bosses against the miners' union (the *Bergarbeiterverband*), which allowed the defendants to expand their original testimony about election pressure to include industrial black-listing. The outcome was the same as the Hilger-Lehnen trial: legal victory—and a political black eye—for the mining industry. Black eyes had consequences that went beyond the cosmetic. During the 1907 election, speakers at every Liberal rally in the Saar felt compelled to affirm the workers' right to organize. The two campaigns, to defend the voter's franchise and to expand the worker's freedom of association and right to unionize, became mutually reinforcing.[34] Most important was the shift in public opinion that these

---

[30] And "Gruß an Koleg Geck," the deputy for whom Schaub lost his job. Adam Schaub to [Wm.] Birckle [? elsewhere spelled Brürkli] on 8 Kassel [n.d., 1890], BAB-L R1501/14668, Bl. 236. Another letter from protesters to party: Wallensen, 2 Mar. 1890, to SD, BAB-L R1501/14668, unnumbered enclosure with protest against 9 Hanover.

[31] E.g., the SD protest against 11 Breslau: AnlDR (1881/82, 5/I, Bd. 2) DS 104: 353–56. Forced investigation: Saxe-Coburg-Gotha's 7-page report in answer to a SD protest. Von Wittney to Bis., 29 Aug. 1888, BAB-L R1501/14685, unpaginated.

[32] So v. Koscielski (P) boasted in the debate on the Rickert Bill: SBDR 15 Jan. 1890: 1027.

[33] Suval, *Politics*, 216f says that the election was invalidated, but Specht/Schwabe, *Reichstagswahlen*, 144, notes that he resigned 25 Feb. 1893, two months before his term expired.

[34] Bellot, *Hundert Jahre*, 107, 214–17, 221, 223–26, citing SBHA 12 and 13 Feb. 1904. The

libel actions implied. For if making free with an employee's vote was not only legal, but also the legitimate prerogative of a bread lord—what was libelous about saying that he had done so?

DEFEATING THE SOCIALIST LAW

The ability of dissenting groups to exploit Germany's legalistic culture helps explain why so many voters were willing to brave their economic and social superiors to cast ballots for them. But what happened when laws themselves were fashioned to prevent their acquiring such supporters? Attempts to create "legal exceptions" to universal rules (*Ausnahmegesetze*) were not insignificant in Imperial Germany: much of the Kulturkampf as well as the government's campaign against the Socialists was based on nothing else. But "legal exceptions" were held in bad odor by everyone; nothing embarrassed those pragmatists who wanted to get the job done more than to hear the label "*Ausnahmegesetze*" applied to their policies. We have already looked at one example of such targeted legislation in chapter 4: the Pulpit Paragraph of 1871, designed to restrict campaigning of the Catholic clergy. Based upon a hopelessly artificial distinction between a priest's spiritual and his personal authority, the Pulpit Paragraph, as we saw, proved unenforceable.

More effective was the law passed, under duress, by the Reichstag in October 1878 and renewed biannually until September 30, 1890: the so-called "Socialist Law," aimed at putting the Social Democrats out of business. Socialist partisans had always suffered harassment, but before 1878 it had been uncoordinated. After 1878 they faced a national interdict on their clubs, meetings, and publications. Between 1878 and 1888, the law was used to shut down 78 local and 17 central trade-union organizations, 20 local and 3 central workers' insurance societies, and 106 political and 108 social organizations. The party's cash assets were confiscated and further contributions were prohibited. Pub owners and booksellers were forbidden to make their establishments available to them.[35] Jail terms were issued amounting to at least 1,000 years. Approximately 900 persons were sent into domestic exile. The Berlin party, with 293 expulsions, was particularly hard hit. It responded by turning the expulsions into occasions for spectacular demonstrations, appearing en masse at the train station to see their condemned comrades off. When police drove them from the waiting room, they countered by buying tickets themselves, their great numbers (in the hundreds) forcing the railway to hitch up additional cars, greatly delaying the departure of

---

immediate charges related to a LT election, but the system was the same. Cf. also the libel action against Johannes Fusangel by two pit foremen in the eighties: Wacker, *Rechte*, 21f; and Mazura, *Entwicklung*, 97, 100. Suits for libel and slander between candidates: *BT* 41/12 (8 Jan. 1912).

[35] E.g., 8 Magdeburg AnlDR (1884/85, 6/I, Bd. V) DS 91: 343f; Singer SBDR 29 Nov. 1888: 62–64. Lidtke, *Party*, Appendix C, 229–45 has a translation of the law.

the victims.[36] It was probably this well-publicized incident that prompted Lenin's famous quip that if, in the midst of revolution, the German Social Democrats ever decided to storm the railway, they would line up and buy platform tickets first. But the legalism that Lenin mocked proved to be Social Democracy's power and its glory. The growth of the Social Democratic electorate under the Socialist Law demonstrated the self-defeating nature of a "rule" designed to apply to only one case, and the futility of "exceptional legislation" within a culture that prided itself upon its rules' universal application. Let us examine how.

Initially the Socialist Law seemed a death blow to any hopes for a significant Socialist Reichstag representation.[37] Would a ballot cast for an outlawed party itself be outlawed? voters wondered. But injunctions, once written down, take on a clarity that their authors can rarely imagine; the very act of excluding some options, enables others. As one Breslau comrade remarked: "Every law and every ordinance has a back door."[38] The German governments now found themselves hoist by Bismarck's own antiparty petard. Hating political parties as he did, the chancellor's election code had ignored their reality, referring only to voters and deputies. His constitution had gone even further toward undermining parties by declaring, in Article 29, that every deputy was a representative of "the whole people." The result of this pointed denial, in the constitution and election code, of any legal standing to parties (a denial that continued in the constitution of the Weimar, but not of the Federal, Republic) was that the door to the Reichstag remained open to any citizen eligible to vote, even an adherent of a party under legal quarantine, since parties were "invisible" to the election law. Similarly, any voter, even a Socialist, could compete as a candidate to represent "the whole people."

Once elected, Socialists, like any deputy, enjoyed the protections of parliamentary immunity. Previous arrests and ongoing trials could be suspended for the duration of the session by a simple vote of the plenum. And it is revealing of the strong parliamentary culture that asserted itself from the very first days of the empire that the deputies did not hesitate to pass the necessary suspensions, even on behalf of their bitterest political enemies. The Liberal-dominated Reichstag did this for Centrum defendants during the height of the Kul-

---

[36] Ernst, *Polizeispitzeleien*, 6, 47. Previous harassment: e.g., in Braunschweig: *HZtg* Nr. 104, Beilage I, 5 May 1871, unpaginated. Pubs and booksellers: 8 Magdeburg AnlDR (1884/85, 6/I, Bd. V) DS 91: 343f; Singer SBDR 29 Nov. 1888: 62–64.

[37] § 28, paragraph 1 added: "This limitation [on meetings] does not extend to meetings called for the purposes of an announced election to the Reichstag or to the diets of the states." However, according to Fhr. v. Marschall, Baden's delegate to the Bundesrat, a motion by the Z *Hospitant* Bruël to declare § 9 of the Socialist Law inapplicable to election rallies was rejected. Marschall SBDR 13 Nov. 1889: 283.

[38] The comrade turned out, however, to be an agent provocateur. Müller, *Geschichte*, 70, 160f. Reinhard Koselleck has demonstrated this "*Paradox des Gesetzwerkes*" for an earlier period in "Staat und Gesellschaft in Preußen 1815–1848," in W. Conze, ed., *Staat und Gesellschaft im deutschen Vormärz 1815–1848* (Stuttgart, 1970), 79–112.

turkampf; the Left-and-Centrum dominated Reichstag did it for the antisemites during the nineties; and majorities in every Reichstag did it for the Social Democrats, even during the period of greatest government persecution. "With what touching care the good Windthorst looked out that not a hair on their dear heads was mussed," a conservative citizen gibed, "and how the stern Richter did thunder if ever, from some oversight, one small hair actually did occasionally get ruffled!" Once they had gained the Reichstag floor, the banned Socialists could proselytize to advantage—for every word spoken in parliament, every figure of speech, however incendiary, was constitutionally protected. A newspaper that would ordinarily have faced the public prosecutor might safely retail the boldest message by the simple expedient of quoting from a Reichstag debate—since the speeches were recorded by stenographers, at public expense.[39]

Of course not all Socialists sat in parliament, sometimes (but rarely) the Reichstag did allow the prosecution of its deputies,[40] and a deputy could be tried whenever the Reichstag was not in session. But even outside parliament the degree of cross-party cooperation is surprising. In Hamburg, bourgeois Progressives formed committees to raise money for the families of 65 men who had been expelled from their metropolis under the Socialist Law, and collected 8,200 marks within the first 6 days. The Centrum's irrepressible deputy for Lippstadt, Theodor Schröder, and its Posnanian-born Karl Eusebius Bernard Stephan, who represented an Upper Silesian constituency, were celebrated defense lawyers for Breslauers prosecuted under the Socialist Law. When Socialists were convicted (which wasn't inevitable), they used the appeal system (*Instanzenweg*) against high-handed local officials, occasionally with success. The harder the authorities tried to enlist the legal system for political ends, the worse the result. In 1889, after a year of preparation, thousands of pages of documents, and a list of 470 witnesses, Prussian prosecutors in Elberfeld launched a spectacular trial of 90 Social Democrats, including their popular and respected leader, August Bebel. The result was a "catastrophe" for the state. Forty-three of the men were acquitted outright, and the hostile publicity raining down on their antagonists was more precious, for the party, than money.[41]

---

[39] Quote: Von Oppen, *Reform*, 5–7. During the 9th LP (1893–98) alone, by my count the RT passed motions to suspend trials on 26 occasions for SDs, on 14, for Antisemites, on 2 occasions for FKs (private libel actions), and once each for members of the K, Alsatians, P, Z, VP, LLs, and Bavarian Farmers' League. Prussia's bill to limit speech in the RT—specifically aimed at SDs, without which, Bismark believed the Socialist Law would be crippled—was severely modified in the BR and then instantly defeated in the RT. H. v. Poschinger, *Bismarck* (1897–1901) 4: 35–40.

[40] E.g., a lèse majesté case in 1899: BAB-L R101/3386, Bl. 187–202.

[41] Kutz-Bauer, *Arbeiterschaft*, 308, also 398, 427f. Schröder-Lippstadt: Müller, *Geschichte*, 93–95. Show trial aspects: H. Asmus, "Entwicklung" (1982), 315. The SD's reference to the simultaneous Z protest against the Dortmund election shows clear signs of collaboration. 6 Arns., Anlage 4, AnlDR (1890/91, 8/I, Bd. 3) DS 292: 2055. Similarly disastrous trials in 1896 and 1903: Hall, *Scandal*, 51f, 56f.

THE POWER OF "ELECTION TIME"

But how was a party under legal ban able to recruit enough voters to get candidates elected to the Reichstag in the first place? By exploiting the unique legal protections of "election time" (*Wahlzeit*), the official period between the *Bundespräsidium*'s announcement of new elections and the proclamation of the winners. During election time, the complex web of rules and regulations governing elections (the *Wahlrecht* and *Wahlreglement*) overrode the claims of all other legislation, lifting candidates, their agents, and their supporters out of the Socialist Law's grasp. Thanks to a series of decisions by the Reichstag and the high courts, during election time any indoor meeting or rally—so long as its conveners named it an election assembly—was *prima facie* legal, regardless of the political affiliation of its sponsors or speakers. The normal requirement that "political" associations deliver a list of their officers to the police within two weeks of forming was suspended—during election time.[42]

A virtual time-out, called on behalf of all participants, "election time" was the salvation of the Social Democrats. The freedom to campaign was buttressed even further by § 17, an amendment to the Voting Law submitted from the floor during the last days of the 1869 session and passed without debate. § 17 declared that anyone who was eligible to vote had the right to prepare for elections by forming district-wide organizations ("election committees" and "election clubs"). The effect of this article on the freedom to campaign, and on freedom of association in general, is incalculable. In Mecklenburg-Schwerin, for example, state law required permission at the *ministerial* level for any political gathering, allowing the grand-ducal government to exclude any political party it considered *non grata* from its realm. But Reichstag threats to invalidate any Mecklenburg election where the government had failed to honor § 17 eventually forced this most reactionary of German states to amend drastically its own Law of Association—in order to conform with the Imperial Voting Law.[43] Although the Reichstag's quarrel with Mecklenburg-Schwerin had been provoked by the travails of the Left Liberals, § 17's greatest beneficiary was Social Democracy. The mere word "*election*" in front of an activity provided a shield of immunity. By the simple expedient of changing its name from "Socialist Worker Committee" to "Worker *Election* Committee," for example, a branch of

---

[42] Limburg-Stirum, Envoy to Weimar, to SM v. Bülow, June 1878, BAB-L R1501/14450, Bl. 100–101. Schmidt, Liebknecht, Rickert SBDR 8 Jan. 1886, Spahn, 13 Jan. 1886: 422, 426, 428, 430, 494. Edg. Loening, "Vereins- und Versammlungsfreiheit," in *Handwörterbuch der Staatswissenschaften* (Jena 3rd ed., 1911) 8: 152–71, esp. 165.

[43] Related in the voluminous correspondence set in motion by the complaints of a journalist and circuit-rider for the F, W. Buddi of Güstrow, to the RKA, 17 Apr. 1890; RKA to Meck.-Schwerin's AA, 2 May 1890, their reply to Caprivi, 9 Jun. 1890; C. to Buddi, 26 Mar. 1891, BAB-L R1501/14693, Bl. 258–60; 281–91; 339–343. Difficulties in determining the extent to which § 17 restricted the govt.: IM v.d. Recke to Hohenlohe, 19 Feb. 1897, BAB-L R1501/14454, Bl. 78. Importance of election committees: "Zu den Wahl-Prüfungen im Reichstage," *Berliner Volksblatt* (1 May 1887), BAB-L R1501/14452, Bl. 227.

the Socialist Party itself became legal—as long as it met indoors and during "election time."[44]

Thus it was the election code, and the special protections of election time, that explain how metropolises like Berlin and Hamburg could at one and the same time be off limits to any known Socialist (via the "state of emergency" [*kleiner Belagerungszustand*] provided by the Socialist Law) and nevertheless continually send Socialist deputies to the Reichstag.[45] As the power of the election code over the Socialist Law became clearer, the government tried to compensate with imposing displays of the very authority it was so powerless to enforce. Although the presence of a known and convicted Socialist at the podium could not be legal grounds—absent any specific, immediate threat to public safety—for shutting down an election assembly, such a speaker might well find himself surrounded by armed policemen wherever he went, escorting him from rally to rally.[46] But the mixed message sent out by these little scenes were less likely to excite fear than laughter.

The right to vote inevitably entailed other civic rights that poked holes in every political restriction. The tethers not only of the Socialist Law, but of the commercial code and the press law (which permitted provisional confiscations in order to prevent a crime or disturbance of the peace) were loosened, especially after an amendment in 1883 exempted not only ballots but any publication designed "for electoral purposes." The exemption provided virtual freedom for pictures, leaflets, and even newspapers that elaborated and explained—and proselytized for—a candidate's program. So what if house searches resulted in the capture of Socialist materials? After a few days, they would almost always be returned, as the police learned that provisional confiscation was illegal *when it hindered an election*. The Socialist Congress in Copenhagen was quick to draw attention to the opening that the 1883 amendment allowed.[47] Comrades could now take the same incendiary pamphlets that would once (even before the Socialist Law) have been confiscated, stamp "Vote Liebknecht!" on the cover, and—so long as it was "election time"—distribute them legally at their election assemblies. Election material of any sort became a ticket-of-leave for Socialist canvassers, granting them access to persons and to public places anywhere in the Reich.[48] But when that sacred "time" expired, so did the ticket.

---

[44] Note complaints of Barmen's Police Commissioner: Tenfelde, *Sozialgeschichte*, 569. Also Amtshauptmann des Amtes Meppen to Clauditz, 26 Sept. 1884, SAO Dep. 62-b, 2379.

[45] See Rickert SBDR 13 Nov. 1889: 273–94 on the way to interpret § 9 of the Socialist Law. I am not saying that the law did not cause considerable difficulties. Kutz-Bauer, *Arbeiterschaft*, 134f.

[46] On A. Geck's well-escorted Baden campaign: Rickert SBDR 11 Nov. 1889, 229; I. Auer's in 17 Saxony: AnlDR (1882/83, 5/II, Bd. 5) DS 154: 522; M. Oppenheimer's in 2 Düsseldorf, AnlDR (1882/83, 5/II, Bd. 6) DS 263: 969f. RT resolution against closing SD election assemblies: Müller, *Geschichte*, 155.

[47] Tzschoppe, *Geschichte*, 58; Müller, *Strömungen* (1963), 195, 434n. 47; Müller, *Geschichte*, 155f. The development was gradual, preceded by a bill of Moritz Wölfel and other liberals, and approved by the BR, to exempt ballots mechanically reproduced from laws on printed matter. Poschinger, *Bismarck* 5: 154.

[48] 2 S-H AnlDR (1884/85, 6/I, Bd. 5) DS 125: 479–82. Cf. SBDR 12 Apr. 1883: 1879–88. BAB-

Civil society itself contracted and expanded depending on whether or not Germany was in "election time."[49]

Election time usually lasted about four weeks. But a runoff election might add two more—and after 1890, more than 40 percent of all elections ended in runoffs. By-elections, which brought precious additional *Wahlzeit* to individual districts, were also frequent: there were 25 by- and repeat elections (*Ersatzwahlen* and *Nachwahlen*) between the general elections of 1884 and 1887, 36 between 1887 and 1890, 50 between 1890 and 1893.[50] They were triggered not only by death, illness, or sudden retirement, but by the promotion of a deputy in the civil service (he was then legally required to resign and seek reelection), and by victories in different districts of the same candidate. Such by-elections became engines for inserting the extraordinary space and freedom of the national *Wahlzeit* into the off-term *Alltag*. Not surprisingly, the government of the German states, with Prussia in the lead, wracked their collective brains to devise ways to make this charmed interval as short as possible. The archives are littered with their vain proposals.[51]

The privileges of election time even worked to disable Germanization efforts in Prussian Poland. When the Prussian government resolved in 1876 to dissolve all Polish assemblies whenever the policeman assigned to surveillance did not command the Polish language, the courts intervened, ruling that the burden lay not with the Poles being surveilled, but with the police authority desiring surveillance, to *supply* Polish-speaking observers. Twenty years later, Chancellor Chlodwig zu Hohenlohe's Minister of Interior, well aware that legal opinions differed, decided to test the waters to see if the court's views had changed. Noting the considerable increase in Polish public assemblies, he reissued the directive dissolving any Polish assembly in which the assigned policeman knew no Polish. (In Lippinek the police official read out the directive and announced

---

L R1501/14451, Bl. 163, 164. § 43, Abs. 3 and 4 of the *Gewerbeordnung* in *Reichstags-Wahlrecht*, 21; *Thätigkeit*, 137f. Excellent on all of the above: Ritter, "Sozialdemokratie" (1995), 122f; Lidtke, *Party*.

[49] SBDR 11 Nov. 1889: 236–43. A LL rally was shut down because the originally announced speaker cancelled: 20 Saxony (1884/85, 6/I, Bd. 6) DS 247: 1101; a VP rally in Munich; protest by liberals in 1 Merseburg AnlDR (1881/82, 5/I, Bd. 2) DS 44: 169–72; by Alsations in Strasbourg AnlDR (1877, 3/I, Bd. 3) DS 174: 494–97.

[50] Statistics on runoffs after 1890: Suval, *Politics*, 40. Figures for the 80s are my own.

[51] E.g., in BAB-L R1501: folders 14451, Bl. 145, 149, 236–39, 246–48, 250–52, 255–57, 259f, 268–74; 14452, Bl. 2–17, 62–70; 14460, Bl. 162–64; 14641, Bl. 2f, 8, 10–19, 53f; 14643, Bl. 42–49, 77f, 95, 120–23, 125, 134f, 142f; 14644, Bl. 36; 14645, Bl. 98f, 106f, 134, 255–58, 260; 14654, Bl. 105–7, 111, 113–17; 14694, Bl. 41f; and BAB-L R43/685, Bl. 140–42, 247f. The public was aware of efforts to manipulate the election dates. Cf. the Interpellation by Rickert et al., signed by the entire LV, AnlDR (V LP, Ausserordentlich. Session, 1883), DS 6, in BAB-L R1501/14451, Bl. 188–188v. Complaints about the government's manipulating timing appear in numerous newspaper and journal articles collected in BAB-L R1501/14460, Bl. 2, 4–6, 101–8, 112–113v, 115. Some of the parties applauded the government's attempt to make use of its ability to set election day: "Reichstagswahlen. Der Termin der Stichwahlen," *Liberale Landtag Korrespondenz* (21 Dec. 1911), BAB-L R1501/14645, Bl. 171. Others were circumspect: T. Heuß, *Die Hilfe*, 18/4 (25 Jan. 1912): 50.

mockingly that though he couldn't speak Polish, if those present didn't know German, they were welcome to speak French.) This time it was the electorate rather than the courts that called a halt to the government's efforts. A chorus of protests to the Reichstag instantly informed the minister of the price—in over-turned elections—he would have to pay. He beat a hasty retreat, reversing his policy (and incidentally reprimanding his tactless man in Lippinek)—all in order to avoid giving the Reichstag "a pretext to cashier perhaps yet another election."[52]

We should not imagine that these legal guarantees were powerful enough to turn "election time" into the "carnival" for voters that British historians have discovered in their own pollings.[53] Germans experienced the "carnivalesque," when at all, during the annual three days between Rose Monday and Ash Wednesday. Even in a law-abiding culture, a law is only as powerful as its beneficiaries' willingness to take transgressors to court. Spontaneously, the au-thorities indicated little eagerness to comply.[54] Although in October 1878 the Reichstag had insisted that the Socialist Law must not be construed to limit election activities merely because the person involved was a Socialist, the depu-ties' logic in outlawing the Socialist Party and then exempting its election cam-paign was a difficult one to convey to middle-level authorities, who knew very well what kind of election results their superiors wanted. Not surprisingly, county and local authorities, whose reputation for ham-handedness was prover-bial, found the distinction between *im*permissible writing and speech aimed at furthering Social Democracy (against which they were to bring down the full force of the Socialist Law) and permissible writing and speech aimed at produc-ing Social Democratic election majorities (which they were to leave alone) even more baffling. In 1889 the Election Commission compiled a list of breaches in

[52] IM v. d. Recke to prefects of Münster, Posen, Königsberg, Danzig, Breslau, and Police-Präsi-dent of Berlin, 28 Oct. 1896; IM v. d. Recke to Chancellor Hohenlohe, 24 Mar. 1897, BAB-L R1501/14454, Bl. 22–25. Cf. also SBDR 29 Mar. 1897: 5359–63; 30 Mar. 1897: 5365–85; Inter-pellation: Czarlinski and Gen. AnlDR (1895/97, 9/IV, Bd. 6) DS 719: 3809. On disparity of legal opinions: the diverse rulings on whether one might post election material *inside* a pub without police permission: *DGZ*, XLIII/33 (13 Aug. 1904): 199.

[53] O'Gorman, "Rituals," 79–115; idem, "Culture," 17–32.

[54] In 1887 the Baden government claimed to have blocked or dissolved every SD assembly, preventing candidate A. Geck from getting a chance to speak. Von Eisendecker to Bis., Karlsruhe, 10 Feb. 1887, BAB-L R1501/14642, Bl. 156. Especially ignored was the right of SDs to hold small committee meetings of 5 to 7 people to prepare for elections, something Hasenclever considered much more significant than whether or not a *voter* assembly (i.e., a rally) was forbidden. Hasen-clever SBDR 5 Feb. 1886: 904. Interpretation of the law took time to sort out: cf. the frantic telegrams between the Kiel police, the *Regierung* in Schleswig, and the Prussian MdI over the confiscation of SD ballots in 1881, at the end of which, faced with conflicts between press law, commercial code, and Socialist Law, the MdI required the confiscated ballots be returned. There was no sign of bad faith; but the polls closed 25 minutes after the arrival of his telegram. The RT voided this election. 7 S-H (Kiel-Altona) AnlDR (1882/83, 5/II, Bd 6) DS 279: 1029–31. The deputies were not always so stringent: 6 Berlin (1880, 4/III, Bd. 4) DS 94: 666–74; 5 Hessen (Offenbach): Singer SBDR 7 Mar. 1888: 1361.

the mesh of legal protections of freedom of association and assembly that had been charged to the police during the election time: 110 in the preceding eleven years.[55] For competitive elections to take place, citizens had continually to protest these abuses; the Reichstag had constantly to reaffirm their rights with instructions to the governments.[56] Even so, violations continued on into the twentieth century.[57]

Socialist ballotteers took care to carry several copies of the Electoral Law with them on their rounds. Scarcely a weapon against apoplectic bosses or policemen, the most palpable effect of waving the Electoral Law in the face of local big men was on the legal consciousness of the ballotteers themselves.[58] (And not only on *Socialist* ballotteers. Centrum chaplains and Polish aristocrats were likewise driven to become legal experts, insisting on being shown the law or ordinance restricting them, demanding the signature of the authorizing magistrate, learning to cite chapter and verse of their own rights, as good as other citizens.) By playing by the rules, the Social Democrats forced the government to take them seriously: not as plotters and bomb-throwers, but as competitors for the support of the citizenry.[59]

Perhaps the period of the Socialist Law (1878–90) is not the watershed that historians have sometimes imagined. In some regions, the police had harassed Socialists unmercifully long before it was passed, driving them out by the spring of 1878.[60] In other parts of the empire, the law itself was barely or

[55] The small number of mandates effectively impugned by violation of these rules is explained by the RT's practice of not investigating when the size of the victory precluded invalidation. SBDR 11 Nov. 1889: 226–43, esp. Rickert, 228 and 230; and AnlDR (1888/89, 7/IV, Bd. 6) DS 251: 1462–73.

[56] WPK motion for invalidity of 4 Arns. on grounds of violation of § 28 of the Socialist Law: AnlDR (1887/88, 7/II, Bd. 4) DS 100: 513–16; highly instructive debate on Rickert motion on right of assembly: SBDR 6 Mar. 1888: 1325–27 and SBDR 29 Nov. 1888: 56–67; Auer, referring to 9 Han. SBDR 3 Dec. 1890: 762.

[57] Korfanty claimed police refused to let the P hold a single rally in Upper Silesia: SBDR 28 Jan. 1904: 542; in Altenburg a rally was forbidden on the basis of the Socialist Law more than a decade after it had expired: Stücklen (SD) SBDR 6 Feb. 1904: 750. Following in AnlDR (1912/14, 13/I): pollwatchers excluded in 7 precincts: 8 Breslau (Bd. 23, DS 1638: 3573); and in spite of LR's and Kreisamt's telegraphed instructions: 5 Merseburg (Bd. 19, DS 840: 1136–39, esp. 1138), 7 Gumb. (Bd. 23, DS 1586: 3402), 8 Hesse (Bd. 16, DS 350: 291f).

[58] H. Kröber, a shoemaker, possessed five copies. 1 Munich (1882/83, 5/IV, Bd. 4) DS 123: 981–89. Especially persistant was the tailor, H. Mahlke of Flensburg: his protest, upheld by the WPK on 2 S-H AnlDR (1884/85, 6/I, Bd. 5) DS 125: 479; and another from 10 Mar. 1887, BAB-L R1501/14664: Bl. 1–8. When the director of the Silesia Works in Paruschowitz removed Franz Sch. from "blocking" the path to the works by distributing election leaflets, Sch. sued him for false arrest. He was himself convicted for false accusations and slander and sentenced to 6 months in prison. *DGZ* 43/20 (14 May 1904): 120. Liebknecht on chikanery of officials in Kiel campaign: SBDR 8 Jan. 1886: 425–28.

[59] As can be seen from the indignant marginalia with which bureaucrats covered the articles of the SD press. E.g., "Zur Rechtlosmachung der Wähler in Reuß," *Vorwärts*, 18 Dec. 1912, BAB-L R1501/14460, Bl. 378.

[60] Schloßmacher, *Düsseldorf*, 133; Kutz-Bauer, *Arbeiterschaft*, 126, 142; *GA* Nr. 160, 12 July 1871, and Nr. 170, 3 Aug. 1871. The same kind of harassment was experienced by other parties,

unenthusiastically enforced.[61] It was, after all, during the reign of the Socialist Law that Social Democracy made its biggest breakthrough. In only three years, between 1887 and 1890, the party doubled its vote, a jump unequaled by themselves or any other party at any other period in the empire.[62] In absolute terms, it displaced the National Liberals as Germany's champion vote-getter (although with a somewhat lower count than the National Liberals had reached in 1874, 1877, and 1887, and the Centrum, in 1874). The comrades registered the new status quo by two departures. Their Central Committee countermanded the resolution of an earlier party congress calling on supporters to abstain from voting in any runoff in which a Socialist was not a candidate. Instead it called on the membership to throw the weight of their ballots behind any candidates who promised to oppose exceptional legislation.[63] Secondly, at the Erfurt Party Congress in 1891 the comrades changed their name. They dropped the old, class-based "Socialist Workers' Party" for the more universalistic "Social Democratic Party," a symbolic shift marking Social Democracy's birth as a mass organization.

From the very beginning, the behavior of the provincial and local authorities had done much to undermine the German workers' confidence in the impartiality of their national "government above parties." Then came the Socialist Law, linking class conflicts at the worksite to the national political system and insuring their perpetuation in yet another "hot family feud" that, like the cultural battle, could neither be ended nor resolved. But the paradoxical combination of discriminatory Socialist Law and egalitarian electoral code had a momentous impact on the political culture of the German workingman. With their own political existence branded as illegal, supporters of the outlawed party became paragons of legalism. Moreover, their fluctuating status within an enforcement system that was both haphazard and frequently reproved and "rectified" by the Reichstag set in motion that undesired, and at first unconscious, fixation on parliamentary elections that (however incongruous in a movement whose ideology relegated politics to "superstructure" and whose eschatology ended in revolution) soon became the defining characteristic of German socialism—and launched it on the long path toward political pragmatism in a pluralistic, parliamentary democracy.

---

though less often. A. Schütte, chairman of the LL Election Committee, in 3 Braunschweig, 12 Mar. 1887, BAB-L R1501/14657, Bl. 13–15.

[61] Essen country: Tenfelde, *Sozialgeschichte*, 531n. 199; Solingen: Bramann, *Reichstagswahlen*, 56; Hessen: White, *Party*, 133; Magdeburg region: Birk, "Entwicklung," 183; Hamburg, until 1886: Kutz-Bauer, *Arbeiterschaft*, 331–33.

[62] Sperber, *Voters*, 39f. The SPD's increase from 1871 to 1874—from 3.2% to 6.8%—is too small in absolute numbers to be considered a breakthrough.

[63] Opposition to the change was vehement, but as it was done in committee, there was no discussion. Blank, "Zusammensetzung," 541–43. The watershed signified by the SD's 1890 count became fully apparent only later. G. A. Ritter, *Arbeiterbewegung* (1959), 80f; excellent on the SDs new psychological uncertainty: 79–106.

THE RULES OF PUBLIC SPEAKING

Not all the rules that affected imperial elections were written down. Campaigns were also governed by a popular conception of what constituted a public political gathering. An advertised *public* meeting, people believed, should not only be open to all comers; a time should also be set aside—and indeed as part of the regular program—for views opposed to those of the principal speakers. This popular conception of the "public" as implicitly controversial was institutionalized in the "discussion-speaker" (*Diskussionsredner*), a person designated to represent the rival party or interest group at the gatherings of its opponents.[64]

In every nineteenth-century franchise regime, parties sent their best spokesmen around the country to speak on behalf of less rhetorically gifted candidates. Peculiar to Germany, so far as I know, was the regular practice of shipping the best debaters to *opponents'* rallies. Although nothing required him to do so, a prospective discussion-speaker was expected to contact the sponsoring organization in advance, making known his intention to appear. He could usually presume upon a good half hour to answer the announced speaker, and woe to the chairman who tried to cut him short at ten minutes.[65] Although the requirements of good form ended there, at some rallies the resulting speeches approximated a formal debate, with the discussant given the opportunity to respond not only to the main speaker's address, but eventually to his rebuttal.[66] The generosity of some conveners extended even further. At a big assembly in the Hamburg suburb of Barmbek, the convening Liberal election club graciously allowed a "mixed podium," elected from Liberals and Social Democrats, to conduct the meeting. Here it was a Social Democrat who gave the main address, and the Liberal, the "counter-address"—and this was in 1878, right after the Kaiser had been gravely wounded in a second assassination attempt and Bismarck was whipping up antisocialist hysteria across the land.[67] Such behavior was not unique. We have reports of Erfurt Social Democrats

---

[64] Examples can be found in the local studies of nearly every district and every election. The implicit rules governing public assemblies were explicitly discussed in a long debate on Liebermann v. Sonnenberg's motion demanding stronger police protection for antisemitic rallies. SBDR 21 Mar. 1906: 2186–2218. Initially even spokesmen for the older elites, although not eager to campaign themselves, felt obligated to represent the antisocialist position at SD rallies. Kulemann, *Erinnerungen*, 24f; Gerlach, *Erlebnisse*, 21f. Contrast Ralf Dahrendorf's view that German political culture smothered conflict. *Society and Democracy in Germany* ([Munich, 1965] New York, 1967).

[65] *Wittener Volkszeitung* (Z) quoted in Nettmann, "Witten," 137, 140. Complaints about only five minutes for the discussant: Schöpflin, Horn, Hoffmann (SD) SBDR 21 Mar. 1906: 2213–15; "Im Wahlkreis Hannover-Linden," *BT* XLI/7, 2. Beiblatt (5 Jan. 1912).

[66] Monshausen, *Wahlen*, 272f.

[67] Kutz-Bauer, *Arbeiterschaft*, 281. Hostility to SDs varied considerably. A major Hagen employer, Commerzienrat Wm. Meckel (NL) declared "the Social Democratic party an absolute necessity and its existence [had] a certain justification." *HVZ* Nr. 4, 6 Jan. 1877, BAB-L R1501/14693, Bl. 13f.

allowing their *invited* antisemitic opponent one and a half hours, and of anti-semites in Bischoffswerda returning the favor.[68]

No law forced the convening party to give the floor to a discussion-speaker. But all parties paid lip service to the notion of the campaign as an instrument of popular education, and all insisted on their own discussant's right, as part of the public, to speak as if that right were the very font of civil liberty.[69] So firmly embedded were these practices in the popular consciousness that any party that tried to exclude or limit discussants met with howls of indignation, and some-times the (mistaken) cry that such limitation was "a quite illegal election influence."[70] Although we may question whether many minds were changed during these forensic exchanges, German campaigns were indeed the scene of genuine debate.

In fact, discussion-speakers were often invited to appear. Some invitations were issued in bad faith, to make the opposing party look weak if it failed to accept the challenge.[71] Yet audiences expected a real debate, and my impression is that most invitations were genuine. In the Second Saxon district, election committees for the Conservatives and the Social Democrats made explicit mutual arrangements to send speakers—on one occasion as many as six!—to each others' public gatherings. Even on the Kaiser's birthday, with political fervor fueled by strong drink, the debate proceeded without incident. The institution had advantages for all sides. Even a notorious mumbler could hope to draw crowds if he could advertise that Wilhelm Liebknecht, a speaker with enormous charisma, was appearing in the lists against him. Since the absence of an opponent could be taken as a sign that the speaker was not really a contender, where no opposing controversialist was to be found, a candidate might put a shill in the crowd to challenge him from the floor.[72]

The mixed audiences that resulted from the institution of discussion-speakers gave it a value for third parties as well. At the bigger and more important venues, their observers gathered arguments to use later against both sides. With an eye to how the event would be reported in the press, outsiders also made tactical choices in bestowing their applause, and when they pronounced on the evening's winners and losers in their columns, they calculated their shadings

[68] Reißhaus (SD) and Zimmermann (Ref.) SBDR 2 Mar. 1906: 2211f.

[69] Rickert SBDR 7 Feb. 1888: 744; Kayser (SD) SBDR 2 Dec. 1882: 590f.

[70] Quote: *GA* Nr. 6, 8 Jan. 1874; protest on 5 Arns. (Bochum) AnlDR (1882/83, 5/II, Bd. 6) DS 292: 1079; criticism of Eisenach antisemites: SBDR 21 Mar. 1906, passim; similarly: "Anti-Semitische Kampfesformen," *Nationalliberale Correspondenz* 39/1 (3 Jan. 1912) BAB-L R1501/14460, Bl. 141; "Aus der Reichstagswahlbewegung," *BT* 41/3 (3 Jan. 1912).

[71] Hagen SD Advertisements "specially invited" their opponents, E. Richter and Julius Funcke: *HVZ* Nr. 4, 6 Jan. 1877, BAB-L R1501/14693, Bl. 14. Stöcker was invited by SDs: M. Braun, *Stoecker* (1912), 157; and he and Richter were invited to appear together in 1881 on the same platform: Ernst, *Polizeispitzeleien*, 50; Hamburg Guelfs invited a SD speaker in 1878. Kutz-Bauer, *Arbeiterschaft*, 281. Fairbairn, "Authority," 825; Müller, *Strömungen*, 196, 208f; Frank, *Stoecker*, 146.

[72] BAB-L R1501/14458, Bl. 128f. Liebknecht's charisma: Bramann, *Reichstagswahlen*, 61. K. E. Sindermann (SD) SBDR 21 Mar. 1906: 2206; Gerlach, *Rechts*, 159f.

with an eye to a future alliance—perhaps in a runoff, perhaps in another district—with one or the other party.[73]

Other "outsiders" (or non-contenders) who made use of the format might be representatives, not of other parties, but of groups with a stake in the election. The Farmers' League was well known for sending interlocutors to election rallies to force the candidate to take a position on tariffs. Catholics, in a Protestant district, and even Jews, on occasion, acted similarly. In the little West Prussian town of Schwetz (now Weichsel), where Poles held a slight demographic edge, the Jewish community had become a crucial component of any "German" success. In 1893, a year when antisemitic parties were winning more seats—seventeen—than any time before the war, Jewish cooperation, and therefore the German seat in Schwetz, was put into question. Rumors surfaced that the two-term "German" incumbent, a local estate owner named Otto Holtz, was antisemitic—not an implausible notion, given that Holtz was a Free Conservative and that both of the conservative parties were playing the antisemitic card. Holtz's agent, a young official attached to the Landrat's office, hurried to the president of the synagogue, the furrier Hirschberg, and assured him that the rumors about Holtz were false. Citing the district's history of friendly inter-confessional relations and pointing to influential Jewish members of the inner circle of the "German" election committee, the man pleaded that "Jewish citizens at least attend our election assembly in order to set the matter straight through interpellations." There indeed the matter was settled. At the rally a Jewish lawyer rose from the floor and demanded to know the candidate's position on antisemitism. Upon receiving a satisfactory answer, Jewish community leaders again came out for the "German"—that is, Free Conservative—incumbent; and he won again.[74]

One group of "outsiders" we have not mentioned. Women were never legally excluded from political clubs and assemblies in Württemberg, Baden, Hessen, Saxe-Meiningen, Saxe-Coburg-Gotha, the Hanse city-states, and some of the other smaller polities. After 1898 their presence was permitted in Bavaria as well.[75] In Saxony, however, women were forbidden to join political associations; and although not explicitly prohibited from attending their assemblies, the police's discretionary authority to ban any meeting held for the purpose of

---

[73] Mixed audiences: *HVZ* Nr. 4, 6 Jan. 1877, BAB-L R1501/14693, Bl. 13f; Nettmann, "Witten," 138f; Romeyk, *Wahlen*, 130, 305, 311, 362; Lepper, ed., *Katholizismus*, 304.

[74] The handful of liberals in the county submitted a protest claiming that the LR's intervention implied a threat to the Jewish community if they did not support Holtz—an interpretation that both the official and the synagogue president denied under oath. 5 Marienwerder AnlDR (1894/95, 9/III, Bd. 1) DS 166: 799f; AnlDR (1895/97, 9/IV, Bd. 2) DS 195: 1259; C. Gamp (FK) SBDR 24 Apr. 1896: 1927.

[75] "Vom Frauenvereinsrecht," *Die Zeit* 2/15 (8 Jan. 1903), 450. A list of almost every German state and its respective law and practice: Jacqueline Strain, "Feminism and Political Radicalism in the German Social Democratic Movement, 1890–1914" (Ph. D. diss., Berkeley, 1964), 55–62. *DGZ* 37/10 (5 Mar. 1898): 59f. Delius, "Die Unterschiede des preußischen und des französischen Vereins- und Versammlungsrechts," *PVB* 26/15 (7 Jan. 1905), 145f, argues that, though controversial, women were no longer excluded in France.

"transgressing against law or morality" was often invoked to keep them away from rallies. As for Prussia, the 1850 Law of Association and Assembly excluded women from any meetings sponsored by political organizations. Jurists equated woman with firearms as providing sufficient cause for shutting a rally down, and in some places even the entry of a landlady to fill up the beer glasses led the gendarme to rise and declare the meeting over.[76] Legally, however, it was not the presence of a woman, but only her refusal to leave that legitimated a closure. And in fact, enforcement of the exclusion varied considerably, not least because whether or not to define the meeting as an impermissible *Vereinsversammlung* (one sponsored by a political organization) or a permissible *Volksversammlung* (popular assembly) was up to the police.[77] In early 1902, the distinction disappeared, and the government, responding to the presence of conservative women at BdL rallies, permitted women to attend even election assemblies so long as some kind of barrier—which might be no more than a line of chalk or a piece of string—segregated the sexes. Already by 1907 the intrepid Lily Braun was traveling by sleigh throughout East Elbia giving speeches at one election rally after another to crowds that were often composed of 30 percent women, with the police present—and no mention of any barrier.[78]

The imperial law of assembly and association of 1908, opening both organizations and rallies to all adults, then opened the floodgates everywhere to women's political participation (and not just surreptitious presence) at this quintessential forum for public controversy. By 1911 the SPD's woman's bureau had scheduled campaign circuits for no fewer than forty-eight women speakers. The Progressives sent out lists of fifteen women speakers to all of their local branches. More important, at the rallies themselves, Liberal women demanded to see women sitting at the podium (*Vorstand*), while Progressive women used the forum to nail candidates down on the issue of female suffrage—which their party's platform had preferred to pass over in silence.[79]

At most gatherings, the candidate himself did not appear, nor was the discussion speaker a celebrity like Wilhelm Liebknecht. Speakers were apt to be local activists, but their rhetorical dexterity was nevertheless often of high caliber. Although one might argue that these stylized duels discouraged independent contributions from ordinary citizens in the audience, it is doubtful whether, in gatherings that sometimes numbered in the thousands, spontaneity was either

[76] Otto Gerland, "Die polizeiliche Beaufsichtigung der Versammlungen," *DGZ* 29/45 (8 Nov. 1890), 263; Tenfelde, *Sozialgeschichte*, 571n. 379. Women were, however, part of the public not only at RT sessions but at city council meetings: *GA* 7 Jan. 1874: 28.

[77] [Köller], *Ungiltigkeit*, 8; "Entscheidungen. Vereins und Versammlungsrecht," *PVB* 20/1 (1 Oct. 1898): 8. Over time the courts limited police discretion: 2. Kammergericht Decisions: *DGZ* 37/17 (23 Apr. 1898): 100. The rules: Hatschek, *Kommentar*, 168, 237f, 248.

[78] Braun, "Agitation" (1907), 200–202. Public mockery of the barrier: "Politische Notizen. Vereinsrecht und Frauen," *Die Zeit* 2/1 (2 Oct. 1902), 1. R. J. Evans, *Movement* (1976), 73.

[79] Skepticism about quality of female speakers: Ludwig Radlof, "Kritisches zur Taktik der Sozialdemokratischen Frauenbewegung," *Sozialistische Monatshefte* 19/1, 7. Heft (10 Apr. 1913), 426. A. Steinmann, "Mitarbeit" (1912), 18; Bertram, *Wahlen*, 196–98.

probable or practicable. As an alternative to spontaneity, the Socialists made a conscious effort to train not only their functionaries but their rank and file in public speaking. The proliferation of potential discussants was not just an advantage to the campaign, but an integral part of the Socialist project of emancipation. What could be more destructive of the system of deference than the ability of common people to speak up for themselves in public? The halting efforts of a small town Demosthenes might cause smiles or yawns among the better spoken, but their impact, commanding the respect owed to courage and fortitude, may have been as great as any Liebknecht's.[80]

During the reign of the Socialist Law, the institution of *Diskussionsredner* was the lifeblood of Social Democracy. It enabled a Socialist activist, in the most unpromising localities, where adherents were too timid or too few to call an assembly of their own, or where no publican would rent them a hall, to attach himself to the meeting of his opponents, and under the very noses of the presiding policeman, proselytize for his candidate, for his party, for his *Zukunftsstaat*. Thus in the Saar, where the bosses prevented workers from *voting* Social Democrat, Socialists nevertheless appeared at the rallies not only of the Centrum, but of Candidate Stumm himself, forcing him to defend his record—and to promise to represent workers in the Reichstag! At least as much as the election code's protections of *Öffentlichkeit* at the polls, it was this popular conception of the "public" as a theater of controversy that ensured that Socialist campaigners would get an audience even in places where the Socialist Law was vigorously enforced.[81]

Political assemblies provided a theater, however, not only of controversy but, like the election itself, of power. And like the election, a principal reason for participating was to let the other side know that you were there. Catcalls and whistles were always a temptation for the less forensically gifted. Social Democrats entertained themselves at Centrum rallies by hooting at every use of the word "God," while Centrum supporters drowned out freethinking opponents with hymns. Some deputies, like the witty Progressive Albert Traeger, were so skilled at the cut and thrust of debate that they could tame the noisiest crowd—which, like Scheharazade's sultan, grew curious about what would come next.[82] Others were not so lucky. The very openness that created a space for outlawed Social Democrats at the gatherings of other parties made it possible for the comrades—or any dissenting spectators—to seize that space for themselves.

---

[80] Göhre, *Three Months*, 90–94. High calibre: see the comments by Carpenter Euler of Bensburg. Müller, *Strömungen*, 241; also 316.

[81] E.g., at a huge Breslau rally at which the advertised speaker was R. Virchow. Müller, *Geschichte*, 75f; also 157f, 302. Stumm's rally: Bellot, *Hundert Jahre*, 183f, 208. Similarly, Z supporters parried the arguments of Hüttendirektor Ott in Pachten and took over his rally: Ibid., 173. In general: Monshausen, *Wahlen*, 341. The value of the institution for the SPD in the Koblenz regency, where halls were denied them even in the decade before the war: Romeyk, *Wahlen*, 68, 70, 81, 130, 134, 222, 225, 290f, 332, 369, 391, 414. One of the SPD's difficulties in penetrating Catholic areas lay in the fact that the Z did not always hold rallies. Ibid., 81.

[82] Severing, *Lebensweg* 1: 28. Nettmann, "Witten," 139f; hymns: Baudert (SD) SBDR 21 Mar. 1906: 2190, 2214; Monshausen, *Wahlen*, 230.

A widespread consensus demanded that public meetings should proceed in a "parliamentary" manner. "Parliamentary" included the expectation that sponsors would let the attending public decide who would chair the assembly, what the agenda would be, and how much time would be allotted to each speaker. Although these practices were not, as was popularly believed, actually required by the various state laws of association, they had acquired the status, in the words of the Christian trade unionist and Centrum man Johannes Giesberts, of "customary law." Thus the moment of maximum danger for any convening party always arrived when the crowd cried "Podium election! Podium election!" (*Bureau-Wahl! Bureau-Wahl!*) When a discussant's battalions outnumbered those of the conveners, they could win the vote on the chairmanship—and take over the meeting. They could then quite decorously call on whomever they pleased, demote the advertised attraction to the rank of discussant, and face those who had come to hear the convening party's address with the choice of either sitting through their own perorations or leaving altogether. Through strategically placed applause and hisses, interlopers could even encroach upon their opponents' nomination process, preventing (at least in that venue) the nomination of a candidate whose sponsors had hoped to present to like-minded citizens for acclamation.[83]

The more open a local party's assemblies, the less confined to notables and clergy, the more vulnerable they became to these tactics. Socialists were the most conspicuous practitioners of the hostile takeover. Their successes in the Berlin assemblies of Adolf Stoecker were well known. (Perhaps because the former Court Preacher's rallies had a quasi-ecclesiastical character, the police seem to have been less vigilant than usual in excluding women, and they too were noisy participants—on both sides.)[84] Socialists also targeted the Christian labor movement, until the latter—especially in Essen—learned how to give tit for tat. Even when a podium vote went against the comrades, they could still make a considerable stir simply by singing the "Workers' Marseillaise." Eugen Richter, for one, got fed up with the Socialists' crying victim in matters of free assembly. By constantly forcing their way into his party's meetings, demanding the floor, and then drowning out the speaker, they were "much worse than the police have ever been in threatening freedom of association." Social Democrats sniffed that the alleged disturbances had occurred only "because the sponsoring party has not allowed the so-called presidium to be elected, in spite of having called a *public* meeting. . . ." Why, Hasenclever wanted to know, should "a

[83] Giesberts SBDR 21 Mar. 1906: 2193; laws: Liebermann v. Sonnenberg: ibid., 2186f. Notorious for disruptions was the flail-wielding clergyman K.F.W. Iskraut: Hoffmann: ibid., 2214, and Severing, *Lebensweg* 1: 27. Baare's hooligans, at a meeting they didn't call: 5 Arns. (Bochum) AnlDR (1882/83, 5/II, Bd. 4) DS 292: 1079. SD attempt to influence the Z's 1877 nomination: Möllers, "Strömungen," 294; their crashing a Z meeting in 1885: Müller, *Strömungen*, 64. Good on this for the Weimar Republic: Chickering, "Mobilization," 307–28; 310, 320.

[84] SDs in Liegnitz: *GA* Nr. 6, 8 Jan. 1874; in Essen in 1877: Paul, *Krupp*, 209f; Müller, *Strömungen*, 64f, 83, 318f. D. v. Oertzen, *Stoecker* (1910) 1: 240; Braun, *Stoecker*, 157f, 163–65; more generally: Romeyk, *Wahlen*, 68, 133, 216, 225. On Stoecker's contribution to the admission of women to the public sphere: Kaiser "Politisierung," 254–71.

majority in a popular assembly let itself be terrorized by the minority of Herr Richter? [i.e., the convening party!] That, gentleman, I can't see as a principle of freedom." Although the Socialist leadership at times pleaded with the members *not* to disrupt the meetings of others, a party memoirist made clear that such interventions constituted a considerable part of the fun of politics— gleefully referring to them as "theater."[85]

The game was open, of course, to anyone. "Majoritizing" an opponent's meeting had probably been "invented" by Berlin Catholics as early as 1869, against the Progressives. Only weeks later, liberals in Baden employed it against the Catholic *Volkspartei*; nearly four decades later, Baden's Left Liberals were packing the meetings of National Liberals.[86] As we have seen, a rural bread lord could commandeer troops of tenants and stable hands to take over a "parliamentary" meeting just as easily as he could march them to the polls. Farmers' Leaguers and antisemites delighted in making these disruptions, the latter eventually driving Berlin Progressives to hire private police (as many as two hundred for a single rally) in order to keep their meetings under their own control.[87] In 1912 National Liberals, shouting, "We are *all* conservative," had the pleasure of wresting a Conservative election assembly from the leader of the Conservative delegation himself—Ernst von Heydebrand, incumbent in one of the safest Conservative districts in the country.

Reaction depended entirely on whose ox was being gored. Newspapers that breathed indignation whenever the rallies of their favorites were captured, would in the very same issue wax sarcastic about their opponents' "martyrdom."[88] During their heyday in the nineties, the antisemitic Reform Party had so exploited these procedures that, especially in the suburbs of Dresden and parts

---

[85] Richter, Hasenclever SBDR 2 Apr. 1878: 675, 677f; "*Schauspiel*": Müller, *Geschichte*, 353; also 302. Richter supporters tried to capture NL meeting: *HVZ* Nr. 4 (4, 6 Jan. 1877), BAB-L R1501/14693, B1. 13f. SD rowdies: v. Friesen SBDR 10 Feb. 1888: 828; 10 Jan 1889: 371. Restrictions on "free speech" punished by withholding runoff support: Frank, *Brandenburger*, 110f. Antisemites: Richter, *Reichstag* (1896) 2: 202f.

[86] "Das Klosterstürmen von 1869," *BK* 1871: 55–124; "Auch Moabitisches," *BK* 1871; "Das Ei des Kulturkampfes," *BK* 1883: 88; *Die Post* Nr. 425, 20 Aug. 1869; Zangerl, "Opening," 187. Z takeover of a nationalist rally called by the steelworks director; and Z and SD rallies, by Stumm's men: Bellot, *Hundert Jahre*, 173, 191.

[87] Richter, *Reichstag* 2: 238–41. Estate owner wielding 70 dependents in Ossa: AnlDR (1885/86, 6/II, Bd. 5) DS 117: 579, 572. Similarly in Rochlitz: 14 Saxony AnlDR (1885/86, 6/II, Bd. V) DS 117: 567, 570–72.

[88] Constrast the gloating "Herr von Heydebrand in seinem Wahlkreis. Das wackelnde Thrönchen der Konservativen," (*BT* 2. Beiheft, Nr. 18, 11 Jan. 1912), describing the NL takeover, with the indignant report in the same issue of agrarian disruptions of a LL assembly in Ploen-Oldenburg: "Wie die Konservativen kämpfen. Das Grammophon als Wahlbegleitung. Ein teuerer Spass." NLs and SDs took over the antisemite W. Bruhn's assembly in Arnswalde-Friedeberg: "Anti-Semitische Kampfesformen," *Nationalliberale Correspondenz* 39/1 (3 Jan. 1912), BAB-L R1501/14460, Bl. 141. Other examples from 1912, by K, NL, and SPD: Bertram, *Wahlen*, 200. In the 80s, SDs had to worry about anarchists taking over *their* meetings (R. C. Sun, "Martyrdom," 55), while they took over K rallies: Müller, *Geschichte*, 302. LL assemblies closed down by antisemites in 1 Saxe-Mein., SBDR 20 May 1886: 2087. FKs forced the police to dissolve a Z meeting in 12 Breslau through continuous cheers for His Majesty: *GA* Nr. 6, 8 Jan. 1874.

of eastern Saxony, their competitors were driven underground. As their star then waned after the turn of the century, the Reformers grabbed at any expedient to prevent these same competitors from doing as they had been done to. They disguised their rallies under misleading monikers (e.g., the "united nationalist parties"); they stopped holding public meetings, instead issuing invitations to individuals in targeted occupations; they posted notices in newspapers and at the doors of their assemblies announcing "No Podium Election. Discussion Time: 15 Minutes," and even "Only voters of the bourgeois (*bürgerliche*) parties are invited" in order to have some legal color with which to institute trespass proceedings against rowdies. But attempts to restrict admission to those presenting invitations could always be thwarted by the designated guests themselves, who passed their tickets on to their friends (or to those who were more interested) and—in the case of Breslau railway workers—even lent them their distinctive work caps (*Dienstmütze*) for disguise. The courts proved anything but obliging to the Reformers' complaints. Miscreants were either acquitted or punished so mildly that one angry Reformer resolved never to trouble himself again.[89]

Sometimes crowds got rowdy. Even in Germany, furniture might get broken and beer mugs go sailing through the air. Social Democrats never forgot that Berlin Progressives had once *spit* in the face of Ferdinand Lassalle. The Centrum asserted territorial rights to the Eifel by appearing at a Social Democratic outdoor gathering with a band whose playing eventually forced the comrades to seek police protection on their way back to the railway station. Especially at the rallies of antisemites, from Court Preacher Stoecker down through a succession of ugly customers, scuffles could break out.[90] But the presence of the policeman went far toward keeping mayhem at a minimum. Conveners were required to make formal seating arrangements for him, usually putting him on the speaker's platform, at a table next to the presidium. Even after the liberalization of the Law of Association in Prussia in 1899, and in the empire as a whole in 1908, the gendarme was visible at every political gathering. Far from protecting conveners from hostile takeovers, the police behaved with infuriating neutrality. There to safeguard public health and fire safety, to see that no law was broken by the presence of women, children, or apprentices, the gendarme might for any one of these reasons, and a wide variety of others over which he exercised nearly unlimited discretion, simply rise and declare the assembly "dissolved." The audience would immediately disperse.

The police's slender tolerance for disorderly conduct delivered enormous

[89] Caps: Müller, *Geschichte*, 353; Liebermann v. Sonnenberg, Raab (RefP), K. Schrader (LL), G. Burckhardt (Christ. Soz.) SBDR 21 Mar. 1906: 2187, 2199; also 2202, 2205, 2210, 2216f.

[90] Hasenclever SBDR 2 Apr. 1878: 677f; "Gerichts-Zeitung. Ein Nachspiel zu einer politischen Versammlungen," *BT* Nr. 14, 1. Beiblatt, 9 Jan. 1912; "Wahlkampf mit Steinen," ibid.; Monshausen, *Wahlen*, 291; *GA* Nr. 17, 21 Jan. 1871: 97; Oertzen, *Stoecker* 1: 240; Romeyk, *Wahlen*, 355f; Möllers, *Strömungen*, 139. G. Malkewitz (K) complained of 1,000 screaming SDs, marching to his house, hurling threats. PAH 11 Feb 1909: 1982–2017, in GStA PK I. HA, Rep. 90a, A.VIII.1.d., Nr. 1/Bd. 9.

power into the hands of even the smallest minority—and put another twist on what it meant to play by the rules. For by making any commotion at all, even a belligerent-sounding shout, an interloper might provoke a nervous peace officer to close down the assembly. The permutations on this game were limited only by the imagination. A pastor or official might show up at a Social Democratic gathering and call for a cheer for the Kaiser—with the sole purpose of seeing the meeting dissolved for the crime of *lèse majesté* when the comrades refused to rise.[91] The worker's party used a similar ploy to deny public space to its numerous opponents—especially during the years immediately after 1878, when local authorities believed (erroneously) that under the new Socialist Law the mere presence of a Socialist speaking sufficed to render a gathering illegal.[92] Standing up in a meeting convened by an opponent, a comrade would recommend the Social Democratic candidate to the audience—with a good prospect of bringing the surveilling gendarme to his feet and thereby "exploding" (*sprengen*) the assembly. For Social Democrats, "exploding" a meeting, or dominating it with their discussion-speaker, were feats of political judo: turning the very strength of their adversary (the state, in the first instance; a rival party in the second) into a weapon against them.

There were many things the parties did not like about the laws governing assemblies—the presence of the police, the exclusion of women, the absence of uniformity among states, to name only a few; but the ability of the public to take over someone else's meetings was not among them. The majority's position became explicit in 1906 when, in the midst of several Reichstag initiatives (*Initiativanträge*) aimed at repealing these exclusions and prescriptions, Liebermann von Sonnenberg submitted a bill designed to enlist the police on behalf of beleaguered conveners. Now a member of the German Social Reform Party, which had united the major antisemitic factions, Liebermann cited the recent by-election in Eisenach, where Social Democrats had broken into the Reformers' invitation-only rally and, after a considerable rumpus, taken it over— but not before doors, windows, and a few heads had been broken. The response of all the parties save the conservatives to Liebermann's motion was a united front of contempt. "Where in the world are there political campaigns without this or that disruptive incident?" a National Liberal wanted to know. Eduard Bernstein, always ready to invoke his years in England, reminded Liebermann that across the channel "the greatest politicians, a Palmerston, a Peel, a Disraeli, a Gladstone," and more recently even a Balfour and a Chamberlain, regularly

[91] Hesselbarth, *Sozialdemokraten*, 41, wrongly implies that the technique was used solely against the SDs. Counter-evidence: Bramann, *Reichstagswahlen*, 50; Romeyk, *Wahlen*, 291, 355f; Rickert SBDR 11 Nov. 1889: 228, and SBDR 13 Nov. 1889: 280; Reißhaus (SD) SBDR 21 Mar. 1906: 2211; Müller, *Geschichte*, 157f; Richter: *Reichstag* 2: 202f.

[92] Illegal to dissolve an assembly solely because the speaker was SD: (on Kiel) Schmidt, Liebknecht, Rickert SBDR 8 Jan. 1886, 422, 426, 428, 430; (on 2 S-H) Spahn, Rickert, Köller (dissenting), Liebknecht, Windthorst SBDR 13 Jan. 1886: 494, 498–500, 503–5. Exchanges between the MdI and the WPK are instructive for how the RT held the government's feet to the fire. Though the WPK voted to validate 2 S-H because the majority was huge and the SD did not make the runoff, the RT invalidated it—because *two* SD assemblies had been forbidden.

exposed themselves to flying objects and got shouted down for their pains, yet never called the police; the English did not even *have* a Law of Assembly. The Lassallean-Progressive skirmishes in Berlin in the sixties were trotted out; as was the Reform Party's irascible Pastor Karl Friedrich Wilhelm Iskraut and his flail-wielding farmers at the "Battle of Spenge"; the Social Democrats' forcible takeover of a Reformer's rally in Lörrach, Baden, in 1890 (in spite of thirteen attending police); a scrimmage between Socialist and antisemitic coal miners in Eisleben that same year; the strong armed "explosion" of rival assemblies in the Dresden suburbs by columns of German-National Shop Assistants on behalf of Reform Party candidates in 1893, and subsequently in Thuringia; their bush-whacking the Social Democratic Professor Neißer's lecture on venereal disease in Stettin; a Centrum-BdL takeover in Geisa, Saxe-Weimar, in 1903; stone-throwing Socialist masons at a Reformer's assembly in Melsungen in Hessen-Nassau (one participant responded by pulling a revolver); the "national" parties' obstructions at a Socialist rally in the Meiningen countryside: the Reichstag's ability to recall each and every election fracas of years past only served to confirm Bernstein's judgment that the German Empire's election broils had been "extraordinarily tiny and harmless." Universal—again excepting the conservatives—was the feeling that the antisemites got what they deserved, not only because their behavior was easily the worst, but also because of their sneaky attempts, in the rallies they called themselves, to exclude the general "public." Johannes Giesberts insisted that bringing order into a rambunctious crowd of a thousand or more was simply not possible with a dozen gendarmes. He spoke for many when he argued that given the alternative of occupying the entire locale with police officials, "I'd rather have a little *Tumult*."[93]

In fact, it would be wrong to exaggerate the manipulation and the mayhem that went on during the campaign. In many, perhaps most, confrontations between opposing parties, the decencies were observed. A British journalist sent to report on the election of 1903 was amazed not only by speeches that lasted two hours but by the "perfect courtesy . . . generally extended to members of the opposition. . . ."[94] It was a far cry not only from the brawls that had earlier been so common in England, but also from the violence that marred political assemblies in Vienna that same decade, especially between Czechs and Germans. It would be easy to explain these differences as the journalist himself did, by referring to the ubiquitous gendarme. But were Viennese rallies really less well policed?[95] Was it really stricter laws that made German meetings more decorous, or was it the respect in which Germans held the law? Whatever the expla-

[93] Quotes: Giesberts, A. Patzig, E. Bernstein SBDR 21 Mar. 1906: 2194, 2196, 2203.

[94] "Working," 275. "Heated fencing" unmarred by insults between the LLs and SDs in Herford-Halle: Severing, *Lebensweg* 1: 28; 3-way exchange between Christ. Soz. (Catholic), SD, and Constantia (Z) in Aachen: Lepper, ed., *Katholizismus*, 291–97; Lepper, *Strömungen* 1: 304. Exceptions: *GA* Nr. 6, 8 Jan. 1874: 33; Müller, *Strömungen*, 197; Bellot, *Hundert Jahre*, 173, 184, 227; "Wahlterrorismus des Zentrums," *BT* Nr. 18, 2. Beiheft, 11 Jan. 1912.

[95] The Viennese contrast is my own, spurred by Boyer's *Culture*, 322f.

nation, although "perfect courtesy" at German election assemblies was far from guaranteed, the odd arrest was generally considered an embarrassment, a discredit to the offending party.

The institution of the discussion-speaker, and the attendant belief that political meetings were little parliaments, profoundly affected the nature of the German campaign. Although at the for-members-only gatherings of some of Germany's ultranationalist, para-political (and marginal) groups a sudsy unanimity was all but scripted (the Pan-German League comes quickly to mind), these were very much the exception.[96] The assumption that the entire "public," rather than simply one's own party faithful, would be present at any election assembly worthy of the name, makes the American term "rally" a somewhat misleading designation for these gatherings. In insisting upon the rights of the discussant, the parties and their audiences paid honor to what was in many precincts still a fiction: the presumption that elections proceeded from the choices of individuals, made after weighing arguments from both sides. Yet these assumptions and this insistence turned the campaign into genuinely democratic contests for the hearts and minds of the German people—even in places where the balloting itself was not yet free.[97]

To make the election itself free, neither the customary understandings of the law nor popular notions of what constituted the "public" were sufficient. Some kind of power was also necessary. Friends, kin, peers of all kinds, as we shall see in the next chapter, and especially clubs and organizations were "social capital" that might empower a citizen to vote "uneconomically."[98] But these same resources had their costs. For it was not only the strictures of the state and the importunities of his betters, but also, and even more continually, those of his equals that bore down upon the German voter. The strength of the community worked two ways: toward providing protection but also toward enforcing conformity. It is to these issues that we now turn.

[96] Pan-Germans: Chickering, *We Men*, 154–58, 173, 175f; membership: 213; similarities with other nationalist societies: 187f; intrusions by opponents: 161; marginality: 110, 135.

[97] E.g., workers pressed the NL candidate in debate in Saarbrücken's 1902 by-election—though bosses still prevented SD *voting*: Bellot, *Hundert Jahre*, 208. Political assemblies might be frequent and lively even when turnouts were low, such as 9 Potsdam in 1877. Frank, *Brandenburger*, 116, 121f.

[98] The importance of intermediary associations for democracy was first noted by Tocqueville, *Democracy* (1830), but it has been the focus of recent discussion. Among many, see: Fish, *Democracy* (1995), esp. n. 31; idem, "Crisis" (1996), 152. Bringing together a wide literature on "social capital": Putnam, "Bowling" (1995) and idem, *Making* (1993), 163–85—an analysis of Italy. Putnam excepts, however, those associations connected with the Catholic Church, which he believes are "negatively associated with good government": a conclusion that points to the danger of generalizing from one case.

CHAPTER TEN

Belonging

A person thinks politically as he is socially.

—*Paul Lazersfeld*, The People's Choice *(1948)*

CONFORMITY

In June 1914 one of Germany's leading novelists penned the following description of a Reichstag election in the imaginary town of Netzig:

> The decision came at three in the afternoon. An alarm whistle rang out in Kaiser Wilhelmstrasse, and everyone rushed to their windows and shop doors to see where the fire was. It was the Veterans Association [*Kriegerverein*; literally: Warriors Association], in full fig . . . Kühnchen was in command, his spiked helmet awry, swinging his sword in a fearsome manner. . . . At the other end of the street, the new colors were presented and received, with thunderous music and proud hurrahs. Reinforced by inexhaustible supplies of patriotic recruits, the procession reached Klappsch's tavern. As they wheeled into formation, Kühnchen gave the order: "Advance to the urns!" Inside, the overseers were waiting in their Sunday best, with Pastor Zillich presiding. In martial tones Kühnchen issued his commands. "Onward, comrades, to the polls! We're electing Fischer!" Whereupon, with crashing music, pivoting from the right wing, they marched into the locale. The entire procession followed the *Kriegerverein*. Klappsch, not prepared for so much enthusiasm, had already run out of beer. Finally, after the national cause seemed to have thrown up all of which it was capable, the mayor, Dr. Scheffelweis, arrived amidst hurrahs. He quite openly allowed a red ballot to be pressed into his hand, and when he returned from the urn, you could see that he was agreeably moved.[1]

Thus did Heinrich Mann satirize the self-importance, the mindless conformity, and ultimately the hypocrisy of small-town patriotism at election time (for thanks to preelection horse trading, having nothing to do with national welfare but everything to do with local economic interests, the warriors' choice had fallen on Napoleon Fischer, head of Netzig's SPD). Although few commentators were so adept at capturing the tones of *Vereinsdeutsch*, that inflated diction characteristic of German Babbitts at play, Mann was joining a chorus of criticism.[2]

---

[1] Mann, *Untertan*, 318f.

[2] E.g., L. E. Schücking's *Reaktion* is *Der Untertan* without the novelistic drapery. Vereinsdeutsch: Chickering, *We Men*, 155.

Beginning in the eighties, it was a rare election that did not produce challenges based on the activities of the warriors associations.[3] Unlike some of the tonier nationalist bodies—the Navy League, the Army League, the Eastern March Society, the Pan-Germans, for example, all peopled by the educated Protestant bourgeoisie—the *Kriegervereine*, founded after the defeat of the French in 1871, were genuinely grass-roots organizations. Open to all those who had seen military service of any sort, the clubs were immensely popular, especially in Protestant stretches of northern and central Germany, where local groups might number from a dozen to somewhat more than one hundred members. By 1889, the various branches could claim roughly a million adherents—about one-tenth of the electorate. Twenty years later, that membership had nearly doubled.[4] The probability that a community would boast a warriors' association was in inverse proportion to its size. In Royal Saxony, they counted more than one member for every five voters. In Prussia, people said, "a village without a *Kriegerverein* was like a cat without a tail."[5] Their privileges allowed the warriors to sponsor festivals, to hold dances outside police hours, and, on special occasions, to march armed. Although their declared aim was to encourage patriotism, they enjoyed a well-deserved reputation as chug-a-lug clubs (*Sauf und Rauf Vereine*). At the same time, their mutual support funds, their collections on behalf of their widows and orphans, and the dues they levied to pay for burials adorned with their own martial presence gave members a financial as well as a social stake in belonging. In the eyes of critics, this combination of economic benefits, which an individual would forfeit with loss of membership, and royal privilege, which the government could withdraw from any branch, constituted potentially coercive political power.

The associations were commonly reckoned an election machine for any party that could claim the mantle of nationalism or the favor of its respective state government. Their by-laws forbade discussing religion or politics, but obligated members to loyalty to Kaiser and Reich. Conservative and National Liberal forces were quick to occupy the space defined by interested interpretations of the words "unpolitical" and "loyal."[6] The associations were especially visible in the campaigns of 1887, 1893, and 1907, dominated by the military budget, a matter deemed dear to the warriors' hearts.

---

[3] E.g., 8 Merseburg AnlDR (1890/91, 8/I, Bd. 3) DS 297: 2081; 8 Hessen AnlDR (1912/14, 8/I, Bd. 16) DS 350: 289; 7 Gumb. AnlDR (1912/14, 13/I, Bd. 23) DS 1586: 3404. Schücking, *Reaktion*, 92f.

[4] Figures: K. Zeitz (NL) SBDR 10 Jan. 1889: 363f; Wolfgang Hartwig, "Bürgertum, Staatssymbolik und Staatsbewußtsein im Deutschen Kaiserreich 1871–1914," *GG* 16/3 (1990): 269–95; 271. Scholarship on the *Kriegervereine* is too enormous to cite. Within the same constellation one could include the Bund Deutscher Militäranwärter, whose chairman, J. A. Schwier, claimed 40,000 members in a letter to Bülow, 15 Jan. 1907. BAB-L R1501/14697, Bl. 193.

[5] Figures extrapolated from Rickert SBDR 10 Jan. 1889: 360; G. Birk, "Kriegervereinswesen" (1982), 266, 271; quote on 273.

[6] Graf v. Hohenthal und Bergen, Zeitz SBDR 10 Jan. 1889: 361, 364. Complaints in 8 Kassel: W. Schmalz, cabinetmaker, date worn away, BAB-L R1501/14468, Bl. 214; elsewhere: unsigned protest, ibid., Bl. 233.

Election proclamations from state or district headquarters typically began by announcing that the leadership would not tell a member how to cast his ballot ("That is solely a matter between your God and your soldier's heart"); moved quickly into the obligation to vote ("The Fatherland that you once shielded with your bodies, and that you are ready at any time to shield again, calls!"); and ended by declaring that there was only one way to treat a member who supported an opponent of our German Empire: "Turn your back on him with contempt!"[7] In 1907, when the ballot was supposed to be protected by envelopes and voting booth, one parent body still asked to be notified if any "duty-forgetting" member campaigned against the government, so that it might request him to resign voluntarily. Such instructions always raised hackles; the progressive *Berliner Zeitung* referred to the veterans as "*Kriechervereine*" (toady clubs). The warriors' reputation for fairness was not improved by the fact that they were sometimes employed to break strikes.[8]

An evening spent toasting the good old days *beim Kommiß* undoubtedly encouraged a beery nostalgia. Whether it actually engendered popularity for nationalist, conservative political positions or merely mirrored tavern sentiment is difficult to determine. Statewide election directives sometimes ran up against local veterans' groups with minds of their own, actively supporting Left Liberal, Centrum, or even Social Democratic candidates.[9] Indeed, in some Braunschweig villages, polling returns in the eighties revealed that fewer than a third of the warriors could have voted *non*-Socialist. In Thuringia, we see rural branches taking over the distribution of Socialist ballots, and one opened its hall to the Socialist candidate—scandalizing higher-ups by turning the portrait of the Kaiser and their Duke to the wall for the speech's duration. Protesters insisted that those branches which too openly flouted headquarters could face disciplinary action. Did awareness of such a possibility produce conformity? At least three branches in Saxe-Coburg-Gotha, after receiving instructions to vote against the Social Democrats, chose instead to withdraw from the parent body.[10]

The political weight of the warriors associations lay not in the powers and privileges of their central organs, but—as Heinrich Mann's Netzig and its unanimously "red" ballots showed—in the ability of the branches to organize and

---

[7] "Kameraden des deutschen Kriegerbundes!" *Thüringer Ztg* 41 (18 Feb. 1887) BAB-L R1501/14664, unpaginated; Gen. v. Spitz [sp.?], Chairman of the Prussian Landes-Kriegerverbandes, to Bülow, 10 Feb. 1903, BAB-L R1501/14695, Bl. 24f. The General sent campaign literature to his counterparts in Saxony, Baden, Hessen, Braunschweig, and 12 smaller states commanding 702,000 members. The letter made the rounds of the entire bureaucracy (I counted 9 signatures) before going to the Kaiser. The RT might or might not consider such influence illegitimate: [Köller], *Ungiltigkeit*, 17f. On 5 Hessen: Hasenclever SBDR 17 May 1887: 621.

[8] Erzberger, *Bilder*, 55f; Köller SBDR 20 May 1886: 2084; Bellot, *Hundert Jahre*, 187.

[9] LLs: *Thätigkeit*, 159; Z: Bellot, *Hundert Jahre*, 227; Horn Report, 24 Feb. 1907, LHAK 403/8806: 4v; Monshausen, *Wahlen*, 337; SDs: ibid., 298, 338; 1 Erfurt AnlDR (1912/14, 13/I, Bd. 20) DS 1160: 2291–98.

[10] Köller SBDR 20 May 1886: 2082, 2093; Zeitz SBDR 10 Jan. 1889: 364f; W. Boch, Reinbaben SBDR 20 May 1886: 2090f; Blos, *Denkwürdigkeiten* 2: 117.

enforce local conformity. Usually this took the form of a resolution calling for a unanimous vote or agreeing to expel those who voted wrong.[11] (Headquarters and membership took it as given that warrior ballots would be recognizable in some way.) "We took a stand against Social Democracy," admitted the head of a steering committee in Hanover, who had passed out ballots at the polls; "Everyone has his free will, but a Social Democrat cannot remain in the club."[12] As in any organization, however, the effectiveness of the threat to exclude was no stronger than the willingness of members to enforce it. In Braunschweig, when the steering committee moved to expel two men who had come out for the Socialist candidate, the 700-man membership voted it down—arguing that politics were not allowed (whereupon the authorities dissolved the branch—and confiscated its treasury of 37–40,000 marks).[13]

The veterans' associations never offered weaker groups effective shelter against the powerful; only rarely did they protect the individual against the group. But they were never really controlled from above. Their sharpest weapon was a declaration that someone was, as one election proclamation put it, "not a comrade [*Kamerad*]." Social Democrats eventually advised their adherents not to waste their time protesting the *Kriegervereine*'s campaign interventions, unless they could prove that secrecy had been violated: "Free men don't let themselves be bothered by such 'orders'; anyone who allows himself to be put in leading strings voluntarily and abdicates his political independence—such a person can't be helped."[14] In small-town Germany, however, to expect a comrade (*Genosse*) to risk expulsion from the comrades (*Kamaraden*) was asking a great deal.

We would miss the point of Mann's satire, however, if we believed that it was limited to the nationalist milieu. The march to the polls of the serried ranks of Netzig (a word with connotations of networks, meshes, and, ultimately, trap) was Mann's metaphor for Wilhelmine society as a whole. Not just the backstairs deals that led the leader of Netzig's notables, Dr. Scheffelweis, to cast a red ballot, but the collective, and implicitly coercive, character of the voting act itself damned a polity in which, as Mann and other intellectuals saw it, political choices were not rational, not individual, and definitely not free. Voting is, after all, the defining mark of modern citizenship. Mann could rely upon his readers' awareness of similar pressures on other voters—in Catholic and Protestant so-

---

[11] F. Sievers, Kleinhändler, SD Protest in 9 Han., 12 Mar. 1887, BAB-L R1501/14664, Bl. 82: Singer, Traeger, Rickert, and Zeitz SBDR 10 Jan. 1889: 353f, 359, 362f, 368; Auer SBDR 3 Dec. 1890: 768. Cf. 1 Saxe-Mein. (1884/85, 6/I, Bd. 6) DS 184: 765f.

[12] Read by I. Baumbach (FK) SBDR 3 Dec. 1890: 764; marked ballots in 9 Han. AnlDR (1890/91, 8/I, Bd. 1) DS 95: 638, 640. Notification that ballots would be "checked": 13 Saxony AnlDR (1887/88, 7/II, Bd. 4) DS 212: 906.

[13] Bock SBDR 20 May 1886: 2090; Blos, *Denkwürdigkeiten* 2: 116f. Similar defense of a liberal shoemaker in 3 Danzig (1882/83, 5/II, Bd. V) DS 80: 348.

[14] Election proclamation, 1 Saxe-Mein. (1884/85, 6/I, Bd. 6) DS 184: 766; *Thätigkeit*, 161.

cial clubs, in artisans' guilds, in trade unions—to bring home his message about the distance between the subject (*der Untertan*, the title of the novel) and the genuine citizen.[15]

Here was a world in which the SPD's humor magazine, *Der Wahre Jakob*, could have a field day with the following advertisement, which had appeared in a Braunschweig newspaper:

> I hereby declare the vote cast by me on the 21st of the month for W. Blos (the only one which the latter received here) null and void. I announce myself free from any responsibility and obligation towards Social Democracy, and now that I have won an entirely different view on the matter, I am joining the National Liberal Party and give my vote retroactively to Herr Alderman Retemeyer.
>
> Schandelah, February 1887
> Emil Opitz, Linen Dealer[16]

It was not only the supporters of Social Democracy who felt vulnerable. When an elderly resident of Rostock sent William II a clipping from his local paper that he believed revealed the "true character" of the SPD, he wanted his own name kept out: "*Majestät! im Interesse dieser Sendung u. Bericht, ist es wohl gut es geheim zu halten.*"

The social penalties for deviance rarely needed to be spelled out. When the ne'er-do-well father-in-law of the upwardly mobile Walter Eickenrot announces, in Ludwig Thoma's mordant comedy, *Die Sippe*, that he finally has a job—on an SPD newspaper—the audience could both laugh at and sympathize with the furious Walter, who immediately foresees the consequence for his reserve officer status: "I might as well take off my uniform right now!"[17]

Assumptions like these, everyone knew, were an iceberg of which the occasional parade to the polls was only the visible tip. Such election-day processions were practiced by every political camp. When they were made up of welders shepherded by factory managers, of stable-jacks and field hands by stewards and squires, of villagers by rural constables, of soldiers by their commanding officers, their coercive function was obvious.[18] When composed of

---

[15] *DA* 21/24 (14 June 1903): 398; *GA* Nr. 6, 8 Jan. 1874: 32; [Köller], *Ungiltigkeit*, 18; in 11 Düsseldorf: Reyscher SBDR 18 Apr. 1871: 270. "Auf zur Wahl!" Meppen, 28 July 1878, in the possession of Dr. Josef Hamacher, Haselünne.

[16] Blos, *Denkwürdigkeiten* 2: 154f. Similar cases in the *Hamburger Echo*: Kutz-Bauer, *Arbeiterschaft*, 162.

[17] "Your Majesty! It is probably a good idea, so far as this mailing and report goes, to keep it secret." Wm. Habermann, Rostock, 20 Dec. 1906, to Wm. II, BAB-L R1501/14697, Bl. 138. *Die Sippe* (Munich, [1913], 1956), 49f.

[18] Among non-agricultural employees, here are just a few of those I found being marched in closed ranks to the polls: quarry workers and miners in Hanover; brewers in Mainz and Berlin; weavers in Saxony; chemical and silk workers in Ludwigshafen; porcelain workers in Meckl.-Strehlitz; loggers in 6 Potsdam and throughout Central Silesia; clay factory workers in the Erzgebirge; mirror factory workers in 10 Breslau; pencil factory workers in Oberfranken; factory workers generally in Rheinbrol and in 6 Magdeburg; more than 100 warders from the Royal Saxon

parishioners strolling behind their priest, village veterans strutting behind the marshals of their warriors association, their ritualized, symbolic function was more apparent.[19] Most ambiguous were the processions of Social Democrats. Credible reports from the party's Saxon heartland complained of the comrades' surrounding voters, passing out ballots, marching them to the polls, and standing over them, just like bosses, as they voted.[20] In communal elections too, trade unions led columns to the polls straight from the foundries and the mines, still covered with soot and still wearing their Davy lamps. The proletarian brigades had to pass through streets lined with union sentries, who followed them to the urn to monitor their voting.[21] Was this solidarity or coercion?

COMMUNITAS OBLIGE

The question is an important one, but impossible to answer. What we can say is that every election procession, regardless of who organized it, pointed to realities and relationships that both preceded and outlasted the choices made on election day. It is to the unequal development and articulation of these relationships that we must look for an explanation for one of the puzzles in our story of the achievement of competitive elections: the relatively greater weakness of the Social Democrats, compared to the Centrum and Poles, when confronted with the hostility of the powerful. The discrepancy is best demonstrated in those mixed districts in the industrializing west where Centrum and Social Democrats both competed with socially and economically powerful National Liberals, and where both were subjected to reprisals.[22] In Bochum-Gelsenkirchen, a largely Protestant district of hundreds of thousands, the total Social Democratic vote in the *first seven national elections combined did not reach 4,000.* In Saarbrücken, where between 30 and 40 percent of the population was Protestant, *Social De-*

Insane Asylum at Colditz; miners, steel and iron workers throughout the Ruhr; soldiers (ineligible to vote!) in Liebenswalde and in 3 Koblenz.

[19] Priests leading congregations: Kühne, *Dreiklassenwahlrecht*, 147. One hundred marching villagers: 5 Oppeln AnlDR (1879, 4/II, Bd. 4) DS 105: 647f. Marching veterans: A. Schütte (L) protest against 3 Braunschweig, 12 Mar., 1887, Bl. 15; Singer SBDR 29 Nov. 1888: 64. Mann as a historical source: Reinhard Alter, "Heinrich Manns *Untertan*—Prüfstein für die 'Kaiserreich-Debatte'?" *GG* 17 (1991): 370–89.

[20] Physical threats in Zwickau: Reimer SBDR 10 Apr. 1874: 697, and Ortsrichter u. Bezirksvorsteher Eduard Würker, to RKA, 28 Jan. 1877 and again 22 Aug. 1878, BAB-L R1501/14693, Bl. 21 and 71; in 15 Saxony, SBDR 17 Jan. 1894, 691–94, esp. 692; "Ein unhaltbares Verfahren bei Wahl-Prüfungen," 27 Mar. 1914, *Hamburger Nachrichten*, BAB-L R1501/14653/1, unpaginated; W. Löwe-Calbe SBDR 11 Apr. 1874: 718; Chemnitz: Göhre, *Three Months*, 107f; Romeyk, *Wahlen*, 62.

[21] "Beantwortungen von Anfragen. J. B., Wahlbeeinflussungen bei Gemeindeverordnetenwahlen; Befugnisse des Wahlvorstandes," *PVB* 27/15 (13 Jan. 1906): 272: 1. Blue-collar bullies working for NLs: 1 Erfurt 1877 AnlDR (1877, 3/I, Bd. 3) DS 113: 359; in 3 Hamburg, Graf v. Arnim-Boytzenburg SBDR 12 Mar. 1878: 482.

[22] Contrast Sieg-Mülheim-Wipperfürth (Catholic) with neighboring (and Protestant) Wiehl: Möllers, *Strömungen*, 180f, 216; similarly, Mülheim: Müller, *Strömungen*, 181, 427n. 106.

mocracy did not get a single recorded vote in any of these first seven elections.
In Stumm's Ottweiler–St. Wendel-Meisenheim, just over 40 percent Protestant,
Socialists were invisible until 1887, scrambled to get 2,591 votes in 1890, and
then all but disappeared again.[23] In all three districts, the Centrum achieved
substantial levels of support—as it did in others similarly burdened by intense
employer pressure, even where Catholics were a minority.[24]

The discrepancy in the success of the three outsider camps cannot be attributed entirely to the continuing effects of the Kulturkampf. No doubt that conflict siphoned off potential Socialist support among working-class Catholics, but
since Social Democracy also carried the anti-Catholic banner, why should the
Kulturkampf have kept their Protestant counterparts away from the Socialist
cause?[25] State persecution, while undoubtedly more severe and more continuous
for the Social Democrats than the Centrum (although not the Poles), also does
not completely bridge the explanatory gap. The Socialist Law was never, or
hardly ever, enforced in Essen County during the twelve years it was on the
books. Even after September 1890 when the law expired, Essen Social Democracy took more than a decade to expand, a failure "all the more astonishing,"
notes Frank Bajohr, because the structural prerequisites there appeared ideal.[26]

The 1878 elections in a working-class suburb of Essen, where Alfred Krupp
ran as candidate for the "national" cause, provide some clues for explaining the
contrast. In the seven precincts of Altendorf, canvassed by no fewer than 339
company "volunteers," resided one-third of all Krupp's steelworkers. Here Candidate Krupp was able to better the count of his National Liberal predecessor by
a factor of seven. In the face of the Krupp juggernaut, the Centrum's vote
plummeted; but Social Democracy vanished altogether—losing almost 96 percent of its previous tally.[27] Revealingly, the Socialists lost the greatest number

---

[23] Molt, *Reichstag*, 186n. 4. In the 12 highly industrialized districts in the Düsseldorf regency, the
SDs in the 1870s and early 1880s were strong only in Elberfeld-Barmen and Solingen. Similarly in
Koblenz regency: Romeyk, *Wahlen*, 408. SDs and urbanization: Ritter, "Sozialdemokratie im Deut-
schen Kaiserreich," 295–362.

[24] Schloßmacher, *Düsseldorf*, 239. In Dortmund-Hörde, where Catholics were 42.6% of the population, the Z threw its support behind the LL Lenzmann. The fact that in 1890 Schorlemer-Alst (Z)
won in Hamm-Soest, with a similar confessional breakdown, suggests that analogous alliances,
rather than successful intimidation, is the explanation for the Z's occasional absences from the
district's election statistics in the 70s and 80s. Specht/Schwabe, *Reichstagswahlen*, 162–72.

[25] *Pace* Rohe, esp. in *Wahlen*, and "Konfession." Newcomer status also does not fully explain SD
backwardness: Kutz-Bauer, *Arbeiterschaft*, 126.

[26] Bajohr, *Krupp*, 25, 27–29; Tenfelde, *Bergarbeiterschaft*, 531n. 199. Harassment of Poles: Stephen SBDR 8 Jan. 1897: 290–97; Jan. 1897: 299–321; v. Carlinski 29 Jan. 1897: 705–33. SPD
willingness to wage Kulturkampf even at the end of our period: Romeyk, *Wahlen*, 140.

[27] Möllers, *Strömungen*, 328–30; Paul, *Krupp*, 44f, 266; Phillips, *Reichstag-Wahlen*, 104. Altendorf was 72% Catholic. I assume that Z voters were entirely Catholic and that "national" and SD
voters together were largely, though not entirely, Protestant. We can never tease out with certainty
the decisions of individuals from precinct statistics (J. Morgan Kousser, "Ecological Regression and
the Analysis of Past Politics," *JIH* 4/2 [Autumn 1973]: 237–62; Bartolini/Mair, *Identity*, 21f; on
changes in turnout, 174). But while eligible voters since the last election had increased, as had

Fɪɢ. 9

Comparison of 1877 and 1878 Elections in Altendorf (pop. 63,328)

Year	Precinct	Centrum Votes	SPD Votes	NL Votes	% Turnout
1877	Frohnhausen	393	16	17	66
1878		382	0	132	80
1877	Holsterhausen	326	63	9	61
1878		344	3	141	75
1877	Altendorf II	424	60	47	63
1878		416	8	222	76
1877	Altendorf I	382	65	48	70
1878		331	0	230	80
1877	Kronenberg II	245	164	67	74
1878		100	9	456	88
1877	Kronenberg I	291	222	85	82
1878		106	9	530	88
1877	Holsterhausen-	199	236	67	65
1878	Schederhof	102	7	543	85

Source: figures extrapolated from Möllers, *Strömungen*, 329f; and Paul, *Krupp*, 44f, 266.

Precincts listed in descending order of Z support. Support for Krupp is negatively correlated with Z support. Precisely the same (ascending) order depicts 1877 support for the SDs.

of votes in precincts where they had the most votes to lose. This might seem logical, but the same was not true of the Centrum. Rather, it was in the precincts where the Catholic party had the fewest supporters that it lost the most votes. Unlike the Social Democrats, from those precincts where it had much, much was *not* taken.

Since the economic opportunities for these two sets of voters must be presumed to be the same, not a different economic calculus, but differences in political homogeneity seem to explain the discrepancies in resistance to the Krupp campaign. The numbers suggest that once a critical mass had been reached, homogeneity was a self-reinforcing mechanism. In fact, Krupp himself recognized this principle when he tried, unsuccessfully, to require Catholics and Protestants in his housing blocks to "live all mixed up together."[28] An activated and homogeneous neighborhood, in Essen as in Netzig, had its own means of enforcing election norms, and its sanctions for nonconformity might be at least as undesirable as the canon king's. *Communitas oblige.* As studies of group behavior during the Third Reich suggest, conformity may be as powerful a force as authority. In an uncertain world, on whom, ultimately, does the work-

precinct turnouts, to explain such a dramatic shift in preferences in one year by people entering and leaving the electorate is implausible.

[28] Paul, *Krupp*, 168. Residential patterns and independence: H. Steffens, "Arbeiterwohnverhältnisse," in K. Tenfelde/H. Volkmann, eds., *Streik* (1981), 124–42; Kutz-Bauer, *Arbeiterschaft*, 168f.

ingman most depend—his bread lord or his brother-in-law? His plant or his neighborhood?

Homogeneity is of course perceived socially and culturally as much as demographically and spatially. We have already seen how the Centrum's and Poles' potential constituency could gather not only in the pews but within a whole associational cosmos beyond the bread lord's sway. Such social space was important precisely in those newly industrializing areas where company housing could be searched at any time, where postal officials collaborated with bosses by violating the mail,[29] where newcomers lacked extensive preexisting childhood or familial connections. Where social space was provided by consciously Protestant sociability, as in the Ruhr, where the Protestant churches established prayer groups, convivial organizations, and even workers' clubs, they were for a long while likely to reinforce the bread lord's "national" election choices.

In some regions, of course, Social Democracy also enjoyed compact residential patterns; it too could tap existing networks of sociability and translate a social-cultural into a political space. In Chemnitz, the party's influence pervaded every aspect of daily life. In Hamburg, the most unchurched city in the empire, a lively plebeian club scene easily took on political coloration. A workers' educational society had existed there for decades; a Lassalle cult, with twenty-six Lassallean glee clubs, as early as 1873.[30] Structures such as these enabled hard-pressed adherents to winter over the storms of employer hostility and police persecution.

But in most places, Socialists had to begin from scratch. The proletarian "class," although a ready-made constituency from the standpoint of Marxist theory, hardly existed in nineteenth-century Germany even as a significant percentage of wage-earners, much less as a community, and least of all as a self-conscious identity.[31] And in the exploding, polyglot population centers of the Ruhr, where preexisting structures of plebeian sociability were lacking, Socialists were slow to build them. The complex associational life that now seems to us the hallmark of the SPD did not appear in most places until the turn of the nineteenth century. And by then it already represented a mass movement conscious of its ascendance, not the hunted sect of the catacombs.[32]

In the meantime, in places like Essen, Social Democrats were the last of the town's groups to translate their message into associations that could create and mobilize politically a larger, culturally defined community. This neglect may have stemmed in part from the demographic characteristics of the movement's early adherents: male, highly skilled, single, and for all these reasons more than usually mobile. At the height of their powers, such men hardly needed the

---

[29] "Cosmos": Mooser, "Vereinswesen," 452; Romeyk, *Wahlen*, 401. Bajohr, *Krupp*, 24f.

[30] Kutz-Bauer, *Arbeiterschaft*, 117, 193; V. Lidtke, *Culture* (1985), 23–29, 37; Chemnitz: Moore, *Injustice*, 223.

[31] Moore, *Injustice*; Rohe, "Introduction: Elections" (1990), 3.

[32] Excellent: Lidtke, *Culture*, esp. chaps. 1 and 7; Guttsman, *Party*, 174–215.

social and self-help organizations sought by the older, the less skilled, the fathers of families—organizations that provided cover for political recruitment as well as the means of political discipline. But the neglect of sociability also grew directly out of the party's own ethos. Mobility, not milieu-building, was the option pushed by the activists, because motion itself, they knew, undermined habit and widened horizons.[33] While the object of Centrum politics was the *defense* of the (Catholic) quotidian, Social Democracy offered itself, as Frank Bajohr has argued, precisely as a way to *emancipate* its adherents from the "chains" of the *Alltag*. Whereas Centrum voting was (at the very least) an affirmation of group identity, Socialist voting, in the early decades, was apt to be an expression of individualistic self-determination. Not only sociability but the "social" itself, as Germans understood the term (i.e., a practical concern for the various problems of the poor), held a low priority for much of the vanguard. Social Democracy on the ground represented far less an agenda for tackling the pressing needs of one's mates than we might have supposed, and far more an individual's aspiration for autonomy, culture, and self-respect—an aspiration that seems, initially at least, to have been peculiarly "unsocial" in its expression.

Thus uplift, not innocent merriment, marked the presence of the committed Social Democrat. *"Bildung," "Geistesbedürfnisse,"* the responsibilities of *"Kulturvölker"* were as central to the Social Democratic as to the Liberal political lexicon. Only when Socialist leisure could be translated into vehicles for self-improvement—into temperance, free-thinker, library, and theatrical societies; into fitness associations of gymnasts, cyclists, and hikers—did party sociability flourish widely, and in some regions this translation took several decades. Even then, the clubs were often disparaged by activists as *"Klimbim Vereine"* (nonsense societies), a distraction from the class struggle.[34] The primacy of politics within the Social Democratic mission, as well as its overwhelming orientation toward the experience of wage-earners, reinforced its character as a men's movement, and—for all the party's message of female as well as male emancipation—may have made it initially difficult for Social Democracy to find a footing in the domestic private sphere. Only belatedly did the comrades recognize that parties not only grow out of a milieu, but can themselves shape and reshape it. This deficit helps explain why Social Democracy, anchored only in the courage of individuals, long remained in many places a diffuse social protest movement, unable to survive forceful employer intervention—and unable to mount a successful attack of its own.[35] Before it could march its voters to the

---

[33] Schönhoven, "Selbsthilfe," 166f; Kutz-Bauer, *Arbeiterschaft*, 126, 134; v. Oppen, *Reform*, 11.

[34] "Culture," "intellectual needs," "civilized nations." Forcefully argued by Bajohr, *Krupp*, 27, 33–37; support in Lidtke, *Culture*, 175; Guttsman, *Party*, 210; and the autobiography of Moritz Bromme, in Kelly, ed., *Worker*, and consonent with v. Saldern, *Wege*.

[35] Rohe, "Introduction: Elections," 11f, 14. One must, of course, be careful of too sweeping contrasts. Unions and craft associations were always encouraged. Lepper, *Strömungen* 1: 152–57. An analogous distaste for relying on the "milieu" was sometimes expressed—with remarkably little self-knowledge—by liberals. "Zum 3. März," *GA* Nr. 53, 3 Mar. 1871: 439.

polls, Social Democracy had first to develop the attributes not only of a party, but of a community.

Extrusion

If kin, friends, and associations of all kinds were among the resources that (along with high employment rates and cultural practices embodied in written and unwritten rules) might empower a beleaguered citizen to vote "uneconomically," kin, friends, and associations (let us call them, without prejudice, the "community") might just as easily, and indeed simultaneously, limit a voter's choices. The contribution of communities to free elections lay not in the experiences of individuals, *qua* individuals, but in the establishment of competition between groups. For here is the paradox of Heinrich Mann's Netzig on election day: serried ranks of quite respectable voters, *free*—through their belonging—to vote for the Social Democratic *Reichsfeind*. Empowerment and limitation were two sides of the safety that came with numbers, the familiarity that came with belonging.

Belonging to a community brings its own vulnerabilities. Once political issues were felt to matter, ostracism was always a possibility facing dissenters. In rural and small-town Germany, the personal consequences might be at least as painful as loss of work, or housing, or *Waldstreu*. During the Kulturkampf, the *Ostseezeitung* reported that in the Posnanian town of Kosten, "no merchant, not even a Protestant or Jewish one, dare[d] sell anything to the pro-state parish priest, even to meet him publicly in a friendly manner." In Prüm in 1907 a pastor announced that any confrère "who did not come out for the Centrum was not worthy of the sun's shining on him"—making even silence uncomfortable.[36] Conservative branches of the Farmers' League were known not only to expel Liberals, but to use their press to make pariahs of Landräte who failed to put the resources of the state at their disposal during elections. Though a victim might sue for defamation of character, and win—as did the Landrat of Flensburg—his local usefulness was over. The reader may remember the unlucky Landrat of County Birnbaum from chapter 6: excoriated by the Farmers' League and challenged to a duel for his political deficiencies, he dutifully (as a civil servant) refused satisfaction—and committed suicide.[37] Like exemplary dismissals, ostracism need not be invoked against every delinquent to be effective. One sufficiently publicized example usually sufficed.

Thus the same sense of identity that could enable "uneconomic" voting, could also enforce it.[38] In Lublinitz-Tost-Gleiwitz, as gendarmes and county officials were impressing upon impoverished constituents the compelling merits

---

[36] Quoted: Rust, *Reichskanzler*, 721; similarly in 10 AL in 1907: Hiery, *Reichstagswahlen*, 420; Definitor Schmitt of Prüm, Horn Report, 24 Feb. 1907, LHAK 403/8806: 4.

[37] Kühne, *Dreiklassenwahlrecht*, 83–87.

[38] Jakob Neureuter, famed pastor of Marpingen, ridiculing parishioners who complied with their (NL) bread lord: 6 Trier AnlDR (1882/83, 5/II, Bd. 6) DS 323: 1329.

of the Free Conservative Duke of Ujest, a correspondent to the Polish-language *Katolik* anathematized all those who would dare vote for the grandee as "true Judases," ready to "sell us out." The editor appended a note instructing his readers to report the names of any "traitors" to his editorial offices, and promised to "requite to each one what he has deserved, without mercy."[39] Considering how puny the powers of the press must have seemed in a rural district where the standard-bearer for the other side controlled in excess of 100,000 acres, it is not surprising that the Reichstag laughed when these lines were read. But the threat of ostracism, especially when phrased in the language of treason and Judas-metaphors, was a powerful one. And it encouraged voters to see the election not as a choice of representatives or a debate over policies but as a war between hostile communities.

Even against the high-born, the threat of extrusion proved effective. Fear of ostracism was why the "Declaration of Rhenish Catholic Nobles" on behalf of the Septennat in 1887 proved of no election value whatsoever to the government—which had undoubtedly engineered it as a weapon against the Centrum. No sooner was the declaration published than Franz Count von Spee-Heltorf announced that it was his "duty" to withdraw his signature "for certain reasons." Two other signers quickly followed suit. Finally even the candidate of the "Septennat Catholics," Landrat von Fürstenberg, withdrew from the race against the Centrum—infuriating those nationalist Protestants whose arms had been twisted to come out for him. The community's leverage against the powerful was best demonstrated in Upper Silesia, when the Catholic press met the open threats of landlords and mine-owners against Centrum voters by organizing public opprobrium against them. Such efforts were undoubtedly behind the Centrum's ability, by 1890, to take every Oppeln election district but one.[40] The grandees had to live in the neighborhood too.

Ostracism and what contemporaries called "election terrorism" were stations along a continuum of communal pressures. A truly protean term, "terrorism" might refer to anything from an employer's intimidation of his dependents to the government's manipulation of public opinion.[41] It was used to denote (and delegitimize) the power of strikers over those who wished to work; the pressure

---

[39] Read by Albrecht SBDR 5 Apr. 1871: 184. The Duke's egregious pressures: AnlDR (1874/75, 2/II, Bd. 4) DS 176: 1122–37; SBDR 21 Jan. 1875: 1153–71; AnlDR (1875/76, 2/III, Bd. 3) DS 195: 722; AnlDR (1876, 2/IV, Bd. 3) DS 72: 665; SBDR 26 Dec. 1876: 844f; Mazura, *Entwicklung*, 99f, 107.

[40] Müller, *Strömungen*, 243, 254; *GA* Nr. 188, 13 Aug. 1871: 1682; Mazura, *Entwicklung*, 55.

[41] "Die kassierte Wahl in Stendhal-Osterburg," *SaaleZ*, 27 Mar. 1914, and *Nationalliberale Correspondenz* 108 (28 May 1914), both in BAB-L R1501/14653/1, unpaginated; "Werksterroristen" in the Ruhr: quoted by H.-O. Hemmer, "Bergarbeiterbewegung," 99; v. Saldern, *Wege*, 59; "Ein Saarabisches Wahlbild," *Saar-Post* 20 (25 Jan. 1912); AnlDR (1912/14, 13/I, Bd. 23) DS 1639: 3610. "Official terrorism" described a government warning to a paper that reprinted a *Kladderadatsch* election poem: 17 Saxony (1882/83, 5/II, Bd. 5) DS 154: 522; a "correction" in a newspaper by the Saxon MdI elicited a protest from Ed. Bauer, typesetter, et al. against this "downright terroristic pressure": 13 Saxony AnlDR (1887/88, 7/II, Bd. 4) DS 212: 907.

of pastors on their bishop; of the organized on the unorganized; of the stupid on the smart; of the majority on the minority (and the minority on the majority!); of parties on the electorate; of one wing of a party on another. If we took the term at face value every time we met it, we would have to conclude that much of Germany lived in a constant state of fear. But in fact "terrorism" referred to any practice—social, religious, economic, physical, and ritual—aimed at effecting a particular political outcome.[42]

Wherever its associational infrastructures were well developed, "terrorism" became associated with Social Democracy.[43] In 1871 a spokesman conceded that "in almost all Saxon districts wherever worker candidates have been put up" the comrades grabbed ballots from voters and forced Social Democratic ones on them. But he shrugged it off: "Whoever does not know how to get hold of another ballot . . . just doesn't deserve to vote."[44] As their influence spread, however, Socialists went beyond threats, monitoring, and hooliganism on election day. Conservatives believed that the dues workers paid to the SPD were treated as insurance premiums for keeping their jobs. They knew that "if they can't demonstrate 'clean underwear,' as the expression has it,' they will, wherever purposeful 'comrades' rule, simply be pushed out of work."[45]

SPD "terrorism" enforced solidarity not only on other workers, but eventually on those outside the "class" altogether. When the notables of Mann's Netzig marched to the polls to vote for Napoleon Fischer, the autocratic chief of the local SPD, they were responding, at least in part, to Fischer's credible threat of a boycott against their businesses. However rare such an event may have been in 1893, when the fictional election took place, by the time Mann penned this passage, the boycott weapon had become, as we shall see, a part of the German electoral scene—and one indelibly (though not exclusively) associated with a now-formidable SPD.[46]

---

[42] Terrorism by strikers: *MK* 34 (26 Aug. 1871): 270; W. Schwarze (Z) SBDR 18 Feb. 1903: 7993; by priests over bishops: "Das Wahlrecht der Geistlichen," 71; by Alsatian press over Alsatian notables: Manteuffel to Wm. I, Straßburg, 3 Nov. 1884 GStA PK I. HA, Rep. 89/211, Bl. 36v; by laity over theologians: Anon., "Zum Katholikentag 1905," *DZJ* 5/35 (28 Aug. 1905), 409–11; by the "ultra-liberal majority" of Elberfeld-Barmen's aldermen over "bürgerlichen circles": "Wahlaussichten für die Rhein Provinz," GStA PK I. HA, Rep. 89/210, Bl. 230v; by minority of First Danzig's K election committee: Rickert SBDR 9 Apr. 1886: 2017; by [party] leaders over the "simple voter": J. Pfeiffer to Wm. II, 1 Mar. 1903, BAB-L R1501/14695, Bl. 97; by Hessen's Young Liberals over a NL count and baron: Freiherr von Saß, "Jungliberaler Terrorismus," *DA* XXVII/41 (10 Oct. 1909): 515–16; by the Z over its Silesian nobility: Leugners-Scherzberg, *Porsch*, 75; by Z agrarians over Z workers: Nipperdey, *Organisation*, 280.

[43] W. Frankenburger (F) SBDR 10 Apr. 1878: 875; BAB-L R1501/14450, Bl. 96; v. Friesen SBDR 10 Jan. 1889: 371; Göhre, *Three Months*, 107f; Nebe, *Grenzboten* 5 Dec. 1907, quoted in Below, *Wahlrecht*, 156n. 158.

[44] R. Schraps (Sächs. VP) SBDR 17 Apr. 1871: 244–50.

[45] "Zur Sicherung des Wahlgeheimnisses," *Die Post* (24 Mar. 1903) BAB-L R1501/14456, Bl. 101f; v. Oertzen (K) SBDR 17 Nov. 1906: 3698.

[46] 15 Saxony, SBDR 17 Jan. 1894: 691–94, esp. 692; 10 AL AnlDR (1905/06, 11/II, Bd. VI) DS 483: 4741; Counterprotest of Eduard v. Flottwell, Kapitan a. D., 14 Saxony AnlDR (1912/13, 13/I, Bd. 19) DS 718: 932f.

Boycott

Extrusion is a weapon effective only in face-to-face communities: a club, a village, a network of aristocrats, an urban neighborhood. The larger and more amorphous the group, the more difficult ostracism is to enforce and the easier it is for those targeted to escape the penalty. The boycott, on the other hand, positively requires a larger arena, because the boycotters themselves will need alternative sources of supply. And because it pinpoints a single relationship, the economic one, the boycott is feasible precisely in populous, plural, urban societies where ostracism would be impossible to enforce on a scale broad enough to make a difference.

Ostracism and the political boycott have another central difference. Ostracism is the sour side of solidarity. Its target is not the opponent, but the faltering friend. By definition, it can only be conducted against someone who conceives of himself as belonging to the community from which he is excommunicated. His extrusion is thus to a considerable extent an extrusion defined subjectively. The boycott, on the other hand, is waged against the outsider: someone who does not belong to the class or milieu. The evil, in the eyes of the world at large, appears all the greater, because a boycott can be imagined as happening to anyone. Socialist election statements occasionally implied that they had a weapon against the employers' threat of dismissal: "The election is free and secret! . . . Should they threaten you with dismissal from work or with other disadvantages, *then tell us*. **We will then take care of the punishment of the guilty**" announced a Braunschweig proclamation in 1878.[47] The boycott did not itself "enable" uneconomic voting among otherwise powerless citizens, but it did allow them to turn the economic calculus into a weapon against opponents. For the small shopkeeper, afterall, even the small consumer was a bread lord.

In using boycotts for electoral purposes, Germans were far from unique. "Exclusive dealing" with businesses that shared one's convictions was a political obligation in Peel's England, endorsed both by *Blackwood's Magazine* and the *Quarterly Review*. In Birmingham, shopkeepers who voted conservative could find crosses chalked on their doors, to warn liberal customers away. In Stockport the marketplace rang, Norman Gash tells us, with cries of "Cobden beef, Cobden potatoes" from stall-owners anxious to assure their customers that they belonged to the popular side.[48] Nevertheless, most of the English examples come from an era when the franchise was a privilege and expressed by voice, not ballot. In Imperial Germany, where every man counted, where the lines between groups were sharper, and the claims of reciprocity less axiomatic, the boycott's felt offense to the election process seems to have been greater. It is certainly harder for the historian to consider the tool as merely a curious example of electoral folkways.

Boycotts were never the exclusive tool of the Social Democrats. Aachen's

---

[47] Quoted in Steinbach, *Zähmung* 2: 683. Emphasis in original.
[48] Seymour, *Reform*, 187; Gash, *Politics*, 137; its universality, 175.

Catholic labor movement used the threat of exclusive dealing against its bourgeois coreligionists in the Centrum election club, Constantia.[49] More than thirty
years later, Catholic farmers in parts of Strasbourg-Land took revenge for the
victory of the Free Conservative Fürst Alexander zu Hohenlohe by boycotting
shopkeepers and refusing to deliver milk to Jews (shouting "Down with Hohenlohe! Down with Protestants and Jews!")[50] Conservatives and Liberals also used
the boycott. The tool was closely associated with the Farmers' League, who not
only blackballed individual businessmen, but put entire towns under interdict, in
one case, in retaliation for the Left Liberal Reichstag candidacy of its mayor.[51]

Did these efforts win elections? For all the weaknesses of the secret ballot,
farmers were not in a good position to monitor voters outside their own communities; and whether most members of the BdL were willing to sacrifice their
convenience, which was also an economic good, to their politics may be
doubted. Nevertheless, the threat of boycott might force a candidate to withdraw—as did the National Liberal bank director, Dr. August Weber, in the face
of Conservative pressure, from his campaign for the Second Saxon district in
1912 (with the result that the SPD won the election).

Most vulnerable to the economic sanctions of his customers, because his
occupation brought him into direct connection with electoral politics, was the
publican. On the one hand, renting his hall to a party meant windfall profits at
the end of a long evening of thirsty speechifying. On the other hand, in addition
to the variety of penalties an unwary innkeeper might suffer from local officials,
a party's enemies—the *Kriegerverein* and the BdL, for example—might retali-
ate by canceling their annual ball.[52] Particularly delicate was the issue of the
Stammtische—those knots of "regulars" whose table was reserved for lunch,
for cards, for club meetings; whose records and equipment might be stored on
the premises; and from whose custom the publican benefited throughout the
entire year. The very premise of the institution was reciprocal loyalty: of
Stammtisch to their "table," of publican to his *Stammgäste*. For a publican to
flout the sentiments of a *Stammtisch* for the sake of the business of "outsiders"
justified, at least in the eyes of the Progressive Eugen Richter, the severest
requital.[53] Most disadvantaged by the pressures on publicans, at least initially,

---

[49] Lepper, ed., *Katholizismus*, 265; and to defend priests: Lepper, *Strömungen* 1: 335.

[50] D.V.C., "Zentrum" (1909); "Ein Stimmungsbildchen," 283f; 10 AL AnlDR (1905/06, 11/II, Bd.
VI) DS 483: 4736; Hiery, *Reichstagswahlen*, 328. The spiraling consequences of reciprocal (nonelection) boycotts between Jews and non-Jews in Bretten, Baden (pop. 4,786), triggered by the
founding of an antisemitic German-Social Association by two Bretten notables: Smith, "Alltag,"
291–93. In 1878 the *SVZ* urged an anti-Jewish boycott in the course of a massive antisemitic
campaign—apparently as part of its editor's attempt to capture one of Breslau's seats, held by a
Jew. Müller, *Kampf*, 128–39, 200.

[51] Geh. Justizrat Diefenbach, "Der reichsländliche Gerichtshof zur Prüfung der Gültigkeit von
Wahlen," *BT* (5 Mar 1914). Morgenblatt, BAB-L R1501/14653, unpaginated.

[52] Bertram, *Wahlen*, 201f; Kühne, *Dreiklassenwahlrecht*, 83f; Monshausen, *Wahlen*, 281.

[53] Richter SBDR 8 May 1880: 1242, 1244; 8 Kassel AnlDR (1877, 3/I, Bd. 3) DS 68: 268–72.
Denial of admittance to the pub because of *Stamm* guests' objections in Querfurt (7 Merseburg):
Petition of Otto Huth et al., turners, 6 (?) May 1990, BAB-L R101/3343, Bl. 199f.

were Social Democrats, who might as a consequence find it impossible to move into unfamiliar territory. In their own neighborhoods, however, the boycott gave them a weapon of last resort against timid tavern-keepers who might otherwise have been reluctant, especially during the reign of the Socialist Law, to rent out their halls. In their own locales, with their own newspapers and journals on the racks, the *Sozis* themselves were *Stammgäste*, with all the weight that implied.[54]

Calculations that first confronted the publican were soon inscribed in the political ledgers of other businessmen. The young seminarian Paul Göhre, down and out in a Chemnitz factory in order to see how the other half lived, noticed in 1890 that "socialism for business reasons is far more widespread in all such industrial centers than is commonly supposed; it is to be found among a great many different kinds of tradespeople." By the turn of the century the conviction that Social Democracy owed much of its strength to the economic calculations of shopkeepers and artisans, and even workers themselves, was widely shared. Stories circulated of Socialist block captains demanding that tradesmen take out subscriptions to *Vorwärts*, lest they be boycotted, and coming around with the "collection plate" (*Klingelbeutel*) at election time, extorting contributions in return for being checked off the list.[55] When Robert Blank published his famous analysis of the Social Democratic electorate in 1905, arguing that at least a quarter of Socialist voters had to be "non-proletarian," some observers may have seen a more sinister explanation than Blank's own optimistic conclusion that the comrades had ceased to be a class party.[56]

What could be done to protect small businessman in the face of pressure? The Chemnitz police, in a more than doubtful interpretation of the imperial penal code, declared themselves ready to charge anyone who appealed in public, in front of a crowd, for a boycott, with a hundred marks fine or fourteen days in jail. The owner of a restaurant at Berlin's Zehlendorf Bahnhof won 4,700 marks in damages against the Berlin SPD in 1906 for ruining his business, not only by its own boycott but because the measures the comrades took to enforce it frightened away his middle-class customers. But his success was unusual. Twenty-two times the Imperial Court refused to consider ostracism and boycott as offenses against public morals. Jurists expressed disappointment with the lack of legal remedies and complained that refusal to prosecute was a form of "class justice," enforced "against the socially better positioned." In 1908 and 1909 the German Jurists' Congress commissioned an investigation into the le-

---

[54] Kurt Koszyk, "Anfänge und frühe Entwicklung der sozialdemokratischen Presse im Ruhrgebiet (1875–1908)," in *Beiträge zur Geschichte Dortmunds und der Grafschaft Mark* 50 (1953): 1–151; esp. 84; Hesselbarth, *Sozialdemokraten*, 41; Romeyk, *Wahlen*, 290.

[55] Göhre, *Three Months*, 96; *DA* 22/43 (23 Oct. 1904): 685–87; O. Fischbeck, SBHA, 19 May 1909: 6846.

[56] Blank, "Zusammensetzung." SPD support among the middle classes: Wm. Kohlsdorf, Bitterfeld, to Bülow, 28 Dec. 1906; anon. to Bülow, Frankfurt a.M., 10 Jan 1907, BAB-L R1501/14697, Bl. 56f, 146; Pohl, *Arbeiterbewegung*, 521f.

gality of the political boycott.[57] And the Prussian and imperial government took
the occasion of the drafting of the new penal code to consider whether to make
the political boycott explicitly illegal, considering penalties of up to a year in
prison for the crime of *Verruf* (ostracism and/or boycott) resulting from an
election. But the objections to criminalization were strong. Such legislation
would open the floodgates to anonymous political denunciations (*Denunzian-
tentum*), it was said. Language against economic intimidation of the voter
would be impossible to formulate without including employers' blacklists; yet
blacklists would be impossible to prove in this age of the telephone. Over the
years the bureaucracy had become aware of the complexities of criminalizing
activities designed to change people's minds, and it hesitated to introduce a
measure that "so far as is known, exists nowhere in foreign legislation."[58] Like
their counterparts in the Reichstag, the civil servants who prepared imperial
legislation always had one eye on the international community of civilized nations, of which they considered themselves members.

Ultimately, the best weapon against the boycott was mutual agreement by the
parties to refrain from it. In the Rhineland's Wetzlar a businessman's letter to
the editor in 1913 pleaded for *all* parties to issue a public declaration "that they
concede to the local . . . business people the free, unlimited exercise of their
vote according to their inner convictions and that they would disapprove of
every economic disadvantage on the part of their adherents." It met with a
positive response by all competing parties except the SPD.[59] Perhaps this mutual disarmament pact signified a genuine cultural turning point, away from
coercive forms of electioneering. But it came very late in the day.

Boycotts were most effective, of course, in the (indirect) Landtag elections,
where in the second stage a small and highly visible group of electors (*Wahlmänner*) determined the outcome in each district.[60] In Reichstag elections, however, where a mass electorate voted directly, the ballot of this or that tradesman
was a drop in the bucket. What then could be the political function of the
boycott there?

The first was agitational. Calls to stop patronizing someone who was enrich-
ing himself from "our" purchases and to buy only from "our own" were an ugly

---

[57] Der Boykott vor dem Kammergericht," *FrZ* 155 (10 Oct. 1909) GStA PK I. HA, Rep. 90a,
A.VIII.1.d., Nr. 1/Bd. 10; A. Meyerowitz, "Streik" (1912), 838–49; esp. 845–49; Chemnitz: Singer
SBDR 11 Nov. 1889: 232f.

[58] IM Bethmann Hollweg to Bülow, 9 Mar. 1907, BAB-L R1501/14645, Bl. 51; discussion
among representatives of Prussian, Saxon, and Imperial governments, 2 Feb. 1912, BAB-L
R1501/14460, Bl. 171–89. Eventually a very divided group agreed to recommend including *Verruf*
among the forms of compulsion to be outlawed under § 119 of the new penal code: BAB-L
R1501/14645, Bl. 226. As late as 1912, bureaucrats were still trying to find ways to amend the code
to prevent "threats with economic disadvantages." BAB-L R1501/14645, Bl. 208. An English liberal referred to the intimidation clause in the Corrupt Practices Act as waste paper. Seymour,
Reform, 386.

[59] Romeyk, *Wahlen*, 363.

[60] "Retributive elections": Kühne's "Elezioni," 41–73, *Dreiklassenwahlrecht*, and "Liberalen."

feature of more than one election campaign, notably (although not exclusively) those waged by antisemites. As such, they were grim precursors of more ominous boycotts in 1933. The function of such boycotts, however, was not merely expressive, an outlet for hostility, but to create and sustain an atmosphere of partisanship and excitement. For this purpose even actions like the SPD's "boycott" of the Berlin Philharmonic—which could hardly have hoped to result in either economic damage or electoral profit—had value.[61] A form of propaganda of the deed, it was a way of waging the election war by other means. Its payoffs lay not in the short run of the current campaign, but in long-term partisan recruitment.

But the boycott had other uses. The SPD might employ it as a way of forcing wary pub-owners to rent them their halls. When the "patriotic" parties used it against Catholic shopkeepers in Duisburg, Gütersloh, and Gelnhausen in the nationalistically charged campaign of 1907, it was not to prevent Centrum victories, since Catholics in these districts (except Duisburg) were already overwhelmingly outnumbered. But boycotts might scare the Catholic constituency into deserting their party's election alliances—in these districts, with the Social Democrats. (In the event, the tactic backfired. Catholics helped the SPD to victory against National Liberals in all three runoffs.)[62]

Parties used the boycotts not only tactically, but also "strategically," as a notable Saxon case demonstrated. In 1893, with nearly three times more votes in Saxony than the antisemites, the Social Democrats had managed to elect only seven deputies, to the antisemites' six—thanks to the dispersal of their voters and hostile runoff alliances. The party moved instantly to showcase this discrepancy, by employing their purchasing power against one of the victors. They boycotted the large distillery owned by the mother of Felix Oskar Hänichen, the freshman antisemitic deputy for the vicinity outside Dresden. In less than two years, they had driven young Hänichen to resign his seat. The word went out that Hähnichen's mother had lost so much money that she could no longer support him while he lived in Berlin. More probably, his brothers, who managed the firm, were unwilling to pay the price for Felix Oskar's political convictions. In the by-election to fill Hänichen's vacated seat, Social Democrats won handily, polling almost twice the votes of the new antisemitic candidate. The success of the Socialist boycott had even larger secondary effects. In deliberations to revise the Saxon state franchise later that year, both the National Liberals and the government insisted on introducing the secret ballot, lest the SPD deploy such "terrorism" in state elections![63]

[61] Meyerowitz, "Streik," 847; Suval, *Politics*, 158; Monshausen, *Wahlen*, 200. "Exclusive dealing" with coreligionists sometimes meant "peaceful segregation" rather than conflict. Smith, "Religion," 283–314.

[62] Pub-owners: Romeyk, *Wahlen*, 290. Catholics: Becker, "Kulturkampf," 76; Specht/Schwabe, *Reichstagswahlen*, Nachtrag: 39, 44, 48; varient runoff policies: Crothers, *Elections*, 168–73.

[63] Retallack, *Notables*, 77, 85; on Hänichen: Reichstags-Bureau, ed., *Amtliches Reichstags-Handbuch. Neunte Legislaturperiode. 1893/98* (Berlin, n.d.), 174; Specht/Schwabe, *Reichstagswahlen*, 222; Ritter/Niehuss, *Arbeitsbuch*, 89; D[elbrück], "Preußische Wahlreform," 191.

The SPD's most famous use of the boycott—during the Landtag elections of 1908, especially but not exclusively in Berlin—was both agitational and strategic. Until the turn of the century, the SPD had all but ignored state elections, where the three-class franchise and oral voting had made defeat a foregone conclusion. In 1898, however, the party began to contest a few seats in the Prussian Landtag. The comrades' triumph in the 1903 Reichstag campaign, revealing them as a "party of three million," encouraged the leadership to expand their assault on the Landtag, by applying their numerical strength against those beneficiaries of election privilege, the wealthier voters (and their delegates) in the first and second classes.[64] The miracle weapon was to be the boycott.

As all of Berlin soon learned, the party's strategy involved the use of massive, self-proclaimed "Social Democratic Terrorism," specifically "the Terror of the Comradesses."[65] Three months before the polling in 1908 a Protestant weekly published a secret document attributed to a "confidential agent of the Social Democratic Women of Germany." In it the women were called upon to monitor the votes of their butchers, their bakers, their greengrocers, their milk, coal, and wood-dealers, and every shopkeeper who was dependent on working-class customers.

Even though women had appeared as speakers as well as listeners at a number of Socialist gatherings during the 1907 campaign, the decision to employ them as shock troops in the spring of 1908 was nevertheless a bold one. For all the visibility of women in Socialist cortèges, the high profile of certain Socialist heroines in nocturnal sorties to hang posters and scribble graffiti, and Social Democracy's belief in women's equality, in 1908 women still comprised only 6 percent of the party's membership nationwide.[66] Even though their share in Berlin must have been considerably larger—in a single precinct, Neukölln, the party employed 262 *paid* female functionaries only four years later—it is impossible to estimate it in 1908 with certainty. The announcement itself acknowledged that the mass of women were still outside the movement. But all the more necessary then that they be mobilized now: "All of these women we must have if our plan is to succeed." The leadership was not above enlisting male authority in the effort, announcing a meeting for the greater Berlin metropolitan area "to which all organized comrades are obligated to send their wives." A certain anxiety among the meeting's planners could be detected in their pointed reminder that "it will be the duty of the comrades this evening to stand back for once, in order to make possible the participation of the women in the discussion."[67]

The strategic boycotters no more wanted to drive the tradesman out of busi-

[64] Parties were aware of the reciprocal relationship between RT and LT campaigns. Romeyk, *Wahlen*, 142.

[65] "Sozialdemokratischer Terrorismus," *Vorwärts* (24 May 1908); "Der Terror der Genossinnen," *Vorwärts* (2 June 1908), both cited by Fischbeck, Berlin (LL).

[66] Müller, *Geschichte*, 110, 114f. Women members: Guttsman, *Party*, 152, 241; difficulties: Kutz-Bauer, *Arbeiterschaft*, 231–34, 237f, 241–43.

[67] "An die organisierten Genossen Groß-Berlins!" quoted in Protest, AnlAH (1908/09, 21/II) DS 579, Anlage A: 6 [the archive's pagination], GStA PK I. HA, Rep. 90a, A.VIII.1.d., Nr. 1/Bd. 9; "Working," 276.

ness than the bread lord wanted to fire his workforce. What both wanted—and here they differed from those who boycotted out of ethnic resentment—was to change behavior. But unlike the action of an employer, who preferred to operate unnoticed by anyone but his targets, a mass action demanded publicity: to intimidate the target, but also to convince, and keep convincing, its own scattered and by no means reliable troops—and to make sure that in a densely populated city like Berlin, with twelve (Landtag) election districts, the boycotts in one precinct were not undermined by purchases made by customers who lived and voted in another.

Therefore, the grisly language: the vows that the women were going to "knock the teeth out of terrorism via terrorism" of their own; the promise to "wage the struggle against all shopkeepers to the point of destroying their existence"; the public demand, by the chairman of the Berlin Social Democratic election association, that Social Democrats use the same methods that Junkers used in the countryside—and "with the greatest harshness [*Schroffheit*]." Therefore the *Neue Zeit*'s smug call for an "eye for an eye, tooth for a tooth."

The Social Democrats won seven Landtag mandates in 1908, six of them from Berlin. The real goal of the boycott strategy, however, was not this handful of urban seats in an otherwise impenetrable Landtag, but (in conjunction with a battery of other techniques—such as deliberately slowing the voting process) to make Prussia's whole system of indirect, two-tier, elections, and especially its open ballot, "uneconomic" for the majority parties. The middle classes would be taught that open voting was by definition "the franchise of terror."[68]

So ran the theory. And much of the public believed it. The secret ballot in Landtag elections had been demanded by some conservative-minded citizens as early as the eighties in order to protect their fellows from economic retaliation in Catholic and industrial areas.[69] A baker's guild eventually sent an open letter to the Prussian government asking for the secret ballot, because otherwise the boycott would force them to vote Social Democratic "if we don't want to lose the few customers [*das bißchen Kundschaft*] that we still have."[70] This sentiment, though never in the majority, was spreading in Conservative and especially conservative Liberal circles in both Saxony and Prussia. One Prussian editor noted that it was precisely "in order to remove the worker from this unbearable pressure" from other workers that the English government had abolished public voting in 1872, with the result that workers were again voting Tory.[71]

Nevertheless most Conservatives realized that the boycott was an urban phe-

---

[68] Quoted by Fischbeck, SBHA, 19 May 1909: 6842–44, 6858; *Neue Zeit* 33 (14 May 1909), "Sozialdemokratischer Terrorismus," *Vorwärts* (24 May 1908), "Wozu der Lärm?" and "Der Terror der Genossinnen," *Vorwärts* (2 June 1908). Berlin V, VI, VII, XII, AnlAH (1908/09, 21/II) DS 579, Anlage B, C, and D: GStA PK I. HA, Rep. 90a, A.VIII.1.d., Nr. 1/Bd. 9, Bl. 280f.

[69] Unnamed (apparently Stoeckerite) writer to Bismarck, 5 Jan. 1884, BAB-L R43/685, Bl. 183–88.

[70] Quoted in Kühne, *Dreiklassenwahlrecht*, 115.

[71] D[elbrück], "Preußische Wahlreform," 191; Below, *Wahlrecht*, 155, 156n. 129.

nomenon. In the countryside, humble voters were hardly in a position to boy-cott men who might be their employers. Secure in their rural fastnesses, most Conservatives were not too sorry to see the boycott threaten the previously safe Landtag seats of their Left Liberal rivals in the metropolises. But they did join with them and the National Liberals in throwing out four of the SPD's six Berlin victories.[72]

Had the "the terrorism of the comradesses" really decided the Berlin Landtag elections? Police investigations after the more haphazard boycott of 1903 had found little evidence of appreciable damage to Berlin businesses. In 1908, when Socialist partisans had gone from business to business, collecting signed prom-ises from men in the second and first class to vote Social Democratic, support for SPD candidates among first- and second-class voters had indeed risen. Yet it appears that most of the targeted tradesmen had responded to the pressure by simply remaining away from the election. At the second stage of the process, in which delegates picked deputies, the evidence for the boycott's effectiveness is stronger. One Conservative shoemaker and nine artisans elected as the Left Liberals switched their allegiance to the Social Democratic candidate, while thirty-one National Liberal and Conservative delegates apparently did not vote at all: sufficient evidence, for outraged Left Liberals, that the threat of boycott had stolen their elections.[73]

Nevertheless the Socialist victories might just as easily be explained by the 1906 reform in the method of income tax reporting, which helped democratize the top two classes by moving a large number of voters up one class: from third to second, and from second to first.[74] Equally important, the comrades had by now already succeeded in turning most of Berlin into a Social Democratic "mi-lieu." The replacement of the party's traditional monthly *Zahlabend* (the section meeting at a local club at which members paid their dues) with door-to-door collections (*Hauskassierung*) can be taken as a marker for the party's transfor-mation from sect to "church"; that is, from an association with a limited, en-tirely voluntary membership of the saved into one in which belonging was as much a function of social location—in this case, the neighborhood—as an act of conversion. In the working-class precinct of Neukölln, Berlin Social Democ-racy was able to employ nearly a thousand agents as dues-collectors, at a com-mission of three pfennigs per member per month (10 percent of the total take), deploying one to every four apartment buildings. Their *Hauskassierung* put the screw on everyone on the block, whatever his class or political affiliation.[75]

---

[72] Differing views: Malkewitz (K) SBHA 11 Feb 1909: 1996, and R. Friedberg (NL) SBHA 19 May 1909: 6851. GStA PK I. HA, Rep. 90a, A.VIII.1.d., Nr. 1/Bd. 9.

[73] Varying glosses on the evidence by H. Schoeler (FrVP) in the *Moabiter Bezirksanzeiger* (27 June 1908), Ströbel (SD) SBHA 19 May 1909: 6819; Fischbeck (FrVP): SBHA 19 May 1909: 6845; the 5th, 6th, 7th, and 12th Berlin, in AnlAH (1908/09, 21/II) DS 579: 7, Anlage B, C, and D: GStA PK I. HA, Rep. 90a, A.VIII.1.d., Nr. 1/Bd. 9, Bl. 281.

[74] Kühne, *Dreiklassenwahlrecht*, 111, 114.

[75] Fischbeck, SBHA, 19 May 1909: 6086; from *Zahlabend* to *Hauskassierung* is in Guttsman (though the gloss is mine), *Party*, 170, 241.

Such an institution could only be effective when a party could credibly claim to encompass an entire milieu. Though such a situation did not rule out involuntary voting by individual dissenters, it suggests that large movements of voters were by and large an accurate expression of the political sympathies of the neighborhood.

The case of Moabit, another working-class quarter and the focus of greatest indignation, is instructive. The night before the 1908 Landtag runoff, lists were posted on shops and apartments of fourteen businesses whose proprietors had failed to support the SPD in the first tier of voting. The reigning opinion in the quarter was clear: roughly the same district had just produced 99,560 votes for the SPD in the *Reichstag* election the previous year (1907)—more than 70 percent of the ballots cast, and this under a barrage of hostile government propaganda and under balloting conditions that were by now as nearly secret as anywhere in the empire. "Let Bülow commandeer from above, we will commandeer from below," Ottilie Baader, the chairwoman of the Social Democratic Women of Germany, proclaimed.[76] But for all the posted lists, for all the efforts of both the SPD's own propaganda machine and of antisocialist public opinion to figure Berlin's women as twentieth-century Madame Lafarges, we may doubt whether many Moabit women really waved threats of economic ruin in the face of their corner butchers and bakers, people whom they saw every day, with whom they had friendly dealings, on whom they might sometime depend for credit until the next payday. The fact that SPD proclamations insisted that "the investigation of the political credo of each tradesman must be done not just by one woman, a great number of women should do it, so that the man becomes anxious in the face of the many customers who could desert" suggests that the leadership feared that rank-and-file women might indeed leave the task of "exercising the strongest conceivable terrorism" to the professionals.[77] The female Social Democrat as hard-bitten harridan, eager to wreak starvation on a hapless shopkeeper who failed to toe the party line, was probably no closer to the complex reality producing election outcomes than the Catholic woman as manipulative "Eve," compelling her husband to do the bidding of the parish priest by withholding marital "favors." Buried within the SPD's bellicose pronouncements are lines that suggest that their understanding of the Berlin women's reality was indeed more nuanced: "Comradesses! Draw forth your entire arts of persuasion, don't let yourself be frightened off by anything!"[78]

[76] Identified by Fischbeck, SBHA 19 May 1909: 6841, 6843, GStA PK I. HA, Rep. 90a, A.VIII.1.d., Nr. 1/Bd. 9. I am comparing the RT's 6 Berlin (Moabit and parts of Wedding) with the LT's Berlin XII (also Moabit and parts of Wedding), though they may not be exactly coterminous. Specht/Schwabe, *Reichstagswahlen*, Nachtrag: 8; Kühne, *Handbuch*, 164f. Impressive membership figures for Neukölln SPD in 1912: Guttsman, *Party*, 241.
[77] "An die organisierten Genossen Groß-Berlins!" quoted in Protest, AnlAH (1908/09, 21/II) DS 579, Anlage A: p. 5 of the archive's copy, GStA PK I. HA, Rep. 90a, A.VIII.1.d., Nr. 1/Bd. 9; female functionaries in Neukölln: Guttsman, *Party*, 241; in Dortmund (6 Arnsberg), SPD growth into a mass party after the turn of the century was partly a result of women's interest. Almost 20 percent of the district's members in 1913–14 were women. Graf, *Entwicklung*, 27.
[78] SPD proclamation read by Fischbeck: SBHA 19 May 1909: 6843f.

The comradess whose courage needed bolstering, whose "arts" of persuasion were enlisted, was unlikely to be someone who was going to force her green-grocer of long standing into bankruptcy. The purpose of the language of terror was to make an actual boycott unnecessary. Nevertheless, the lengths to which the movement would go to enforce a boycott are apparent in the trade union resolution, passed shortly before the election, to expel any member who continued to patronize a boycotted pub.[79] If boycotts were to be enforced by the same kinds of monitors who enforced strikes, would proletarian women have dared to cross the picket line? The SPD's intimidating rhetoric seems to have been aimed at the faltering comradess as much as her tradesmen.

Some Left Liberal and Centrum deputies objected to the Landtag's eagerness to accept as proven the existence of "terror" in order to throw out the SPD's new Berlin mandates. "One really doesn't need to burden the struggle against the three-class voting system with sensitivities," Naumann argued.[80] Urban liberals had themselves a long record of economic intimidation, and Social Democrats had no trouble proving that their critics used different standards depending on whose victory they were judging. But the SPD's own past outrage over economic terrorism in Reichstag elections told against them now. The boycotts lost the SPD moral capital, as some Socialists soon perceived: witness their lame efforts to argue that no boycott strategy actually existed; that the boycott notices had been posted by Left Liberals—a dirty trick designed to get SPD victories invalidated![81]

It is this loss of moral capital, not the six Social Democratic seats in Berlin (five of which were thrown out and four rewon), that makes the long-run impact of the SPD's boycott movement significant. Whether or not the Berlin petty bourgeoisie voted Social Democratic out of conviction or fear, outside the great metropolitan centers those shopkeepers and artisans whose perceptions of the party were not softened by a previous history of friendly relations with Socialist customers could read in their newspapers, on the best Left Liberal authority, how the SPD was throttling their liberties. They could imagine themselves in the position of the delicatessen owner Seela, confronted with a boycott list that reappeared on his store sign no matter how many times he tore it down, whose wife was afraid to help him out in his—now empty—store, who was ready to break his lease and move out of town. They could cringe at the jeremiads of Otto Fischbeck, Berlin's Left Liberal city councilman, who proclaimed that "never has power been brought to bear anywhere so starkly and brutally" as it was against Berlin's small tradesmen, who had "to dance to the

---

[79] Kühne, *Dreiklassenwahlrecht*, 115n. 70.

[80] "Die Ungültigen Landtagsmandate," *Die Hilfe* 15/22 (30 May 1909): 338. After an outraged Fischbeck read aloud bloodthirsty passages Reinhard (Z) warned against believing everything that appeared in *Vorwärts*. SBHA 19 May 1909: 6852, GStA PK I. HA, Rep. 90a, A.VIII.1.d., Nr. 1/Bd. 9.

[81] Counter Protest by H. Borgmann (SD): AnlAH (1908/09, 21/II) DS 579, GStA PK I. HA, Rep. 90a, A.VIII. 1. d., Nr. 1/Bd. 9; H. Ströbel (SD), SBHA 19 May 1909: 6810–23.

pipe of Social Democracy, and when they don't do it, then they may have to—
as the pretty threat says—die of hunger."

It did not take Fischbeck beating the drum of worker-*Mittelstand* antagonism
to convince the anxious small businessman that Social Democrats were dangerous people. The radical wing of the Sozis' own party did it for them. Robert
Leinart's campaign flyer in Hanover's Linden had boasted that "shopkeepers
will be forced, in their own interest, to vote for Social Democratic electors,
whether they want to or not; they will have to, in order to keep their working-
class customers, *for hunger hurts!*"[82] When a decade later Leinart presided over
the General Congress of Workers and Soldiers Soviets, chaired the Central Soviet (*Zentralrat*) of the short-lived German Socialist Republic, and then in 1919
led Prussia's Constitutional Assembly, we should not be too surprised that
many members of this same *Mittelstand* were suspicious of the state that ensued—especially as Leinart himself was president of Prussia's Landtag during
the Weimar Republic's first years (1920–24). When Paul Hirsch, the winner in
Berlin VII, boastfully accepted the charge in 1908 that "we are delivering these
people up to starvation," small wonder that when he presided over Prussia's
democratization, as Minister President between 1918 and 1920 and Deputy
Mayor of Berlin-Charlottenburg between 1921 and 1925, some of those he had
been once willing to "deliver up" felt that the country was now in the hands of
class enemies who would stop at nothing.[83] And the fact that Hirsch's chief
antagonist in 1908, the outraged Otto Fischbeck, would himself serve (as a
member of the new German Democratic Party, the DDP) in Hirsch's cabinet as
Minister of Trade, was less likely to produce reassurance than cynicism. However we assess its success in gaining SPD seats in the Landtag, precisely because its aim was to draw the greatest possible attention to Social Democracy's
ability to wield extra-parliamentary power, the boycott was a short-sighted
strategy that burdened Germany's transition from bureaucratic monarchy to
democratic republic, a transition that—unknown to its participants—was only
ten years away.

Subverting the Rules: Gerrymandering from Below

In 1907 a chauffeur in a Berlin suburb overheard a conversation that started the
rumor mills working. Waiting outside Tübbecke's Tavern, where his employer
was attending a Conservative election rally, the chauffeur mingled with the
spillover crowd of Social Democrats who had turned out to greet Wilhelm
Liebknecht, the advertised discussant. The talk turned to the SPD's prospects
here in Potsdam City–Spandau–East Havelland. "Not to worry," boasted one of
the comrades, "we're getting hefty reinforcements from Berlin." To the ques-

[82] Fischbeck, quoting Leinart, SBHA, 19 May 1909: 6843f, GStA PK I. HA, Rep. 90a A. VIII. 1.
d., Nr. 1/Bd. 9. *Vorkosthändler* Seela: Kühne, *Dreiklassenwahlrecht*, 114.
[83] Hirsch quoted in *Vorwärts*: AnlAH (1908/9, 21/II) DS 579, GStA PK I. HA, Rep. 90a,
A.VIII.1.d., Nr. 1/Bd. 9, Bl. 280. Leinert and Hirsch in Mann, *Handbuch* (1988), 182f, 241.

tion, "How so?" the insider replied, "We've bunked down 1,800 men from Berlin in Spandau." A newcomer naively asked, "Wouldn't these people be needed in Berlin?" The smug reply: half the Social Democratic voters in Berlin VI could leave, and the party would still have plenty for victory.[84]

Rumor, even in an age of mass communication, still played an important, if often undiscoverable, role in political perceptions. Peculiarly persistent in the German Empire was the report that armies of workingmen were being mustered out of their customary quarters and bivouacked in an adjacent district. There they would rent a bed for a night or two (sometimes twenty to a room), notify the police, as the law required, of their new location (the *Meldepflicht*), put their names on the voting lists—and vote Social Democrat. Particularly in a by-election, such a sudden concentration of voting power could overwhelm an unsuspecting foe. Even in a general election, if a race were close—and Berlin I in 1912 was decided by nine votes—the deployment of surplus voters from a safe district to a vulnerable one could be decisive.

At least since 1878 rumors of such tactics had been heard around many of the larger cities: Berlin, Hamburg, Altona—even Stuttgart.[85] In 1903 a group of liberal workingmen in Bremen wrote to Bülow, warning him that Social Democrats from Hamburg and the industrial regions of Hanover were now pouring into their town for the elections. (And in fact, the SPD did take Bremen from the Left Liberals that year.) Socialist movement was also reported in Hessen.[86] The truth of at least some of these rumors was undeniable. The old town of Leipzig—like Bremen, a liberal bastion—was inundated by working-class voters from its solidly Social Democratic suburbs during the election of 1912. Wilhelmsburg was also targeted, but the police were alerted in time to take defensive action.[87] Signs of similar activity appeared in Dresden, Düsseldorf, and Frankfurt am Main.[88] These human waves of Socialist workers gave the concept of "mobilization" (*Mobilmachung*) a whole new dimension.

People were voting where they did not belong. And not only Social Democrats. The Buderus firm promoted a large number of its officials and relocated them at company expense in Betzdorf, Rhineland, in order to pack a liberal

[84] Deposition of Paul Dammer, 5 Feb. 1907: BAB-L R1501/14458, Bl. 126f, 128f.

[85] Voter [illegible] to RKA, Münster, 22 July 1878, BAB-L R1501/14693, Bl. 53f; Richter SBDR 8 May 1880: 1245f; 1 Württ. AnlDR (1894/95, 9/III, Bd. 2), DS 268: 1144–54.

[86] Anon. to Bülow, 18 Jun. 1903, BAB-L R1501/14703, Bl. 002ff; B. to Bremen Senate 29 June 1903; "Verzeichniße zu den Akten über Wahlfälschungen vom 1903–1904": BAB-L R1501/14703; Dr. Wagner, Kreisamt Dieburg, to Hessen SM, 8 Jan. 1913, on 1903: BAB-L R1501/14461, Bl. 118.

[87] Dr. Wagler, Leipzig Police, 26 Sept. 1912: BAB-L R1501/14460, Bl. 364f; Wilhelmsburg: Stoltz (?), MdI to BH 23 Apr. 1913, BAB-L R1501/14461, Bl. 54f.

[88] Supreme Court in Dresden, BAB-L R1501/14461, Bl. 110–112v; RdI to Saxon AA, and reply, re Letter of 10 Dec. 1912, BAB-L R1501/14460, Bl. 459–69. In Dresden, the Election Commission sent upwards of 600 communications to local communities instructing them on preventing and detecting double voters. Samples revealed no systematic fraud. Koettig, Dresden Police, to Kreis-hauptmannschaft Dresden, 1 Feb. 1913, ibid., Bl. 460–67. Haupt OBM for Stadtrat Freiburg, in Saxony, 14 Jan. 1913, to Kreishauptmannschaft in Dresden, ibid., Bl. 468f. Elsewhere: Bertram, *Wahlen*, 202.

nominating assembly there.[89] And in Berlin, five of whose six Reichstag districts were solidly Social Democratic, two resourceful "bourgeois" voters, the bank director Max Hirschberg and a student, Wilhelm Busse, hit upon the same scam in 1912. Although they lived in Berlin VI—whose voting population numbered nearly 220,000—they were (in the student's words) "not so dumb as to vote there." So they took sleeping quarters in nearby Berlin I, whose eligible voters hovered around 13,000, thereby contributing to the nine-vote margin that kept this silk-stocking district in Left Liberal hands.[90] Catholics also took a leaf from the Reds' book. In Bergheim-Euskirchen, a district so black that challengers to the Centrum had been routinely overwhelmed since 1874, the Catholic Workingman's Association urged its members to cast their ballots in nearby Cologne, where the Social Democrats were mounting a strong challenge to the Catholic party's dominance. The invasion of Cologne was foiled only by the mayor's office, which informed the workers (erroneously, in fact) that their plan was illegal.[91]

In the Saar, clerical sermons were credited with shifting as many as 4,000 Catholic miners and metalworkers from Merzig-Saarlouis, a safe Centrum district in which Catholics made up 96 percent of the population, into Saarbrücken and Ottweiler–St. Wendel-Meisenheim where, with much lower percentages of the faithful, the Centrum had never managed to budge the "national" parties. Contrary to rumor, however, it was not the clergy, but an enterprising activist by the name of Peter Schmidt, an agent for the *Saar-Post*, who was responsible for the maneuver. He had the *Post* reproduce a complete residential registration form in its pages, with instructions to the subscriber on how to cut it out, fill in the blanks, and designate *him*, Schmidt, as executor, should the unorthodox *Meldeschein* be rejected by the police. Lest his project be frustrated by faulty memories, Schmidt even journeyed out into the villages to get the birth dates of the 3,000-some voters he was hoping to enroll. Only then were the parish clergy brought in, to do the house-to-house legwork, informing workers of their "new" voting opportunities.

Liberals immediately undertook countermeasures against this "systemic ambush."[92] Disinformation flyers were circulated claiming (falsely) that those who voted in the district would also be assessed local taxes. Prefect and Landräte issued instructions to village mayors not to cooperate with boarders who requested changes on their *Meldeschein*. The renowned Professor Paul Laband of Strasbourg was enlisted to provide legal window dressing for the local authorities' stonewalling. (Laband aired his personal and political misgivings about the transport of voters, but his two opinions also dutifully cited Reichstag rulings in

[89] Monshausen, *Wahlen*, 67.

[90] AnlDR (1912/13, 13/I, Bd. XVII) DS 450: 414, 416. Statistics in Michael Erbe, "Berlin im Kaiserreich, 1871–1971," in Wolfgang Ribbe, ed., *Geschichte Berlins. 2 Bde. Von der Märzrevolution bis zur Gegenwart* (Munich, 1987) 2: 691–792; 770–73.

[91] Stoltz (?), MdI, to BH, 23 Apr. 1913, BAB-L R1501/14461, Bl. 54f.

[92] Dr. Bretschneider to NL agents, AnlDR (1912/14, 13/I, Bd. 23) DS 1639: 3575–3612; quote: 3582; debate SBDR 19 May 1914: 9080f; Bertram, *Wahlen*, 203.

1879 and 1898 that condoned voting outside one's legal residence: a noteworthy victory for scholarship over political conviction.) In the end, the redoubtable Schmidt took his case all the way to the Ministry of Interior, which responded with telegraphed corrections to Landräte, prefects, and mayors, requiring them to accept these last-minute enrollees. Schmidt's efforts did not succeed in dislodging the Liberals. But they did cost Ernst Bassermann, Saarbrücken's winner, a nervous month before the election and (thanks to a Centrum challenge) two years of anxiety afterward, before his election was eventually confirmed.[93]

Such mobilizations were by no means peculiar to Germany. They had been deployed in the United States at least since 1854, when invading voters had contributed the term "Bleeding Kansas" to America's political lexicon—and to the origins of the Civil War. Even after meaningful registration requirements were adopted in most American states, "colonization," as it was called, remained a favorite tactic of urban bosses until the First World War.[94] In the Kaiserreich, however, the phenomenon was a by-product not only of party development, but of an industrialization that had spawned proletarian colonies outside the municipal boundaries of the big cities and, as in the Saar, at a workplace far from homes that could be visited only at weekly or fortnightly intervals. For these men to vote in the same place they worked put many under the thumb of their employers—which is why the Centrum had once proposed that citizens be required to vote where they kept their families and paid their taxes, a measure it hoped might pry the pocket borough of Neunkirchen from Baron von Stumm's steely grip. From Left Liberal to Conservative, the parties of the employers had responded that any residency requirement would make voting difficult for migrant and commuting workingmen (especially, they might have added but did not, because elections took place on workdays). It would thus thwart the clear intent of the voting law's framers, which had been to open the franchise to as many as possible.[95] They would soon have cause to regret their position. The conservative parties' shift in favor of a residency requirement grew with the Socialist vote. A mere two-year residency, it was calculated (especially when coupled with a similar requirement for the candidates themselves), would have wiped out half of Social Democracy's troops.[96] But the

---

[93] Laband, letters of 20 Dec. 1912 and 10 Mar. 1912, in AnlDR (1912/14, 13/I, Bd. 23), DS 1639: 3603f; AnlDR (1879, 4/II, Bd. 5) DS 166: 1346f; Dr. Weiß, "Wohnbegriff in Reichstagswahlen," *PVB*, 28/13 (29 Dec. 1906): 248. Jurists acknowledged that "residence" as defined by the RT and voting law was broader than that of the penal code: Gurwitsch, *Schutz*, 38; Ludwig Koerner, *Wohnsitz und Wahlrecht* (diss., Heidelberg, 1910).

[94] Argersinger, "Perspectives," 672, 675, 683; Harris, *Administration*, 19. Connections with plural voting: Seymour/Frary, *World* 1: 260f.

[95] Steffens, "Arbeiterwohnverhältnisse;" 6 Trier AnlDR (1890/91, 8/I, Bd. 3), 346: 2212f, 2217. The pro-employer majority thus overturned earlier RT rulings: on 4 Meck.-Schw. AnlDR, (1879, 4/II, Bd. 5) DS 166: 1346–54, and AnlDR (1880, 4/III, Bd. 4) DS 186: 948–61; on 1 Saxon-Anhalt (1884/85, 6/I, Bd. 5) DS 135: 509–12.

[96] v. Oppen, *Reform*, 11f; A. Putschke to Bülow, Zittau, 19 Jan. 1907, BAB-L R1501/14697, Bl. 210–14.

various proposals bruited by the government and the Right always ran up against obdurate Reichstag resistance.[97]

The movement of Social Democratic voting brigades from their suburban workplaces into the urban metropolis in the seventies and eighties suggests that, at least in some regions, the protections that the Centrum had sought through residency requirements might also be acquired through voter mobility. After the turn of the century, however, the direction of voter migration seems to have reversed. Rather than escaping the suburban or rural workplace, some brigades seemed to be targeting them. The Centrum's efforts in Saarbrücken in 1912, although denounced as an "invasion" by its opponents, in reality simply voted the workers who were already there: the so-called "bunkers and boarders" who slept during the work week at their place of employment.[98] With greater guarantees of secrecy, a seller's market for labor, and effective party organizations, the decision to change one's voting place was no longer defensive but offensive. The worm had turned.

Police despaired of stopping the hordes: it seemed scarcely possible to check whether each of the "departing overnighters" (*abgemeldeten Schlafburschen*) from the outskirts of town had genuinely changed residences. To try to deal with these cases through the imperial court system was an exercise in futility. And even when the invaders had failed in their object—turning the election— most of the authorities believed that it was only a matter of time and better planning before they would succeed. Without an amendment to the voting law linking the franchise to a stable residence, their hands would be tied.[99]

By international standards, Germany's election law was breathtakingly liberal. In an age in which precisely the humblest classes were the most mobile, residency requirements were the easiest way to restrict the franchise without appearing to be hostile to democratic equality, as France had demonstrated in 1850. There a conservative legislature, not wishing to incur the onus of retreating from manhood suffrage, had imposed instead a stringent three-year residency requirement and at a stroke reduced the French electorate by a third.

[97] Tiedemann (FK) AnlDR (1905/6, 11/II, Bd. 2) DS 70: 1785, in BAB-L R1501/14457, Bl. 94; MdI to Bülow, 7 Apr. 1907, BAB-L R1501/14458, Bl. 124; Dr. Ayrer, Leipzig Kreishauptmannschaft, to Saxon MdI, 2 Oct. 1912, BAB-L R1501/14460, Bl. 352; "Ein Attentat auf unser Recht!!" *Mecklenburgische Volkszeitung* (hereafter *MVZ*) 61 (22 May 1898); MdI (Meck.), "Berichtigung," 23 May 1898; "Wie das Großherzogliche Mecklenburgische Ministerium berichtigt!" *MVZ* 63 (25 May 1898); MdI (Meck.), "Berichtigung," 25 May 1898; "Das mecklenb. Ministerium des Innern, das liberale Stadt-Regiment in Rostock und das Wahlrecht der Saisonarbeiter," *MVZ* 63 (27 May 1898): all in BAB-L R1501/14694, Bl. 195–97.

[98] "Achtung! Schlafhausbewohner und Quartierleute!" *Saar-Post* 294 (23 Dec. 1911), AnlDR (1912/14, 13/I, Bd. 23) DS 1639: 3601. "Invasion": *Nationalliberale Correspondenz*, 39/1 (3 Jan. 1912) BAB-L R1501/14460, Bl. 140v.

[99] Quote: Dr. Wagler, Leipzig Police, 26 Sept. 1912. BAB-L R1501/14460, Bl. 364f; "Der Schutz der Wahlhandlung nach § 108 St. G. B. in der Judikatur des Reichsgerichts," *Archiv für Öffentliches Recht* (Tübingen, 1906) 20/2: 285–301; LR v. Wilms to RP in Potsdam, 11 Feb. 1907, BAB-L R1501/14458, Bl. 125–27; MdI to Chancellor, 7 Apr. 1907, BAB-L R1501/14458, Bl. 124; Dr. Ayrer, Leipzig Kreishauptmannschaft, to Saxon MdI, 2 Oct. 1912, BAB-L R1501/14460, Bl. 352.

Britain's tough residency requirements might require a newcomer to wait as long as twenty-nine months before being admitted to the polls. And in Germany, voting for the village council was restricted to ten-year residents.[100] But the Reichstag's Election Law dealt with residency only as an administrative convenience. The requirement that the voter "reside" in the precinct whose voting lists contained his name (§7), absent any definition of what "reside" actually meant, left everything open.[101]

The liberality of the Election Law, buttressed by a particularly strong Reichstag interpretation in 1898, became the Magna Carta of the SPD, who invoked it whenever local potentates tried to exclude migrant harvesters and beet-workers from the voting rolls. All motions for change were requited with motions of their own to sharpen penalties for election misconduct. The Centrum swung into line, dropped its 1890 proposal for residency requirements, and petitioned the government to instruct its mayors that they *must* accept any voter on their lists who had sleeping quarters in their precinct.[102] And the imperial government felt compelled to go along. When the government of the diminutive principality of Reuß (Older Line), faced with a sudden by-election hard on the heels of the general election of 1912, instructed panel chairmen not to accept ballots from voters whom they knew had arrived since the first polling, there was hell to pay in the SPD press. The Chancellor's office was forced to spring into action, becoming the sheepdog for the SPD, herding wayward Reuß back into the constitutional fold.[103]

The problem of residency opened up a range of issues that would have considerable impact on Germany's future. The terms employed by its victims to describe popular gerrymandering ("invasion," "ambush," "colonization," "vagabondage") implied that belonging itself—in this case to the constituency, a collectivity of legitimate voters—constituted some normative value. Yet as parties and interest groups began to take over many of the functions of communities, constituting themselves not only as real local milieux but as "imaginary" trans-local communities, the question of boundaries and of "belonging," and the relationship of both to the organization of political representation, became fraught with difficulty. In fact, the future—as we shall see in the next section—

---

[100] R. Huard, *Suffrage* (1991), 54f, cited in M. Kreuzer, *Institutions* (2000); Seymour/Frary, *World* 1: 149; Richard J. Evans, *Death in Hamburg: Society and Politics in the Cholera Years, 1830–1910* (New York, 1987), 48.

[101] Some places seem to have required that voters bring proof that their names had been removed from the list in their legal (as defined by the commercial and civil codes) residency, but most apparently did not, for if they had, the anxieties about double-voting would have evaporated. Stoltz (sp?), MdI to BH, 23 Apr. 1913, BAB-L R1501/14461, Bl. 54f; Haupt, OBM for Stadtrat of Freiberg [Saxony], to Kreishauptmannschaft Dresden, 14 Jan. 1913, BAB-L R1501/14460, Bl. 460–67. Usually the most that was demanded was proof of the voter's name. Demanding the Anglo-American system: Unsigned to Bis., Naumburg (?), 5 Mar. 1890, BAB-L R1501/14693, Bl. 234.

[102] Bill of Dr. Frank to amend § 120 of the Penal Code, 23 Jan. 1912, in BAB-L R1501/14645, Bl. 220; *Rheinisch-Westfälische Zeitung*, quoted in "Politische Schieberkunst," *Nationalliberale Correspondenz* 39/1 (3 Jan. 1912), BAB-L R1501/14460, Bl. 140v.

[103] Correspondence and clippings in BAB-L R1501/14460, Bl. 378f, 393–99, 400–403, 409–21.

was not going to tie voters more closely to their districts, but to loose them from the bonds of territoriality altogether.

How significant were the migrating hosts of partisans, as opposed to those hapless voters whose work simply forced them to vote far from home? The chancellor's office, spurred by an indignant Liberal press, conducted investigations into the rumors of invading legions after the elections of 1903, 1907, and 1912 and urged its partner governments to do the same.[104] Were they chasing phantoms? The phenomenon probably occurred less frequently and certainly less effectively than either the authorities or the Cassandras in the press feared. Although some alarmists went so far as to trace, however improbably, the explosive growth of the Berlin suburb of Niederbarnim to an SPD election strategy, little evidence was uncovered to suggest that election outcomes were significantly determined by citizens gerrymandering with their feet. (By 1912, even a hermetically sealed Niederbarnim would have produced an SPD victory.)[105] But even if the rumors had proved correct, the government felt helpless to suggest a remedy. A residency requirement would have necessitated materially amending the Election Law, a prospect that it was realistic enough to admit was "probably, given the current situation [in the Reichstag], quite out of the question."[106] Moreover, any initiative that put the existing law in question opened up a can of worms from which the Right and its supporters could expect little good for their own cause, and incalculable undesirable consequences as other reforms slithered out. Not least of these wrigglers was the long-standing demand for redistricting.[107] It took no great insight to see that the Social Democrats felt justified in gerrymandering from below because the existing boundaries of election districts constituted a de facto form of gerrymandering from above. It is to this issue that we shall now turn.

WHO IS MY NEIGHBOR? THE IMAGINED COMMUNITY AND THE DEMAND FOR PROPORTIONAL REPRESENTATION

Two considerations have historically served to legitimate the requirement that a citizen actually live in the district in which he voted. The first was practical. A

[104] Bülow to federated governments, 7 July 1903, BAB-L R1501/14703, Bl. 2–7; Delbrück (for BH), to federated governments, 1 Nov. 1911 BAB-L R1501/14460, Bl. 132; and again on 10 Dec. 1912, ibid., Bl. 363.

[105] Replies to the BH's inquiry: BAB-L R1501/14460, Bl. 459–69; 475–78; BAB-L R1501/14461, Bl. 54f, 113f, 118–20, 125–44. Frank, *Brandenburger*, 97–103.

[106] MdI to Bülow, 7 Apr. 1907, BAB-L R1501/14458, Bl. 124; quote from v. Wilms, LR in Nauen, to RP in Potsdam, 11 Feb. 1907, ibid., Bl. 126f. Cf. Dr. Ayrer, Leipzig Kreishauptmannschaft, to Saxon MdI, 2 Oct. 1912, BAB-L R1501/14460, Bl. 352.

[107] To keep this can closed, Bismarck pressed government to forego desired reforms that would have changed administrative boundaries. Cf. correspondence from Mar. 1877 through 1880: BAB-L R1501/14450, Bl. 14, 16–18, 82, 83–85, 205v-206, 213–17; BAB-L R1501/14653, Bl. 58–60, 70; and again in 1887: BAB-L R1501/14452, Bl. 162, 164f, 222f; as did his successors in 1893–94 BAB-L R1501/14453, Bl. 169f, 173, 211.

residency requirement is a convenient means of verifying that the voter is who he says he is: a barrier against fraud, particularly against plural voting.[108] Although police responses to government inquiries sometimes elided the distinction between mobile voters and fraudulent ones, outright party-sponsored fraud was not really a problem.[109] "Personators" were almost always ingenuous men from the humbler classes who had learned of someone who either would not or could not vote, and acted on their own initiative, motivated by a desire to let no political opportunity go to waste.[110] Foreign voters were usually "easterners," Polish workers and Jewish businessmen with doubtful claims to naturalization, but with the same desire to "count" politically.[111]

Even if all of the suspicions ever voiced were true, the figures did not approach the 25,000 illegal voters credited to Tammany Hall's naturalization mills in the late nineteenth century. The Tübingen jurist Carl Schneidler, in his 1888 study of election misconduct, considered fraud on the scale of even hundreds of votes "probably scarcely conceivable." And while massive fraud in turn-of-the-century American elections has led to some skepticism about the reigning ethno-cultural historiography that interprets votes as "essential vehicles of cultural expression," the handful of cases of plural or illegal votes alleged in each German election actually fortifies a cultural interpretation of the significance of the vote as a mark of self-respect and intensity of political commitment.[112] The shoemaker Max Bruno Falz voted outside his district, so that no one would know that, as a poor relief recipient, he was ineligible to exercise this mark of

---

[108] Note from G.[allenkamp? civil servant], 2 July [1903], BAB-L R1501/14703, Bl. 3f; "Reichstagswahlrecht und Wohnsitzveränderung," *Königsberg Hartungsche Ztg* (20 Dec. 1912). BAB-L R1501/14460, Bl. 379; "Tages-Rundschau," *Abendblatt der FrankZ* 355 (23 Dec. 1911); also the *Neue Politische Correspondenz* (12 Dec. 1911). BAB-L R1501/14645, Bl. 184f.

[109] Responses to Bülow's inquiry suggested few cases of proxy voting, personations, or similar irregularities: BAB-L R1501/14703, Bl. 121–24, 240, 245f; ibid., 14705, Bl. 33–38, 54–77, 96–107. In 1903, however Jos. Herzfeld, a lawyer and SD deputy for Rostock, was convicted of voting in both Rostock and Berlin. Oddly, the court set the penalty at only 14 days' jail, acquitting him of "a dishonorable intention" (*Gesinnung*) because he acted out of "party zeal" and in an important question of principle (the election). Ruling of the Royal Landesgericht Berlin, 1 Dec. 1903, BAB-L R1501/14703, Bl. 288–319. SS of MdI to SS of RJA, Jul. 1904, BAB-L R1501/14705, Bl. 1–4. A handful of cases of double voting, often in good faith: BAB-L R1501/14703, Bl. 39–42, 79–82, 140.

[110] E.g., Court judgment on Jos. Braun, BAB-L R1501/14461, Bl. 98–101. Other cases from 1912: Bl. 149–51, 155f, 157–64, 167, 169–74; BAB-L R1501/14460, Bl. 475f.

[111] Cf. 1 and 2 Berlin (1882/83, 5/II, Bd. 5) DS 29: 266f and 3 Königsberg (1879, 4/II, Bd. 6) DS 232: 1524–26. Accusations that ca. 60 Swiss were allowed to vote K in Gut Gollmitz bei Prenzlau: 4 Potsdam AnlDR (1912/14, 13/I, Bd. 22) DS 1435: 2953. In general: "Wahlfälschung bei Reichstagswahlen," *Annalen des Reichsgerichts* 1 (1880): 458f; 4 (1881): 355f.

[112] Schneidler, "Die Delicte gegen das öffentliche Wahl- und Stimmrecht. R. St. G. B. §§. 107–109," *Der Gerichtssaal. Zeitschrift für Strafrecht, Strafprozeß, Gerichtliche Medicin, Gefängniskunde und die gesamte Strafrechtsliteratur* 40 (1888): 1–28; quote on p. 15. Argersinger, "Perspectives," 672. Some scholars date the classic age of U.S. urban electoral corruption *after* World War I. Tweed fraud and complaints against eleven other big cities: Allen/Allen, "Fraud," 159, 162—who, however, dissent from the picture of widespread corruption.

citizenship.[113] When the agricultural laborer Hermann Stern of Groß Sibsau confessed to voting twice, he had not been the tool of a party machine. But, he explained, "he would rather go to jail [*Strafe leiden*] than let the Poles pull through."[114] The dishonesty of these men was individual, and—unlike those bribed plural voters of Boss Tweed's New York—a sign not of venality but of political will.

As for the parties themselves, although they took advantage of legal loopholes to move their constituents, respect for the rules deterred them from seizing these same loopholes to vote them twice. I have even found cases in which SPD poll watchers turned in Social Democratic voters whom they detected voting twice or impersonating another—scruples that would have amazed party activists in some other countries.[115] A bemused Eduard Bernstein recounted how a Labour Party agent in London had tried to register him to vote, even after he insisted that he was not a British citizen. It was up to his opponents to discover that, the agent replied, and to petition to get Bernstein's name *off* the voting lists. In Germany, even the liberal press, indignant about the SPD's migrating voters, did not charge them with voting twice. Liberals denounced migrating voters not for election fraud (*Wahlfälschung*) but for producing a "fraudulent picture of the election" (*Wahlbildfälschung*).[116]

The second historical legitimation of the requirement that the citizen be resident in the community in which he voted has been ideological. In some traditions, Anglo-American ones especially, it was territory (conceived as reflecting "interests"), not "unmeaning population," that was held to be the object of representation. The residency requirement was the most obvious means of insuring that the voters electing the representative had some connection to the territory and to each other. (As Laband put it: without such a requirement the "purpose and effect of the legal division into election districts would be frustrated.")[117] Even when territories themselves had some historical substance, however, the affinities of populations have rarely corresponded precisely with their boundaries, and politicians, inspired by the desire to see their own party advantaged, have often redrawn them accordingly—most famously, the Massachusetts governor Elbridge Gerry, whose salamander-shaped election district in 1912 gave "gerrymandering" its name. Yet Gerry's tendentious boundary-making, while subverting the substance, preserved the form of territorial representation.

But Professor Laband to the contrary not withstanding, a territorial concep-

---

[113] BAB-L R1501/14460, Bl. 464–66; ibid., 14461, Bl. 110–112v. One woman cast a proxy vote for her husband because she did not want the *Schlepper* to tell people that he was in jail. Ibid., Bl. 108f.

[114] BAB-L R1501/14461: Bl. 15f; and Bl. 122–24.

[115] BAB-L R1501/14460, Bl. 464f; ibid., 14461, Bl. 110–112v.

[116] "Politische Schieberkünst," *Nationalliberale Correspondenz* 39/1 (3 Jan. 1912) BAB-L R1501/14460, Bl. 140v. Dr. Wagler of the Leipzig Police, however, did consider the SPD action fraud. Ibid., Bl. 364.

[117] Quoted in Liberal protest: 5 Trier AnlDR (1912/14, 13/I, Bd. 23) DS 1639: 3585, 3604.

tion of representation, after its appearance in the Frankfurt Assembly, rarely shows up in German discussions of the franchise, even as an ideal.[118] Reichstag districts were from the very beginning constructed from several counties shoved together and had only the weakest claims to being a definable community whose connections extended into the past. German deputies, unlike American congressmen, were never required to reside in the district they represented, and some never showed their face. (Windthorst, widely known as the "Pearl of Meppen," graced his Meppen "setting" only twice in twenty-three years.) The farther to the Left a party stood, the more likely its candidate would come from outside the district, a fact not lost on contemporaries.[119] And party luminaries, as we know, ran multiple candidacies, sometimes choosing their constituency only after all the returns were in. The greatest blow to the concept of territorial representation was Article 29 of the imperial constitution, which declared a deputy the representative of "the whole people," one on whose conscience no particular interest could have a claim.

This understanding of representation as cut loose from any particular territory had powerful consequences when demographic changes began to make some election districts much more populous than others. The law clearly intended some rough equality in representation, prescribing as a norm one deputy for every 100,000 people. But an early government proposal to adjust the boundaries between districts with every new census was defeated in the Constituent Reichstag by the Left. The experience of 1856, where the Prussian government had redrawn sixty-one oppositional districts, had not been forgotten, and the deputies feared for their seats if the administration were empowered to redistrict at regular intervals.[120] Yet already by 1871 the huge discrepancy between the largest constituency (Pleß-Rybnik) and the smallest (Schaumburg-Lippe) was exciting the comment of statisticians, who accurately predicted that the unfairness would grow worse in years to come. By the eighties the largest district, Berlin VI, had a population more than twice the legally stipulated norm (and eight times that of Schaumburg-Lippe), and the oppositional press was taking pleasure in calculating these inequities with the regularity of the righteous.[121]

---

[118] Exceptions: Prussian LT in 1849, Hatschek, *Kommentar*, 133; the Prussian cabinet in the early 60s: v. Selchow [Votum] to SM . . . 28 Oct. 1864, Bis. to SM, 23 Dec. 1864, BAB-L R43/685, Bl. 2–7, 11f; Pollmann, *Parlamentarismus*, 72; Kühne, *Dreiklassenwahlrecht*, 222f. Laband's own opinion has to be seen in the context of the contemporary debate over redistricting—a debate in which he was weighing in on the conservative side. Groups often thought that the boundaries of *precincts*—where people voted—should represent some sort of "belonging." *Der Köcherbote* (Gaildorf) 93 (6 Aug. 1878) BAB-L R1501/14693, Bl. 62.

[119] A. Putschke to Bülow, Zittau, 19 Jan. 1907, BAB-L R1501/14697, Bl. 210–14.

[120] "Die Ungleichheit der Wahlkreise: II," *BrZ* (F) 25 Mar. 1885: BAB-L R1501/14451, Bl. 303; Hatschek, *Kommentar*, 134–40.

[121] Knorr, "Statistik," cols. 313–18; *Hannoverscher Kurier* (4 Oct. 1881), and "Reichswahlgesetz und Wahlkreis Einteilung," *Hannoverscher Kurier* (7 Nov. 1884) both in BAB-L R1501/14451, Bl. 64 and 242; "Die Eintheilung der Reichstags-Wahlkreise," *BT* (2 Apr. 1887) BAB-L R1501/14452, Bl. 224.

The Reichstag was urged to compensate the cities by increasing the number of deputies—and before the projected new Reichstag building went up, since Paul Wallot's design made room for only 400 seats. Eventually demands for redistricting became more insistent, some claiming that there was "no more urgent state necessity, no greater national question than this demand."[122] Nevertheless, although the wording of the Imperial Election Law made clear that the initial district boundaries were provisional, constituencies were never redrawn. By 1912, Schaumburg-Lippe had still grown very little, while Teltow-Charlottenburg's population topped a million, making a Schaumburg-Lippe vote twenty-five times as powerful as one from Teltow-Charlottenburg.[123]

Germany was not the only country where aspirations to democracy conflicted with constituency boundaries that delivered unequal voting power to different citizens. Even after the 1885 Redistribution Act, Britain's largest district had thirty times the population of Dublin University, which sent two members to the House of Commons—a ratio worse than any in Germany. Britain's inequities also had political consequences—for example, for the future of Ireland, when in the general election of 1886, the Liberals (generally for Home Rule) won the popular vote by 65,000, but the Conservatives took over the government, disposing of a huge majority of 104 seats in the House of Commons. Although never quite so glaring again, such discrepancies between the popular vote and the distribution of seats continued as long as the German ones did—that is, until the reforms at the end of the First World War. But there was one big difference: British election law made no pretense to equality. The number of times a man might vote was limited only by the number of districts in which he held property at the requisite value. The Liberal Unionist Joseph Chamberlain, who voted in three constituencies, claimed to know someone who voted in twenty-three, and another who voted eighty times. Some British constituencies were swamped with property-holding nonresidents, making a mockery of the whole notion of territorial representation. The Tories, who were said to gain between forty and eighty seats in each election thanks to plural voters, made sure that before 1918 all

---

[122] Review of E. Cahn, *Das Verhältnis-Wahlsystem in den modernen Kulturstaaten* (Berlin, 1909) in W. Heile, "Mehrheitswahl" (1909), 482–84. On demands to redistrict or increase numbers of deputies: Bis. to Forckenbeck, 9 Dec. 1876, BAB-L R101/3342, Bl. 230–230v; Antrag Blos/Most AnlDR (1878, 3/II, Bd.2) DS 67: 550; Antrag Rittinghausen/Sonneman, Jan. 1882, BAB-L R1501/14451, Bl. 290–92; Wallot design: SBDR 9 Jun. 1883, 24 Jan 1885; Petition of (Berlin) Workingman's Precinct Assoc. of Lausitzer Platz and Viereck motion: 3 Mar. 1884 AnlDR (1884/85, 6/I, Bd. 6) DS 228: 945; Election Club (F) of Berlin VI, 14 Jun. 1890, and District Club of Hamburger Vorstadt zu Berlin, BAB-L R1501/14453, Bl. 79, 82–86, 144f; W. Gannert, Chair of the Berlin Workingman's Assoc., 18 Feb. 1907, BAB-L R1501/14458, Bl. 138f; "Handlungen des Dritten Deutschen Städtetages am. 12 Sept. 1911 zu Posen betr. Neueinteilung der Reichstags Wahlkreise," "Das 'gleiche' Wahlrecht," *Leipziger Volkszeitung* 218 (20 Sept. 1911) both in BAB-L R101/3360, Bl. 28.

[123] Huber, *Verfassungsgeschichte* 3: 874; Steinbach, *Zähmung* 1: 35f. Schaumburg-Lippe is unrepresentative of the problem, however, because it was as apt to elect a LL as a FK. Cf. also "Das Reichstag Wahlrecht-ein Pluralwahlrecht," *Vorwärts* 19 (25 Feb. 1911) BAB-L R101/3360: Bl. 7–9.

attempts at ending the system went down to defeat by using their power in that least democratic assembly of all—the House of Lords.[124]

Nor were the injustices of Germany's territorial representation of the magnitude of the U.S. Senate, where as of 1999 the state of Wyoming, with almost 500,000 residents, elected as many senators as the state of California, with nearly 33.5 million—that is, 67 times as many: a discrepancy that seems to bother no one. The U.S. Electoral College, a ghostly institution of whose existence citizens have to be periodically reminded, and which exists only to represent territory, has twice given Americans a president who had been defeated in the popular vote.

What was special about the German system was not its inequities, but the immense attention they attracted. Journalists found the question endlessly fascinating, claiming to see in the system's rural bias a perverse distribution of power proportionate to "backwardness." The Left argued that failure to redistrict amounted to "a repeal, for residents of big cities and industrial centers, of equal suffrage." The fact that the east Elbian flatland remained closed to Socialist efforts meant that, on average, it took 75,800 votes for the comrades to elect one of their own, while a Conservative needed a mere 17,700.[125] Since geographical discrepancies reinforced partisan advantage, calculating the putative composition of the Reichstag according to criteria that more accurately reflected the distribution of the population became a national pastime.[126]

All boundaries, however, are in some sense arbitrary. This recognition led some who had initially favored reform to draw back, fearing the enormous power that it would put in the hands of any redistricting government.[127] The question of boundaries, moreover, raised the fundamental issue of belonging. Every border made those majoritized by it feel that they were on the "wrong" side, displaced from their true political "home." The *"reichstreue"* voters of Gaildorf were so tired of their demographically foreordained defeats at the hands of the Centrum that after years of complaints they issued a public declaration announcing their boycott of Reichstag elections until the boundaries of their district (13 Württemberg) had been redrawn: a patent attempt to pressure the imperial government.[128] And where populations were mobile, every district might seem gerry-

---

[124] Seymour/Frary, *World* 1: 151–55, 166–69, 177f; Blewett, "Franchise," 44–51, is less sure of systematic bias.

[125] Quotes: F. Naumann, "Ungleiches Wahlrecht," 580–82; Rittinghausen/Sonnemann motion, Jan. 1882 BAB-L R1501/14451, Bl. 290–92. Merkt, "Einteilung," cols. 50–67. Numbers: Falter, *Wähler*, 131; different numbers, but same message: *Vorwärts* 86 (13 Apr. 1907), BAB-L R1501/14458, Bl. 130.

[126] *Pace* Suval, *Politics*, 41. "Die Ungleichheit der Wahlkreise," *BrZ* (F), 23 and 25 Mar. 1885, BAB-L R1501/14451, Bl. 301, Bl. 303.

[127] Bis. to Ministry, 23 May 1866, BAB-L R43/685, Bl. 15; "Die Ungleichheit der Wahlkreise: II," *BrZ* (F) 25 Mar. 1885: BAB-L R1501/14451, Bl. 303.

[128] Amtspfleger Haaf to Herbert Bismarck, 6 Aug. 1878 (enclosure: *Der Köcherbote* Nr. 93, 6 Aug. 1878, and "Reichstagswahl," *Der Köcherbote* Nr. 121, 13 Oct. 1881, BAB-L R1501/14693, Bl. 58–62; 84).

mandered. Changing the boundaries of individual constituencies would not make the Reichstag more representative, argued a manager for a printing shop in Brandenburg's Beeskow in a letter to Bismarck.[129]

For those who identified less with a territory than with other collectivities, the single-member constituency left them—if they were in the minority—feeling disenfranchised. If the deputies did not, as Article 32 of the constitution asserted, represent the "territory" that elected them, but the entire nation, then what justification could there be for privileging the majorities of 397 separate election districts—and robbing local minorities of the voting power that their numbers, nationwide, deserved? Beginning in the seventies voters began writing to the chancellor making precisely this point: the injustice of a Reichstag drawn from hundreds of districts, each decided by its own majority, with no way of compiling "lost" votes. Alternative systems, both complicated and simple, were suggested—not just by political theorists, but by dissatisfied doctors, lawyers, merchants, priests, rich men, poor men, bureaucrats, artisans, and factory owners. From Hamburg and Berlin to Karlsruhe, Regensburg, and smaller towns and villages across Germany the suggestions came. Sometimes the object was to give minority opinion its due. Sometimes, but not always, the purpose of a proposal was to obviate the need for political parties altogether, or at least parties representing interests the proponent perceived to be "narrow."[130] Some felt that an occupational franchise would be fairer.[131] As time went on, the only just solution seemed to be to give up on the idea that the voter "belonged" anywhere, territorially or occupationally, and to accept a mode that would atomize the electorate. Territorial boundaries would disappear, seats would be distributed among parties proportional to their entire popular vote, and individuals would be counted equally. This system of radical proportional representation had been publicized by the British political scientist Thomas Hare, and

[129] H. Prelipper (Trelipper?), to Bis., 19 Nov. 1884, BAB-L R43/685, Bl. 227–30.

[130] Against parties: the attorney Fr. Hofnockel to Bis. (essay enclosed), Weiden in Oberpfalz, 15 Nov. 1881, BAB-L R1501/14693, Bl. 97–99 (acknowledged with thanks, 29 Nov. 1881, Bl. 101). Adolph Laewi (sp.?) said that he wanted to *encourage* great political parties, "similar to those in other countries." Laewi to Bis., Regensburg, 10 Mar. 1890, ibid., Bl. 235–40. Other suggestions: Dr. Otto Ringk, surgeon and midwife, "Entwurf zur Einfuhr eines neuen Wahlgesetzes," Berlin, 1884, ibid., Bl. 117–19; T. Moeller, Pastor in Gr. Trebbow bei Schwerin, to B., 24 Feb. 1886, ibid., Bl. 147–52; Deputy Pastor Fischer to Ministry, Rengersdorf, Kr. Sagan, 9 Feb. 1898, BAB-L R1501/14694, Bl. 141f; W. Staelin to Bis., Hamburg, 16 Nov. 1884, BAB-L R43/685, Bl. 221f; Geh.RR Dr. Ritzhaupt to B., 25 Nov. 1881, Karlsruhe, enclosing copy of his article, "Zur Frage der Wahlreform," *Zeitschrift für badische Verwaltung und Verwaltungs-Rechtspflege* 14 (7 July 1869), ibid., Bl. 28–31. Newspaper discussion: "Die Ungleichheit der Wahlkreise," BrZ, 23 and 25 Mar. 1885, BAB-L R1501/14451, Bl. 301, 303; "Das Reichstags Wahlrecht-ein Pluralwahlrecht," *Vorwärts* 19 (25 Feb. 1911), BAB-L R101/3360, Bl. 7–9.

[131] "Kaufmännischer Lesezirkel," *Deutsche Buchhändler Ztg*, 35 and 36 (2 Sept. 1884): 122; "German Men!" Printed announcement against the "one-class voting system," signed by Fr. Krupp, jr., Privatier, Bonn, 22 Nov. 1884, sent to Bis. BAB-L R43/685, Bl. 231f; memorandum to Wm. II from Aug. Roese, printer, Swinemünde, 6 Mar. 1890, in BAB-L R1501/14693, Bl. 245–56; Adolph Laewi to Bis., 10 Mar. 1890, ibid., Bl. 235–40; Jul. Pfeiffer to Wm. II, 1 Mar. 1903, BAB-L R1501/14695, Bl. 93–105v.

through the work of the legal scholar Johann Caspar Bluntschli, was already well known in Germany.[132]

The emerging consensus in favor of a radically individualistic voting system may seem paradoxical among a people so accustomed to voting as communities. Yet the idea of abstracting voters from their visible communities and reckoning them to those invisible, imagined communities to which each, by his ballot, declared he really belonged met few critics. It was a sign of how rapidly the parties, as new foci of identification, had taken hold. Spokesmen for all points on the political spectrum, at one time or another, argued for the justice of proportional representation, beginning with a statistician for the Prussian government, who noted during the constitutional conflict of the sixties that the Conservatives, with more than 30 percent of the popular vote, had been getting only 10 percent of the Landtag's seats.[133] By the eighties liberals were singing the same tune.[134] PR's proponents even included, on occasion, the Centrum: a party whose compact constituency gave it the least to hope and the most to fear nationally from such an arrangement—but which, in state parliaments such as Württemberg, might bet on coming out ahead.[135] But as population flowed from country to town and from east to west, it became apparent that the SPD, of all parties, would benefit most from the change. The argument for PR shifted from the needs of representing a minority, hitherto described as "raped" by majoritarian rule, to the needs of fully realizing the potential of the majority—as the SPD aspired to be. From the passage of the 1891 Erfurt Program on, the SPD's tom-toms beat a constant PR refrain.

Indeed, most commentators expected PR to mean a sharp shift to the left. Figure 10, on the next page, gives an idea of the changes they expected. The results of these calculations caused its Left Liberal author to crow: "With that [i.e., PR], the Power and the Glory of the Conservatives-Clericals-and-Poles is finally over." Few of these triumphalists seem to have been troubled by the possibility that their projections, based on the claim to a more thoroughgoing democracy, might have been thwarted under a system of representation that corrected the inequities not only of geography but also of gender. Yet what we know of voting in the Weimar Republic suggests that preferences of women for those parties most sympathetic to the churches—that is, the Con-

---

[132] Ritzhaupt to Bis., 25 Nov. 1881, BAB-L R43/685, Bl. 28–31; H. Prelipper (Trelipper?) to B., 19 Nov. 1884 (a bureaucratic pencil noted: "recommends the well-known Hare system"), ibid., Bl. 227–30. Bluntschli, *Allgemeinen Staatsrechte* 1, Buch 5, Chap. 7, quoted in Fr. Hofnockel to Bis., 15 Nov. 1881, BAB-L R1501/14693, Bl. 97–99.

[133] E. Engel, "Die Ergebnisse der Urwahlen . . . ," cited in Ritter/Niehuss, *Arbeitsbuch*, 138.

[134] Even as they were benefiting from partisan "geometry" in Bavaria and Baden. *Die bayerische Wahlkreis-Geometrie von 1881/87 in ihren Wirkungen und in ihrer Tendenz beleuchtet von einem Freunde der Wahlfreiheit und des Rechts* (Regensburg and Amberg, 1887); X.Y.Z., *Badische Wahlkreis-Arithmetik nebst einigem Nichtarithmetischen das dazu gehört* (Freiburg i. Br., 1895).

[135] "Zentrum und Reichstagswahlrecht," *KVZ* (28 Jan. 1904) BAB-L R1501/14457, Bl. 7; Schofer, *Erinnerungen*, 85, 87; Below, *Wahlrecht*, 112; Blackbourn, *Class*, 130. Polish complaints about RT *Wahlkreisgeometrie* in 4 Marienwerder: v. Koscielski SBDR 7 Mar. 1888: 1359.

FIG. 10

The Effects of the Single-Member, Majoritarian Constituency Compared to PR
as of 1907

Parties	Seats in Maj. System	Seats in PR System
Conservatives	60	39
Free Conservs	24	17
Farmers' League	8	8
Südd. BB	0	2
Antisemites	21	9
	113	75 Conservatives: minus 38
National Liberals	54	60
Fr. Vgg	14	13
Fr. VP	28	27
Südd VP	7	5
Danes	1	0
	104	105 Liberals: plus one
Centrum	105	79
Poles	20	16
Guelfs	1	2
Alsace-Lorraine	7	3
	133	100 Clericals/
		Particularists: minus 33
Social Democrats	43	117 Social Democracy: plus 76
Other	4	0

Source: Taken from E. Cahn, *Das Verhältnis-Wahlsystem in den modernen Kulturstaaten,* reviewed by Heile in "Mehrheitswahl," 482–84. Totals are mine.

servatives, Centrum, and Poles—might well have counterbalanced their losses
to proportional representation.

But in the meantime? By 1900 support for PR had progressed to the point that
it was introduced in communal elections in Bavaria (1903), Württemberg
(1906), and Oldenburg (1908); in state elections in Württemberg and Hamburg
(1906); and was being discussed in the Reichstag for the proposed labor-man-
agement elected Chambers of Labor as well as for the revamped boards administering sickness insurance funds, a visible trend that contributed to the growing
scholarly discussion of the technique internationally.[136]

The redistricting debate also had implications for our own story. For it was in
the context of the widespread *de*legitimizing of constituency boundaries, the
sense that their elections were being stolen, that the Social Democratic "inva-
sions" took place. Since the boundaries of election districts, and most especially
those blurred by industrial development, urban sprawl, and commuting popula-

[136] "Biographie von Prof. R. Siegfried," BAB-L R1501/14474, Bl. 229v; Vogel et al., *Wahlen,*
135.

tions, had no *felt* legitimacy—then why be limited by them? If the boundaries could not be shifted, then the voters could. The militant response to the state's stony refusal to redistrict "from above" was a redistricting, as opportunity offered, from below. Urged on by local Social Democrats, whose national leadership claimed that the government's failure to redistribute seats constituted "systematic election fraud" (*Wahlfälschung*), the migrant working population, in Berlin, Hamburg, Offenbach, Leipzig and their suburbs, did their own gerrymandering, with their feet.[137]

To commit voters and then physically move them across district boundaries for even a short time required even more organization than the massive May Day and franchise demonstrations that so impressed contemporaries: teams of party workers to fill out the change-of-address forms for new arrivals, and money for beds in flophouses, for change-of-address fees, and for the fines incurred when an election soldier was caught making out an official notification of a "move" that he had not in fact made. In Leipzig in 1912 these penalties, all told, amounted to 1,000 marks—which the SPD was able to pay immediately.[138] Competitive elections require parties, and parties depend not only upon the freedom of voters, but on money and organization. How German parties acquired both is the question to which we shall now turn.

[137] This is my interpretation. "Systematic election fraud": Vorstand der Sozialdemokratischen Partei, *Handbuch* (1911), 755.

[138] Dr. Wagler, Leipzig Police, to Royal Kreishauptmannschaft Leipzig, 26 Sept. 1912, BAB-L R1501/14460, Bl. 364–65v; Koettig, Dresden Police, to Kreishauptmannschaft Dresden, 1 Feb. 1913, ibid., Bl. 460–67.

CHAPTER ELEVEN

Organizing

> In all parliaments elected by universal and equal suffrage, the entry
> of money for the financing of election organizations brought a funda-
> mental transformation, changing the deputies from "masters" of the
> voters to "servants" of the party leadership.

> —*Peter Molt (1963)*

> No idea has ever made much headway without an organization be-
> hind it.

> —*Samuel H. Barnes (1955)*

MILLIONS of individuals, however democratic their sentiments and however
free their ballots, cannot exercise control over a state. Their views are too various, their desires, too fleeting. The sweeping statements of principle, vague
constituencies, weakly differentiated interests, and inchoate organizational
structures so characteristic of the old notable politics, on the one hand, and the
hyper-democracy of "movement" politics, on the other, cannot make any real
claims on a state, because the spokesmen associated with them are not able to
"deliver." Elections without genuine parties produce amorphous legislatures
that offer no security that those doing the talking actually speak for anyone
outside the room. Incapable of disciplined action, such bodies are doomed to
impotence, no more able to define and carry out an agenda than the average
faculty senate. For popular choices to have an impact, they must be funneled
through organizations capable of aggregating interests and giving them the kind
of stable embodiment that would make it worthwhile for the state to cooperate.
Such organizations, which presuppose the presence of "civil society," but do
not follow automatically from it, were quick to emerge in the German Empire.[1]

How do organizations acquire the ability to "aggregate interests"? We have
already seen how, thanks to the Kulturkampf, German politics quickly developed a clear, sharp cleavage that could "structure the vote," a task that is the
minimum function of political parties in new democracies. And we have seen
how religious identity (Catholic and, dialectically, Protestant) provided a basis
for that sense of mutual obligation, horizontal and vertical, that makes a genu-

---

[1] Fish, *Democracy*, 61, to whose ideal type of "civil societyishness" (43–42) and illuminating
analysis of post-Gorbachevian Russia (57, 133) I owe this paragraph.

ine party possible. A similar sense of obligation ("solidarity norms," in Claus
Offe's phrase) enlivened regional, ethnic, and eventually class identities, enabling the parties that represented them to acquire resources of time and money
from their supporters and—as they faced the outside world—to command sufficient sway over their adherents to bind the latter to positions on issues often
only "imaginatively" related to their personal concerns.[2] The financial effort
involved in electing and supporting a candidate reinforced the theme of "sacrifice" (*Opfermut*), with which we are already familiar. And this sense of shared
sacrifice knotted the moral filaments connecting the deputy, often serving without compensation, to the party member digging deep to make his donation or to
pay his dues, to the voter in the precinct, who might risk material disadvantages
with every ballot cast.

In the following chapter, we will extend this discussion by examining the
ways and means of Germany's political parties: how they gathered these resources and extended these networks; how they connected their constituents to
themselves and to each other; and how the imperatives of getting and spending
affected the very concept of representation.

BALLOTS, PARLIAMENTARY ALLOWANCES, AND RAIL PASSES

The amount of money required to obtain a seat in parliament is rightly considered a clue to the openness of a political system. At two key points where one
might have expected the German conception of representation as a state function to have led to public funding—at the beginning of the electoral process,
with the printing and distribution of ballots, and at the end, with salaries for
representatives—candidates were in fact thrown back on their own resources.
Ballots themselves were relatively cheap, running to about 100 marks per district in 1907; but distributing them could be expensive. Even in the eighties, the
safest seat in a rural Catholic district might require well over fifty agents to
distribute 25,000 ballots. By the late nineties, in an urban district like Mülheim,
100 campaign workers were necessary even to make a showing.[3] Acquiring
funds sufficient to support a man (and his family) while he served in the Reichstag was an even bigger task. It was the need to make good these two deficits
that provided the most urgent spur to the creation of professional party organizations, a development that might have emerged more slowly—as it did in
France and the United States—had the state been willing to take over these
expenses itself.[4]

[2] "Structuring the vote": Leon D. Epstein, cited in Fish, *Democracy*, 77, as is Offe, 54.
[3] Table of 56 Meppen agents, with addresses and occupations, Oct. 1884. Frye to Meppen agents
(form letter), June 1878; Frye to Heyl, 30 Jun. 1878, asking for a personal canvass; Windthorst to
Heyl, 5 July 187. In private hands. R. Clauditz to agents, 18 Sept. 1884; W. to Clauditz, 18 Oct.
1887. SAO Dep. 62-b, 2379. Müller, *Strömungen*, 368. NLs, however, had only 250 agents in all of
Hanover in 1902. G. Vascik, "Conservatism" (1993), 246.
[4] France had granted an annual salary of 2,500 francs from 1852, raised by 1900 to 12,500

That the people's representatives should serve without pay was by no means obvious to most Germans. In every state legislature in Germany, deputies received a *per diem* or some other compensation for their work.[5] Only Reichstag members were banned, by Article 32 of the imperial constitution, from receiving any form of remuneration. Bismarck had insisted on the ban as a necessary correlate to the uniquely egalitarian imperial franchise. Even more than the desire to freeze out candidates who might not share the outlook of the propertied classes, the chancellor wanted to prevent the emergence of professionals who would make parliament their "business"—and acquire the expertise and collective identity to challenge his authority.[6] He responded to the deputies' repeated protests against Article 32 by offering to amend it at any time—but only at the price of an "organic" (read: anti-democratic) revision of the entire Election Law.[7]

Supporters of the ban on stipends, in the minority, could cite similar provisions in Italy, Spain, and especially Britain, where MPs worked without compensation until 1911.[8] Far from being mere curiosities for the comparative historian, precedents from the Mother of Parliaments, with telling quotations from liberals like Mill, were incorporated into the arguments of the Right, leading their opponents to complain bitterly about the use of "English relationships" to justify the undemocratic elements in Germany's status quo.[9] Motions to repeal or amend Article 32 were passed fourteen times between 1871 and 1904: a record, surely, of consensus coupled with persistence, and on the face of it surprising in a body whose own social composition, at least in its first decades,

---

francs. Compensation for representatives was established in the first article of the U.S. Constitution. Meyer, *Wahlrecht*, 214f, 465, 506f; 512f.

[5] Meyer, *Wahlrecht*, 180, 500f, 507–9; Stauffenberg [F] and Hänel [F] SBDR 26 Nov. 1884: 17, 28. Unfortunately, Hermann Butzer's massive study, *Diäten und Freifahrt im Deutscher Reichstag: Der Weg zum Entschädigungsgesetz von 1906 und die Nachwirkung dieser Regelung bis in die Zeit des Grundgesetzes* (Düsseldorf, 1999) appeared too late for me to use.

[6] Bismarck: *"gewerblicher Parlamentarismus"* (5 May 1881), in *Gesammelte Werke* Bd. 12: 262ff, cited in Huber, *Verfassungsgeschichte* 3: 893 (quote), 894f; Richard Augst, *Bismarcks Stellung zum parlamentarischen Wahlrecht* (Leipzig, 1916), 149. Meyer, *Wahlrecht*, 514–16, quotes from the RT debate in a way that suggests that the initial opposition to per diems came from the federated governments; in Mar. 1867, Bis. remarked that compensation could be introduced via legislation should problems develop. Quoted by Hänel SBDR 26 Nov. 1884: 28; Bis.'s response: ibid., 33.

[7] Graf Schwerin in 1867, quoted by Stauffenberg; Bis. and an unidentified K, cited by Graf v. Stolberg-Wernigerode; and B.'s offer of an "organic" revision: SBDR 26, Nov. 1884: 17, 21, 26.

[8] Until 1858, a landed estate worth £600 per annum was required for English and Welsh county members, and £300 for borough members. Overseers' fees might (between 1868 and 1880) run from £4 to well over £1,000 in England and Wales. Scotland did not have a property qualification and its official fees were paltry. Gash, *Politics*, 108–9; Gwyn, *Democracy*, 22–28, 206–28. The higher quality of RT (compared to LT) personnel was attributed to the "winnowing" process imposed by the absence of stipends. Kulemann, *Erinnerungen*, 53f.

[9] Quoting Mill: K. A. Baumbach (F) SBDR 12 Jan. 1892: 3574. Complaints: A. Reichensperger to Jörg, 3 Nov. 1881, in Jörg, *Briefwechsel*, 471; Stauffenberg SBDR 26 Nov. 1884: 17. Germans found England's "privatization" of public business a scandal. Meyer, *Wahlrecht*, 465, 506–7, 512f; on the constituent RT: 517.

vastly overrepresented the well-to-do. But opinion was strong that the national parliament should be a "photograph" of the nation itself.[11] More important, compensation for deputies was, as Peter Spahn put it, "a question of the prestige of the Reichstag."[11]

The financial burden that followed from Article 32 was considerable. In order to maintain a second residence in Berlin and absent himself eight months a year from his normal occupation, it was estimated that a deputy would need an annual income of 6,000 marks: a figure that in 1884 excluded over 99 percent of the population of Prussia.[12] Reichstag delegations kept their eyes open for well-heeled aspirants who could pay their own way, a search that often involved lengthy negotiations among hopefuls representing different local factions. Short of electing the wealthy, however, where could such monies be found? A variety of expedients were grasped. Some deputies agreed to accept subsidies from committees of voters within their districts; others (especially Conservatives) received generous presents from grateful individuals. Eventually deputies who edited party newspapers or served in other party capacities were given inflated salaries. The most reliable device, however, was to tap richer districts like Berlin and Hamburg to support candidates in poorer ones, a mechanism that pushed activists toward forming continuous, statewide party organizations and led to greater and greater centralization of fund-raising efforts within the boundaries of the individual states. The result of such measures was that the German understanding of "party" rapidly changed from a gathering of men connected by affinity, to an affinity connected by an organization.[13]

Social Democrats were the first to develop permanent constituency organizations with formal memberships. By 1878 they had acquired nearly 40,000 dues-paying members and were able to pay their Reichstag deputies 80 to 100 marks a month. By the nineties, the SPD's budget included 105,000 marks for stipends alone, their deputies' allowances had risen to 3,000 marks annually (with an additional 3,000 marks for the delegation's cochairmen), and Bebel was bragging that even if his party had won 100 Reichstag seats, instead of only 35, they

---

[10] Bis. promised a "photograph" in 1867. Cited by Reichensperger, as was Miquel's answer: that "every suggestion was wrong that led to making a caricature of the photograph." SBDR 1 Feb. 1888: 675. Similar metaphors: Kayser SBDR 9 Dec. 1885: 245; Singer (SD) SBDR 3 Feb. 1888: 693; Geh. RR Dr. Ritzhaupt, "Zur Frage der Wahlreform," *Zeitschrift für badische Verwaltung und Verwaltungs-Rechtspflege* 14 (7 July 1869) BAB-L R43/685, Bl. 28–31.

[11] Quoted in Bachem, *Vorgeschichte* 6: 261f. Although Stöcker supported stipends (SBDR 12 Jan. 1892: 3584), many Ks and some NLs resisted to the end: Anon., "Zur Diäten-Frage," *Deutsches Wochenblatt* 7 (1894): 229f; "Diäten. Verfassung. Wahlrecht," *Grenzboten* 63/1 (1904): 306f; O. Arendt (FK), "Das Diätenwesen im Reichstag und im Landtag," *Der Tag* Nr. 145 (1911); Kulemann, *Erinnerungen*, 50–54. A middle position: Meyer, *Wahlrecht*, 518f.

[12] Hänel, Stauffenberg, Auer SBDR 26 Nov. 1884: 17f, 22, 29; Rickert SBDR 10 Dec. 1885: 257.

[13] Hasenclever SBDR 17 Feb. 1886: 1940. The SPD, however improbably, also benefited from contributions and bequests of wealthy patrons. Hall, *Scandal*, 145. Huber, *Verfassungsgeschichte* (1963) 3: 893; Nipperdey, *Organisation*, 152, 227, 383; Jaeger, *Unternehmer*, 113, 113nn. 24, 25; Jörg, *Briefwechsel*, 403. Until 1899 the Law of Association forbade political organizations to unite across regional or state boundaries.

would have no difficulty supporting the delegation—and "could sustain a significant portion of our honored colleagues" as well![14]

The solidarity preached by the Social Democrats meant turning even children's festivals into profit-making ventures. It also meant sacrifice—a word repeated over and over. Local branches were expected to put aside funds to subsidize rural areas or the party as a whole. In big cities, this might be more than 10 percent of their income, but the practice was common, at a lower level of munificence, even in quite small towns. Opponents tried to get propaganda mileage from toting up what the poor Socialist owed in weekly dues to union and precinct committees (ten pfennige for men, five for women in the early twentieth century), what he paid at the pub at monthly *Zahlabende*, what he gave for newspaper subscriptions, what he shelled out in admission fees.[15] Admittedly, sacrifices that could not be shared among many sometimes drove members away. When the twenty-some activists in Göttingen's little organization (about a tenth of its formal membership) doubled party dues from twenty to forty pfennige in order to cover expenses, membership plummeted. The comrades were driven to discuss paying bounties for each new recruit. Yet Social Democracy as a whole, from the late nineties on, was taking in roughly a million marks a year.[16] It was common wisdom that all the parties together did not spend half the money that the SPD was able to employ for political purposes.[17]

The prospect of the Socialists disposing of limitless resources concentrated the minds of the other parties wonderfully. National Liberals immediately recognized the nature of the Socialists' fiscal challenge, but were unable to move beyond a confidential canvassing of known sympathizers for a "once-and-for-all contribution."[18] Eugen Richter's Left Liberals, on the other hand, followed the Socialist lead. Although they shied away from obligatory dues until 1903, by the mid-eighties the *Freisinnigen* had enrolled at least 20,000 active members, founded approximately 200 local branches, and managed to establish a war chest of 50,000 marks to subsidize deputies who did not live near Berlin. The

[14] Bebel SBDR 12 Jan. 1892: 3580; Müller, *Geschichte*, 306; R. H. Dominick, *Liebknecht* (1982), 263, 331, 385. Fears that without stipends the middle parties would disappear, leaving only "the aristocracy and the money matadors on the farthest right and the SDs on the farthest left": Stauffenburg SBDR 16 Nov. 1884: 17f. See also Ritter, *Arbeiterbewegung*, 58–62, 228–31; Nipperdey, *Organisation*, 383.

[15] "Sacrifice": Koettig, Dresden Police, to Kreishauptmannschaft Dresden, 1 Feb. 1913, BAB-L R1501/14460, Bl. 462; Göhre, *Three Months*, 99–103, 114. SD confirmation: Keil, *Erlebnisse* 1: 85. Dues: Müller, *Geschichte*, 139; somewhat different figures: 351; for women: Guttsmann, *Party*, 273. Rural work: Hesselbarth, *Sozialdemokraten*, 46. SDs' "spirit of sacrifice" stressed by the Catholic Volksverein: Heitzer, *Volksverein*, 160.

[16] V. Saldern, *Wege*, 43f, 55, 57; Nipperdey, *Organisation*, 306; Ritter, *Arbeiterbewegung*, 51, 61f; Guttsmann, *Party*, 169–74.

[17] "Agitationsgelder, sozialdemokratische," Siebertz, *Abc-Buch*, 21f; *DA* 9/12 (22 Mar. 1891): 194–96; *DA* 27/6 (7 Feb. 1909): 95; Lefèvre-Pontalis, *Élections*, 111; Molt, *Reichstag*, 279; v. Saldern, *Wege*, 159–63, 164f.

[18] Wehrenpfennig to Forckenbeck, 20 Feb. 1877, GStA PK I. HA, Rep. 92, Nachlass Forckenbeck, Bd. B, Bl. 4.

stipends were independent of a deputy's personal wealth—although the rate (lower than the Social Democrats') was only 500 marks a session.[19]

One might have thought that for a deputy to accept subsidies from individuals or groups would have been unacceptable in a culture where traditionally public servants were conceived as members of the "universal estate," beholden to nothing and no one but the common good. Certainly the practice at least implicitly contradicted Article 29 of the constitution, charging deputies with representing "the whole people," and declaring them bound to no "instructions or commissions" either from constituents or party. But the practice swiftly took hold, and men who accepted allowances from their constituents or their party suffered neither social nor political penalties for doing so.

Herein lay an important difference between German and English parliamentary culture. Macaulay had once remarked ruefully that "without a competence it is not very easy for a public man to be honest; it is almost impossible for him to be thought so. . . ." When Richard Cobden accepted a subscription raised by his supporters to enable him to continue in office, the shadow on his reputation made it impossible for the Whigs to take him into their government. As late as 1901 even the fledgling Labour Party had difficulties establishing a Labour Members' Maintenance Fund. It was Ireland, that incubator of mass politics, not England, that provided the precedents for German practices. The "O'Connell Tribute," which began a long tradition of supporter-funding for nationalist deputies, found its German analog in 1888 when voters presented Richter with 100,000 marks on his fiftieth birthday to use in any way he chose on behalf of the political cause.[20] Some eyebrows were raised (particularly by those colleagues within his party who felt Richter had enough power already), but accepting the money did him no political harm.

What saved the impecunious Reichstag member from the mortification of his English counterpart (whose need for a subsidy "lay him open to the suspicion of being actuated . . . by the lowest motives") was the fundamental constitutional difference between the German and the British parliament: the absence in Germany of any direct connection between Reichstag majorities and "places" within the executive. Because of Germany's "dualism," no cabinet position could grow out of a deputy's political activity.[21] However much he and his party might influence proceedings at the "law factory," he would never—here like

---

[19] C. Graf Stolberg-Wernigerode (FK) SBDR 16 Nov. 1884: 21; K. Baumbach, "Der Diätenfonds der Fortschrittspartei," *Die Nation* 1 (1883–84): 78–80.

[20] Gash, *Politics*, 107–9; Gwyn, *Democracy*, 127, 144, 159–66, 179, 205. Nipperdey, *Organisation*, 208.

[21] Quote: Gash, *Politics*, 108. The illuminating analysis of Shefter, "Party," does not mention this constitutional/structural factor. Although Hohenlohe, chancellor from 1896 to 1900, had sat in the RT during its first decade, his was a bureaucratic career, which even before 1871 had culminated in the Minister Presidency of Bavaria. The Prussian Ministers of Finance and Trade, J. Miquel and T. Möller, respectively, had once served as NL deputies, but their move to cabinet office was independent of party. The "offer" of a cabinet post to Bennigsen in the late 70s failed precisely because Bis. refused to concede that any constitutional consequences would arise from it. When G. v. Hertling (Z) accepted the Minister Presidency of Bavaria in 1912, however, the public correctly saw a constitutional watershed.

the O'Connellites and Parnellites, but unlike Whigs and Tories—get his hands on public patronage. Consequently, far from being suspect as a "placeman," seeking office in order to further his fortune, the man who agreed to run for a Reichstag seat could expect to hear his sacrifices extolled.[22] Even those deputies who already held administrative posts when they entered the Reichstag—the Landräte, the prefects, and the judges—were largely protected from any imputation of trying to advance their careers. For law required that upon promotion they automatically lost their seat. To continue to sit in the Reichstag, they would have to resubmit themselves to the electorate—always a chancy operation, and one that no government could desire for its supporters.

Accusations that a candidate was getting financial help from abroad were potentially more damaging. Such allegations were never implausible, given the many affinities between political groupings across state boundaries. Thousands of pounds, after all, were funneled from North America into Parnell's Home Rule Party. Dominique Antoine, the Reichstag deputy for Metz, was accused by his opponents of receiving election help from revanchists in France. Rumors likewise circulated that Germany's *Freisinnigen*, die-hard free traders, were taking money from England's Cobden Club.[23] Social Democrats, whose commitment to international organization was explicit and who openly solicited support from comrades in other lands, were the most frequent target for such charges. Prussia's Ministry of Interior, which monitored appeals in Socialist publications, would relay information about foreign subscriptions in support of Socialist candidates to the latter's opponents, suggesting that they make of it "whatever use seems appropriate."[24] In 1887 government outlets reported that Socialists had accepted over 52,000 marks from supporters in France. Bebel dismissed the allegation with the greatest *sang froid*: 52,000 marks covered *total* foreign support for their campaign; most of that money had come from the United States: "from France, unfortunately, all told, only 300 francs."[25]

More credible than the government's dark warnings about foreign influence were misgivings about the powerful instrument for conformity that party-funded allowances put in the hands of the leadership. Did not a deputy who accepted a mandate under these terms "in effect sell himself to his party?"[26] The chaffing of Left Liberals under the "tyranny" of Richter, who used his control of the purse to keep his colleagues in line, suggested the potential for abuse.[27] But the Social Democrats, whose discipline was much tighter than the Left

---

[22] A. Reichensperger to Jörg, 3 Nov. 1881, in Jörg, *Briefwechsel*, 471; "Auf zur Wahl!" KVb, 28 July 1878; "Meppen . . . ," *KVb.*, 13 Feb. 1887.

[23] On Antoine: 14 AL AnlDR (1884/85, 6/I, Bd. 6) DS 185: 767–69; "English gold": Rickert SBDR 10 Dec. 1885: 256. Gwyn, *Democracy*, 135.

[24] RdI to G. A. Schlechtendahl, FK Committee of Barmen, 19 Feb. 1887, Schlechtendahl to RdI, 27 Feb. 1887, BAB-L R1501/14693, Bl. 164f, 173–75.

[25] Friesen, Bebel SBDR 10 Jan. 1889: 372, 376.

[26] Quoted by Stolberg-Wernigerode SBDR 16 Nov. 1884: 21. Huber agrees: *Verfassungsge-schichte* 3: 893f.

[27] Meyer, *Wahlrecht*, 520; Nipperdey, *Organisation*, 203f, 383. Viscount Gladstone's similar suggestions about the connection between party allowances and party discipline: Gwyn, *Democracy*, 120–23.

Liberals, mocked the suggestion that anyone in *their* party would be so "child-ish" as to say to a colleague, "If you don't vote the way I do, you'll get no allowance."[28] If party stipends enforced discipline, that discipline was already, at least in principle, acceptable to its supporters. We have few examples of a constituency nominating a candidate against the declared will of his party's leadership, and no examples of which I am aware of any deputy's being able to ignore the leadership and still retain his seat: as good a sign as any that the ties between voters and parties were truly binding.[29]

Constitutionally, these party-funded subsidies were as illegal as any govern-ment stipend, and Bismarck threatened to have anyone who was proven to have accepted an allowance expelled from parliament. But as the Reichstag alone had the authority to rule on the legitimacy of its members, the chancellor's threat proved to be hot air. When the government invoked anti-bribery laws to prosecute four Social Democrats and three *Freisinnigen* in the notorious "Sti-pend Trials," it got a black eye for its pains. The courts dismissed charges against all seven—providing tacit legitimation of the practice.[30] Although the government was upheld on appeal, and party stipends were ruled unconstitu-tional, contrary to Bismarck's threat no one was expelled. The imperial treasury claimed the right to confiscate the stipends, but it could hardly take each deputy to court every year. In fact, as jurists immediately recognized, the government's claim proved unenforceable.[31]

Additional links in the chain connecting party and voter were forged by a measure passed in 1874: the free railway pass. Initially intended only to equal-ize the burdens among members who lived at varying distances from the capi-tal, the rail pass was quickly perceived by activists as a way to send their paladins into sleepy or moribund constituencies to raise money and enthusiasm for less adept local candidates. As Ian Kershaw has shown elsewhere to such effect, "charisma," rarely occurring spontaneously, always depends upon a rela-

---

[28] Hasenclever SBDR 17 Feb. 1886: 1095. Bebel, however, announced that the SPD would pay no attention to § 29, which declared "members of the RT . . . not bound by any commissions and instructions." He and his comrades were prepared at any time to give an accounting to their voters. SBDR 10 Dec. 1885: 280.

[29] E.g., Solingen: Blos, *Denkwürdigkeiten* 2: 112–14, 118. However, contrary to Molt, *Reichstag*, 275, who says *no* candidates were nominated against the will of the leadership, Stötzel's first victory in Essen in 1877 was against the Z's official nominee, and Juliusz Szmula and Franz Strzoda (1893) in Upper Silesia likewise ran against Z-endorsed candidates. On victory, all three joined the Z delegation. Harry K. Rosenthal, "National Self-Determination: The example of Upper Silesia," *Journal of Contemporary History* 7/3–4 (Jul.–Oct. 1972): 231–42; 233–35. In 1907 in 2 Arns., J. Becker (Z), defeated the Z incumbent, J. Fusangel. I do not know which had the leader-ship's backing. On this race: Loth, *Katholiken*, 124n. 100.

[30] Bismarck SBDR 26 Nov. 1884: 26; Rickert SBDR 10 Dec. 1885: 254; Hasenclever SBDR 17 Feb. 1886: 1095. Compensation from party coffers for expenses and loss of income for electors (*Wahlmänner*), although it sometimes caused a victory's nullification, was very early common prac-tice in Prussian LT elections. Kühne, *Dreiklassenwahlrecht*, 76, and 76nn. 101, 102, 103.

[31] Tzschoppe, *Geschichte*, 59–63; M. v. Seydel, *Commentar*, 215–17. Seydel's earlier defense of party stipends: "Der deutsche Reichstag," *Annalen des Deutschen Reichs* (1880): 352–433; esp. 404f, and 405n. 5.

tionship between leader and group that, far from superseding organization, presupposes it. Thanks to the pass, the indefatigable Richter and the dashing Heinrich Rickert became indispensable figures at Left Liberal rallies in the most far-flung reaches of the empire. In 1879 alone Richter traveled from Posen to Kiel, from Kassel to Stettin, then to Tilsit, Memel, Insterburg, and many other, quite tiny communities throughout East Prussia. In 1881 he spoke in Bielefeld, Potsdam, and all across provincial and royal Saxony.[32] The pass enabled Windthorst to spend a fortnight in 1881 traveling to constituencies from the Ruhr to Lake Constance. Eventually his itinerary expanded well beyond the Catholic heartland. Rising in the middle of the night to catch the train, giving as many as three addresses at three different places in a single day, Windthorst became—thanks initially to the rail pass—such a staple at Centrum rallies that local leaders would advertise his appearance before telling him of it. "Someone," he complained about a rally in Münster, "simply wrote into the world that I was coming too. . . ."[33] A Conservative critic mockingly compared the diminutive Centrum leader to the titan Antaeus, always drawing new energy from the soil, the *Volk*.[34] The metaphor conveyed a truth not only about Windthorst, but about the parties generally: a tide of strength (money, support, and connectivity) was flowing upward, giving the delegations their power to "aggregate interests."

The populism of these leaders had its limits. Neither Windthorst nor Richter, Bebel nor Stoecker devoted much time to kissing babies or shaking hands. They gave their speeches in halls rather than on stumps—sometimes speaking to audiences of 8,000 or more. Nevertheless in their reliance on the railroad, their campaigning showed striking similarities to developments in England, France, and America. They were taking politics "out of doors," not only out of parliament, but outside the small gatherings of prominent "friends" whose endorsements in less democratic days had been all that was necessary to mediate a candidate's relationship with the electorate. And just as British opinion wondered at the propriety of Gladstone's Midlothian campaign of 1879–80, and French opinion, at the glad-handing of a Gambetta, a Clemenceau, and finally a Boulanger, so too did some Germans, especially but not only on the Right, sniff that extramural campaigning discredited the candidate who engaged in it.[35] Rudolf von Bennigsen, a man of such reserve that when he walked into a room the "windows froze," declined every request by his Liberal colleagues "to play the agitator like Eugen Richter or Rickert."[36] But those happy warriors refused to apologize. When Ernst von Köller, Landrat for Kammin (and Conservative

[32] Richter, *Reichstag* 2: 142, 237; Poschinger, *Bismarck* 2: 381–83.

[33] Windthorst to Reuss, 8 Oct. 1882, BAT 105/1493; W. to R. 29 Aug. 1884, BAT 105/1523 Stöcker may also have benefited from the railway pass: Braun, *Stoecker*, 83.

[34] Helldorf SBDR 10 Dec. 1885: 276. Windthorst to Heyl, 22 Oct. 1881; Extrablatt des *Katholischen Volksboten*, 22 Sept. 1884. Both courtesy of Dr. Josef Hamacher, Haselünne.

[35] Köller SBDR 2 Dec. 1882: 595; BAB-L R1501/14641, Bl. 163. Size of rallies: 5 Arns. (Bochum) AnlDR (1882/83, 5/II, Bd. 6) DS 292: 1075. Bendikat, *Wahlkämpfe*, 96, 106, 123, 147, 164, 214, 234, 254.

[36] Oncken, *Bennigsen* 1: 290; 2: 492, 613. Lasker too had expressed misgivings about unrestricted passes. Quoted by Stolberg-Wernigerode SBDR 26 Nov. 1884, 20.

tactician), charged Richter with invading his Baltic constituency, Richter retorted that the objection had only made him resolve "to do more for Pomerania
than I have until now been able to do." Precisely because so many deputies still
felt bound by the cozy conventions of *Honoratiorenpolitik*, the free rail pass
played a crucial role in political mobilization, allowing the brassy few to make
up the deficits of the dignified many.[37]

The out-of-doors campaigning of Gladstone, Gambetta, Clemenceau, and
Boulanger has recently been described as "bonapartist," even "caesarist."[38] This
seems an odd characterization. For the political figure in Germany to whom
these labels were usually applied was not, of course, Richter, or Bebel, or
Windthorst, but the campaigner who never left home: Otto von Bismarck. So
long as he was chancellor, Bismarck (whose high-pitched voice was unimpres-
sive) confined his speechifying to parliament. And Bismarck was determined to
level the playing field. Although the rail pass law had granted deputies the right
to travel during the session and eight days before and after "in all directions,"
the chancellor complained that one deputy had used his pass to travel 12,000
kilometers within a single eight-month period, while another (probably Richter—although rumor fingered Field Marshall von Moltke, and Bismarck himself blamed Social Democrats) had actually surpassed 17,000 kilometers. Between the main election and the runoffs of 1884, the chancellor was able to get
the Bundesrat to produce new passes that were limited to travel to and from the
deputy's residence and Berlin. The restrictions lasted until 1906.[39]

But by then, the damage had already been done. Those who had tasted the
fruits of mass politics could not be pushed back into the tiny Edens of semi-
public meetings among the locally like-minded. Parliamentary leaders had become used to spending their weekends on the campaign trail, sounding the
political waters in this district and that, submitting themselves to challenges
about legislation. The ten years of unrestricted rail passes between 1874 and
1884 had gone far to nationalize the political arena, linking local groupings to
nationally known figures. Like the great speed of the locomotive itself, the rail
pass—born of the government's refusal to grant parliamentary allowances—
had "condensed geography."[40]

The rail pass was not the only expedient developed to lessen the burden of
the unpaid deputy. The Reichstag also managed to force through *per diems* for
those serving on the time-consuming Justice Commission—an exception to Ar-

[37] Richter SBDR 2 Dec. 1882: 595. The reluctance of many Z deputies, especially before 1900, to
campaign in their districts: Heitzer, *Volksverein*, 159.

[38] Bendikat, *Wahlkämpfe*, 15, 98, 208, 341, 384, 400. Max Weber on Gladstone's "caesaristic-
plebiscitarian" Midlothian campaign: "Politik" ([1921], 1958), 523.

[39] Bis. SBDR 26 Nov. 1884: 24; Auer, ibid.; Kayser SBDR 9 Dec. 1885: 249; Blos, *Denkwürdigkeiten* 2: 123. Cf. Meyer, *Wahlrecht*, 517; Poschinger, *Bismarck* 2: 383; 5: 200. Molt, *Reichstag*,
"Caesarist demagogy" was ascribed to Bis. by liberals like H. Baumgarten. Mommsen, *Weber*
([1959], 1984), 6f.

[40] The phrase is Wolfgang Schivelbusch's: *The Railway Journey: Trains and Travel in the Nineteenth Century* (New York, 1979), 42. The influence of E. Lieber's speaking Sundays with voting
groups on the Z's position on Caprivi's military bill: Bachem, *Vorgeschichte* 5: 273.

ticle 32 that the Bundesrat actually allowed to stand. Parties also encouraged Reichstag deputies to run for state parliaments, in order to use state allowances to fund their Reichstag careers.[41] Dual mandates undoubtedly alleviated some of the financial pinch—which explains Bismarck's plan in the eighties (never carried out) to change the constitution to disallow it.[42] As late as 1907, 65 percent of the Centrum's Reichstag delegation and 25 percent of the Social Democrats' (with the other major parties ranged between) held concurrent seats in state legislatures. But when the prerequisite for accepting the seat in the democratic national body becomes election to a state legislature whose franchise is manifestly *un*democratic, the egalitarian promise of manhood suffrage has been considerably compromised.[43]

One effect of the ban on stipends was to skew for several decades the composition of the Reichstag sharply in favor of the rich—and of state and communal officials, army officers and judges, professors and clergymen, all of whom could take a leave of absence while continuing to collect their salaries.[44] A far more serious consequence was absenteeism. The 100-man Centrum—with its heavy south German contingent—sometimes disposed of only twenty deputies.[45] As late as the 1903–7 session, the Social Democrats' treasurer encouraged any Socialist deputy who was not indispensable to skip the midweek sessions, simply in order to keep the party's *per diem* costs down. By the 1890s, the Reichstag's lack of a quorum was described as "almost permanent." A joke went around that the greatest spectacle at the grand opening of the North Sea Canal was the sight *in Kiel* of the Reichstag in full force.[46] The empty back benches in Berlin undoubtedly made *intra*-party life simpler for the leadership; it also contributed to their ability, so necessary in parliamentary systems, to work together across party lines. But in what sense could one still speak of popular control when the decisions of these leaders were routinely made without even being discussed by their own delegations? Did not the reduction of parliament to roughly fifty active members, the passage of national legislation by sometimes

[41] Stauffenberg SBDR 26 Nov. 1884: 19; Molt, *Reichstag*, 47; Kühne, *Dreiklassenwahlrecht*, 353.

[42] "Vorschlag des Min-Präs., betr. Vorlage eines Gesetz-Entwurfes, daß Reichstags-Mitglieder nicht Abgeordnete des Landtages sein können," 14. Feb. 1883, GStA PK I. HA, Rep. 90a, A.VIII.1.d., Nr. 1/Bd. 5, unpaginated.

[43] In the Württ. LT deputies received 10 marks a day, allegedly keeping those holding double mandates from doing their duty in the RT. Siebertz, *Abc-Buch*, 489.

[44] Guaranteed by Art. 78 of the Constitution. An excellent survey of the RT's social composition: Schumacher, "Wahlbewerbungen," 353–75. Also Molt, *Reichstag*, esp. 38–48; Sheehan, "Leadership," 515, 517n. 19, 518n. 21; Meyer, *Wahlrecht*, 479f; Rosenbaum, *Beruf*, 62; Willy Kremer, *Der soziale Aufbau der Parteien des Deutschen Reichstages von 1871 bis 1918* (diss. Cologne, 1938), 28; Rudolf Morsey, "Die deutschen Katholiken und der Nationalstaat zwischen Kulturkampf und Erstem Weltkrieg," in G. A. Ritter, ed., *Deutsche Parteien* (Cologne, 1973), 270–98; figures on 286; Stauffenberg SBDR 16 Nov. 1884: 18.

[45] Voters did not like it. The absenteeism of Jos. Krebs threatened to split the Essen Z: Möllers, *Strömungen*, 227. Lack of *per diems* was not the sole cause of Z absenteeism, however. Geo. to Anna v. Hertling, 30 Oct. 1874, BAK Nachlass Hertling, 9, Bd. I.

[46] Hänel SBDR 7 Feb. 1888: 749; James F. Harris, *A Study in the Theory and Practice of German Liberalism: Eduard Lasker, 1829–1884* (New York, 1984), 127; v. Oppen, *Reform*, 3, 16–20.

as few as twenty assenting deputies, attenuate the meaning of democratic representation beyond recognition?

Such a situation could continue only so long as the leaders of the various delegations cooperated in keeping quorum-calls to a minimum, which for many years they did. But after the turn of the century the Social Democrats broke ranks, making the quorum-call a favorite tactic for sinking or delaying unloved bills, especially in tax debates. Far from encouraging shorter sessions, as Conservatives had once hoped, the absence of publicly funded stipends made it difficult to gather together even enough deputies to pass a motion to adjourn.[47] Nor did the increase in party-funded "professional" politicians solve these problems, since the very fact that they were professionals meant that their time was much in demand outdoors: in political organizing, in fund-raising, in journalism. When Bülow finally approached the Kaiser to amend Article 32, he had two irresistible arguments on his side: the impossibility otherwise of getting Centrum support for the government's naval and financial bills, and the Reichstag's debilitating absenteeism. Both arguments, in their different ways, acknowledged the indispensability of parliament.

The Bundesrat finally acceded to stipends in the spring of 1906—to the tune of 3,000 marks a year (less 20 marks for each sitting the deputy missed). By then, the high levels of organization so characteristic of German political life had long been established.[48] Reichstag deputies were already men who, in Max Weber's phrase, were living "from politics." Far from preventing the development of a professional political class, as Bismarck had hoped, the unintended consequence of the ban on compensation was to force men who wanted to serve in parliament to make politics a career.

MACHINEWORK

It was not usual for candidates to canvass voters personally in Germany, although newcomers, such as Otto Böckel (the antisemitic Reform Party) in the eighties and Friedrich Naumann (National Social Party) in the late nineties were forced to canvass in order to break into a game in which other parties had been familiar players for two decades. The distribution of ballots, however, albeit by the candidate's surrogates, took on the aspects of a canvass, and was an automatic spur to higher levels of organization.[49]

Every candidate rejoiced when he could rely on unpaid partisans for this

---

[47] Meyer, *Wahlrecht*, 519; *Thätigkeit*, 143; Bachem, *Vorgeschichte* 6: 261, 304; Kulemann, *Erinnerungen*, 41, 45, 50–54; Molt, *Reichstag*, 310, 312–14.

[48] Lerman, *Chancellor*, 64, 80. Text of the Gröber bill to amend Art. 32: *Reichstags-Wahlrecht*, 36. The constitutional amendment of 21 May 1906 continued to forbid a salary, but did offer compensation. Huber, *Verfassungsgeschichte* 3: 895. Jaeger, *Unternehmer*, 101, gives a higher figure: 400 Marks a month.

[49] As British liberals foresaw, predicting that the ballot would lead to the supremacy of political associations. Seymour, *Reform*, 431. German liberals' skepticism about universal suffrage limited their capacity to imagine the consequences of organizational details: Pollmann, *Parlamentarismus*, 88, 89n. 116.

chore. In the flatland the Conservative parties (and in some places, their Liberal counterparts) could call upon the considerable apparatus of state—from Landräte and gendarmes to teachers and village headmen—to expedite the distributions and keep costs low (an estimated 500 to 1,000 marks a district), although at the risk of invalidation if they won.[50] The Centrum, with their priests and catechumens, was even better situated. In cities, however, the parties themselves rose to the challenge of organization. By 1877, the Centrum had put at least one agent on each side of every Düsseldorf street (street agents, they were called); and Socialists in Hamburg disposed of a genuine "machine." By the end of the eighties they had enveloped the city in a network of precinct captains (*Bezirksführern*), each at the head of some twenty to fifty additional party members. With roughly seven hundred voters to a precinct, one might encounter a member, ballot sack in hand, among every twenty people one met. In Hamburg's industrialized but still quite rural suburbs, Liberals had preceded them by a decade, dividing each precinct into subsections of twenty voters and delegating volunteers to ferry groups of ragged workers back and forth to the polls all day long in their elegant carriages, a device that produced turnouts of 90 percent.[51] Given the dependent status of the voters, these signs of condescension in Hamburg may well have been the functional equivalent of the forced march to the polls that we have seen in face-to-face communities. Even so, any evidence of bread lords stooping to conquer is worth noting, so contrary are both the condescension and the high levels of organization to our usual picture of liberals in Bismarckian Germany.

The task of distributing ballots was a time-consuming one, and the enthusiasm of unpaid volunteers, rarely sufficient. In Munich the cobbler Heinrich Kröber, given 6,000 addressed envelopes containing Bebel ballots, spent three days delivering 2,000 of them gratis until he felt he could no longer leave his business unattended. He hired Sebastian Kraft to deliver the rest. Stopped by a policeman, Kraft, on poor relief and ineligible to vote ("on account of which I don't bother myself about political party-life"), claimed not even to know the contents of the envelopes he was delivering. Hundreds of peddlers in Chemnitz coupled ballot distribution with a sideline in watch-charms, matchboxes, and scarfpins with pictures of Bebel, Liebknecht, and the Socialist city's own favorite son, Dr. Max Schippel.[52] In localities where a party was weak, however, it was caught in a double bind. With few members, it dared not call on their services too often, for fear the burdens would drive them away. But to ask loyalists to find the resources to hire agents ran similar risks. At least for Social Democrats, as we have seen, the development of a supportive "milieu" often

[50] Bennigsen SBDR 15 Dec. 1888, quoted by Richter 3 Feb. 1888: 684. Nipperdey, *Organisation*, for NLs: 151–55; LLs: 200–204, 208, 220f, 226f, 235f; SPD: 306, 308, 313, 319, 322f, 325, 327, 341, 368, 370, 372, 383; K costs: Molt, *Reichstag*, 260.

[51] Schloßmacher, *Düsseldorf*, 53, 70, 207, 213f, 223, 241; Kutz-Bauer, *Arbeiterschaft*, 116, 130 and 130n. 60, 132.

[52] 1 Munich AnlDR (1884, 5/IV, Bd. 4) DS 123: 983f; Göhre, *Three Months*, 97; Czapliński, "Presse," 30f; unpaid: Keil, *Erlebnisse* 1: 84; Möllers, *Strömungen*, 78; Nipperdey, *Organisation*, 306; Bergsträsser, "Geschichte," 250.

followed party organization and election success, rather than vice versa. The way to jump-start the process was to transfer resources and manpower from the haves to the have-nots, from the hubs of party organization to the frontiers, with predictable consequences for local autonomy. Not surprisingly, such "centralization" was pushed most loudly not by those at the center, enjoying positions of strength, but by those—such as the Social Democrats in the university town of Göttingen—on the peripheries of party activity.[53] Bebel was not happy with the implications of increasing professionalization: "There has been a complete change during the past ten years in the way in which the party works," he complained to Victor Adler in 1911. "There is little trace of the old willingness to make sacrifices. Today all services are to be paid, and paid well at that."[54] Yet far from being incompatible with the ethos of Social Democracy, the principle of payment for work was intimately tied up with the gospel of self-respect preached by the labor movement: this laborer too was worthy of his hire.

How much money was spent? In 1887 Socialists paid an agent about twenty marks to distribute ballots and campaign literature—hardly a princely sum given the risks and aggravations attendant upon the chore. Twenty years later an agent in Marburg working for the *Freisinnige Volksvereinigung* made ten marks more. (In England, £200 was felt to be a fair salary for a principal election agent for most of the nineteenth century, although some did considerably better.)[55] Paying a mercenary had its perils, since another party could always offer more: as the *Freisinnigen* discovered when one of their distributors sold his ballots to their opponent's agent for ten marks.[56] The greatest dangers, however, were run by the distributors themselves, since any excuse or none might be used by hostile local authorities to destroy their ballots, box their ears, jail them for two weeks, or drag them to the edge of town and kick them over the line— in at least one case, threatening to beat them to death.[57] It seems clear that most of these balloteers, even when paid, worked for love as well as money.

As we know, in Germany the responsibility for voter "registration," that is, for keeping an official, up-to-date list of eligible voters, fell not on the citizen but on local governments: a departure from Anglo-American practice with important consequences. In Britain the intricacies of the property qualification made keeping an accurate list of those eligible to vote such a chore that localities

---

[53] Göttingen's nonsocialist Workers' Associations organized many more workers than the SPD. V. Saldern, *Wege*, 129; also 46, 50, 56, 84, 231, 235. Magdeburg: Asmus, "Entwicklung," 317.

[54] Guttsman, *Party*, 269n. 37; Bebel quote: 241f. Cf. Saul, "Kampf," 172f. Yet in 6 Berlin, 800 volunteers showed up to work gratis for the SPD on election day. Lefèvre-Pontalis, *Élections*, 124.

[55] From this, he probably hired additional staff. Gwyn, *Democracy*, 37n. 1. Agents: 5 Hessen AnlDR (1887/88, 7/II, Bd. II) DS 155: 673. LLs: Waldeck-Pyrmont AnlDR (1907/9, 12/I, Bd. 20) DS 736: 4627.

[56] 20 Saxony AnlDR (1884/85, 6/I, Bd, 6) DS 247: 1102. Similarly, in 3 Baden: Amtsvorstand St. Blasien to MdI, 24 June 1893, GLA 236/14901, 3/b; 1 Koblenz: Monshausen, *Wahlen*, 70.

[57] Protest of Bochum Z, 20 Jan 1891, BAB-L R1501/14668, Bl. 189; M. Dietz, K. Grehs, and F. Pröbstl, Election Protest of 12 Mar. 1887 (Munich II), BAB-L R1501/14656, Bl. 14f; 20 Saxony (1884/85, 6/I, Bd. 6) DS 247: 1103.

frequently neglected it. It was up to the voter to prove his eligibility, a task so complicated that it often required a defense in court. Radicals complained that "the franchise of the people [had been] . . . emptied into an attorney's brief bag." Registration kept perhaps 2.5 million otherwise eligible British men from voting. No doubt the task of keeping an accurate register was much easier in authoritarian Germany, thanks to the *Meldepflicht*, the obligation to notify the police of one's residential comings and goings. Even so, in a place like Hamburg, with its highly mobile population, it took 170 clerks working full time to put together the city's lists in 1887. By making the government responsible for keeping accurate lists, German law both guaranteed the franchise for the ordinary voter and (compared to Britain) substantially lowered the costs of the election for candidates and their parties.[58]

Each citizen had the right to inspect the lists during the eight days before the election to insure that he had not been left off. In Hamburg 68 percent of the eligible voters in 1887 made use of their right.[59] Berliners were just as conscientious, with 206,898 persons coming to check their names for the election of 1907—as a measure of civic consciousness, a figure at least as impressive as the city's high turnout on election day.[60]

Was a voter permitted to check the lists on behalf of another as well? And could he make copies—which included addresses and occupations—to take away with him?[61] We have seen in chapter 3 how overseers and other representatives of the authorities made use of the lists to summon their contingents to the polls. But already in the seventies, Progressives in Berlin and Breslau, and Socialists in Kiel, Altona, and royal Saxony had adopted the same practice in order to target their own constituencies.[62] It was twenty years, however, before the Reichstag officially reversed an earlier position and, supported by Germany's jurists, agreed that universal access to *all* the names in the list was

---

[58] British astonishment that in Germany "registration is the duty of the state": "Working," 274. Seymour, *Reform*, 5, 134–40, 167, 352f, 361, 364–68, 370, 373f, 381–83; quote: 368n. 2; Hanham, *Elections*, 399–402; Blewett, "Franchise," 35–43; 43n. 65. Bills to amend the system were defeated. Seymour/Frary, *World* 1: 163f.

[59] Kutz-Bauer, *Arbeiterschaft*, 120. In Breslau, 7,000 persons checked the lists in 1890. Müller, *Geschichte*, 352.

[60] The SPD distributed forms with which to protest being left off the list. 13,000 were submitted in 1903 in Berlin alone. Kühne, *Dreiklassenwahlrecht*, 122f. Party bureaus made their own lists available to voters long after city hall had closed its books—especially helpful in a city with 832 different polling places. "Lokales u. Vermischtes. Das Wahllokal," *BT*, Nr. 15, 1. Beiblatt, 9 Jan. 1912 (Abend).

[61] A party's answer was always "interested." F. Buht u. Gen. (K), Emden, 5 Aug. 1878, BAB-L R1501/14693, Bl. 57; KP on 2 Frankfurt AnlDR (1881/82, 5/I, Bd. 2) DS 103: 252; Reimer SBDR 10 Apr. 1874: 696; SD on 8 Magdeburg AnlDR (1881/82, 5/I, Bd. 2) DS 91: 333–36 and 2 Düsseldorf AnlDR (1882/83, 5/II, Bd. 6) DS 263: 971; against denial of right to copy lists: KP on 2 Berlin AnlDR (1881/82, 5/I, Bd. 2) DS 44: 120–22; v. Donimirski et al., 4 Marienwerder, 12 Mar. 1887, to RT, BAB-L R1501/14665, Bl. 82–86. In general: Hatschek, *Kommentar*, 157–61.

[62] H. H. Wachs (NL) SBDR 10 Apr. 1874: 697; Kayser SBDR 8 May 1878: 1248. A 10-page list from 1881 with 675 Meppen voters, 534 of them checked off, in columns assigned to Z agents, is in the SAO Dep. 62-b.

FIG. 11
Election Week in Hamburg (1887): Voters
Checking the Lists

Day	Persons
Monday	1,716
Tuesday	6,717
Wednesday	9,826
Thursday	10,878
Friday	10,494
Saturday	10,297
Sunday	22,985
Monday	10,467
	83,380

Source: H. Kutz-Bauer, *Arbeiterschaft* (Bonn, 1988), 120.

imperative (since "I am not inspecting the list because I am a voter of the Bahnhof Strasse or of the Bismarck Strasse or of the Sperling Gasse, but because, as an active citizen . . . , I participate in the legal consequences of the entire election").[63]

Any party that could afford it made multiple copies, for the *Schleppers*, male and female, not to mention those fleets of cyclists poised to fetch potential supporters, were unimaginable without them.[64] Their value had been demonstrated in a Hamburg by-election as early as 1883; the lists from one precinct had made the difference.[65] For all the technique's "modernity," a coercive impulse could still be heard behind the *Schlepper*'s knock. In Halberstadt, a National Liberal *Schlepper* greeted each householder with the following announcement: "Herr Tannery Owner Kühne and Merchant Heinzius send their compliments, and you should come to the election and sign here on this list indicating your intention to do so." We should not be surprised that by 1907

[63] Felix Stoerk, "Die Oeffentlichkeit der Wählerliste nach preußischen Verfassungs- und Verwaltungsrecht," *DGZ* 37/48 (26 Nov. 1898): 289–91. Vigorous debate broke out over the practice in Prussian LT and local elections, since the lists contained confidential tax information. Ferd. Nöll, "Ueber die Entnahme von Abschriften der ausgelegten Wahllisten seitens der Wähler," *PVB* 21/21 (24 Feb. 1900): 225–27; "Ungültigkeit der Wahlen zur Stadtverordnetenversammlung" (1901), 276f; [Georg] Strutz, "Die Oeffentlichkeit der Wählerlisten für die Wahlen zum Abgeordnetenhause und zu den Gemeindevertretungen," *PVB* 20/10 (3 Dec. 1898): 97–99; SBHA (1907–8, 20/IV): 2867ff. In 1881 the WPK had ruled that it was permissible for Berlin's City Council to allow LLs but not SDs access to the lists. AnlDR (1880, 4/III, Bd. 4) DS 94: 669. Similar case in 1890: *Thätigkeit*, 165. FVp agents barred from lists: 4 Potsdam AnlDR (1912/14, 13/I, Bd. 22) DS 1435: 2948f, 2952.

[64] 5 Arns. AnlDR (1882/83, 5/II, Bd. 6) DS 292: 1081; Kühne, *Dreiklassenwahlrecht*, 126; "Working," 276; "Politik und Presse" *DA* 21/27 (5 Jul. 1903): 443–45; esp. 444; Koettig, Dresden Police, to Kreishauptmannschaft Dresden, 1 Feb. 1913, BAB-L R1501/14460: Bl. 462.

[65] Kutz-Bauer, *Arbeiterschaft*, 127n. 50, 136, 269.

Germany's turnout had reached nearly 85 percent—only six points lower than Austria's, where voting was compulsory.[66]

The parties did not limit themselves to an assured clientele. By the eighties, Berliners were receiving ballots and leaflets from every party, mailed to them directly, sometimes two or three times during a single campaign. Richter caused a sensation when he used the mails to penetrate villages on estates outside Greifswald. Each laborer received an envelope (postmarked Berlin) addressed to him by name, delivered by the imperial postman—with a Progressive ballot inside. How did the party get these names and addresses? Someone must have gotten access to the Greifswald lists! How could they have possibly paid for it? Richter's feat created an uproar among the Pomeranian gentry.[67]

Keeping your lists accurate and up-to-date was a never-ending task, and for Social Democrats, whose target group was noted for its mobility, a matter of life and death.[68] The logistical challenges were daunting. In the first elections, the eligible voters of all six Berlin districts had been kept on a single list, making extended access for more than one person at a time practically impossible. By 1878, the situation had reversed itself—perhaps for the worse, since the capital now had 18,000 separate lists, the result of each householder and apartment-owner being required to draw up a list of his tenants, whose numbers might equal that of an entire precinct in a rural constituency. Checking for accuracy was always necessary, since many landlords—especially Progressives—only bothered to list those on the first two floors and *parterre*, shirking their duty to climb up to the attic or down to the cellar to get the names of their poorer tenants.[69] Since it took hundreds of clerks working feverishly to produce legible copies for the precinct panels, voters or parties had little time left to make copies of their own. Social Democrats soon began pressuring the municipalities to duplicate the precious lists, at cost, for any party that requested them, a demand that pitted them against obdurate (usually Progressive) city fathers.[70]

---

[66] SD Protest against NLs in Halberstadt: 8 Magdeburg AnlDr (1881/82, 5/I, Bd. 3) DS 91: 335; complaint of Emden KP against liberals, 5 Aug. 1878, BAB-L R1501/14693, Bl. 57. 14 Saxony AnlDr (1912/13, 13/I, Bd. 19) DS 718: 927; Birle to Jörg, 12 Jan. 1877: Jörg, *Briefwechsel*, 439; Koettig, Dresden Police, to Kreishauptmannschaft Dresden, 1 Feb. 1913, BAB-L R1501/14460; 467. A sunnier view of the role of *Schleppers*: Suval, *Politics*, 244. Boyer, *Culture*, 89.

[67] Behr-Behrenhoff SBDR 1 Feb. 1888: 655; Richter SBDR 3 Feb. 1888: 682f. The SDs had already used direct mailing in Munich. AnlDR (1884, 5/IV, Bd. 4) DS 123: 983. Two years earlier, during the Prussian LT elections, the MdI had secretly attempted to mail campaign leaflets to every home in the kingdom. Kühne, *Dreiklassenwahlrecht*, 69. Bergsträsser, "Geschichte," 249, supposed that the use of the postal system by the nonsocialist parties for last-minute flyers and ballots was new.

[68] "Die Wiederwahl Kaempfs," *BT* 6 Nov. 1912. The blue pencil marks on the article indicate that the significance of obsolete lists for defeating SDs did not escape RdI bureaucrats. BAB-L R1501/14645, Bl. 269. Outdated lists could provoke embarrassing interpellations: Bötticher to SM of Weimar, 23 Feb. 1895, BAB-L R1501/14453, Bl. 254.

[69] Reimer SBDR 10 Apr. 1874: 696; Kayser SBDR 8 May 1880: 1245; 6 Berlin AnlDR (1880, 4/III, Bd. 4) DS 94: 672.

[70] Richter, Löwe SBDR 8 May 1880: 1245f, 1250; Möllers, *Strömungen*, 92; SPD protest, 6 Berlin AnlDR (1880, 4/III, Bd. 4) DS 94: 669–72.

By the turn of the century, however, most cities were doing so as a matter of course. When Richter requested that the government make this service obligatory across the land, however, it refused.[71] Access for all, favor for none was the most that the government would guarantee. Candidates who lacked the energy or organization to make their own copies paid the penalty.

EDUCATING THE ELECTORATE

Contrary to what we might expect from elections elsewhere, spectacle and pageantry were not important aspects of the German campaign. In small communities whose networks of authority and conformity were still intact, festivity was hardly necessary to the task of mobilization. In larger, more heterogeneous, more "modern" locales, where parties already determined the agenda, mass assemblies were indeed held to generate enthusiasm, dishearten opponents, and lay claim to the public space: that is, to display power. But power was conceived not festively but forensically: as the rhetorical display of correct opinions, rendered irresistible by armies of facts. Few eggs were dodged (and thrown); tableaux vivants, graced by local pulchritude, were reserved for very special occasions; and virtually no one was hanged in effigy. The silent presence of the note-taking gendarme no doubt helped keep behavior generally decorous, but—just as important—an unspoken consensus about what was appropriate to political decision-making ensured that spectacle would play a subordinate role to other modes of persuasion, and that campaign rituals would be verbal rather than visual.[72]

The democratic heartbeat of Social Democracy was nowhere more evident than in the long hours dedicated to turning each member into a local Demosthenes, prepared, at least in theory, to go to the barricades of public debate. The major part of each branch meeting was devoted to speeches and discussion from the floor. As the president of the Social Democratic Election Club of Chemnitz announced to his forty-odd regulars: "It is desired that everyone should take part, and that everyone should express an opinion. No matter how poorly this is done, everyone may be sure of not being laughed at, since we meet each fortnight for precisely the purpose of training ourselves to cope successfully with the arguments of our opponents in larger assemblies." From eight until twelve, weavers, master-mechanics, and laborers had their say. Even "if they spoke the most arrant nonsense," an observer noted, they were accorded the utmost attention, "with a gravity almost childlike." Although some of these speeches were presentable, more frequently they were crude and ungrammatical, betraying "a fearful jumble of knowledge and ignorance, practical experience and total inability to grasp the situation, with often such extravagance of

[71] Richter to IM v. Hammerstein, 16 May 1903; Kitzing to Bülow, 19 May 1903; Kitzing to Richter, 19 May 1903, BAB-L R1501/14456, Bl. 173f.
[72] Contrast England's "Politics of Sight": Vernon, *Politics*, 107–16. Also O'Gorman, "Rituals."

views as startled the more cautious and practical members of the club. . . ."[73]
Yet the encouragement of everyman's participation fortified self-respect and
sealed the participant's loyalty to the party—a small price to pay for
the impression of amateurism that dogged some of Social Democracy's early
appearances.

Nevertheless, the exigencies of forensic competition demanded speakers
of proven quality. Social Democrats quickly established formal training programs for their spokesmen. By 1876 they were employing 8 fully salaried
speakers, 14 part-timers, and 123 trained (but not yet salaried) "professionals."
This team expanded exponentially over time, allowing the party to work not
just the major urban centers, but suburbs and small towns. By 1890 the party
was even going after the Centrum's constituency, a challenge that produced an
immediate and analogous response: the founding of the "*Volksverein* for Catholic Germany." The *Volksverein*'s goal was to turn Catholic workers into "adult
citizens," able to take a knowledgeable, active interest in public affairs—and to
be able to stand up for themselves in public assemblies. Instruction manuals
encouraged prospective speakers to read a daily paper, to underline, clip, and
organize articles, filing them in labeled folders as a source for future speeches.
The *Volksverein*'s classes set their sites not only on the eloquent few, but on the
taciturn many, hoping that even workers who might never become gifted at the
podium would at least be able to offer a comment from the floor—and at the
workplace.[74] Thus competition continually raised the standards of political argument, which in turn reinforced the tendency toward the nationalization of campaign organizations.

The Progressives had less need for training programs, but were equally quick
to professionalize their rallies. By 1880 they had put together a list of sixty-four
well-known spokesmen available for districts in need. Further to the Right,
party culture was more resistant to such professionalization. Believing, as they
did, that political legitimacy derived from preexisting authority, conservatives
found speech-making that went beyond the promise to do one's best for king
and country ideologically repugnant. The very act of making arguments implicitly contradicted the "naturalness" of the order they were resolved to preserve,
for if authority really is natural, then the less said, the better. National Liberals
were also slow to employ professional speakers, waiting until the end of the
century, when they were galvanized by the explosion of Social Democracy.
Even then both Liberals and conservatives were apt to "subcontract" their
campaigns to nationally based interest groups (who had their own training
schools)—a different kind of professionalization.[75] In 1907 the Imperial Asso-

---

[73] Göhre, *Three Months*, 90–94. Father Cronenberg tried to encourage similar skills in his Paulus
Verein in Aachen, but the charismatic nature of his authority undermined efforts at democracy.
"Minutes . . . of the Chr. Soz. Party" 1877, in Lepper, ed., *Katholizismus*, 208.

[74] Although technically not part of the Z, and officially contributing no funds to it, the VV was
founded by Windthorst and its board was always staffed with Z leaders. Heitzer, *Volksverein*, 144–
91, 246f, 259–63.

[75] "Subcontracted" is Eley's insight: *Reshaping*, 28. Excellent on Diederich Hahn's impact on

ciation for Combating Social Democracy offered orators for fifty marks an appearance. Cadres of Africa veterans, sponsored (and probably paid for, at least indirectly) by the government, provided additional drawing cards for gatherings on the Right.[76] Professionalization was not incompatible with democratization. When the BdL began putting large resources earmarked for public-speaking at the disposal of favored candidates, one consequence was that ordinary farmers suddenly began running for the Reichstag.[77]

The election was conceived as an educational institution.[78] Consequently a much bigger item in campaign budgets than speakers and rallies was the flood of print that inundated the land of poets and thinkers. Not for Germans the colorful posters that in France played so large a role in the campaign, giving it "a burlesque physiognomy" and leaving the walls of public buildings looking "like a multicolor tapestry."[79] In Bavaria and Saxony one might find posters, but in Prussia the Press Law of 1851 forbade the posting of pictures, proclamations, or advertisements, except for public entertainments, sales, and items lost and found. Social Democratic vandals sometimes painted the walls of houses with the names of their favorites the night before the election, but placards, largely confined to written texts, were restricted to a limited number of officially designated pillars—or sandwich-board men walking around Berlin.[80] The illustrated broadsheet was not entirely unknown. In 1887, National Liberals distributed charts showing French troops massing on the border and garish depictions of how they might deal with German women when they arrived. But most German propagandists seemed to believe that one word was worth a thousand pictures.[81]

Much more common, then, were the handbills, crowded with text, and continually updated in order to answer a rival's charges or to give tactical advice to supporters. In 1877 Social Democrats distributed well over a million pieces of literature in Berlin alone; Richter, more than a million copies of a single flyer the following year.[82] By 1907, the SPD was turning out 55,500,000 leaflets; by 1914, the *Volksverein* was rebutting them with 89 million of its own: this in a

BdL agitation: Vascik, "Conservatism," esp. 252, and on antisemites: Levy, *Downfall* and Eley, "Anti-Semitism." See also: Richter, *Reichstag* 2: 89, 98, 109, 169–71; Nipperdey, *Organisation*, 154, 200, 306; Bergsträsser, "Zur Geschichte," 248, 252; v. Saldern, *Wege*, 85.

[76] "Working," 277; Nipperdey, *Organisation*, 152; Erzberger, *Bilder*, 46–53.

[77] Molt, *Reichstag*, 117.

[78] Steinbach, *Zähmung* 1: 57.

[79] Lefèvre-Pontalis, *Élections*, 30, 120.

[80] §§ 9, 10, and 41 of the Prussian Press Law quoted in SBDR 6 Mar. 1888: 1317; *Thätigkeit*, 138; [Köller], *Ungiltigkeit*, 12; M. Hagen, "Werbung und Angriff: Politische Plakate im Wandel von Hundert Jahren," in H. Bohrmann, ed., *Politische Plakate* (Dortmund, 1984). Thanks to Julia Sneeringer for this reference. When Lefèvre-Pontalis, *Élections*, 112, says that 600,000 antisemitic placards were distributed in Berlin, although the party won only 46,000 votes, he must mean handbills. Posters in Leipzig (beyond Prussian law): Guttsman, *Party*, 173; in 10 AL: AnlDR (1905/06, 11/II, Bd. VI) DS 483: 4739f; in Bavaria: *GA* Nr. 12, 15 Jan. 1874: 68.

[81] Grafitti and broadsheets: Müller, *Geschichte*, 110, 182, 353.

[82] Richter, *Reichstag* 2: 67–69; Ullstein, *Richter*, 43–45; Nipperdey, *Organisation*, 200, 306; Möllers, *Strömungen*, 318.

country whose *entire* population numbered under 70 million![83] Those with less well developed organizations, such as the antisemites, would recycle the same leaflet in each constituency by rubber-stamping a different candidate at the head.[84] As time went on, leaflets became increasingly refined in their targets. The Centrum published a series entitled "What has the Reichstag Centrum done for the _____?" finishing the sentence with Businessman, Artisan, Agriculture, and Worker, respectively. All of this was accompanied by satires, campaign songs, and doggerel, as well as the inevitable endorsements signed by local *Prominenten* that were standard features of every campaign.[85]

Yet voters were assumed to be great readers, whose appetites could scarcely be satisfied by a mere handbill or leaflet. Books, large and small, were an essential part of the political process. Deputies had published "accountings" of their activities (*Rechenschaftsberichte*) as early as 1848, and by the seventies, these accountings were taking very substantial form.[86] The Centrum's deputy for Cleve published between hard covers a *Report to His Voters* that ran to 113 pages, bound together with a 222-page collection of speeches by his colleagues, complete with footnotes and a detailed index. The author described himself as feeling "pressured" to "give a short [!] accounting to my mandataries [*Auftrag-gebern*]" of the highlights of the parliamentary term. He chose print, he said, primarily in order to reach "*all* of my voters"; but also because experience had taught him that the authorities would shut down Centrum rallies at the most trivial provocation and that "every unconsidered word" made both speakers and listeners vulnerable to prosecution (this was 1877, and the Kulturkampf was in full force).[87] Probably few deputies put out entire books to justify their reelection, relying on those published by and for his party.[88] But culturally driven expectations discouraged the production of mere ephemera. Hellmut von Gerlach warned his agent: "Don't distribute anything whose format makes it suita-

---

[83] Crothers, *Elections*, 153; Klein, *Volksverein*, 63. See also v. Saldern, *Wege*, 57f; Nettmann, "Witten," 120–22.

[84] Bergsträsser, "Geschichte," 251. The technique was pioneered by SDs by 1884. BAB-L R1501/14702, Bl. 42.

[85] A. Wolfstieg/K. Meitzel, *Bibliographie* (1896) 2: 142. Satirical: [A. Reichensperger], *Phrasen* (1872); Anon., *Humoristisch-satirisches Bilderbuch* (1881) (antisemitic); H. Chalkeus, ed., *Lied* (1899) (vs. Eugen Richter).

[86] Dr. C[arl] G[ustav] Kries, *Wähler* (1851); Major Dr. H[einrich] Beitzke, *Wähler* (1859); *Rechenschaftsbericht des Reichstagsabgeordneten und ersten Vicepräsidenten des deutschen Reichstags Fürsten Chlodwig von Hohenlohe-Schillingsfürst*, cited by H. Gollwitzer, *Standesherrn* (1964), 421; Ketteler, "Centrums-Fraction"; L. Müller (F), "Aus dem Reichstage," an interim report to his constituents on the first eight days of the new RT, *GA* Nr. 38, 14 Feb. 1874: 117. The sickness of the LT deputy Dr. Paux was cited to explain the interruption of his regular reports: *GA* 32, 7 Feb. 1874: 180.

[87] Virnich, *Fraction*. Although this report was for the LT, RT speeches were bound in the same volume.

[88] E.g., A. Bebel, *Die parlamentarische Thätigkeit des Deutschen Reichstages und der Landtage und die Sozialdemokratie von 1871 bis 1873. Nebst einem Anhang* (Leipzig, 1873). An edition with the same title covered 1874–76. Also Vorwärts's *Thätigkeit*; M. Erzberger, *Zentrumspolitik* (1904 through 1913).

ble for wrapping paper! Sell little books! Even ten years from now, perhaps, you will find them in the farmer's library."[89]

Just as the British agent "nursed" his constituency between elections with good works and public benefactions, so too did the German parties fortify the voter's allegiance with improving literature of all sorts: from collections of speeches (Richter clearly believed that any speech worth making was worth publishing) to discussions of technical issues (the tobacco monopoly, the military budget) to celebrations of party heroes, with whom the voter was encouraged to identify.[90] "*Our* Virchow," "*Our* Bebel," "*Our* Windthorst," "*Our* Bismarck" were offered to the faithful. Voters smoked their tobacco in pipes graced with their heros' face; treated sore throats with patent medicines boasting their names.[91] The parties presented their champions as *Erzieher*, a term whose literal meaning is "educator," but "educator" with the moral penumbra bestowed by a culture that held education sacred. The influential works by Nietzsche in the seventies ("Schopenhauer as Educator") and Julius Langbehn in the nineties (*Rembrandt as Educator*) have long seemed characteristic of the Empire; and where else but in the German *Kulturraum* could we find such campaign titles as "Bennigsen as Educator," "Windthorst as Educator," "Moltke as Educator," "Bismarck as Educator?"[92] "The political ignorance of the masses is our worst enemy," proclaimed a campaign booklet aimed at the Bavarian "citizen and husbandman." Where education was so valued, it was inevitable that the parties would stake their own claim.[93]

---

[89] H. v. Gerlach, "Wahlgeplauder" (1903), 148–51.

[90] Speeches: E.g., *Gegen die Konservativen. Rede des Abg. Eugen Richter, gehalten im Bezirksverein der Hamburger Vorstadt für den 3. Berliner Landtagswahlkreis* (Berlin, 1898); L. Windthorst, *Ausgewählte Reden, gehalten in der Zeit von 1851 bis 1891 3 Bde* (Osnabrück, 1901/2). At least three collections of Moltke's speeches were issued: *Reden des Abgeordneten Grafen Moltke. 1867–1878* (Berlin, 1879); *Graf Moltke als Redner. Vollständige Sammlung der parlamentarischen Reden Moltkes. Chronologisch geordnet . . .* (Berlin, Stuttgart, [1889]); *Reden des General-Feldmarschalls Grafen Helmut von Moltke* (Berlin, 1892).

[91] H. Steinitz, *Unser Rudolf Virchow. Ein Lebensbild* (Berlin, 1884); "Unserem August Bebel zum 70. Geburtstag" (poem), in Illustrierte Unterhaltungs-Beilage of the *Wahren Jacob*, 1910, Nr. 615; *Unser Bismarck. Leben und Schaffen des Deutschen Reichskanzlers Fürst Otto von Bismarck in kurzgefaßter Entwicklung dem deutschen Volke vorgeführt* (Leipzig and Berlin, 1885); the oversized, copiously illustrated coffee table book by Christian W. Allers, *Unser Bismarck* (Berlin, Stuttgart, Leipzig, n.d. [1896]); "Unser Windthorst! Windthorst-Meppen" (poem for Windthorst Day, 28 Sept. 1884), courtesy of Dr. Joseph Hamacher, Haselünne—as are the advertisements for Windthorst Chest Medicine, Windthorst Tobacco, Windthorst Pipes. The sheer volume of popular biographies of political figures is overwhelming. To get some idea: Wolfstieg/Meitzel, *Bibliographie*.

[92] [Max Harden], "Bennigsen als Erzieher," *Zukunft*, Bd. 3 (1893): 373–79; H. H. Mönch, *Windthorst als Erzieher* (Trier, 1893); "Moltke als Erzieher," *Simplicissimus* (Munich, 1900–1901) V/39, title page—one of the few *Simplicissimus* drawings not meant satirically. P. Dehn, *Bismarck als Erzieher*, reviewed in "Politische Notizen. Bismarck als Erzieher," *Die Zeit* II/15 (8 Jan. 1903): 449. In 1892 the *Deutsches Adelsblatt* printed an article entitled "Der König als Führer und Erzieher des Volksthums," *DA* 10/1 (3 Jan. 1892): 3. The Austrian Christian Socials put out an "[Albert] Gessmann als Erzieher." Boyer, *Culture*, 650. On Langbehn's best-seller *Rembrandt als Erzieher*, see Fritz Stern's *Politics of Cultural Despair* (Berkeley, 1961), 116–36.

[93] Epigram to forward in Siebertz, *Abc-Buch*. The point is also made by Rohe, "Introduction: Elections," 14.

If politicians were "educators," then voters were expected to become students. The most characteristic, if not the largest selling, items of German campaign literature were political encyclopedias, jokingly referred to as "bibles." Beginning modestly with such titles as the "Little Election Book," the "Election Catechism," the "Election Calendar," the "Vademecum," the "Parliamentary Handbook," and especially the "Political ABC," political expertise soon took its place on the growing shelf of nineteenth- and early twentieth-century self-help literature.[94] In 1879 Richter produced what would become the classic of the genre, the *ABC Book for Radical Voters: A Lexicon of Parliamentary Questions and Controversies of the Day*. By its third edition Richter's *ABC* had grown to 544 pages, covering everything from coffee duties to Count Moltke's self-contradictions on the subject of war (under "M"), and setting a standard for election propaganda that his competitors struggled to meet.[95] The Centrum was the last to follow suit, but finally in 1900 it published its own *ABC*. Beginning with "*Abkommandieren*" (the charge that the Centrum leadership ordered its backbenchers to absent themselves so that Reichstag compromises the party officially opposed would nevertheless be sure of passage), moving to "*Bebel's Villa*" (alleged to have cost a half million marks), all the way to "Württemberg deputies' attendance record" (an attack on the Volkspartei), the Centrum loyalist was provided with nearly seven hundred pages of political ammunition.[96]

Print and the spoken word combined in the climactic ritual of every political rally worth its name: the dual between a featured orator and the discussants. Conversions were probably rare; but it was a matter of self-respect for a party to be able to defend itself with facts and arguments. The young Schwabian schoolteacher Matthias Erzberger launched his Centrum career by appearing regularly at Socialist and Liberal rallies and dazzling fellow Catholics with the barrage of information he was able to hurl at speakers twice his age and boasting years of parliamentary experience.[97] The fat little *ABCs*, small enough to fit

---

[94] A sample: [Koester], *Das wohlgemeinte Wahlbüchlein. Eine Ansprache an die schlesischen Urwähler und Wahlmänner vom Lande* (Berlin, 1848); F. Harkort, *Wahl-Katechismus pro 1852 für das Volk von Friedrich Harkort* (Braunschweig, 1852); Anon., *Politisches Wahl-Büchlein zum 28. April und 6. Mai 1862 für Jedermann* (Nordhausen, 1862) (F); Anon., *Der liberale Wähler oder Was man zum Wählen wissen muß. Handbüchlein nach dem ABC geordnet* (Berlin, 1879); Anon., *Des braven Wählers ABC. Aus dem schätzbaren Zukunfts-Material eines vergangenen Wahlministers zu Tage gefördert und der Gegenwart nutzbar bemacht von XYZ* (Berlin, 1888); *A-B-C für konservative Wähler. Hrsg. unter Mitw. namhafter Konservativer* (Berlin, 1881); *A-B-C für konservative Wähler hrsg. unter Mitw. sächsischer Reichstagabgeordneten* (Berlin, 1884); *Vademecum zur Landtags-Wahl 1888.* Hrsg. von dem Wahlverein der Deutschen Conservativen (Berlin, [1888]); L. M. v. Hausen, ed., *Konservativer Kalender* (Charlottenburg, 1908); *Politisches A-B-C- Buch für bayerische Landtagswähler mit Programm der vereinigten Liberalen und Demokraten Bayerns und Landtagswahlgesetz nebst Wahlkreiseinteilung* (Munich, n.d. [1907]).

[95] *Neues ABC-Buch für freisinnige Wähler. Ein Lexikon parlamentarischer Zeit-und Streitfragen* (Berlin, 1884); *Politisches ABC-Buch. Ein Lexikon parlamentarischer Zeit- und Streitfragen von Eugen Richter, Mtgl. des Reichstags und Abgeordnetenhauses* (Berlin 7th ed., 1892). (It appeared first for the Prussian LT elections of 1879 under the title: *Der liberale Urwähler oder Was man zum Wählen wissen muß.*) Richter, *Reichstag* 2: 142.

[96] Siebertz, *Abc-Buch.*

[97] Klaus W. Epstein, *Erzberger* (1959), 9. For SPD: v. Saldern, *Wege*, 127.

into a pocket, ready to be whipped out should its owner wish to fortify himself inconspicuously before stepping forth in debate, were made for the Erzbergers of the world.

Newspapers and democratic elections were also made for each other. Before the polling, the papers were the eyes of the campaign, communicating to partisan foot solders, blind in their local trenches, the larger picture of the assaults and feints of the foe. Subscribers became stringers, sending in reports from the front to the "Political Overview" section, with no reward except the pleasure of appearing in print. The *Berliner Tageblatt* reported hundreds of such contributions from readers in 1912—too many to publish.[98] Voters were assumed to care about every race, and papers would devote pages and pages to listing *every* candidate for every district; and then do it again for the runoff.[99] The total audience was a large one. In 1880 an estimated 60 percent of the literate population read a newspaper. By 1891 Germans boasted 800 dailies, as many as England, and they supported more newspapers of every kind (5,500) than any other European country. (The expression for doing the unnecessary became "to carry newspapers to Berlin.") Although nearly half of these papers were either trade organs or what Germans call *Käseblättchen*—local advertisers, whose destiny it was to wrap cheese, not form minds—all but a handful of the other papers were not only political, but tied to a specific party.[100] Every pub, tavern, and inn in Germany subscribed to at least one paper for its customers. A subscription was a declaration of political identity—which is one reason why those in authority, in church, in state, in mine, in shop—tried to control them.

Since their readership was assumed to comprise the committed, the self-denying tone of apparent impartiality that we demand of our own respectable press was the ideal of no one. In reporting the activities of their opponents, newspapers from all points on the political spectrum employed the full range of *ars rhetorica*—exaggeration, sarcasm, and the ironic feigning of doubt. To get perspective, a conscientious Social Democrat would subscribe not just to his own party's press, but to several papers of his opponents, for only so could he master the arguments of the enemy.[101] This dedication explains why, in overwhelmingly Socialist Chemnitz, where the Left Liberals had celebrated their last victory in 1871, and where their party had not had a significant presence since 1884 (when it came in third), the Left Liberal *Neueste Nachrichten* could fly on its masthead the sobriquet "Most Widespread Chemnitz Newspaper" and boast in 1898 a paid circulation of 57,000—an incredible 28 percent of the

[98] Severing, *Lebensweg* 1: 26; "Aus der Reichstagswahlbewegung," *BT* 41/18 (8 Jan. 1912).

[99] A sample for 1912: BAB-L R101/339. The same phenomenon on a lesser scale appeared as early as 1874: *Katholischer Volksbote* (Meppen), Extrablatt for 14 Jan. 1874, printed election results by Amt and precinct, along with those from Z districts in Cologne, Crefeld, Essen, Düsseldorf, etc.

[100] Keil, *Erlebnisse* 1: 93; Asmus, "Entwicklung," 317. Readership: August Lammers, cited by Smith, *Nationalism*, 80f; numbers of papers in 1891: *DA* 9/12 (22 Mar. 1891): 194–96, which gives 3,000 papers for England, of which 800 were dailies; France had 2,800, and 700, respectively. Breakdown between political and nonpolitical is from E. R. May, *The World War and American Isolation* (Cambridge, 1959), 98f. "Newspapers to Berlin": de Jonge, "Parlament," 210.

[101] Göhre, *Three Months*, 96–98.

entire population of men, women, and children, and more than all of Chemnitz's eligible voters combined.[102]

Many of Germany's chief publicists were themselves members of state and national parliamentary delegations: men like Richter, Rickert, and Naumann among Left Liberals; Eduard Müller, Georg Dasbach, Julius Bachem, Theodor Wacker, and Matthias Erzberger in the Centrum; Otto Böckel, Max Liebermann von Sonnenberg, and Oswald Zimmermann (Antisemites), Georg Ratzinger (Bavarian Farmer's League), Georg Oertel (BdL) and Otto Arendt (Free Conservative) on the Right; Wilhelm Liebknecht, Eduard Bernstein, Karl Kautsky, Gustav Noske within Social Democracy—one could name many more in every camp. The Conservatives, with less interest in propaganda, were a partial exception, but some of their best-known leaders, such as Stoecker and Wilhelm von Hammerstein, disposed of their own press organs.[103] The type was not unknown in other franchise regimes—Georges Clemenceau comes immediately to mind, and in fact thirty-one members of the 1898 Chamber of Deputies were journalists.[104] But in no other country did the masters of the written word play so significant a parliamentary role as in Germany. In Britain, where the popular press was concentrated in the hands of a very few, the parties were put in the undignified position of courting the favor of the great publishing magnates with honors and titles.[105] The closest German equivalents to the British press lord was Rudolf Mosse, one of the richest men in Prussia, and perhaps the five Ullstein brothers; but unlike the British press magnates, no one ever thought they might bring a government down. More than the growth of party bureaucracies, which was slow even within Social Democracy and outside it almost invisible by British standards, it was the journalist in Germany who connected party and electorate, who provided continuity between elections, and who most exemplified "politics as a vocation." In the view of Max Weber, "the political publicist, and above all the journalist, is nowadays the most important representative of the demagogic species."[106]

Always risking prosecution by the government or lawsuit from their opponents, political editors, even those with no parliamentary mandate, often became folk heroes. Notorious or celebrated, depending on one's politics, was the onetime schoolteacher Karol Miarka, founder of the illustrated Silesian weekly *Katolik*, who was jailed seven times during 1871–72, incarcerated nine months

---

[102] "Leichenreden," *Neueste Nachrichten. Verbreitetste Chemnitzer Ztg* 10/148 (30 Jun. 1898), BAB-L R1501/14694, Bl. 215; Specht/Schwabe, *Reichstagswahlen*, 229.

[103] Molt, *Reichstag*, 176–82, 228, makes the same point, with different publicists.

[104] Of 581 deputies. Lefèvre-Pontalis, *Élections*, 33. In contemporary San Francisco it was "hard to find a political leader who had not at one time owned or edited a newspaper. Running a newspaper and running for office . . . were similar and deeply intertwined activities." Ethington, *City*, 21.

[105] G. H. Searle, *Corruption* (1987), 80–99; G. A. Ritter, "Parlamentarismus" (1962), 22.

[106] Weber, "Politik," 513. Bavaria in 1910 exemplifies the extreme: 19 LT deputies each controlled his own local Z newspaper (2 of them controlled 2)—in addition to the LT delegation's official paper. Möckl, *Prinzregentenzeit*, 556n. 4. Nipperdey, *Organisation*, 327, 369. English impression of absence of bureaucracy: "Working," 275.

the second year, and suffered violence in 1874.[107] Miarka's writing, aimed at Upper Silesia's hard-pressed cotters and miners, and suffused with grievance against liberals, Protestants, and Jews, had the character less of news articles than of jeremiads, in which confessional, social, and Polish nationalist themes were impossibly entangled.[108] The conjunction of Kulturkampf with democratic electoral contests was a godsend to Miarka's style of journalism. Within four years of its founding in 1869, *Katolik*'s circulation had soared to the third highest in the province. And since (not least through Miarka's efforts) Upper Silesia's elections were subject to continual challenges (twelve between 1871 and 1887) and therefore to constant repeat- and by-elections, Miarka always had grist for his mill. By the end of the seventies, *Katolik*'s sales equaled the best that *Germania*, the Centrum's "national" paper, would ever attain. Ultimately *Katolik* surpassed *Germania* more than threefold, with an estimated circulation of 20,000 by the late eighties and a readership of roughly 340,000 by the war. But Miarka's articles reached deeper into Silesia's Polish-speaking constituency than either his subscription figures or Polish literacy rates suggest. In 1925 an eighty-five-year-old Upper Silesian recalled how

> Every week we assembled, usually after Sunday mass, in the village inn or in one of the roomier farmhouses, where one of our neighbors who knew how to read would read aloud the current articles in the *Katolik*. We followed the presentations on Church-state issues with greatest interest. Even on the way home the excitement about this or that measure of the government against the Catholic Church continued to vibrate in us all to such an extent that almost always we would resolve to meet again, even in the evening, here and there, in order to debate about it even further. And whenever it happened that more than one opinion was expressed among us, whoever wanted to push his own views through had only to declare: 'that's what Miarka said'—for everyone else immediately to agree.

Journalists like Miarka and Georg Dasbach, his counterpart in the Eifel and Saar who also associated the social and the religious cause with resistance to "Jewish" oppressors, although clearly identified with a party, could become regional powers in their own right. (*Katolik*'s shift from Centrum to Koło Polskie at the end of the century was a major event in capturing the region for Polish nationalism.)[109] Giants locally, such men were not restrained by national

[107] Mazura, *Entwicklung*, 81. L. Müller, *Kampf*, 174–75n. 4; Trzeciakowski, *Kulturkampf*, 147f.

[108] Miarka's columns were given national attention when Bis., assuming (wrongly) that M. was a priest, used them to indict the clergy for stirring up social, religious, and ethnic violence, notably in the Königshütte strike of June 1871. Bis. SBHA, 9 Feb. 1872: 700. Rioters had looted stores (largely Jewish-owned), set fire to buildings, and forced Beuthen's mayor to flee for his life. Even after order was restored, the town remained under occupation for two months. See nrs. 149–52, 154, 159, 162f, 168, 171–73, 189 in GA from 29 June through 15 Aug. 1871.

[109] Accounts differ on where *Katolik* was published: Mazura, *Entwicklung*, 80–81n. 6 (quote), 82; Trzeciakowski, *Kulturkampf*, 27, 30; Franzke, *Industriearbeiter*, 109; Müller, *Kampf*, 175, 191. Czapliński, "Die polnische Presse," 23, 24, 28, 31f, says that it was first published biweekly, later thrice weekly. Rust, *Reichskanzler*, 621; Leugers-Scherzberg, *Porsch*, 78, 103. *Katolik* was probably behind E. Müller's victories in 1871 and 1872 in Pleß-Rybnik.

and parliamentary standards of respectable discourse, and were embarrassments to the national delegations. Yet they lay beyond the leadership's effective control.[110]

In places where editors were less resourceful, intermediating institutions were necessary before the press could become the crucial link between the ephemera of local campaigns and the long-term process of political socialization. Here as in so many aspects of party development, Left Liberals were pioneers. In 1877 Eugen Richter and Ludolf Parisius established a monthly *Parliamentary Correspondence* to make the Progressives' doings in Berlin available to friendly editors in the provinces. By 1881 the *Parliamentary Correspondence* had a circulation of almost 20,000.[111] The *Correspondence* was a tremendous force for nationalizing campaigns (it would change its name to *Election Correspondence* the fortnight before an election, at which point it appeared several times a day), not least by forcing imitation. "Parliamentary bureaus," with the task of feeding reports of Reichstag debates to sympathetic press organs throughout the country, soon became universal among the parties. Even the government had its press bureau, the *Reichskorrespondenz*, run out of the Ministry of Interior, using the Wolff wire services, paid for by the confiscated funds of the Guelf royal house, and supplying 400-odd county gazettes (*Kreiseblätter*)—gratis.[112]

Never have so many been asked to read so much by so few. The assumption that the German voter craved instruction, that the franchise was a call to seriousness, was shared by all participants. A perusal of election propaganda leaves the inescapable impression of a widespread yearning for a mastery of the science of politics that was as much a part of the nineteenth-century rise of respectability as hygiene and chastity. Social Democrats rejoiced in the knowledge that "as long as the earth has existed, there has never been such an educated *lowest class* in any nation as there is in our day in Germany . . . a thinking, reading, reflecting, criticizing people."[113] The "Party of the Book,"

---

[110] On Windthorst's difficulties with Dasbach: W. to Alexander Reuß, 28 Apr. 1833, 16 May 1883, BAT 105/1512: II, Bl. 296f, 307f; Hermann Mosler to Reuss, 4 Feb. 1884; Reuß to Mosler, 7 Feb. 1884, BAT 105/1522, Bl. 14a, 80; W. to Reuß, 18 Nov. 1884, BAT 105/1523, Bl. 269.

[111] L. Parisius and E. Richter, *Aus der deutschen Fortschrittspartei. Parlamentarische Korrespondenz.(Organ der Partei für Mitteilungen des Central-Wahlkomité's und des geschäfts-führenden Ausschusses)* (Berlin, 1877–83); Bergsträsser, "Geschichte," 247; Nipperdey, *Organisation,* 322. The Z followed Richter's lead and established an information bureau and reporting service for member papers in May 1878, but it was never successful in controlling local press satrapies.

[112] Richter, *Reichstag* 2: 69f, 72, 172; Richter on the *Reichskorrespondenz:* SBDR 10 Dec. 1885: 256; Ullstein, *Richter,* 62–64, 103f, 185f; Pflanze, *Bismarck* 3: 52; Steinbach, *Zähmung* 1: 59, 97. The government also published the *Provinzial Korrespondenz,* which was distributed by Landräte, given gratis to private persons, and used as a source for county gazettes. Schorlemer: SBHA 6 Dec. 1878: 212f; Robert Nöll v. der Nahmer, *Bismarcks Reptilienfonds. Aus Geheimakten Preußens und des Deutschen Reiches* (Mainz, 1968), 98, 107. *The Norddeutsche Allgemeine* received in later years 30,000 M a year from the government, but subscriptions hardly extended beyond official circles.

[113] C. v. Massow, *Reform oder Revolution!* (Berlin, 1895), 20f. See also v. Saldern, *Wege,* 56f; critically evaluated: 235f. Criticism of Richter for being "schoolmasterly": Ullstein, *Richter,* 227.

Thomas Nipperdey dubbed Imperial Germany's Socialists, but the term applies with scarcely diminished accuracy to their contemporary rivals—and to the Socialists' own offspring today. During the October 1994 national elections, the SPD was still issuing thick campaign "bibles," now with each entry printed separately on a flash card rather than between the covers of a book, while the atmosphere of embarrassed levity that accompanied the efforts of the rock stars at its rallies testified to the persistence of a political culture more at home with print than with pageantry. "Modern demagoguery . . . makes use of oratory," Weber conceded in 1918, "but the printed word is more enduring."[114]

How did the voter respond to all of these closely printed pages with which he was inundated? All we have to go on is the evidence of the market: the stuff sold. Like the rallies, the print campaign was self-supporting. Hellmut von Gerlach admonished his agents not to make presents of any of his campaign literature, but to put a price on each item, however cheap. "The countryman is frugal, gives nothing away, and therefore respects nothing that is for free, but rather considers it worthless and tosses it out. What he has paid for, on the other hand, he holds in honor."[115] The political press, far from draining the parties' resources, ultimately provided them with an ongoing source of income, as candidates moved from printing leaflets to founding newspapers to establishing their own publishing houses. Richter, who began by distributing his speeches and ended with far-flung publishing ventures that magnified enormously his power within the party, was only the most famous of a long line.[116]

The close connection between publishing and parliament helps explain Germany's high levels of campaign spending—but also how the parties were able to afford it. Social Democrats were sustaining forty-seven editors as early as 1878. By 1913 the number had grown to 367. Publishing formed the backbone of the central headquarters' finances. The contribution to Social Democratic funding from *Vorwärts*, its daily paper, was higher, on average, than all local contributions to the party put together, excepting those from Berlin and Hamburg.[117] By the mid-seventies Wilhelm Liebknecht, between his numerous jail terms, was earning between 250 and 400 marks a month for editing *Vorwärts* and the weekly *Die Neue Welt*: about six times the income of the average worker. By the mid-eighties, his publishing and agitational enterprises were bringing him 7,000 marks a year, making him, in the words of his biographer, "among the highest-paid people in the nation." Of course, not every newspaperman did so well. Karl Fentz, printer, editor, and distributor of Mannheim's *Volksstimme*, circulation 6,000, earned a scant twenty-four marks for a seven-day week in 1890—and nothing at all when sales were down. Liebknecht's

[114] "Politik," 513. Weber also referred to "the work of education, which it carries out among the masses." "Bemerkungen," 550–53. Nipperdey, *Geschichte* 2: 558.

[115] Gerlach, "Wahlgeplauder," 148–51; Hesselbarth, *Sozialdemokraten*, 42.

[116] Nipperdey, *Organisation*, 198, 204. Not all of Richter's ventures were profitable or even self-supporting. Ullstein, *Richter*, 116–19.

[117] Ritter, *Arbeiterbewegung*, 60; Molt, *Reichstag*, 229.

income, however, had risen to 10,000 marks by 1890, enabling him to afford an apartment in fashionable Charlottenburg. Although such riches could hardly compare to those of, say, Baron Wilhelm von Hammerstein, who was taking in 40,000 marks annually as editor-in-chief of the Conservative *Kreuz-Zeitung*, the sums provoked consternation among the comrades and glee among SPD's opponents. Not surprisingly, lampoons satirizing the Social Democrat who feasted at chic restaurants on oysters and *Veuve Cliquot*, ordering *"just* one more course" before heading off to a rally to collect the "worker's mite," became a staple in the campaign arsenals of rival parties.[118] The lesson we should draw, however, was not that Social Democracy was corrupt but that in a culture as political *and* as bookish as Germany's, a really successful politician-journalist could scarcely avoid getting rich.[119]

POWERS OF THE PURSE: BIG MONEY, PARTY, AND NEO-CORPORATIVISM

A German national election "does not cost much less than a million marks a side," estimated Britain's representative in Berlin in 1881. That figure was a vast exaggeration—and it was also dramatically below the going rate in Britain, where in 1880, among a voting population only a fraction the size of Germany's, well over two million *pounds* changed hands.[120] But the trajectory of British campaign spending was about to fall, while Germany's was rising rapidly. By 1910 the total costs of a British general election had declined to just under £1,300,000—largely thanks to the disappearance of bribery; while expenditure in the empire's last election was said to have reached nearly ten million marks.[121]

Campaign spending can be taken as a "marker gene"—not a cause, but a sign—of political organization. By the eighties all parties had begun to connect their regional strongholds and to move out into new territory. Bipolar contests ceased to be the norm by 1881; by 1893, four competitors per district had become more frequent than three: a sign that campaigns were now genuinely national. The progress of Social Democracy, although hobbled by repressive legislation, was spectacular. In 1871 Socialists had sometimes held rallies at

[118] Fentz: Keil, *Erlebnisse* 1: 92–94. "Der Sozialdemokrat" (election poem), *Hettinger Ztg* 15 Feb. 1887, in Nettmann, "Witten," 123. Hammerstein: Hall, *Scandal*, 153.

[119] Dominick, *Liebknecht*, 263, 331, 384f, 407f. Bebel's income included an annual 3,600 mark retainer from *Die Neue Zeit*, for which he wrote little. Glee at Liebknecht's salary, quoted at 7,200 M: *DA* 12/44 (4 Nov. 1894): 839–41; "Nagelneues vom Zukunftstaat," *Wittener Ztg* (NL), 5 June 1898, reprinted in Nettmann, "Witten," 133. *"Our* Wilhelm" as opposed to Berlin's *other* Wilhelm, continued to be venerated by the rank and file: Lefèvre-Pontalis, *Élections*, 124. V. Saldern, *Wege*, 171.

[120] Sir John Walsham, 21 May 1881, Granville Survey Nr. 1, reporting on the 1878 election. The F had spent a mere 16,000 marks; even in 1881 they spent only ca. 206,000 marks. Nipperdey, *Organisation*, 201.

[121] Gwyn, *Democracy*, 37, 51; Searle, *Corruption*, 85; Bertram, *Wahlen*, 190–93; "Konservative Industriejunker," *Die Hilfe* 15/48 (28 Nov. 1909): 6f. German spending was considerably ahead of Austria's. Boyer, *Culture*, 92.

which only the speaker himself showed up—a proceeding described (with obvious *Schadenfreude*) by Progressive rivals as "characteristic for all of Thuringia."[122] By 1887 they were able to field candidates in 69 percent of all districts. Three years later, the number had risen to 89 percent. The multiplication of candidacies allowed previously invisible supporters to be counted. Socialists were rewarded for this organizational feat with nearly 20 percent of the vote in 1890, increasing their share by a whopping 95 percent, a jump unequaled by themselves or any other party at any other election in the empire.[123]

The techniques of getting and spending had been demonstrated to all with eyes to see and energy to follow. By the 1912 election, total costs for all parties had increased tenfold since 1882, although the electorate (now over fourteen million voters) had grown not much more than a third. In part these expenses reflected the larger number of candidates competing for a single seat. But the average cost per candidate in 1912 was also punishing: an estimated 25,000 marks. Although in hopeless districts challengers would spend less, in symbolically important ones, they might spend very much more. National Liberals put well over 100,000 marks into capturing rural Ragnit-Pillkallen from the Conservatives in a 1913 by-election, as part of their "Charge into East Elbia": a level of spending, some contemporaries believed, that signaled the Americanization of the German campaign.[124] Others, however, such as the young political scientist Ludwig Bergsträsser, tied spending to very German themes. Deeply moved by the enormous sacrifices in time and money that his fellow citizens, small as well as great, proved willing to make to realize their views, he concluded that although every campaign doubtless had its unedifying sides, its indoctrinations and exaggerations, still "we see here also something good and beautiful: the spirit of sacrifice, the dedication to an ideal, the work for the whole."[125]

The spirit of sacrifice was indeed in evidence. Yet clearly not all of this smoney was coming from the grass roots. Reports of big contributors abounded, and fueled unease about what such largesse meant for popular representation. From the first, the social geography of left liberalism, concentrated as it was in towns, with wealthy supporters in a few metropolitan constituencies, made it partic-

---

[122] "Politische Übersicht," *GA* Nr. 128, 4 June 1871: 1135; Lidtke, *Party*, 17; Fenske, *Wahlrecht*, 108ff. Molt, *Reichstag*, 185, dates the decisive monitarization of election campaigns from 1882 to 1895.

[123] Sperber, *Voters*, 39f. Percentages calculated from the data in Ritter/Niehuss, *Arbeitsbuch*, 40. Steinbach, "Entwicklung," 5; Ritter, "Sozialdemokratie" (1995), 120–46; here, 122.

[124] Kühne, *Dreiklassenwahlrecht* 566n. 35 and 36. Other statistics on candidates: Fenske, *Wahlrecht*, 108ff; Bertram, *Wahlen*, 190–93, 256, gives 10,000–15,000, discounting the 20,000–30,000 mark figures given in Nipperdey, *Organisation*, 91; Molt, *Reichstag*, 261n. 9. But since Nipperdey in 1992 again asserted the 25,000 figure, and only such an average approaches the 10 million mark, I take it as authoritative. *Geschichte* (1992) 2: 518, 579. Spending in general: Nipperdey, *Organisation*, 220n. 4, 226f, 227n. 7. Changes in electorate extrapolated from Ritter/Niehuss, *Arbeitsbuch*, 39, 42.

[125] Bergsträsser, "Geschichte," 252f.

ularly vulnerable to ugly rumors. The evidence of Left Liberals' superior organization—the shifting of resources from big city to small town—emboldened
the conservative press to mutter darkly about corruption, and particularly about
"Jewish" corruption. The Jews of Berlin were indeed generous contributors to
the Left Liberal cause, especially in the early eighties, when they recognized in
Richter's party their only committed champions against Stoecker's "Berlin
movement," then making efforts to expand beyond the capital.[126] Similar
charges of corruption, also associated with Jewish campaign contributors, plagued British Liberals, although not until after the turn of the century. Significantly, they were able to deflect these much more colorable allegations by simply tarring their accusers with the sin of antisemitism. Richter's defense against
all insinuations, on the other hand, was to make a point of regularly publishing
an accounting of his party's campaign finances; indeed for a while his was the
only party to do so.[127] Even so, the support of Berlin's Jews, along with the
stories, perhaps apocryphal, of mysterious financiers bringing in their favorites
in out-of-the-way districts, combined with Richter's organizational and publicistic feats to give the Progressives a reputation for nearly unlimited ways and
means. When Progressives were joined in 1884 by the free trade Secession
from the National Liberals (to form the new *Freisinnige* Party), the popular
association between left liberalism and wealth was given added fuel. Prominent
among the Secessionists were Ludwig Bamberger, Karl Schrader, and Georg
Siemens, all former or sitting members of the board of the Deutsche Bank, the
"red" bank of Berlin.[128] Stories of a banker who had dropped 50–100,000 marks
in East Prussia's Sensburg-Oertelsburg in 1881 in order to bring in a Left Liberal were dug up once again. The rumors were supported by no evidence, but
whatever their truth, the *Freisinnigen* became known as the "Money-bags Delegation" (*Fraktion Goldsack*), a label that stuck long after the resources of the
eighties had become only a memory.[129]

Every party had its Mycenases, even the Social Democrats. Within the delegations themselves, some deputies were in a position to fund not only their own

[126] "Die reichlich jüdischen Korruptionsmittel," in *DA* 11/41 (8 Oct. 1893): 770; E. Hamburger,
"Wähler" (1978), 351, 357; Nipperdey, *Organisation*, 201, 234.

[127] Britain: Searle, *Corruption*, 3, 206f; Ullstein, *Richter*, 66. The SPD was similarly accused by
the *KrZ*, which cited an alleged contribution of 300,000 marks by Leo Arons. *Vorwärts* responded
that the party's audit books were open to inspection. Hall, *Scandal*, 145. Bis.'s Jewish banker, G.
Bleichröder, was said to have contributed 10,000 marks to the Ks' campaign in return for their
forcing the antisemites to stop running in Berlin. The antisemitic journalist Jos. Cremer was accused of pocketing the money. Frank, *Stoecker*, 207.

[128] L. Gall, "Bank" (1995), 83–93, 108f.

[129] Apostata [Maximilian Harden], "Fraktion Goldsack," *Die Zukunft*, Bd. 3 (1893): 333–36. Not
that the term was used exclusively for LLs. Cronenberg's Christian Socials announced themselves
opponents of the "Geldsacks," meaning fellow Catholics in the Constantia. Lepper, ed., *Katholizismus*, 105, 126. The SPD referred to *all* of their opponents as "money bags parties."
Thätigkeit, 113. Drop in funding: Nipperdey, *Organisation*, 201. 7 Gumb. in 1881: J. v. Mirbach
(K), P.A.W. Meyer (F), W. Hegel (K) SBDR 6 Mar. 1888: 1307, 1309. The banker was not identified except that he was *not* Bleichröder; in 1887 the same man bestowed his favors on a Kartell
candidate *against* the LL. Traeger SBDR 13 Feb. 1886: 1050.

campaigns, but to help out their colleagues—a process that reinforced their own power within the party. In the Centrum, the Fulda manufacturer Richard Müller and Count Franz von Ballestrem, the latter with a vast fortune based on Silesian coal, iron, and zinc, were important deputies as well as major contributors.[130] Among the National Liberals, regular infusions to the party's war chest became a kind of self-imposed tax on the leadership. Eduard Bartling, the mining, steel, and paper industrialist, and Robert Friedberg, a professor whose wife belonged to a Breslau Jewish banking family of great wealth, bankrolled much of the Prussian Landtag delegation's activities. In the Reichstag, Count Waldemar Oriola, a Hessen landowner, Cornelius von Heyl, the Worms leather manufacturer, and Ernst Bassermann, whose own family millions in Baden were enhanced by his wife's banking connections, performed a similar role.[131] Occasionally misgivings were heard that the party was growing dependent on "a few dozen potent men." In this Germany's Liberals were no different from Britain's, who financed their efforts in the 1900 and 1906 general elections largely from the contributions of twenty-seven benefactors, eighteen of them businessmen from northern England and Scotland.[132]

Money alone, however, never guaranteed anyone's election to the Reichstag. Georg Siemens's three failures to take Schweinitz-Wittenberg from the Conservatives in the 1870s demonstrated that there were powers greater than money in the Saxon flatland. Ernst Bassermann's difficulties in finding a district that would elect him were proverbial.[133] And if money was sometimes of no avail even with the backing of a political party, it was useless without one—as Baron Carl Friedrich von Fechenbach found to his disgust. Deep pockets had enabled Fechenbach to make a political splash in many ways. He could dash off memoranda to the chancellor and the Kaiser and presume on receiving a reply. He could publish pamphlets retailing his thoughts on every issue, and ensure (through well-placed subsidies) a wide echo for his views in the antisemitic and pro-guild press—even, by suborning their journalists, in papers officially committed to the Conservatives. He could pay an agent to concoct petitions with thousands of signatures thanking him for his work on behalf of the artisan movement, in order to represent himself to public opinion as its leader—a ruse sufficient to establish his reputation as a social reformer, at least among some historians. But the well-heeled baron, who at various times announced himself as a National Liberal, a Conservative, and a Centrum man, found his ambition of sitting in the Reichstag frustrated at every turn—because none of the parties would have him. Offered the financial support of this busy megalomaniac, the leadership of all three of the parties in question kept their distance. Even in his

---

[130] For these and other big Z donors: Jaeger, *Unternehmer*, 111; Stegmann, *Erben*, 30, 241, 451, 472–73, 492.

[131] Martin, *Machthaber*, 448, 452, 454f; White, *Party*, 42f, 129.

[132] Kulemann, *Erinnerungen*, 152; Nipperdey, *Organisation*, 152, 220; Searle, *Corruption*, 112.

[133] Siemens: Phillips, *Reichstags-Wahlen*, 64; Gall, "Bank," 84. Bassermann: Martin, *Machthaber*, 448; 5 Trier AnlDR (1912/14, 13/I, Bd. 23) DS 1639: 3602.

home district of Miltenberg in Lower Franconia, the answer to the baron's hopeful queries about a possible nomination was a polite no.[134]

More plausible than the fears of this or that big spender were anxieties about "organized interests." The growth of large industrial organizations, which at the turn of the century were increasing at twice the rate of the population as a whole, paralleled the curve of campaign spending—raising suspicions about a possible connection.[135] In this the Germans were scarcely alone. In every franchise regime, voices were expressing alarm at the threat that "organized money," as the Americans called it, posed to democratic processes. In France, the Panama Scandal of 1892–93, in which 150 deputies and senators were accused of taking bribes, so discredited parliament that some predicted the collapse of the Third Republic.[136] In the United States, perceptions of political corruption were powerful enough to get the Federal Corrupt Practices Acts passed in 1910–11—although never powerful enough to get them enforced. In Edwardian and Georgian Britain, tangible exchanges were part of political life: MPs held dummy company directorships, honors-trafficking was the coin of every election campaign, and in an endless search for leverage with the "media," parties in power hastened to bestow peerages on the owners of newspaper chains lest their rivals do so first.[137] Scandal was the inevitable result of an explosion of wealth that was outrunning any consensus on what constituted conflict of interest. But with equal inevitability, the suspicion that public men and public decisions were for sale called the parties, and ultimately parliamentary institutions themselves, into question.

Imperial Germany was spared the scandals that plagued the powers to its west. Members of parliament did not sell their votes for cash or campaign contributions. The absence even of *talk* about a need for a Corrupt Practices Act is telling. The colloquial term for corruption remained "Panama" right to the end; homegrown varieties of corruption were too insignificant to replace it with a term domestically coined.[138] Just as the strength of local pressures, from his peers as well as his betters, made the bribery of voters either superfluous or

---

[134] H. Lange to Fechenbach 1 Jul. 1881; *Ostsee-Ztg und Börsen-Nachrichten der Ostsee* (Stettin), 11 Jan. 1884; Fechenbach to Jörg, 19 Apr. 1885; v. Schauensee to F., Würzburg, 18 Oct. 1884; v. Regner to F., Würzburg, 22 Dec. 1884; Pastor Potthoff to F., Dresden, 5 Jun. 1885; Ernst Jaeger to F., Speyer, 2 Oct. 1886, and 4 Jul. 1887. By 1890 Fechenbach was drawing up prospectuses for a "Deutsche Arbeiterpartei"; on 21 Dec. 1891 he sent a memorandum to Caprivi for a prospective "Neue Partei (National-Partei)." BAK, Nachlaß Fechenbach.

[135] Molt, *Reichstag*, 185. Large firms ("*Grossbetriebe*") were defined as employing 50 or more. Fears: Stegmann, *Erben*, 256.

[136] Most famously, Fr. Engels, but he was not alone. Searle, *Corruption*, 423.

[137] John T. Noonan, Jr., *Bribes* (New York, 1984), 626–28. Searle, *Corruption*, 40–45, 80–102, 350–432.

[138] E.g., police bribes in Cologne were referred to as "a real *Polizeipanama*." Hall, *Scandal*, 102—a book that, tellingly, never even mentions bribes of deputies. Though the SPD press claimed that a military procurements scandal was the equal of Panama, it involved ministerial favoritism (toward Krupp), not votes in parliament. Ibid., 183–86; see also 172f.

ineffective, analogous cultural attitudes seem to have inhibited attempts on the individual deputy's virtue. The importunities of "organized money" appeared in Germany not as backstairs bribes in return for secret quid pro quos, but took the form of more or less open campaign contributions—and threats to cut them off.

To many Germans, this was bad enough. The sheer number of organizations clamoring to get into the political act, some offering money, others promising the votes of their huge memberships, aroused alarm. The case of *Justizrat* Kehren, National Liberal candidate for Düsseldorf, although probably not typical, became a byword for the problem. Kehren was pressured for commitments by his provincial consumer's union, by the Düsseldorf's Foremen's Association, by the Leipzig-based *Mittelstand* Association, by the candy industry, the antivaccinationists, and the Scientific-Humanitarian Committee of Berlin. Kehren rejected these demands as "outrageous," citing as his model Count Arthur Posadowsky, who had refused even to discuss their programs, because "a deputy who bound himself in such a manner was no longer the representative of the people, but rather only the agent of individual groups."[139] Posadowsky won, but Kehren lost his election.

The financial resources of organized interests were bound to become part of the calculus of campaigning, increasingly important as economic issues loomed larger on the Reichstag's agenda. The Farmers' League, which had been a major force in bringing down Caprivi in 1894 and contributed to the fall of Bülow in 1909, demonstrated for everyone the vulnerability of the election process to the interventions of a powerful lobby.[140] Between 1898 to 1914, the League succeeded in securing commitments to their program from never fewer than seventy-eight deputies. Taken together, the League's protégés, although dispersed among several parties, made up the largest delegation in the Reichstag during two of the last four legislature periods. In 1907, with 138 deputies, their numbers surpassed those of any previous delegation in the history of Imperial Germany, with the single exception of the National Liberals after their landslide in 1874. The message to other interests who wanted to exert similar influence was clear: Go thou and do likewise.[141]

Germany's industries set out to duplicate the Farmers' League's success. By 1908 the various lobbies could count 12,000 branch associations capable of offering campaign help to friendly candidates via paid apparatchiks. Lobbyists themselves entered parliament. Gustav Stresemann, director of the Association of Saxon Manufacturers, chairman of the League of German Industrialists (BdI), and connected to a variety of other organizations representing light industry, signaled this new type. After acquiring a considerable reputation in Saxon state politics through his skillful use of business interests to help capture Conservative Landtag seats for his fellow National Liberals, in 1907 Stresemann entered the Reichstag. There he continued his intermediary role, keeping

[139] "Abgelehnte Wunschzettel," *BT* 14, 2 Beiblatt (7 Jan. 1912).

[140] Nipperdey, *Geschichte* 2: 586–88.

[141] This conclusion was Max Maurenbrecher's in "Die Ethik der Reichstagswahl," *Die Zeit* 2/31 (30 Apr. 1903): 136–39.

his colleagues informed of the interests of manufacturing, and his manufacturing sponsors informed of the *interna* of commission meetings and his party's caucuses.[142]

The importunities of the lobbies were resented by everyone. Cornelius von Heyl zu Herrnsheim, the leader of the National Liberals' right wing, himself employer of thousands, a man whose power in Worms, where he was "the notable of notables," equaled that of Krupp in Essen and King Stumm in the Saar, fumed at the "insolence" of the exigent Henry Axel Bueck, chairman of the Central Association of German Industrialists (*Centralverband deutscher Industrieller*, hereafter: CV), who set conditions for heavy industry's support. Calling him "one of those hirelings of the trade associations," von Heyl compared Bueck's profession unfavorably to that of a trade-union secretary.[143] But for all their mutual indignation, Bueck's lobbying was a natural response to the logic of competitive elections. We need only remember the prescient Free Conservative, who had pointed out in 1871: "The very signature of this franchise is exert yourself, exercise your influence as much as you can."[144]

The visible signs of corporate power raised three troubling issues. On the most general level, was not the ultimate effect of the lobbies to drain significance from the electoral process? A cursory glance at the campaign proclamations proved to one disgusted observer that elections were not between the parties but between the great economic organizations: "Party membership actually makes up only a threadbare little cloak out of which peeks the jacket of the Farmer's' League 'or the belt of the Hansa [*Bund*] or some other economic interest."[145] Where was the business of representation actually done—in the public deliberations of the duly constituted forum of the nation, or in private negotiations between interests, candidates, and parties, which the Reichstag merely ratified after the fact? Yet representation of the public legitimately takes place through a range of institutions: the courts and the executive, churches and voluntary societies, economic associations and elected deputies. The frontier delimiting the political from the social is a complex one, in which memberships and competencies inevitably overlap. The untidy ambiguities of such "pluralism" is deemed, at least by some political scientists, to contribute to the stability of modern democratic systems.[146] For citizens of the Kaiserreich, however, only just emerging from a corporatist society, these multiple claims to represen-

---

[142] Molt, *Reichstag*, 197, 294; Warren, *Kingdom*, 83f. Stresemann was preceded as deputy-cum-lobbyist by Diederich Hahn, regional and then national director of the BdL, who entered the RT in 1893. Vascik, "Conservatism," 229–61.

[143] Quotes: Warren, *Kingdom*, 10, 29. White, *Party*, 42f, 129.

[144] Behr SBDR 17 Apr. 1871: 240. Kulemann (*Erinnerungen*, 165–67), whose 1898 candidacy in Saarbrücken was scotched by Stumm and whose 1903 candidacy in Göttingen by the agrarian wing of the NLs, expressed an understandably jaundiced view of the role of economic interests in the election process. But Stumm's power was based on far more than his ability to bankroll elections, and the agrarians' weight within any given party was based on their votes, not their money.

[145] Quoted in Stegmann, *Erben*, 256, without source or attribution.

[146] Pitkin, *Concept* (1967), 221f.

tation were much more likely to be perceived as threats to parliament's own authority to speak for the people.[147]

Yet fears about parliament's loss of significance were surely exaggerated. Tariffs and guild regulation, mass transit and public utilities, social insurance and factory inspection, tax distribution and redistribution: all of these objects of lobbying interest required legislation, and therefore, enhanced the role of the deputies. As Thomas Nipperdey has argued, "To govern against or even without the Reichstag became increasingly impossible."[148] It was inevitable that once political parties acquired, however indirectly, powers over the economy, the forces of the economy would demand representation within the councils of the parties. And then the question is not whether, but how; and by and for whom? The devil lurked in the details.

Underlying the uneasiness caused by the organized interests was a second anxiety, the fear that powerful lobbies could override the electorate and neutralize its egalitarian constitution. The unmediated relationship between voter and representative that had been the democratic promise of the Reichstag franchise, its chief advance over the state election laws and its guarantee of equality, seemed to fade as bodies not accountable to the public inserted themselves into the processes of nominating and electing candidates. Did not a deputy who accepted such help obligate himself to those who gave it—to the material disadvantage of others whom he was also legally bound to "represent?" The disquiet had been prefigured in the seventies, when Centrum deputies seemed to many Germans mere lobbyists for the Catholic Church, abusing the very process designed to represent all the people. Similar misgivings arose in the eighties that the Left Liberals were becoming an arm of the Central Association of German Citizens of Jewish Faith. Such problems—insoluble from the standpoint of democratic theory—are inherent in the whole notion of "representation," in which part must stand for whole.[149]

In modern democracies, it is the party that makes good the weaknesses of the individual by gathering together the like-minded and giving them weight. By

---

[147] *FrankZ* (18 Oct. 1909) BAB-L R1501/14645, Bl. 78; E. Lederer, "Parteien" (1912): cols. 329–38; idem, *Die wirtschaftlichen Organisationen* (Leipzig/Berlin, 1913). Dissenting: Kaelble, *Interessenpolitik*, 123. Wehler seems to agree with Lederer: "Unmistakably, power migrated from parliament to those informal decision-making collectives hovering outside, so that often nothing more was left for the elected representatives of the voting public than the ratification of their resolutions." *Gesellschaftgeschichte* 3: 674. Nipperdey (*Geschichte* 2: 576, 593–95) acknowledges the "normality" of interest-group activity, its "democratizing effect," and its difference from "corporatism," but emphasizes its retarding influence during the Empire. Pluralism: S. M. Lipset, "Introduction: Ostrogorski" (1964), lvii–lix, lxiii; Philippe Schmitter, "Still the Century of Corporatism?" *Review of Politics* 36/1 (1974), 85–131.

[148] Nipperdey, *Geschichte* 2: 471–75; analysis and quote on 474. Wehler sees the growing need for economic intervention "irresistably raising the value" both of the RT (*Gesellschaftsgeschichte* 3: 669, subsection 2) *and* of the *"authoritarian* state." (673). H.-P. Ullmann, *Interessenverbände*, 84f.

[149] Pitkin, *Concept*, 8f. Resentment at the relationship between the *Centralverein deutscher Bürger jüdischen Glaubens* and the LLs: *Zukunft* (1893), 145–51, quoted, along with figures, in Hamburger, "Wähler," 356f. The *Centralverein*'s complaints when the LLs ran *baptised* Jews: Nipperdey, *Organisation*, 234.

the same token the party it is that provides a buffer protecting candidate and deputy against the overweening lobby. And the party makes possible the packaging of policies that bring organized interests into at least rough-and-ready accommodation with each other, something that the lobbies, designed to advocate *one* interest, could never do for themselves. As John Vincent has reminded us, "Party is a civilizing thing: it has to unite many people, and overcome many conflicts, before it can even begin to be divisive in turn itself."[150] Political scientists call this civilizing process "interest aggregation."

The aggregation of diverse agendas into legislative positions that are both responsible and not too incoherent is never a simple task. Ninety years of hindsight and continued practice—on both sides of the Atlantic—have not made it any easier today. The necessity of mediating between exigent claimants and reconciling their demands with each other and with the party's *un*organized constituencies put Wilhelmine parties under constant strain. Conservatives and Social Democrats, whose corporate sponsors, the organizations of agriculture and labor, respectively, were fairly homogeneous, felt these strains the least. The Centrum, which presumed to speak across the whole economic spectrum, felt them much more.[151] And the liberal parties, lacking the cement of religion or a target economic constituency, felt them to the point of pain. What made the integrative tasks of imperial Germany's parties especially difficult, however, was less the might of the lobbies than the empire's constitutional dualism, which denied party leaders their greatest incentive for enforcing discipline and compromise: the prospect of executive power. In Germany, the will to integration had to be supplied by ethos alone—a complex mix of ideology, ethics, personal and communal loyalties, and pure partisanship.

But the frustration of voters whose economic and other interests lacked extramural organization gave birth to a persistent malaise, a sense that the parties were obscuring rather than reflecting the full variety of legitimate interests.[152] It was in the context of this malaise that the idea of a parliament elected by occupations exerted a continuing attraction. Already in the eighties some voters were urging it on the government as an alternative to the Reichstag. The idea was picked up by a number of businessmen, annoyed that the existing system did not give them the weight they felt was their due.[153] By 1906 the occupational parliament, the most fundamental challenge to the liberal faith in a common representation, had found advocates not only within the boardrooms of the smokestack industries but was being proposed, with some reservations, by a

[150] Vincent, *Pollbooks*, 30.

[151] Sheehan, "Leadership," 523; Loth, *Katholiken*.

[152] Cf. the call for the commercial classes (*Handelsstand*) to elect one of their own in every district and their disgust with "party discipline," in the "Kaufmännischer Lesezirkel," *Deutsche Buchhändler Ztg*, Nrs. 35 and 36 (2 Sept. 1884): 122.

[153] E.g., "German Men!" Printed announcement against the "one-class voting system," signed by Fr. Krupp, Jr., Privatier, Bonn, 22 Nov. 1884, and sent also to Bis. BAB-L R43/685, Bl. 231f; Aug. Roese, printer, to Wm. II, Swinemünde, 6 Mar. 1890, in BAB-L R1501/14693, Bl. 245–56; A. Laewi to Bis., Regensburg, 10 Mar. 1890, BAB-L R1501/14693, Bl. 235–40; Jul. Pfeiffer to Wm. II, 1 Mar. 1903, BAB-L R1501/14695, Bl. 93–105v.

figure such as Georg Jellinek, the leading liberal constitutional theorist of his day. It would continue to haunt German politics as a ghostly alternative even after war and revolution had transformed the conditions that gave it birth.[154]

And what was the practical significance of the great sums of money the "organized interests" were pouring into German campaigns? This brings us to the third concern raised by corporate spending: its effect on the concrete legislative positions of the deputies within their orbit. Donors certainly believed that they would get something for their money or they would hardly have given so much. But the conflicts of interest so blatant in Edwardian politics were less clear in Germany.[155] The terms set by even the most notorious industrial lobby for its financial support took care that at least the decencies were preserved. The CV demanded that the candidate receiving its help promise to treat trade and agriculture equally, that when considering social legislation he not forget Germany's competitive position abroad, and that he relay industry's views to the appropriate Reichstag committees.[156] Conditions as general as these could hardly have strained the conscience of the most scrupulous Social Democrat.

A deputy's obligations to his backers were of course not necessarily exhausted by explicit promises. And even without the spur of money, he would scarcely forget the ties wrought by inclination and association. Georg Siemens, on the board of the Deutsche Bank, assured a colleague who complained that his parliamentary activities took time away from the firm that, on the contrary, precisely in the Reichstag he could "be useful to the bank . . ."; otherwise, he would never have indulged his "private wish" for a seat. Almost the entire parliamentary leadership of the National Liberals, the Free Conservatives, even the *Freisinnige Vereinigung* enjoyed in the final decade of the Reich some con-

---

[154] Jellinek cited in Lederer, "Parteien," col. 336; and in Dr. Weiß, "Besprechungen von Neuigkeiten des Buchhandels. Leo von Savigny, *Das parlamentarische Wahlrecht im Reich und in Preußen und seine Reform* (Berlin, 1907), *PVB*, 28/20 (16 Feb. 1907): 378. Some support in Z: Blackbourn, *Class*, 126f, 131. Even in the Weimar Republic, a parliament based on occupations found broad support. Fenske, *Wahlrecht*, 28. On occupational franchises: Kühne, *Dreiklassenwahlrecht*, 473–75. The industrialists' demand was in glaring contrast to their resistance, citing liberalism's commitment to the whole society, to demands from below for occupational representation in the process of candidate selection. Ibid., 369f. Kaelble, *Interessenpolitik*, 119 argues that the CV did *not* favor an occupational parliament, 123; the opposing position: Stegmann, *Erben*, 113–28 (a history of the discussion of the occupational parliament, which exaggerates the influence of the Z's aristocratic wing), and 283–92. Dirk Stegmann "Between Economic Interests and Radical Nationalism: Attempts to Found a New Right-Wing Party in Imperial Germany, 1887–94," in *Between Reform, Reaction, and Resistance. Studies in the History of German Conservatism from 1789 to 1945*, ed. by L. E. Jones and J. N. Retallack (Providence, Oxford, 1993), 157–85, is an excellent overview.

[155] Many deputies held company directorships, including Bassermann and Stresemann, but no shadow seems to have been cast on their integrity. Epstein, *Erzberger*, 110. No conflict of interest scandals are mentioned in Hall, *Scandal*.

[156] "Bericht der Geschäftsführung der Wahlfondskommission des CVDI über die Reichstagswahlen von 1912," Appendix 5, Kaelble, *Interessenpolitik*, 215–22, esp. 218.

nections to finance or industry.[157] It would be naive to believe that a deputy's behavior was never influenced by the pressures of his financial backers; but it would be difficult if not impossible in most cases to distinguish those influences from those of class, inclination, conviction, and the needs of inner-party harmony.[158]

One indicator of the integrity of the deputies was the mounting dissatisfaction of the lobbies themselves. Certainly when the Reichstag increased grain tariffs by nearly 40 percent in 1902, the efforts of the Farmers' League appeared to have paid off. But even the might of this most successful of pressure groups should not be exaggerated. Itself "riven with cleavages" as well as "bitter personal quarrels and vendettas within the leadership," the extremity of its demands often put it on poor terms with both the government and with the majority of the Reichstag, since those deputies who were not its particular friends were usually its enemies. The limits of the BdL's power were exposed sharply in 1903. Angry at the Conservatives for compromising with Bülow on grain tariffs twenty to thirty-five marks lower than they had demanded, the Farmers tried to circumvent the parties altogether and take agriculture's case directly to the electorate. It put up fifty-five candidates of its own—and saw all but four of them defeated. By 1912, the power of the Farmers' League was in decline, less than a third of its candidates surviving the runoffs.[159]

The perennial question "Who, whom?" was raised most forcefully by corporate Germany's most notorious intervention in an election campaign—during the "Hottentot" elections of 1907. At the initiative of Bülow, a cross-lobby, cross-party "Patria Committee" was established to win the election for the government. Bülow made it a point to secure the support of the giants of commerce, finance, and industry. Richard Vopelius, Bueck's colleague at the CV, took charge of collecting the money. The committee's long list of distinguished supporters included the bankers Robert von Mendelssohn and Paul von Schwabach, each of whom subscribed 30,000 marks. Its heaviest contributors, however, were not individuals at all, but corporations, who were asked to donate one mark for every employee. The Mining Association (*Bergbaulicher Verein*) and the Northwestern Group alone accounted for 230,000 marks.[160] Not all of the committee's monies went to particular candidates. Some, for example, went

[157] Siemans quoted in Gall, "Bank," 85. NLs: Anthony J. O'Donnell, "National Liberalism and the Mass Politics of the German Right, 1890–1907" (Ph.D. diss., Princeton, 1973), 57–62.

[158] An important argument, based on roll-call analysis, that, far from being the plaything of interest groups, party membership was "by far the main influence" RT votes: W. Smith and S. Turner, "Legislative Behavior" (1981), 3–29. Also Kaelble, *Interessenpolitik*, 20. Cf. Stegmann, *Erben*, 128. Nipperdey, *Organisation*, 152, 154f; idem, *Geschichte* 2: 529. Arguing for considerable deputy dependency on contributions: Fricke, "Imperialismus," 538–76; Jaeger, *Unternehmer*, 13; Kulemann, *Erinnerungen*, 152, 155; Eley, *Reshaping*, 27f.

[159] Barkin, *Controversy*, 211–52. Vascik, "Conservatism," 252–56; quote on 230. Slightly different figures: Stegmann, *Erben*, 259. BdL candidacies: Nipperdey, *Geschichte* 2: 339, 587.

[160] Molt, *Reichstag*, 264f.

to the Navy League, whose propaganda was expected to contribute to a general atmosphere favorable to the government's cause.[161]

But if business's massive financial contributions in 1907 is the smoking gun that convicts the political system of subservience to corporate interests, one has to ask: where is the corpse? Bülow was the winner in this election; corporate Germany was not. The chancellor's strategy, after all, was to encourage preelection agreements sharing out seats among all parties running against the Centrum, Social Democracy, and the Poles—parties ranging from the Left Liberals to the antisemites. Competition, the source of any consumer's leverage, was thus replaced by a government-sponsored oligopoly, and industry's purchasing power correspondingly declined. Industry's pleasure at seeing Social Democratic seats nearly halved (dropping from eighty-one to forty-three) was offset when it learned that preelection agreements dividing up the constituencies actually funneled some of the Patria Committee's monies to candidates that corporate contributors actively disliked. Only ten men personally employed in industry were elected, while two CV officers actually lost their seats. Albert Ballin, the shipping magnate, complained that the number of deputies who worked in heavy industry, high finance, and trade "could all be driven home in a single wagon." Another disgusted spokesman described the results of the election as "a complete disfranchisement of business."[162] But the absence of direct representation was only half of the bad news. Having paid the pipers, the lobbies found themselves unable to call their tune. Once the election was over, the National Liberal leader, Ernst Bassermann, rejected the CV's overtures "in the brusquest possible manner," its trade organ noted angrily; and his delegation showed "not the slightest inclination" to come to terms.[163] Apparently one *could* eat someone's bread without singing his song.

Feeling used by the government and the parties, a number of lobbies resolved never to be taken in again: "For National Liberal Reichstag deputies of the ilk of Bassermann, Stresemann *e tutti quanti*—not a penny!" announced the *Deutsche Volkswirtschaftliche Correspondenz* in 1908: a threat that gained notoriety when it was quoted on the Reichstag floor. Alexander Tille, spokesman for the Saar mining industry, set up discussions aimed at founding a separate "Employers' Party."[164] Short of that, the CV established a war chest to support its

---

[161] Interpellation on the matter: SBDR 25 Feb. 1905; AnlDR (1907, 12/I) DS 120, BAB-L R1501/14645, Bl. 8; Bülow SBDR 26 Feb. 1907: 63. Consternation over how to handle interpellation: Posadowsky to Bülow, 1 Mar. 1907, B. to P., 1 Mar. 1907, BAB-L R1501/14458 Bl. 109ff. Jaeger, *Unternehmer*, 185, 185n. 97; Fricke, "Imperialismus," 554–62, 567f; Martin, *Machthaber*, 226; Hall, *Scandal*, 172f.

[162] Quotes in Stegmann, *Erben*, 147, 152.

[163] Between 1907 and 1910 the CV's *Deutsche Industriezeitung* ran a series of articles attacking the NLs. The situation improved only right before the war. Kaelble, *Interessenpolitik*, 198, and 198n. 471.

[164] Fricke, "Imperialismus," 563; Stegmann, *Erben*, 150–59 ("and all the others—not a penny" is from "Der Fall Stresemann," *DVC* 20 [10 Mar. 1908], quoted on 150), 228ff; quoted again in the RT: Jaeger, *Unternehmer*, 119; A. Tille, *Die Arbeitgeberpartei und die politische Vertretung der deutschen Industrie* (Südwestdeutsche Flugschriften in Nr. 5, Saarbrücken, 1908).

own candidates in the future. Every member association was "taxed" .05 percent of its annual wage bill; that is, fifty pfennige for every 1,000 marks it paid in wages.[165] At the same time, it put a temporary halt on any contributions to National Liberals. Instead the CV worked behind the scenes to encourage the Liberals' right wing to detach itself from the party and join the Free Conservatives, perhaps in a new party organization. To stimulate these contacts, the CV appointed Johannes Flathmann, formerly General Secretary of the National Liberal Party in Hanover and a man considerably to the Right of most of his party's Reichstag delegation, to manage its Campaign Fund. Similarly, National Liberal press organs were encouraged to champion the "spirit of Bennigsen," an implicit critique of Bassermann. The CV made no secret that its aim was to combat "democracy," that "illiberal conception of the state under which . . . such a large part of our people today seem to have fallen."[166]

The CV's Campaign Fund immediately attracted unfavorable public comment. Alluding to the certificate of good behavior that Ruhr chimney barons issued to their workers, Friedrich Naumann denounced the fund as simply "the parliamentary form of the *Arbeiternachweis*."[167] Bassermann and Stresemann themselves had no illusions about the danger. "When once we bow down before the financial power of Westfalian industry, we will have lost our moral raison d'être," Bassermann told Eugen Schiffer. A dismayed Stresemann confided that he was "coming more and more to the view that our party is gradually being bought out by the Central Association of German Industrialists. . . ." The CV had

> proceeded quite systematically, distributing the money not only for individual election districts, but also for entire provinces . . . and our party secretaries will gradually accustom themselves to turning to Herr Flathmann with their financial needs. The consequence is that they [the party secretaries] will demand right-wing National Liberal deputies or candidates, the Central Association takes over the financial leadership, and with it buys the soul of the National Liberal Party.[168]

Hellmut von Gerlach—a not disinterested observer—mocked the "National Miserables," waffling, or so he said, at the prospect of the long purses that might or might not be opening for them at the next election. But for all the Liberals' miseries, at the party congress Bassermann's supporters were able to get him reelected leader of the Reichstag delegation by acclamation—a maneuver that perforce left the CV's supporters within the party "speechless from

---

[165] The date the fund was founded varies, sometimes within the same book: Kaelble, *Interessenpolitik*, 19f, 28–30, 120f; Jaeger, *Unternehmer*, 126–28; Stegmann, *Erben*, 159–66, 391; Ullmann, *Interessenverbände*, 85. The CV itself had spent only 96,000 M in 1907, most of industry's money being funneled through member associations, and going to parties rather than individual candidates.

[166] Kaelble, *Interessenpolitik*, 28–30; the Election Fund Commission's "autobiography" is in Appendix 5: 215–22; Stegmann, *Erben*, 222f and 222n. 80. Stegmann notes Paul Reusch's marginal comment: "For the time being, don't pay."

[167] *FrankZ* (18 Oct. 1909), in BAB-L R1501/14645, Bl. 78; Naumann, "Konservative Industriejunker," 6–7.

[168] Quoted in Stegmann, *Erben*, 222, 307f; on Flathmann, ibid., 211.

harmony."[169] Turmoil and intrigue between Left and Right wings continued, but Bassermann kept his party on a course that industry's most outspoken heralds opposed: cooperation with the Left Liberals and the Hansabund (which had now established its own campaign chest), rejection of a *Sammlung* with the Conservatives against the Social Democrats, and support for at least moderate political reforms to strengthen popular representation (such as redistricting Reichstag constituencies and reforming the Prussian franchise) in a more egalitarian direction.[170] Humorists jibed that the National Liberals were afraid of their own courage, and the quivering bourgeois was as much a trope in depictions of their party as the swinish priest was for the Centrum. On pp. 388–89, we see *Simplicissimus* mocking the night terrors suffered by a Liberal deputy after swinging a deal with the SPD to collaborate on a Reichstag vote. But for all its jibes at the party's alleged spinelessness, the strip implicitly acknowledged that the angst that moved the party was internally generated. The message here was that, while it might vote with the Social Democrats, the National Liberal conscience remained monarchist. It is remarkable that none of *Simplicissimus*'s many gibes at the Liberals ever suggested corruption, nor that its night terrors stemmed from the pressures of contributors.

During the 1912 campaign, the CV's fund spent more than a million marks and backed 120 candidates. If these candidates had been successful, the CV would have underwritten more than a third of the Reichstag. Some deputies—Bassermann, for example—long suspected that the ultimate goal of the chimney barons was repeal of the franchise that was proving so frustrating[171]. But the industrialists were in for another disappointment. In spite of the vast infusions of money into their campaigns, only 41 of the 120 CV-backed candidates came through. The numbers of seats personally held by entrepreneurs and lobbyists were halved.[172]

Thus the dream of heavy industry, that it might exert the same election influence on urban districts as the Farmers' League in rural ones, began to fade. Where the Farmers won elections, they did so not just with money, but with organization and the conviction of their supporters. Outside of agricultural districts, the lobbies were no match for the parties in either attribute. By 1914 even the National Liberals, slow though they had been to undertake constituency organization, were able to boast a membership of nearly 300,000—and 50 pro-

[169] Quoted in Stegmann, *Erben*, 224; Gerlach quote on 227.

[170] Stegmann, *Erben*, 222; also 230f, 239. Funds: Nipperdey, *Organisation*, 153.

[171] Yet 74 of these CV-backed candidates were on the "Left"—that is, FVP and Left NLs! Stegmann, *Erben*, 260.

[172] Stresemann too was without a seat. "Aus der Reichstags Wahlbewegung," *BT* 41/11 (7 Jan. 1912). Jaeger, *Unternehmer*, 118 (Bassermann's fears from 1908), 185n. 97; Fricke, "Imperialismus," 565f; Sheehan, "Leadership," 521, 523; Molt, *Reichstag*, 203, 294; Kaelble, *Interessenpolitik*, 121, 123, 225; Nipperdey, *Geschichte* 2: 579. The *Reichsdeutscher Mittelstandsverband* was able to count 203 deputies who had promised to support their program, but the worth of such promises may be measured by the lobby's continued pessimism. Stegmann, *Erben*, 262. Total election costs: Bertram, *Wahlen*, 256.

vincial and central party secretaries to keep track of them.[173] So long as campaign muscle was measured in bodies rather than marks, the true analogs in industrial districts to the Farmers' League in rural ones were not the lobbies of businessmen, but the trade unions of workers. In 1913 the Reichstag took up—and defeated—a measure especially dear to industrialists' hearts, and one that we may take as a barometer of the CV's (lack of) success: a motion to outlaw the picket line. Of the entire National Liberal delegation, only one deputy voted yes.[174]

What explains the failure of the industrialists to achieve their goals? Leverage implies alternatives. But if a deputy or his party ignored the directives of his corporate sponsors, where were the backers to go? In today's America, lobbies can punish a wayward protégé by switching their support the next time around. But in the Kaiserreich, by 1903 at the latest, political choices within any given election district were so polarized that few lobbies had that option, for the protégé's opponent was certain to be someone they liked even less. Forced to find candidates in urban or mixed districts in which either Social Democracy or the Centrum was a strong presence, the industrialists had to cut their coat to fit their cloth. So long as the imperial franchise remained intact, even those corporate interests most dissatisfied with the parties were forced to submit their agendas to an electorate the parties had organized. Chaffing against the chains of the party system, they continued to discuss other options, but in practice they recognized the hopelessness of trying to go outside party-controlled channels. The parties certainly needed money, but money needed the parties even more. This basic fact of political life goes far to explain developments that would have been inconceivable had neo-corporatism really got what it felt it had paid for: for example, the refusal in 1912 by the Duisburg National Liberals, in the very heart of the Ruhr, to run the candidate that the CV's Campaign Fund pressed on them. Or National Liberal willingness, in Bochum that same year, to accede to miners' demands that they nominate a miner as their standard-bearer.[175]

The staunchness of the liberal parties—for those were the CV's main targets—in the face of pressure is worth noting. "Very many more deputies friendly to industry would have been elected," the management of the Campaign Fund reported after the election of 1912, had not "the liberal parties formed a firm, compact fighting group against all elements farther to the Right." The result was that "a series of candidates from the Right, willing and able to represent the interests of industry, and consequently supported by the Campaign Fund, were left at the starting gate." Although nearly sixty of the CV's can-

[173] Nipperdey, *Geschichte* 2: 520f, 528, 555.

[174] And although the Hansabund announced the results of the 1912 election as a big success, the analysis by the management of CV's Campaign Fund shows the HB's success to have been limited to bringing in *Social Democrats*! "Bericht der Geschäftsführung der Wahlfondskommission des CVDI über die Reichstagswahlen von 1912," in Kaelble, *Interessenpolitik*, 215–22, esp. 218f. Stegmann, *Erben*, 271; 259f for 1912 election losses for industry and Junkerdom.

[175] Kühne, *Dreiklassenwahlrecht*, 365. Cf. Stegmann, *Erben*, 227–30.

NATIONAL LIBERAL NIGHTMARES

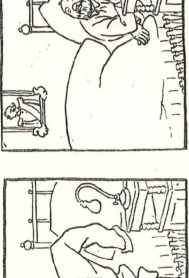

"So, we pulled it off."

"and actually gave Bebel our vote for once—"

"actually, it's ludicrous—"

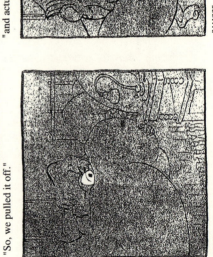

"??!!!???"

"!!!!!??"

"...!!!..."

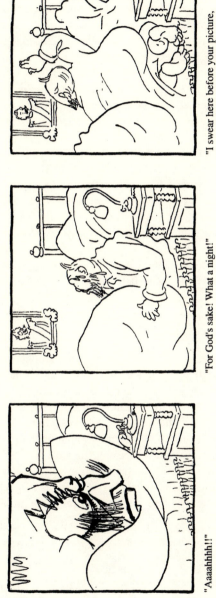

"Aaaahhh!!"

"For God's sake! What a night!"

"I swear here before your picture,
Your Majesty, never to fall away from
the national path!!!"

Fig. 12. T. T. Heine, *Simplicissimus* XVI/2 Nr. 50 866.

didacies were still active at the runoffs, the *Freisinnige Volkspartei*'s preference for Social Democrats over any candidates associated with the Right sealed their fate.[176] The year 1912 marked the unambiguous victory of party over lobby.

As the parties' own organizations continued expanding by leaps and bounds, the ability of any economic interest to influence elections at constituency pressure points diminished accordingly. The existence of 397 geographically bounded, single-member constituencies gave the parties considerable protection, allowing them to fob off impossible demands by citing the necessity of integrating diverse interests. Unfortunately, the parties themselves fatally misperceived this structural source of strength. In the last years of the empire, they began to place themselves in the service of the increasingly vociferous demands for a "fairer" election system: that is, one based on proportional representation. And as Emil Lederer predicted so presciently in 1912, proportional representation would necessarily strengthen the influence of the interest groups over the parties, "indeed would inexorably lead to their complete domination by the interest organizations."[177] The Weimar Republic's system of proportional representation drew Reichstag delegations not from constituencies but, in an order established before the election, from party lists, leaving the parties with no alibis in facing the lobbies and their contributors. Until then, however, the parties on the receiving end of a donor's largesse could still, with considerable honesty, repeat the proverbial boast of the Count de Mirabeau, President of the French National Assembly in 1791: "I can be paid, but I can't be bought."[178]

THE PROFESSIONALS

"Democracy" is related to "the cost of politics"—but more ambiguously than is sometimes assumed.[179] The high price of elections does not prevent "democracy" so much as determine the kind of "democracy"—that is, the kind of representation—a country will have. In England the high cost of obtaining a seat was a major force in keeping parliament the preserve of a highly privileged elite until well into the twentieth century. In Germany, although personal wealth continued to be a factor in the election of a candidate, the rules of the game fostered a diverse political class, recruited in part from modest levels of society. Although the Centrum, the Poles, Alsatians, and conservatives still continued to draw upon local notables, by the twentieth century the composition of the other

---

[176] "Bericht der Geschäftsführung der Wahlfondskommission . . ." in Kaelble, *Interessenpolitik*, 219. Somewhat inconsequentially, however, the report cites only 8 constituencies where the SPD-F alliance defeated a fund-supported candidate.

[177] Lederer, "Parteien," col. 335. A good survey of the literature on PR: Nohlen, *Wahlrecht*. Skeptical about industry's political power after the decline of notables: Jaeger, *Unternehmer*, 129; Kaelble, *Interessenpolitik*, 20, 122; more negative: Molt, *Reichstag*, 307; Ullmann, *Interessenverbände*, 120–22.

[178] Cf. exchange on bribery between Liebermann v. Sonnenberg and O. Zimmerman (Ref.) SBDR 27 Feb. 1907: 99, 114.

[179] Cf. the title of Gwyn's book, *Democracy and the Cost of Politics*.

delegations had been transformed. The social openness in the German system was indeed connected to the "cost of politics"—to the fact that many of the technical costs of elections were borne by state, but also, and especially, to the feedback mechanisms that, as campaigns themselves became increasingly expensive, rewarded good organization with more money and more voters.[180]

The expense of elections, including the support of the winner, drove in turn the inexorable professionalization of the German political class. If not full-time parliamentarians, many, perhaps most, Reichstag deputies were full-time politicians. Politics itself proved to be a route of upward social mobility, the basis for increased social status, personal esteem, and financial reward. Every important trade union leader, for example, eventually took a seat in the Reichstag.[181] Growing professionalization in other occupations, moreover, reinforced the trend toward professionalization in politics. As the tasks of public administration became so demanding as to chain the civil servant to his desk, the Landrat, who had once turned up as every tenth or eleventh deputy in the Prussian Landtag, after 1900 appeared only half as frequently—if that much.[182] As for busy businessmen, the diminution of their numbers was noted with head-shaking by both contemporaries and historians, although an additional cause of their disappearance—that voters didn't want them—is frequently forgotten.[183] For all these reasons, Bismarck's nightmare of a Reichstag made up of a class of men who made their living "off" politics came true.

But professionalization, which tends to increase the respect in which other vocations are held, appears to diminish elected officials in the esteem of the public they are chosen to represent. The Iron Chancellor's disdain for the professional politician was taken over by critics of the empire, left and right, where it fed into the antiparty discourse that has been the companion of representative institutions throughout their history. In Germany, this universal distaste for the professional politician was strongly inflected by an idiom of decline that was a commonplace, especially in conservative circles, by the end of the century.[184] The two discourses came together in 1918 when Max Weber, taking stock of

[180] Overseers' fees" in England and Wales, 1868–80, ran from £4 to over £1,000 per district. Gwyn, *Democracy*, 21–28.

[181] Molt, *Reichstag*, 237; tables on party and trade union functionaries in the RT; 230f. Retallack, *Notables*, 232f. About 70% of the SPD delegation were men employed in the workers' movement. Nipperdey, *Organisation*, 383; also 103; Huber, *Verfassungsgeschichte* 3: 893.

[182] Extrapolated from Kühne, *Dreiklassenwahlrecht*, 87f; the change was spurred by the IM himself: Saul, "Kampf," 196n. 138. A corrective against exaggerating the political fallout of professionalization: Witt, "Landrat," passim.

[183] Sour grapes: "The nation's best energies have no desire to sit in the circle of the German Reichstag." *DA* 21/27, 5 Jul. 1903: 444. A welcome exception: Hartmut Berghoff and Roland Möller, "Unternehmer in Deutschland und England 1870–1914," *HZ* 256/2 (Apr. 1993), 381. Cf. also Kaelble, *Interessenpolitik*, 116f, and tables on 223–25; Gall, "Bank," 83. The Ruhr elites' interest in local elective office, where the franchise was in their favor, also declined. Spencer, *Management*, 61.

[184] E.g., *DA* 21/27 (5 Jul. 1903): 444. Stegmann, *Erben*, 116, gives a number of citations from the nineties. Even in France, where party activity was still conducted by local committee, critics deplored the professional politician as a sign of *décadence*. Lefèvre-Pontalis, *Élections*, 12.

Germany's professional politicians, described a breed of subalterns staffing "a parliament with a deeply sunken intellectual level." Denied the possibility of executive power or responsibility, these men, he decided, were animated by "guild instincts"—that is, the desire for self-perpetuation. Organization, it would seem, at least in the context of German dualism, demanded mediocrity: among those "who made these petty posts their lives, it was impossible for any man who was not of their hue to rise."[185] Weber's complaint that the Reichstag had lost its ability to attract the best political energies, has been echoed by admirers who should have known better ever since. Bound to their organizations, lacking the discipline of responsibility, "the stature of deputies and party leaders" in the Wilhelmine Reichstag, we hear from a recent commentator, "was pretty mediocre."[186] To which we must ask: compared to whom? In what sense did Erzberger and Scheidemann fall short of Windthorst and Bebel? Why should Bassermann, Naumann, and Stresemann be considered the epigoni of Bennigsen, Rickert, and Richter? The answer is not at all obvious.[187] Weber's wartime lament that his country, now near defeat, had failed to produce the "leaders" that so distinguished its parliamentary enemies might have been less impassioned had he lived in France when Clemenceau was rusticated for his involvement in the Panama scandals, or in England when its high-living Prime Minister was dubbed, and with good reason, "£loyd George." It would certainly have been less impassioned had the war in Europe gone the other way. Instead, the opening up of the Wilhelmine political class, of which the democratization of the Reichstag was but one part, has been described by one of Weber's most distinguished followers as a sign of "craving for recognition, the need for prestige, and the vanity of the middle-class careerist."[188] In Germany, upward mobility has never found a good press.

Yet ambivalence about the professional politician as a type has roots deeper than Bismarck, broader than snobbery. Ever since Cincinnatus left his plough, saved the country, and returned to his labors when the job was done, the model of the lay legislator has exercised a powerful attraction, against which the "pol" can have little appeal. The lay ideal presupposed, of course, a particular style of campaigning—or, more accurately, of not campaigning. It implied that the virtues of the candidate could be sufficiently well known as to need no advertisement. It assumed a public whose legitimate interests were sufficiently homogeneous for wisdom and integrity in a candidate to be qualifications enough, making instructions from his constituents both undesirable and unnecessary. In

---

[185] Quoted: Weber, "Parlament," 308; "Politik als Beruf," 530. Germans were not alone in their belief in "decline." Ostrogorski gave voice to similar feelings when he remarked that "as soon as a party, even if created for the noblest object, perpetuates itself, it tends to degeneration." M. Ostrogorski, *Democracy* ([1902] 1964) 1, quote on ix.

[186] Nipperdey (quoted), *Geschichte* 2: 575; Molt, *Reichstag*, 29.

[187] A 1910 book entitled *German Powerholders* ranks Bassermann as more powerful than Bennigsen in his day, and includes (in addition to Bebel) Erzberger, Peter Spahn (Z), H. E. Müller (Meiningen) (FrVP), as well as the BdL director and former NL Diederich Hahn: Martin, *Machthaber*, 447, 456.

[188] H. Rosenberg, quoted in Molt, *Reichstag*, 109.

Germany, this ethos was enshrined in Article 29 of the imperial constitution, which declared the deputy the representative of the whole nation, on whose conscience no *particular* interest—and therefore no binding promises (the so-called "imperative mandate")—could have a claim. It was Article 29, as we have seen, that provided the opening for Social Democrats to campaign for Reichstag seats after their party had been outlawed in 1878. The ethos it proclaimed was appealing to liberals and conservatives alike, in England as well as in Germany. Its tones ring out in the Duke of Ratibor's indignant rejection of the demand of Pleß-Rybnik's Catholics in 1871 that he outline his position on church-state controversies: "I won't have peasants sticking a pistol to my chest!"[189] We can hear it in Westminster, where J. S. Mill made it a condition of his nomination that he not be required either to campaign or to make promises. The same ethos was behind the Liberal Association of Düsseldorf's announcement in 1878 that their nominee had "refrained for moral reasons" from appearing before them: "He did not want to importune as candidate." When some of those assembled objected to voting for a man who had submitted no program, the board replied that the candidate could "not bind himself in advance; such is not to be presumed of a man of honor."[190]

Everywhere throughout the European and Atlantic world, *vox populi*, when it demanded prior commitments, sounded illegitimately coercive to those who considered their own independence a major qualification for public office.[191] But if a voter cared more for the positions than for the person of his representative, if indeed he had ideas of his own about the proper course of state action, how else than through such queries and demands was he to insure that his vote would actually support the policy of his choice? The lay ideal spoke more strongly to abstract convictions, and to the social conventions of local elites, than to the realities of the developing national political culture. With large and diverse election districts, the ideal's demands on both the local celebrity of the candidate and the harmony among his constituents were simply too great. Party organizations were needed to mediate the connection between candidates and constituents, and the imperatives of party, which demanded discipline, ran counter to the individualism at the heart of the lay ideal. Sometimes the parties themselves were slow to recognize this fact—as the case of the Düsseldorf Liberal Association in 1878 shows. The Social Democrats, on the other hand, who made no bones about offering the electorate a binding program, were always poised to exploit any opponent's refusal to "give an accounting or a report

---

[189] Quoted in Rust, *Reichskanzler*, 621.

[190] Schloßmacher, *Düsseldorf*, 219; also 222, in 1879 LT election. Cf. also Forcade de la Biaix (Z), who declined, as a judge, to express a partisan standpoint outside of parliament: Möllers, *Strömungen*, 265–67. Nipperdey, *Organisation*, 37.

[191] The literature on the "mandate-independence controversy," which Pitkin calls "undoubtedly the central classic controversy in the literature of political representation," is endless. Representative: Felix Stoerk, *Das verfassungsmässige Verhältnis des Abgeordneten zur Wählerschaft* (Vienna, 1881). Excellent: Pitkin, *Concept*, chap. 7, quote: 145; and Kühne, *Dreiklassenwahlrecht*, 51, 173, 177, 234, 318, 577.

to his voters." The Centrum, although it claimed to exercise no compulsion over its deputies' votes, was equally hard-nosed about enforcing commitments on the religious issues dear to Catholic hearts.[192]

We should beware, therefore, of reading too much into the celebrated victory of Count Posadowsky, who in 1912 had agreed to run only on the condition that he "remain free of all party ties and . . . not be expected to campaign." A recent and justly famous Chief of the Imperial Office of Domestic Affairs; a conservative who enjoyed the endorsement of the progressive "Society for Social Reform"; a Protestant known for his efforts at Catholic inclusion: the Count was in a position to stipulate conditions about his candidacy that were both credible and at the same time scarcely possible to lesser men. Posadowsky's election was less a sign of the continuing viability of the unbound "lay" deputy than a throwback to an era in reality long gone.[193]

Nevertheless, it would be wrong to dismiss the continued hold of the ideal of the lay representative on the popular imagination as a piece of "ideology," a palatable disguise for the continued political claims of traditional elites. For such a dismissal ignores the fact that the age of mass organization, of parties and of interest groups, creates its own privileges. It is not mere ideology to yearn for an openness in the system that would allow, at least occasionally, a Mr. Smith to go to Washington, a Herr Schmidt to go to Berlin.[194] The recognition that some element of the democratic ideal is lost when an ordinary—or at least unorganized—citizen can never dream of adding his *individual* voice to those of his country's legislators has been a powerful and enduring current in western democracies. We hear it not only in the distaste of nineteenth-century notables for parties and professional politicians, but also in the demand for term limits that arose among Green voters in the Federal Republic in the 1980s and among so many voters of both parties in the United States today. It underlies the suspicions of reformers and theorists, like Robert Michels, who was convinced that "organization . . . gives birth to the domination of the elected over the electors, of the mandataries over the mandators, of the delegates over the delegators," and concludes: "Whoever says organization says oligarchy."[195]

Oligarchy is a misleading term for a group of men who are, after all, peri-

---

[192] SD's: Schloßmacher, *Düsseldorf*, 232; Z: *MK* 16 (22 Apr. 1871): 115; unnamed priest to Windthorst, 30 Aug. 1882, and W. v. Schorlemer-Vehr to Ziner, 13 Aug. 1889, BAK, Kleine Erwerbung Nr. 596.

[193] *Pace* Sheehan, "Leadership," 524. Bertram, *Wahlen*, 140–42, notes that even Posadowsky withdrew his refusal to give speeches; cf. also 153f. In LT elections, the ideal of the unbound representative lived on (juxtaposed to its tradition-based opposite, the person chosen as spokesman for his "corporation"), especially among liberals. Listing of refusals by candidates to accept an imperative mandate: Kühne, *Dreiklassenwahlrecht*, 234n. 14, 370. On the *Gesellschaft für Soziale Reform*: Molt, *Reichstag*, 304f, 305n. 57.

[194] There were "wild" deputies even in the RT as late as 1893 (27), 1898 (37), 1903 (22), 1907 (12), and 1923 (25), although some of them probably represented interest groups. Table 31 in Molt, *Reichstag*, 355.

[195] Quoted as an epigram by Lipset in "Introduction: Ostrogorski," i. I have changed "who" to "whoever."

odically subject to popular recall. But it is not misleading to see professional politicians as forming a class of their own. French commentators spoke of candidacies being monopolized by "a new race, the politicians."[196] The famous golf match between the Liberal Lloyd George and the Conservative Bonar Law at the height of the Home Rule crisis has been used to make a similar point about Georgian Britain. Some commentators have credited precisely this easy sociability, reinforced by considerable social homogeneity, within the French and the English political class with stabilizing their parliaments' collective norms and thereby strengthening their ability to assume political responsibility. The professionalization of the Reichstag, in this view, was insufficient to overcome the social, regional, and ethnic diversity attendant on democratization. This diversity is said to have made it harder for Germany's representatives to achieve that consensus on fundamentals which successful parliamentary government demands.[197]

But the Lloyd George–Bonar Law golf game, the proof text for the continued vitality of the House of Commons's collective esprit, gives a misleading impression of the governability of prewar Britain—so at least George Dangerfield has argued.[198] And anyone familiar with the Reichstag in its first, less democratic, decade should be skeptical about the cohesion provided by common membership in the *Honoratiorenstand* when great matters are at stake. This was the Reichstag, after all, in which the Right Honorable Higher Court Judge Peter Reichensperger smashed a lectern in two, and in which Count Ballestrem was nearly called out by Prince Bismarck.[199]

The German parliament in fact developed its own forms to overcome social diversity. If every Social Democrat was a "Comrade," within the National Liberal delegation, members made a point of addressing and referring to each other, regardless of the normally compulsory titles distinguishing noble rank or high office, as "Colleague."[200] The prewar Reichstag may have lacked the easy sociability of Britain's "club" and France's "republic of pals," but if so, the cause lay far more in its political than in its social diversity. And even that political diversity, reinforced by an election law that encouraged a multiparty system that reflected the economic, ethnic, religious, and ideological cleavages in German society, did not prevent the development of significant patterns of

---

[196] Lefèvre-Pontalis, *Élections*, 12.

[197] G. A. Ritter, "Deutscher und Britischer Parlamentarismus" (1962), 30; Molt, *Reichstag*, esp. 279f; Sheehan, "Leadership," 525f. Golf: Searle, *Corruption*, 127, 189.

[198] *The Strange Death of Liberal England* (New York, 1935). Where small groups of people controlled so much, the hobnobbing of political enemies encouraged suspicions of bad faith, which in wartime led to conspiracy theories that Britain's leaders were under enemy control. Searle's *Corruption*, 241–93, shows how the very conditions promoting the resilience of the British system under one set of circumstances, under another (adverse news in wartime) led to its fragility—very suggestive for the German historian.

[199] Reichensperger: Julius Bachem, *Erinnerungen eines alten Publizisten und Politikers* (Cologne, 1913), 71.

[200] The exception: Bennigsen, who remained *Herr von*, and later *Exzellenz*. Kulemann, *Erinnerungen*, 62f.

cross-cleavage cooperation. Memoirists affirm, with some astonishment, that the mutual execrations of the campaign stopped at the Reichstag door; that good personal relationships, respect, and even sympathy developed between members of the most antagonistic parties. The National Liberal Wilhelm Kulemann got to know Herr and Frau Wilhelm Liebknecht at an international conference and considered them both "magnificent human beings"—and the Liebknechts were not the only Socialists with whom he began to hobnob. Even on the hustings, good humor might reign. In 1912 Eugen Schiffer and August Strosser, rival Liberal and Conservative candidates for the same seat, shared an automobile ride from Berlin to their district with complete cordiality. Carl Bachem paints a similar picture and gives the impression that, at least for the Centrum, even the SPD was not beyond the pale.[201] A roll-call analysis of voting behavior in the Wilhelmine Reichstag concludes that in its ability to integrate diverging interests and viewpoints legislatively, the German parliament "does not appear to have been qualitatively different from most other legislatures."[202] It seems in fact as true of the Kaiser's Germany as of France's Third Republic that, in Robert de Jouvenel's famous *mot*, there was "less difference between two deputies, one of whom is a revolutionary and the other not, than between two revolutionaries, one of whom is a deputy and the other not."[203]

German deputies were also not lacking in allegiance to their parliament as an institution—witness their collective insistence on stipends, over four decades and encompassing the entire political spectrum except for the far Right. Witness as well the willingness of almost the entire National Liberal delegation in 1912 to put aside class allegiance, partisan conviction, and the anger of their wealthiest supporters in order to accord to Social Democracy the recognition due its numerical weight by electing Philipp Scheidemann First Vice President of the Reichstag.[204] Witness the Social Democrats' willingness to vote war credits in August 1914.

But the very rise of the professional politician in Germany was a sign that competing class interests, confessional claims, and national demands had become institutionalized in highly articulated party structures, structures whose strength was owed to their ability to mobilize and reinforce, at the grass roots, political identities that were, by definition, in conflict. Even in the far more

---

[201] Cf. Bachem's sympathetic description, as an unintentional accident, of the scandalous incident in which the SD delegation "refused" to rise for the cheer for the Kaiser. *Vorgeschichte* 5: 384. Shared ride to 5 Magdeburg: Bertram, *Wahlen*, 204. Kulemann's relationship with Liebknecht and the SPD: *Erinnerungen*, 225–27, compared to Kartell RT: 79–82 and 187; easy relationships among nonsocialist parties: 43f; President of the LT, v. Kröcher (K) defended the SDs' constitutionalism against his K colleague: SBHA 10 Feb 1909: 1950–77, GStA PK I. HA, Rep. 90a, A.VIII.1.d., Nr. 1/Bd. 9, Bl. 1968; friendliness of Hessen's Grand Duke to Socialist leader: White, *Party*, 176; between deputies and members of the BR: 90. Contrast Fairbairn, *Democracy*, 261.

[202] Smith/Turner, "Behavior," 28, rebutting Molt's picture.

[203] *La République des Camarades* (Paris, 1914), quoted in Sheehan, "Leadership," 525f.

[204] NL support for Scheidemann was controversial and put the fraction, and Bassermann's leadership, under severe strain: "Ueber die Wahl des Reichstagspresidiums," *Die Parteien*, Heft 1 und 2 (1912) 124, 212, 304; White, *Party*, 194; Gall, "Bank," 436.

homogeneous Prussian Landtag, the institutionalization of these conflicts at the constituency level reacted on legislation in ways that made the deputies' hard-bought efforts at compromise a Sisyphean labor.[205] In English constituencies, such party allegiance was less firmly anchored, at least since the Liberal Secession of 1886, in the identities of voters than it was in Germany. And in France, structures tying national parties to local identities at the constituency level existed barely at all.

On the other hand, when the bonds of obligation were strong, they might tie constituency as well as delegation. As the legal requirement that a victor win an absolute majority increasingly forced candidates into runoff elections, all parties, including those in third and fourth place, were forced into negotiations with each other—across cultures, across election districts, and sometimes even across legislative bodies. The necessity of so many runoff alliances helped counter the entrenchment of hostile identities by habituating voters to supporting the candidate of a rival party. And the deputy so elected found himself bound by commitments not only to his own party, but to the parties of at least *some* of his opponents.[206] If this is not "aggregating interests," an important function not only of parties but of parliaments, it is hard to imagine what is.

The tension between the democratization of the electorate and the ability of parliament to do its job is no invention of mid-nineteenth-century Liberal/Conservative ideology, any more than the connection between the mobilization of the electorate and the displacement of parliament's decision-making into the hands of party oligarchies was a figment of the mugwump imagination. Democratization implies publicity, publicity demands money, money requires organization, and organizations—in our case, parties—inevitably develop hierarchies and rationales that take on a life of their own. With the increasing visibility of such organizations, it was equally inevitable that perceptions would grow that "party organizations are not democratic reflections of popular will, but powerful instruments for dominating the electorate, for imposing officials, opinions, and policies on the public." Social scientists, from the Russian-born Moisei Ostrogorski to the Italian economist Vilfredo Pareto to the onetime German Social Democrat Robert Michels, added their voices to this popular disquiet when they argued that organization inevitably led to rule by an elite. The tensions between the demands of the individual for representation and the need for mass organization, between democracy and party, never has been, and never can be, resolved. Lord Ampthill was surely right in 1922—after debate in Britain had chased for two decades endlessly around the same circle of money and party, organization and representation—when he insisted, "You cannot choose between parliamentary government and party government . . . they go together."[207]

---

[205] Their consequences for the LT's difficulties in reforming the Prussian franchise: Kühne, *Dreiklassenwahlrecht*, 445f, 449.

[206] A point made by Kühne, *Dreiklassenwahlrecht*, 210, 236, about the LT, but in principle as true for RT elections—as G. A. Ritter noted decades ago in "Parlamentarismus," 42.

[207] Ostrogorski paraphrased by Lipset in his "Introduction" (1964), lvii; Ampthill in Searle, *Corruption*, 348.

CHAPTER TWELVE

Conclusions

> The franchise turns the servant into the master. At first only for one election day. But when used sensibly and by everyone, soon into master for ever—more correctly: to a free man.
>
> —*Vorwärts (1876)*

> Democratic societies are populated not by freely acting individuals, but by collective organizations that are capable of coercing those whose interests they represent.
>
> —*Adam Przeworski (1991)*

IN autumn 1918, after three and a half years of total war and with defeat certain, the authority of the Kaiser's government collapsed. After the forced abdication of the monarch, the revolution that established the subsequent Weimar Republic was a moderate one. It reconfigured executive and legislative power to eliminate the dualism that had been the defining feature of the imperial constitution. And it instituted reforms similar to those enacted in many Western countries at the end of the war: women's suffrage, proportional representation, and an end to all remaining elements of plutocracy, such as Prussia's three-class voting system. For a long time it was customary to deplore this moderation as another example of Germany's "failure" at the business of revolution. But as Heinrich August Winkler has argued, a half century of universal suffrage meant that Germany's "level of democratization" was simply too high for an upheaval in the French or Russian mode. "Accustomed to the Reichstag's universal suffrage, a phase of revolutionary dictatorship would have appeared to the overwhelming majority of Germans as a loss rather than a gain in participation, as a step backward rather than progress." The most widely shared demand of the citizenry, including the majority of the representatives of the workers and soldiers' councils, was for national elections, the sooner the better.[1] After fifty years of going to the polls, Germans assumed that democracy was both desirable and inevitable.

---

[1] Winkler, *Revolution* (1984), 19–23, 30f, 53; the same in idem., *Sozialdemokratie* (1979), 11–20; idem, *Weimar* (1993), 13. Contra Wehler, *Gesellschaftsgeschichte* 3: 1041: a fortiori, decades of manhood suffrage explains why Germans raised no mass movement analogous to English chartism—aimed at precisely that.

This chapter will try to explain why this was so by reviewing the features of the election process that had turned the German Empire, by 1914, into "a partly democratic country."[2] Then it will reflect, briefly, on the legacies of the Kaiserreich for the successor generation. But before we begin, we must consider more systematically than we have so far the role of the government, and why it proved unable to benefit from the franchise that Bismarck had so optimistically bestowed.

WEAK GOVERNMENT, STRONG STATE: THE PARADOXES OF OFFICIAL POWER

A window on the changes that had—and had not—taken place over the last half century is provided by the last imperial election in Nordhausen, Prussian Saxony. Critics charged that provincial officials, from the Landrat to the most humble factotum, had worked furiously to defeat Otto Wiemer, the Left Liberal incumbent. In one hamlet, where the village steward lay sick, his wife had buckled on his saber, donned his service cap, and gone out to deliver anti-Wiemer circulars herself. The Landrat's blue stamp had adorned the leaflets of a coalition of conservative groups, headed by the antisemitic Economic Union, all of which conveyed the same message: Wiemer must be brought down. Reserve officers had passed the word to the *Kriegervereine*, and warrior branches that had recently been disciplined for voting Social Democratic were promised their colors back if Wiemer were defeated. A turnout of 98.8 percent for the first ballot—setting the all-time record for the Empire—had demonstrated the contest's enormous symbolic significance: for Left Liberals had held Nordhausen for thirty years, and Wiemer was the *Fortschrittliche Volkspartei*'s national leader. Wiemer was indeed brought down, but the election was overturned on grounds of government influence.

The reader who has followed our story from the beginning may be excused for feeling a sense of *déja vu*. Here, in the last prewar election, was the traditional *Obrigkeitsstaat*, intervening down a chain of command that had been familiar since 1848. Even the use of women was an old story. But with the name of the victor, we are brought up short. The candidate on whose behalf the state, the conservatives, and the antisemites had lavished their efforts was a Social Democratic fire-eater named Oskar Cohn, a man who stood on the Left of his leftist party.[3]

The whys and wherefores of this strange constellation—to which we shall return—did not interest those pushing for invalidation. When pressed, they ac-

---

[2] Winkler, *Weimar*, 601.

[3] 1 Erfurt AnlDR (1912/14, 13/I, Bd. 20) DS 1160: 2291–98; SBDR 28 Nov. 1913: 6067–71. Turnout: Hiery, *Reichstagswahlen*, 326n. 93. Cohn joined the USPD during the war. Other unlikely elections impeached for government influence: 3 Marienwerder (P), AnlDR (1984/85, 6/I, Bd. 4) DS 273: 1176–78; Saxon-Altenburg (SD): SBDR 16 Mar. 1904: 1871–82.

knowledged that nothing so crude as a telegram announcing "Sovereign Wants Cohn!" had arrived at the Landrat's office. But nevertheless, they insisted, here was a "ministerial candidacy."[4] Within the man-bites-dog story in Nordhausen lie conflicting narratives of power and weakness. The fact that the Reichstag overturned the Social Democrat's victory reveals that in the eyes of many, even in 1912, government power still constituted a threat to free elections. From our own perspective, however, nothing demonstrates official impotence more dramatically than the corner into which a half century of democratic practices had painted the servants of the Hohenzollern: the alternative between "wanting Cohn"—or another five years of the leader of the Progressives.

How had it come to this?

Bismarck had intended, in introducing the democratic franchise, to create an overwhelming advantage for his government. Like all contemporaries, he was impressed with the franchise's effectiveness in Napoleon III's France. It was "bonapartism," and its apparent reconciliation of representation with authoritarianism, that leant manhood suffrage its glamour for the future chancellor— and its menace for nearly everyone else.[5] "Ministerial candidates"—men whose election the bureaucracy explicitly promoted—were the hallmark of the French system, and Prussian cabinet deliberations in the sixties revolved around ways to adapt the idea to German conditions. Ingenious possibilities were tossed about—such as reckoning every eligible voter who stayed away from the polls to the official candidate's total. But juridical objections prevailed. To treat abstentions as votes was an "untenable fiction."[6] Procedures that might delegitimize the results of a process whose function was to confer legitimacy would not fly. Moreover, the clarity and simplicity that first recommended ministerial candidacies to Prussia's leaders—the division of the contest between government and opposition—ultimately raised misgivings. What might come of repeatedly putting the crown's prestige so directly on the block?[7] Hovering in the background of this discussion, ever present but unacknowledged, was the recognition that explicit ministerial candidacies would dispel the aura of a government "above parties" and, by bridging the gap between executive and legislature, end the dualism that shielded the crown's prerogatives from parliament's grasp. In the end, while adopting Napoleon's suffrage, the cabinet dropped his

---

[4] Neumann-Hofer SBDR 28 Nov. 1913: 6070.

[5] Zeldin, *System* (1958), 81; Jones, *Politics*, 221. "Bonapartism" and "caesarism" were used interchangeably. Pollmann, *Parlamentarismus*, 93, 101n. 41; Steinbach, *Zähmung* 1: 110f.

[6] Bis. to SM, and the more scrupulous responses of Bodelschwingh (quoted): 26 May 1866, and Roon, "Votum," 27 May 1866, BAB-L R43/685, Bl. 13–19, 21–25. Eulenberg: Pollmann, *Parlamentarismus*, 98, 99n. 35, 100n. 39. Voters came up with the same idea! BAB-L R1501/files: 14693, Bl. 235–40; 14694, Bl. 137–42; 14695 unpaginated; 14696, Bl. 15–17. The Dutch government had used the same "fiction" in reckoning abstentions in Flanders in the 1820s. Kenneth Barkin, private communication.

[7] Excellent: Pollmann, *Parlamentarismus*, 72, 94f, 95nn. 15, 16, 96–101; Steinbach, *Zähmung* 1: 31.

official candidacies. Bismarck admitted that "Germans can't be governed in the same manner as the French."[8]

Nevertheless, while the ministry did not back individuals, the organs of government did not remain on the sidelines.[9] And each time they intervened—whenever a provincial administrator brokered a candidacy, whenever a county gazette (*Kreisblatt*) published "informational" commentary on an election—the cry went up that here was a "ministerial candidacy."[10] One marvels at the studied ignorance behind this indignation. By the eighties at the latest, it was surely no secret to anyone which parties the government preferred. A system that might impeach an election if the Landrat's endorsement had graced the winning candidate's leaflet, yet allowed the Landrat himself to stand for election (and in his own county!) baffled outsiders. It relied upon a distinction between public and private activity so fine as to be undetectable to even the Gallic mind.[11] Yet while the pejorative term "ministerial candidacy" lived on in election challenges right up to the victory of Oskar Cohn, the genuine article, *à la française*, never, ever, made an appearance in Germany. Why not?

French ministerial candidacies were founded on a premise that was shocking for many Germans even to contemplate: patronage. "Bonapartism," and later, rural republicanism, was anchored in "a thousand trifling subsidies." The *maire* delivered his commune's votes to the candidate (often with a list of names, and the notation that a roof was needed here, livestock "losses" required replacement there). The candidate, through his access to the ministry, delivered goods and services to the voters. The heart's-blood of the electoral circulatory system, however, was not individual favors, but public works: roads, canals, bridges—

---

[8] Cf. Bis. to SM, 23 May 1866, BAB-L R43/685, Bl. 16.

[9] Note the form letter sent 21 Oct. 1884 to a Prussian minister (probably Puttkamer) and other high-ranking bureaucrats, from the chairman of the K campaign committee in 1 Berlin, Fhr. v. Hammerstein, urging that civil servants be granted leave and be put at the disposal of 41 election bureaus, to fetch tardy voters and man polling places. BAB-L R1501/14693, Bl. 137. His candidate, Adolf Wagner, lost.

[10] Von Bunsen SBDR, 29 Mar. 1871: 43; Wehrenpfennig SBDR 17 Apr. 1871: 237; Rickert SBDR 9 Apr. 1886: 2015; protest of Ed. Bauer, typesetter, and Theo. Werner, file cutter, against "an *official* or government candidate in the worst *French* sense:" 13 Saxony AnlDR (1887–88, 7/II, Bd. 4) DS 212: 907; Delsor SBDR 21 Apr. 1903: 8925f. Pejorative references to ministerial candidacies and to the French system predated the empire: "Der Minister des Innern," 431–34. Arguing that Napoleon's control over elections has been exaggerated: Zeldin, *System*, 11, 45, 63, 119, 135f, 137f; and that it indirectly contributed to rooting democratic ideas in the public: 98f.

[11] Lefèvre-Pontalis, *Élections*, 122, 126; Leser, "Untersuchungen." Government bafflement as to what the RT would and would not tolerate began at least as early as the Poschinger Report in 1879. BAB-L R1501/14450, Bl. 158. It continued as late as 1917, when Bethmann Hollweg, a man with surely more pressing things on his mind, had his staff look into the history of IM Puttkamer, still a byword for improper influence three decades after his fall. BH was obviously preparing a response to the Constitutional Commission's proposal to speed up scrutinies by allowing the RT to gather information directly. Von Zahn, "Äusserung über die Ungültigkeitserklärung der Wahl des Rittergutsbesitzers Puttkamers. . . . 24 May 1917, and "Das Wahl-Prüfungselend," *Weser-Ztg* 10 May 1917, both in BAB-L R1501/14653, unpaginated.

and especially railway branch lines (*lignes électorales*), whose bewildering configuration represented terrible economics, but great politics.[12]

Neither during Prussian cabinet deliberations in the sixties nor at any later time did Germany's leaders contemplate using public works systematically for electoral purposes—and the colonial secretary's apparent departure from these norms in 1907 did indeed cause "stupefaction," and not only among his fellow bureaucrats. Structural differences between the two countries may help explain the omission. The French system of electoral patronage was encouraged by a simplifying bipolarity—the centralization of decision-making in Paris and the poverty of isolated rural communes—that was missing in Germany, with its complex federalism and its dense north-south belt of prosperous towns. But the most important difference was probably cultural. An "unobjective"—that is, political—use of the state's resources offended German notions of propriety.[13] Here is a newspaper from the Ems flood plain, rebutting suggestions that voters dared not elect Windthorst, known for his friendship with the deposed Guelf dynasty, because he was *persona non grata* to the Hohenzollern:

> Do you think that the election of such a man would kill the construction of a canal or a street for your district or commune? Believe it—the government of His Majesty does not wage canal politics. You could elect a Red and you would still not have to fear *on that account* that the government would, out of revenge, act otherwise than the *objective* circumstances demanded.[14]

I am not suggesting that the *Ems-und Hase Blätter*'s confidence in the objectivity of the state's decisions was universally shared. To the peasant mind it was probably inconceivable that the government would *not* follow the way of the world and do as it was done by. But suspicions, without explicit support from the government itself, could not be turned into election victories. The 1879 Landtag election in Gummersbach-Waldbröl was a case in point. When the national camp tried to overcome its internal divisions by nominating the Minister of Public Works, Albert von Maybach, arguing that with Maybach, Gummersbachers could be assured of being included in the railroad network, local advertisers responded by denying that the minister would be able to do any more for his own district than for any other. The electorate seems to have agreed, because the first polling produced no clear winner within the national camp, and Maybach withdrew.[15]

The contrast between Germany and France was made explicit in 1884, when

---

[12] Jones, *Politics*, 295–97 (quote), 299, 301f, 306; Lefèvre-Pontalis, *Élections*, 11, 31n.1; *lignes électorales*: Sydney Pollard, *The Peaceful Conquest. The Industrialization of Europe, 1760–1970* (Oxford, 1981), 132, 160. After 1877, with parliament and government aligned, the term "ministerial candidate" dropped out of usage. The designation "republican" sufficed. Charnay, *Les scrutins*, 117.

[13] Bennigsen contrasted to France the "good German tradition" that the bureaucracy worked for the whole: Fenske, "Landrat," 454.

[14] "Reichstags-Wahlangelegenheit," *Ems-und Hase Blätter* 25 Aug. 1867.

[15] Müller, *Strömungen*, 117–20, 123, 129; H. v. Gerlach, "Wahlprüfungspraxis und Wahlprüfungspraktiken," *Die Nation* 24 (1906/7), 118f.

the Viceroy of Alsace-Lorraine, Edwin von Manteuffel, excused his region's poor showing in elections by referring to the Reichsland's "French" expectations:

> The French government made the communes responsible for their votes in elections. A commune that voted according to the wishes of the government received the greatest possible consideration for their petitions; a commune that voted according to the wishes of the opposition never got their petitions granted. The communes of Alsace-Lorraine grew up under this system, and since the German administration never entered onto this path, but still decides on petitions only according to objective considerations, the communes feel free of any fear that their votes could have disadvantageous consequences for themselves, and fall under the influence of agitators who make promises to them.
>
> In order to remedy this disadvantage, in the future those requests from communes that are based not in law, but rather request preferential treatment, will be handled by considering their behavior in the election.[16]

Manteuffel had indeed discovered the secret of the French government's success with universal suffrage. But his announcement of a like policy was bluster. A military man, the viceroy had no understanding for the legalism of his bureaucracy—with whom he was always on the worst terms. Given this legalism, Manteuffel's exclusion of decisions "based in law" from his threatened system of *quid pro quos* reduced the scope of his proposal to the vanishing point. I have seen no evidence that he even tried to put it into effect.[17] Although individual instances of political favoritism occasionally turn up, no historian will ever bestow upon the German Empire or its components the moniker accorded the Third Republic—a "milk cow state."[18]

If using the state's carrot to influence German voters was unthinkable, what about its stick? Certainly the threat of disadvantage was one of the messages conveyed by the gendarme's ubiquitous presence on the campaign trail, recording who attended the rallies, quoting the give-and-take of discussion, noting whose name came first during the ritual three cheers at the end—the Kaiser's, the candidate's, or the pope's.[19] Undercover informants provided additional de-

---

[16] M. to Wm. I, Straßburg, 3 Nov. 1884, GStA PK I, HA, Rep. 89/211, Bl. 36–37v. Government influence under French rule: Delsor SBDR 21 Apr. 1903: 8925f.

[17] Hiery's searching examination into election influence, in *Reichstagswahlen*, does not mention it, which must be decisive.

[18] I am not claiming that K and NL candidates did not allude to benefits they might bring their district. They sometimes did, and when they did not, local and county officials might do it for them. But hints of favor lacked the specificity of their French counterparts: a significant difference. Promises to bring desires for a branch line to the attention of Berlin: LR Fhr. v. Riedesel of 8 Kassel (and Mb of LT), 30 Jul. 1891, BAB-L R1501/14667, Bl. 148–51; LR in 7 Gumb. AnlDR (1912/14, 13/I, Bd. 23) DS 1586: 3394f; promises satirized by J. Cremer, SBHA, 1888, quoted in Kühne, *Dreiklassenwahlrecht*, 354. Not surprisingly, the few cases approaching French patronage that I have found were mostly in AL. 7 AL, AnlDR (1880, 4/III, Bd. 4), DS 126: 775–79. "Milk cow": Jones, *Politics*, 295, 306.

[19] Horn Report, 24 Feb. 1907, LHAK 408/8806, Bl. 12. Other surveillance: Turban to Grand Duke Friedrich, 31 Mar. 1887, GLA 60/494; and IM Eisenlohr, 14 Jun. 1993 to regional officials,

tails, all of which were summarized by the prefect and sent to the provincial governor. The police also passed information to private employers—although not as much or as often as the latter wished.[20] The German *Obrigkeitstaat* was hardly unique in its thirst for political information. French authorities also kept their *fiches*. As late as 1919 the leader of the Radical Socialists, Eduard Herriot, charged the Ministry of the Interior, then a Radical fiefdom, with being "an organ of the political police; there elections are made; there orthodoxy is put under surveillance."[21] But in France, information was used to reward and punish. It became the key to unlocking the votes of whole communes. The German governments, in contrast, did nothing. And without making their information "operational" against the district, what was the good of even the most perfect surveillance?

Indeed, since surveillance rarely went undetected, its impact was less to threaten than to make the government look ridiculous. What impression must it make when a speaker stared at an informant and said, "Go ahead, take down everything I say and send it to the Landrat"?[22] As early as 1882 people joked about the hosts of police hovering around the Progressive Moses Oppenheimer at every public appearance. "Moses' guardian angels," they quipped.[23] If, as Conservatives argued, every Reichstag election injured existing authority, then the mockery provoked by authority's hamhandedness injured it most of all.

Of course lower officials could and did act independent of any cabinet-level policy. We have already seen that the Landrat might influence tax assessments. "Little Bismarcks" in the form of mayors threatened their villages with corvée for disloyal voting.[24] "The power of the state is powerful . . . even in the hand of the last night watchman and rural constable," Lasker insisted;[25] and the parade of evidence of partisanship against especially the *gendarmerie* compel us to agree.[26] But petty tyranny had existed before the democratic franchise, and by putting bullying into a wider political context, the elections now encouraged resistance.

Ultimately, it was only the states' own personnel that surveillance could in-

---

with replies: GLA 236/14901 (Baden); Göhre, *Three Months*, 102f. Sometimes citizens themselves sent in evidence of disloyal sentiment: Aug. Michaelis, Hotelier in Neubrandenburg, to Bötticher [19 Feb. 1890], BAB-L R1501/14693, Bl. 228; Oberingeneur Fr. Ruppert to Bülow, Chemnitz, 10 Jan. 1906 (*sic*), BAB-L R1501/14697, Bl. 141.

[20] Wm. Funcke to Puttkamer, Hagen, 23 Dec 1881, BAB-L R43/685, Bl. 42, 43–47v.

[21] Quoted in Charnay, *Les scrutins*, 101.

[22] Horn Report, 24 Feb. 1907, LHAK 408/8806; open criticism by small businessman: Onrod (sp.?) to BR, Beelitz, 30 June 1903, BAB-L R1501/14696, Bl. 20f.

[23] 2 Düsseldorf: AnlDR (1882/83, 5/II, Bd. 6) DS 263: 969f. Mockery of surveillance: Ernst, *Polizeispitzeleien*, 6; Fontane, *Stechlin*, 145–48, 166, 228–30, 262; Hall, *Scandal*, 54. Complaints: "Wahlaufruf" 30 Sept. 1906 (sent 1907), BAB-L R1501/14697, Bl. 109f.

[24] 17 Han., AnlDR (1881, 4/IV, Bd. 4) DS 104: 622, 624–26. "Bismarck im Kleinen": Seyffardt, *Erinnerungen*, 241.

[25] Quoted in Poschinger Report, 11 Feb. 1879, BAB-L R1501/14450. Similar views: Schücking, *Reaktion*, 99; v. Saldern, *Wege*, 175, 183; Müller, *Geschichte*, 184; Hall, *Scandal*, 24, 54, 92f.

[26] Sachse (SD) on Bochum, SBDR 10 May 1912: 1828–30; AnlDR (1912/13 13/I, Bd. 17) DS 403: 346–48.

timidate in large enough numbers to influence outcomes. Railway, postal, and shipyard workers were subjected to intense pressure.[27] Higher up, each civil servant was made to feel personally responsible for the turnout and tallies of the unit under his purview. And if a Landrat himself should run and lose, his suitability for his post was called into question.[28]

But it is well to put these pressures in perspective. Germany's were not the only public employees subjected to election intimidation; nor were they ever required, as in some locales in the United States, to cough up an informal tax on their salaries in the form of a "contribution" to the government party's campaign chest.[29] The weight of government pressure on civil servants, moreover, was not always retrograde. When Baden officials learned of the presence of gymnasial teachers at antisemitic rallies (a "truly sad sign of the times," the informant commented, "that so many educated men find pleasure in antisemitic hooliganism"), they forbade their participation—with success. The government of Hessen, encouraged by its grand duke, who hated "the persecution of the Jews," also took steps in 1892 to ensure that none of its teachers participated in antisemitic politics, and saw that they were stringently enforced.[30]

And no government succeeded in enforcing complete conformity. Dissent cropped up in the most unlikely places. Take the teacher in Elbing-Marienburg who was summoned to his Landrat's office in 1884 after the latter learned that he had failed to stand up when a cheer was offered for the Conservative candidate—a brother of the Interior Minister. The teacher spoke with a lawyer and decided not to appear. It did not belong to his duties, he declared, to have to cheer for Herr von Puttkamer.[31] By the nineties it was taken for granted that many middle- and lower-level government workers were voting Left Liberal or SPD.[32] After 1902, as civil servants began to feel the pinch of higher food prices brought on by the "Bülow" tariffs, some were so bold as to let the chancellor know their dissatisfaction in the form of an explicit threat not to support the government at election time.[33] A united front behind the Conserva-

[27] Shipyards: 3 Danzig, AnlDR (1882/83, 5/II, Bd. 5) DS 80: 338–49; SBDR 16 June 1882: 541–43 and 2 Dec. 1882: 582–602; President of RT to Bis., 15 June 1882; Bis. to Adm. v. Stosch, 16 June 1882, Rear Adm. Livonius to Bötticher, 16 June 1882; B.[ötticher?] to Stosch, Nov. 1882; Stosch to B[ötticher?], 27 Nov. 1882; B[öttischer?] to Stosch 2 Dec. 1882, BAB-L R1501/14641, Bl. 147f, 151, 153–55. Bebel, Gröber SBDR 26 Feb. 1907: 60, 125.

[28] Bis. to Hohenlohe, Straßburg, n.d. [Feb. 1887], BAB-L R1501/14643, Bl. 2f; *Amtsvorstand* Tauberbischofsheim to Baden MdI, 16 Jul. 1893, GLA 236/14901, Bl. 14c; Horn Report, 24 Feb. 1907, LHAK 408/8806. Threats to seminary director (2 Gumb.), "Zwei Fragen an die königliche Staatsregierung," *NL Correspondenz* 49/1 (3 Jan. 1912), BAB-L R1501/14460, Bl. 140. "Wie Bismarck" 1/5: 11; "Wahlaussichten für die Provinz Pommern" and "Wahlaussichten für die Provinz Brandenburg": GStA PK I, HA, Rep. 89/210, Bl. 215, 237.

[29] US naval yard: Argersinger, "Perspectives," 682; tax: Seymour/Frary, *World* 1: 258.

[30] Smith, "Alltag," 284; Levy, *Downfall*, 137–41.

[31] Rickert SBDR 9 Apr. 1886: 2015f; Möllers, *Strömungen*, 332.

[32] Ulrich, Oberrevisor, to Graf [Caprivi], Dessau, 27 June 1893, BAB-L R1501/14694, Bl. 39; in Saxony: Retallack, "Antisocialism," 69; Hanover: Ehrenfeuchter, *Willensbildung*, 211ff; "Working," 271, 279.

[33] Wm. Kohlsdorf, Bitterfeld, to Bülow, 28 Dec. 1906, BAB-L R1501/14697, Bl. 56f; Anon. to

tive candidate was sometimes missing even among higher, "political" officials.[34] Although most dissident officials were careful to keep their politics to themselves, after 1888 (and the fall of the egregious "Minister of Elections," Robert von Puttkamer), the state was equally quiet about disciplining them. Exemplary punishments were out of the question. For unlike other bread lords, government employers faced real penalties if word of retaliation got out: at the very least, an embarrassing outcry, and potentially, an overturned election.[35]

The significance of these facts for the fate of Bismarck's project cannot be overestimated. By refusing to calibrate material benefits and (large-scale) penalties according to voting behavior, the German state denied itself the very tool that made the French franchise "work"—thus eliminating the main rationale for manhood suffrage in an authoritarian system. What could Bismarck have thought was left? The royalism of the rural population is emphasized by the older literature, although just how far Bismarck, so unsentimental himself, relied on the sentiment of others may be doubted. The potential for bureaucratic manipulation has been emphasized in modern accounts. Certainly the Prussian cabinet thought long and hard about ways to stack the deck; the notion of "ambulatory election panels," for example, which would increase "participation" by going from house to house to collect the ballots of indolent voters, was one idea that kept turning up. But the recognition that such measures would carry a "strong police-state aftertaste" defeated them all.[36]

Not in manipulation, but in organization: there lay the government's opportunity under the new election law. Before Socialists and Progressives dreamt of building their political machines, before the Catholic clergy demonstrated that they already had one, the state was there. In a traditional society, the state's ability to coordinate, communicate, and distribute would immediately advantage any candidate it favored. The larger the electorate, the greater the advantage—especially when the replacement of indirect with direct elections ended its opponents' ability to target a few limited pressure points. A massive expansion of the electorate, voting directly, in a world that was still dispersed, rural, and small scale: *this* was to be the secret of manhood suffrage for a bureaucratic state.

The state's infrastructural advantage was indeed formidable. But it was an advantage that, as we have seen, disappeared almost overnight: thanks to the efforts of the clergy in Catholic districts, thanks to competitive party organization in urbanized areas elsewhere. And outside rural East Elbia, where the provincial administration remained a significant auxiliary for conservatives, the

---

B., Frankfurt a.M., 10 Jan. 1907, ibid., Bl. 146. T. Barth, "Erziehung zur Heuchelei," *Die Zeit* II/50 (12 Sept. 1903): 741–44.

[34] LR Köller's candidacy, for example, was opposed by the prefect! "Wie Bismarck" 1/5: 11.

[35] Fairbairn makes this point forcefully: *Democracy*, 69–109, 247. Cf. Suval, *Politics* (1985), 44. Bodewig, *Wahlbeeinflussungen*, 138; L. v. Bar, "Wahlrecht und Beamtenverhältnis," *Das Recht. Rundschau für den deutschen Juristenstand* 14/1 (10 Jan. 1910), cols. 1–4.

[36] Roon, "Votum," 27 May 1866, BAB-L R43/685, Bl. 23. Bis. had broached the matter in 1864: B. to SM, 23 Dec. 1864, ibid., Bl. 11f.

state's infrastructure, since its successes might provoke invalidation, was a wasting asset.

A second advantage the German government is said to have enjoyed was its power to respond to a defeat in parliament by dissolving the Reichstag, thereby setting the theme of the ensuing campaign.[37] Five times—in 1878, 1887, 1890, 1893, and 1907—it did just that. These elections have been considered "plebiscites," a term that carries authoritarian overtones. Yet although it is sometimes argued that the mere threat of a dissolution allowed the chancellor to "discipline" a wayward Reichstag, that threat played a much more powerful role in parliamentary Britain, where parties and candidates, not the state, as in Germany, had to bear an elections' administrative costs. Indeed, these five elections bear a closer resemblance to the polling that follows a dissolution of the House of Commons, when a defeated government takes its case to the people, than to an authoritarian plebiscite, where an otherwise silenced public is offered a single choice.[38]

In 1907 Bülow actually made the case for the executive's unprecedented level of campaigning by citing his counterparts in England and France, a parallel that provoked the inevitable rejoinder that *those* statesmen were also party leaders.[39] It was an important distinction—but one that pointed to the weakness of the German government, not to its strength. For even as the logic of the electoral process was eroding the strict dualism dividing executive and legislature, and conservative citizens were urging Bülow to "step down among the people," the government was caught within a set of traditional and constitutional expectations that led it to continue to insist that it was "no party government," that it pursued "the goals . . . that His Majesty the Kaiser has prescribed. . . ."[40] Unfortunately for the chancellor, the opposition agreed that "the heaviest reproach that can be made to any government is the reproach of being a party government."[41] As long as this shared conception persisted, Bismarck and even Bülow, unlike Gladstone and Asquith, was condemned to campaign via surrogates: warriors' associations and patriotic leagues, certainly, but ulti-

[37] Michael Stürmer, *Regierung und Reichstag im Bismarckstaat, 1871–1880: Cäserismus oder Parlamentarismus* (Düsseldorf, 1974): 114; Wehler, *Empire*, 57. More nuanced: Steinbach, *Zähmung*, esp. 3: 1973.

[38] Anthony Trollope's *Phineas Finn* (1869) vividly portrays the impecunious British MP's fear of a possible dissolution. Pollmann suggests that 1867 was the most genuinely plebiscitary of German elections: *Parlamentarismus*, 102, and 102n. 50. C. zu Hohenlohe described elections in AL as having a "fully plebiscitary character." 3 May 1893, GStA PK I, HA, Rep. 89/211, Bl. 182–86. Citizens themselves sometimes asked for a plebiscite: Prof. Dr. A. Müller, Chemnitz, to Wm. II, 16 Dec. 1894, BAB-L R1501/14694, Bl. 60f.

[39] Wiemer (FVp) SBDR 27 Feb. 1907: 82.

[40] Mangler, "Die Anfechtung von Reichstags Wahlen," *DN* (25 Feb. 1912), BAB-L R1501/14653, unpaginated; and quotes: Ernst Krieger (pseudonym?), Lt. a.D., to Bülow, Bad-Kreuznach, 5 Jan. 1907, BAB-L R 1501/14697, Bl. 105f; Bötticher SBDR 2 Dec. 1882: 602.

[41] Lasker SBDR 2 Dec. 1882: 584; also Rickert ("above parties") SBDR 2 Dec. 1882: 584, 595. For the SPD, however "the question whether or not the government is a *party government* simply leaves us cold." Kayser, ibid., 591. Disagreeing that the government could not constitutionally take part in elections: Zoepfl, *Grundsätze* 2: 282–83n. 1.

mately through friendly political parties. By 1893 at the latest, however, no party was truly reliable. The Conservatives and the National Liberals, although eager to draw on the state's resources, had agendas of their own, not all of them desired by the chancellor. And about those other "block" parties elected during Bülow's 1907 "plebiscite"—Left Liberals and antisemites—the imperial government could only have the gravest misgivings.

But there is an even more telling reason why the "plebiscitary" option offered the executive no real way to gain control of the Reichstag. Unlike a genuine plebiscite, which a government might win, these plebiscitary campaigns were always a lose-lose proposition. It is true that when Bismarck appeared in the streets after dissolving the Reichstag in December 1886, he was greeted with cheering crowds throwing their hats into the air. Bülow's December 1906 dissolution produced a similar response. And it is also true that three of these "plebiscites"—1878, 1887, and 1907—returned a Reichstag whose majority claimed to support the government's line. But in each case, participation in the campaign politicized the very crown that the dualistic constitution was intended to shield. The interventions of the King of Saxony and the Grand Duke of Baden may have led the way here.[42] But most conspicuous was William II, who allowed nationalist pressure groups and rightist politicians to turn his person into a political mascot.

We see this most clearly in 1907, when the first balloting fell on the eve of William II's birthday. Hearts swelling at their monarch's "courage" in dissolving parliament, supporters of the government made a point of describing any vote against the Centrum, the Social Democrats, the Guelfs, or the Poles as a birthday present for their Kaiser. They swarmed into Berlin's streets to cheer him as he appeared on his balcony to greet the results of the polling. Telegrams, letters, and cards—from old and young, men and women, workers and doctoral students—congratulated him on "his" victory. So close was the association between the "plebiscite" and the monarch's person that correspondents from as far away as Vienna, Amsterdam, Paris, Pau, Eastbourn, Essex, New York, and even Blomfontain sent him passionate election greetings. To many of these well-wishers, the Kaiser sent his personal thanks.[43]

Some of these missives were harmless enough, such as the postcard trumpeting the defeat of Magdeburg's SPD incumbent, designed by a champagne salesman, Hermann Spannuth, and graced with the self-important slogan *"Nur Muth, sagt Spannuth!"*[44]

[42] Telegrams to Bavaria's king: Dönhoff to Bis., Dresden, 23 Feb. 1887, BAB-L R1501/14642, Bl. 173. On the grand duke: Singer SBDR 11 Nov. 1889: 230.
[43] There are 120 in the unpaginated Beiheft of Rep. 89. Additional congratulations are in Königliches Geh. Civil-Cabinet, in GStA PK I, HA, Rep. 89/215. LR Fhr. v. Lauer of Ottweiler, Trier, to Wm. II, 7 Feb. 1907, asking permission to allow the press of the national parties to publish the Kaiser's telegram to him, to use against the Dasbach (Z) press. Reply: "No objection." GStA PK I, HA, Rep. 89/213. Fr. Krupp founded the *Süddeutsche Korrespondenz* in order to supply South Germany with a *"ganz auf die Person des Kaisers ausgerichtetes Blatt."* Jaeger, *Unternehmer*, 184. The trend is satirized in Mann, *Der Untertan*.
[44] "Just have courage," says Spannuth. GStA PK I, HA, Rep. 89/215.

WILHELM KOBELT.

Nur Mut, sagt „Spannuth"
da wurde sogleich Herr Fleischermeister **Wilhelm Kobelt** zum
Reichstags-Abgeordneten der Stadt „Magdeburg" gewählt.

RESULTAT:
Wilhelm Kobelt (Lib.) . . . . **26,222** Stimmen
Pfannkuch (Soz.) . . . . **24,257** do.
(bisheriger Abgeordneter)

Hermann Spannuth, Magdeburg
Vertreter der
Sectkellerei CHR. ADT. KUPFERBERG & Co., Hoflieferanten, MAINZ

Fig. 13. Souvenir postcard celebrating victory of master butcher Wilhelm Kobelt
(lib.) over the SPD incumbent in Magdeburg, 1907, paid for by Hermann Spannuth,
champagne merchant. The reverse side prints Bülow's response to the victory
telegram of Magdeburg's "national" parties, thanking them for their dedication and
unity. Spannuth mailed the postcard "out of joy" to the Kaiser, using the occasion
respectfully to introduce himself.

Others were less benign. Of the many poems sent to William to commemorate his "heroic" victory, one urged:

Majesty, Majesty, just don't flinch
Although Berlin be ever so *red*,
All of these fellows are going to be lynch'd:
Long live the Black-White-Red.[45]

Associating itself with such partisanship destroyed the crown as a symbol of national unity. Many citizens found their government's connivance at the vicious attacks on the opposition "nauseating."[46] Bebel claimed that he got 100,000 extra votes every time the Kaiser gave a speech. This disgust, as much as anything else, helps explain the discouraging story told by the popular vote, even in the "plebiscites" that produced spectacular "wins," in terms of seats, for the government.[47] In 1887, the victorious Kartell won only 47.3 percent of the vote; the even broader coalition of Bülow Bloc parties in 1907, only 38.9 percent. That meant that 61.1 percent of the country had voted for the opposition.

Each plebiscitary campaign, moreover, encouraged the very mobilization that was drawing wider and wider sections of the population into the orbit of the parties and destroying the consensual political culture for which many older Germans so longed—and on which the monarch's authority ultimately depended. In 1907, the Poles and Centrum, whose finite constituencies were already highly mobilized, nevertheless added hundreds of thousands of new voters: an "absolutely colossal gain," a contemporary noted. The SPD, even as it lost seats, added a quarter million voters. At best, plebiscitary victories were quick fixes, with every artificial high invariably and immediately followed by a crash that left the pro-government total in the next election even lower than its pre-plebiscite starting point—and leaving it fewer unmobilized reserves for the future.[48] The three successful campaigns of 1878, 1887, and 1907 were therefore only bumps of air on a curve of support that otherwise sank continuously from 1871 to 1912.

As for a chancellor's other electoral assets, these were penny ante indeed. The county gazettes, which got his position out (though at the price of continual protests);[49] a "reptile" press, surviving on secret handouts (and very little re-

---

[45] Stammtisch Müller, Dresden. Ibid.

[46] Amicus to Bülow, n.d. (shortly before 1907 balloting), BAB-L R 1501/14697, Bl.107f. A call for peace and moderation between government and SPD (with a promise to "tell the same to Herr Bebel"): No Name (*"thut nichts zur Sache!"*) to Bülow, Berlin, 3 Jan. 1907, ibid., Bl. 73.

[47] Noted by Le Maistre, Darmstadt, to Bismarck, 23 Feb. 1887. BAB-L R1501/14642, Bl. 177. Bebel: Hall, *Scandal*, 155.

[48] Quote: "Beschämende Zahlen," *Die Neue Gesellschaft* 3/19 (6 Feb. 1907): 217. The percentage of votes cast for K, FK, and NL parties in 1881 was 6.4% below their totals in 1877; in 1890, 4.3% below their totals in 1884; and in 1912, 1.5% below those of 1903. Calculated from Ritter/Niehuss, *Arbeitsbuch*, 38–42. Sperber's similar point: *Voters*, 268f.

[49] BAB-L R1501/14694, Bl. 196; 13 Saxony AnlDR (1887–88, 7/II, Bd. 4) DS 212: 907; Zangerl, "Opening," 276f; Fenske, "Landrat," 446–52. MdI secret subsidies and *Kreisblätter* policy: Müller, *Strömung*, 57–62.

spect);[50] subsidies for groups that might prove disruptive to the government's enemies (75,000 marks went to Father Eduard Cronenberg, a thorn in the side of Aachen's Centrum in the seventies—but one unable to bring it down).[51] The military could call up the reserves right before an election—which might, it hoped, increase the tendency of the men to vote "patriotic" when they returned home.[52] And under Interior Minister Puttkamer, as we have seen, the state made life easier for the government's allies by interpretations of the law that kept precincts as small—and voting as transparent—as possible.[53] Notorious was the state's capacity to harass editors and balloteers, to shut down (temporarily) political rallies, to prosecute criticism under the guise of *lèse majesté*—invoked by 1900 against almost 300 citizens annually. Individual officials could also chill free speech by initiating libel actions. Bismarck is said to have been personally responsible for almost 10,000.[54] But the law, which might empower the state, also restricted it—as we have also seen.

Finally, the chancellor could use administrative discretion to *time* elections and runoffs in ways calculated to work to the government's advantage.[55] But even here legal and technical considerations left little wiggle room.[56] In the end, no tinkering with timing could overcome the lack of good choices, as was clear in 1912 when the imperial government chose to hold runoffs on three different days, spread over a five-day period. It was this decision that holds the key to the strange events in Nordhausen with which we opened. Although local Rightists had initially promised Otto Wiemer their runoff support, presumably because of assurances he had made, Wiemer had also, as chief of the Progressives, negotiated a series of bargains for his party, nationwide, with the SPD. The arrangement was guarded in strictest secrecy, but the first two sets of runoffs revealed to one and all which way the Progressive wind was blowing. When Wiemer's own runoff occurred, on the fifth day, the Right requited what they saw as a betrayal by executing an abrupt *volte face*, throwing their support

[50] Lerman, *Chancellor*, 116–18; Saul, "Kampf," 191–95. Cf. Napoleon III: Zeldin, *System*, 112f.

[51] Lepper, ed., *Katholizismus*, esp. 177f, 186f, 194–99.

[52] Done in Saxony: Dönhoff to Bis., Dresden, 23 Feb. 1887, BAB-L R1501/14642, Bl. 173f.

[53] Puttkamer to the RPen, 7 Sept. 1884, BAB-L R1501/14642, Bl. 9, 39.

[54] Libel: Hall, *Scandal*, 66–70. Suval, *Politics*, 42; LR Fhr v. Riedesel, 30 Jul. 1891, BAB-L R1501/14667, Bl. 51v; 3 yrs. for lèse majesté: 1899, BAB-L R101/3386, Bl. 187–202.

[55] See chap. 9, n. 51; LR Seydewitz of Görlitz, n.d. ca. 1881, quoted in "Wie Bismarck" 1/5: 9. Citizen requests to Bis. about timing: unsigned, Königsberg, 9 June 1878; unsigned, Dresden, 13 June 1878: BAB-L R1501/14693, Bl. 34f; Große Carnevals-Gesellschaft zu Cöln, 17 Jan. 1887, Gelbke v. Benedictus to RdI, Dresden, 17 Feb. 1887; Bis. to Puttkamer, 14 Feb. 1887: all in BAB-L R1501/14642, Bl. 105f, 124, 147; B. Gehle (worker) to Bis., Munich, 4 Jan. 1907: BAB-L R1501/14697, Bl. 91f.

[56] Protocols of SM and memo on the same: BAB-L R1501/14460, Bl. 121. The public cottoned on to the advantages of various election dates: Rickert et al., Interpellation 29 Aug. 1883, BAB-L R1501/14451, Bl. 188. Discussion about timing throughout 1902 in *VossZ, SchlZ, Danziger Ztg, Berliner Börsen-Ztg, Deutsche Tageszeitung, FrZ, Berliner Neueste Nachrichten, Badische Landes-Ztg, National-Ztg, Reichsbote.* BAB-L R1501/14455; and again in 1911 (BAB-L R1501/14460): *Deutsche Tageszeitung, VossZ, BT, Deutsche Juristen Ztg, Der Tag.*

behind the Social Democrat.[57] It was to this—the chancellor's decision not to hold runoffs simultaneously—rather than to the influence of the local bureaucracy that Oskar Cohn really owed his "governmental" victory.

It comes as no surprise that a government so hamstrung by its constitutional premises should continually contemplate changing the law that deprived it of the majorities it needed to carry out its work. Over the years imperial officials researched, deliberated, and debated a number of ideas, including those suggested by friendly voters.[58] But any alteration, however slight, risked triggering a discussion of first principles that might snowball into comprehensive legislation that would sweep away the government's few remaining bastions of support.[59] Moreover, no reform that benefited the pro-government parties would ever pass the Reichstag. Awareness of this absolute barrier was what led some on the Right to contemplate abolishing the democratic franchise altogether. The *Staatsstreich*, as we saw in chapter 8, was a temptation to which successive German chancellors were repeatedly drawn, but ultimately knew they must resist.[60] For the only feasible alternative to becoming a parliamentary monarchy was to keep alive the imperial government's claim to being "the State": that is, the embodiment of the law, or at least the impartial administrator of it. Partisanship was corrosive enough to this idea—something the government uneasily sensed, even as it continued to intervene in partisan ways. Illegality of any kind would kill it. For all the fears of Max Weber and others about "caesarism," as far as elections were concerned the appropriate metaphor for the government was not Caesar, but Gulliver.[61]

Yet we must be careful. For if the government was weak, the state was strong. Its strength lay not in the power to determine outcomes, but in its ability to maintain the default settings, the essential framework, in which election contests could take place. Dankwart Rustow, in his "dynamic model" of democratic transitions, noted only one aspect of this framework: clear geographical boundaries that are recognized by most citizens. In confining his "preconditions" for democracy to this one point, Rustow sold the state short. For it is not just the solidity of boundaries, but the strength of the state and the assumptions it estab-

---

[57] Teased out of Bertram, *Wahlen*, 224–34, 241f. In 4 S-H the BdL refused to honor its runoff agreement with NLs under similar circumstances. Hof SBDR, 28 Mar. 1912: 1137.

[58] E.g., on compulsory voting: Reichskanzlei to SS des I, 21 Jan. 1907, BAB-L R1501/14458, Bl. 65; MdI to SS des AAs, 4 May 1907, ibid. Bl. 67; T. L[ewald?], Ministerialdirektor, ibid., 14460, Bl. 191–98. Newspaper articles on same: ibid., 14459, Bl. 84, 86–8y.

[59] See chap. 10, n. 107. Also: Puttkamer to Bis., and his reply: 25 Mar. 1887, BAB-L R1501/14452, Bl. 221–23.

[60] Some voters were also tempted: BAB-L R1501/files: 14693, Bl. 36f; 14697, Bl. 144f; BAB-L R43/685, Bl. 219f. Others, however, advised unambiguous support for the RT franchise: BAB-L R1501/files: 14694, Bl. 191f; 14697, Bl. 76f, 91f. D[elbrück], "Auflösung," 184–87.

[61] "Caesarism": Mommsen, *Weber*, 7. I found no signs in the elections that *Chancellor* Bismark disposed of any charisma; such charismatic authority as he wielded developed in his retirement. Contrast Wehler, *Gesellschaftsgeschichte* 3: 483f, 849 (where he uses the much more apt description, "Great Coordinator"), 8651, 1293. I rate the fairness of the Germany's courts more highly than does Hall, *Scandal*, 70–75. Supporting evidence: Ernst, Polizeispitzeleien, 50, 64–67, 75.

lishes—within its staff and within the population at large—that allow conflict to become competition in the first place. To borrow from James Madison: a government must be able to control the governed as well as be obliged to control itself.[62] A state must be able to ensure a minimally honest count and, especially, to preserve public order. We have not discussed these requisites much in the preceding pages, for it is always their absence rather than their presence that commands the notice of contemporaries.[63] There are of course no absolute criteria for ascertaining when a state is strong "enough." The German official was notorious (in some circles) for his arrogance and hair-splitting observance of red tape; he was also celebrated (in others) for representing the "rights of those whom he is administering, even against the state." We need swallow neither the critique nor the mystique in order to acknowledge that the German *Obrigkeitsstaat* protected its voters better than the English liberal state at mid-century or the American and Italian states at its end—when broken heads were a common accompaniment of the polling; nor to suspect that it may have been better equipped to foster habituation to democratic procedures than even the more peaceable regions of the American "party state" of the same period—whose bureaucracy, police, and judiciary were often acknowledged partisans, and grand juries, run as partisan machines, sometimes refused to indict election officials for voting fraud.[64]

We have seen in these pages that the state's men could be maddeningly unfair. But the ideal of universal procedures enforced by an impartial civil service established a standard that tended not only to discipline the contenders, but to curb the state's own personnel. Consequently, even among the most high-handed officials, there were clear limits. Poll watchers were thrown out of polling places; but no German of whom I am aware was ever seriously injured for campaigning, much less beaten to death. Police and local officials felt only too free to confiscate oppositional ballots from distributors, even to snatch them from a voter's hand. But no ballots, so far as I am aware, were ever destroyed by the police once they were cast; and the police allowed no one else to do so either.[65]

If we are going to stress, with Rustow, Przeworski, and other theorists, de-

---

[62] "You must first enable the government to control the governed; and in the next place oblige it to control itself." *Federalist*, quoted in Huntington, "Meaning," 24.

[63] Hooliganism at election time was not unknown: Hörde (bosses' thugs vs. SDs), AnlDR (1890/91, 8/I, Bd. 3) DS 292: 2055, 2057; 7 Gumb. (Ks vs. NLs), AnlDR (1912/14, 13/I, Bd. 23) DS 1586; Harburg in 1878: Kutz-Bauer, *Arbeiterschaft*, 133. Troops were summoned to Darmstadt in 1884 after SDs broke up two F rallies: White, *Party*, 132. There were fracases at victory celebrations, especially when losers felt robbed, as Poles did in Schwetz and as Z supporters did in Saarbrücken. Bertram, *Wahlen*, 203. But these were exceptional—and police powers were invoked instantly.

[64] A. Ernst v. Ernsthausen, *Erinnerungen eines Preußischen Beamten* (Bielefeld and Leipzig, 1894), 287 (quote); Otto Hintze, "Der Beamtenstand," *Vorträge der Gehe-stiftung zu Berlin* 3 (Leipzig, 1911): 1–78; esp. 69, 72, 74, 76; Argersinger, "Perspectives," 682. Ernst, *Polizeispitzeleien*, 50. When SDs argued that the MdI put provocateurs in their midst, the courts on occasion backed them. Ibid., 64–67, 75.

[65] Reported misdeeds were prosecuted. BAB-L R1501/14703, Bl. 271–86. Hamburg contrasted to Prussia: Kutz-Bauer, *Arbeiterschaft*, 368–70, 381–85, 413f, 414n. 289.

mocracy "as a matter primarily of procedure rather than of substance," of "institutionalizing uncertainty," then the ability of a state to guarantee the stability of its procedures, the certainties within which "uncertainty" can fruitfully operate, becomes *the* crucial component in providing channels for the conflicts that are the substance of political life.[66] The German state proved both willing and able to enforce the rules, even against itself. The Imperial Office of Domestic Affairs, and the chancellors, were enlisted, ex officio, by parliament to insure that refractory member states abide by the election codes. Even Bismarck found himself drawn in, forced to pursue the cause of a Mecklenburg gardener, surely the last chick in the rural pecking order, who had been improperly deprived of his vote. The iron chancellor finally succeeded in getting Mecklenburg to discipline its election official—but only by threatening the duchy not to defend it against a Reichstag interpellation.[67] That this was the threat that proved so compelling is itself not without significance.

HIERARCHY, COMMUNITY, AND COMPETITION

Much of our discussion in these pages has concerned itself with barriers to exercising a free vote. Those that Germans confronted most continually, however, came from a quarter that was all but impossible for the state to reach: from entrenched local hierarchies and from relations founded on economic and social need. We have seen how big men expected to decide on nominations and determine balloting, and how they enforced these expectations. Often just as exigent when the outcome was foreseeable as when the race hung by a thread, their motives had little to do with utility and everything to do with authority.

For it was the nature of the imperial franchise to turn every contest into a challenge to authority. On election day, "even the most miserable and downtrodden person, who sees himself oppressed and enslaved year after year, gets a feeling of humanity, of human dignity, and says to himself: for once I too am a man who counts for something. I, the poorest man and the most oppressed day laborer, count for as much as the Herr Estate-Owner. . . ."[68] This change in subjectivity is universal suffrage's most telling consequence. The "moral status" it confers, argue Martin Harrop and William Miller, "acts as a further shield. . . . a source of self-respect which is the most important limit on exploitation of

---

[66] "Procedure": Rustow, "Transitions," 345, "uncertainty": Przeworski, *Democracy*, 15, 26, 32.

[67] Anderson, "Voter," 1474. Hohenlohe used the same threat when Württ. failed to hold an election immediately after the death of an incumbent. H. (signed by Posadowsky) to Württ. SM, 30 Mar. 1898, BAB-L R1501/14454, Bl. 118–20. Denying that the imperial government had a legal obligation to enforce the *RT's* interpretation of the electoral laws, even as he affirmed that it would continue to do so: Dr. Schulze in RdI, n.d. [ca. 1912] BAB-L R1501/14460, Bl. 412f.

[68] Kayser SBDR 9 Dec. 1885: 245f (quote); similarly, Helldorf SBDR 9 Dec. 1885: 243; and 3 Feb. 1888: 699—but then he retreated: 747. Quoted (along with Rauchhaupt [K] SBHA, 6 Dec. 1883) by Rickert SBDR 7 Feb. 1888, 743f; Joh. Geo. Allen, Dresden, to Wm. II, 1 Mar. 1903, BAB-L R1501/14695, Bl. 93–105; Treitschke deplored the franchise for giving the masses a "fantastic overestimation of their own power and own value." Kühne, *Dreiklassenwahlrecht*, 400.

all."[69] That Germans cherished their new dignity is proved not only by turnouts that eventually topped 80 percent (for some of these men, as we have seen, had no choice but to vote), but especially by the reluctance of the poor to accept public relief, because to do so would disenfranchise them.[70] For little men too, the vote was charged with meaning out of all proportion to any foreseeable impact on policy.

Not surprisingly, therefore, the "Day of Equality" for the worker became a "Day of Horror" for the master.[71] As one citizen confided in a letter to the Kaiser, "the simple voter reasons, if I can decide the fate of the state, if I have as much political power as the Herr Pastor or the Herr Baron, then I must be entitled to eat as well as the pastor or the baron." This conclusion may not, as the correspondent believed, have led directly to "communism." But it did establish a cognative dissonance that encouraged a critical spirit, a condition of "continual latent revolution."[72]

The impact was visible in the behavior of the candidates. On election day, "even His Grace, the Herr Count, or His Highness the Prince, must 'kindly condescend' to step down among his constituents," Bebel gloated.[73] The evidence was there as early as 1872, when the Duke of Ratibor, who only the year before had refused even to reply to questions from his constituents, began to "kindly condescend" in his effort to recapture his seat from the Centrum. Recognizing that impoverished Upper Silesian voters were not likely to identify with *him*, the duke now went to considerable lengths to insist that he identified with *them*. "I was born among ye," he proclaimed (in fact he was born in Rotenburg Castle in Hessen). "Speaking as one brother to another," he contrasted his own thirty-year domicile in the district (sharing "thick and thin") to the Berlin residency of his opponent, a man who spoke, he noted pointedly, "not a word of Polish."[74] But although his own Polish was pretty good, the duke's invocations of community fell flat, because democratic politics were already beginning to divorce the sense of community from mere physical proximity. "Why should we vote for a man who does not even live here?" citizens in the adjacent county asked, referring to the Duke—and voted again for the Berlin chaplain, Eduard Müller. With the criterion for public office palpably shifting from natural superiority over the voter to identity with him ("even the name of a man like 'Miller' offers a greater guarantee"),[75] the subversive implications of the new franchise were clear.

The significance of the challenge was demonstrated by the intensity of the elite's response. But as we have seen, a growing economy cushioned the impact

[69] *Elections*, 260f.

[70] Tennstedt, *Sozialgeschichte*, 205; also Warren, *Saxony*, 67.

[71] Kayser, glossing Minnigerode's pamphlet of 1881, SBDR 9 Dec. 1885: 245f.

[72] Joh. Geo. Allen, Dresden, to Wm. II, 1 Mar. 1903, BAB-L R1501/14695, Bl. 93–105.

[73] SBDR 10 Dec. 1885: 281; also Singer SBDR 3 Feb. 1888: 692.

[74] Ratibor's birthplace: Rust, *Reichskanzler*, 609; quotations: 623, 625f. Trzeciakowski, *Kulturkampf*, 29.

[75] Quoted by Schröder from a survey he made in the district: SBDR 22 Nov. 1871: 433f.

of threats, evictions, and dismissals, while the parties themselves, in a remarkably rapid display of organizational energy, exerted counterpressures. The earliest protections for the dissident voter, however, lay not in the parties, but in the communities, especially when, as in Saxony and parts west, a dense confluence of intermediate associations could give "community" some institutional form. In rural Protestant East Elbia, on the other hand, not least because of the weakness of such institutions, large numbers of voters remained at the mercy of their betters to the very end of the Reich. But elsewhere, one consequence of imperial elections was to undermine, locally, the bread lords' political and social power. As for the authority of the Catholic cleric, it was not diminished, but it was transformed, by being put in the service of a party whose national policy-makers were laymen.

The strength of these solidarity ties in the face of vertical pressures did not come automatically. It was the product of the Kulturkampf and of the class struggle that developed in the Empire's first decades. These were the "hot family feuds" that Dankwart Rustow argues an "infant democracy requires."[76] Both originated in a complex set of processes, but the new democratic franchise and the anxiety it triggered were significant components. The ensuing polarizations fueled a politics of identity that reinforced the hold of the community over its members. Historians of Imperial Germany, conceiving democratization as "emancipation" rather than empowerment, have had few good words to say for communities, whose toughness lay precisely in the degree to which individuals were *not* "emancipated" from them. Yet it was often these communal bonds that enabled the citizen to transcend the calculus of material advantage characteristic of both coerced voting and classic clientelism, and to vote "uneconomically."

The result was hardly a "political mass market," for the voter rarely acted as a consumer acts, expressing his taste as an individual. It was not in the exercise of individual freedom, but in competition between groups, that democratic practices took hold in Germany. And a process that was genuinely competitive at the national level was often the reflection of multitudes of precincts where competition was nonexistent. Although a strong element of horizontal solidarity acquits many, perhaps most, of these precincts of the charge of clientelism, it hardly exempts them from the description "elections without choice."[77]

Community was not, as we have seen, a stable entity. As regional and national organizations took on more and more electoral functions, they contributed to a process of abstraction, in which the community was redefined into something trans-local: confession, class, and, in most cases, party. It was with abstractions such as these that the voter eventually identified.

The consequences were significant. Through such abstractions people whose experiences were in large part still rooted in parishes, villages, and small towns, "learned," as Werner Frauendienst put it, "to think in the categories of the

[76] "Transitions," 355.

[77] Cf. Rouquié's argument (based on Latin America and Africa) about "gregarious voting." "Controls," 22–27.

Reich."[78] The jelling of identity politics, visible in the "Bebel caps" and "Bebel hair" worn by Social Democrats and in the Kaiser-mustaches of nationalists, was what enabled Germany's nascent political parties, at a much earlier stage than their counterparts in France, to "structure the vote."[79] It also allowed the parties to develop those disciplined constituencies that were so essential if they were to take advantage of the runoff elections that by 1912 decided every second race. The strength of the individual's identification with these abstractions made it possible for parties to demand the sacrifice of the voter's relative preference, in the real, existing *local* community, for the sake of a strategy aimed at producing the maximum number of seats nationally: the kind of sacrifice that produced Nordhausen's conservative, antisemitic support for Oskar Cohn in 1912.[80] Finally, it was these ties of identity that gave the parties their credibility as agents of intermediation between their own constituencies and other parties, and, acting with these parties, between the public and the government; that allowed them to perform the task of aggregating interests, without which no constructive legislation is possible.[81] It was to the strength of these ties—and to the members' growing parliamentary experience—that the Reichstag owed the muscle that it showed from the 1890s on.

There is no denying that these advantages for the abstract community exacted a stiff price in local conformity.[82] The threat of ostracism and boycott is no less coercive than eviction and dismissal. But enforced conformity was not unique to elections in imperial Germany. Any interest association—union, lobby, church, political party—if it is going to be able to act on behalf of its members, must be able to follow through on deals made in its name: to "deliver." And that means, as Adam Przeworski and others have pointed out, that they must be able to sanction members who attempt "to advance their particular goals at the cost of the collective interest. To have market power, unions must be able to punish workers who are eager to replace their striking colleagues; to have a strategic capacity, employers' associations must be able to control competition among firms in a particular industry."[83] Parties too can be effective only to the degree that they can maintain discipline among their adherents—in the Reichs-

---

[78] Frauendienst, "Demokratisierung," 742.

[79] "Structuring the vote": Leon D. Epstein, quoted in Fish, *Democracy*, 72f.

[80] Bertram, *Wahlen*, 225–32, has subjected Carl Schorske's argument in *German Social Democracy, 1905–1917: The Development of the Great Schism* (New York, 1955) that the LLs were not able to "deliver" on their election bargains with SDs, to searching, and I think convincing, criticism, rejecting (232n. 1) Schorske's conclusion that "the elections of 1912 revealed that the cleavage in public opinion followed the divide of middle class and workers, not that of Junkers and middle class." Statistics: Suval, *Politics*, 40.

[81] A point Nipperdey makes regarding the Z: *Geschichte* 2: 492; and Fish, pointing to its absence in Russia: *Democracy*, 79.

[82] It is the resistance of the empire's "subcultures" to dissolving into a "pluralistically open society," not skepticism about the power of the RT, that leads Dieter Langewiesche to question the empire's democratization. "Das Deutsche Kaiserreich-Bemerkungen zur Diskussion über Parlamentisierung und Demokratisierung Deutschlands," *Archiv für Sozialgeschichte* 19 (1979): 628–42, 640f.

[83] *Democracy* (1991), 12.

tag, certainly, but also, in a system that necessitated runoffs, in places like Nordhausen and a hundred other constituencies. It is this uncomfortable reality that makes *just* tolerable, from the perspective of democratic theory, the pressures communities exerted on its adherents. The key term here is "adherent." For free elections also demand, on any theory of democracy going, that self-defined outsiders be protected from these same sanctions. How to square this circle? Only through a genuinely secret ballot.

DEMOCRACY'S APPRENTICES

In any society where, like Imperial Germany's, the governors are honest but the citizens are dependent, and where the penalties for dissent, whether exacted by one's masters or one's peers, are real, the protection of the ballot's secrecy becomes the overwhelming issue, as weighty for the development of free elections as the fight against bribery in England and fraud in the United States. Consequently, the debate over the democratic franchise that Germans missed in the sixties, when the *right* of the poor man to vote was bestowed from above, broke out in the eighties, in the struggle to *protect* the poor man's vote. Ambivalence about this protection was as strong in Germany as ambivalence about ending corruption in England. It pervaded society from top to bottom, since every stratum had an interest in monitoring voters and every party benefited from being able to penetrate the legally prescribed veil of secrecy. The institutional framework in which German elections took place, however, made protests easy, because the government bore the cost. And when protests by individuals against the violation of their ballots were brought before the Reichstag, the logic of party competition—under the glare of publicity provided by a burgeoning partisan press—forced all sides (except East Elbian conservatives, largely exempt from the discipline of competition) to join in demanding protections: ballot envelopes and voting booths.

The deputies' defense of the integrity of election procedures had deeper unintended consequences. For the logical corollary to any demand that the election be conducted according to the election code was an acknowledgment that all groups who were elected by these procedures had a legitimate place in the Reichstag. Thus the more the deputies insisted on procedures, the more deeply they became enmeshed in the defense of the franchise itself, and in its explicit egalitarianism. Ultimately they found themselves committed, rhetorically, to key aspects of democracy: equality, tolerance of dissent, an open society.[84] My argument that election competition forces antagonists into more and more democratic modes of behavior and argument was borne out as early as 1898, when the SPD and the Centrum vied in defense of the Reichstag franchise, making it the central issue of the campaign. Left Liberals joined the competition, as did, eventually, most of the National Liberals, whose Reichstag leadership now be-

---

[84] For analogous unintended consequences in Vienna: Boyer, *Culture*, 288.

gan to move decisively to the Left. The fact that by 1912 the Conservatives felt it necessary to make their support for "an unweakened Kaiser-power" their election theme shows us how far the balance had tipped in favor of parliament.[85]

The public defense—and enforcement—of the franchise by the majority of the deputies did not mean that all of them wished that the Reichstag become yet more perfectly representative. Nor did it mean that they longed to see the same system of direct, equal, and secret balloting extended to other arenas. Although in the decade before the war most of the German states reformed their franchises and—with the exceptions of Lübeck, Hamburg, and Saxony—in a dramatically democratic direction, elections to Prussia's Landtag and to most of the city halls remained unreformed.[86] Left Liberals would have lost out, following democratization of the municipal and Prussian franchises, to Social Democrats and Conservatives; National Liberals, to Social Democrats and the Centrum.[87] The Centrum, in the event of redistricting and Prussian Landtag reform, would have lost seats to the Left. And Left Liberals and Social Democrats—although this outcome often went unsaid—would have lost seats in any general enfranchisement of women.[88] The reluctance of any party to commit political suicide should not surprise. The penchant of historians for distinguishing between idealistic and self-interested reform proposals, between democrats and "democrats," obscures the obvious fact that nowhere in the world have political actors ever sponsored a franchise reform without calculating its probable partisan consequences. What is important is that competition pushed all political actors to cast those reforms that self-interest could tolerate (such as redistricting and PR, in the case of Left Liberals; such as the Reichstag franchise for municipalities, in the case of the Centrum) in an idiom that could only be a democratic one: that is, in an argument that invoked the popular will as the legitimate arbiter of public affairs.[89]

Further evidence of the leveling effects of competition can be seen when we look at the question of women's suffrage. Women already had the right to vote in some local bodies: as property owners in the rural communes and county diets of most places except the Prussian Rhineland and Bavaria west of the

[85] K Proclamation for 1 Frankfurt, AnlDR (13/I, Bd.) DS 480: 529. 1898 campaign: Kühne, *Dreiklassenwahlrecht*, 456.

[86] The southern states did introduce PR in some city and communal elections. Helmut Croon et al., *Kommunale Selbstverwaltung im Zeitalter der Industrialisierung* (Stuttgart, 1971), 47f. Dates of state franchise reform: Kühne, *Dreiklassenwahlrecht*, 25f.

[87] Richter in 1894 threatened resignation to force his FrVp to reject an extension of the RT franchise to communal elections. In Kiel, when the numbers of worker votes climbed too high for comfort, the LL majority in the city council raised the census. Only in 1910 did the united LLs—the FtVp—support the RT franchise for communal elections. Gagel, *Wahlrechtsfrage*, 143f, 158; Kühne, *Dreiklassenwahlrecht*, 407.

[88] Bebel realized it; Lily Braun did not. R. J. Evans, *Movement* (1976), 9; Braun, "Agitation," 201f.

[89] Even the conservatives conceded in 1910 the secret ballot for LT elections—discarding the alpha and omega of their previous policy—to solidify their new alliance with the Z, and in exchange for the Z's support for indirect voting. NL fury at the theft of their own political clothes gave the government an excuse to thwart the parliamentization implicit in the Blue-Black bid, and table the reform. Kühne, *Dreiklassenwahlrecht*, 550–56, 567f.

Rhine; and as wage-earners in elections choosing the boards administering state-regulated insurance funds. They were a presence in national election campaigns from the start. Some of their participation was not, strictly speaking, legal: they "bribed" voters with cake and beer, they rented bunks to floating voters who had falsified their residence papers, they voted as proxies for husbands (even a widow did this). But they had also participated legally: in audiences, usually with their husbands, at outdoor political addresses (even before the liberalization of the law of association and assembly in 1908); as composers of songs for victory celebrations; as signers of election protests and witnesses in investigations; as distribution points for leaflets and ballots; and in thinly disguised auxiliaries for the parties. Already in 1907 Lily Braun, comparing herself to the "ancient Teutons" on the warpath, had hit the campaign trail in search of SPD votes, proving herself the happiest of warriors.[90] With the formal liberalization of 1908, women's participation in the work of all parties increased tremendously.

Initially many Germans probably agreed with Robert von Mohl, who had remarked in 1874 that "the complete exclusion of the feminine sex can scarcely meet a reasonable doubt, even among those who see participation in state elections as a natural right. Even they would have to see that bringing females into political life is against their nature and would have the most ruinous consequences for everyone."[91] Social Democrats did not mention women's suffrage in their Eisenach Program in 1869, and when Bebel moved it at the Gotha Congress in 1875, he was voted down, with the argument that women did not yet have sufficient education. Bebel countered, in an argument remarkably like Dankwart Rustow's—and ours: "A right must be practiced [geübt], and there must be the opportunity to do it, if we want to see the effects. . . . [Education] will happen precisely by our giving them the franchise, so that they become practiced in exercising it."[92] Only in 1891, at its Erfurt Congress, did the majority of the SPD adopt Bebel's thinking, and only in 1895 did it submit a motion to that effect to the Reichstag.

But what is remarkable is not that the SPD was slow to take up women's suffrage. They were in line with progressive opinion elsewhere, and certainly not behind the vast majority of German women themselves, who began to organize on behalf of the suffrage only in 1894. Rather, what is worth noticing is the rapidity with which the logic of competitive democratic politics led other parties to see the same light.[93] That same year, 1895, Adolf Stöcker was demonstrating his openness to women's issues. In 1903, noting that women were al-

[90] Braun, "Agitation," 200–202.

[91] "Erörterungen" (1974), 539. A rundown of states in which independent women who were rich enough could vote in communal elections: Evans, *Movement*, 10.

[92] Quoted in E. Altmann-Gottheiner, "Parteien" (1910), 596. The continued antifeminism of some: ibid., 597f.

[93] This is the point of Altmann-Gottheiner's "Parteien," which demonstrates pragmatic openness toward women's suffrage across the political spectrum, with differences within parties as great as those between them; also Wally Zeppler, "Frauenbewegung," *Sozialistische Monatshefte* 29, 2 Bde., 14 Heft (14 July 1913), 53–57.

ready voting in Australia, he warned the Free Church–Social Congress "not to dismiss new things out of hand as unrealizable. . . . Full women's suffrage is in today's modern culture already an entirely normal condition."[94] By 1912 National Liberal women in Cologne not only staffed the party's phone lines, they sent their own delegates to the provincial party congress—and pressed their interests on party elders by referring to the competition of Social Democrats, Centrum, and Left Liberals for women's support.[95] And though political equality posed the same challenge to Catholic teaching on authority within the family as it did to the bread lord's at the workplace, even theologians, such as Munich's Cardinal Faulhaber, came around.[96] We see here the working of the Rustowian model. Whatever their theoretical objections, all sides acknowledged that women's activity had become important to their own success.[97] The result was that male public opinion kept pace with women's own rapidly growing desire for the vote, creating a wide consensus on the inevitability of female suffrage even before the war and insuring its effortless enactment at the end.[98] We should not take this development for granted. In France, birthplace of the Rights of Man, where the theoretical objections were surely less weighty than those of Germany's Conservative pastors or Catholic prelates, but where party development—and thus election competition—was considerably weaker, it was 1946 before women were brought in.

By the 1890s the Reichstag's expanding commitments brought it into increasing conflict with the desires of the emperor, producing what some have described as a chronic crisis. Yet under tremendous pressure from the Imperial and Prussian ministers, the deputies stood fast. The most important constitutional developments of the decade are to be found in what did *not* happen. The Reichstag— and the Prussian Landtag—refused to pass three bills aimed at fundamentally curtailing the rights of labor and of Social Democrats. And it did so at a time when labor conflict was growing, prominent employers were vociferously demanding remedies, and the threat of a royal *Staatsstreich*, with the express aim of producing a legislature more amenable to these proposals, hung in the air. The rejection of the Sedition Bill, the Little Socialist Law, and the Penitentiary Bill are measures of how much the Reichstag's respect for civil liberties—and its nerve!—had stiffened since the days when it had waged its culture wars and repeatedly passed exceptional laws against Socialists. And both the respect and the nerve were measures of the democratizing consequences of the franchise—

[94] Kaiser, "Politisierung," 268.

[95] Steinmann, "Mitarbeit," 13, 18–20; many articles on the political role of women in the *Schlesische Freikonservative Parteikorrespondenz* in 1913–14.

[96] In Nov. 1917 he reassured Cologne's Felix Hartmann, noting that the Kaiser, Chancellor Hertling, and the Z supported the "inevitable expansion of the vote to women." Cremer, "Cross," 242f.

[97] E.g., LL women: "Der Wahlkampf in Groß-Berlin," BT 41/7, 4 Jan. 1912; "noble ladies" (K) in 1 Köslin, *FrankZ* Nr. 60, 1 Mar. 1903, BAB-L R1501/14456. Bl. 3; use of women in 1912: Bertram, *Wahlen*, 196–99.

[98] Altmann-Gottheiner, "Parteien," 584f.

a consequence that we can see even more clearly when the same issues returned in autumn 1910, after street fighting broke out between strikers and strike-breakers in the Berlin district of Moabit. France's use of troops to break railway strikes that October had made a big impression on the Kaiser, and he noted that Premier Aristide Briand had been supported by the French chamber: "That's the way it's got to be with us too!" But the Imperial Justice Department, after reviewing the dismal fate of the Sedition and Penitentiary Bills, concluded that no similar measure had a chance of passing. Elections were coming up. "The majority parties, especially the Centrum, will not be inclined to worsen their campaign position vis-à-vis Social Democracy, which is already bad enough, by bringing through such a bill." Moreover, it warned, the bill's predictable defeat would affect the government's own election prospects very unfavorably—especially as the SPD would exploit the measure in its campaign.[99] Democracy was moving forward, and not only by convinced democrats.

The second thing that did not happen over the course of these struggles was a plebiscite. Unlike Bismarck in 1878, who punished the liberal majority for rejecting his first draft of the Socialist Law by dissolving the Reichstag and taking his case to the country, the government in the nineties held fire. It knew it could not win. The calculation shows how much, since the 1870s, the electorate's respect for civil liberties had grown.

The third thing that did not happen was a *Staatsstreich*. This was the most important absence of all. For however much other aspects of imperial life may have resembled contemporary Britain and the United States, in one respect Germany was truly *sonderbar*. British and American representatives never had to conduct their daily business in the face of continual "indiscretions" suggesting that their government was about to suspend the constitution that had elected them. In France, the closest analogy was the affair of *Seize Mai* (May 16) in 1877, when President MacMahon dismissed Premier Jules Simon without consulting the Chamber of Deputies. MacMahon's misstep, denounced by Victor Hugo as a "demi-coup," became a milestone in the history of the Third Republic as Republicans rallied to defend their own understanding of the constitution.[100] In Germany, however, the issue was never finally joined in this dramatic fashion. For in the event, the imperial government gave up without a fight.

It was certainly no accident that the idea of a *Staatsstreich* kept recurring in the nineties, and in an increasingly public way. But it was also no accident that a *Staatsstreich* was never attempted. After two decades the Reichstag was simply too formidable, too broadly and deeply anchored in the esteem of the public and its institutions. Caesarism, if indeed it had ever been a serious option, had ceased as an option by 1898. In the twentieth century, although rumors occasionally surfaced in the press, and there was no shortage of cabinet discussions about legal ways the franchise might be amended, the *Staatsstreich* was dead.[101]

[99] K. Saul, *Staat* (1974), 309.
[100] Thanks to my colleague Susanna Barrows for this information.
[101] E.g., Votum des MdI on Prussian WR Reform: 7 Nov. 1909, GStA PK I. HA, Rep. 90a, A.

As Hans Delbrück noted in 1907, "Those crazies who are still talking about the necessity of a *Staatsstreich* today . . . don't need to be taken seriously."[102]

What *had* happened in the nineties was that parliament, in the presence of these threats to the democratic franchise, had insisted on *increasing* the power of the electorate—which it did by persisting in its demands for protections of the ballot.[103] Victory came in 1903, when the Bundesrat finally agreed to the Rickert Bill, and harnessed the state's own machinery behind the new safeguards. What accounts for the government's decision for reform over another revolution from above? Was it uncertainty, about the consequence of both reform and of refusal to reform? The ingrained traditions of bureaucratic *Korrektheit* (especially clear in the case of Posadowsky)? The sense, among Germany's ruling elite, that they were part of a wider world—a world of franchise regimes—in which their peers were not the Tsar and the Sultan, nor even the Austrian Emperor, but Belgium, England, France, and (with no little sniffing) the United States?[104] Surely it was all three.

In the imperial government's agreement to the ballot reform, we can recognize "that very act of alienation of control over outcomes of conflicts," not only on the part of the parties, but among key figures within the state, that Adam Przeworski has designated "the decisive step towards democracy."[105] The step was not inevitable. The Social Democrats need not have been such optimists, putting just enough wary trust in the Reichstag and in the electoral process to enable the other parties to treat with them. The government need not have been such pessimists, fearful of the deluge—perhaps in violence, certainly in loss of prestige and public confidence—should legality be violated. The liberals, Centrum, and Poles need not have opted for the integrity of elections and the power of parliament *with* the SPD in preference to a united front against it. The repeated decision to accept procedures and rules for controlling conflict over any alternative were conscious choices. They give the lie to a widely shared contention that "through its position and development the Reichstag of the empire was fully unsuited to becoming the first step [*Vorstufe*] of a democratic parliament."[106] They were indeed based upon the kinds of cost-benefit calculations recently stressed by political theorists in their discussions of transitions to democracy. But we should not underestimate also the psychological predispositions estab-

---

VIII. 1. d., Nr. 1/Bd. 10, Bl. 99–125. Continued rumors: *Die neue Gesellschaft* 3/10 (6 Feb. 1907): 217; Crothers, *Elections*, 148n. 120; Saul, *Staat*, 15f, 34–36.

[102] D[elbrück], "Die Auflösung," 187. Voters also warned against any "Staatsstreich" or exceptional legislation. A. Putschke, businessman, Zittau, to Bülow, 19 Jan. 1907, BAB-L R1501/14697, Bl. 210–14. Though the *desire* continued to be expressed by reactionaries (Stegmann, *Erben*, 263n. 46, and ff; Saul, *Staat*, 306ff), Kühne dismisses "the ubiquitous threats of a Staatsstreich," for which there were no concrete plans, as "Redensarten." *Dreiklassenwahlrecht*, 402f, 406.

[103] Cf. complaints in "Diäten," 306f.

[104] R. Martin attributed Bethmann's instruction to the MdI to allow open-air democratic and SPD demonstrations to the "French and English newspaper vote"! *Machthaber*, 524f.

[105] Przeworski, "Problems," 58.

[106] Molt, *Reichstag*, 328.

lished by a decades-long learning process. In this war of nerves with the government, the deputies showed their mettle, their willingness to take risks for principle and power.[107]

I don't want to exaggerate the progressive features of Germany's electoral politics. The inequality and intimidation that lived on in eastern Prussia—of particular gravity since East Elbian votes could determine legislation in the Prussian Landtag, and that Landtag, in turn, the Bundesrat—provoked smoldering fury. Demands to reform the Prussian franchise that made this domination possible preoccupied public opinion—and the government—in the decade before the war, but a consensus on the character of the necessary changes proved elusive. From the bitterness of the debates about this issue we can draw two conclusions: first, the extreme difficulty of reform where entrenched interests were at stake; and second, the degree to which democratic participation had become established as the norm against which all other political questions were measured.

The situation produced by the survival, until 1918, of Prussia's three-class voting system, in a decade that produced franchise reforms in seventeen other German states, has been described as an "exception, unique in national as well as international comparison."[108] Every situation bears unique features, but the ability of a regional elite to use its power in an undemocratic Periphery to exert a stranglehold over developments in the more democratic Center is no *unicum*. The American South was much like East Elbia in being a geographically isolated and relatively poor region that was able both to quarantine itself from progressive developments occuring in the rest of the country and to exercise a veto over much of national politics. The absence of electoral competition in the "solid South"—where turnouts were sometimes no more than 2 percent—and Congress's rules allocating powerful committee chairmanships according to a member's seniority, enabled the South to control what legislation reached the floor of the Senate, long after that institution had ceased (in May 1913) to be elected indirectly by the state legislatures. Only in the 1960s, after violent resistance and loss of life, did the national Center exercise the political will to insist that this regional Periphery, too, join American democracy.

The German Empire was also not unique in having—in the Prussian Landtag and the Bundesrat—an undemocratic "upper house," able to veto legislation passed by the more democratic parliament.[109] Only in May 1911, after a constitutional struggle that gripped parliament, but hardly seemed to trouble the electorate, was Britain's hereditary House of Lords' stranglehold on legislation broken, its power reduced to a suspensive veto—beating the reform of the Prussian

---

[107] Cost-benefit: Przeworski, *Democracy*; Rustow, "Transitions." Insofar as the explanation for the durability of German dualism up to the end of the war lies with the actions of the Reichstag, I find it not in the "failure of the parliamentarians," their "unwillingness to take risks," (864, 1039f), or their shrinking from an "existential trial of strength," but in the Empire's precocious party development. Contrast Wehler, *Gesellschaftsgeschichte* 3: 864f, 1039f, 1287.

[108] Kühne, *Dreiklassenwahlrecht*, 25.

[109] Ibid., 458.

franchise by a mere seven years. Even then, the continued opposition of the Lords to Irish Home Rule meant that Britain's underlying constitutional crisis remained fatefully unresolved. Its conclusion, in 1920–22, with the partition of Ireland, came only after a bloody recourse to arms.

HABITUATION

Institutions and laws were not the only motors in the "process of institutionalizing uncertainty" so characteristic of a practicing democracy. Culture—that mysterious power that "tells people what to want; . . . informs them what they must not do; . . . [and] indicates to them what they must hide from others"— played, as we have seen, a central role in the process: in demarking the Empire's first, and arguably most important, political cleavage; in the unwritten rules that defined the public sphere as necessarily contested; and—perhaps most fundamentally—in structuring the German citizenry's extraordinarily legalistic expectations of their state.[110] If we have said much, however, in previous chapters, about the culture's impact on electoral politics, we have said little about electoral politics' impact on political culture. Did Germany, in the Rustowian terminology we have have been employing, move beyond the stage at which political leaders make conscious choices that institutionalize uncertainty to a point at which the population itself has also become to "habituated" to open conflict that it takes for granted these procedures for regulating it; to the point at which painful compromises hammered out in the parliament can be accepted by a diverse public? If, as we have been arguing (and as contemporaries also argued), democracy is a learning experience, can we say that by the end of our period, Germans had "learned" democratic values?[111]

One answer was given in 1918–19, in the spontaneity with which the public turned to elections rather than to other modes of effecting the changes they desired.

But even earlier, an acceptance of democratic procedures can be inferred: from the growing majorities with which the parties that supported measures like the Rickert Bill were returned to parliament; from the insistence on a discussion speaker at political rallies—a recognition that in a true "public" there is more than one point of view; even from the prestige enjoyed by the Reichstag.[112]

---

[110] The definition of culture: Przeworski, *Democracy*, 24. "Institutionalizing uncertainty": ibid., 15, and idem, "Problems" (1986), 58; 60—a function somewhat broader than the one emphasized by Kaltefleiter/Nißen, *Wahlforschung*, 26, of insuring the chance of innovation. The public's insistance on debate contrasts sharply with Norbert Elias's belief that German culture *devalued* "the art of verbal debate through argument and persuasion"! Michael Burleigh, review of Elias, *The Germans* (Oxford, 1996), in *TLS*, 29 Mar. 1996: 5.

[111] Cf. Windthorst SBDR 9 Feb 1888: 798. "Joint learning experience": Rustow, "Transitions," 358. See also Fish, "Russia's Crisis," 159. Cf. Wehler, *Gesellschaftsgeschichte* 3: 1039, 1287.

[112] Symbolized by Windthorst's obsequies, in which members of parliament *and* government, BR,

True: the explosive growth of political Catholicism and Social Democracy outraged many and bothered even more, leading some to question the wisdom of precisely *this* democratic franchise. But judging from the suggestions they sent to Kaiser and chancellors—evidence all the more persuasive because of the sample's built-in conservative bias—most of the critics favored amending rather than repealing it. Many of these suggestions, not surprisingly, showed scant regard for democratic values. There were proposals for the exclusion of certain parties or parts of the population: the Centrum, SPD, Poles, Alsatians, tax delinquents, recipients of private charity.[113] There were calls for property or age restrictions, open balloting, or an appointed "economic" parliament to balance the elected Reichstag.[114] Some were breathtakingly naive, such as Franz Pieczonka's plea for a lottery, or the demand that admission to the polls be dependent on passing an exam.[115] But *most* of these citizen-advocates seem to have put their hopes in an increase rather than a reduction of popular participation. Some proposed making voting obligatory, an idea that drew on a tradition going as far back as Stein's municipal ordinance of 1808 and current in the rhetoric of voting obligation.[116] Others wanted to reward voting with a tax break.[117] Others requested absentee ballots for commercial travelers—or at least free rail passes home.[118] Others wanted the franchise extended to military personnel—or to women.[119] Some suggested that nonvoting be punished (perhaps

and delegates of the reigning monarchs conspicuously participated—to the indignation of F. Hartung: *Geschichte*, 219f.

[113] Voter suggestions, complaints, and comments, as well as those appearing in newspapers, occupy nine fat files in the archives of the RdI. Vs. Z: BAB-L R1501/files: 14697, Bl. 4; 14693, Bl. 42–46; vs. SPD: BAB-L R101/3353, Bl. 317; BAB-L R1501/files: 14697, Bl. 118f; 14696, Bl. 36–39; vs. P and Alsations: BAB-L R1501/14693, Bl. 187f. Taxes, charities: BAB-L R1501/files: 14693, Bl. 21; 14694, Bl. 34f, 63f.

[114] BAB-L R1501 files: Property: 14693, Bl. 27f, 32f; Bl. 234; 14697, Bl. 58. Age: 14453, Bl. 91; 14694, Bl. 307f. Open voting: 14693, Bl. 39–41; 14695, Bl. 211; 14696, Bl. 65f; 14697, Bl. 167f. *Volkswirtschaftsrat*: 14693, Bl. 96, 245–56; 14695, Bl. 12. BAB-L R43/685, Bl. 231f. For an occupational parliament: BAB-L R1501/files: 14453, Bl. 311–24; 14695, Bl. 93–105. Call for abolition of the RT franchise without suggestions for replacement: "Zur Reichstagswahl," *Würzburger Presse mit Bayerischer Volkszeitung*, 10 Oct. 1881, Nr. 239. BAB-L R1501/14693, Bl. 80. BAB-L R1501/files: 14451, Bl. 243f; 14453, Bl. 76f.

[115] BAB-L R1501/14693, Bl. 110, and 1494, Bl. 269–74, respectively.

[116] BAB-L R1501 files 14694, Bl. 214f; 14696, Bl. 18f; 15696, Bl. 216; Liebermann v. Sonnenberg SBDR 27 Feb. 1907: 98. *Berliner Times-Korrespondent*, quoted in GA Nr. 15, 18 Jan. 1874: 81; *Reichsbote*, quoted in "Deutsches Reich. Die Wahlfälschungen," *Vorwärts* 22 Jan. 1903, BAB-L R1501/114455, Bl. 158. The government's investigation into possible consequences of obligatory voting: SS des Innern to Bülow, 14 July 1908, BAB-L R1501/14459, Bl. 124–38. Obligatory voting: 14 Saxony, AnlDR (1912/13, 13/I, Bd. 19), DS 718: 934; 7 Gumb., AnlDR (1912/14, 13/I, Bd. 23) DS 1586: 3424; advocated for LT elections (with secrecy): Porsch (Z), SBHA 15 Feb 1903: 913; opposed by Ernst Radnitzky, *Die Parteiwillkür im öffentlichen Recht* (Vienna, 1888), 38f; rhetoric of *Wahlpflicht*: Nettmann, *Witten*, 134, and Hahne, "Reichstagswahl," 119.

[117] RKA's comment, 28 July 1877: an "idea that is no more new than it is fruitful." BAB-L R1501/14693, Bl. 30.

[118] BAB-L R1501/files: 14693, Bl. 49–51, 171; 14694, Bl. 36f.

[119] BAB-L R1501/files: 14694, Bl. 304; 14695, Bl. 12; 14696, Bl. 159f, 217f.

by tripling the delinquents' income tax, or by publishing their names). Still others advocated plural voting for those with greater taxes or greater age.[120] And finally some citizens, as we saw in chapter 10, insisted that only proportional representation would encourage those in demographically hopeless districts to vote.

My impression of the spread of democratic assumptions is reinforced by trends in the press. If the success of British Conservatives can be measured by the circulation figures of conservative dailies like the *Daily Express* (ca. 500,000) and the *Daily Mail* (1,000,000), then the failure of the German Right is no less clear. The officially Conservative *Kreuz-Zeitung* counted only 12,000 subscribers in the years before the war; the Free Conservative's *Post*, half that figure. The *Berliner Neueste Nachrichten* and the *Deutsche Zeitung*, also conservative, sold to 12,000 and 14,000, respectively—and this in a country of some sixty million. In Saxony, the *Dresdner Neueste Nachrichten*, edited by a group of moderate, "English"-style nobles, was drawing circulation away from its hard-line Conservative rival, the *Dresdner Nachrichten*. Somewhat more successful was Böckel's biweekly *Reichsherold*. During its brief moment of glory in the early nineties it boasted 15,000 subscribers. The most successful of all the papers on the Right, the *Deutsche Tageszeitung*, the BdL's "serious" daily, with a secure base among farmers, still reached only 22,000. Although sales figures may be smaller than readership, they may also be larger. They gain weight by comparison with those of the democratic press: *Tägliche Rundschau* (48,000); *B.Z. am Mittag* (60–100,000); *Berliner Tageblatt* (180,000); and *Berliner Morgenpost* (360,000).[121] If one added the SPD, Left Liberal, and Centrum press, the impression of democratic movement would be even more overwhelming. If public opinion can be found in published opinion, then it seems clear that, in the popular mind, the Right was becoming marginalized.

Marginalization encouraged radicalization—and vice versa. This truism can be illustrated in the fortunes of the Pan-German League, which declined from an organization whose respectability seemed guaranteed by the presence of some liberal imperialists of note, such as Max Weber and Ernst Bassermann, to an unpopular group of racist cranks. Its membership peaked in 1902 at not quite 23,000, mostly men who signed on after hearing a rousing speech, but whose involvement often went no further.[122] The Catholic *Volksverein* on the eve of the war numbered more than thirty-six times as many members, the SPD in 1907

---

[120] Tax penalty: BAB-L R1501/files: 14693, Bl. 115f; 14697, Bl. 197f, 210–14; plural voting: BAB-L R1501/14693, Bl. 230f, 302f, BAB-L R1501/14696, Bl. 24f. I uncovered nothing that suggests that Germans were longing for a charismatic *"Führer"* (*Pace* Wehler, *Gesellschaftsgeschichte* 3: 1285).

[121] Statistics for all papers except *Reichsherold*: Martin, *Machthaber*, 522f. Similar description, but judging the discrepency between the flourishing "liberal" (in the broadest sense) press and the conservative-cum-radically nationalist rivals to be another of the Empire's "paradoxes:" Wehler, *Gesellschaftsgeschichte* 3: 1243–49; 1283. Levy, *Downfall*, 56, 115, estimates that the three largest-circulation antisemitic papers together had only 25,000 subscribers in the 1890s, although since other papers often reprinted their articles, resonance was considerably broader.

[122] Says Chickering, *We Men*, 110, 134f, 214, 221, 323.

counted more than forty-four times as many (530,466)—and nearly doubled *that* figure by 1914. Hemorrhaging membership brought the Pan-Germans to the brink of dissolution, from which they were rescued only by the contributions of industrialists. Within nationalist circles, they were dismissed as "sparrows among National Liberal starlings."[123]

More typical of nationalist opinion in the early twentieth century was the Navy League. But so far from being necessarily on the Right, the Navy League was likened to a "Young Liberal Conventical."[124] The League's dimensions, which topped 300,000, were a sign of the continuing strength of "national" topoi among middle-class Protestants—and of the weakness of such themes in recruiting beyond the bournes of class and confession that had set effective limits on liberalism for decades. Enthusiasm for the fleet did not win elections; but by revealing the popularity of the imperialist variant of nationalism in the early years of the century, it did suggest the reservoir of sentiment available for radicalization once international events enabled nationalism to trump other issues.

LEGACIES

"Democracy" has, and will always have, normative connotations. Although in the past decade triumphalists have claimed that democratic institutions provide the most rational way of allocating power and resources, few of us would want to rest our support for democracy on this putative (and perhaps very temporary) efficiency. We value democracy because we value the human dignity that it seeks to uphold. But do these values necessarily follow the procedural flag? The institutionalists, in choosing procedures as their starting point, imply that they do, and our own story has provided some empirical support for this assumption.

By now the skeptical reader will surely ask, Is it not panglossian to assign such positive weight to the empire's nasty, bitter, unresolved conflicts (Rustow's innocuously labeled "hot family feuds") as motors forcing groups to compact on procedural *modi vivendi*? Should not any historian, and certainly any historian of Germany, be suspicious of the Rustowian political theodicy—where good comes out of evil, where effective parties and "interest aggregation" grow out of Kulturkampf and class struggle? Did not elections, under *these* conditions, work not only to uncover the latent conflicts within society, but also to amplify, extend, and reinforce them? Does not the institutionalist emphasis on democracy "as a matter primarily of procedure rather than of substance" run the danger of overlooking the proverbial six-ton elephant in the room: the destruc-

---

[123] *KrZ* quoted in Eley, *Reshaping*, 281; also 366; Stegmann, *Erben*, 296–300; SPD: Moore, *Injustice*, 183.

[124] Eley, *Reshaping*, 262, 279, 280n. 88, 357. Fairbairn notes the League's "curious invisibility . . . in mass electoral politics," and asks "how effective can social imperialism have been if it did not much affect elections?" *Democracy*, 247.

tive *feelings*—anger, contempt, self-righteousness, even hatred—that accompanied these conflicts and were fostered by them?

One measure of whether institutions were encouraging the values we associate with a democratic civic culture—equality, mutual respect, tolerance—is a society's stance toward those minorities too small to be represented directly in the electoral process. In Germany's case, this means the Jews, whose persecution and destruction in later decades have cast a long shadow, and rightly, over all our judgments on the Kaiserreich.[125] The sources employed in this study have been less vocal about their attitudes toward Jews than toward Catholics, Socialists, and even Poles, and any conclusions drawn from them must remain tentative.[126] My *impression* is that popular feeling against Jews was strongest in the empire's first decades: in the seventies and early eighties among Catholics, and in the eighties and early nineties, among Protestants. In the very first election, Catholics expressed fears that liberal proposals for school reform (ending the use of local clergy as school inspectors, integrating the denominations, but retaining mandatory religious instruction) would jeopardize their children, by making it possible for them to be taught by Jews.[127] Traditional religious prejudices were reinforced by the evident enthusiasm for the Kulturkampf among prominent Jewish-owned newspapers and two of the Reichstag's highest-profile deputies, Lasker and Bamberger. The *Germania* and the *Schlesische Volkszeitung*, but especially smaller papers with more localized circulations, complained vigorously about the dangers that emancipated and irreligious Jews allegedly posed to Christian civilization.[128] Among Protestants, on the other hand, especially artisans and farmers, it was not the cultural conflicts of the seventies but the economic crisis of the eighties and early nineties that leant desperate plausibility to the arguments of Stöcker, Böckel, and their imitators that linked obvious Jewish successes to their own, equally obvious, failures.

Elections magnified the publicity these men gave to the "Jewish question," as nervous campaign managers in other parties began to scramble for low ground. Yet even in the early eighties we can find examples of public stands against

[125]Excellent, but differing, recent accounts: Helmut Berding, *Moderner Anti-Semitismus in Deutschland* (Frankfurt a. M., 1988), and Alan S. Lindemann, *Esau's Tears. Modern Anti-Semitism and the Rise of the Jews* (Cambridge, UK, 1997), which has a transnational perspective.

[126] However, we do have testimony from 1 Minden in AnlDR (1877, 3/I, Bd. 3) DS 187: 515–26 and SBDR 2 Apr. 1878: 677–82, and from 1 Berlin AnlDR (1881–82, 1/II, Bd. 2) DS 44: 117–20: the two hearts of the Stöcker movement. Also: 2 Han. AnlDR (1884, 6/I, Bd. 5) DS 148: 539; Frank, *Brandenburger*, 60. I found only one proposal that might have disenfranchised Jews: C. (?) Jul. Schulz, Greiz (Reuß a.L.), to Bülow, 1 Jul. 1903, BAB-L R1501/14696, Bl. 36–39. Fritz Pieske, rentier of Charlottenburg, the only correspondent who was exclusively or even primarily antisemitic, wanted the Kaiser to make Jews ineligible for the RT. 24 June 1903, ibid., Bl. 32f.

[127] 7 Oppeln, AnlDR (1871, 1/I, Bd. 2) DS 69: 164f.

[128] E.g., Eduard Müller's *Bonifacius Kalender*; the publications of G.F. Dasbach; the *Gladbacher Merkur*; the *Reichszeitung* (Bonn). "Abgeordneter Carl Bachem und die Juden," Historisches Archiv der Stadt Köln, Bachem Nachlaß, 1006, Nr. 65b. Cf. also Blaschke, "Herrschaft," 246–67. Olaf Blaschke's *Katholizismus und Antisemitismus im Deutschen Kaiserreich* (Göttingen, 1997), arrived on my desk too late for me to use.

antisemitism. It happened in Witten in the Ruhr, when eighty-seven citizens (including eighteen factory owners and directors, eight higher-level civil servants, eight school directors and teachers, and twenty-two artisans, foremen, and workers) responded to a Stöcker speech by signing an invitation to the public to discuss (read: refute) the court preacher's allegations.[129] Thus while the electoral process initially brought latent hostility toward Jews to light, it is not clear that it reinforced these feelings. Local Jewish leaders refused to allow conservative candidates to get away with fellow-traveling. They appeared at election assemblies and forced them to take a position against antisemitism. And the pressures of electoral competition made strange bedfellows. In 1887 Bamberger was reelected in Alzey-Bingen *only* because the Centrum "campaigned like hell" for him, he said, and because thousands of Catholic voters gave him their support.[130]

As for the "climate," there were signs that hostility to Jews began to lose ground. The Association for Defense against Antisemitism (*Abwehr-Verein*), established in 1890 by prominent non-Jewish Left Liberals, set up branches in districts where antisemites were agitating. And the Central Association of German Citizens of Jewish Faith (*Centralverein*), founded three years later, let no antisemitic argument go unrebutted.[131] Moreover, the public stand against antisemitism taken by individuals who were revered among social groups known to be prejudiced against Jews—Richter and Theodor Mommsen (Protestant *Mittelstand* and university); Windthorst and Ernst Lieber (Catholics); Crown Prince (later Kaiser) Friedrich, Grand Dukes Ernst Ludwig of Hessen and Friedrich I of Baden, and Chancellor Caprivi (officials)—helped to deny respectability to the antisemitic cause.[132] It is hard not to see in the Empire's second generation of leaders a growing awareness of antisemitism as a positive evil. Thus, while the most respected figure in the Catholic episcopate of the seventies, Bishop (and Baron) Emanual von Ketteler, shared with many of his estate negative stereotypes about Jews, and the revered Bishop Konrad Martin, imprisoned during the Kulturkampf, subscribed to the most bloodthirsty medieval legends, the most powerful prelates of the eighties and nineties, Cologne's Cardinal Philipp Krementz and Breslau's Cardinal Georg Kopp—men on opposite ends of the Catholic political spectrum—were both hostile to antisemitism.[133] The first leader of the National Liberals, Rudolf von Bennigsen, had as a young man referred to the "usual failings of the Jewish nation" and as an old man saw

---

[129] Monshausen, *Koblenz*, 71f. Nettmann, *Witten*, 116f. The Catholic *SVZ* ended its vituperative campaign against Jews in 1881 after Jewish businessmen not only withdrew their own advertisements, but got non-Jewish advertisers to boycott the paper. Müller, *Kampf*, 137.

[130] 5 Marienwerder, AnlDR (1894/95, 9/III, Bd. I) DS 166: 799f, and AnlDR (1895/97, 9/IV, Bd. 2) DS 195: 1253, 1259; Le Maistre to Bis., Darmstadt, 23 Feb. 1887, BAB-L R1501/14642, Bl. 176; Anderson, *Windthorst*, 356. Catholics had already helped elect Bamberger in 1881.

[131] Levy, *Downfall*, 146, 181; on the deterrent effects of the Abwehr Verein's "pouncing" on any party that used antisemitism in its campaigns: 188.

[132] Crown Prince: Margarethe Edle v. Poschinger, *Kaiser Friedrich III, 1870–1888* (Berlin, 1900), 288. Others: Levy, *Downfall*, 138–41.

[133] Blaschke, "Herrschaft," 263n. 80.

much to recommend in the writings of Houston Stewart Chamberlain.[134] He was succeeded by Ernst Bassermann, no less nationalist, but—like his colleagues in the Liberal leadership, Stresemann and the Reichstag's vice-president, Hermann Paasche—married to a woman of Jewish descent and connected to Jewish as well as Christian worlds.

Recent research suggests that the traditional picture of cynical politicians using antisemitism as a way to integrate voters behind economic and social programs—a picture inspired by the example of Stöcker in Berlin in the early eighties—may be misleading. More frequently, especially as time went on, we see antisemites offering social and economic programs as a way to gather people behind their otherwise uncompetitive parties.[135] By the late nineties, these parties were already in decline, and the day when their campaigners sought publicity by such stunts as leading dogs through the streets with posters saying "Don't vote for Jews" (as they did in Berlin in 1881) had passed.[136] Whatever people's prejudices, the "Jewish" issue did not draw crowds. In 1906 antisemitic organizers were accused of hiding their antisemitism in order to attract audiences by pretending to be National Liberals.[137] Thanks to the trade-offs they enjoyed with other parties in the "national" bloc, seventeen antisemitic candidates were elected to the 397-man Reichstag the following year. But the success of these alliances had been dependent upon muting their antisemitism. In the end, their candidates "had not won elections because of their antisemitism, but in spite of it."[138]

I do not want to go beyond the evidence. The rhetoric of agrarian groups, Catholic and Protestant, was suffused with antisemitic resentment. Stereotypes about Jews continued to be taken for granted, popping up in the most unlikely places. The appendix of the 1907 text edition of the election code, for example, intended for the instruction of election panels, reprinted a sample voting list, with blanks for each voter's name, age, occupation, and residence, as well as examples of why someone might be denied the vote. Along with such entries as "Arnold, Ludwig; 25; tenant farmer," and (under "remarks") "not yet twenty-five years old," the short sample of names includes "Cohn, Hirsch; 39; tradesman; in bankruptcy."[139] But I have seen no convincing evidence that the salience

---

[134] Oncken, *Bennigsen* 1: 100; 2: 623f.

[135] See Smith, "Alltag," 284. On the failure of antisemitism to "integrate" Catholics and Protestants: idem, "Religion," 310–12, and esp. 310n. 93.

[136] For such modes, "the time was not yet ripe," as a dissertation of 1933 commented ambiguously. Frank, *Brandenburger*, 60.

[137] Baudert (SD), Patzig (NL), Raab (Reform), Liebermann v. Sonnenberg SBDR 21 Mar. 1906: 2190, 2092, 2096, 2199, 2216.

[138] Levy, *Downfall*, 228, 233.

[139] *Reichstags-Wahlgesetz*, Anlage A. Note also the title page cartoon in *Simplicissimus* VII/26 (1907–3): 210, "The Polanizing of West Prussia," which depicts three ugly *Ostjuden*, surrounded by rabbits, hopping all over each other. The caption: "Soon we'll be the only ones here still speaking Joiman (*daitsch*)." The article on "Antisemitism, Antisemitic Party" by Siebertz, editor of the *Bayerischer Kurier* (Z), which condemns antisemitism, is not free from antisemitism itself. *Politisch-Soziales Abc-Buch*, 49–56.

of these stereotypes was increasing.[140] Antisemitic campaigners were never able to do what their rivals did: command the sacrifices from voters of time and money necessary to sustain them as effective parties.[141] By the last imperial Reichstag, antisemitic deputies had declined to six. Observers at home and abroad had stopped taking their "movement" seriously.[142] As long as the empire lasted, the practice of democracy did not encourage lasting victories for anti-semitic demagogues. On the contrary, competitive elections set in motion a process that educated Germany's political elites in the hatefulness of antisemi-tism and that habituated the rank and file to the kinds of compromises that discouraged fanaticism.

Nevertheless, to the question of the beneficence of conflict, there can be no final answer. Some conflicts may be too powerful for even the institutions of democracy to contain. The Polish-German antagonism, which intensified during the decade before the war, seems to have been one of these, although even here I would not want to rule out the importance of contingent decisions—such as the Prusso-German government's resumption of aggressive germanization poli-cies. (The culmination—Prussia's 1908 Expropriation Law—was indeed loudly supported by some extra-parliamentary groups, notably the Eastern Marches Society. But the law was tied up in the courts until 1912, and when Bethmann Hollweg finally did implement it, he was roundly condemned by a Reichstag majority—a "humiliation" that "in a fully parliamentized system would have forced his resignation.")[143] Elsewhere, violent labor unrest proved to some that the class divide was growing—although massive demonstrations on behalf of

[140] Contrast Blaschke, whose belief in a "sharply increasing antisemitism in the Empire" (in "Wider die 'Herrschaft,'" 237), reflects considerable scholarly opinion, with: on Baden, Smith, "Alltag"; on Breslau, Till van Rahden, "Mingling, Marrying, and Distancing. Jewish Integration in Wilhelminian Breslau and Its Erosion in Early Weimar Germany," in *Jüdisches Leben in der Weimarer Republik. Jews in Weimar Germany*, ed. by W. Benz et al. (Tübingen, 1998), 193–217; esp. 216; on Frankfurt, Roth, *Stadt*, 341. About the unpolitical *Alltag*, historians will never achieve certainty, for even hundreds of local studies would not guarantee against false positives—and false negatives.

[141] Lack of monetary contributions: Theodor Fritsch's *Antisemitische Correspondenz und Sprech-saal für innere Partei-Angelegenheiten (Wird nur an zuverlässige Parteigenossen versandt)*, Leipzig, Dec. 1882, Nr. 2; Levy, *Downfall*, 119f, 285n. 21. Cf. the NLs "whose members . . . have brought every necessary sacrifice in time, energy, and money for the good cause." Le Maistre to Bis., Darmstadt, 23 Feb. 1887, BAB-L R1501/14642, Bl. 177.

[142] Lefèvre-Pontalis, *Élections*, 112f, contrasted the German failure to the Austrian success; Ernst (SD) contrasted the present favorably with the eighties. *Polizeispitzeleien*, 60.

[143] Hagen, *Germans*, 210. Elections themselves may have softened intra-ethnic conflict by encour-aging cooperation. In the Ruhr the *Wittener Volkszeitung* (Z) printed the Z's proclamation in 1878—covering the whole front page—in Polish. Z rallies featured Vicar Rupinski from West Prussia, who would address his "countrymen" in Polish after addresses by the main speaker and discussant. The fact that Poles stayed until the end of a long, German-speaking evening for his remarks bespeaks some goodwill. NLs despaired of challenging Z elections: "There'll still be some ultramontane polack or other who, as soon as someone hands him 3 marks and a bottle of denatured spirits, will take responsibility for all Christian-Catholic election heroics [*Wahlheldentaten*]." Nettmann, *Witten*, 140, 144, 147. In spite of calls that German advertisers boycott Polish papers, advertisements for German firms made up about 80%–90% of the latter's income. Czapliński, "Presse," 29.

Prussian franchise reform suggested to others that the gulf was a simpler one, between the privileged few and the unprivileged many. As for anti-Catholicism, its resurgence was apparent even before Bülow's deliberate decision in the 1907 elections to worry the confessional wound. The alarm at the "power" of the Catholic clergy after 1900 demonstrates how lessons learned under one set of circumstances—in this case, a grudging tolerance in the 1880's—have to be learned again when conditions change. Dislike of Catholic difference, as we saw in chapter 5, increased with the democratization of the southern states and with the growing authority of the Reichstag—since both of these developments meant more power for the representatives of the Catholic minority. "We had fed the heart on fantasies, / The heart's grown brutal from the fare; / More substance in our enmities / Than in our love."[144] These lines, written by a near-contemporary about a society that also enjoyed many democratic institutions, might apply to the Kaiserreich as well.

The mutual distrust so characteristic of the empire's politicized communities made it difficult for Germans to "invent a people" on whose judgments they could feel secure. Small wonder than that while demands for the democratization of the Prussian franchise captured everyone's attention, demands for constitutional changes that would have given full power to the "people"—that is, to a simple majority of the representatives elected by the *various* German peoples—found no comparably widespread articulation. Contemporaries seem to have sensed what the political scientist Arend Lijphart has subsequently argued: that in highly "plural" societies, majority rule, on classic English lines, "is not only undemocratic but dangerous," spelling "civil strife rather than democracy." Such societies need institutional arrangements that emphasize consensus instead of victory, that include rather than exclude, and that work to maximize the number of "winners" by forcing coalitions. Lijphart terms such arrangements, found in varying forms in many successful democracies today, "consensus democracy."[145]

But contemporary theorists perceived the alternative to monarchical authority only in terms of the classic majoritarian model and expended tragically little thought on how the goal of democratic responsiveness—broad participation and broad agreement on the policies of the government—might best be realized, constitutionally, under German conditions.[146] Nor in their postwar haste to institutionalize PR, did Germans realize that the imperial system, even as it ritualized hostilities, had also worked to deflect them, not least because of the rules—single-member districts and absolute majorities—that made coalitions a predictable part of every party's future. Election pacts had forced Germans to vote across every cleavage line: Alzey-Bingen's Catholics, as we have seen, for the *Kulturkämpfer* Bamberger; Nordhausen's antisemites, for the Socialist Jew, Oskar Cohn. Patrollers of the confessional divide were treated in Neuwied-

---

[144] W. B. Yeats, "Meditations in Time of Civil War," from *The Tower* (1928).

[145] Lijphart considers the majoritarian (Westminster) and the "consensus" models as "diametrically opposite models of democracy." *Democracies*, 3, 22f.

[146] So argues Ritter, "Parlamentarismus," 33f.

Altenkirchen to an alliance between the Centrum and the county chairman of the anti-ultramontane Protestant League.[147] Commentators on the class war in Essen had to digest the Social Democrats' choice of their millionaire boss, Friedrich Krupp, over the former metalworker Gerhard Stötzel, on the Centrum's left. Left Liberals, whose hatred of antisemitism is beyond doubt, traded support with the antisemitic parties in 1907.[148] The "aha's!" historians sometimes express when they uncover this or that impure election alliance miss the point: in this system, no party was "*ausgegrenzt*."[149] And the same competitive process that led antisemites after the turn of the century to drop the "Jewish question" from their election appeals, led Social Democrats to soft-pedal the class struggle.[150] "Culture," with its confessional and class animosities enforced by watchful communities, continued to tell the voter that cleavage was paramount. The rules of the imperial electoral system responded: not always, and not now.[151]

In ritualizing Germany's conflicts, elections kept them within nonviolent bounds. Yet such rituals aroused a not unreasonable suspicion that the parties' interest lay not in resolving conflicts, but in perpetuating them. The perception that the parties were battening off of Germany's divisions helped keep antiparty sentiment, typical of the early stages of representative institutions everywhere, alive in Germany on into the Weimar Republic, where it would haunt and burden German politics.

Confessional and class animosities—much exacerbated by events immediately following the war—continued to structure decisions in the postwar years, often in fateful ways. In the 1925 presidential election, a coalition of democratic parties, with its standard-bearer chosen from the Centrum, was norrowly defeated by a retired field marshall representing a coalition of the Right: because Bavarian Catholics refused to vote for anyone with SPD support, and because some Protestant liberals preferred the reactionary Paul von Hindenburg to an "ultramontane." Had either of these groups behaved differently, world history might have been different.

The practices of imperial politics—the habits of voting coupled with the

[147] Kühne, *Dreiklassenwahlrecht*, 295–98.

[148] Even George Winter, the VP of the *Abwehr-Verein*, threw his support behind antisemites in Eisenach in order to prevent an SPD victory in 1907—for which he was forced to resign. Levy, *Downfall*, 148f.

[149] Other strange bedfellows: Z and F anticlericals throughout the 80s; antisemites/K helping SDs in Breslau (1881) and in Magdeburg (1884); Z and SPD in 1907. See "Political Carnival" and "At the Run-off"—in which one Bavarian peasant explains to another why they must vote SDP: "because religion is in danger!" *Simplicissimus* XI-II/2 (Oct. 1906–Mar. 1907): 749, and 783. Cf. H. W. Smith's trenchant comments: "Religion," 306 n. 77. Similarly (with more pessimistic conclusions): Fairbairn, *Democracy*, 261.

[150] Crothers, *Elections*, 149n. 121. The revisionist controversy (SPD) and the *Zentrumsstreit* were signs of the same pressures.

[151] Of course what a culture "said," even about itself, was not always true. The SPD's "alternative culture" was less a Marxist culture, than a more liberal, democratic, and humane version of mainstream culture; many workers remained members of *bürgerliche* social organizations, moving between both "cultures." Lidtke, *Culture*, 45, 194f.

habits of not having to rule—had left both Centrum and Social Democrats better equipped to defend subcultural cohesion than to take responsibility for governing—as became clear during the crisis of 1917 and, even more trag- ically, in the terminal crisis of the Republic that began in 1930. Although for most of these years the Centrum (unlike its Bavarian offshoot) dutifully shoul- dered the sorts of compromises that helped keep the Republic afloat, it was unfortunate that German democracy had to depend upon a party whose *raison d'être* was anchored in the quite different needs of a universal church. The "incommensurability of Church and State" meant that in the post-war world the party was itself always on the point of dissolution.[152] As for the SPD, it had thrived on the Empire's dualism. Its ethos and idiom were tailored to heroic opposition.[153] But the very labor conflicts that had reinforced its cohesion in opposition, undermined it in power. Dissolve, it did not, but the Weimar SPD proved unable to keep its most distressed constituents within the fold—losing them at key junctures to more radical parties on Left and Right.

The diminishing strength of these two once mighty parties, draining away at precisely those moments when they had to translate strength into responsibility, suggests that the enormous prestige enjoyed by the prewar Reichstag was itself a function of the empire's constitutional dualism. In confrontation with a united monarchical authority—in the struggle for the secret ballot, for example, or over stipends for deputies—the deputies could unite. It was within this unity—which would disappear once parliament itself supplied both government and opposi- tion—that the Reichstag could appear to embody the entire "German people."

And yet: although not everything that Germans learned while practicing for a parliamentary democracy was benign, Imperial Germany's worst legacy to the next generation was not its political culture, but its war: the "seminal catastro- phe," in George Kennan's phrase, of the twentieth century. It was war that turned ethnocentric nationalism into mass pathology. It was war that made para- noid styles of reasoning seem cogent.[154] It was war, and its devastating conse- quences, that raised the stakes of every domestic conflict beyond what any loser—however democratic his habits of mind—might peacefully be willing to pay. It was war that ended the authority and capacity of the state to insure that rules would be enforced, that contracts—explicit and implicit—would be hon- ored, that citizens would be protected from violence, and that violence would not go unpunished. When we read Max Weber in 1918 pointing to the *journal- ist* as "the most important representative of the demagogic species," and reflect on Röhm's street theater, on Albert Speer's techno-pageantry, on Hitler's ha- rangues, we realize that we are indeed in a different world.[155]

---

[152] Becker, "Ende," 361. Responsibility: Leugers-Scherzberg, *Porsch*, 222–87; Ulrich v. Hehl, *Wilhelm Marx 1863–1946* (Mainz, 1987).

[153] As Winkler points out, however, France's Socialists, except during the *Union Sacrée*, also preferred the pleasures of non-responsibility. *Weimar*, 599.

[154] Searle, *Corruption*, 241–70, 299f demonstrates this, including its antisemitic consequences, brilliantly for Britain.

[155] For some startling continuities, however: Chickering, "Mobilization."

What would have happened had there been no war—the war that Germany's governors, although not solely responsible, did so much to bring about? Although the southern states had to all intents and purposes become parliamentary democracies by 1914, some kind of "jump" would surely have been necessary at the national level to have moved Germany from dualism to a parliamentary regime. The jump need not have been violent. Perhaps the death of the Kaiser at eighty-three would have sped a regime change—in 1941—analogous to Spain's at the death of Franco at the same age in 1975. We cannot know. We do know, however, that after the disasters of the next decades, Germans in 1945 did not begin with nothing. Where they were able to act freely, the old cleavages, somewhat blurred, reasserted themselves, along with a vigorous party system, a deeply ingrained respect for procedures, and a tradition of participation. Any story of democracy must be a story without an end—because there is always something provisional about democracy, and even professed democrats are always only "practicing." Democracy is never a destination, a resting place; it is always a work in progress, an unfinished search for justice and human dignity.

*BIBLIOGRAPHY**

BUNDESARCHIV BERLIN-LICHTERFELDE (BAB-L)

R 43 (*Reichskanzlei*) Nr. 685
R 101 (*Reichstag*) Nrs. 3342–3404
R 1501 (*Reichsamt des Innern* until 1879: Reichskanzleramt)
Nrs. 14450–61; 14474–76; 14641–46; 14653–70; 14672; 14674; 14676–79; 14682–91;
   14693–97; 14702–6; 14708

GEHEIMES STAATSARCHIV PREUSSISCHER KULTURBESITZ (GStA PK)

I. HA, Rep. 89 *Geheimes Zivilcabinet, Jüngere Periode*
   Nrs. 210–14   Reichstag, 1866–1918
   Nr. 215   Reichstag, Beiheft, ohne Datum (Huldigungstelegramme)
I. HA, Rep. 90a *Staatsministerium*
A. VIII.1.d.,   Nr. 1   *Bildung des Hauses der Abgeordneten, Verordnungen und Regle-
                   ments zur Ausführung der Wahlen und Festsellung der Wahl-
                   bezirke*
            Bde. IV–XIII, 1868–1922
I. HA, Rep. 92 Forckenbeck Papers

BISTUMSARCHIV TRIER (BAT)

Alexander Reuß Papers, Abt. 105, Nrs. 1490 through 1660
Bishop Michael Korum Papers, Abt. 108, Folder 817

BUNDESARCHIV KOBLENZ (BAK)
Kleine Erwerbung
Friedrich Carl von Fechenbach Papers

GENERALLANDESARCHIV KARLSRUHE (GLA)

60/494 Turban an Großherzog Friedrich
236/14901 "Wahlagitation der Geistlichen, 1883–1904"
236/14882 "Wahlen zum Reichstag. Hier Agitation der Geistlichen, 1884–1890"

LANDESARCHIV KOBLENZ (LHAK)
403/8806 "Verhalten der Geistlichen . . . bei den Wahlen, 1851–1911"

NIEDERSÄCHSISCHES STAATSARCHIV OSNABRÜCK (SAO)

Dep. 62b, 2379

*Except in rare cases, only works cited more than once in the text are listed.

U.S. NATIONAL ARCHIVES, WASHINGTON, D.C.

Politisches Archiv des Auswärtigen Amts. Originals are in Bonn. I used the following microfilms: I.A.A.b.102 vol. 1 Deutschland. RT: Acta betr. der Angelegenheiten des Reichstags und die Reichstagswahlen (T-149, Reel 281 ACP, frames 416–846); and Preussen 3 Nr. 2, Landtagswahlen Bd. 1.9.1888–31.12.1905, pp. 449–558 (T-149, reel 251). Cited as US NA/AA/RT and US NA/AA/LT, respectively.

REFERENCE WORKS

Albrecht, Dieter, and Bernhard Weber, eds. *Die Mitarbeiter der Historisch-Politischen Blätter für das katholische Deutschland 1838–1928. Ein Verzeichnis.* Mainz, 1990.

Haunfelder, Bernd, and Klaus Erich Pollmann, comps. *Reichstag des Norddeutschen Bundes 1867–1870. Historische Photographien und biographisches Handbuch.* Düsseldorf, 1989.

Hirth, Georg, ed. *Deutscher Parlaments-Almanach.* Munich and Leipzig, 1877, 1887. As of 1890 this becomes: Reichstags-Bureau, ed. *Amtliches Reichstags-Handbuch.* Berlin, 1890, 1893, 1898, 1902, 1903, 1906, 1907.

Hirth, Georg. "Die Mitglieder des Deutschen Reichstags. Biographische Notizen." *Annalen des deutschen Reiches* (1872): cols. 191–286.

Hohorst, Gerd, Jürgen Kocka, and Gerhard A. Ritter, comps. *Sozialgeschichtliches Arbeitsbuch. Bd. II. Materialien zur Statistik des Kaiserreichs 1870–1914.* Munich,[2] 1978.

Königliches Statistisches Bureau. *Die Gemeinden und Gutsbezirke des Preussischen Staates und Ihre Bevölkerung. Nach den Urmaterialien der allgemeinen Volkszählung vom. . . .* Berlin, 1873, 1874 ff.

Landau, Fabian. *Die Wahlen zum Deutschen Reichstage seit 1871.* Hamburg, 1905.

Mann, Bernhard, et al. *Biographisches Handbuch für das Preussische Abgeordnetenhaus 1867–1918.* Düsseldorf, 1988.

Parlamentarisches Handbuch für den deutschen Reichstag und Preußischen Landtag. Ausgabe für die XII. Legislatur-Periode des Preußischen Landtags, edited by Friedrich Kortkampf. Berlin, 1874.

Phillips, A[dolph], ed. *Die Reichstags-Wahlen von 1867 bis 1883. Statistik der Wahlen zum konstituierenden und Norddeutschen Reichstage, zum Zollparlament sowie zu den fünf ersten Legislatur-Perioden des deutschen Reichstages.* Berlin, 1883.

Ritter, Gerhard A., with Merith Niehuss. *Wahlgeschichtliches Arbeitsbuch. Materialien zur Statistik des Kaiserreichs 1871–1918.* Munich, 1980.

Rowell, Chester H. *A Historical and Legal Digest of all the Contested Election Cases in the House of Representatives of the United States from the First to the Fifty-Sixth Congress, 1789–1901.* Washington, D.C., 1901.

Schwarz, Max. *MdR. Biographisches Handbuch der Reichstage.* Hanover, 1965.

Wolfstieg, August, and Karl Meitzel. *Bibliographie der Schriften über beide Häuser des Landtags in Preussen auf Veranlassung der Bibliotheks-Kommission des Hauses der Abgeordneten.* Berlin, 1915.

Reichstags-Wahlgesetz vom 31. Mai 1869 und Wahlreglement in der Fassung der Bekanntmachung vom 28. April 1903 nebst den Anlagen und dem Bericht der Wahlprüfungs-Kommission über die Ergebnisse der Wahl-Prüfungen in der Legislatur-Periode 1893 bis 1908. Textausgabe mit Sachregister. Munich, 1907.

Reichstags-Wahlrecht. Wahlverfahren. Wahlprüfungen. Zusammenstellung der sämtlichen gesetzlichen Bestimmungen hierüber, nebst den Grundsätzen der Wahlprüfungskommission betreffs der Giltigkeit und Ungiltigkeit von Wahlen. Berlin, 1903.

Schuster, Rudolf. *Deutsche Verfassungen.* Munich, 1992.

Specht, Fritz, and Paul Schwabe, *Die Reichstagswahlen von 1867 bis 1907.* Berlin, 1908.

Statistisches Jahrbuch für das Deutsche Reich. Herausgegeben vom kaiserlichen Statistischen Amt. Berlin, 1880 ff.

Statistisches Reichsamt. *Statistik des Deutschen Reichs.* Berlin, yearly.

NEWSPAPERS AND PERIODICALS

Berliner Tageblatt
Bonifacius Kalender
Deutsches Adelsblatt. Wochenschrift für die Aufgaben des christlichen Adels. Organ der Deutschen Adelsgenossenschaft
Deutsch-evangelische Blätter
Deutsche Gemeinde-Zeitung
Deutsche Juristenzeitung
Ems-und Hase-Blätter. Oeffentliches Organ für den Obergerichts-Bezirk Meppen
Evangelische Kirchen-Zeitung
Fliegende Blätter
Schlesische Freikonservative Parteikorrespondenz
Germania
Görlitzer Anzeiger
Hallische Zeitung
Die Hilfe
Historisch-Politische Blätter
Katholischer Volksbote
Lingen'sches Wochenblatt
Märkisches Kirchenblatt
Nationalliberale Blätter
Die Neue Gesellschaft
Das Neue Jahrhundert. Organ der deutschen Modernisten
Die Post (Berlin)
Preußisches Verwaltungs-Blatt
Simplicissimus
Sozialistische Monatshefte
Der Staatsbürger. Halbmonatsheft für Politische Bildung
Die Wahrheit
Die Zeit. Nationalsozialistische Wochenschrift
Das Zwanzigste Jahrhundert

CONTEMPORARY PRINTED SOURCES

Altmann-Gottheiner, Elisabeth. "Die deutschen politischen Parteien und ihre Stellung zur Frauenfrage." *Zeitschrift für Politik* 3, nos. 3–4 (1910): 581–98.

B., J. "Wahlbeeinflussungen bei Gemeindeverordnetenwahlen; Befugnisse des Wahlvorstandes." *Preußisches Verwaltungs-Blatt* 27, no. 15 (13 Jan. 1906): 272.

Bamberger, Ludwig. "Die erste Sitzungsperiode des ersten deutschen Reichstags." *Jahr-*

buch für Gesetzgebung, Verwaltung und Rechtspflege des deutschen Reiches 1 (1871): 159–99.

Below, Georg von. *Das Parlamentarische Wahlrecht in Deutschland.* Leipzig, 1909.

Berdrow, Wilhelm, ed. *Krupp. A Great Business Man Seen Through His Letters.* New York, 1930.

Bergsträsser, Ludwig. "Zur Geschichte der parteipolitischen Agitation und Organisation in Deutschland." *Vergangenheit und Gegenwart. Zeitschrift für den Geschichts-Unterricht und Staatsbürgerliche Erziehung in allen Schulgattungen* 4 (1912): 241–53.

Bernstein, Eduard. "Wahlprüfungen durch Richter." *Sozialistische Monatshefte* 19, no. 8. (24 Apr. 1913): 471–78.

Bismarck, Otto von. *Die gesammelten Werke.* Bde. 6c, 9, 14. Berlin, 1929.

Blos, Wilhelm. *Denkwürdigkeiten eines Sozialdemokraten.* 2 Bde. Munich, 1914–19.

Blaustein, Arthur. Review of *Die Reichstagswahlen von 1867 bis 1903* . . . by Fritz Specht and Paul Schwabe. *Zeitschrift für Politik* (Berlin) 1, no. 3 (1908): 549–50.

Bodewig, Hartmann. *Geistliche Wahlbeeinflussungen in ihrer Theorie und Praxis dargestellt.* Munich, 1909.

Boelcke, Willi, ed. *Krupp und die Hohenzollern. Aus der Korrespondenz der Familie Krupp 1850–1916.* Berlin (East), 1956.

Braun, Lily. "Auf Agitation." *Die Neue Gesellschaft* 3, no. 17 (1907): 200–202.

Brentano, Lujo. "Das Arbeitsverhältnis in den privaten Riesenbetrieben." *Verhandlungen des Verein für Sozialpolitik* 116 (1906): 135–51.

Campe, [Rudolf] von. "Die geistliche Wahlbeeinflussung und das neue Strafgesetzbuch." *Nationalliberale Blätter* 24, no. 40 (1912): 6–10; no. 41 (1912): 36–38.

Cohn. "Schutz der Wahl- und Stimmfreiheit gegen Mißbrauch kirchlicher Zuchtgewalt." *Das Freie Wort. Frankfurter Halbmonatsschrift für Fortschritt auf allen Gebieten des geistigen Lebens* 7 (1907–8): 578–82.

Csekey, Stefan von. "Ein Beitrag zur Wahlprüfungsorganisation." *Blätter für Vergleichende Rechtswissenschaft und Volkswirtschaftslehre* (Berlin, 1912): 43–48.

"Das Verbot des Jesuitenordens. (Reichsgesetz vom 4. Juli 1871)." *Annalen des deutschen Reiches* (1872): cols. 1171–1234.

"Die Jesuiten-Petitionen im Reichstag (Mai 1871)." *Annalen des deutschen Reiches* (1872): cols. 1121–70.

Die Thätigkeit des Deutschen Reichstags von 1890 bis 1893. Mit einem Anhang enthaltend: Die wichtigsten Beschlüsse der Wahlprüfungs-Kommission, die für die Agitation und die Wahlen wesentlichsten Bestimmungen des Strafgesetzes und des Wahlgesetzes für den Reichstag nebst Wahlreglement. Berlin, 1893.

D[elbrück, Hans]. "Die Auflösung des Reichstags." *Preußische Jahrbücher* 127 (Jan.–Mar. 1907): 184–90.

———. "Preußische Wahlreform." *Preußische Jahrbücher* 130 (Oct.–Dec. 1907): 188–91.

Delius. "Das unentgeltliche Vertheilen von Druckschriften u.s.w." *Preußisches Verwaltungs-Blatt* 19, no. 29 (16 Apr. 1898): 297–98.

———. "Das Verbot von Volksversammlungen am Aufenthaltsorte des Kaisers und Königs sowie am Sitze der Parlamente." *Preußisches Verwaltungs-Blatt* 28, no. 14 (5 Jan. 1907): 253–55.

"Diäten. Verfassung. Wahlrecht." *Grenzboten* 63, no. 1 (1904): 306–7.

"Die Worte 'kauft oder verkauft' im § 109 des RStGB . . ." *Annalen des Reichsgerichts* 5 (1882): 398–400.

Ditscheid, Ägidius. *Matthias Eberhard, Bischof von Trier im Kulturkampf.* Trier, 1900.

Drenkmann. "Ueber die Wahlvergehen. Ein Beitrag zur Revision der §§ 84–86 des Strafgesetzbuchs." *Archiv für Preußisches Strafrecht* 17 (1869): 168–79.

"Ein Stimmungsbildchen aus dem 'nicht-konfessionellen' Zentrum." *Das Neue Jahrhundert* 3, no. 24 (11 June 1911): 283–84.

Elble, Otto. *Der Kanzelparagraph (§130a St.-G.-B.)* Diss. Heidelberg, 1908.

"Entscheidungen. Durch die Vorschriften des Vereinsgesetzes ist die Anwesenheit von Frauen bei allen von politischen Vereinen veranstalteten Versammlungen (Konferenzen usw.) verboten." *Preußisches Verwaltungs-Blatt* 26, no. 22 (25 Feb. 1905): 387–88.

"Entscheidungen. Sozialdemokratische Vereine." *Preußisches Verwaltungs-Blatt*, 28, no. 29 (20 Apr. 1907): 549–50.

Ernst, Eugen. *Polizeispitzeleien und Ausnahmegesetze 1878–1910. Ein Beitrag zur Geschichte der Bekämpfung der Sozialdemokratie.* Berlin, 1911.

Erzberger, Matthias. *Bilder aus dem Reichstagswahlkampf 1907. Die Agitation der Zentrumsgegner beleuchtet nach deren Wahlschriften.* Berlin, 1907.

Fontane, Theodor. *Der Stechlin.* [1898], Goldmann Klassiker Taschenbuchausgabe, Munich, n.d.

Freudenthal, Berthold. *Die Wahlbestechungen.* Strafrechtliche Abhandlungen, Heft 1, Breslau, 1896.

Friedrich, Julius. *Das politische Wahlrecht der Geistlichen.* Giessen, 1906.

Georgius. "Darf ein katholischer Geistlicher liberaler Parteimann sein?" *Die Wahrheit* 48, no. 3 (1 Apr. 1909): 389–96.

Gerlach, H[ellmut] von. "Wahlgeplauder." *Die Zeit* 2, no. 31 (30 Apr. 1903): 148–51.

———. "Die sogenannte Wahlurne." *Die Nation* 22, no. 44 (1904/5): 692–95.

———. "Die Wahlprüfungs-Verschleppungskommission." *Die Nation* 23, no. 15 (1905/6): 229–230.

———. "Wahlprüfungspraxis und Wahlprüfungspraktiken." *Die Nation* 24, no. 8 (1906/7): 118–19.

———. *Die Geschichte des preußischen Wahlrechts.* Berlin, 1908.

———. *Meine Erlebnisse in der Preußischen Verwaltung.* Berlin, 1919.

———. *Von Rechts nach Links.* Zurich, 1937.

———. *Erinnerungen eines Junkers.* Berlin, n.d.

"Glossen über 'Verquickung von Politik und Religion.'" *Die Wahrheit* 43, no. 10 (15 Feb. 1909): 289–95.

Göhre, Paul. *Three Months in a Workshop. A Practical Study* ([*Drei Monate Fabrikarbeiter*, Leipzig, 1891]. London and New York, 1895.

Gore, James Howard. *Political Parties and Party Policies in Germany.* New York, 1903.

Gurwitsch, Girsch. *Der strafrechtliche Schutz des Wahlrechts. (§§ 107–109 R St.-G.-B.)* Diss. Heidelberg, Leipzig, 1910.

Hatschek, Julius. *Kommentar zum Wahlgesetz und zur Wahlordnung im deutschen Kaiserreich.* Berlin and Leipzig, 1920.

Heile, Wilhelm. "Mehrheitswahl oder Verhältniswahl?" *Die Hilfe* 15, no. 31 (1 Aug. 1909): 482–84.

Henning, Max, ed. *Der 'rote Kaplan.' Zum Andenken an Dr. Heinrich V. Sauerland. Eine Auswahl seiner im 'Freien Wort' pseudonym erschienenen Arbeiten.* Frankfurt a. M., 1910.

Herrfurth, L. "Der Zeitpunkt der Neuwahl des Reichstags und des Preußischen Abgeordnetenhauses." *Deutsche Juristen-Zeitung* 3, no. 1 (1 Jan. 1898): 1–5.

Hirth, Georg. "Zusammentritt des Reichstages und Prüfung der Wahlen." *Deutscher Parlaments-Almanach.* Leipzig, 1893, 62–81.

Jellinek, G(eorge). "Sprechsaal. Zur Verantwortlichkeit des Reichskanzlers. Ein Epilog." *Deutsche Juristen-Zeitung* 14, no. 9 (1 May 1909): cols. 532–33.

"Die Jesuitenpetitionen." *Grenzboten* 49, no. 4 (1890): 393–404.

[Jörg, Joseph Edmund]. "Das deutsche Reich von der Schattenseite im Reichstag." *Historisch-Politische Blätter* 67 (1872): 763–75; 852–68.

————. *Briefwechsel 1846–1901*, comp. by Dieter Albrecht. Mainz, 1988.

Jonge, Moritz de. "Parlament und Wahlprüfungsjustiz." *Grenzboten* 71, no. 2 (1912): 207–10.

"Der katholische Geistliche auf der politischen Arena. (Von einem römisch-katholischen Priester)." *Das Neue Jahrhundert* 1, no. 8 (12 Feb. 1909): 90–94.

Keil, Wilhelm. *Erlebnisse eines Sozialdemokraten.* 2 Bde. Stuttgart, 1947.

Kelly, Alfred, ed. *The German Worker. Working-Class Autobiographies from the Age of Industrialization.* Berkeley, 1987.

Ketteler, Wilhelm Emmanuel Freiherr von. "Die Centrums-Fraction auf dem ersten Deutschen Reichstage." Mainz, 1872. In *Schriften, Aufsätze und Reden, 1871–1877*, Bd. 4 of *Sämtliche Werke und Briefe*, edited by Erwin Iserloh and Christoph Stoll. Mainz, 1977.

Knorr, Julius. "Statistik der Wahlen zum ersten deutschen Reichstag." *Annalen des deutschen Reiches* (1872): cols. 287–364.

[Köller, Ernst M. von]. *Die Ungiltigkeit von Reichstagsmandaten und deren Verhütung. Rathgeber bei der Abhaltung von Wahl-Versammlungen und Wahlen für den Reichstag.* Herausgegeben von dem Wahlverein der Deutschen Conservativen für seine Mitglieder. Berlin, n.d. (1897).

Korn. "Wandlungen der Reichsverfassung." *Das Recht. Rundschau für den deutschen Juristenstand* 14, no. 1 (10 Jan. 1910), cols. 26–27.

Kötzschke, Hermann. *Offener Brief an den Herrn Reichstagsabgeordneten Geheimen Kommerzienrat Freiherrn von Stumm und Genossen.* Leipzig, 1895.

Kulemann, Wilhelm, *Politische Erinnerungen. Ein Beitrag zur neueren Zeitgeschichte.* Berlin, 1911.

Lachner, Carl von. *Grundzüge einer Beurteilung der Unvereinbarkeit von Priesteramt und Abgeordnetenmandat unter besonderer Berücksichtigung des Deutschen Reiches. Eine politische Studie.* Diss. Heidelberg, 1908.

Lederer, Emil. "Parteien und Interessentenorganisationen." *Der Staatsbürger* 3, no. 8 (1912): cols. 329–38.

Lefèvre-Pontalis, [Germaine Antonin]. *Les Élections en Europe à la Fin du XIXe Siècle.* Paris, 1902.

Leser, Guide. *Untersuchungen über das Wahlprüfungsrecht des deutschen Reichstags. Zugleich ein Beitrag zur Frage: Parlamentarische oder richterliche Legitimationsprüfung?* Diss. Heidelberg, 1908.

M., K. "Zum Schutz des Wahlrechts." *Grenzboten* 44, no. 1 (1885): 157–59.

Mahlert. "Zum polizeilichen Überwachungsrecht bei Versammlungen." *Juristische Wochenschrift* 42, no. 7 (1913): cols. 358–64.

Mann, Heinrich. *Der Untertan.* [Leipzig, 1918] Nördlingen, 1964.

Martin, Rudolf. *Deutsche Machthaber.* Berlin and Leipzig,[4] 1910.

Mayer, Max Ernst. "Bekämpfung der Wahlumtriebe durch das Strafrecht." *Zeitschrift für Politik* 3 (1910): 10–29.

Merkt, Otto. "Die Einteilung der Reichstagswahlkreise." *Der Staatsbürger* 3, no. 2 (1912): cols. 50–67.

Meyer, Georg. *Das parlamentarische Wahlrecht*. Berlin, 1901.

Meyerowitz, Artur. "Streik, Aussperrung, Boykott und Verruf in der Rechtsprechung des Reichsgerichts." *Juristiche Wochenschrift* 42, no. 16 (1912): 838–49.

"Der Minister des Innern und die Wahlen zum Abgeordneten Hause." *Berliner Revue* 26, no. 13 (27 Sept. 1861): 431–34.

Mittermaier, Karl Josef Anton. "Ueber die Bestrafung der bei Wahlen verübten Vergehen." *Archiv des Criminalrechts* (N.F., 1849): 338–67.

Mohl, Robert von. "Kritische Erörterungen über Ordnung und Gewohnheiten des Deutschen Reiches." *Zeitschrift für die gesamte Staatswissenschaft* 30 (1874): 528–663.

"Momentbild aus der Zentrumsagitation." *Das Neue Jahrhundert* 2, no. 2 (9 Jan. 1910): 21.

Naumann, Friedrich. "Ungleiches Wahlrecht." *Die Zeit* 2, no. 19 (5 Feb. 1903): 580–82.

———. "Auf dem Wege zum Bonapartismus." *Die Zeit* 2, no. 20 (12 Feb. 1903): 626–29.

———. "Im Automobil." *Die Hilfe* 13, no. 6 (10 Feb. 1907): 83–84.

———. "Das Zentrum." *Die Hilfe* 13, no. 8 (24 Feb. 1907): 114–15.

———. "Konservative Industriejunker." *Die Hilfe* 15, no. 48 (28 Nov. 1907): 6–7.

Oppen, Hans von. *Zur Reform des Reichstags-Wahlrechts. Ein Vorschlag zur Güte*. Berlin, 1895.

Ostrogorski, Moisei. "Women's Suffrage in Local Self-Government." *Political Science Quarterly* 6, no. 4 (Dec. 1891): 677–710.

Pachmann, Theodor. "Ueber politische Clerikal-Vertretung—ein altes Thema neu bearbeitet." *Österreichische Vierteljahreschrift für Rechts- und Staatswissenschaft* 10 (1862): 106–20.

Poschinger, Heinrich von. *Fürst Bismarck und der Bundesrat*. 5 Bde. Stuttgart and Leipzig, 1897–1901.

Prengel, Th. "Beiträge zur Wahlprüfungsstatistik des deutschen Reichstages 1871–90." *Annalen des deutschen Reiches* (1892): 1–90.

"Religion und Politik." *Das Neue Jahrhundert* 3, no. 47 (19 Nov. 1911): 556–60.

Report on the Practice Prevailing in Certain European Countries in Contests for Election to Representative Legislative Assemblies: 1881, Presented to both Houses of Parliament by Command of Her Majesty. London, 1881.

Richter, Eugen. *Im alten Reichstag. Erinnerungen*. 2 Bde. Berlin, 1884 and 1896.

[Richter, Eugen], *Neues ABC-Buch für freisinnige Wähler. Ein Lexikon parlamentarischer Zeit- und Streitfragen*. Berlin,[3] 1884.

Saarbrücker evangelische Pfarrkonferenz. *Freiherr von Stumm-Halberg und die evangelischen Geistlichen im Saargebiet. Ein Beitrag zur Zeitgeschichte*. Göttingen, 1896.

Saß, [Georg Friedrich] Frhr. von. "Politik und Presse. Die Sozialdemokratie proklamiert den 'Terror.'" *Deutsches Adelsblatt* 26, no. 23 (7 Jun. 1908): 325–26.

———. "Jungliberaler Terrorismus." *Deutsches Adelsblatt* 27, no. 41 (10 Oct. 1909): 515–16.

———. "Die Ungültigkeitserkärung der sozialdemokratischen Mandate im preußischen Abgeordnetenhause. Die Sozialdemokratie proklamiert den 'Terror.'" *Deutsches Adelsblatt* 27, no. 20 (16 May 1909): 259–60.

Schloss, Heinrich. "Parlamentarische oder richterliche Wahlprüfung?" *Der Staatsbürger* 3, no. 4 (1912): cols. 156–62.

Schmoller, Gustav. "Die preußische Wahlrechtsreform von 1910 auf dem Hintergrund des Kampfes zwischen Königtum und Feudalität." *Jahrbuch für Gesetzgebung, Verwaltung und Volkswirtschaft im Deutschen Reich* 34, no. 3 (1910): 349–67.

Schofer, Joseph. *Erinnerungen an Theodor Wacker.* Karlsruhe, n.d. [1922].

Schücking, Lothar Engelbert. *Die Reaktion in der inneren Verwaltung Preußens.* 1908[4], Berlin-Schöneberg.

Sello, Friedrich Wilhelm. *Der Schutz der öffentlichen Wahlen nach dem Reichsstrafgesetzbuch (§§ 107–109).* Diss. Greifswald, Berlin, 1908.

Severing, Carl. *Mein Lebensweg.* 2 Bde. Cologne, 1950.

Seydel, Max von. *Commentar zur Verfassungs-Urkunde für das Deutsche Reich.* Freiburg i.B. and Leipzig,[2] 1897.

Seyffardt, Ludwig Friedrich. *Erinnerungen.* Leipzig, 1900.

[Sickenberger, Otto]. "Zum Katholikentag 1905." *Das Zwanzigste Jahrhundert* 5, no. 35 (28 Aug. 1905): 411–14; no 36 (3 Sept. 1905): 421–24.

Siebertz, Paul. *Politisch-soziales Abc-Buch. Ein Handbuch für die Mitglieder und Freunde der Zentrumspartei. Auf Grund authentischen Quellenmaterials.* Stuttgart, 1900.

Siegfried, [Richard]. "Wahl," *Meyers Konversationslexikon* 19 (Jahres-Supplement 1898–99).

Siegfried, R[ichard]. "Die verschwiegene Wahlurne." *Annalen den Deutschen Reichs* (1906): 735–60.

Steinmann, Adelheid. "Mitarbeit der Frau in der Nationalliberalen Partei." *Nationalliberale Blätter* 24, no. 40 (1912): 13–20.

Stenographische Berichte über die Verhandlungen des . . . deutschen Reichstags. Abbreviated SBDR.

Stenographische Berichte über die Verhandlungen des preußischen Hauses der Abgeordneten. Abbreviated SBHA.

Stier-Somlo, F[ritz]. "Die Wahlprüfungen im Reichstage." *Das Recht* 11, no. 2 (25 Jan. 1907): cols. 89–95.

Sybel, Heinrich von. "Klerikale Politik im neunzehnten Jahrhundert." In *Kleine Historische Schriften* 3: 376–454. Stuttgart, 1880.

Techlenburg, A. "Sprechsaal. Ungültigkeit von Stimmen wegen ihres Inhalts." *Preußisches Verwaltungs-Blatt* 26, no. 10 (3 Dec. 1904): 169.

"The Working of a German General Election." *Blackwood's Edinburgh Magazine* 151 (Feb. 1907): 266–81.

Treue, Wolfgang, ed. *Deutsche Parteiprogramme seit 1861.* Göttingen, [1954] 1968.

Tzschoppe, W. von. *Geschichte des Deutschen Reichstags-Wahlrechts.* Leipzig, 1890.

"Ungültigkeit der Wahlen zur Stadtverordnetenversammlung, weil einem Wähler nicht gestattet wurde, sich Notizen aus der offen gelegten Liste zu machen. Entscheidung des Oberverwaltungsgerichts, II. Senats, vom 2. Juli 1901 (II. 1110)." *Preußisches Verwaltungs-Blatt* 23, no. 18 (1 Feb. 1902): 276–77.

Virnich, Winand. *Die Fraction des Centrums in der zwölften Legislaturperiode des preußischen Landtages 1873–1876. Ein Bericht an seine Wähler und alle Freunde des Centrums.* Münster, 1876.

Vorstand der Sozialdemokratischen Partei. *Handbuch für sozialdemokratische Wähler. Der Reichstag 1907–1911.* Berlin, 1911.

Wacker, Theodor. *Die Rechte der abhängigen Wähler von der Cartell-Mehrheit mit Füßen getreten. An der Hand der Wahlprüfungs-Verhandlungen des Reichstages 1887–1890.* Freiburg i.B., 1890.

"Das Wahlrecht der Geistlichen," *Das Zwanzigste Jahrhundert* 5, no. 7 (12 Feb. 1905): 70–72.

Weber, Max. *Die Verhältnisse der Landarbeiter im ostelbischen Deutschland.* Leipzig, 1892.

———. "Bemerkungen im Anschluß an den vorstehenden Aufsatz." *Archiv für Sozialwissenschaft und Sozialpolitik.* 20 (N.F. Bd. 2), 2. Heft (1905): 550–53.

———. "Diskussionsreden auf den Tagungen des Vereins für Sozialpolitik (1905, 1907, 1909, 1911). Debatterede zu den Verhandlungen des Vereins für Sozialpolitik in Mannheim 1905 über das Arbeitsverhältnis in den privaten Riesenbetrieben." In Max Weber, *Gesammelte Aufsätze zur Sociologie und Socialpolitik*, 394–97. Tübingen, 1924.

———. "Parlament und Regierung im neugeordneten Deutschland (Mai 1918)." In *Gesammelte politische Schriften*, 294–431. Tübingen,[2] 1958.

———. "Politik als Beruf." In *Gesammelte Politische Schriften.* 493–548. Tübingen,[2] 1958.

———. "Wahlrecht und Demokratie in Deutschland." In *Gesammelte Politische Schriften*, 233–79. Tübingen,[2] 1958.

"Wie Bismarck und Puttkamer konservative Wahlen machten." *Das freie Wort. Sozialdemokratisches Diskussionsorgan* 1, no. 4 (Oct. 1929) 1–15; 1, no. 5 (Nov. 1929): 8–16.

Zentrums-Album des Kladderadatsch 1870–1910. Berlin, 1912.

Zoepfl, Heinrich. *Grundsätze des Gemeinen deutschen Staatsrechts mit besonderer Rücksicht auf das Allgemeine Staatsrecht und auf die neuesten Zeitverhältnisse.* Part 2 Leipzig and Heidelberg 1863, reprinted in Scriptor Reprints, Scriptor Verlag Kronbert/Ts. 1975.

"Zum Katholikentag 1905." *Das Zwanzigste Jahrhundert* 5, no. 35 (28 Aug. 1905): 409–11.

SECONDARY SOURCES

Allen, Howard W., and Kay Warren Allen. "Vote Fraud and Data Validity." In *Analyzing Electoral History: A Guide to the Study of American Voter Behavior*, edited by Jerome M. Clubb et al., 153–94. Beverly Hills and London, 1981.

Anderson, Margaret Lavinia. *Windthorst: A Political Biography.* Oxford, 1981.

———. "The Kulturkampf and the Course of German History." *Central European History* 19 (Mar. 1986): 82–115.

———. "Voter, Junker, *Landrat*, Priest: The Old Authorities and the New Franchise in Imperial Germany." *American Historical Review* 98, no. 5 (Dec. 1993): 1448–74.

———. "The Limits of Secularization: On the Problem of the Catholic Revival in 19th Century Germany." *Historical Journal* 38, no. 3 (1995): 647–70.

Anderson, Margaret Lavinia, and Kenneth Barkin. "The Myth of the Puttkamer Purge and the Reality of the Kulturkampf." *Journal of Modern History* 54 (Dec. 1982): 647–86.

Argersinger, Peter H. "New Perspectives on Election Fraud in the Gilded Age." *Political Science Quarterly* 100 (Winter 1985/6): 669–87.

Asmus, Helmut. "Die politische Entwicklung in Magdeburg vom Ausgang des 18. Jahrhunderts bis zum ersten Weltkrieg, unter besonderer Berücksichtigung der Geschichte der Magdeburger Arbeiterbewegung." In *Bauer und Landarbeiter im Kapitalismus in der Magdeburger Börde*, edited by Hans-Jürgen Rach and Bernhard Weissel, 299–324. Berlin (East), 1982.

Bachem, Karl. *Vorgeschichte, Geschichte und Politik der deutschen Zentrumspartei.* 9 Bde. Cologne, 1927–32.

Bade, Klaus J. "'Kulturkampf' auf dem Arbeitsmarkt: Bismarcks 'Polenpolitik' 1885–1890." In *Innenpolitische Probleme des Bismarck-Reiches*, edited by Otto Pflanze, 121–42. Munich and Vienna, 1983.

Bajohr, Frank. *Zwischen Krupp und Kommune. Sozialdemokratie, Arbeiterschaft und Stadtverwaltung in Essen vor dem Ersten Weltkrieg.* Essen, 1988.

Baranowski, Shelley. *The Sanctity of Rural Life. Nobility, Protestantism, and Nazism in Weimar Prussia.* Oxford, 1995.

Barkin, Kenneth D. *The Controversy over German Industrialization 1890–1902.* Chicago, 1970.

———. "Germany and England: Economic Inequality." *Tel Aviver Jahrbuch für deutsche Geschichte* 26 (1987): 200–11.

———. "A Case Study in Comparative History: Populism in Germany and America." In *The State of American History*, edited by Herbert J. Bass, 373–404. Chicago, 1970.

Bartolini, Stefano, and Peter Mair. *Identity, Competition, and Electoral Availability. The Stabilisation of European Electorates 1885–1985.* Cambridge, 1990.

Becker, Josef. "Das Ende der Zentrumspartei und die Problematik des politischen Katholizismus in Deutschland." In *Von Weimar zu Hitler*, edited by Gotthard Jasper, 344–76. Cologne, 1968.

———. *Liberaler Staat und Kirche in der Ära von Reichsgründung und Kulturkampf. Geschichte und Strukturen ihres Verhältnisses in Baden 1860–1876.* Mainz, 1973.

Becker, Winfried. "Kulturkampf als Vorwand: Die Kolonialwahlen von 1907 und das Problem der Parlamentarisierung des Reiches." *Historisches Jahrbuch* 106, no. 1. Halbband (1986): 59–84.

Bellot, Josef. *Hundert Jahre politisches Leben an der Saar unter preussischer Herrschaft (1815–1918).* Bonn, 1954.

Bendikat, Elfi. *Wahlkämpfe in Europa 1884 bis 1889. Parteiensysteme und Politikstile in Deutschland, Frankreich und Großbritannien.* Wiesbaden, 1988.

Berghahn, Volker. *Germany and the Approach of War in 1914.* New York, [1973] 1995.

Bertram, Jürgen. *Die Wahlen zum Deutschen Reichstag vom Jahre 1912. Parteien und Verbände in der Innenpolitik des Wilhelminischen Reiches.* Düsseldorf, 1964.

Bessel, Richard. "Formation and Dissolution of a German National Electorate: From Kaiserreich to Third Reich." In *Elections, Mass Politics, and Social Change in Modern Germany. New Perspectives*, edited by Larry Eugene Jones and James Retallack, 399–418. Cambridge, England, 1992.

Biernacki, Richard. *The Fabrication of Labor: Germany and Britain, 1640–1914.* Berkeley, Los Angeles, London, 1995.

Birk, Gerhard. "Das regionale Kriegervereinswesen bis zum ersten Weltkrieg, unter besonderer Berücksichtigung des Kreises Wanzleben." In *Bauer und Landarbeiter im Kapitalismus in der Magdeburger Börde*, edited by Hans-Jürgen Rach and Bernhard Weissel, 265–97. Berlin (East), 1982.

———. "Zur Entwicklung des regionalen Vereinswesens, unter besonderer Berücksichtigung des Kreises Wanzleben." In *Bauer und Landarbeiter im Kapitalismus in der Magdeburger Börde*, edited by Hans-Jürgen Rach and Bernhard Weissel, 163–214. Berlin (East), 1982.

Blackbourn, David. *Class, Religion and Local Politics in Wilhelmine Germany: The Centre Party in Württemberg before 1914.* New Haven, Conn., 1980.

———. "Progress and Piety: Liberals, Catholics and the State in Bismarck's Germany." In *Populists and Patricians. Essays in Modern German History*, 143–67. London, 1987.

———. *Marpingen. Apparitions of the Virgin Mary in Bismarckian Germany*. Oxford, 1993.

Blank, R[obert]. "Die soziale Zusammensetzung der sozialdemocratischen Wählerschaft Deutschlands." *Archiv für Sozialwissenschaft und Sozialpolitik* 20 (N.F. Bd. 2) no. 2 (1905): 507–50.

Blanke, Richard. *Prussian Poland in the German Empire, 1871–1900*. Eastern European Monographs, Boulder, Colo. 1981.

Blaschke, Olaf. "'Wider die 'Herrschaft des modern-jüdischen Geistes.' Der Katholizismus zwischen traditionellem Antijudaismus und modernem Anti-Semitismus." In *Deutscher Katholizismus im Umbruch zur Moderne*, edited by Wilfried Loth, 236–65. Stuttgart, 1991.

———. "Die Kolonialisierung der Laienwelt. Priester als Milieumanager und die Kanäle klerikaler Kuratel." In *Religion im Kaiserreich. Milieus-Mentalitäten-Krisen*: edited by Olaf Blaschke and Frank-Michael Kuhlemann, 93–135. Gütersloh, 1996.

Blessing, Werner K. *Staat und Kirche in der Gesellschaft. Institutionelle Autorität und mentaler Wandel in Bayern während des 19. Jahrhundert*. Göttingen, 1982.

Blewett, Neal. "The Francise in the United Kingdom, 1885–1918." *Past and Present* 32 (Dec. 1965): 27–56.

Boll, Friedhelm. "Arbeitskampf und Region. Arbeitskämpfe, Tarifverträge und Streikwellen im regionalen Vergleich 1871–1914." In *Der Aufstieg der deutschen Arbeiterbewegung. Sozialdemokratie und Freie Gewerkschaften im Parteiensystem und Sozialmilieu des Kaiserreichs*, edited by Gerhard A. Ritter, 379–414. Munich, 1990.

Boyer, John W. *Culture and Political Crisis in Vienna: Christian Socialism in Power, 1897–1918*. Chicago, 1995.

Bramann, Wilhelm. *Die Reichstagswahlen im Wahlkreise Solingen 1867–1890*. Cologne, 1973.

Braun, Max. *Adolf Stoecker*. Berlin, 1912.

Briggs, Asa. *Victorian People*. New York, 1955.

Burke, Albie. "Federal Regulation of Congressional Elections in Northern Cities, 1871–94." *American Journal of Legal History*, 14 (Jan. 1970): 17–34.

Burnham, Walter Dean. "Political Immunization and Political Confessionalism: The United States and Weimar Germany." *Journal of Interdisciplinary History* 3 (1972): 4–13.

Büsch, Otto, ed., *Wählerbewegungen in der deutschen Geschichte*. Berlin, 1978.

Charnay, Jean-Paul. "L'église catholique et les élections français." *Politique. Revue Internationale des Doctrines et des Institutions* 19–20 (Jul.–Dec. 1962): 257–306.

———. *Les scrutins politiques en France de 1815 à 1962. contestations et invalidations*. Cahiers de la Fondation nationale des Sciences politiques. Paris, 1964.

———. *Le Suffrage Politique en France. Élections parlementaires, élection présidentielle, référendums*. Paris, 1965.

Chickering, Roger. *We Men Who Feel Most German. A Cultural Study of the Pan-German League, 1886–1914*. London and Sydney, 1984.

———. "Political Mobilization and Associational Life: Some Thoughts on the National Socialist German Workers' Club (e.V.)." In *Elections, Mass Politics, and Social Change in Modern Germany*, edited by Larry Eugene Jones and James Retallack, 307–28. Washington, D.C., 1992.

Cowling, Maurice. *1867: Disraeli, Gladstone, and Revolution: The Passing of the Second Reform Bill.* Cambridge, 1967.

Cragoe, Matthew. "Conscience or Coercion? Clerical Influence at the General Election of 1868 in Wales." *Past and Present* 149 (Nov. 1995): 140–69.

Cremer, Douglas J. "Cross and Hammer: The Catholic Workingmen's and Workingwomen's Associations in Southern Germany, 1848–1934." Ph.D. diss., University of California, San Diego, 1993.

Croon, Helmut. "Die Stadtvertretungen in Krefeld und Bochum im 19. Jahrhundert. Ein Beitrag zur Geschichte der Selbstverwaltung der rheinischen und westfälischen Städte." In *Forschung zu Staat und Verfassung. Festgabe für Fritz Hartung*, 289–306. Berlin, 1958.

Crothers, George Dunlap. *The German Elections of 1907.* New York, 1941.

Czapliński, Marek. "Die polnische Presse in Oberschlesien um die Jahrhundertwende (1889–1914)." *Zeitschrift für Ostforschung* 39, no. 1 (1990): 20–37.

Dardé, Carlos. "Fraud and the Passivity of the Electorate in Spain, 1875–1923." In *Elections before Democracy. The History of Elections in Europe and Latin America*, edited by Eduardo Posada-Carbó, 201–22. London, 1996.

Deas, Malcolm. "The Role of the Church, the Army and the Police in Colombian Elections, c. 1850–1930." In *Elections before Democracy. The History of Elections in Europe and Latin America*, edited by Eduardo Posada-Carbó, 163–80. London, 1996.

Dominick, Raymond H. *Wilhelm Liebknecht and the Founding of the German Social Democratic Party.* Chapel Hill and London, 1982.

Dülffer, Jost. "Historische Wahlforschung." *Neue Politische Literatur* 2 (1988): 432–40.

Ehrenfeuchter, Bernd. *Politische Willensbildung in Niedersachsen zur Zeit des Kaiserreichs. Ein Versuch auf Grund der Reichstagswahlen von 1867 bis 1912, insbesondere seit 1890.* Diss. Göttingen, 2 Parts, 1951.

Eley, Geoff. *Reshaping the German Right. Radical Nationalism and Political Change after Bismarck.* New Haven and London, 1980.

————. "Anti-Semitism, Agrarian Mobilization, and the Conservative Party. Radicalism and Containment in the Founding of the Agrarian League, 1890–93." In *Between Reform, Reaction, and Resistance. Studies in the History of German Conservatism from 1789 to 1945*, edited by Larry Eugene Jones and James Retallack, 187–228. Providence and Oxford, 1993.

Epstein, Klaus W. *Matthias Erzberger and the Dilemma of German Democracy.* Princeton, 1959.

Ethington, Philip J. *The Public City. The political construction of urban life in San Francisco, 1850–1900.* Cambridge, 1994.

Evans, Richard J. *The Feminist Movement in Germany, 1894–1933.* London and Beverly Hills, 1976.

Fairbairn, Brett. "Authority vs. Democracy: Prussian Officials in the German Elections of 1898 and 1903." *Historical Journal* 33, no. 4 (1990): 811–38.

————. "Interpreting Wilhelmine Elections: National Issues, Fairness Issues, and Electoral Mobilization." In *Elections, Mass Politics, and Social Change in Modern Germany. New Perspectives*, edited by Larry Eugene Jones and James Retallack, 17–48. Cambridge, England, 1992.

————. Fairbairn, Brett. *Democracy in the Undemocratic State. The German Reichstag Elections of 1898 and 1903.* Toronto, 1997.

Falter, Jürgen W. *Hitlers Wähler.* Munich, 1991.

Farr, Ian. "Populism in the Countryside. The Peasant Leagues in Bavaria in the 1890s."

In *Society and Politics in Wilhelmine Germany*, edited by Richard J. Evans, 136–59. New York, 1978.

Fenske, Hans. *Wahlrecht und Parteiensystem. Ein Beitrag zur deutschen Parteienge-schichte.* Mainz, 1972.

———. "Der Landrat als Wahlmacher. Eine Fallstudie zu den Reichstagswahlen von 1881." *Die Verwaltung* 28 (1979): 433–56.

Fischer, Hubertus. "Konservatismus von unten. Wahlen im ländlichen Preußen 1849/ 52—Organisation, Agitation, Manipulation." In *Deutscher Konservatismus im 19. und 20. Jahrhundert*, edited by Dirk Stegmann, Bernd-Jürgen Wendt, and Peter-Christian Witt, 69–127. Bonn, 1983.

Fish, M. Steven. *Democracy from Scratch: Opposition and Regime in the New Russian Revolution.* Princeton, 1995.

———. "Russia's Crisis and the Crisis of Russology." In *Reexamining the Soviet Experience: Essays in Honor of Alexander Dallin*, edited by David Holloway and Norman Naimark, 139–66. Boulder, Colo., 1996.

Fohrmann, Ulrich. *Trierer Kulturkampfpublizistik im Bismarckreich. Leben und Werk des Preßkaplans Georg Friedrich Dasbach.* Trier, 1977.

Frank, Robert. *Der Brandenburger als Reichstagswähler. 1867/71 bis 1912/14.* Diss. Berlin, 1933.

Frank, Walter. *Hofprediger Adolf Stoecker und die christlichsoziale Bewegung.* Berlin, 1928.

Franz, Günther. *Die Entwicklung der politischen Parteien in Niedersachsen im Spiegel der Wahlen 1867–1949.* Bremen, 1951.

Franzke, Karl. *Die Oberschlesischen Industriearbeiter von 1740–1886.* Breslau, 1936.

Frauendienst, Werner. "Demokratisierung des Deutschen Konstitutionalismus in der Zeit Wilhelms II." *Zeitschrift für die Gesamte Staatswissenschaft* 113, no. 4 (1957): 721–46.

Fredman, L. E. *The Australian Ballot: The Story of an American Reform.* East Lansing, 1968.

Fricke, Dieter. "Der deutsche Imperialismus und die Reichstagswahlen von 1907." *Zeitschrift für Geschichtswissenschaft* 9, no. 3 (1961): 538–76.

Fridenson, Patrick. "Herrschaft im Wirtschaftsunternehmen. Deutschland und Frankreich 1880–1914." In *Bürgertum im 19. Jahrhundert. Deutschland im europäischen Vergleich*, Bd. II, edited by Jürgen Kocka, 65–91. Munich, 1988.

Gagel, Walter. *Die Wahlrechtsfrage in der Geschichte der deutschen liberalen Parteien 1848–1918.* Düsseldorf, 1958.

Gall, Lothar. "Die Deutsche Bank von ihrer Gründung bis zum Ersten Weltkrieg. 1870–1914." In *Die Deutsche Bank 1870–1995*, edited by Lothar Gall et al., 1–137. Munich, 1995.

Garber Marie, and Abe Frank, *Contested Elections and Recounts: vol. I Issues and Options in Resolving Disputed Federal Elections; vol. II A Summary of State Procedures for Resolving Disputed Federal Elections* (Washington, D.C., 1990).

Gash, Norman. *Politics in the Age of Peel: A Study in the Technique of Parliamentary Representation, 1830–1850.* New York, 1953.

Götz von Olenhusen, Irmtraud. "Die Ultramontanisierung des Klerus. Das Beispiel der Erzdiözese Freiburg." In *Deutscher Katholizismus im Umbruch zur Moderne*, edited by Wilfried Loth, 46–75. Stuttgart, Berlin, and Köln, 1991.

Graf, Hans. *Die Entwicklung der Wahlen und politischen Parteien in Groß-Dortmund.* Hanover and Frankfurt a.M., 1958.

Graf, Wolfgang. *Kirchliche Beeinflussungsversuche zu politischen Wahlen und Abstimmungen als Symptome für die Einstellung der katholischen Kirche zur Politik (Allgemeiner Zeitraum: Deutschland von 1848 bis zur Gegenwart)*. Diss. Mainz, 1971.

Grofman, Bernard, and Arend Lijphart, eds. *Electoral Laws and Their Political Consequences*. New York, 1986.

Gross, Friedrich. *Jesus, Luther und der Papst im Bilderkampf 1871 bis 1918. Zur Malereigeschichte der Kaiserzeit*. Marburg, 1989.

Guttsman, W. L. *The German Social Democratic Party, 1875–1933*. London, 1981.

Gwyn, William B. *Democracy and the Cost of Politics in Britain*. London, 1962.

Hagen, William W. *Germans, Poles, and Jews: The Nationality Conflict in the Prussian East, 1772–1914*. Chicago, 1980.

Hahne, Peter. "Die Reichstagswahl 1903 im Wahlkreis Minden-Lübbecke." *Mitteilungen des Mindener Geschichts- und Museumvereins* 42 (1970): 107–32.

Hall, Alex. "By Other Means: The Legal Struggle Against the SPD in Wilhelmine Germany, 1890–1900." *Historical Journal* 17, no. 2 (1974): 365–86.

——. *Scandal, Sensation and Social Democracy. The SPD Press and Wilhelmine Germany, 1890–1914*. Cambridge, London, New York, and Melbourne, 1977.

Hamburger, Ernst. "Jüdische Wähler und bürgerliche Parteien." In *Wählerbewegung in der deutschen Geschichte*, edited by Otto Büsch et al., 345–61. Berlin, 1978.

Hamerow, Theodore S. "The Origins of Mass Politics in Germany 1866–67." In *Deutschland in der Weltpolitik des 19. und 20. Jahrhunderts. F. Fischer zum 65. Geburtstag*, edited by I. Geiss and B. J. Wendt, 105–20. Düsseldorf, 1973.

Hanham, H. J. *Elections and Party Management. Politics in the Time of Disraeli and Gladstone*. London, 1959.

Harris, Joseph P. *Registration of Voters in the United States*. Washington, D.C., 1929.

——. *Election Administration in the United States*. Washington, D.C., 1934.

Harrop, Martin, and William L. Miller. *Elections and Voters: A Comparative Introduction*. Basingstoke and London, 1987.

Hartung, Fritz. *Deutsche Geschichte 1871–1919*. Leipzig, 1952.

Heitzer, Horstwalter. *Der Volksverein für das katholische Deutschland im Kaiserreich 1890–1914*. Mainz, 1979.

Henke, Josef. "Die Hochburgen der 'katholischen Parteien.' Materialien zum Wahlverhalten vom Kaiserreich bis zur Bundesrepublik Deutschland." In *Deutschland in Europa. Kontinuität und Bruch. Gedenkschrift für Andreas Hillgruber*, edited by J. Dülffer, B. Martin, and G. Wollstein, 348–73. Berlin, 1990.

Hermet, Guy, Richard Rose, and Alain Rouquié, eds. *Elections Without Choice*. New York, 1978.

Hesselbarth, Hellmut. *Revolutionäre Sozialdemokraten, Opportunisten und die Bauern am Vorabend des Imperialismus*. Berlin (East), 1968.

Heyl, Arnulf von. *Wahlfreiheit und Wahlprüfung*. Diss. Tübingen, Berlin, 1975.

Hiery, Hermann. *Reichstagswahlen im Reichsland. Ein Beitrag zur Landesgeschichte von Elsaß-Lothringen und zur Wahlgeschichte des Deutschen Reiches 1871–1918*. Düsseldorf, 1986.

Hirschmann, Günther. *Kulturkampf im historischen Roman der Gründerzeit 1859–1878*. Munich, 1978.

Hombach, Heinz-Jürgen. *Reichstags- und Landtagswahlen im Siegkreis sowie in den Kreisen Mülheim/Rhein, Wipperfürth, Gummersbach, und Waldbröl 1870–78*. Diss. Bonn, 1963.

Hoppen, K. Theodore. *Elections, Politics, and Society in Ireland, 1832–1885.* Oxford, 1984.

———. "Priests at the Hustings: Ecclesiastical Electioneering in Nineteenth Century Ireland." In *Elections before Democracy. The History of Elections in Europe and Latin America,* edited by Eduardo Posada-Carbó, 117–38. London, 1996.

Huber, Ernst-Rudolf. *Deutsche Verfassungsgeschichte seit 1789.* Vols. 3 and 4. Stuttgart, 1963, 1969.

———. *Dokumente zur Deutschen Verfassungsgeschichte. Bd. II Deutsche Verfassungs- dokumente 1851–1918.* Stuttgart, 1964.

Huntington, Samuel P. "The Modest Meaning of Democracy." In *Democracy in the Americas. Stopping the Pendulum,* edited by Robert A. Pastor, 11–28. New York, London, 1989.

Jaeger, Hans. *Unternehmer in der deutschen Politik (1890–1918).* Bonn, 1967.

Jensen, Richard J. *The Winning of the Midwest: Social and Political Conflict, 1888–96.* Chicago, 1971.

Jones, P. M. *Politics and rural society. The southern Massif Central c. 1750–1880.* Cambridge, London, New York, New Rochelle, Melbourne, and Sydney, 1985.

Kaelble, Hartmut. *Industrielle Interessenpolitik in der Wilhelminischen Gesellschaft. Centralverband Deutscher Industrieller, 1895–1914.* Berlin, 1967.

Kaiser, Jochen-Christoph. "Zur Politisierung des Verbandsprotestantismus. Die Wirkung Adolf Stoeckers auf die Herausbildung einer evangelischen Frauenbewegung um die Jahrhundertwende." In *Religion und Gesellschaft im 19. Jahrhundert,* edited by Wolf- gang Schieder, 254–71. Stuttgart, 1993.

Kaiser, Renate. *Die politischen Strömungen in den Kreisen Bonn und Rheinbach, 1848– 1878.* Bonn, 1963.

Kaltefleiter, Werner and Peter Nißen. *Empirische Wahlforschung. Eine Einführung in Theorie und Technik.* Paderborn, Munich, Vienna, and Zurich, 1980.

Kalyvas, Stathis N. *The Rise of Christian Democracy in Europe.* Ithaca and London, 1996.

Kammer, Karl. *Trierer Kulturkampfpriester. Auswahl einiger markanter Priester- Gestalten aus den Zeiten des preußischen Kulturkampfes.* Trier, 1926.

Kissling, Johannes H. *Geschichte des Kulturkampfes im Deutschen Reiche.* 3 Bde. Freiburg i.B., 1911.

Klein, Gotthard. *Der Volksverein für das katholische Deutschland (1890–1933). Ge- schichte, Bedeutung, Untergang.* Paderborn, Munich, Vienna, and Zürich, 1996.

Kocka, Jürgen. *Arbeitsverhältnisse und Arbeiterexistenzen. Grundlagen der Klassen- bildung im 19. Jahrhundert.* Bonn, 1990.

Kousser, J. Morgan. *The Shaping of Southern Politics. Suffrage Restriction and the Es- tablishment of the One-Party South, 1880–1910.* New Haven and London, 1974.

Kreuzer, Marcus. *Institutions and Political Innovation: Mass Politics, Political Organi- zation, and Electoral Institutions in France and Germany, 1870–1939.* Ann Arbor, 2000.

Kühne, Thomas. "Le elezioni del parlamento prussiano e il diritto elettorale delle tre classi 1867–1918." *Ricerche di Storia Politica* 8 (1993): 41–73.

Kühne, Thomas. "Wahlrecht-Wahlverhalten-Wahlkultur. Tradition und Innovation in der historischen Wahlforschung." *Archiv für Sozialgeschichte* 33 (1993): 481–547.

———. *Dreiklassenwahlrecht und Wahlkultur in Preußen 1867–1914.* Düsseldorf, 1994.

———. *Handbuch der Wahlen zum Preußischen Abgeordnetenhaus 1867–1918. Wahl- ergebnisse, Wahlbündnisse und Wahlkandidaten.* Düsseldorf, 1994.

Kühne, Thomas. "Die Liberalen bei den preußischen Landtagswahlen im Kaiserreich." In *Liberalismus und Region. Zur Geschichte des deutschen Liberalismus im 19. Jahrhundert*, edited by Lothar Gall and Dieter Langewiesche, 277–305. Munich, 1995.

Kulczyncki, John J. *The Foreign Worker and the German Labor Movement. Xenophobia and Solidarity in the Coal Fields of the Ruhr, 1871–1914*. Oxford and Providence, RI, 1994.

Kutz-Bauer, Helga. *Arbeiterschaft, Arbeiterbewegung und bürgerlicher Staat in der Zeit der Großen Depression. Eine regional- und sozialgeschichtliche Studie zur Geschichte der Arbeiterbewegung im Großraum Hamburg 1873 bis 1890*. Bonn, 1988.

Langewiesche, Dieter. *Liberalismus in Deutschland*. Frankfurt a. M., 1988.

Lepper, Peter Herbert Heinrich. *Die Politischen Strömungen im Regierungsbezirk Aachen zur Zeit der Reichsgründung und des Kulturkampfes, 1867–1887*. 3 Bde. Diss. Bonn, 1968.

———. "Kaplan Franz Eduard Cronenberg und die christlich-soziale Bewegung in Aachen 1868–1878." *Zeitschrift des Aachener Geschichtsvereins* 79 (1968): 57–148.

———, ed. *Sozialer Katholizismus in Aachen. Quellen zur Geschichte des Arbeitervereins zum hl. Paulus für Aachen und Burtscheid 1869–1878(88)*. Mönchengladbach, 1977.

Lerman, Katharine Anne. *The Chancellor as Courtier. Bernhard von Bülow and the Governance of Germany, 1900–1909*. Cambridge, 1990.

Leugers-Scherzberg, August-Hermann. *Felix Porsch. 1853–1930. Politik für Katholische Interessen in Kaiserreich und Republik*. Mainz, 1990.

Levy, Richard S. *The Downfall of the Anti-Semitic Political Parties in Imperial Germany*. New Haven and London, 1975.

Lidtke, Vernon L. *The Outlawed Party; Social Democracy in Germany 1878–1890*. Princeton, 1966.

———. *The Alternative Culture; Socialist Labor in Imperial Germany*. Oxford and New York, 1985.

Liebert, Bernd. *Politische Wahlen in Wiesbaden im Kaiserreich (1867–1918)*. Wiesbaden, 1988.

Lijphart, Arend. *Democracies. Patterns of Majoritarian and Consensus Government in Twenty-One Counties*. New Haven and London, 1984.

Lipset, Seymour Martin. "Introduction: Ostrogorski and the Analytical Approach to the Comparative Study of Political Parties." In Moisei Ostrogorski, *Democracy and the Organization of Political Parties. Vol. I: England*, abrd. ed., New York, 1964. ix–lxv.

Loth, Wilfried. *Katholiken im Kaiserreich. Der politische Katholizismus in der Krise des Wilhelminischen Deutschlands*. Düsseldorf, 1984.

———. "Soziale Bewegungen im Katholizismus des Kaiserreichs." *Geschichte und Gesellschaft* 17 (1991): 279–310.

Mallmann, Klaus-Michael, and Horst Steffens. *Lohn der Mühen. Geschichte der Bergarbeiter an der Saar*. Munich, 1989.

Manchester, William. *The Arms of Krupp; 1857–1963*. Boston, 1968.

March, James G., and Johan P. Olsen. "The New Institutionalism: Organizational Factors in Political Life." *American Political Science Review* 78, no. 3 (Sept. 1984): 734–50.

Mazura, Paul. *Die Entwicklung des politischen Katholizismus in Schlesien. Von seinen Anfängen bis zum Jahre 1880*. Diss. Breslau, 1925.

McLeod, Hugh. "Weibliche Frömmigkeit—männlicher Unglaube? Religion und Kirchen im bürgerlichen 19. Jahrhundert." In *Bürgerinnen und Bürger. Geschlechterverhält-nisse im 19. Jahrhundert*, edited by Ute Frevert, 134–56. Göttingen, 1988.

Menne, Bernhard. *Blood and Steel: The Rise of the House of Krupp*. New York, 1938.

Mielke, Gerd. "Des Kirchturms langer Schatten: Konfessionell-religiöse Bestimmungs-faktoren des Wahlverhaltens." In Rainer-Olaf Schultze et al., comps. *Wahlverhalten*, 139–65. Stuttgart, Berlin, Cologne, 1991.

Möckl, Karl. *Die Prinzregentenzeit. Gesellschaft und Politik während der Ära des Prinz-regenten Luitpold in Bayern*. Munich, 1972.

Möllers, Paul. *Die politischen Strömungen im Reichstagswahlkreis Essen zur Zeit der Reichsgründung und des Kulturkampfes. (1867–1878)*. Diss. Bonn, 1955.

Molt, Peter *Der Reichstag vor der improvisierten Revolution*. Cologne and Opladen, 1963.

Mommsen, Wolfgang J. *Max Weber and German Politics, 1890–1920*. [Tübingen, 1959] Chicago and London, 1984.

———. "A Delaying Compromise: The Imperial Constitution of 1871." In *Imperial Germany, 1867–1918*, 20–40. London and New York, 1995.

Monshausen, Theo. *Politische Wahlen im Regierungsbezirk Koblenz 1880–1897*. Diss. Bonn, 1969.

Moore, Barrington. *Injustice: The Social Bases of Obedience and Revolt*. White Plains, N.Y., 1978.

Moore, David Cresap. *The Politics of Deference. A Study of the mid-nineteenth century English Political System*. Hassocks, Sussex, and New York, 1976.

Mooser, Josef. "Das katholische Vereinswesen in der Diözese Paderborn um 1900. Ver-einstypen, Organisationsumfang und innere Verfassung." *Westfälische Zeitschrift* 141 (1991): 447–61.

Morgan, Edmund S. *Inventing the People: The Rise of Popular Sovereignty in England and America*. New York, 1988.

Müller, Klaus. *Politische Strömungen in den Rechtsrheinischen Kreisen des Regierungs-bezirks Köln (Sieg, Mühlheim, Wipperfürth, Gummersbach und Waldbröl) von 1879 bis 1900*. Diss. Bonn, 1963.

Müller, Klaus. "Zentrumspartei und agrarische Bewegung im Rheinland 1882–1903." In *Spiegel der Geschichte. Festgabe für Max Braubach zum 10. April 1964*, edited by Konrad Repgen and Stephan Skalweit, 828–57. Münster, 1964.

Müller, Leonhard. *Der Kampf zwischen Katholizismus und Bismarcks Politik im Spiegel der Schlesischen Volkszeitung. Ein Beitrag zur schlesischen Kirchen- Parteien- und Zeitungsgeschichte*. Breslau, 1929.

———. *Nationalpolnische Presse, Katholizismus und katholischer Klerus. Ein kirchen-und zeitungsgeschichtlicher Ausschnitt aus den Tagen des Großkampfes zwischen Deu-tschtum und Polentum in den Jahren 1896–1899*. Breslau, 1931.

Müller, Theodor. *Die Geschichte der Breslauer Sozialdemokratie*. [Breslau, 1925], Glashütte im Taunus, 1972.

Nettmann, Wilhelm. "Witten in den Reichstagswahlen des Deutschen Reiches 1871–1918." *Jahrbuch des Vereins für Orts- und Heimatkunde in der Grafschaft Mark, mit dem Sitz in Witten an der Ruhr [Wittener Jahrbuch]* 70 (1972): 77–165.

Neubach, Helmut. "Schlesische Geistliche als Reichstagsabgeordnete 1867–1918. Ein Beitrag zur Geschichte der Zentrumspartei und zur Nationalitätenfrage in Oberschle-sien." *Archiv für Schlesische Kirchengeschichte* 26 (1968): 251–78.

———. "Zu den Reichstagswahlen im Wahlkreis Ratibor-Oberschlesien, 1871–1918." *Zeitschrift für Ostforschung* 26, no. 1 (1977): 117–22.

Neugebauer-Wölk, Monika. *Wählergenerationen in Preussen zwischen Kaiserreich und Republik. Versuch zu einem Kontinuitätsproblem des protestantischen Preussen in seinen Kernprovinzen.* Berlin, 1987.

Nipperdey, Thomas. *Die Organisation der deutschen Parteien vor 1918.* Düsseldorf, 1961.

———. "War die Wilhelminische Gesellschaft eine Untertanen-Gesellschaft?" In *Nachdenken über die deutsche Geschichte*, idem. Munich, 1986.

———. *Deutsche Geschichte. 1866–1918. Bd. II. Machtstaat vor der Demokratie.* Munich, 1992.

Nohlen, Dieter. *Wahlrecht und Parteiensystem.* Leverkusen, 1986.

Nord, Philip. *The Republican Moment: Struggles for Democracy in Nineteenth-Century France.* Harvard, 1995.

Nossiter, T. J. *Influence, Opinion and Political Idioms in Reformed England. Case Studies from the North-east, 1832–74.* Sussex, 1975.

Oertzen, Dietrich von. *Adolf Stoecker. Lebensbild und Zeitgeschichte*, 2 Bde. Berlin, 1910.

Olbrich, Karl. "Der katholische Geistliche im Volksglauben." *Mitteilungen der schlesischen Gesellschaft für Volkskunde* (Breslau) 30 (1929): 90–105.

Oncken, Hermann. *Rudolf von Bennigsen*, 2 Bde. Stuttgart, 1910.

———. "Aus dem Lager der deutschen Whigs." *Historisch-Politische Aufsätze und Reden*, 265–302. Munich and Berlin, 1914.

Ostrogorski, Moisei. *Democracy and the Organization of Political Parties. Vol. I: England*, abrd. ed. 1902, New York, 1964.

O'Donnell, Guillermo. "Transitions to Democracy: Some Navigational Instruments." In *Democracy in the Americas: Stopping the Pendulum*, edited by Robert A. Pastor, 62–75. New York and London, 1989.

O'Gorman, Frank. "Campaign rituals and ceremonies: the social meaning of elections in England, 1780–1860." *Past and Present* 135 (May 1992): 79–115.

———. "The Culture of Elections in England: From the Glorious Revolution to the First World War." In *Elections before Democracy. The History of Elections in Europe and Latin America*, edited by Eduardo Posada-Carbó, 17–32. London, 1996.

O'Leary, Cornelius. *The Elimination of Corrupt Practices in British Elections, 1868–1911.* Oxford, 1962.

Olschewski, Bernd-Dietrich. *Wahlprüfung und Subjektiver Wahlrechtsschutz. Nach Bundesrecht unter Berücksichtigung der Landesrechte.* Berlin, 1970.

Paul, Johann. *Alfred Krupp und die Arbeiterbewegung.* Düsseldorf, 1987.

Perkins, J. A. "The German Agricultural Worker, 1814–1914." *Journal of Peasant Studies* 11, no. 3 (1984): 3–27.

Pflanze, Otto. *Bismarck and the Development of Germany* (2d ed., Princeton, 1990. Vol. I, *The Period of Unification, 1815–1871*; vol. II, *The Period of Consolidation, 1872–1880*; vol. III *The Period of Fortification: 1880–1898*).

Pitkin, Hanna Fenichel. *The Concept of Representation.* Berkeley, 1967.

Poguntke, Thomas. "Parties in a Legalistic Culture: The Case of Germany." In *How Parties Organize. Change and Adaption in Party Organizations in Western Democracies*, edited by Richard S. Katz and Peter Mair, 185–215. London, Thousand Oaks Calif., and New Delhi, 1997.

Pohl, Karl Heinrich. *Die Münchener Arbeiterbewegung. Sozialdemokratische Partei, Freie Gewerkschaften, Staat und Gesellschaft in München 1890–1914.* Munich, 1992.

Pollmann, Klaus Erich. *Parlamentarismus im Norddeutschen Bund 1867–1870*. Düsseldorf, 1985.

Pollock, James Kerr. *German Election Administration*. New York, 1934.

Pomper, Gerald M. *Elections in America. Control and Influence in Democratic Politics*. New York and Toronto, 1968.

Posada-Carbó, Eduardo. "Elections before Democracy: Some Considerations on Electoral History from a Comparative Approach." In *Elections before Democracy. The History of Elections in Europe and Latin America*, idem, ed., 1–17. London, 1996.

———. "Limits of Power: Elections under the Conservative Hegemony in Columbia, 1886–1930." *Hispanic American Historical Review* 77, no. 2 (1997): 245–79.

Poschinger, Margarethe Edle von. *Kaiser Friedrich. III. 1870–1888*. Berlin, 1900.

Przeworski, Adam. "Some Problems in the Study of the Transition to Democracy." In *Transitions from Authoritarian Rule*, edited by Guillermo O'Donnell, Philippe C. Schmitter, and Laurence Whitehead, 47–63. Baltimore and London, 1986.

———. *Democracy and the Market. Political and Economic Reforms in Eastern Europe and Latin America*. Cambridge, England, 1991.

Przeworski, Adam, and John Sprague. *Paper Stones: A History of Electoral Socialism*. Chicago, 1988.

Puhle, Hans-Jürgen. *Agrarische Interessenpolitik und preußischer Konservatismus im wilhelminischen Reich (1893–1914)*. Hanover, 1966.

———. Putnam, Robert D. *Making Democracy Work: Civic Traditions in Modern Italy*. Princeton, 1993.

———. "Bowling Alone: America's Declining Social Capital." *Journal of Democracy* 6, no. 1 (Jan. 1995): 65–78.

Puttkamer, Albert von. *Staatsminister von Puttkamer. Ein Stück preußischer Vergangenheit 1828–1900*. Leipzig, 1928.

Reiber, Hans Joachim. *Die katholische deutsche Tagespresse unter dem Einfluß des Kulturkampfes*. Diss. Leipzig, 1930.

Reif, Heinz. *Die verspätete Stadt. Industrialisierung, städtischer Raum und Politik in Oberhausen 1846–1929*. Cologne, 1993.

Retallack, James N. *Notables of the Right. The Conservative Party and Political Mobilization in Germany, 1876–1918*. London, 1988.

———. " 'What Is To Be Done?' The Red Specter, Franchise Questions, and the Crisis of Conservative Hegemony in Saxony, 1896–1909." *Central European History* 23, no. 4 (Dec. 1990): 271–312.

———. "Antisocialism and Electoral Politics in Regional Perspective: The Kingdom of Saxony." In *Elections, Mass Politics, and Social Change in Modern Germany. New Perspectives*, edited by Larry Eugene Jones and James Retallack, 49–71. Cambridge, England, 1992.

Richter, Ludwig. " 'Auseinanderstrebendes Zusammenhalten'. Bassermann, Stresemann und die Nationalliberale Partei im letzten Jahrzehnt des Kaiserreiches." In *Gestaltungskraft des Politischen. Festschrift für Eberhard Kolb*, edited by Wolfram Pyta and Ludwig Richter, 55–86. Berlin, 1998.

Ritter, Gerhard A. *Die Arbeiterbewegung im Wilhelminischen Reich. Die sozialdemokratische Partei und die freien Gewerkschaften 1890–1900*. Berlin, 1959.

———. "Deutscher und Britischer Parlamentarismus. Ein verfassungsgeschichtlicher Vergleich." In *Recht und Staat in Geschichte und Gegenwart*, Heft 242/243, 3–56. Tübingen, 1962.

Ritter, Gerhard A. "Zu Strategie und Erfolg der sozialdemokratischen Wähler-rekrutierung im Kaiserreich." In *Wählerbewegungen in der Deutschen Geschichte*, edited by Otto Büsch et al., 313–324. Berlin, 1978.

———. *Social Welfare in Germany and Britain. Origins and Development.* English trans. of 1983 work: Leamington Spa, New York, 1986.

———. "Die Sozialdemokratie im Deutschen Kaiserreich in sozialgeschichtlicher Perspektive." *Historische Zeitschrift* 249 (1989): 295–362.

———. "The Social Bases of the German Political Parties, 1867–1920." In *Elections, Parties, and Political Traditions. Social Foundations of German Parties and Party Systems, 1867–1987*, edited by Karl Rohe, 27–52. New York, 1990.

———. "Das Wahlrecht und die Wählerschaft der Sozialdemokratie im Königreich Sachsen, 1867–1914." In *Der Aufstieg der deutschen Arbeiterbewegung*, edited by idem, 49–101. Munich, 1990.

———. "Die Sozialdemokratie und die Reichstagswahlen 1877–1890. Der Durchbruch der Partei zur Massenbewegung in der Zeit des Sozialistengesetzes." In *Geschichte als Möglichkeit. Über die Chancen von Demokratie. Festschrift für Helga Grebing*, edited by Karsten Rudolph and Christl Wickert, 120–46. Essen, 1995.

Rohe, Karl. "Konfession, Klasse und lokale Gesellschaft als Bestimmungsfaktoren des Wahlverhaltens. Überlegungen und Problematisierungen am Beispiel des historischen Ruhrgebiets." In *Politische Parteien auf dem Weg zur parlamentarischen Demokratie in Deutschland. Entwicklungslinien bis zur Gegenwart*, edited by Lothar Albertin and Werner Link, 109–26. Düsseldorf, 1981.

———. "Wahlanalyse im historischen Kontext. Zur Kontinuität und Wandel von Wahlverhalten." In *Historische Zeitschrift* 234 (1982): 337–357.

———. "Introduction: German Elections and Party Systems in Historical and Regional Perspective." In *Elections, Parties and Political Traditions: Social Foundations of German Parties and Party Systems, 1867–1987*, edited by Karl Rohe, 1–26. New York, 1990.

———. "Political Alignments and Re-alignments in the Ruhr 1867–1987: Continuity and Change of Political Traditions in an Industrial Region." In *Elections, Parties, and Political Traditions*, idem, 107–44. New York, 1990.

———. *Wahlen und Wählertraditionen in Deutschland.* Frankfurt a. M., 1992.

Röhl, John C. G. *Germany Without Bismarck. The Crisis of Government in the Second Reich, 1890–1900.* London, 1967.

Rösch, Adolf. "Der Kulturkampf in Hohenzollern." *Freiburger Diözesan-Archiv*, N.F. 16 (Freiburg i.B., 1915): 1–128.

Röttges, Otto. *Die politischen Wahlen in den linksrheinischen Kreisen des Regierungsbezirks Düsseldorf 1848–1867.* Kempen, 1964.

Rokkan, Stein. "Towards a Generalised Concept of Verzuiling." *Political Studies* 25 (1977): 563–70.

Romeyk, Horst. *Die Politischen Wahlen im Regierungsbezirk Koblenz 1898 bis 1918.* Diss. Bonn, 1969.

Rose, Alexander. *Deutsche und Polen in Oberschlesien.* Berlin, 1919.

Rose, Richard. "Is Choice Enough? Elections and Political Authority." In *Elections Without Choice*, edited by Guy Hermet, Richard Rose, and Alain Rouquié, 196–212. New York, Rose, 1978.

Rosenbaum, L[ouis]. *Beruf und Herkunft der Abgeordneten zu den Deutschen und Preußischen Parlamenten 1847 bis 1919. Ein Beitrag zur Geschichte des deutschen Parlaments.* Frankfurt a. M., 1923.

Rosenberg, Hans. *Grosse Depression und Bismarckzeit. Wirtschaftsablauf, Gesellschaft und Politik in Mitteleuropa.* [1967], Frankfurt a. M., 1976.

Ross, Ronald J. *Beleaguered Tower: The Dilemma of Political Catholicism in Wilhelmine Germany.* South Bend and London, 1976.

———. "Enforcing the Kulturkampf in the Bismarckian State and the Limits of Coercion in Imperial Germany." *Journal of Modern History* 56 (Sept. 1984): 456–82.

———. *The Failure of Bismarck's Kulturkampf: Catholicism and State Power in Imperial Germany, 1871–1887.* Washington, D.C., 1998.

Roth, Anni. *Politische Strömungen in den Rechtsrheinischen Kreisen Mülheim, Wipperfürth, Gummersbach, Waldbröl und Sieg des Regierungsbezirks Köln 1900–1919.* Diss., Bonn, 1968.

Roth, Ralf. *Stadt und Bürgertum in Frankfurt am Main.* Munich, 1996.

Rouquié, Alain. "Clientelist Controls and Authoritarian Contexts." In *Elections Without Choice*, edited by Guy Hermet, Richard Rose, and Alain Rouquié, 19–35. New York, 1978.

Rust, Hermann. *Reichskanzler Fürst Chlodwig zu Hohenlohe-Schillingsfürst und seine Brüder.* Düsseldorf, 1897.

Rustow, Dankwart. "Transitions to Democracy: Toward a Dynamic Model." *Comparative Politics* 2, no. 3 (Apr. 1970): 337–63.

Saldern, Adelheid von. *Auf dem Wege zum Arbeiter-Reformismus: Parteialltag in sozialdemokratischer Provinz Göttingen (1870–1920).* Frankfurt a. M., 1984.

Sartori, Giovanni. "Sociology of Politics and Political Sociology." In *Politics and the Social Sciences*, edited by Seymour Martin Lipset, 65–100. Oxford, 1969.

———. *Parties and Party Systems. A Framework for Analysis.* Cambridge, England, 1976.

———. "The Influence of Electoral Systems: Faulty Laws or Faulty Method." In *Electoral Laws and Their Political Consequences*, edited by Bernard Grofman and Arend Lijphart, 43–68. New York, 1986.

Saul, Klaus. *Staat, Industrie, Arbeiterbewegung im Kaiserreich. Zur Innen- und Aussenpolitik des Wilhelminischen Deutschland, 1903–1914.* Gütersloh, 1974.

———. "Der Kampf um das Landproletariat. Sozialistische Landagitation, Großgrundbesitz und preußische Staatsverwaltung 1890 bis 1903." *Archiv für Sozialgeschichte* 15 (1975): 163–208.

Schauff, Johannes. *Das Wahlverhalten der Deutschen Katholiken im Kaiserreich und in der Weimarer Republik. Untersuchungen aus dem Jahre 1928.* (Cologne, 1928), Mainz, 1975.

Scherzberg, Lucia. "Die katholische Frauenbewegung im Kaiserreich." In *Deutscher Katholizismus im Umbruch zur Moderne*, edited by Wilfried Loth, 143–63. Stuttgart, Berlin, and Köln, 1991.

Schloßmacher, Norbert. *Düsseldorf im Bismarckreich. Politik und Wahlen. Parteien und Vereine.* Düsseldorf, 1985.

———. "Der Antiultramontanismus im Wilhelminischen Deutschland. Ein Versuch." In *Deutscher Katholizismus im Umbruch zur Moderne*, edited by Wilfried Loth, 164–98. Stuttgart, Berlin, and Köln, 1991.

Schönhoven, Klaus "Selbsthilfe als Form von Solidarität." *Archiv für Sozialgeschichte* XX (1980): 147–93.

Schmädeke, Jürgen. *Wählerbewegung im Wilhelmischen Deutschland*, 2 Bde. Berlin, 1995.

Schmidt, Martin. *Graf Posadowsky. Staatssekretär des Reichsschatzamtes und des Reichsamtes des Innern 1893–1907.* Diss. Halle and Saale, 1935.

Schmidt, Paul. *Die Wahlen im Regierungsbezirk Koblenz 1849 bis 1867/69*. Bonn, 1971.

Schmitt, Karl. "Religious Cleavages in the West German Party System: Persistence and Change, 1949–1987." In *Elections, Parties, and Political Traditions*, edited by Karl Rohe, 179–203. New York, 1990.

Schulte, Wolfgang. *Struktur und Entwicklung des Parteisystems im Königreich Württemberg. Versuche zu einer quantitativen Analyse der Wahlergebnisse*. Diss. Mannheim, 1970.

Schulze, Winfried. "Peasant Resistance and Politicization in Eighteenth-Century Germany." Unpublished paper delivered at the AHA, Dec. 1987.

Schumacher, Martin. "Agrarische Wahlbewerbungen zum Reichstag 1912–1920/22. Ergebnisse einer Auszählung." In *Probleme politischer Partizipation im Modernisierungsprozeß*, edited by Peter Steinbach. Stuttgart, 1982.

Schwidetzky, Ilse. *Die polnische Wahlbewegung in Oberschlesien*. Breslau, 1934.

Searle, G. H. *Corruption in British Politics, 1895–1930*. Oxford, 1987.

Seymour, Charles. *Electoral Reform in England and Wales: The Development and Operation of the Parliamentary Franchise, 1832–1885*. New Haven, 1915.

Seymour, Charles, and Donald Paige Frary. *How the World Votes: The Story of Democratic Development in Elections*, 2 vols. Springfield, Mass., 1918.

Sheehan, James J. "Political Leadership in the German Reichstag, 1871–1918," *American Historical Review* 74, no. 2 (Dec. 1968): 511–28.

———. *German Liberalism in the Nineteenth Century*. Chicago, 1977.

Shefter, Martin. "Party and Patronage: Germany, England, and Italy." *Politics and Society* 7 (1977): 403–51.

Smith, Helmut Walser. "Alltag und politischer Antisemitismus in Baden, 1890–1900." *Zeitschrift für die Geschichte des Oberrheins* 141 (N.F. Bd. 102) (1993): 280–304.

———. "The Learned and Popular Discourse of Anti-Semitism in the Catholic Milieu of the Kaiserreich." *Central European History* 27, no. 3 (1994): 315–28.

———. "Religion and Conflict: Protestants, Catholics, and Anti-Semitism in the State of Baden in the Era of Wilhelm II." *Central European History* 27, no. 3 (1994): 283–314.

———. *German Nationalism and Religious Conflict: Culture, Ideology, Politics, 1870–1914*. Princeton, N.J., 1995.

Smith, Woodruff, and Sharon Turner. "Legislative Behavior in the German Reichstag, 1898–1906." *Central European History* 14 (Mar. 1981): 3–29.

Spencer, Elaine Glovka. *Management and Labor in Imperial Germany: Ruhr Industrialists as Employers, 1896–1914*. New Brunswick, N.J., 1984.

Sperber, Jonathan. *Popular Catholicism in Nineteenth-Century Germany*. Princeton, 1984.

———. *Rhineland Radicals: The Democratic Movement and the Revolution of 1848–1849*. Princeton, 1991.

———. *The Kaiser's Voters: Electors and Elections in Imperial Germany*. Cambridge, 1997.

Steffens, Horst. "Arbeiterwohnverhältnisse und Arbeitskampf. Das Beispiel der Saarbergleute in der großen Streikzeit 1889–1893." In *Streik. Zur Geschichte des Arbeitskampfes in Deutschland während der Industrialisierung*, edited by Klaus Tenfelde und Heinrich Volkmann, 124–42. Munich, 1981.

Stegmann, Dirk. *Die Erben Bismarcks. Parteien und Verbände in der Spätphase des Wilhelminischen Deutschlands*. Cologne, 1970.

Steil, Hans Willi. *Die Politischen Wahlen in der Stadt Trier und in den Eifel- und Mo-selkreisen des Regierungsbezirkes Trier 1867–1887*. Diss. Bonn, 1961.

Steinbach, Peter. "Die Entwicklung der deutschen Sozialdemokratie im Kaiserreich im Spiegel der historischen Wahlforschung." In *Der Aufstieg der deutschen Arbeiter-bewegung. Sozialdemokratie und Freie Gewerkschaften im Parteiensystem und Sozialmilieu des Kaiserreichs*, edited by Gerhard A. Ritter et al., 1–35. Munich, 1990.

———. *Die Zähmung des politischen Massenmarktes. Wahlen und Wahlkämpfe im Bis-marckreich im Spiegel der Hauptstadt- und Gesinnungspresse*, 3 Bde. Passau, 1990.

———. "Reichstag Elections in the Kaiserreich: The Prospects for Electoral Research in the Interdisciplinary Context." In Larry Eugene Jones and James Retallack, eds., *Elections, Mass Politics, and Social Change in Modern Germany. New Perspectives*, 119–46. Cambridge, UK, 1992.

Steinmetz, George. *Regulating the Social: The Welfare State and Local Politics in Impe-rial Germany*. Princeton, 1993.

Stern, Leo, ed. *Der Kampf der deutschen Sozialdemokratie in der Zeit des Sozialisten-gesetzes 1878–1890. Die Tätigkeit der Reichs-Commission*, 2 Bde. East Berlin, 1956.

Sun, Raymond C. "Misguided Martyrdom: German Social Democratic Response to the Haymarket Incident, 1886–87." *International Journal of Labor and Working Class History* 24 (Spr. 1986): 53–67.

———. *Before the Enemy Is Within Our Walls*. Washington, D.C., 1999.

Suval, Stanley. *Electoral Politics in Wilhelmine Germany*. Chapel Hill, 1985.

Tenfelde, Klaus. *Sozialgeschichte der Bergarbeiterschaft an der Ruhr im 19. Jahrhun-dert*. Bonn, 1981.

Tennstedt, Florian. *Sozialgeschichte der Sozialpolitik in Deutschland. Vom 18. Jahrhun-dert bis zum Ersten Weltkrieg*. Göttingen, 1981.

———. *Vom Proleten zum Industriearbeiter. Arbeiterbewegung und Sozialpolitik in Deutschland 1800 bis 1914*. Cologne, 1983.

Thränhardt, Dieter. *Wahlen und politische Strukturen in Bayern, 1848–1953*. Düsseldorf, 1973.

Trischler, Helmuth. "Gewerkschaftliche Sozialreform und bürgerliche Sammlungspolitik. Die Volksversicherung im Wilhelminischen Deutschland." In *Von der Arbeiterbewe-gung zum modernen Sozialstaat. Festschrift für Gerhard A. Ritter zum 65. Geburtstag*, edited by Jürgen Kocka et al., 618–33. Munich, 1994.

Trzeciakowski, Lech. *The Kulturkampf in Prussian Poland*. New York, 1990.

Ullmann, Hans-Peter. *Interessenverbände in Deutschland*. Frankfurt a. M., 1988.

Ullstein, Leopold. *Eugen Richter als Publizist und Herausgeber. Ein Beitrag zum Thema "Parteipresse"*. Diss. Leipzig, 1930.

Vascik, George. "Agrarian Conservatism in Wilhelmine Germany. Diederich Hahn and the Agrarian League." In *Between Reform, Reaction, and Resistance. Studies in the History of German Conservatism from 1789 to 1945*, edited by Larry Eugene Jones and James N. Retallack, 229–61. Providence and Oxford, 1993.

Verba, Sidney, Norman Nie, and Jae-on Kim. *Participation and Political Equality. A Seven-Nation Comparison*. Cambridge and New York, 1978.

Vernon, James. *Politics and the People. A Study in English Political Culture c. 1815–1867*. Cambridge, UK, 1993.

Vincent, John. *Pollbooks. How Victorians Voted*. Cambridge, 1968.

Vogel, Bernhard, Dieter Nohlen, and Rainer-Olaf Schultze. *Wahlen in Deutschland. Theorie-Geschichte-Dokumente 1848–1970*. Berlin and New York, 1971.

Wagner, Franz, and Fritz Vosberg, *Polenspiegel. Die Aktivitäten der Polen in Deutsch-

land nach ihren eigenen Zeugnissen. [1908] Veröffentlichung aus der Reihe *Ostpolitische Studien,* Bd. II, Struckum, 1988.

———. *Polenspiegel. Die Umtriebe der Polen nach ihrer eigenen Presse* (3d and 4th revised and expanded edition of *Polenstimmen*), published for the Deutsche Ostmarkenvereine. Berlin, 1908.

Walker, Mack. *German Home Towns: Community, State and General Estate, 1648–1871.* Ithaca, 1971.

Warren, Donald Jr. *The Red Kingdom of Saxony. Lobbying Grounds for Gustav Stresemann, 1901–1909.* The Hague, 1964.

Weber, Christoph. *"Eine starke, enggeschlossene Phalanx." Der politische Katholizismus und die erste Reichstagswahl 1871.* Essen, 1992.

Weber, Eugen. *Peasants into Frenchmen. The Modernization of Rural France, 1870–1914.* London, 1977.

Weber, Paul. *Die Polen in Oberschlesien. Eine Statistische Untersuchung.* Berlin, 1913.

Webersinn, Gerhard. "Prälat Karl Ulitzka. Politiker im Priester." *Jahrbuch der Schlesischen Friedrich-Wilhelms-Universität zu Breslau* 15 (1970): 146–205.

Wehler, Hans-Ulrich. *The German Empire.* Göttingen, 1973, Leamington Spa, G.B. 1985.

———. *Deutsche Gesellschaftsgeschichte; II. Von der Reformära bis zur industriellen und politischen "Deutschen Doppelrevolution," 1815–1845/49* Munich, 1987; *III. Von der 'Deutschen Doppelrevolution' bis zum Beginn des Ersten Weltkrieges, 1849–1914.* Munich, 1996.

Weinandy, Klaus. *Die politischen Wahlen in den rechtsrheinischen Kreisen Sieg, Mülheim, Wipperfürth, Gummersbach und Waldbröl des Regierungsbezirkes Köln in der Zeit von 1849 bis 1870.* Diss. Bonn, 1956.

White, Dan S. *The Splintered Party. National Liberalism in Hessen and the Reich, 1867–1918.* Cambridge, Mass., and London, 1976.

Whyte, J. H. "The Influence of the Catholic Clergy on Elections in Nineteenth-Century Ireland." *English Historical Review* 75, no. 295 (Apr. 1960): 239–59.

Wichardt, Hans-Jürgen. "Die Polenpolitik Preußens und die Vereins- und Versammlungsfreiheit in der Rechtssprechung des königlich Preußischen Oberverwaltungsgerichts." *Zeitschrift für Ostforschung* 27, no. 1 (1978): 67–78.

Winkler, Heinrich August. *Die Sozialdemokratie und die Revolution von 1918/19. Ein Rückblick nach sechzig Jahren.* Berlin and Bonn, 1979.

———. *Von der Revolution zur Stabilisierung. Arbeiter und Arbeiterbewegung in der Weimarer Republik 1918 bis 1924.* Berlin and Bonn, 1984.

———. *Weimar 1918–1933. Die Geschichte der ersten deutschen Demokratie.* Munich, 1993.

———. "Die deutsche Abweichung vom Westen. Der Untergang der Weimarer Republik im Lichte der 'Sonderwegs-These.'" In *Gestaltungskraft des Politischen. Festschrift für Eberhard Kolb,* edited by Wolfram Pyta and Ludwig Richter, 127–37. Berlin, 1998.

Winkler, Jürgen R. *Sozialstruktur, Politische Traditionen und Liberalismus. Eine Empirische Längsschnittsstudie zur Wahlentwicklung in Deutschland 1871–1933.* Opladen, 1995.

Witt, Peter-Christian. "Der preußische Landrat als Steuerbeamter 1891–1918. Bemerkungen zur politischen und sozialen Funktion des deutschen Beamtentums." In *Deutschland in der Weltpolitik des 19. und 20. Jahrhunderts,* edited by Immanuel Geiss and Bernd Jürgen Wendt, 205–19. Düsseldorf, 1973.

Wölk, Monika. "Wahlbewußtsein und Wahlerfahrungen zwischen Tradition und Moderne." *Historische Zeitschrift* 238, no. 2 (Apr. 1984): 311–51.

Wollstein, Günter. *Theobald von Bethmann Hollweg. Letzter Erbe Bismarcks, erstes Opfer der Dolchstoßlegende*. Göttingen and Zurich, 1995.

Woods, C. J. "The general election of 1892: the catholic clergy and the defeat of the Parnellites." In *Ireland under the Union. Varieties of Tension. Essays in Honour of T.W. Moody*, edited by F.S.L. Lyons and R.A.J. Hawkins, 289–320. Oxford, 1980.

Zangerl, Carl H. E. "Baden's Opening to the Left: A Study of Regional Politics, 1904–1909." Ph.D. diss., University of Illinois at Champaign-Urbana, 1974.

———. "Courting the Catholic Vote: The Center Party in Baden, 1903–1913." *Central European History* 10, no. 3 (Sept. 1977): 220–40.

Zeldin, Theodore. *The Political System of Napoleon III*. London, 1958.

Ziekursch, Johannes. *Hundert Jahre Schlesische Agrargeschichte*, 3 Bde. Leipzig, 1925.

———. *Politische Geschichte des Neuen Deutschen Kaiserreiches. III. Bd., Das Zeitalter Wilhelms II. (1890–1918)*. Frankfurt a. M., 1930.

Zwahr, Hartmut. "Die deutsche Arbeiterbewegung im Länder- und Territorienvergleich 1875." *Geschichte und Gesellschaft* 13 (1987): 448–507.

Grafenecke (Counts' Corner), 163–64
Graudenz-Strasburg (3 Marienwerder), 126
Graudinger, Pastor, 143n. 146, 147n. 162
Greece, 5, 27
Green Party, 394
Greifswald (2 Stralsund), 29, 361
Groß, Ludwig, 206
Gröber, Adolf, 52n. 83, 243n. 11, 251
Groß Munzel, 47
Groß Sibsau, 337
Groß Strehlitz-Kosel (3 Oppeln), 165
Grossblock, 138
Grote, George, 58
Guelfs (Hanoverian legitimists), 39n. 17, 61,
   103, 116n. 45, 177, 241, 296n. 71, 371, 403,
   409
Gumbinnen, regency, 9n. 20, 26n. 19, 47n. 58,
   176, 177, 184n. 109, 194, 197n. 156, 280n.
   11; Gümbinnen-Insterburg (3 Gumbinnen),
   47, 51, 194
Gummersbach-Waldbröl, Landtag election dis-
   trict, 100n. 118, 403
Gündelwangen, 137
Gustavus Adolphus Association, 135
Gutach, 283
Guteborn, 168
Gutehoffnungshütte, 214
Gutenberg, Johann, 85
Gütersloh, 146, 323
Guttsman, William, 241

Haarmann, Gustav, 218
Haeckel, Ernst, 135
Hagen (4 Arnsberg), 295n. 67, 296n. 71
Hagenau (10 Alsace), 140
Hahn, Diederich, 363n. 75, 379n. 142, 392n.
   187
Halberstadt, 360
Halle (4 Merseburg), 182
Hamburg, 43, 244, 255, 270, 330, 341, 344,
   348, 372; as socialist stronghold, 261, 263n.
   77, 264n. 81, 266, 267n. 92, 290, 314; lib-
   erals in, 257, 288; suffrage changes in, 343,
   420
Hamburg Universal Sickness and Death Bene-
   fit Fund for Metalworkers, 274
Hameln-Linden Land-Springe (9 Hanover), 47,
   204–5, 207
Hammerstein, Wilhelm von, 369, 373
Hammerstein-Loxten, Baron Hans von, 249
Hamm-Soest (7 Arnsberg), 321 n. 24
Hanau-Gelnhausen (8 Kassel), 27, 146
Hanham, H. J., 171
Hänichen, Felix Oskar, 323

Hanover, 47, 98, 183, 191, 207, 208, 213, 279,
   309, 310n. 18, 330, 346n. 3, 385. *See also*
   Guelfs
Hare, Thomas, 341, 342n. 132
Harburg (17 Hanover), 280n. 11, 414n. 63
Harpener Bergbau-AG, 214
Harrop, Martin, 11n. 33, 415
Hartmann, Cardinal Felix (archbishop of Co-
   logne), 422n. 96
Hartung, Fritz, 247n. 23
Hasenclever, Wilhelm, 40, 155, 281, 283,
   292n. 54, 300
Haspe, 48
Hasselmann, Wilhelm, 45
Haym, Rudolf, 90
Heidenheim, 207
Heilbronn (3 Württemberg), 282n. 22
Heimpel, Hermann, 13
Heise, factory director in Freden, 208
Helldorf-Bedra, Otto von, 181
Henckel von Donnersmarck, Guido, Count
   (later Fürst), 69
Henrici, Ernst, 187
Hergenroether, Franz Josef, 75, 116
Herriot, Eduard, 403
Hersfeld (6 Kassel), 188
Hertling, Georg Freiherr von, 350n. 21, 422n.
   96
Herzfeld, Josef, 336n. 109
Hessen, 63, 94, 177, 191, 196–97, 262, 308n.
   7, 330, 416; antisemites in, 185, 187, 188,
   304, 406; constitutional arrangements in, 4,
   31, 297; political Catholicism in, 98, 104,
   111, 116, 116n. 43, 123n. 72
Heydebrand, Ernst von, 301
Heyl zu Herrnsheim, Cornelius von, 228n. 84,
   376, 379
Hibernia, steel firm, 214
Hilger, Ewald, 285
Hindenburg, Paul von, 435
Hirschberg, Jewish furrier, 297
Hirschberg, Max, 331
Hitler, Adolf, 436
Hitze, Franz, 125, 125n. 80
Hoesch, Albert, 214–15
Hof (1 Oberfranken), 183
Höfen, 39
Hohenlohe clan, 165–66
Hohenlohe-Ingelfingen, Karl von Koschintin,
   Prinz zu, 165
Hohenlohe-Oehringen, Erbprinz Christian
   Krafft zu, 165–66, 172n. 68
Hohenlohe-Oehringen, Hugo Fürst zu, Duke of
   Ujest, 45, 165, 317